Reducing Inflation

Studies in Business Cycles
Volume 30

National Bureau of Economic Research
Conference on Research in Business Cycles

Reducing Inflation

Motivation and Strategy

Edited by   Christina D. Romer and
David H. Romer

The University of Chicago Press

Chicago and London

CHRISTINA D. ROMER is professor of economics at the University of California, Berkeley, and a research associate of the National Bureau of Economic Research. DAVID H. ROMER is professor of economics at the University of California, Berkeley, and a research associate of the National Bureau of Economic Research.

The University of Chicago Press, Chicago 60637
The University of Chicago Press, Ltd., London
© 1997 by the National Bureau of Economic Research
All rights reserved. Published 1997
Printed in the United States of America
06 05 04 03 02 01 00 99 98 97   1 2 3 4 5
ISBN: 0-226-72484-0 (cloth)

Library of Congress Cataloging-in-Publication Data

Reducing inflation : motivation and strategy / edited by Christina D. Romer and David H. Romer.
     p.   cm. — (Studies in business cycles; v. 30)
    Includes bibliographical references and index.
    ISBN 0-226-72484-0 (cloth : alk. paper)
    1. Inflation (Finance) 2. Monetary policy. I. Romer, Christina.
II. Romer, David. III. Series.
HG229.R42 1997
332.4′1—dc20   96-44811
                                                 CIP

Contents

Acknowledgments

This volume grew out of a National Bureau of Economic Research conference on monetary policy and low inflation held in Islamorada, Florida, in January 1996. We are grateful to many people who made the conference and the resulting volume possible. The Bradley Foundation and Chase Manhattan Bank provided generous financial support. Kirsten Foss Davis and Lauren Lariviere managed all of the logistics of the conference with their usual care and good cheer, and Deborah Kiernan efficiently and patiently oversaw the preparation of the volume for publication.

Martin Feldstein provided not only the initial idea for the conference, but also excellent advice and ceaseless support. Needless to say, we are very grateful to him. Finally, we would like to thank the contributors to the volume, many of whom branched outside their usual fields of research to provide a fresh perspective on monetary policy. We are truly grateful for the exceedingly hard work and excellent research they provided.

Introduction

Christina D. Romer and David H. Romer

In recent years, a consensus has emerged among economists and central bankers that low inflation should be the key goal of monetary policy. In the 1980s and early 1990s, country after country endured depressed output and high unemployment to reduce its rate of inflation. Despite this consensus and concerted action, however, the economic rationale and policy implications of low inflation are only partly understood. For example, while there is ample evidence that high inflation harms economic growth and stability, there is remarkably little research on the costs and benefits of reducing inflation from, say, 3% to 1%. Similarly, there is little research on the least disruptive way to reduce inflation.

This volume, which grew out of a conference held in Islamorada, Florida, in January 1996, seeks to fill this gap in our understanding of low inflation. In a series of related but independent papers, sixteen distinguished economists analyze the appropriateness of low inflation as a goal for monetary policy and discuss possible strategies for reducing inflation. In considering the strategies for reducing inflation, the authors analyze both day-to-day issues in the conduct of monetary policy and fundamental reforms of monetary institutions.

Perhaps the most unusual feature of this collection of papers is the wide range of data and analytical techniques that they employ. One paper analyzes an original survey to detect attitudes toward inflation; another uses detailed panel data to investigate the effects of inflation on the wages of individual workers. Several papers use narrative evidence on historical episodes to analyze the successes and failures of monetary policies in the past, while others rely on sophisticated econometric analysis of macroeconomic indicators. An-

Christina D. Romer is professor of economics at the University of California, Berkeley, and a research associate of the National Bureau of Economic Research. David H. Romer is professor of economics at the University of California, Berkeley, and a research associate of the National Bureau of Economic Research.

other paper puts together a detailed data set to analyze differences in institutions and inflation across countries. And one paper even employs the novel approach of searching for key words in the *Wall Street Journal*.

While the methods of analysis differ greatly across the papers, two things unite them. Most obviously, all of the papers seek to answer important questions about the wisdom and methods of reducing inflation. More subtly, each paper mixes frontier economic research with concern about pressing policy issues. This is truly a volume that should be read by anyone who studies or conducts monetary policy.

The Effects of Inflation

The first four papers deal with the motivation for reducing inflation from its already low level to one even lower. A large number of central banks have committed themselves to achieving price stability. Is this a wise policy, or are the costs of reducing inflation likely to exceed the benefits?

Robert Shiller, in his paper "Why Do People Dislike Inflation?" analyzes one of the most important but least understood costs of inflation: the unhappiness that it causes ordinary people. Shiller conducts an extensive survey of attitudes toward inflation in the United States, Germany, and Brazil. One fact that he documents overwhelmingly is that people in each country hate inflation. For example, 84% of Americans strongly agree or agree somewhat with the statement "The control of inflation is one of the most important missions of U.S. economic policy"; in Germany, 94% of those surveyed agree with a similar statement.

Shiller goes on to probe why people dislike inflation so. He finds that a common perception is that inflation erodes standards of living. The model that appears most prevalent among the public is that inflation results from the greed and incompetence of businesses and public officials, and that it does not produce any compensating increases in nominal wages. He also finds that people in all countries fear that inflation lowers national prestige.

Shiller also compares the responses of the public with those of economists. He finds that economists are dramatically less concerned about inflation than ordinary people, and that they have a much different view of the costs of inflation. These differences could suggest that widespread economic education might reduce some of the unhappiness caused by inflation. Until that happens, however, policymakers must remain cognizant of the fact that reductions in inflation appear to have substantial benefits in terms of the public's satisfaction with life and the cohesiveness of society.

David Card and Dean Hyslop, in their paper "Does Inflation 'Grease the Wheels of the Labor Market'?" analyze a potential cost of low inflation. It is often argued that, in a world where nominal wage cuts are rare, inflation can be very useful in allowing equilibrating changes in real wages. Card and Hyslop use panel data from the Current Population Survey and the Panel Study of

Income Dynamics on individual wages to analyze whether this positive effect of inflation exists.

The authors find that many workers' nominal wages do not change from one year to the next, and that the fraction of workers with rigid nominal wages is much higher when inflation is lower. Card and Hyslop go on to estimate what the distribution of wage changes would look like in the absence of nominal rigidities, and then use these counterfactual wage distributions to calculate the effect of reducing inflation on real wage growth. They calculate that a 1 percentage-point decrease in the inflation rate increases the rate of real wage growth by about 0.06%. While this cost of reducing inflation may sound small, it is far from trivial. These estimates suggest that a decline in inflation of 5 percentage points (a common amount of disinflation in the 1980s) raises real wages by 0.3%; if labor demand is unit elastic, this rise in real wages leads to a reduction in employment of 0.3%.

Card and Hyslop supplement their analysis of individual wages with an analysis of real wages and employment by state. While they find that local employment exerts a strong influence on local wage determination, they find little evidence that the rate of local wage adjustment is faster in a higher-inflation environment. They take this finding as evidence that the efficiency gains from the "greasing the wheels" effect of inflation in the labor market are likely to be modest.

Opponents of price stability can easily point to a large cost of this policy: the recession that would be needed to drive inflation to zero would involve significant output losses. One weakness of the existing case for price stability is that no clear large offsetting benefit has been identified. In his paper "The Costs and Benefits of Going from Low Inflation to Price Stability," Martin Feldstein argues that price stability in fact has a clear benefit that is much greater than the cost of achieving it.

The benefit that Feldstein focuses on is the reduction in tax distortions. Previous work by Feldstein and others has shown that the U.S. tax system penalizes saving and subsidizes owner-occupied housing, and that higher inflation increases these distortions. In the present paper, Feldstein begins by carefully computing the magnitudes of these distortions and their responsiveness to inflation. He finds that the distortions are large and quite responsive to inflation. For example, at 4% inflation the U.S. tax system effectively taxes consumption at age seventy relative to consumption at age forty at a rate of 330%; lowering inflation by 2 percentage points would reduce this tax rate to 270%.

The next step is to find the welfare benefits that would result from the reduced distortions brought about by lower inflation. Using existing estimates of such parameters as the intertemporal elasticity of substitution and the elasticity of substitution between housing and other consumption, Feldstein finds that the steady-state welfare benefits of a reduction in inflation of 2 percentage points are close to 1% of GDP. This estimate is only moderately sensitive to reasonable changes in the parameter values. When combined with a plausible discount rate, these figures imply that (neglecting the issue of how quickly the welfare gains would reach their steady-state levels) the present value of benefits from reduced distortions swamp the roughly 5% of a year's GDP that would have to be sacrificed to bring about the reduction in inflation.

While Feldstein calculates the welfare gains from the reduced distortions in a partial equilibrium framework, in his comments on the paper, Andrew Abel redoes these calculations using a calibrated general equilibrium model. He takes Feldstein's estimates of the implicit tax rates and subsidies on saving and owner-occupied housing and their responsiveness to inflation, constructs a general equilibrium model of the economy, chooses plausible values for its parameters, and calculates the resulting steady-state welfare gain from a reduction in inflation of 2 percentage points. His baseline results are quite similar to Feldstein's. He then goes on to investigate the sensitivity of the results to various changes in the assumptions and parameter values.

Laurence Ball, in his paper "Disinflation and the NAIRU," argues that achieving price stability may depress output not just during the transition period, but over the long term. Specifically, he argues that a period of disinflation may increase an economy's normal unemployment rate.

Normal unemployment rose sharply in many industrialized countries in the 1980s. These increases are often attributed to a combination of a decline in the demand for low-skilled labor and labor market institutions that prevent reductions in real wages. But Ball is unable to find any evidence of a relation between increases in normal unemployment in the 1980s and any of a wide range of measures of labor market distortions. He finds instead that there is a strong relationship between increases in normal unemployment and the size and length of the disinflations that countries undertook. He also finds that the impact of disinflations on normal unemployment is larger in countries with greater labor market distortions. These results are consistent with theories of hysteresis in labor markets.

These findings have several important implications beyond simply suggesting that the costs of disinflations are higher than previously believed. First, they suggest that if a country needs both to disinflate and to reform its labor markets, it should undertake the labor market reforms first. Second, they suggest that disinflations should be done quickly. And finally, the findings call into question policies, such as more generous unemployment benefits in recessions, that attempt to lessen the burden of cyclical unemployment.

While these four studies of the costs and benefits of lower inflation move the discussion very far, they do not yet provide decisive evidence on the optimal rate of inflation. Shiller's and Feldstein's studies point to price stability as a sensible goal for policy. Card and Hyslop's paper provides evidence that inflation improves the efficiency of the labor market at least a small amount. And Ball's paper suggests that the tight policy needed to bring about disinflation may have substantial negative effects on the equilibrium unemployment rate. Given that policymakers have to choose some rate of inflation, the ambiguities of these studies suggest that more research in the same vein is desperately needed.

Improving the Conduct of Monetary Policy

The second group of papers moves beyond the goals of policy to consider the difficulties facing central bankers in their conduct of policy. Even if policymakers are sure that they want to achieve low inflation, there may be obstacles to the realization of that goal. For example, policymakers may lack timely information about economic conditions or they may not possess the tools necessary to target inflation successfully. The papers in this section look at several important obstacles to achieving the desired rate of inflation.

Douglas Staiger, James Stock, and Mark Watson analyze a crucial obstacle to effective monetary policymaking in their paper "How Precise Are Estimates of the Natural Rate of Unemployment?" The natural rate, or the NAIRU as it is often called, is a frequently used indicator in the formulation of monetary policy. For example, if a central bank wishes to hold the inflation rate steady, it is exceedingly useful to know the level of unemployment at which inflation starts to accelerate. Despite its frequent use, the statistical accuracy of our existing measures of the natural rate is largely unknown. Staiger, Stock, and Watson seek to remedy this situation.

The authors examine two types of models of the natural rate. One is the standard expectations-augmented Phillips curve common in the literature. The other is a univariate model of unemployment based on the assumption that unemployment returns to the natural rate in the long run. In each case, Staiger, Stock, and Watson look for evidence that the natural rate has changed over time and pursue the daunting empirical task of deriving standard errors for estimates of the natural rate.

The findings of this empirical analysis are not encouraging for proponents of the usefulness of the natural rate. Staiger, Stock, and Watson find that the natural rate can be measured only very imprecisely. For example, they find that a typical estimate of the natural rate in 1990 is around 6%, with a 95% confidence interval of roughly 5 to 7%. Since this imprecision is characteristic of all the models they consider, the authors conclude that the natural rate is unlikely to be a useful tool in the formulation of monetary policy. Indeed, the imprecision of the estimates and the fact that the estimates vary substantially over time may suggest that mistaken or outdated views of the natural rate could lead to serious mistakes in policy.

"America's Peacetime Inflation: The 1970s" by J. Bradford De Long considers one episode where the obstacles to good policymaking appear to have been insuperable. As De Long points out, the 1970s are the only peacetime period in modern U.S. history when prices rose by a substantial amount for a sustained period. In his paper, De Long considers numerous explanations for what went wrong in this decade.

One explanation that he debunks is the role of oil price shocks. Many have claimed that the 1970s were largely a period of bad luck rather than bad policy. De Long shows that wage inflation was already high before the oil price shock of 1973 and that oil price shocks appear to have had little effect on the growth rate of nominal wages. From this, he concludes that, while the supply shocks had substantial effects on both prices and output at times during the 1970s, they were not the fundamental cause of the sustained inflation.

De Long sees the fundamental cause of the inflation of the 1970s in economists' imperfect understanding of how the economy operated. He argues that the Great Depression left economists and policymakers with the view that unemployment must be controlled at all costs and with the incorrect belief that permanently lower unemployment could be bought with higher inflation. According to De Long, this view was a recipe for disaster: sooner or later policymakers were going to try to exploit the trade-off. While he believes that a period like the 1970s was bound to happen, De Long also suggests that the decade of inflation had the beneficial effects of showing that there was not a long-run trade-off between inflation and unemployment, and of building a consensus for low inflation.

In his paper "Do 'Shortages' Cause Inflation?" Owen Lamont examines whether a novel variable might prove to be a useful guide to the conduct of monetary policy. It is sometimes asserted that inflation is at least partly the result of bottlenecks or shortages in the economy: an increase in nominal demand may have a particularly strong effect on prices because of disequilibrium in the adjustment of prices and quantities. Lamont seeks to test this assertion by deriving an innovative measure of shortages and then examining its empirical relationship to inflation.

The measure of shortages that Lamont uses is the number of times in a given month that the word "shortage" appears on the front page of the *Wall Street Journal* and the *New York Times*. He then tests whether this indicator of disequilibrium is a useful predictor of inflation. Lamont's finding is that references to shortages are indeed highly correlated with future inflation. This innovative and admittedly slightly wacky variable appears to capture information not found in traditional predictors of inflation such as commodity prices, monetary aggregates, and interest rates. The usefulness of "shortages" in predicting inflation may suggest that economists should direct more attention to market imperfections in considering the effects of changes in aggregate demand. It may also suggest that policymakers should rethink the methods and variables that they use to predict inflation.

The Contribution of Monetary Institutions

While some of the obstacles to low inflation occur in the conduct of policy, still others may be inherent in the institutions set up to determine policy. For example, numerous theoretical analyses suggest that an independent central bank may be an important precondition for achieving low inflation. The three papers in the final section of the volume seek to assess the contribution of different institutions to the success of monetary policy in the United States and abroad.

In our paper "Institutions for Monetary Stability," we look systematically at the various sources of failures in monetary policy. We argue that dynamic inconsistency—the fact that optimizing policymakers have an incentive to expand once expectations are set—has been overrated as a cause of inflation. We suggest instead that imperfect understanding of how the economy functions on the part of economists, central bankers, elected leaders, and voters has been a much more common source of monetary policy mistakes. We support this view with numerous examples of policy failures in the United States and abroad over the last century.

We go on to analyze what this view of the source of policy failures implies about the desirability of different monetary institutions. We find that the institutions that can best deal with the problems caused by imperfect understanding are often quite different from those that can best deal with the problems caused by dynamic inconsistency. For example, limited professional knowledge about the effects of policy suggests that it would be unwise to tie policymakers to a rule that could turn out to be incorrect. In contrast, the surest way to deal with dynamic inconsistency is precisely to bind policymakers to a fixed rule.

After considering institutional solutions to dynamic inconsistency and various types of imperfect understanding, we discuss a combination of institutions that deals with as many of these concerns as possible. The most novel aspect of this institutional framework is a two-tier structure that insulates the central bank from political control, while still allowing the actual policymakers to be removed rapidly if they turn out to be incompetent. We then compare this institutional framework to the recent reforms in New Zealand and France and the proposed European Central Bank. While some of the reforms, such as those in New Zealand, come quite close to our framework, we argue that serious consideration of the importance of limited knowledge would lead to some modifications and extensions of even this carefully crafted reform.

Marta Campillo and Jeffrey Miron, in their paper "Why Does Inflation Differ across Countries?" use cross-country data to assess the role of various factors in explaining the international variation in inflation performance. In contrast to the many previous studies that have focused primarily on the role of central bank independence, Campillo and Miron consider a broad range of institutional and structural features that could affect national inflation experiences. For example, in addition to the standard legal indices of central bank independence, the authors consider institutional factors such as the exchange rate arrangement of each country. Among the structural characteristics of each country that they analyze are the degree of openness, political instability, and the government's ability to collect taxes. They also include prior inflation experience as a possible determinant, since high inflation in the past may lead to a national consensus in favor of low inflation in the present.

Campillo and Miron estimate the relationship between average inflation over the period 1973–89 and all of these variables for a sample of sixty-two countries. Their main finding is that structural features are far more important than institutional features in determining national inflation experiences. Indeed, they find that, when a wide range of variables is included and a broad sample of countries is considered, the conventional finding that central bank independence is important essentially vanishes. Instead, structural features that affect the size of the dynamic inconsistency problem, such as openness and political instability, appear to be more important. The need and the ability that a country has to tax also turn out to be crucial determinants of whether a given country uses inflation to generate government revenue.

This study has important implications for policymakers and economists concerned about inflation. Most obviously, it suggests that economists' focus on central bank independence as the key to low inflation is misplaced. Countries concerned abut inflation may be better served by reforming their fiscal structure rather than their monetary institutions.

When it comes to low inflation, no country has been as successful in the post–Bretton Woods period as Germany. Richard Clarida and Mark Gertler try to figure out the keys to Germany's success in their paper "How the Bundesbank Conducts Monetary Policy." One of the first facts that the authors show is that, in its design and independence, the Bundesbank is essentially indistinguishable from the U.S. Federal Reserve. Therefore, any differences in inflation performance between Germany and the United States must be due to differences in the way policy is conducted, rather than in the institutional framework.

Clarida and Gertler then go on to examine German monetary-policy practices in detail. This analysis contains both a narrative description of how the Bundesbank has behaved since 1973 and empirical estimation of a sophisticated reaction function. What comes out of this analysis is the surprising conclusion that the Bundesbank has behaved since 1973 in much the same way that the Federal Reserve has operated under Alan Greenspan. Since 1973 the Bundesbank has been very concerned about inflation, but has also been willing to risk some inflation when unemployment is high.

This portrayal of the behavior of the Bundesbank raises the very interesting question of how the Germans got smart so much sooner than the rest of the world. While Clarida and Gertler do not explicitly address this question, they do provide some clues. One difference that they note between the behavior of the Bundesbank and the Federal Reserve even under Greenspan is that the Bundesbank makes explicit inflation targets. While these targets are not binding, Clarida and Gertler believe that having to publicly explain deviations from the inflation target has served to discipline German central bankers. Perhaps this one small difference in policymaking strategy is what helped the Bundesbank avoid some of the errors made by other central banks in the 1970s.

As we hope these brief descriptions of the individual papers make clear, this volume contains a wealth of information about the motivation and strategies for attaining low inflation. While we will not claim that the ten papers here are the final word on inflation and monetary policy, they have undoubtedly moved the analysis forward by many steps. We hope that both economists and policymakers will be challenged by these essays to learn even more about the optimal inflation rate and the best way to achieve it.

I   The Effects of Inflation

1   Why Do People Dislike Inflation?

Robert J. Shiller

1.1   Introduction

The purpose of this study is to try to understand, using public survey methods, why people are so concerned and dismayed by inflation, the increase in the price level, and decline in value of money. Studying public attitudes toward inflation may help government policymakers better understand the reasons that they should (or should not) be very concerned with controlling inflation, and may help the policymakers better understand issues concerning exchange rate policies. A study of public attitudes toward inflation may also help us learn whether differences across countries in attitudes toward or understandings of inflation might explain any differences across countries in inflationary outcomes.

With the help of several students, I designed the surveys reported here to discover in some detail what people see as the origins of inflation and what real problems people see inflation as causing. Discovering this means asking a lot of questions, to find out what things people associate with inflation, what theories they have about the mechanism of inflation, what their information

Robert J. Shiller is the Stanley B. Resor Professor of Economics at the Cowles Foundation for Research in Economics, Yale University, and a research associate of the National Bureau of Economic Research.

This research was supported by the U.S. National Science Foundation and the National Bureau of Economic Research. The author thanks the numerous people who filled out the questionnaire. Questionnaire design and translation and survey management were undertaken with the help of Michael Krause in Germany and Jose Carlos Carvalho in Brazil. The cooperation of the Institute of World Economics in Kiel, Germany, and of Harmen Lehment there is much appreciated. The author also thanks Moshe Buchinsky, Giancarlo Corsetti, Robert Faulstich, Benjamin Friedman, Ilan Goldfajn, Anil Kashyap, Miles Kimball, Alvin Klevorick, Gregory Mankiw, William Nordhaus, Christina Romer, David Romer, Matthew Shapiro, Virginia Shiller, and conference participants for helpful suggestions. Aslak Aunstrup, Mylene Chan, Paulo Freitas, John Lippman, Chris Malloy, and Daniel Piazolo provided excellent research assistance.

sets regarding inflation are, and what their preferences are with regard to inflationary outcomes. One thing stressed in this study is learning the kinds of models of inflation that people have, ideas people have as to the causes of inflation and the mechanisms whereby inflation has its effects. We shall see from the results that people have definite opinions about the mechanisms and consequences of inflation, and that these opinions differ across countries, between generations in both the United States and Germany, and, even more strikingly, between the general public and economists.

This paper begins with a characterization of the problem of defining popular understandings of inflation. The first steps in this study, section 1.3, consisted of informal interviews with people, attempting to learn directly from them what they thought about inflation. Following these interviews, questionnaires A, B, and C were designed, to be distributed to large groups of people to allow some quantitative measure of the attitudes we thought we discerned in the informal interviews (section 1.4). Questionnaire A was short, asking people to write short answers in their own words. Questionnaire B was used to compare a random sample of people in the United States with professional economists, and questionnaire C was used for intergenerational and international comparisons. In section 1.5, the answers written by the respondents on questionnaire A are described. In section 1.6, the results about public concerns with inflation from questionnaires B and C are presented. The issues studied are the importance of inflation for the standard of living, why people think inflation affects their standard of living, other concerns besides the standard of living, psychological effects of inflation, concerns that opportunists use inflation to exploit others, morale issues, concerns about political and economic chaos caused by inflation, and concerns about national prestige and prestige of the currency. Differences are found across generations and across countries and between economists and noneconomists in some very basic assumptions about inflation. In section 1.7, further analyzing questionnaire B and C results, I discuss some general notions about the origins of public opinions about inflation and reasons why such opinions differ across groups of people. International as well as intergenerational differences in information about inflation are documented. Evidence is given of the importance of perceptions that expert opinion supports the public's concern with inflation, and of public beliefs that there is a social contract in which a commitment to fighting inflation is a requirement of all public figures. In section 1.8, I conclude, offering broad interpretations of the results. The appendix discusses sample design and survey methods.

1.2   Defining the Problem: The Study of Inflation in Popular Culture

The word "inflation" appears to be the most commonly used economic term among the general public. Table 1.1, column 1, shows how often the word has been used, in comparison with other economic terms, based on a computer search of news stories in the ALLNWS (all news) section of the Nexis system,

Table 1.1   **Number of Stories That Use Various Economic Terms on Nexis General News Search Facility, Level 1**

	ALLNWS	CURNWS (last 2 years)
Inflation	872,004	255,987
Unemployment	602,885	161,939
Productivity	376,775	103,507
Infrastructure	331,888	148,354
Economic growth	322,888	106,354
Poverty	316,995	114,190
Monopoly	231,370	72,103
Price index	179,911	50,278
Communism	150,000	35,139
Price increase	147,877	35,115
Money supply	104,498	24,005
Diversification	89,034	21,300
Consumer price index	74,054	21,096
Trade barriers	59,101	18,053
Risk management	46,979	19,646
Price level	38,086	8,130
National debt	37,771	11,818
Job opportunities	36,816	12,129
Industrial policy	24,316	5,433
Technological innovation	15,971	4,638
Public investment	15,946	5,137
Real interest rate	15,447	3,710
International competitiveness	15,170	3,949
Public goods	12,998	4,586
Economic efficiency	11,741	2,962
Deflation	11,584	3,141
Indexation	10,550	2,564
Productive capacity	9,263	1,988
Income distribution	7,884	2,171
Human capital	7,102	2,604
Price gouging	6,427	1,850
False advertising	6,219	1,851
Cost of living allowance	4,595	762
Market incentives	4,037	1,270
Index bonds	3,398	869
Externality	2,985	1,169
Potential output	1,353	449
American Economic Association	1,289	324
Game theory	1,292	551
Economics profession	1,136	271
National economic strategy	810	99
Real business cycle(s)	127	55
Indexed annuity	59	23

Source: Compiled by the author using the Nexis on-line service.

an electronic search system for English-language news publications (and including some broadcasts) around the world. The word "inflation" appeared in 872,004 stories, far outnumbering the stories containing any other economic term.[1] Only "unemployment" comes even close, with 602,885 stories. The term "inflation" even outranks the word "sex," for which Nexis ALLNWS produced only 662,920 stories.

At this time of relatively low inflation among most of the major countries of the world, "inflation" still appears to be the most commonly used economic term. The Nexis system, in its current news section CURNWS which covers the last two years only, still produced more stories using the word "inflation" than using any other economic term; see table 1.1, column 2.

Because the word "inflation" is so much a part of everyday lives, it has many associations and connotations to ordinary people. Moreover, because shopping, and thereby noticing prices, is an everyday activity for ordinary people, thinking about prices is also a major part of people's thinking, and the subject of inflation is one of great personal interest for most people.

Inflation, when it is substantial or shows the risk of becoming substantial, is clearly perceived as a national problem of enormous proportions. This fact is also evident in the constant attention that inflation is given in the media and in the fundamental role it plays in many political elections. News about inflation seems to have serious consequences for approval ratings of presidents and for outcomes of elections.[2] Public-opinion polls have shown that inflation (or something like inflation) has often been viewed as the most important national problem.[3]

The great public concern with inflation has certainly had an impact on the economics profession. We must ask whether the extent of public concern with inflation really makes sense, or whether the economics profession has been influenced from without into devoting too much attention to inflation.

Studying so complex a public concept as inflation will not be easy. To attempt to learn about it at some depth, I have followed here a sequential proce-

---

1. The coverage of the Nexis ALLNWS section gradually tapers off as one goes back in time; many publications are indexed back to the early 1970s. A search for the word "inflation" as an indicator of public interest in consumer price inflation carries some risk: the word has other uses as well. However, a sampling of the stories turned up by Nexis shows that the great majority of the stories using the word "inflation" are talking about the phenomenon of aggregate price increase. In a sample of one hundred stories, ninety-four referred to the phenomenon of aggregate price increase. Two referred to specific price inflation, such as land price inflation, but these stories also referred to aggregate inflation. Five of the one hundred referred to figures "adjusted for inflation," but did not specifically say anything about the phenomenon of inflation. One of the one hundred referred to the inflation of automobile air bags.

2. See Cartwright and DeLorme 1985; Parker 1986; Golden and Poterba 1980; Cuzan and Bundrick 1992; and Fair 1978, 1994.

3. The Gallup Poll has asked in the United States since 1935 "What do you think is the most important problem facing this country [or this section of the country] today?" Those citing inflation or the high cost of living as the most important problem have usually represented a significant percentage of respondents. The percentage was usually over 50% from 1973 to 1981, when inflation was higher than it is today.

dure, involving first informal conversations with people, allowing me and my students to use our judgment as much as possible, and then a questionnaire survey.

1.3   First Steps of This Study

I asked student research assistants to interview random people in the United States and Germany informally, with a list of suggested interview questions, and to give me their impressions; I interviewed some people as well. I then discussed with these students what people seemed to be saying.

When asked why they dislike inflation, people often protest that they are not experts, and they need to be prodded to respond. When they do respond, it is often with what seem to be incompletely thought-out ideas and vague associations about inflation, yet a conviction that inflation is important. Most people seemed to be vulnerable to fundamental confusions about inflation, and in spite of their convictions as to the importance of inflation, seemed not to have given really serious thought to it.

Several students came back to me independently of each other and told me, as a result of their interviews, that it was very easy to see why people dislike inflation: people think inflation erodes their standard of living. For example, my student Michael Krause, who interviewed in Germany, wrote:

> If you ask people in conversation why they think that people dislike infla-
> tion, everybody says it is because of the increase in the cost of living, the
> fall in real income. This is particularly relevant for those who live from
> pensions or social security transfers, where inflation corrections lag behind
> (at least when the inflation rate has unexpectedly increased). Several times
> I indicated that nominal incomes would be adjusted to inflation. It was said
> that it was uncertain that an adjustment would take place, or when it will
> take place, at least there is uncertainty about whether this adjustment would
> be sufficient.

Conducting these interviews inclined us to a hypothesis that the main issue for the public with regard to inflation is just that people do not see the connection between inflation and increases in income that might be associated with it. We must try to understand why people would think that there might be little connection between the inflation rate and the changes in their own income. Simple reflection on the mechanism of inflation suggests that there are likely to be many people who benefit from it, rather than harmed by it, but no one reported hearing an interviewee volunteer that he or she benefited from inflation. There is something of a puzzle here why the answers should so uniformly assume that inflation is harmful to the respondent.

Many other issues were also raised regarding inflation, issues that seemed to suggest concerns along very different lines. Some of these appear poten-tially very important too, even if people did not bring them up first in our conversations. These other concerns will be described below in the answers to various questions. They may even turn out to be the most important issues for policymakers' trying to decide whether or how much to fight inflation.

1.4   Questionnaire Design

To give quantitative force to our impressions about what people thought, various of their ideas were put into questionnaires, to be distributed to large samples of people who could indicate the extent of their agreement with these ideas.

I decided to use three questionnaires because there were too many questions to expect any one respondent to answer them all with patience and thought-fulness. Separating the questions into three questionnaires also gave us some opportunity to avoid suggesting ideas that might bias answers elsewhere in the same questionnaire.

Questionnaire A is very short and emphasizes open-ended questions where respondents are given space to write a paragraph to answer. The questionnaire, distributed to a random sample of people in the United States, is so short that it occupies both sides of a single sheet of paper; the text of this questionnaire is reproduced in section 1.5. We felt that people could not be expected to write thoughtful answers if the questionnaire were too long. By omitting from this questionnaire many of our other questions that we could not pose without putting ideas into their heads, we got some fairly pure responses. The disadvantage of this questionnaire is that, by not putting ideas into respondents' heads, we cannot influence what people will choose to talk about in their answers, and we may not learn what we want to learn from them.

Questionnaire B is longer, six pages, three sheets on both sides, with multiple-choice questions aimed at basic concepts and theories about inflation. This questionnaire was distributed both to a random sample in the United States and to economists, whose professional opinions were to be contrasted with those of the public.

Questionnaire C is another six-page questionnaire with multiple-choice questions. It contains questions to elicit intergenerational and international differences in attitudes toward inflation, and in public knowledge and popular ideas about inflation. Questionnaire C is the only one translated into foreign languages. It was distributed in the United States in English, in Germany in German, and in Brazil (with E-mail via Bras-net) in Portuguese.

Germany was selected because of its reputation as a country with extreme inflation aversion and low historical inflation rates. Brazil was selected as a country that has had a history of very high inflation and continues to have very high (by U.S. standards) inflation. The questionnaires included an age question; we tabulate results separately here for older people in the United States and Germany. There is a popular theory that those who experienced the troubles in Germany around World War II, or who were closer to the German hyperinflation of the early 1920s, are more troubled by inflation, and with these results we can confirm whether this is so.

Results from all of the questionnaires should be interpreted with some caution. There may be problems with translation; some of the words may be more loaded with meanings, or have different connotations, in the different languages. Although we used the back-translation method to produce nearly identical questionnaires in English and German, there are still potential problems.[4] Moreover, apart from the translation problem, the questions often have multiple interpretations, as indicated by some of the comments written on the questionnaires. One should be cautious in interpreting apparent public agreement with a statement made on the questionnaire; people might agree to a lot of things that are not really in their own minds, if in reading them they merely like the sound of them.

There are also issues of selection bias in our answers: we have responses only from those who chose to answer. The selection-bias issues are perhaps most important with questions about how important inflation is (people who think inflation is important are more likely to fill out the questionnaire) and with questions about the extent of public information (people who know more about inflation are more likely to fill out the questionnaire). Selection bias is likely to be most extreme with our Brazil results, since the Brazil survey was conducted using E-mail, whose users tend to be young and, presumably, sophisticated; often they are students and faculty currently living outside of Brazil. Time and budget constraints prevented our doing a mail survey to a random sample in Brazil; it was decided to accept the higher risk of selection bias rather than have no results from Brazil at all. I will indicate the places where I am particularly concerned with issues of interpretation and of selection bias, but the reader is encouraged to keep these issues in mind at all times in judging the results.

The standard errors of the sample proportions should also be kept in mind, so that small differences in answers are not overinterpreted. Recall that the standard error for a sample proportion equal to 0.5 is, with one hundred observations, 0.050, and with fifty observations, 0.071; the standard error for a sample proportion equal to 0.9 or 0.1 is, with one hundred observations, 0.030, and with fifty observations, 0.042. Sample size here is generally clearly adequate for broad statements about proportions, though we should not make much of a difference, for example, between proportions of 0.5 in one sample and 0.6 in another.

---

4. The questionnaire was first written in English. When translating it into German, if difficulties in conveying the precise meaning with similar wordings arose, the question was rewritten in German, and then back-translated into English. The process was iterated until we felt we had identical questionnaires in the two languages. The attentive reader may discern some subtle word oddities in the English versions of the questions that arose in this way. The Portuguese version was produced directly from the English questionnaire, without back-translation.

1.5   Results with the Short Open-Ended Questionnaire (Questionnaire A)

Text of Questionnaire A, with Results of 120 Questionnaires in Brackets

Questionnaire: Opinions on Inflation

This is a questionnaire about your views on inflation. By inflation, we mean a steady increase of the average of all prices, and thus of the price level.

A1. Do you think that controlling inflation should be a high priority for the US government and its agencies?

[Circle one number]

1. Yes, strongly agree	[59%]	[*n*=118]
2. Yes, agree somewhat	[33%]	
3. Neutral or no opinion	[1%]	
4. No, disagree somewhat	[4%]	
5. No, strongly disagree	[3%]	

A2. Do you find, when you hear or see news stories about inflation, that you personally find these stories interesting?

[Circle one number]

1. Yes, very interesting	[47%]	[*n*=119]
2. Yes, somewhat interesting	[42%]	
3. No or no opinion	[11%]	

A3. Some people think that news about inflation is boring technical stuff, that they can't relate to. Can you explain to them why they should find it interesting?

[space for answer]

A4. Do you have worries that if inflation rises too high, then something really bad might happen?

[Circle one number]

1. Yes, very much	[47%]	[*n*=118]
2. Yes, somewhat	[43%]	
3. No or no opinion	[10%]	

A5. If you answered yes to the above, what are you worried might happen?

[space for answer]

A6. When inflation gets very high, what do you think is the reason?

[space for answer]

A7. When you go to the store and see that prices are higher, do you sometimes feel a little angry at someone?

[Circle one number]

1. Yes, often	[38%]	[$n=120$]
2. Yes, sometimes	[48%]	
3. Never	[15%]	

A8. [If you said yes above] Who do you tend to feel angry at and why?

[space for answer]

A9. Think about how much your income (measured in dollars per month) went up (or down) in the past five years. What do you think are the most important factors that account for the change in your income? (Please try to list all the relevant factors that apply to you):

[space for answer]

Income went 1. up	[53%]	
2. down	[47%]	[$n=94$]

A10. Try to imagine how things would be different if the United States had experienced higher inflation over the last five years, so that prices of things you buy had risen to higher levels than we actually see today. How different do you think your income (the total dollars you earn in a month) would be now, in comparison with your actual income now, if we had had the higher inflation?

[Circle one number]

[$n=114$]

1. My income (in dollars per month) would be lower.   [28%]
2. My income (in dollars per month) would be about the same.   [35%]
3. My income (in dollars per month) would be higher.   [31%]
4. No opinion   [6%]

Thank you very much. Please return this questionnaire to Prof. Robert Shiller, Cowles Foundation for Research in Economics, Yale University, Box 208281, New Haven, CT 06520-8281   Reference Number _____

The short open-ended questionnaire distributed only in the United States seems to have succeeded in encouraging participants to give their concerns about inflation without imposing much structure on their answers; people often wrote a lot. Often there were substantial essays crammed onto the page, and reading responses does seem to convey a picture of how people think about inflation. The answers to multiple-choice questions are tabulated in the questionnaire, but the written answers, which can only be described incompletely here, are perhaps more significant.

The results appear to confirm that most people think that inflation is an important national policy issue: 92% strongly agreed or agreed somewhat in question A1. Moreover, people report that they are interested in news reports on inflation: 89% chose "very interesting" or "somewhat interesting" (question A2). Of course, these results must be discounted somewhat, since there is likely a selection bias at work here: people who are more interested in inflation are more likely to fill out the questionnaire.

What is perhaps most significant are the reasons people give for being interested in inflation news, question A3. They seem most often to be saying that they are interested in inflation because they think it hurts their standard of living, although they were usually not completely clear. I divided the answers (from the 105 people who answered this question) into five categories: (1) those who seemed to be trying to say directly that inflation hurts their standard of living (33%), (2) those who referred to the fact that inflation lowers the buying power of the dollar (responding essentially with the definition of inflation; 23%), (3) those who said just that inflation is something one must know for planning and budget purposes (8%), (4) those who said that inflation hurts the economy in general (10%), and (5) those who stated only that inflation was important without giving reasons or who wrote something that was tangential to the question (26%).

Here are some excerpts from answers to question A3 that I categorized as asserting that inflation hurts people's standard of living, category 1.

It affects their life and lifestyle.

Inflation governs the way we live. It's simple: raise the prices, get less for your money.

Every individual is personally affected in his lifestyle, comfort, health, etc., by whatever is happening about inflation. How can they not be interesting?

Inflation can rob a person of income.

Their saving for retirement and college fund for their children will be evaporated when they need them the most.

Inflation has a strong impact on an individual's pocketbook and on one's standard of living.

As a retired senior citizen, inflation has most definitely lowered my purchasing power.

It affects everyone's standard of living and their lives.

Because it is directly related to their income.

Because it affects the wages they receive and the price they pay for houses, cars, groceries and everything else they buy. In short, it affects their standard of living.

Our very being depends on this.

Right now it is killing US.

Here are some excerpts from answers to question A3 that I put in category 2, as asserting little more than that inflation lowers the buying power of the dollar.

Inflation reflects everyday prices of all goods, services, and products.

I have a simple statement: inflation is directly related to your pocketbook.

Although these answers are sometimes perhaps nothing more than re-statements of the definition of inflation, it would seem that these statements, entered in answer to a question why inflation news is interesting, suggest that the respondent feels that inflation erodes his or her income. That this is the meaning of these statements is suggested by the answers in category 1 that include sentences like these as well.

It is possible, on the other hand, that not all of the category 2 answers imply that the standard of living is generally eroded by inflation, only that one must be knowledgeable about it to live within a budget. There were a few answers that seemed to say that knowing the inflation rate is helpful in planning, category 3. Here are some excerpts from these answers to question A3.

Inflation rate is a gauge to measure the value of today's dollar against its value in time to come, and also, the true return on investments. It is necessary knowledge in future planning.

Inflation is the barometer for your pocketbook. Certainly, it is important in gauging your spending. I would explain that inflation or deflation affects your spending and savings directly. Therefore, you should know the inflation rate at all times.

People need to learn fast due to economic world change rapidly and it is the most keen fact that influences their own life. Just makes it easier to understand.

Here are some answers to question A3 that I categorized as suggesting systemic problems of inflation, more than just the direct effect of higher prices on their ability to buy, category 4.

It is an indicator of future events to occur economically.

The stability of the economy is important, as it facilitates one's ability to buy and save. A stable economy encourages investment and growth.

There were, however, few such answers.

The impression that people are worried about the effects of inflation on their standard of living is further supported by their responses to questions A4 and A5. In answering question A4, whether they are worried that something really bad might happen if inflation rises too high, 90% said "yes, very much" or "yes, somewhat." What is striking is the dramatic nature of some of the answers to the following question about just what might happen. The most common answers concerned fears of depression and/or a dramatic drop in overall standard of living.

That I, and millions like me, will be forced into poverty—perhaps not like the "great depression," but close.

If inflation rises too high, more people will be forced to seek assistance, e.g., welfare, food stamps, charity, etc.

We wouldn't be able to afford anything. Our wages wouldn't be high enough.

I will not be able to live within my weekly paycheck.

There will be more homeless and starving people.

A few reported fears of political instability.

1. Political nightmare, 2. riot, 3. big incidents.

Hyperinflation can cause governments to fall and individuals' savings may be lost causing chaos throughout the land.

A few reported general fears of damage to the economy.

High inflation affects all aspects of business and investing. It is unhealthy for business, failures will result.

If too high the economy would collapse.

A financial collapse, followed by a depression.

A few seemed to refer to the effects on their pension checks or other investments.

I will not have enough money to manage my older years independently.

Buying power in retirement might be significantly reduced at a point where a relatively fixed income would occur.

People on fixed incomes would be hard pressed to meet mortgage payments or car payments or even rent.

A few spoke of changes in the income distribution.

Increase in people with high levels of income. Decrease in number of people in middle-class levels of income. Increase in number of people in poverty levels of income.

That the gap between the rich and the poor will become so great that there will no longer be a middle income group or even the potential of one.

Answers to question A6, asking people to list the causes of inflation, reveal that people haven't any clear sense what is causing inflation; there are very many different factors that they think might be responsible. The most common cause cited was greed. The word "greed" or "greedy" was volunteered by 17 (16%) of the respondents. There were also a lot of nonspecific references to the government as a cause (16 respondents). The next most commonly mentioned cause was that people borrow or spend too much (11), and after that the Federal Reserve and interest rates (10), big business and corporate profits (9), followed by the money-supply increase (8), government deficit (7), politicians in general (5), high demand (4), and welfare (3). Causes cited by 1 or 2 respondents each included cost increases, lack of price controls or regulation, the dollar decline, unemployment, lack of saving by the public, hoarding of goods, the shrinking middle class, the rest of the world, shortages, labor unions, management caving in to wage demands, taxes too high, fraud and corruption, over-confidence in the continuing inflation, balance of payments, corporate executives overpaid, Republicans in power, and just plain stupidity.[5]

While people appear to be in great disagreement why inflation occurs, they do tend nonetheless to be angry at someone when they see prices rise: in answer to question A7, 38% reported feeling angry often, and an additional 48% reported feeling angry sometimes. There was little agreement on the answer to question A8, on who they are angry at. The government was mentioned by 18 respondents, manufacturers by 15, store owners by 6, business in general by 6, wholesalers by 4, executives by 3, the U.S. Congress by 3, and greedy people by 3. Also mentioned were institutions, economists, retailers, distributors, middlemen, conglomerates, the president of the United States, the Democratic Party, big-money people, store employees (for wage demands), "my employer" (for not increasing my salary), and myself (for being ignorant of matters).

Question A9, in which the respondent is asked to list all relevant factors in explaining how his or her income changed in the last five years, was inspired by Katona's report (1975, 140) that people tend to see the causes of their income increases in personal terms, rather than as due to inflation: "survey respondents with gains in income were asked the puzzling question, 'How come that you make more than five years ago?' In reply most people spoke of their own accomplishments and progress. Only a very small proportion of people referred to inflation." Question A9 was included to see if we could confirm his report, but we were operating under a handicap in doing so at the end of this questionnaire: the question is asked following eight questions about inflation, which surely ought to put the idea of inflation in people's minds. Still, only 16 of 47 who wrote an answer, 34%, mentioned inflation, which seems an important omission in a five-year period when prices went up 13%. Of course, it is probably true that for most people the most important factor accounting for income change in this interval was not inflation, and the tendency for most people to omit it as among the leading factors might be forgiven.

What is more striking are the answers to the hypothetical in question A10, about what would have happened to incomes had there been more inflation. People seem to have no idea: answers are about equally distributed among the three possibilities, income would be lower, about the same, or higher. From the answers to this question, it would appear that there is practically no recognition of a response of income to inflation, and thus there would appear to be a strong presumption that inflation hurts real incomes.

It is worthwhile noting what was *not* mentioned, or only rarely mentioned, on a questionnaire that gave plenty of space for people to write open-ended answers. Not a single respondent volunteered anywhere on the questionnaire that he or she benefited from inflation. There was little mention of nominal contracts; only four respondents mentioned these. There was little mention of the fact that inflation redistributes income from creditors to debtors; only one

---

5. Katona (1975) also concluded that the public has no clear ideas as to the causes of inflation.

respondent clearly stated this. Not a single respondent clearly mentioned the inconveniences created by inflation, such as making more trips to the bank.

1.6   Public Concerns with Inflation: Results from Questionnaires B and C

1.6.1   Confirmation of Importance of Inflation and Its Effects on Standards of Living

Answers to some of the questions on questionnaire B (distributed to randomly selected people in the United States and to economists) and questionnaire C (distributed to randomly selected people in the United States and Germany, and via E-mail in Brazil) confirm the central importance in public perceptions of inflation and of the standard-of-living concern. These closed-end questionnaires give more precise description of our conclusions, since the wording of the answers is the same for everyone, and allows accurate comparisons across groups.

The respondents in all three countries, and among both the younger and the older in the United States and Germany, were very concerned with inflation.[6]

C1. Do you agree with the following statement? "The control of inflation is one of the most important missions of US [German, Brazilian] economic policy."

	1 Fully agree	2	3 Undecided	4	5 Completely disagree	
US all	56%	28%	7%	7%	2%	$n=123$
Born < 1940	69%	13%	11%	4%	2%	$n=45$
Born > 1950	44%	38%	2%	13%	2%	$n=45$
Germany all	76%	18%	5%	1%	0%	$n=174$
Born < 1940	90%	8%	1%	1%	0%	$n=77$
Born > 1950	51%	40%	7%	2%	0%	$n=55$
Brazil	56%	32%	2%	4%	7%	$n=57$

Concern with inflation is high everywhere. The Germans tend to agree with this statement more often than the others, but it is striking that no group of respondents chose 1 or 2 less than 80% of the time.[7] The older people (born

---

6. Words in brackets in the questions shown here are the word corresponding to the country of the respondent.

7. The breakdown of categories by birth year was chosen so that the older group would be people who clearly experienced World War II and the post–World War II inflation in Germany,

before 1940) were more likely to agree fully than the younger people (born in 1950 or later). The differences between German and U.S. respondents are much stronger for the older group than for the younger group; this is a pattern that recurs in answers to other questions below. Note that our Brazilian sample of E-mail users is approximately comparable in age to our younger group: 91% of our Brazilian respondents were born in 1950 or later. There is not a large difference between the Brazilians and the younger German or U.S. respondents in answers to this question.

Another way to gauge public concern with inflation, and to see whether there are international differences in this concern, is to ask people whether they would accept inflation if it were necessary in order to curb unemployment, that is, to ask them how they would choose between two points on a Phillips curve. The question presumes the existence of a Phillips curve trade-off, and so is asking directly about preferences with regard to inflation and unemployment.

> C8. Imagine that you faced a choice for the United States [Germany, Brazil] between the following two extreme possibilities, which would you choose?
>
> 1. The US [Germany, Brazil] would have in the next 10 years an inflation rate of only 2% a year, but an unemployment rate of 9%, thus about 12 million [3.5 million, 6 million] unemployed.
>
> 2. The US [Germany, Brazil] would have in the next ten years an inflation rate of 10% a month, but an unemployment rate of only 3%, thus about 4 million [1.2 million, 2 million] unemployed.

	1	2	
U.S. all	75%	25%	$n=113$
Born < 1940	79%	21%	$n=38$
Born ≥ 1950	72%	28%	$n=43$
Germany all	72%	28%	$n=153$
Born < 1940	66%	34%	$n=65$
Born ≥ 1950	84%	16%	$n=49$
Brazil	54%	46%	$n=50$

The results show that most people in all countries would choose low inflation even if it meant that millions more people would be unemployed. The Brazilians more often choose 2 than people in other countries, possibly since having lived through it they have learned ways of enduring it, and possibly since Brazil does not have as developed a social safety net for the unemployed. But there

---

and the younger group would be people who are clearly postwar and would not remember the inflation. People born in the 1940s were excluded from either group, but included in the figures from the "All" group, along with people who refused to reveal their age on the questionnaire.

is less difference across countries in answers to this question than I expected. There is little difference between the German and U.S. respondents overall, and so the popular theory that Germans have a greater distaste for inflation is not confirmed here. The difference between the age groups within Germany is much bigger than the difference overall between Germany and the United States. The absence of a large difference between the German and U.S. respondents suggests that the differences between the two countries might be more in their understandings of the unemployment consequences of inflation, rather than differences in pure preferences regarding inflation.

While the general public appears to dislike inflation everywhere, results from questionnaire B show that economists do not generally agree.

B1. Do you agree that preventing high inflation is an important national priority, as important as preventing drug abuse or preventing deterioration in the quality of our schools?

	1 Fully agree	2	3 Undecided	4	5 Completely disagree	
U.S. all	52%	32%	4%	8%	4%	n=117
Economists	18%	28%	11%	26%	18%	n=80

The fraction of our U.S. respondents who fully agreed was nearly three times as high as the fraction of economists who fully agreed. This question also shows some indication of the magnitude of the public concern with inflation; with about half of the public choosing 1, one might say that the problem of high inflation appears to be viewed by the public (though not by economists) as on par with the drug problem or the problems of our schools.

In confirming that people think that inflation is a very important issue, it is helpful to see whether people see the inflation process, the surprise in inflation, as causing a problem, or the effects of the new price level itself. One way of giving information on this is to ask people if they would like to go back to earlier prices if they could.

B18. Do you agree with the following statement? "If the government were to make a mistake next year, such as printing too much money, and created prices that are 20% higher than they are today, I think that they should try to reverse their mistake, and bring prices back down where they are today."

	1 Fully agree	2	3 Undecided	4	5 Completely disagree	
U.S. all	46%	22%	22%	4%	6%	n=113
Economists	0%	3%	5%	28%	64%	n=76

There is here a very sharp difference between the economists' answers and the public's: the public seems to be at odds with the fundamental economists' notion that we should accept base drift in the price level.

Why is there such a difference between the economics profession and the general public about the importance of inflation or price level changes? The general public in the United States clearly thinks differently from professional economists about the costs of inflation, and are far more likely to think of inflation as lowering standard of living.

B9. Which of the following comes closer to your biggest gripe about inflation:

1. Inflation causes a lot of inconveniences: I find it harder to comparison shop, I feel I have to avoid holding too much cash, etc.

2. Inflation hurts my real buying power, it makes me poorer.

3. Other _____

	1	2	3	
U.S. all	7%	77%	15%	$n=110$
Economists	49%	12%	40%	$n=78$

Over six times as many in the general public chose 2, that inflation hurts real buying power, indicating that economists think in very different terms about inflation. One may conjecture that the favored answer from economists here reflects concerns about the process of inflation, the frictions that accompany it, rather than the change in the price level itself, while the favored answer from the general public would reflect suffering caused by the new higher price level in the face of fixed nominal incomes.

Consistent with this popular impression that inflation hurts standard of living, the general public tends to see inflation as hurting most people, while economists see about 50% as being hurt (50% would be the fraction hurt if inflation caused a random redistribution of income among people).[8]

B5. What percent of the population do you think is hurt when there is sudden, unexpected, high inflation?

_____%

U.S. all	69% (mean)	$n=108$
Economists	48%	$n=73$

The majority among the general public in all the countries studied here except Brazil fully agree that high inflation can reduce the growth and economic progress of a country.

C11. Do you agree with the following statement? "Inflation rates over 30% to 40% a year can reduce the growth and economic progress of a country, especially in comparison with countries where inflation is under 5% a year."

---

8. Katona (1975) tabulated a similar question to the general public.

	1 Fully agree	2	3 Undecided	4	5 Completely disagree	
U.S. all	57%	30%	7%	3%	3%	$n=122$
Born <1940	67%	24%	7%	0%	2%	$n=45$
Born ≥1950	48%	34%	9%	5%	5%	$n=44$
Germany all	69%	19%	9%	1%	1%	$n=173$
Born <1940	78%	11%	9%	0%	3%	$n=76$
Born ≥1950	60%	33%	5%	2%	0%	$n=55$
Brazil	40%	28%	12%	9%	11%	$n=57$

Note that the opinion that inflation harms economic growth is weakest among the Brazilians, but even among the Brazilians, 68% chose either 1 or 2.[9] Full agreement with this statement is a little higher for the German than the U.S. respondents, and higher for older people in both countries.

1.6.2 Why Do People Think Inflation Hurts Their Standard of Living?

To understand why the general public thinks inflation hurts their standard of living, let us first recognize that we cannot get a good understanding until we learn what people think causes inflation. Inflation is best regarded as an endogenous variable, which reflects a number of causal forces just as does the standard of living, and so we may not view inflation as itself the ultimate cause of anything.

We saw from our questionnaire A results that people cite a wide variety of causes of inflation, no single cause. Although the disagreement about the causes of inflation seemed to be so high that it is difficult to make any general statement about what people are thinking, the public often seemed ready to put down inflation as caused by bad behaviors, motivated by greed or other low impulse. Respondents described inflation as caused by big businesses pursuing profits, the Fed erroneously increasing the money supply, people borrowing or spending too much, the politicians letting the government deficit get out of hand. If there is any common story about causes of inflation among many of these people, it would seem to be that the causes are tied up with people's

---

9. In a pilot study for this paper, as part of another survey of a random sample of U.S. institutional money managers in the spring of 1995, I asked: "What effect do you think a strongly and steadily inflationary national policy would have on long-run economic growth? Please answer by writing in the change in the growth rate of U.S. Gross Domestic Product (GDP) that would accrue if we allowed the consumer price index inflation rate to rise above 10% and left it above 10% for a long time. If you think that real economic growth would be x% less per year, write $-x\%$. If you think that real income growth would be x% more per year, write $+x\%$. If you think that there would be no change, write 0: Change in annual real GDP growth rate:——%" There were seventy-five respondents to this question; the median answer was -2%. Thus, this sample of people expected that inflation can have very serious impact on growth.

acting badly. There is a tone of moral indignation when people tell of businesses trying too hard to pursue profits, the Fed behaving stupidly, people trying to live above their means, or politicians trying too hard to get reelected. It is important to realize this, since some economists have speculated that when people speak of inflation they mean nothing more than the decline of the standard of living itself, such as might have been caused by a negative technology shock or an oil price increase. I should admit, though, that my conclusion about the nature of these causes is due to my rather subjective interpretation of written answers.

But, if we accept this interpretation of the public's ideas about causes of inflation, why do people think that inflationary shocks from these causes hurt their standard of living? Perhaps their thinking arises from an observed correlation, that inflation tends to come at times when other factors are harming their standard of living, and so people are influenced by the perceived correlation between inflation and their problems. The oil price shocks of 1973 and 1979 apparently precipitated both inflation and recession and occurred when the uptrend of productivity was ending in many countries, yet people may not remember the oil price shock as a cause, thinking instead of the inflation. The German hyperinflation of the early 1920s, an event widely alleged to have shaped German public opinion regarding inflation, occurred at a time of heavy reparation payments, as the German government resorted to inflationary finance to make the reparation payments, and Germans may have confused the lowered standard of living due to the export of real resources as reparations with a consequence of inflation itself.

But any such impressions as to correlations between inflation and other economic variables would not translate well into impressions of causality from inflation to the other variables were there not some kind of model, some kind of story, that inclines people to see inflation as causing declines in living standards. Some clues as to the nature of such popular stories or, let us say, popular models of the economy, emerged from our discussions with people, and led us to formulate questions about them.

An important factor that emerged from our conversations is that most people seem to fail to think of the models that come naturally to economists about the competitive pressures that shape their wages and salaries; they tend to see any feedback of inflation on wages and salaries as working through the goodwill (or lack thereof) of their employer. This was confirmed by the answers to question B12.

> B12. Please evaluate which of the following theories about the effects of general inflation on wages or salary relates to your own experience and your own job: [Circle one number]
>
> 1. The price increase will create extra profits for my employer who can now sell output for more; there will be no effect on my pay. My employer will see no reason to raise my pay.

2. Competition among employers will cause my pay to be bid up. I could get outside offers from other employers, and so, to keep me, my employer will have to raise my pay too.

3. A sense of fairness and proper behavior will cause my employer to raise my pay.

4. None of the above or no opinion.

	1	2	3	4	
U.S. all	26%	11%	21%	43%	$n=112$
Economists	4%	60%	11%	25%	$n=75$

Only 11% of the U.S. respondents chose 2, that, in effect, market forces will cause a raise in pay, while 60% of the economists chose this.

People do not tend to see inflation as a process that naturally tends to affect wages and salaries as well as goods prices. In one of our conversations, a respondent said she always had deep worries about real income after hearing some long-term projection of prices. I thought that economists probably have a very different perspective on the significance of such long-term projections, and the comparison of the public with economists on question B6 bears this out.

B6. Do you agree with the following statement? "When I see projections about how many times more a college education will cost, or how many times more the costs of living will be in coming decades, I feel a sense of uneasiness; these inflation projections really make me worry that my own income will not rise as much as such costs will."

	1 Fully agree	2	3 Undecided	4	5 Completely disagree	
U.S. all	66%	20%	7%	6%	1%	$n=116$
Economists	5%	15%	9%	30%	41%	$n=80$

It is hard to imagine a more striking difference between two groups of respondents than we observe here: only 5% of the economists agreed fully with this statement, while 66% of the U.S. respondents did.

The tendency of economists to see a much more tenuous connection between inflation and the development of real wages led me to suppose that economists would tend much more than the public to agree in question B7.

B7. Do you agree with the following statement? "Inflation is a sort of units of measurement thing and little more: the dollar is a yardstick by which we measure value, and the length of this yardstick (value of the dollar) is changing through time. All we have to do is make sure we are taking full account of the length of the yardstick, and inflation will have little effect on us."

	1 Fully agree	2	3 Undecided	4	5 Completely disagree	
U.S. all	12%	8%	32%	20%	27%	$n=114$
Economists	23%	28%	6%	27%	15%	$n=78$

Over half the economists chose 1 or 2 here, while only 20% of the public did.

A similar question was asked on questionnaire C, to allow international comparisons of the notion that inflation is expected to be corrected.

C5. Do you agree with the following statement? "It makes no sense to pay attention to the development of the inflation rate, because a pretty accurate inflation correction in my income is to be expected anyway."

	1 Fully agree	2	3 Undecided	4	5 Completely disagree	
U.S. all	2%	1%	3%	30%	65%	$n=122$
Born <1940	5%	0%	5%	30%	61%	$n=44$
Born ≥1950	0%	2%	2%	20%	75%	$n=44$
Germany all	5%	4%	11%	11%	69%	$n=169$
Born <1940	7%	5%	14%	7%	68%	$n=74$
Born ≥1950	2%	0%	9%	13%	76%	$n=54$
Brazil	0%	0%	5%	25%	70%	$n=57$

There is a striking tendency to disagree that inflation corrections can be expected in all countries sampled.

People tend to think that their income may not be corrected for inflation, at least for many years.

C6. Imagine that next year the inflation rate unexpectedly doubles. How long would it probably take, in these times, before your income is increased enough so that you can afford the same things as you do today? In other words, how long will it be before a full inflation correction in your income has taken place? [Please mark only one answer.]

1 ____ Up to a month
2 ____ Until the next negotiation with my employer within a year
3 ____ Several years
4 ____ Never will be restored
5 ____ Do not know

	1	2	3	4	5	
U.S. all	0%	7%	39%	42%	11%	$n=123$
Born <1940	0%	2%	36%	48%	14%	$n=44$
Born ≥1950	0%	11%	44%	33%	11%	$n=45$
Germany all	0%	8%	40%	40%	12%	$n=171$
Born <1940	0%	8%	41%	35%	16%	$n=74$
Born ≥1950	0%	5%	40%	42%	13%	$n=55$
Brazil	2%	19%	17%	28%	34%	$n=53$

Over three-quarters of respondents in all groups in both the United States and Germany chose 3 or 4, that it will take years for real income to be restored or that it will never be restored. Even in Brazil, with its indexation, 45% chose 3 or 4.

Of course, the hypothetical question asked here—concerning a sudden change in the inflation rate—raises difficult intertemporal issues that a careful answerer might find challenging. In fact, the inflation rate is changing all the time, and it would seem that there must be times when there is no inflation but wages are increasing to catch up to past inflation, so that wages may be increasing because of inflation even when there is no inflation. The public probably lacks the quantitative skills to model the response of their pay to inflation, which economists might cast in terms of distributed lags or the like. There may be little to be gained by trying different versions of this question, with different hypothetical time paths of inflation, since the public cannot easily answer any such questions, beyond just giving some vague impressions that the pay will substantially fall behind.

The notion that wages lag behind prices is very old: as early as 1895 it was stated that "the prices of what wage earners have to buy respond far more promptly to changes in the quantity of money than do wages—the prices at which labor is sold. Hence, whenever money is getting better, though nominal wages may tend to decrease, wage earners are constantly getting more goods in exchange for the money they actually get for their labor; and whenever money is getting poorer, though nominal wages may tend to increase, wage earners are constantly getting less of the necessaries and comforts of life in return for the wages they receive."[10] General Domingo Perón, the Argentinean populist dictator, had a colorful way of describing this hypothesis: "Until now, prices have gone up on the elevator, and wages have had to use the stairs" (quoted in Cavallo 1983, 318). (He sought to reverse the situation.)

Whether this wage-lag hypothesis is valid was the subject of discussion of many economists in the early to midpart of this century; the outcome of the discussion was essentially that there was no evidence for the hypothesis. Claims for evidence in support of the wage-lag hypothesis were vigorously challenged by Alchian and Kessel (1960) and Cargill (1969). Bach and Stephenson (1974) found that periods of higher inflation in 1950–71 tended to be periods when wages as a share of national income *rose,* rather than fell. Of course, the general public cannot be expected to know of this research.

Most professional economists today are probably well aware from experience that it is difficult to estimate the lag of incomes on prices from the data, and are likely to imagine that actual relations are complicated and elusive. Economists are familiar with long time-series plots showing the consumer price index and other nominal series marching up through the years in seeming tandem. We are accustomed to expecting that, over long time periods of substantial inflation as economists define it, other things equal, any nominal series

10. John De Witt Warner, *Sound Currency,* October 1, 1895.

would move overall pretty much like the aggregate price level. The general public has not had much experience of studying time-series economic data.

One notion that we thought that we discerned among some of the people we talked with is some idea that people will always be behind when there is inflation, because their wages are fair only in the time of the year when their wages are set, and that they will fall behind within the year. We had great difficulty in formalizing this into a question that people would understand, but did include the following on questionnaire B:

B13. Think about times when your income for next year is decided by your employer (or your last employer, if you are no longer employed). Which of the following do you think is closer to what your employer does:

1. "I think that my employer has in mind, to the extent that fairness is a consideration, making my wage higher at the beginning than would seem fair and equitable, in comparison with prices and other people's wages, to allow for the fact that prices and other people's wages will rise through the year due to inflation, in order that my wage is still reasonably fair and equitable later in the year."

2. "I think that my employer has in mind, to the extent that fairness is a consideration, making my wage fair and equitable at the beginning of the year, despite the fact that inflation will make it compare somewhat unfavorably later in the year."

3. Neither or no opinion.

	1	2	3	
U.S. all	12%	26%	62%	$n=110$
Economists	14%	30%	55%	$n=76$

Most of the responses were "neither or no opinion," but there is a suggestion that our impressions from our conversations were right, since of those who did answer the question, most chose 2 over 1, meaning that they think that they have a fair wage only at the time of the year when wages are set. The implication is that higher inflation means real wages will be on average less fair.

1.6.3 It's Not Just Standard of Living: Other Important Concerns about Inflation

The results until now suggest that the public is concerned with inflation primarily because of its presumed effect on their standard of living, and that this concern is substantially due to ill-conceived ideas of the lagged effects of inflation on wages and salaries. But there appear to be many more concerns than just such effects of inflation on real income.

That there are other important concerns is shown by the answer to question B2, which immediately followed question B1 about whether preventing inflation is as important a national priority as preventing drug abuse or preventing deterioration in the quality of our schools.

B2. (If you circled 1 or 2 in the preceding question) Would you still agree if the type of inflation being prevented caused incomes to rise at the same rate as prices, so that the inflation would have no effect on living standards?

1. Yes, I would still agree in the preceding question.

2. No, I would disagree in the preceding question.

	1	2	
U.S. all	65%	35%	$n=98$
Economists	63%	37%	$n=38$

Most of the public, and the economists, agree that preventing inflation would still be such an important national priority.

It is interesting, too, that when presented with a similar pair of questions about unemployment, we get analogous responses.

B3. Do you agree that preventing economic recessions (times of high unemployment and low sales for business) is an important national priority, as important as preventing drug abuse or preventing deterioration in the quality of our schools?

	1 Fully agree	2	3 Undecided	4	5 Completely disagree	
U.S. all	55%	25%	8%	8%	4%	$n=114$
Economists	38%	38%	8%	15%	3%	$n=80$

B4. (If you circled 1 or 2 in the preceding question) Would you still agree if you were told that the method of preventing economic recessions had an absolutely equal impact on economic booms (times with lots of job opportunities, and lots of sales for firms), preventing really good times just as much as it prevented really bad times?

1. Yes, I would still agree in the preceding question.

2. No, I would disagree in the preceding question.

	1	2	
U.S. all	83%	17%	$n=92$
Economists	84%	16%	$n=56$

We had conjectured that most public desire for economic stabilization policy was formed from an impression that such policy can promote a higher average level of income, and we thought that most of the public would not agree on B4. However, both economists and the general public are generally supportive of stabilization policy that is just that, preventing really good times just as much as really bad times.

Answers to another question reveal that a substantial minority of the public (though not economists) would like to see inflation contained even if it meant a major reduction in economic growth.

B11. Do you agree with the following statement? "Keeping inflation low is so high a priority that I would not like to see a national policy that caused the inflation rate to double from where it is today even if that policy were sure to double the real (inflation-corrected) growth rate of the economy."

	1 Fully agree	2	3 Undecided	4	5 Completely disagree	
U.S. all	21%	15%	38%	18%	10%	$n=114$
Economists	4%	3%	5%	17%	71%	$n=79$

If there are other concerns about the effects of inflation than just the effects on real incomes, what are they? The other concerns explored here are the psychological effects of inflation, the use of inflation by opportunists to take advantage of others, the moral and morale effects of inflation, the effects of inflation on political stability, and the effects of inflation and currency depreciation on national prestige.

1.6.4   Psychological Effects of Inflation

Shafir, Diamond, and Tversky (1997), based on experimental evidence of various sorts, found that people seemed to base their sense of satisfaction in their earnings partly on nominal earnings, rather than just on real earnings. This is a form of "money illusion." I tried to replicate their results in a very unsubtle way, that of merely asking people directly about the Shafir-Diamond-Tversky premise. If people answered as if they were unaware of such an effect, it would not be evidence contrary to their premise; such feelings may be subconscious or difficult to express. However, people (excluding economists) did not report that they were unaware of such feelings.

B17. Do you agree with the following statement? "I think that if my pay went up I would feel more satisfaction in my job, more sense of fulfillment, even if prices went up just as much."

	1 Fully agree	2	3 Undecided	4	5 Completely disagree	
U.S. all	28%	21%	11%	14%	27%	$n=112$
Economists	0%	8%	3%	13%	77%	$n=79$

The public's answers here are spread all over the range from 1 to 5, but one might say that the fact that about half of the U.S. sample picked 1 or 2 reveals some perceived benefits of inflation, rather than costs.[11] But connected with this feeling there may be some perception that the apparent satisfaction is illusory or the result of tricks. "Inflation is like a narcotic. For a while it puts us in a high mood, glorifies the world, and helps us forget our problems, but an awakening follows inevitably" (Karl Schiller, 1970).[12] This leads us to consider

11. Consistent with this interpretation of the answers to B17, it has been found that consumption expenditures respond positively to inflation; see Branson and Klevorick 1969.
12. Gemeinschaft zum Schutz der deutschen Sparer 1990, 21, our translation. Schiller was German economics minister, 1967–72, and finance minister, 1971–72, and was architect of the *Stabilitätsgesetz* (stabilization law) 1967.

the possibility that there is some concern among the public that inflation is a sort of deception, or that it facilitates deception by some people.

1.6.5   The Use of Inflation by Opportunists to Exploit Others

Popular discussions suggest that people apparently dislike inflation because it enables people to play tricks on them. "Only a healthy money is an honest money" (Otmar Emminger, 1979).[13] "In a society that wants to give a lot of room to individual freedom and responsibility, the stability of the value of the currency represents principles and values like security of one's rights, honesty, credibility, and consistency, and so represents what is generally expressed by the word *Währung* (currency)" (Sachverständigenrat, 1967).[14]

That inflation gives opportunities for some to take unfair or dishonest advantage of others is clearly a concern in the United States. I tried to ask about such concern in a rather more concrete way than is suggested by the above quotes, asking about specific examples of such bad behavior.

> B10. Do you agree with the following statement? "One of the most important things I don't like about inflation is that the confusion caused by price changes enables people to play tricks on me, at my expense. For example, my boss can 'forget' to raise my pay, and, if (s)he does, than I am taking a real pay cut. The government can 'forget' to change the tax brackets, and so I wind up paying higher taxes."

	1 Fully agree	2	3 Undecided	4	5 Completely disagree	
U.S. all	51%	21%	11%	11%	6%	$n=113$
Economists	28%	33%	9%	16%	15%	$n=80$

This statement apparently struck a sympathetic chord among the public, and moreover the economists tended to agree with it, though less strongly.

1.6.6   Moral or Morale Effects of Inflation

That somehow national morale, or a sense of moral behavior in others, is compromised by inflation seemed to be a factor in our informal discussions with the public. There is also a suggestion of such a factor in the popular press. For example, in the February 1995 *Reader's Digest,* the lead article by Jude Wanniski, reprinted from the *Wall Street Journal* and entitled "You Call This a Good Economy?" was substantially an article about inflation and its relations to morality or morale. *Reader's Digest* is the most widely read magazine in the world, with 28 million copies sold each month, and so the editors appear to

---

13. Gemeinschaft zum Schutz der deutschen Sparer 1990, 20, our translation. Emminger is the author of many books on the D-Mark and the international monetary system.

14. Ibid. The Sachverständigenrat is a German government-appointed standing blue-ribbon panel that provides advice about major national issues. We did not translate *Währung* here, since we think it has untranslatable connotations. *Währung* is usually translated as "currency," yet the word has connotations of "quality," "value," or "guarantee," not shared by *currency*. The impression that inflation is a thing to be avoided seems to have infiltrated German thinking in subtle ways.

have a good sense about what interests the general public; it is significant that they chose this article as the lead article in the issue, and even to offer, at the end of the article, reprints in bulk. One must try to read this sympathetically, to try to understand why this article was regarded by the editors of *Reader's Digest* as so noteworthy. The tone of the article is inspirational, as if the writer was pointing out some sham or temptation, and exhorting us to keep our senses and values about us.

This article is especially noteworthy to us, since it appears to contain substantially more than just a claim that inflation has caused a decline in our standard of living. The article dwells at some length on prices themselves. One might think that long-run inflation paths would be a boring topic for most people; inflation has to do with changes in units of measurements, a seemingly dry academic topic. Wanniski enlivens the topic by interspersing words with moral tone among recollections about price changes:

> In the period between 1950 and 1970 it was the rule—rather than the exception—that an ordinary family, without higher education, could sustain itself decently on the income of a single breadwinner. In 1955, when I was 19 and living in Brooklyn, N.Y., my father, who had a sixth-grade education, maintained our family of five on a wage of $82 a week as a bookbinder. My mother taught us fairness and compassion; my father, discipline and enterprise.
>
> With my younger brother and sister, we lived in a small apartment in a relatively new building. The monthly rent in 1954 was under $90, gas and electricity another $7 to $10. We had a 1949 Plymouth that my father had bought new for $1200.
>
> My first good suit, bought for my 1954 high-school graduation, was $30. In the summer of 1950 I worked as an office boy on Wall Street for 75 cents an hour, the minimum wage. In the summers from 1951 to 1953, I labored in the bindery for $1 an hour, with time and a half for overtime. . . .
>
> *Where did this good economy go? It was inflated away.* (49–51)

The story goes on, with many more prices from that time quoted. An economist may ask, what is the point of this personal history and list of prices from the 1950s?

One conceivable exegesis of the long list of prices is the purely economic one that the author is reminding ignorant readers that, if both prices and wages are low, then one's living standard isn't affected by their lowness. This point may well be contained in the passage, but it is clearly not the motivation for including this list of prices. If this were only an article about units of measurement, then it would be no more interesting to readers than an article reminding people about the relation between metric and avoirdupois systems. No, there is something more here.

It is clear that there is a moral tone to this writing; interspersed among the prices are words like "discipline and enterprise." Wanniski does not say he was paid $1 per hour in the bindery, but that he "labored" for it. Also interspersed among these prices is perhaps a sense that the family was happy with what it got, that it spent purposefully, buying a suit for a high school graduation, rather than spending money for frivolous purposes. It would appear that the list of individual prices presented in association with such moral judgments is an effective literary device because these individual price changes are tied up with such judgments in people's memories.

It is difficult to capture just what those we talked to seemed to be thinking about morale or morality. The following question was placed on questionnaire C to try to capture some notion of this concern:

C4. Do you agree with the following statement? "When a country has too high an inflation rate, society loses its cohesion and feeling for the common good."

	1 Fully agree	2	3 Undecided	4	5 Completely disagree	
U.S. all	44%	21%	19%	12%	3%	$n=122$
Born <1940	62%	16%	13%	7%	2%	$n=45$
Born ≥1950	31%	27%	22%	13%	7%	$n=45$
Germany all	36%	13%	32%	12%	7%	$n=168$
Born <1940	49%	15%	24%	8%	4%	$n=75$
Born >1950	19%	13%	42%	19%	8%	$n=53$
Brazil	26%	37%	12%	11%	14%	$n=57$

About half of the older Germans and half of the U.S. respondents fully agreed with this statement, and the overall result from all countries is that very few strongly disagree.[15] The Brazilians are less likely to agree strongly than are the German or the U.S. respondents. One might suppose that the difference arises because Brazilians have experienced high inflation and society did not fall apart. But note that the Brazilians picked 1 about as often as the younger U.S. and German respondents together did; the strong intergenerational differences in answers are the striking result here, not the international differences.

In talking to people about the issues raised by the *Reader's Digest* article, I also got the impression, curiously, that people think that differences in prices between now and long ago are somehow a reflection of a fundamental change in values and the nature of our society, rather than a reflection of purely economic forces. Tied up with this opinion, there seemed to be an odd sense that

---

15. In the pilot study for this paper, as part of another questionnaire survey I was conducting in the spring of 1995 with institutional investment managers, I asked the following questions about the moral dimension in inflation: "What effect do you think that a strongly and steadily inflationary national policy would have on the nation's feeling of morale and sense of shared social purpose? 1. very harmful 2. mildly harmful 3. neutral 4. mildly beneficial 5. very beneficial." Of the eighty-seven respondents to this question, 77.2% chose 1, 19.3% chose 2, none chose 3, 3.4% chose 4, and none chose 5.

some break with the past occurred, and that in getting here from there was not a continuous path. Odd as this impression seemed, I decided to try to follow up on it with a question.

B14. Do you agree with the following statement? "The fact that prices are nearly three times as high as they were twenty years ago is due to a fundamental change in the nature of the economy, not due to the gradual accumulation over the years of the annual inflation, inflation which has generally been far below ten percent a year."

	1 Fully agree	2	3 Undecided	4	5 Completely disagree	
U.S. all	21%	21%	23%	21%	15%	$n=110$
Economists	5%	1%	0%	12%	82%	$n=77$

A substantial minority of the public circled 1 or 2, confirming at least that the statement sounds right to a lot of people, but the economists did not, and feedback suggested that the economists were perplexed by the question.

1.6.7   Political and Economic Chaos Caused by Inflation

Reading the popular literature suggests that there is widespread concern that the effects of inflation may be so severe as to cause a breakdown in the political and economic conditions in a country. It is easy to find quotes supporting this idea; there are very many. The following 1919 passage from Keynes is so widely cited as almost to be a cliché:

Lenin is said to have declared that the best way to destroy the capitalist system was to debauch the currency. By a continuing process of inflation, governments can confiscate, secretly and unobserved, an important part of the wealth of their citizens. By this method they not only confiscate, but they confiscate *arbitrarily;* and, while the process impoverishes many, it actually enriches some. The sight of this arbitrary rearrangement of riches strikes not only at security, but at confidence in the equity of the existing distribution of wealth. Those to whom the system brings windfalls beyond their deserts and even beyond their expectations and desires, become "profiteers," who are the object of hatred of the bourgeoisie, whom the inflationism has impoverished, not less than of the proletariat. As the inflation proceeds and the real value of the currency fluctuates wildly from month to month, all permanent relations between debtors and creditors, which form the ultimate foundation of capitalism, become so utterly disordered as to be almost meaningless, and the process of wealth-getting degenerates into a gamble and a lottery.[16]

Similar themes can be found more recently.

---

16. Keynes [1919] 1979, 147–48. Subsequent commentary on this passage has raised questions whether Lenin ever said this.

Unstable money destroys the public-spirited and social foundation of every free state's order. (Ludwig Erhard, 1955)[17]

Without good money, there is no healthy economy and no healthy social conditions. (Karl Blessing, 1957)[18]

Freedom of the individual, which we all idealize, can only be assured through good money. (Fritz Butschkau, 1968)[19]

The consequences of the international [inflationary] spiral go far beyond economics: they include a sharpening of social divisions and a shaking of values, as inflation rewards speculators while penalizing thrift. The ultimate threat is that inflation will eventually weaken confidence in democratic governments and institutions and prepare the way for sharp violent shifts to the radical right or left. (*Reader's Digest* [condensed from *Time*], July 1974, 50)

Helmut Kohl, the German chancellor, has quite recently, in the context of the debate over European Economic and Monetary Union, made the effects of inflation on democracy an important part of his message to the public: "From bitter historical experience, we know how quickly inflation destroys confidence in the reliability of political institutions and ends up endangering democracy."[20] Kohl argued that we should not let the current atmosphere of cooperation in Europe encourage complacency, and argued against those who say that his concerns are exaggerated: "To anyone who says this is inadmissible histrionics, I ask this question: Who among us five years ago would have believed that the Balkans would have fallen so rapidly into fratricidal war, to ethnic hounding, to rape, murder and death?"[21]

To try to test whether the public is indeed concerned that inflation can cause economic and political chaos, the following question was included in questionnaire C:

C3. Do you agree with the following statement? "If inflation in a country rises out of control it can lead to economic and political chaos."

	1 Fully agree	2	3 Undecided	4	5 Completely disagree	
U.S. all	74%	17%	3%	2%	3%	$n=123$
Born <1940	84%	11%	0%	2%	2%	$n=45$
Born ≥1950	71%	20%	2%	0%	7%	$n=45$

17. Gemeinschaft zum Schutz der deutschen Sparer 1990, 21, our translation. Starting as German economics minister in 1948, Erhard became known as the "father of the German economic miracle." He was West German chancellor 1963–66.

18. Ibid., our translation. Blessing was president of the Deutsche Bundesbank.

19. Ibid., 20, our translation. Butschkau was a German bank president (Deutscher Sparkassen- und Giroverband).

20. Quoted in Alan Cowell, "Kohl Casts Europe's Economic Union as War and Peace Issue," *New York Times,* October 17, 1995, A10, col. 1.

21. Quoted in ibid.

	1 Fully agree	2	3 Undecided	4	5 Completely disagree	
Germany all	77%	18%	3%	2%	0%	$n=173$
Born <1940	89%	8%	3%	0%	0%	$n=76$
Born ≥1950	69%	27%	2%	2%	0%	$n=55$
Brazil	41%	31%	7%	14%	7%	$n=58$

There is a lot of agreement with this statement, suggesting that this concern about inflation is a major one. It is perhaps surprising that there is not much difference between the United States and Germany on answers here. When comparing the United States and Germany, the difference is more intergenerational than international. Only the Brazilians did not fully agree in the majority with this statement, presumably reflecting the fact that the Brazilians have had a lot of inflation and have not experienced economic and political chaos. Even so, a majority of Brazilians chose 1 or 2.

To further consolidate our understanding of the public support of the proposition that inflation causes economic and political chaos, it is useful to confirm whether the public really thinks that the line of causality runs only from inflation to chaos, and not the other way around.

C12. Do you agree with the following statement? "Political instability in a country will likely have a very high inflation rate as a consequence."

	1 Fully agree	2	3 Undecided	4	5 Completely disagree	
U.S. all	26%	30%	34%	5%	5%	$n=122$
Born <1940	36%	27%	30%	2%	5%	$n=44$
Born ≥1950	23%	30%	34%	9%	5%	$n=44$
Germany all	39%	27%	26%	4%	4%	$n=171$
Born <1940	53%	19%	24%	1%	3%	$n=75$
Born ≥1950	20%	47%	25%	4%	4%	$n=55$
Brazil	21%	25%	23%	14%	18%	$n=57$

The impression that such reverse causality is a factor is less strong, and only about half of the older Germans are in full agreement. Still, the majority of people in the United States and Germany choose either 1 or 2 here.

1.6.8 Concerns for Prestige and the Currency

National prestige is presumably an important factor in its own right, and the general public appears to be concerned that we must keep inflation low in order to preserve such prestige: "The inflation rate has proven to be the best indicator for the ability of a country, not to postpone or cover up its problems, but to solve them" (Sachverständigenrat, 1981, in Gemeinschaft zum Schutz der deutschen Sparer 1990, 22).

Inflation is by definition a depreciation of the currency against the consumer market basket; it may also be associated, if the inflation is high, with a depreciation of the currency against other nations' currencies. The decline in value of the currency seems to raise other emotional issues. "Nothing is quite so striking a symbol of national prestige as a currency."[22] Another example, from Germany:

> Until today, the history of Germany after the war is a history in which the D-mark is of great importance. This is valid for the rise of the German currency from the child of the occupation to a world star as well as for the German fears that are associated with the coming European currency. For this Germany, there is much truth in what the great economist Schumpeter wrote, namely, that there is reflected in the monetary situation of a nation everything that this nation wants, does, suffers, and is, and that at the same time the currency of a nation has a substantial influence on its economic affairs and on its fate altogether. . . . Before the federal republic was founded, before there was a national flag, the really leading philosophy of life was predetermined by [Ludwig] Erhard's economic and monetary reform, by the D-Mark.[23]

It is common in Germany to refer to countries whose exchange rate has been declining as *Weichwährungsländer* (soft-currency countries). Now, there are certainly potentially many ways to group or describe countries: one could refer to less-developed countries, or high-population-growth countries, or many other categorizations. To an economist, referring to countries in this manner is not natural unless one is referring to their exchange rates. But, apparently, the word is commonplace and used in much broader contexts. Thus, in a sense the German language itself has changed to incorporate certain assumptions about the correlates of weak exchange rates. To compare with English-speaking countries, I did a Nexis search on the term "soft-currency country" or "soft-currency countries" on CURNWS (25 August 1995). Only twenty-two entries were found, and in about two-thirds of these, the stories were also connected in one way or another to either Germany or Switzerland, suggesting that use of this term may have crept into English from the German sources. Thus, the term "soft-currency countries" does not appear to have the significance in English that *Weichwährungsländer* does in German.

This concern with prestige was confirmed by results from questionnaire C.

> C13. Do you agree with the following statement? "When a country has too high an inflation rate, it can lose international prestige."

---

22. Karen Pennar, "Is the Nation State Obsolete in a Global Economy?" *Business Week,* July 17, 1995, 80.

23. Jürgen Jeske, *Frankfurter Allgemeine Zeitung,* July 1, 1995, 1, our translation.

	1 Fully agree	2	3 Undecided	4	5 Completely disagree	
U.S. all	46%	36%	10%	5%	3%	$n=121$
Born <1940	56%	35%	5%	0%	5%	$n=43$
Born ≥1950	36%	36%	16%	7%	5%	$n=44$
Germany all	51%	29%	13%	6%	1%	$n=171$
Born <1940	62%	21%	12%	5%	0%	$n=76$
Born ≥1950	36%	42%	15%	7%	0%	$n=55$
Brazil	54%	21%	12%	7%	5%	$n=57$

There appears to be a strong belief that such prestige loss is at stake with high inflation. Again it is the older respondents from the United States and Germany who are more likely to fully agree.[24]

In writing this question, we were concerned that international differences in concerns with prestige might have more to do with the consequences of loss of prestige than with the association of prestige with inflation, and so the following question was added to the questionnaire immediately after the above:

C14. Do you agree with the following statement? "Even if a country loses prestige because of high inflation, it doesn't matter. There are no really serious consequences to such a loss of prestige."

	1 Fully agree	2	3 Undecided	4	5 Completely disagree	
U.S. all	2%	6%	10%	39%	44%	$n=122$
Born <1940	5%	7%	9%	23%	57%	$n=44$
Born ≥1950	0%	7%	11%	45%	36%	$n=44$
Germany all	8%	12%	21%	21%	37%	$n=169$
Born <1940	11%	12%	23%	12%	42%	$n=74$
Born ≥1950	4%	7%	11%	38%	40%	$n=55$
Brazil	5%	9%	7%	16%	63%	$n=57$

Very few agreed with this statement, and moreover, no large international differences were found in opinions on the seriousness of loss of prestige: people in all countries tend to think that maintaining national prestige is important.

24. I asked the institutional investors, as part of the above-mentioned pilot-study questionnaire: "What effect do you think that a strongly and steadily inflationary national policy would have on U.S. international prestige? 1. very harmful 2. mildly harmful 3. neutral 4. mildly beneficial 5. very beneficial." Of the eighty-eight responses to this question, 85.2% chose 1, 10.2% chose 2, 1.1% chose 3, 1.1% chose 4, and 2.3% chose 5.

Contrary to expectations, it was the Germans who appeared most likely to agree.

This line of questioning was then rephrased in terms of the value of the currency rather than of the inflation rate.

C17. Do you agree with the following statement? "It is too bad, when the exchange rate of the dollar [D-Mark, Real], the value of the dollar [D-Mark, Real] in comparison with currencies of other countries, falls. Therefore, an important symbol of our economic strength is weakened."

	1 Fully agree	2	3 Undecided	4	5 Completely disagree	
U.S. all	50%	23%	15%	6%	6%	$n=122$
Born <1940	59%	23%	14%	2%	2%	$n=44$
Born ≥1950	41%	27%	11%	11%	9%	$n=44$
Germany all	47%	18%	16%	13%	6%	$n=173$
Born <1940	52%	16%	18%	8%	6%	$n=77$
Born ≥1950	40%	22%	15%	18%	5%	$n=55$
Brazil	12%	25%	16%	16%	32%	$n=57$

About half the people in the United States and Germany are in full agreement with this statement. Presumably Brazilians, who have seen their currency fall so much and a recent renaming of their currency, have lost such hopes for prestige of their currency.

1.6.9   Opinions about Simple Theories of Inflation and Its Consequences

Opinions about the costs of inflation may differ among groups due to differences of opinion about some very simple economic relations that usually are not discussed. I first tried to see whether the public agrees with conventional economic reasoning as regards the effects of inflation on the exchange rate and on inflation rates, and to compare their answers with those of economists.

B15. If the price level goes up a lot more in the United States than it does in other countries, then the dollar will tend to:
[Circle one number]

1. Go up in value abroad (foreigners will have to pay more of their money if they want to exchange their money for a dollar)

2. Stay the same

3. Go down in value abroad (foreigners will have to pay less of their money if they want to exchange their money for a dollar)

4. No opinion

	1	2	3	4	
U.S. all	30%	5%	55%	9%	$n=110$
Economists	4%	0%	92%	4%	$n=78$

B16. If the inflation rate goes up, then interest rates will tend to:
[Circle one number]

1. go up

2. stay the same

3. go down

4. No opinion

	1	2	3	4	
U.S. all	72%	4%	21%	3%	$n=112$
Economists	97%	1%	0%	1%	$n=79$

It appears here that the public and economists are in general agreement on both of these basic theoretical models. The public usually answers correctly (to question B15) about the effects of inflation on the exchange rate, though their answers to this question are wrong about a third of the time. Perhaps more people would have answered correctly if the question had explained the situation a little more or if the question were put in the context of a particular situation. The public does even better on the effects of inflation on interest rates, answering correctly (to question B16) nearly three-quarters of the time. This theory is very important in judging the impact of inflation on our standard of living, since it is consistent with the view that people living off their savings invested in short-term debt are not necessarily harmed by inflation. (Question C11B [see section 1.7.1] draws out whether the public is aware of this line of reasoning.)

It is not clear from the public's partial success in answering what the effects of inflation are on the exchange rate whether people can carry this line of reasoning much further. It is plausible that they would be influenced by a theory that price inflation in our own country harms our competitiveness abroad, and indeed we heard such theories in our conversations before writing the questionnaire. A question that tried to see how often such a theory about inflation and competitiveness is held was included on questionnaire C.

C16. Do you agree with the following statement? "One reason the US [Germany, Brazil] loses from inflation is that the goods that we sell abroad get ever more expensive, therefore our exports fall and jobs get lost."

	1 Fully agree	2	3 Undecided	4	5 Completely disagree	
U.S. all	42%	30%	15%	7%	6%	$n=122$
Born						
<1940	48%	27%	16%	5%	5%	$n=44$

	1 Fully agree	2	3 Undecided	4	5 Completely disagree	
Born						
≥1950	30%	34%	16%	9%	11%	$n=44$
Germany all	58%	16%	13%	5%	8%	$n=169$
Born						
<1940	68%	12%	11%	3%	7%	$n=76$
Born						
≥1950	40%	25%	21%	8%	8%	$n=53$
Brazil	5%	15%	16%	9%	55%	$n=55$

Now, it is apparent the theory does indeed have some sway over people's thinking, at least outside of Brazil. This is an important result, indicating that even though most people are aware of the effect of inflation on the exchange rates, they do not put this awareness together with a theory about international competitiveness, and are likely to want to oppose inflation for a reason that most economists would probably consider very strange. Of course, the public in Germany may be thinking about exchange rate restrictions within the European Economic and Monetary Union, and all respondents may be thinking about some very short-run effects on exchange rates that might be resisted by central banks. Brazilian respondents were relatively more successful in giving what I consider the correct answer, and this could be either because Brazil has experienced such enormous price-level movements that people must have learned that the exchange rate adjusts, or because of the bias of our E-mail sample in Brazil toward more sophisticated people.

Another popular theory about the behavior of inflation that could well have an important role in public thinking, and concerns, about inflation news is a sort of foot-in-the-door theory: if inflation ever gets started, then there is a risk of explosive inflation. Such a theory is described in popular accounts; for example, "with inflation, one can make no easy compromise—if one extends her a finger, she quickly grabs the whole hand (and if one flirts with her, one will end up married to her)" (Otmar Emminger, 1979, in Gemeinschaft zum Schutz der deutschen Sparer 1990, 21). Belief in such a theory would create a reason for extreme vigilance regarding inflation, and so I included a question about it.

C2. Do you agree with the following statement? "If the inflation rate is ever allowed to get above some threshold, it can happen that it gets out of control and prices rise faster and faster."

	1 Fully agree	2	3 Undecided	4	5 Completely disagree	
U.S. all	53%	31%	9%	5%	2%	$n=124$
Born						
<1940	58%	33%	4%	2%	2%	$n=45$
Born						
≥1950	44%	24%	20%	7%	4%	$n=45$

	1 Fully agree	2	3 Undecided	4	5 Completely disagree	
Germany all	69%	18%	9%	1%	3%	$n=171$
Born <1940	77%	16%	7%	0%	0%	$n=74$
Born ≥1950	56%	21%	15%	2%	5%	$n=55$
Brazil	49%	33%	4%	9%	5%	$n=57$

This foot-in-the-door theory is popular in all countries. Germans, especially the older Germans, are more likely to agree fully with the statement.

In talking with our subjects before writing the questionnaires, another view was noted that seems very strange to economists, but that was held with some conviction: people seemed to be saying that there is a potential for a serious problem with inflation, even if it is steady, because eventually the currency will become worthless. It seemed that they were thinking that the exponential decay function $y = e^{-x}$ actually hits the x-axis at some point, rather than being asymptotic to it, or as if they did not understand that the units of measurement, the number of zeros that we put on prices, really do not have any significance. I tried to capture this view in a question, to present both to the general public and to economists.

B19. Do you agree with the following statement? "We can live with moderate, steady inflation for a while, but sooner or later there has to be an alarming problem with steady inflation: if the inflation continues long enough then eventually the dollar will be practically worthless."

	1 Fully agree	2	3 Undecided	4	5 Completely disagree	
U.S. all	44%	20%	15%	14%	7%	$n=110$
Economists	0%	3%	10%	16%	71%	$n=73$

None of the economists agreed fully with this bizarre statement, which provoked annoyed comments from some of them on the questionnaire, but nearly half of the public did.[25]

I sought to find, finally, some sense that there are different impressions as to the validity of the Phillips curve over wide ranges of inflation rates, thinking that in Brazil, at least, the higher inflation might be associated with a view that there are benefits to such inflation.

C7. A number of countries have had inflation rates over 10% a month (that means approximately a tripling of prices in a year). Do you agree with the following

25. Perhaps the question is not worded clearly enough to reveal the misconception that I thought was at work in people's thinking, but I felt that if the statement were made with mathematical precision then people would not react to it with their accustomed patterns of thought, and might accept it as a logical challenge instead. It is in practice difficult to document the nature of common mental confusions, and this question is only a weak attempt at doing so.

statement? "One can say that these countries in a certain sense have been lucky despite the inflation, because with the high inflation there were probably also more jobs."

	1 Fully agree	2	3 Undecided	4	5 Completely disagree	
U.S. all	2%	0%	14%	25%	60%	$n=124$
Born <1940	4%	0%	18%	11%	67%	$n=45$
Born ≥1950	0%	0%	13%	31%	56%	$n=45$
Germany all	1%	6%	27%	11%	54%	$n=171$
Born <1940	3%	5%	32%	15%	45%	$n=74$
Born ≥1950	0%	2%	20%	2%	76%	$n=55$
Brazil	0%	2%	16%	19%	63%	$n=57$

The answers to this question did not come as I had expected. It was in fact the older Germans, not the Brazilians, who least disagreed.

1.7   Causes of Differing Public Attitudes toward Inflation

1.7.1   Differing Public Information Sets

An impression how and why opinions differ across countries or across groups can be produced by our exploring what information people have in the various countries, and the differences across countries in terms of information sets. For example, the anti-inflation bias in Germany is thought by many to be a result of people there remembering the hyperinflation in the 1920s, or remembering the high inflation immediately following World War II. People in other countries, if they do not know of such events, are not likely to reach the same opinions about what may happen in the future. For other examples, differences in opinions about inflation may come about because of different prominence in people's memories of such facts as the effects of inflation on debts. We attempted to find out what people hear about inflation by running the following battery of questions in questionnaire C:

The following are questions for which you should indicate how often you have heard the statement approximately. This is not a question about whether the statement is true or false, but only how familiar such a statement seems to you.

C11A. "An important reason for Hitler's rise to power was the extremely high inflation in Germany in the 1920s."

I have heard this:	1. Often	2. Sometimes	3. Never	
U.S. all	22%	33%	45%	$n=121$
Born <1940	25%	34%	41%	$n=44$
Born ≥1950	16%	28%	56%	$n=43$
Germany all	44%	41%	15%	$n=170$
Born <1940	50%	36%	14%	$n=74$
Born ≥1950	39%	44%	17%	$n=54$
Brazil	34%	45%	21%	$n=56$

C11B. "High inflation is unfair for many people since their savings lose value because the interest rates are not really high enough to compensate for the inflation."

I have heard this:	1. Often	2. Sometimes	3. Never	
U.S. all	51%	36%	13%	$n=122$
Born <1940	57%	36%	7%	$n=44$
Born ≥1950	41%	34%	25%	$n=44$
Germany all	62%	28%	9%	$n=169$
Born <1940	66%	26%	8%	$n=74$
Born ≥1950	52%	35%	13%	$n=54$
Brazil	45%	39%	16%	$n=56$

C11C. "People who are in debt, for example when they buy a house, have an advantage when the inflation rate increases, because the real value of their debt falls."

I have heard this:	1. Often	2. Sometimes	3. Never	
U.S. all	21%	43%	35%	$n=122$
Born <1940	23%	48%	30%	$n=44$
Born ≥1950	18%	45%	36%	$n=44$
Germany all	33%	40%	28%	$n=169$
Born <1940	38%	38%	23%	$n=73$
Born ≥1950	20%	43%	37%	$n=54$
Brazil	26%	37%	37%	$n=54$

C11D. "Working people often find it hard to make ends meet because of inflation."

I have heard this:	1. Often	2. Sometimes	3. Never	
U.S. all	70%	26%	4%	$n=122$
Born <1940	75%	20%	5%	$n=44$
Born ≥1950	61%	32%	7%	$n=44$
Germany all	49%	36%	15%	$n=168$
Born <1940	58%	34%	8%	$n=74$
Born ≥1950	37%	39%	24%	$n=54$
Brazil	91%	9%	0%	$n=56$

C11E. "Retired people can't afford to buy so much because of inflation, because their pensions do not keep up with inflation."

I have heard this:	1. Often	2. Sometimes	3. Never	
U.S. all	83%	15%	2%	$n=122$
Born <1940	93%	5%	2%	$n=44$
Born ≥1950	66%	30%	5%	$n=44$
Germany all	58%	27%	15%	$n=169$
Born <1940	71%	19%	11%	$n=75$
Born ≥1950	39%	37%	24%	$n=54$
Brazil	89%	9%	2%	$n=56$

C11F. Remarkable stories about life in times of very high inflation are told. For example, people are said to have tried to spend their money as fast as possible, and stores are said to have raised prices extremely often.

I have heard this:	1. Often	2. Sometimes	3. Never	
U.S. all	22%	33%	45%	$n=121$
Born <1940	34%	32%	34%	$n=44$
Born ≥1950	11%	34%	55%	$n=44$
Germany all	44%	28%	28%	$n=172$
Born <1940	40%	36%	23%	$n=77$
Born ≥1950	39%	24%	37%	$n=54$
Brazil	75%	21%	4%	$n=56$

C11G. "Chile has had lower inflation in the last decade than Argentina has."

I have heard this:	1. Often	2. Sometimes	3. Never	
U.S. all	0%	11%	89%	$n=119$
Born <1940	0%	18%	82%	$n=45$
Born ≥1950	0%	5%	95%	$n=43$
Germany all	2%	12%	86%	$n=164$
Born <1940	4%	18%	78%	$n=72$
Born ≥1950	0%	4%	96%	$n=53$
Brazil	22%	33%	44%	$n=54$

Reading these responses, one is led to suspect that people interpreted very loosely what it means to hear these statements; the frequencies reporting hearing some statements seem high for the general population. Still, comparing answers in this battery of questions across countries and age groups, we learn various things. Overall, the statements people reported hearing most often are those about the difficulty of living with inflation, C11B, C11D, and C11E.

Comparing C11B with C11C, we see that people in all countries apparently hear more about negative effects on creditors than about positive effects on debtors, although most people in all countries claim to have heard at least sometimes that debtors can be made better off by inflation. This result confirms the impression from our personal interviews, and from the responses to open-ended questions on questionnaire A, that the awareness of potential advantages of inflation to debtors are not so strongly recognized.

Results for C11A and C11F show that there are important international differences in hearing about some famous hyperinflation episodes. The statement C11G was included just to give a suggestion to what extent news about inflation is transmitted regionally, to what extent people hear more about countries that are near neighbors rather than distant neighbors: Chile has had dramatically less inflation in the last decade than Argentina has; it has escaped the hyperinflation experience of Argentina. If people in Latin American countries tend to hear about the inflation experience of other Latin American countries rather than that of European countries, then this would create some tendency for similar opinions across Latin American countries, and hence perhaps similar inflation experience. This hypothesis appears to be born out; 55% of the Brazilian respondents reported hearing this fact about Chile and Argentina at least sometimes, compared with only 11% of the U.S. respondents and 14% of the Germans. (Unfortunately, this result might be compromised by selection bias, as E-mail respondents may be more knowledgeable.)

Most people in all countries and age groups, except for the younger U.S. respondents, say they have heard at least sometimes that high inflation was an important reason for Hitler's rise to power. It seems a little surprising to me that so many people report hearing this. Perhaps people are thinking back on vague recollections about some chaos in the Weimar Republic leading to Hitler's power, and thinking that it is plausible that inflation played some role in it.

Economic commentators often attach credence to the notion that living through the German hyperinflation in 1923, or having closely associated with people who did, accounts for the national aversion to inflation in Germany today, and that therefore older people in Germany are more conservative regarding inflation. If this is the case, then one might expect that Germans will gradually forget their aversion to inflation, and return to more normal inflation behavior in the future.

Why should living through the inflation of 1923, or remembering talking to people who did, make such an impression? Brazilians today have lived through hyperinflation, but we have seen above that they are less worried about the consequences of inflation. The answer may lie in the differences in the Brazilian experience, and differences in what people remember. The critical differences are that in Germany in 1923 the inflation got further out of control than did the more recent Brazilian inflations, and that the loss of control in Germany then coincided with real political chaos, and with Hitler's initial efforts to control Germany.

A fact that is probably little known to young people today, even in Germany, is that the final collapse of the mark in 1923, when the mark's inflation reached astronomical levels (inflation of 35,874.9% in November 1923 alone, for an annual rate that month of $4.69 \times 10^{28}\%$), came in the same month as Hitler's Beer Hall Putsch, his Nazi Party's armed attempt to overthrow the German government.[26] This failed putsch resulted in Hitler's imprisonment, at which time he wrote *Mein Kampf*, setting forth an inspirational plan for Germany's future, suggesting plans for world domination. Another coincidence that probably few remember today: the Kapp Putsch, which resulted in Berlin's temporary capture in March 1919 by the Freikorps, occurred immediately after a sudden, temporary burst of inflation: prices rose 34.2% in February 1919 (annual rate of 3,297.8%), and 56.4% in January 1919 (annual rate of 21,358.5%) though prices increased only 1.4% in March itself.[27]

Most people in Germany today probably do not clearly remember these events; this lack of attention may be because their memory is blurred by the more dramatic events that followed (the Nazi seizure of power and World War II). However, to someone living through these historical events in sequence, to whom the association of the 1923 putsch and the Kapp Putsch with the hyperinflation would be obvious, these putsches may have been remembered as vivid evidence of the potential effects of inflation. Our single question, C11A, about the inflation of the 1920s does not confirm a huge intergenerational difference in Germany in terms of information about hyperinflation. Perhaps what persists is a memory, that older Germans shared a strong conviction produced by experience that inflation may breed political chaos, even though their reasons for believing this are now largely forgotten.

What tends to be remembered from generation to generation may be a combination of stories of vivid events and impressions of conventional wisdom, and not complicated arguments for inferring causality. Stories about vivid events are much easier to remember and natural to transmit to others.

We find indeed that hearing such vivid stories (question C11F) about life in times of high inflation is reported most often by Brazilians, not surprising since their hyperinflation is so recent, and, less obviously, more often by Germans than by the U.S. respondents. We are a little surprised that the older Germans do not report hearing such stories significantly more often than do the younger Germans, suggesting that perhaps such stories, to the extent that they are still told, are part of a national culture in Germany that circulates through all age groups.

1.7.2   Influence of Media and Professionals

An important transmitter of public attitudes toward inflation is found in society and the media. The real reasons for public concern with inflation may have largely to do with how opinion leaders treat the issue. Columnists, politicians,

26. German wholesale price data, from the Statistisches Reichsamt; see Cagan 1956, 102–3.

27. The communist Spartacist Revolt in Berlin in January 1919 also came at a time of high inflation, 6.9% in January 1919 (annual rate of 134.6%), a rate that must have appeared high by comparison with inflation rates in Germany during World War I. There are of course other times when high inflation corresponded to revolutions. For example, Chile had a dramatic increase in inflation in 1973 (to over fourfold price increase in the year) when General Augusto Pinochet Ugarte overthrew the Marxist government of Salvador Allende Gossens, leading to over fifteen years of military government.

and other public figures have learned that the word "inflation" is already loaded with associations and assumptions, and they may reinforce these associations and assumptions by trying to exploit them to make their own words have more effect. According to the German economist Günter Schmölders (1969, 202, our translation):

> In the case of a developed, high inflation, one has to consider the phenomenon of social infection, beyond mere individual motivations. This is because inflations are in the first place social processes. The individual reactions of economic agents will be guided by group interactions, because people watch each other's behavior and to a certain extent control each other. In this context the behavior of the press is of particular importance because it is a sociological group that reacts to crises and the associated events in a pointed manner and that can propagate its opinions effectively through the appropriate media. Part of the atmosphere of the crisis of 1966/67 probably has not just economic origins but also political and journalistic origins. Frequently, the way events are reported creates an artificial reality that becomes real through social-psychological feedback processes. This is a phenomenon that is made very clear by the Anglo-Saxon expression "self-fulfilling prophecy."

As with any phenomenon that is widely discussed publicly, inflation is likely to be associated with the sort of herd effects described by Bikhchandani, Hirshleifer, and Welch (1992) or Banerjee (1992). People have learned through experience to imitate others when in doubt, particularly those who are perceived as experts, since other people's actions may well be based on some information. The problem with such behavior is that information cascades can get started: people may be imitating others who are in turn imitating others who are imitating others. The overall results of such information cascades may be a sense of public opinion, of received wisdom, that may in fact have little basis.

The fact that so many of the differences we see in answers to our question are intergenerational rather than international suggests that the influence of the media is very large. There appears to be a culture of opinions about inflation that is shared by people in the same generation in both the United States and Germany, yet one must doubt that there has been much direct communication between people in the United States and people in Germany. The communications are probably mostly managed by the media. Because these media have been so important in reporting current events, older people in the United States today may be influenced by events in Germany before 1950 more than are younger Germans; this is supported by the results from question C11F, though not those from C11A.

The people who manage the mass communications media must be aware of the abiding public interest in inflation, and at the same time they are, in writing the usual news stories about current events, probably not themselves interested in obtaining a deep understanding of the phenomenon. The incentives these people are under, therefore, is to give publicity to economists who repeat conventional wisdom regarding inflation; since media people are often pretty well aware of opinions expressed in news media in other countries, they may tend to promote a world as well as a national culture regarding inflation. The outcome of this media process is that the general public seems to have the impression that the experts are confirming their impressions as to the importance of inflation.

In this connection, it is very significant that the results from questionnaire B show that much of the public thinks that the media attention given to inflation is at the urging of economists, a far higher proportion than of economists who themselves think so.

> B8. Which is the better explanation why inflation is reported so regularly in the news:
>
> 1. Economists tell reporters that the monthly inflation numbers are very important news, and so reporters feel that they ought to give the inflation numbers a lot of coverage.
>
> 2. The general public is regularly interested in inflation news, and reporters cover inflation to boost the number of viewers or readers.
>
> 3. Neither or no opinion

	1	2	3	
U.S. all	39%	30%	31%	$n=110$
Economists	18%	56%	26%	$n=77$

About twice as many from the public chose 1; it appears that the public imagines that expert opinion shapes media attention to inflation more than the economists themselves think it does.

1.7.3 Perceptions of the Social Contract

It appears likely that the public perceives to some extent a sort of social contract that governments must resist inflation, a contract that we are all born into, and that we as individuals cannot change, any more than we can change the constitution. To the extent that there is such a public perception, anyone who takes public office must feel that he or she is in a position of public trust, and is under pressure to live up to public expectations. Those in public office may choose political battles, on issues that matter a lot to them, and they may try to fight popular misconceptions, but are not likely to have the time or energy to fight the public impressions on such long-debated background issues as basic policy toward inflation. I sought to determine whether there is any agreement that such a social contract exists.

> C15. Do you agree with the following statement? "Despite some opinion differences, US [German, Brazilian] politicians have always promised to keep inflation

down. Especially for this reason, politicians today are morally obligated to be against inflation."

	1 Fully agree	2	3 Undecided	4	5 Completely disagree	
U.S. all	27%	26%	17%	19%	12%	$n=121$
Born <1940	48%	14%	16%	11%	11%	$n=44$
Born ≥1950	14%	35%	12%	28%	12%	$n=43$
Germany all	65%	19%	10%	4%	2%	$n=171$
Born <1940	82%	9%	8%	1%	0%	$n=76$
Born ≥1950	41%	28%	15%	9%	7%	$n=54$
Brazil	34%	16%	23%	9%	18%	$n=56$

Here we see some striking differences between Germany and the other countries, which would work in the direction of preserving low inflation policy there even if there were no differences in understandings of the mechanism of inflation. This question reflects the biggest difference, in all our questionnaire results, between the German and U.S. respondents overall in the proportion who fully agree. We also see here the sharpest difference between *younger* German and U.S. respondents; 41% of the younger Germans fully agree, compared with only 14% of the younger U.S. respondents.

The results from this question suggest that perceptions of the social contract contain the most important differences between Germans and people in other countries, rather than differences in tastes, opinions, or information sets. Because the differences extend to the younger generation, they appear likely to be important for a long time. More research should be done to consolidate our understanding of the international differences in social contract.

1.8 Summary and Interpretation of the Results

To summarize the main perceived costs of inflation briefly, the concerns people mention first regarding inflation are that it hurts their standard of living, and a popular model they have that makes such an effect plausible apparently has some badly behaving or greedy people causing prices to increase, increases that are not met with wage increases. This might be called a bad-actor–sticky-wage model. That people think wages are sticky is particularly supported by the results for questions C5, C6, B6, and B12 (section 1.6.2). There also appear to be popular notions that inflation harms the standard of living by inhibiting economic growth, through some unspecified systemic factors (question C11, section 1.6.1). Other concerns are that inflation makes us feel good (question B17, section 1.6.4), but ultimately deceives us, or allows opportunistic people to deceive us (question B10, section 1.6.5), that the social atmosphere created by inflation is selfish and harmful to national morale (question C4, section 1.6.6), that high inflation can cause political chaos or anarchy (question C3, section 1.6.7), and that inflation and decline of currency value are harmful to national prestige (questions C13 and C17, section 1.6.8).

The list of concerns that noneconomists aired to us in conversation, in their answers to the open-ended questionnaire A, and in their choice of answers on the other questionnaires sound very different from the list of real effects of inflation that Fischer and Modigliani (1978) gave in their treatise on the costs of inflation. Fischer and Modigliani divided the costs of inflation into six categories: (1) those that would persist even in a fully indexed economy, (2) those due to nominal government institutions, (3) those due to nominal private institutions and habits, (4) those due to existing nominal contracts, (5) those due to effects of uncertainty about future inflation, and (6) those due to government endeavors to suppress inflation. The effects listed under category 1 are the "shoe-leather" or "trips to the bank" costs produced when people try to economize on currency and the "menu costs," the cost of changing prices, such as printing new menus. Question B9 (section 1.6.1) asked about these costs, the inconveniences of inflation, versus the effects of inflation on the standard of living, both of economists and the general public, and there was a striking difference in the answers; the public was much more fixated on the supposed direct effects of inflation on the standard of living, and relatively indifferent to the inconveniences of inflation. In noneconomists' answers to the open-ended questionnaire, there were hardly any references (only four people) to the effects of the nominal institutions, habits, or contracts referred to by Fischer and Modigliani under their causes 2 through 4, nor was there any mention of the effects of uncertainty about future inflation or about effects of governments' efforts to suppress inflation.

The different sound of the complaints does not necessarily mean, however, that the concerns expressed by the general public are entirely orthogonal to those of economists. Some of the public's concerns are surely caused by their experience with nominal contracts. Some (seven people) did mention at their own initiative on questionnaire A that their retirement income was being eroded by inflation, and moreover, most were aware that this was an effect when asked directly about it (question C11E, section 1.7.1). The vast numbers of nominal contracts that we have today were made in a sense of trust that the government would not allow massive inflation, and these concerns are shared by economists and the public.

The issues of inflation-generated opportunities for deception (question B10, section 1.6.5), and the effects of inflation on national cohesion and international prestige (questions C4, section 1.6.6; C13, section 1.6.8) are curious for economists, and do not appear on the Fischer-Modigliani list. Perhaps it is here that we should listen carefully to what the public is telling us. A feeling that opportunities for profit through deception are being willingly created by an inflationary policy, possibly to the benefit of certain interest groups, might well promote a feeling of relative detachment from society and a tendency toward less concern for others, especially since inflation is a real concern and object of interest for most people. Moreover, we should also listen to concerns about national prestige, given the attachment in modern culture of prestige to countries with low inflation and strong exchange rates. People's concern for their national prestige is tied up with their feelings of self-esteem, and their trust in their national institutions.

In answering questions about what is really important and what our national leaders really ought to pay attention to, people may tend to rely on some deep intuition derived from life's experiences. The word "intuition" may be wrong here; perhaps what I mean with regard to inflation is that they have dim memories of having concluded that highly inflationary times were times when there was arbitrary injustice, arbitrary redistributions, and social bitterness, and they have memories of social situations in which morale and a sense of cooperation was lost.

Those who implement national policy toward inflation have to sort out which concerns they share with the public and which they do not. They need not share all of these concerns, however, to share a conviction that inflation is to be avoided. There will probably always be a communications gap between economists and the public, at least because professional economists devote their time to studying economic phenomena such as inflation, and earn their keep by being ahead of the public in knowledge and theories about economic phenomena. But there appears to be rather more of a gap than most of us would have expected. The public's models of the economy are fundamentally different from those of economists (recall, for example, questions B12, section 1.6.2; B14, section 1.6.6; and B19, section 1.6.9). The communications gap is all the wider because many people think that the prominence given inflation in the news is due to the economists, while economists often feel differently (question B8, section 1.7.2).

The German respondents are, as hypothesized, rather different from the U.S. respondents in a number of attitudes toward inflation. The Germans tend more often to believe that there is a sort of social contract that authorities must resist inflation (question C15, section 1.7.3), and the German respondents are more often concerned that their policymakers deal with inflation (question C1, section 1.6.1). Moreover, there are important differences between German and U.S. respondents in terms of their reported information sets (questions C11A through C11D, section 1.7.1). All of these differences extended to the younger German and U.S. respondents as well as the older. The Germans seem to show a greater tendency to believe models that imply a high cost to inflation (recall, particularly, questions C2, section 1.6.9; and C11, section 1.6.1). In most of our other questions, though, there were not great differences between German and U.S. respondents, and the differences were often very small when comparisons were made between younger people in Germany and the United States.

For example, Germans do not make notably different decisions than do the U.S. respondents when asked to choose between high inflation and high unemployment (recall question C8, section 1.6.1).

The study also appears to confirm (subject to considerations of the weaknesses of the E-mail sampling method used in Brazil) the hypothesis that the Brazilians have somewhat different opinions about inflation than either German or U.S. respondents. This difference appears to make it more likely that politicians or monetary authorities might find it in their political interest to be tolerant of inflation. If one seeks to explain why inflation is persistently higher in Brazil than in Germany, one might say that the Brazilians are less likely to think that inflation will cause economic and political chaos (question C3, section 1.6.7), less likely to think that inflation will be harmful to economic growth (C11, section 1.6.1), less likely to think that inflation will harm their international competitiveness (C16, section 1.6.9), less likely to think that a decline in the exchange rate harms their international prestige (C17, section 1.6.8), and more likely to choose high inflation if that will reduce unemployment (C8, section 1.6.1). Despite these differences, it is also striking that the Brazilians often did not answer much differently than the young people in either the United States or Germany.

What should we make of the similarity internationally on answers to many questions? In part, the similarity probably reflects the pervasiveness of a sort of world culture; opinion leaders in each country read what people in other countries are saying, and convey the ideas to people in their own countries. On the other hand, the survey results may in many cases underestimate the extent of international differences. The differences reported here may not be very small when compared with differences commonly observed in questionnaire surveys of attitudes on national issues; there seems often to be substantial noise in answers on difficult questions (see Converse 1970, for example), which may dilute actual differences in attitudes in the survey results. Possibly, the international differences would have been bigger if the survey had been directed at opinion leaders or knowledgeable people, rather than a random sample.

This study confirms that the high concern with inflation in both Germany and the United States is in large measure a phenomenon confined to people born before 1940. A striking finding of this study is that intergenerational differences are usually of more importance than international differences (on questions that are not about information, that is, excluding questions C11A through C11G, and looking only at the United States and Germany, where we have intergenerational results). Within Germany and the United States the differences between the younger and older people on attitudes toward inflation tend to be bigger than the differences between the two countries overall.

Since the results reported in this paper were all collected at the same time, fall 1995, there is no way to discern whether the intergenerational differences are due to the age of the respondent (perhaps all people get more concerned with inflation as they age) or to the birth cohort of the respondent (perhaps living through events of the first part of this century inspires more concern with inflation). My interpretation is that the intergenerational differences are due mostly to the birth cohort differences. It would seem that opinions about the mechanism and costs of inflation, or the social contract regarding inflation, are complex phenomena that must have been formed by shared experiences within birth cohorts, and are not due to the aging process itself. That opinions about economic matters are mostly cohort-specific rather than age-specific is supported by the work of Inglehart (1985), who concludes that one's basic values throughout life reflect the conditions that prevailed in one's preadult years. Inglehart has collected data on economic opinions, including opinions on inflation, for over twenty years; see also Inglehart and Abramson (1994).

If the relatively low level of concern of younger people can be expected to remain the same through time, then the public concern with inflation in both Germany and the United States might be expected to decline in coming decades for demographic reasons. The people in our sample born before 1940 are now at least fifty-six years old; those in public life are probably at the peak of their influence or of declining influence. Their ability to prevent a resurgence of inflation must be waning. People who must evaluate the long-term outlook for inflation (such as those investing in long-term bonds) should bear this in mind, before concluding (as many seem to have concluded) that we are entering a new regime of steady low inflation in coming decades.

Appendix

Sample Design

For the United States, we purchased three lists of four hundred names and addresses from Survey Sampling, Inc., Fairfield, Connecticut, a company that specializes in producing high-quality random samples. Each of the three lists was drawn at random from the white pages of all phone books in the United States. Such a sampling method oversamples males, since married couples usually list only the husband's name. However, a letter accompanying the questionnaires invites the recipient to pass the questionnaire to someone else, and this should tend to offset the tendency to oversample males. We ask respondents to indicate their sex; see table 1A.1.

For Germany, we purchased our list of names from the Stuttgart firm Schober GmbH, which specializes in producing random samples. We used a method of defining the sample that seemed to us as closely comparable as possible to that which we used in the United States. Schober had the names categorized by sex and predicted income levels. We had them select approximately 120 females and 280 males from each of their three predicted income groups, low, middle, and high, distributed according to the proportions they

Table 1A.1 Breakdown of Responses by Sex and Age

Questionnaire	Number Mailed	Usable Responses	Male	Female	Decade of Birth 19___ <10	10s	20s	30s	40s	50s	60s	70s+
A U.S. all	400	120	—	—	—	—	—	—	—	—	—	—
B U.S. all	400	118	84	29	4	7	8	16	24	34	16	3
B economists	200	80	67	8	0	1	4	5	20	19	28	0
C U.S. all	400	124	89	29	1	8	11	25	31	25	17	3
C Germany	437	176	128	42	3	8	29	40	37	27	20	8
C Brazil	—	59	42	15	0	0	1	0	4	12	28	12

have in their lists in each of these three income groups, from North Rhine–Westphalia. Within each of these six income-sex groups, they chose a random sample from listed names in telephone directories. We chose fewer females than males because fewer female names are listed in telephone directories, and those that are listed may be unrepresentative of all females, tending to be single or elderly women. As in the U.S. surveys, the second letter accompanying the questionnaire invites anyone in the household to fill out the questionnaire, and so we might expect to see more females answering than our sample proportions would indicate. We chose North Rhine–Westphalia as representative of Germany; it is the most populous *Land* in Germany and includes a mixture of both major urban and rural areas. It includes the cities of Bonn, Düsseldorf, Münster, and Cologne.

For Brazil, we E-mailed questionnaire C, translated into Portuguese, to the Brazil node of Bras-net, a network for Brazilian nationals. Bras-net, a free service managed by São Paulo State University, has about five thousand subscribers who use the service to receive information (such as a daily survey of Brazilian newspapers), and to chat with each other about Brazilian topics. Many of the subscribers live outside Brazil. By E-mailing only to the Brazil node, we hoped to get mainly people living in Brazil, though certainly many who had their E-mail forwarded from Brazil also received our questionnaire. Those who use E-mail are not a random sample of Brazilians; this sampling technique was undertaken because of budget and time constraints, given that the only alternative was to omit Brazil from the study altogether. The letter accompanying the questionnaire was different from those sent in the United States and Germany, based on our sense that a request for help via E-mail should be different to succeed well. The letter was less formal, less like the dignified letter that would accompany a professional survey, evoking instead the camaraderie of network users. This letter also referred directly to the fact that international comparisons were being made, while the letter accompanying the United States and German questionnaires suggested this only by mention of both Yale University and the Institut für Weltwirtschaft. It was felt that, with a questionnaire E-mailed from the United States to Brazil, it would be better if we told them what we were after, to be sure that they didn't have the misconception that we wanted them to try to give American answers.

For economists, two hundred copies of questionnaire B were distributed by stuffing faculty mailboxes in U.S. economics departments at Boston University, Columbia University, Northwestern University, Harvard University, Princeton University, University of California at Berkeley, and Yale University. Again, the accompanying letter to economists was different from the others. The letter explained this project, that questions were intended to capture the thoughts of noneconomists, and apologized that some questions might appear ill-posed or unusual to professional economists.

Survey Method

Our method of handling the survey for random samples of the population in the United States and Germany followed fairly closely that recommended by Dillman (1978). An initial mailing was made to about four hundred people for each questionnaire country.[28] Included with the questionnaire was a short letter, indicating that inflation was an important public policy issue, and telling respondents that their cooperation in the survey would help policymakers frame national policy. We might have preferred not to put the idea in their heads that inflation is an important national policy issue, but we felt it was necessary to refer to this in order to get a good response on our survey. Those who conduct surveys have found that a good response rate depends on an apparent social purpose for the questionnaire; most people are very skeptical of questionnaires and inclined to suspect a concealed profit motive for the questionnaire. We tried to write the letter in such a way that there was no suggestion why the inflation rate should be an important national policy issue. A week after the questionnaire and letter were mailed, a postcard was sent out to all, reminding them of the importance of the study.

On the back page of each questionnaire we wrote a number indicating the respondent, and so we were able to compile a list of people who had responded. Three weeks after the first mailing, a second letter, similar to the first, was mailed to those who had not yet responded, accompanied by a replacement questionnaire, in case they had lost the first.

In the United States, 8% of the twelve hundred letters sent out in the first mailing were returned for insufficient or incorrect address or deceased. Since we received 362 usable responses (see table 1A.1), this works out to be a response rate from the good addresses of about a third. The response rate in Germany was somewhat higher: of the 437 letters mailed, we received usable responses from 176, or 40%, and the actual response rate would be somewhat

---

28. In fact, 382 letters were sent out in the first mailing. When an error was discovered in the address list they gave us, oversampling by 55 low-income females, we were given a new sample of 55 respondents, and letters were sent to these; no second mailing went to the 55 low-income females.

higher if it were figured from the base of correct addresses. (We are lacking a count of the letters returned in Germany for insufficient or incorrect address or deceased.)

The methods used for Brazil and for economists were more simple. For economists, the questionnaire and letter were sent only once, by asking colleagues in the eight universities to stuff mailboxes of professors at the economics departments. Each department was sent twenty-five questionnaires, with the request that these be distributed first and, if there are not enough professors in residence, the remainder to advanced graduate students. Presumably, there was little involvement of graduate students in the survey, since most of these departments have twenty-five professors or more. The response rate from economists was 40%. For Brazil, an E-mail message was sent three times, with a letter in the second and third times telling how many responses were received to date and appealing for more responses to make the sample more informative. The responses amount to about 1% of the subscribers to Bras-net; however, this figure should not be interpreted as a response rate, since we have no information on how many of the subscribers were logged on or read the E-mail message.

References

Alchian, Armen, and Reuben A. Kessel. 1960. The Meaning and Validity of the Inflation Induced Lag of Wages behind Prices. *American Economic Review* 50 (March): 43–66.

Bach, G. L., and James B. Stephenson. 1974. Inflation and the Redistribution of Wealth. *Review of Economics and Statistics* 56 (February): 1–13.

Banerjee, Abjijit V. 1992. A Simple Model of Herd Behavior. *Quarterly Journal of Economics* 107 (August): 797–817.

Bikhchandani, Sushil, David Hirshleifer, and Ivo Welch. 1992. A Theory of Fashion, Custom, and Cultural Change. *Journal of Political Economy* 100 (October): 992–1026.

Branson, William H., and Alvin K. Klevorick. 1969. Money Illusion and the Aggregate Consumption Function. *American Economic Review* 59, no. 5: 832–49.

Cagan, Phillip. 1956. The Monetary Dynamics of Hyperinflation. In *Studies in the Quantity Theory of Money,* ed. Milton Friedman, 25–117. Chicago: University of Chicago Press.

Cargill, Thomas F. 1969. An Empirical Investigation of the Wage-Lag Hypothesis. *American Economic Review* 59 (December): 806–11.

Cartwright, Phillip A., and Charles D. DeLorme, Jr. 1985. The Unemployment-Inflation Voter Utility Relationship in the Business Cycle: Some Evidence. *Southern Economic Journal* 51 (January): 898–905.

Cavallo, D. 1983. Comment on Indexation and Stability from an Observer of the Argentinian Economy. In *Inflation, Debt, and Indexation,* ed. Rudiger Dornbusch and Mario H. Simonson. Cambridge: MIT Press.

Converse, Phillip E. 1970. Attitudes and Non-Attitudes: Continuation of a Dialogue. In

The Quantitative Analysis of Social Problems, ed. Edward R. Tufte, 168–89. Reading, MA: Addison-Wesley.

Cuzan, Alfred G., and Charles M. Bundrick. 1992. Selected Fiscal and Economic Effects on Presidential Elections. *Presidential Studies Quarterly* 22 (January): 127–34.

Dillman, Don A. 1978. *Mail and Telephone Surveys: The Total Design Method.* New York: Wiley-Interscience.

Fair, Ray C. 1978. The Effect of Economic Events on Votes for President. *Review of Economics and Statistics* 60 (May): 159–73.

———. 1994. The Effect of Economic Events on Votes for President: 1992 Update. Cowles Foundation Discussion Paper no. 1084. Yale University.

Fischer, Stanley, and Franco Modigliani. 1978. Towards an Understanding of the Real Effects and Costs of Inflation. *Weltwirtschaftliches Archiv,* 114, no. 4: 810–33.

Gemeinschaft zum Schutz der deutschen Sparer. 1990. *Zitate zur Stabilitätspolitik.* Bonn: Gemeinschaft zum Schutz der deutschen Sparer.

Golden, David G., and James M. Porterba. 1980. The Price of Popularity: The Political Business Cycle Reconsidered. *American Journal of Political Science* 24 (December): 696–714.

Inglehart, Ronald. 1985. Aggregate Stability and Individual-Level Flux in Mass Belief Systems. *American Political Science Review* 79, no. 1: 97–116.

Inglehart, Ronald, and Paul R. Abramson. 1994. Economic Security and Value Change. *American Political Science Review* 88 (June): 336–54.

Katona, George. 1975. *Psychological Economics.* New York: Elsevier.

Keynes, John Maynard. [1919] 1979. *The Economic Consequences of the Peace.* In *The Collected Writings of John Maynard Keynes,* vol. 2. Cambridge: Cambridge University Press.

Parker, Glenn R. 1986. Economic Partisan Advantages in Congressional Contests: 1938–1978. *Public Opinion Quarterly* 50 (fall): 387–401.

Schmölders, Günter. 1969. *Der Umgang mit Geld im privaten Haushalt.* Berlin: Dunker and Humblot.

Shafir, Eldar, Peter Diamond, and Amos Tversky. 1997. On Money Illusion. *Quarterly Journal of Economics,* forthcoming.

Comment   N. Gregory Mankiw

I very much enjoyed reading this paper. The more I reflect on it, however, the less clear I am about *why* I enjoyed reading it. Robert Shiller's surveys produced many intriguing results, but I am not at all sure in what direction they should push either economic theory or economic policy.

Taken as a whole, the results lead to three broad conclusions: (1) People widely believe what might be called the inflation fallacy—the view that inflation per se erodes living standards. (2) People have largely similar views of inflation in different countries with substantially different inflation experiences. People of different ages also have largely similar views of inflation. Although the paper does report some significant differences among the groups,

N. Gregory Mankiw is professor of economics at Harvard University and director of the Monetary Economics Program of the National Bureau of Economic Research.

most of these differences are small. Put simply, people are people. (3) Economists aren't people. To be more precise, economists view inflation very differently than laymen do. Certainly, the differences between economists and laymen are far larger than the differences among Americans, Germans, and Brazilians.

In my comments, I want to focus on the inflation fallacy. When you ask laymen about the effects of inflation, they say inflation makes them poorer. That is perhaps the principal finding of this paper. It is tempting for economists to snicker at this answer. Such a reaction gives us a sense of superiority, and it offers an opportunity to reciprocate the low regard in which much of the public holds the economics profession.

But is the public's view of inflation as fallacious as it first seems? I am not so sure. I suspect that an important difference between economists and laymen is that, to some extent, we speak different languages. When we economists hear the term "inflation," we naturally start thinking about helicopters dropping money over the countryside. We imagine a continuing change in the unit of account that alters all nominal magnitudes proportionately.

By contrast, the public has not been brainwashed into thinking that inflation is always and everywhere a monetary phenomenon. Let me try to translate the issue, as seen by the public, into a language that economists understand. Consider this question: "A shock hits the economy. One result of the shock is a higher cost of living, as measured by the consumer price index. What is the likely effect of this shock on your standard of living?" Put in this way, the issue goes beyond inflation as merely a change in the units of measurement. In particular, one is naturally drawn to think about different kinds of shocks that might cause inflation. As every well-trained undergraduate knows, inflation is sometimes and in some places a supply-shock phenomenon. And, of course, inflationary supply shocks can also lower living standards.

To judge whether this is a plausible view for laymen to hold, I ran a simple regression aimed at summarizing the public's common experience with inflation. I regressed the percentage change in nominal GDP (a broad measure of nominal income) on the percentage change in the GDP deflator (a broad measure of the price level). The data were annual from 1959 to 1994. If inflation were driven solely by monetary shocks and if money were neutral, the coefficient in this regression would be 1. If monetary shocks cause real output and prices to move in the same direction, the coefficient would tend to be greater than 1. In fact, the coefficient was 0.64 (with a standard error of 0.14). That is, when inflation is high, growth in nominal income is also high, but not by enough to compensate fully for the change in prices. Shocks to aggregate supply seem a natural explanation for this result.

To the extent that supply shocks are the cause of inflation, it is easier to see why people talk about "greed" as the underlying problem. When the oil-producing countries cartelize in the form of OPEC, or when workers exert market power through an aggressive union, they induce a shock to aggregate supply that raises prices and reduces other peoples' living standards. If these actors were less greedy, or less successful at satisfying their greed, inflation would be lower, and real incomes would be higher.

It is also possible that such supply shocks lead to persistent, monetary inflation. In the 1970s, for example, the central bank accommodated adverse supply shocks and allowed them to become built into inflation expectations. One can explain such accommodation of supply shocks with the Barro-Gordon model of monetary policy. For example, suppose that an increase in union power raises the natural rate of unemployment. For quadratic preferences over inflation and unemployment, the central bank now has more incentive to produce price surprises, so the equilibrium inflation rate rises. In this case, it might seem natural for laymen to associate inflation and reduced living standards, for they arise from the same underlying shock.

Another way in which such an association might arise is by shocks to general governmental competence. Bad policymakers tend to produce a variety of bad policies, with inflation being only one of the consequences. That is probably why inflation reduces people's sense of national prestige. Inflation is a sign that the country is poorly run.

In all of these examples, inflation arises from some adverse shock that has real (as well as possible monetary) implications. We monetary economists may be tempted to say that this is not really inflation. By "inflation," we mean rising prices resulting from persistent monetary growth. But this definition, while natural from our standpoint, does not correspond to the layman's definition. Without the benefit of training in classical monetary theory, the layman defines inflation to be increases in prices, regardless of the cause.

When I was an undergraduate, I spent two summers working as an intern in the Congressional Budget Office. During the second summer, in 1980, I was assigned to a group called the Inflation Impact Unit. One might expect that such a group would have something to do with monetary policy, but that was not the case at all. Our charge was to prepare Inflation Impact Statements, which were modeled loosely on Environmental Impact Statements. These statements evaluated how pending legislation, such as regulatory reform of the trucking industry, would affect the inflation rate. Although monetary economists may view such an approach as peculiar, it makes more sense from the perspective of laymen, which in this case means Congress. To make this CBO unit more intelligible to monetary economists (but less intelligible to Congress), it should have been called the "aggregate-supply impact unit."

So far I have suggested that the great disparity between economists and the public arises partly from differing interpretation of the term "inflation." But this is probably not the only source of the disparity. Years of studying economics does produce a somewhat better understanding of the economy. To some extent, therefore, the public's perceptions about inflation must be attributable to ignorance about economics in general and monetary economics in particular.

If ignorance is in fact pervasive, how should that fact alter economic theory and policymaking? The most optimistic answer is not at all. Since people cannot influence the inflation rate, ignorance about the causes of inflation may be a reasonable strategy in the presence of information costs. (Dr. Watson once expressed surprise that Sherlock Holmes did not know that the earth revolved around the sun, rather than the other way around. Holmes explained that he had little use for this knowledge and, thus, chose to keep his limited mental faculties free for more practical information.) None of the survey evidence presented in this paper indicates that ignorance about monetary economics leads to mistakes in private decision making. It is possible, therefore, that this ignorance should not affect the models we build or the policy advice we give.

One might argue that ignorance about inflation supports Alan Blinder's view (espoused in his book *Hard Heads, Soft Hearts*) that policymakers should not give much weight to the public's fervent distaste for inflation. Scientists, rather than public perception, determine public policy toward approval of new drugs and standards for food safety. For the same reason, perhaps economists' views on inflation should be given greater weight in determining monetary policy. Because most economists view inflation as more benign than the public does, policy need not take as hard a line against inflation as it otherwise might.

One can also make the opposite argument. Because people do not understand inflation, inflation may induce people to make mistakes in personal financial planning, which in turn makes inflation more costly than economists usually suppose. There are fragments of evidence that misunderstanding of inflation has real effects. Modigliani and Cohn (1979) argued a while ago that the stock market confuses real and nominal interest rates when discounting future cash flows. In a more recent paper (1995), Canner, Weil, and I showed that popular advice about portfolio allocation is more easily explained with the distribution of nominal, rather than real, returns. The tax system is, without doubt, an important institution that fails to account for inflation. If the accountants and tax lawyers who write the tax rules get confused by inflation, how likely is it that everyone else in the economy somehow manages to get things straight?

Recently, I had the pleasure of being a member of a Harvard University faculty committee that was reconsidering the faculty pension plan. When discussing the effects of inflation with other committee members (who were not economists), I came to appreciate two facts. First, they all thought that inflation was terribly important to take into account. Second, most of them had no idea *how* to take it into account. Presumably, the general public is not much better at this than the Harvard faculty.

The implication for policy, therefore, may be that inflation is undesirable precisely because it is misunderstood. Zero inflation is the right rate because then people do not have to think about inflation. As Sherlock Holmes was well aware, thinking time is a scarce resource. A policy of price stability is desirable because it diverts our thoughts from monetary economics toward art, science, and other socially useful activities.

References

Blinder, Alan. 1987. *Hard Heads, Soft Hearts: Tough-Minded Economics for a Just Society.* Reading, MA: Addison-Wesley.

Canner, Niko, N. Gregory Mankiw, and David N. Weil. 1995. An Asset Allocation Puzzle. NBER Working Paper no. 4857.

Modigliani, Franco, and Raymond Cohn. 1979. Inflation, Rational Valuation, and the Market. *Financial Analysts Journal* 35:24–44.

2 Does Inflation "Grease the Wheels of the Labor Market"?

David Card and Dean Hyslop

2.1 Introduction

One of the basic tenets of Keynesian economics is that labor market institutions tend to prevent nominal wage cuts—even in the face of high unemployment. An implication of this downward rigidity hypothesis is that inflation can ease labor market adjustments by speeding the decline in wages for individuals and markets buffeted by negative shocks.[1] According to this argument a modest level of inflation may serve to "grease the wheels" of the labor market and reduce frictional unemployment. In sharp contrast, an emerging orthodoxy among many economists and central bankers is that *stable* aggregate prices reduce labor market frictions and lead to the lowest possible levels of equilibrium unemployment.

In this paper we attempt to evaluate the evidence that relative wage adjustments occur more readily in higher-inflation environments. We focus on two types of evidence. First, at the individual level, we use panel microdata to examine the evolution of individual real wages over time.[2] According to the downward rigidity hypothesis, individual wage changes should exhibit significant asymmetries, with a greater degree of asymmetry, the lower the inflation rate. Second, at the market level, average wages in a local labor market should fall faster in response to a given negative shock in a high-inflation envi-

David Card is professor of economics at Princeton University and a research associate of the National Bureau of Economic Research. Dean Hyslop is assistant professor of economics at the University of California, Los Angeles.

The authors thank Christina Romer, David Romer, and John Shea for comments and suggestions, and John DiNardo for many helpful discussions on the material and methodology in this paper. They also thank David Lee for extraordinary research assistance.

1. This hypothesis is spelled out in Tobin 1972, for example.

2. Previous studies of the extent of nominal rigidity in individual wage data include McLaughlin 1994 and Kahn 1994. See also Lebow, Stockton, and Wascher 1995.

ronment than in low-inflation environments. This implies that the slope of the "cross-sectional Phillips-curve"—a graph of the relationship between market-specific real wage growth and the market-level unemployment rate—will be flatter in periods of low inflation, and steeper in periods of high inflation.

Our microlevel analysis is based on two complementary sources of data: rolling two-year panels constructed from matched Current Population Survey (CPS) files from 1979 to 1993, and multiyear panels from the Panel Study of Income Dynamics (PSID). The CPS provides relatively large and broadly representative samples, while the PSID provides better detail on job changing and enables us to examine the extent of nominal rigidity over longer time frames (one, two, and three years). Simple tabulations of both data sets lead to three basic conclusions. First, measured year-to-year changes in individual wages are quite variable, even for people who remain in the same job. In a typical year during the 1980s, 15–20% of non–job changers had measured nominal wage declines, and a similar fraction had nominal wage increases in excess of 10%.[3] Second, the *most likely* nominal wage change is zero: on average during the 1980s, about 15% of non–job changers report rigid nominal wages from one year to the next. Third, the fraction of workers with rigid wages is strongly negatively related to the inflation rate, with each percentage-point reduction in inflation leading to a 1.4 percentage-point increase in the incidence of nominal rigidity.

The presence of a large "spike" at zero in the distribution of measured nominal wage changes—or at minus the inflation rate in the distribution of real wage changes—leads to the question of what the distribution would look like in the absence of nominal wage rigidity. We use the simple assumption of symmetry to construct "counterfactual" distributions of real wage changes in the absence of rigidities. We then use the counterfactual distributions to measure the fraction of negative real wage changes "prevented" by nominal wage rigidities, and the net effect of nominal rigidities on average real wage growth. This exercise suggests that downward nominal rigidities in a typical year in the 1980s held up the real wage changes of workers by a maximum of about 1 percentage point per year.

Our market-level analysis uses state-level average wages and unemployment from 1976 to 1991. The wage data are constructed from the annual March CPS and are adjusted to reflect the varying composition of the workforce in each state in different years. Consistent with most of the recent literature on regional labor markets (e.g., Blanchflower and Oswald 1994, we find that local unemployment exerts a strong influence on local wage determination: real wages fall in states with higher unemployment (relative to national trends), while real wages rise in states with lower unemployment. However, we find little evidence that the rate of wage adjustment across local markets is faster in a higher-

---

3. Of course, some fraction of this measured variation is attributable to survey measurement error.

inflation environment. Taken in combination with our microlevel findings, these results imply that nominal rigidities have a small effect on the aggregate economy, and that any efficiency gains from the "greasing" effect of higher inflation are probably modest.

2.2 Descriptive Analysis of the Distribution of Individual Wage Changes

2.2.1 Data Sources

Our analysis of individual-level wage changes is based on information from two data sources that collectively span the period from 1976 to 1993. Our first source consists of the "merged monthly earnings files" from the 1979 to 1993 CPS. Each month, the CPS collects hourly or weekly earnings information from employed workers in the one-quarter of the sample frame who will not be interviewed in the next month.[4] One-half of this group (or approximately one-eighth of all wage and salary workers in the overall sample) will be interviewed again in twelve months and asked the same earnings questions. The other half were interviewed twelve months earlier and provided comparable earnings data at that time. By matching individuals from consecutive CPS samples it is therefore possible to construct a series of "rolling panels" with two years of wage information. A typical panel contains about 60,000 individuals, of whom roughly 50,000 report data on either their hourly or weekly wage in both years.[5]

For most of our analysis of the CPS data we restrict attention to the roughly 50% of individuals who report being paid by the hour in both years of the panel.[6] Ideally, since most models of nominal wage rigidity pertain to workers who stay in the same job, we would like to distinguish between individuals who changed employers and those who did not. Unfortunately, the CPS does not regularly collect information on job tenure or on the identity of specific employers. As a crude approximation, we distinguish between individuals who report the same (two-digit) industry and occupation in the two years, and those who report a change in industry or occupation.[7] Finally, in order to minimize the confounding effects that institutionally determined minimum-wage rates

4. The data pertain to the individual's main job as of the survey week, and are not collected for self-employed workers.

5. Details of the matching algorithm and other information on the CPS samples are presented in appendix 2A. We do not use imputed wage data that are allocated in the CPS files to nonrespondents.

6. This fraction is quite stable over the sample period. The advantage of using hourly-rated workers is that we can be sure their payment method is the same in both years. The CPS lumps all other payment periods (weekly, monthly, annual, and commission) into a single "other" category.

7. Many of the observed industry or occupation switches are presumably attributable to misclassification errors (see Krueger and Summers 1988). Changes in the industry and occupation coding system introduced between 1981 and 1983 necessitate slightly different procedures in these years—see table 2A.1, note a.

may have on the analysis of nominal rigidities, most of our analysis also excludes observations that are directly affected or potentially affected by minimum wage regulations.[8]

Our second source of data is the PSID. We constructed two four-year panels of wage observations from the PSID, for the period from 1976 to 1979, and from 1985 to 1988.[9] Although the PSID has far fewer observations than the CPS panels and tends to overrepresent certain groups (such as older workers), it has several other advantages that enhance its usefulness as a data source. First, individuals' wages and labor market experiences can be followed for several years in the PSID, while only consecutive-year matches are possible with the CPS. Second, the PSID questionnaire collects information on firm-specific (or job-specific) tenure, allowing us to draw a cleaner distinction between job movers and stayers.[10] Third, the PSID follows individuals who change addresses, while the CPS cross-sections can be matched only for people who remain at the same address. Finally, the PSID provides us with data from the mid-1970s, a period of high inflation that can be compared to the mid-1980s, when unemployment rates were similar but inflation rates were substantially lower.

2.2.2   The Distribution of Individual Wage Changes

We begin our analysis by presenting a series of histograms representing the distributions of year-to-year changes in real log hourly wage rates for the CPS and PSID samples described above. Figure 2.1 contains the histograms for the fourteen pairs of matched years from the CPS samples, based on wage changes for hourly-rated workers reporting the same industry and occupation in each year. For scale reasons we have censored the log real wage changes at ± 0.35: the masses at the upper and lower extremes represent the cumulative fractions in the respective tails of the distribution. A vertical line at minus the annual inflation rate $(-\pi_t)$ is drawn for each year to identify the real wage change associated with fixed nominal wages.[11]

The histograms show that real wage changes tend to be centered around

---

8. DiNardo, Fortin, and Lemieux (1996) present evidence that minimum wages exert a major influence on the lower tail of the wage distribution. We consider a worker who is observed in periods $t - 1$ and t to be affected by the minimum wage if his or her wage is less than or equal to the contemporaneous minimum in either period. We consider a worker to be potentially affected if the wage in period $t - 1$ is below the minimum for year t.

9. We decided to use two separate panels of four years each, rather than a single panel of individuals who were in the PSID sample from 1976 to 1988, in order to reduce the attrition caused by changing household composition, labor force entry and withdrawal, and the aging and refreshing of the PSID sample.

10. Brown and Light (1992) note that the PSID tenure data contain errors that affect measured job changes. We adopt their recommended strategy of assuming that a job change has occurred whenever reported tenure is less than elapsed time since the previous interview.

11. Throughout the paper we measure inflation by the change in the logarithm of the CPI-U-X1. This series differs from the "official" CPI-U during 1979–82, since it uses a rental equivalence measure of housing cost comparable to the post-1982 CPI-U.

zero, with a prominent "spike" at $-\pi_t$ (i.e., at the point corresponding to fixed nominal wages). The size of the spike tends to be greater during periods of lower inflation: in the late 1970s when inflation was around 10%, the fraction of rigid nominal wages was 7–8%; in the mid to late 1980s, when inflation was at or below 5%, 15–20% of workers had constant nominal wages. Interestingly, it appears that there is a *deficit* in the distribution of wage changes to the left of $-\pi_t$, suggesting that the distribution of real wage changes is being "swept up" to the floor imposed by rigid nominal wages. Nevertheless, a considerable fraction of non–job changers report nominal wage cuts in any year—typically 15–20%.

Figure 2.2 presents the corresponding histograms of real wage changes for the PSID samples of hourly-rated workers in the same job in each year.[12] Despite some differences in the way the wage data are collected in the PSID and CPS surveys, and the more precise delineation of non–job changers in the PSID, the wage change distributions from the two data sources are fairly similar.[13] In particular, the PSID data also show a prominent spike in the distribution of real wages changes at $-\pi_t$. The spike is in the order of 10% during the high-inflation period 1976–79, and about 20% during the low-inflation period 1985–88. As in the CPS data, the wage change distributions in figure 2.2 show a deficit to the left of the spike, suggesting that the real wages of some workers who might otherwise experience nominal wage cuts are "held up" by downward rigidities.

Two earlier studies—by Kahn (1994) and McLaughlin (1994)—present comparable analyses of the extent of nominal rigidity in wage data derived from the PSID. Kahn uses data from 1970 to 1988 on non-self-employed household heads who have the same employer in consecutive years. Kahn's graphs of the distributions of wage changes are very similar to those presented in figure 2.2, leading her to conclude that there is significant downward nominal rigidity, and some evidence of "menu cost" effects (see below). McLaughlin uses data from 1976 to 1986 on household heads who report a wage or salary in consecutive years. Over this sample period he finds that about 7% of individuals have rigid nominal wages (see his figure 4). Nevertheless, McLaughlin concludes that there is little evidence of nominally induced asymmetries in the distribution of *real* wage changes. We believe that this conclusion arises from McLaughlin's decision to pool real wage changes from different years. As shown in figures 2.1 and 2.2, the spike in the distribution of real wage changes occurs at $-\pi_t$, which ranges from -2 to -11% in McLaughlin's

12. The measures of job tenure used in the two panels of the PSID differ: for the 1976–79 panel job tenure refers to the *position,* while for the 1985–88 panel it refers to the *employer.*

13. Appendix figure 2A.1 shows the distributions of wage changes for *all workers* in the PSID who report wages in each year—that is, including non-hourly-rated workers and those who change jobs. The patterns are similar to those in figure 2.2, except that the size of the spike is smaller—approximately one-half of the size observed for hourly-rated non–job changers—and there is more mass in the tails of the distribution.

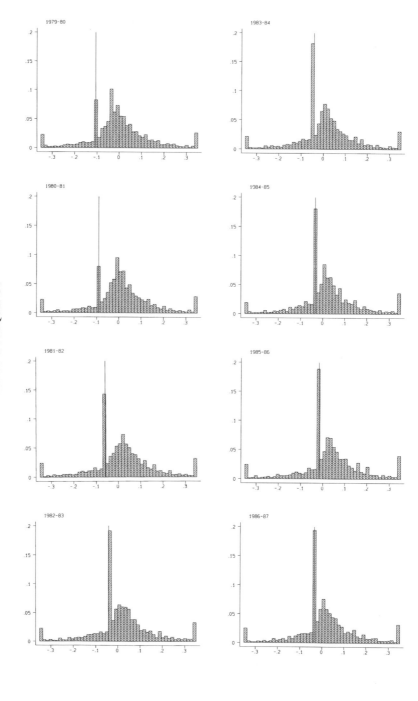

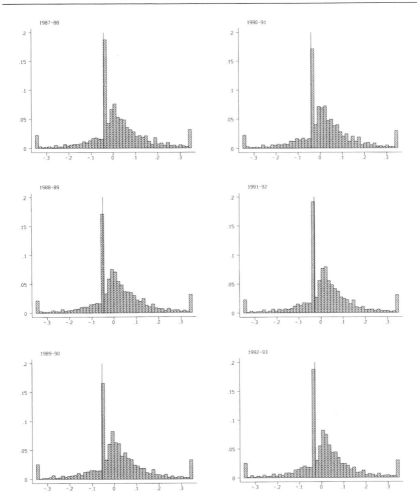

Fig. 2.1   Histograms of the distribution of log real wage changes, matched CPS samples from 1979–80 to 1992–93

sample. Pooling the data for different years thus obscures the spike in the real wage change distribution in any particular year.[14]

While most discussions of nominal wage rigidity implicitly focus on a yearly time frame, the degree of wage rigidity (either downward or upward) is clearly a function of the time horizon over which wage changes are measured. For example, we would expect to see a very high degree of nominal rigidity in week-to-week wage changes (at least in the U.S. labor market), but very little

14. Lebow, Stockton, and Wascher (1995) use PSID data for 1970–88 to measure rigidities among hourly- and non-hourly-rated workers. Their estimate of the fraction of workers with rigid nominal wages and nominal wage cuts is similar to ours.

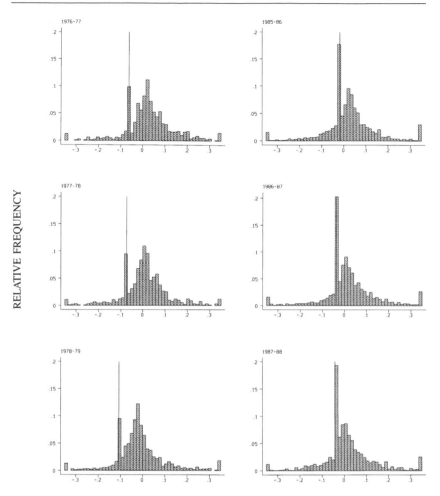

Fig. 2.2   Histograms of the distribution of log real wage changes, PSID samples 1976–79 and 1985–88, hourly-rated workers, same employer

rigidity in decade-to-decade wage changes. To get a sense of the effects of different time frames, figure 2.3 presents histograms of real wage changes over two- and three-year time horizons for hourly-rated workers in the PSID who remain with the same employer. These histograms have the same basic character as the year-to-year histograms in figure 2.2, although the magnitude of the spike corresponding to rigid nominal wages is smaller. During the low-inflation period 1985–88, about 10% of hourly rated non–job changers had constant wages over two years, compared with only 3% in the high-inflation period 1976–79. Over a three-year horizon, the fraction of observations with rigid wages is about 5% in the low-inflation era, and about 1% in the late 1970s. Some degree of nominal wage rigidity clearly persists more than a year.

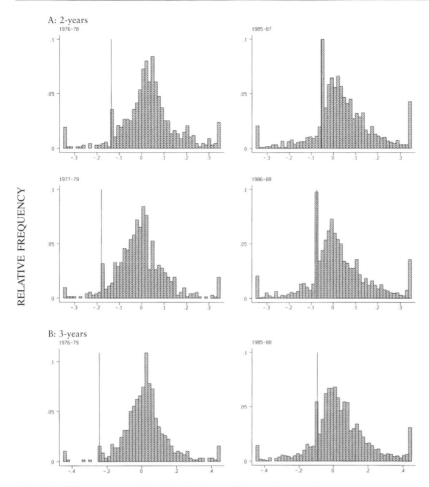

Fig. 2.3   **Histograms of the distribution of log real wage changes, over two-year (A) and three-year (B) horizons, PSID samples, hourly-rated workers, same employer**

Furthermore, long-term rigidity is more pervasive during low-inflation periods than during high-inflation periods.[15]

Tables 2.1 and 2.2 summarize some of the information contained in the histograms in figures 2.1–2.3. Table 2.1, which pertains to our CPS samples of hourly-rated workers, presents the annual inflation rate, the unemployment rate,[16] the median nominal wage change for all hourly-rated workers, the frac-

15. Appendix figure 2A.2 contains the histograms for two- and three-year wage changes for all workers from the PSID samples. These figures again show similar, although smaller, rigidity effects to those for hourly-rated non–job changers, closely matching the patterns for single-year wage changes.

16. Measured as the average unemployment rate during the ending year of each change.

Table 2.1   **Characteristics of Wage Change Distributions in CPS Samples**

	Aggregate Data		Median Nominal Wage Change	% of all Hourly Workers with[b]		% Rigid (exclude min. wage)[c]
	Inflation Rate[a]	Unemployment Rate		Nominal Cut	Rigid Wage	
1979–80	10.6	7.1	9.5	11.6	7.3	7.5
1980–81	9.1	7.6	9.4	12.1	7.2	7.8
1981–82	5.9	9.7	7.2	16.4	13.0	10.9
1982–83	4.1	9.6	4.9	17.7	17.1	14.8
1983–84	4.2	7.5	4.6	17.8	16.7	14.9
1984–85	3.5	7.2	4.4	18.4	16.4	15.2
1985–86	1.8	7.0	4.2	19.1	17.1	15.6
1986–87	3.6	6.2	4.1	19.1	17.3	16.1
1987–88	4.1	5.5	4.5	18.0	16.4	15.4
1988–89	4.7	5.3	4.7	17.2	15.5	14.8
1989–90	5.3	5.5	5.1	17.3	14.3	14.6
1990–91	4.1	6.7	4.9	18.2	14.9	15.7
1991–92	3.0	7.4	3.9	18.9	17.4	17.1
1992–93	2.9	6.8	3.6	20.3	17.1	16.6

Notes: Based on matched CPS samples. See text and appendix A for description of samples.

[a]Inflation rate is one hundred times the change in the log of the CPI-U-X1.

[b]Individuals who report being paid by the hour in both years, and who report the same two-digit industry and occupation in both years, except for 1982–83, 1983–84, and 1988–89. See table 2A.1, note a.

[c]Sample excludes individuals whose first-year wage does not exceed the minimum wage in either year, or whose second-year wage does not exceed the minimum wage in the second year.

tion of workers with measured nominal wage declines, and two estimates of the fraction of workers with zero nominal wage changes—one for all hourly-rated workers, and a second for the subsample of workers unaffected by minimum-wage regulations. Table 2.2 pertains to the PSID data, and shows the inflation rate and the fraction of workers with rigid nominal wages over one-, two-, and three-year time frames in the 1976–79 and 1985–88 periods. For comparison purposes we report both the overall fraction of workers with rigid nominal wages (columns 2 and 5), and the fraction of hourly rated non–job changers with rigid wages (columns 3 and 6).

Taken as a whole, we believe that the data in figures 2.1–2.3 and tables 2.1 and 2.2 present a reasonable prima facie case for the existence of downward wage rigidity for a significant fraction of workers. Although many non–job changers report nominal wage declines, the most likely outcome is for no change in nominal wages: between 6 and 17% report exactly the same nominal wage in one year as the next.[17] Furthermore, the extent of the rigidity is higher,

17. Note that any measurement error in wages is likely to lead to an overstatement of the probability of nominal wage declines and an understatement in the probability of rigid nominal wages. We consider the effects of measurement errors in more detail below.

Table 2.2   **Characteristics of Wage Change Distributions in PSID Samples**

| | Inflation Rate[a] | % Rigid | | | Inflation Rate | % Rigid | |
| | | All | Hourly[b] | | | All | Hourly[b] |
Year	(1)	(2)	(3)	Year	(4)	(5)	(6)
One-Year Wage Changes							
1976–77	6.3	7.4	9.3	1985–86	1.8	8.8	15.6
1977–78	7.3	6.2	7.8	1986–87	3.6	10.1	16.5
1978–79	10.3	6.8	7.8	1987–88	4.1	10.6	16.0
Two-Year Wage Changes							
1976–78	13.6	2.4	3.1	1985–87	5.4	4.7	7.9
1977–79	18.1	1.9	2.1	1986–88	7.6	5.3	8.4
Three-Year Wage Changes							
1976–79	24.4	0.9	1.2	1985–88	9.5	2.8	4.7

Notes: The unemployment rates during the respective periods are 1977, 7.1%; 1978, 6.1%; 1979, 5.8%; 1986, 7.0%; 1987, 6.2%; 1988, 5.5%.

[a]Inflation rate is one hundred times the change in the log of the CPI-U-X1 over the relevant time period.

[b]Individuals who report being paid by the hour in the beginning and ending years, and report no change in "position" (1976–79) or "employer" (1985–88).

the lower the rate of inflation. A regression of the fraction of workers with rigid wages in table 2.1 on the inflation rate yields a coefficient of -1.39 ($t = 12.1$) with an R^2 coefficient of 0.92. This implies that each percentage-point decrease in the inflation rate increases the incidence of rigid wages among hourly-rated nonmovers by 1.4 percentage points. Finally, inspection of the histograms in figures 2.1–2.3 suggests that some of the mass at the rigid-wage spike represents workers who would have experienced even bigger real wage cuts in the absence of a nominal wage floor. In section 2.4 we present a more formal analysis of this issue. Before turning to this analysis, however, we consider two auxiliary questions: whether the extent of wage rigidity is systematically different for hourly-rated versus other workers; and whether the extent of measured nominal rigidity is affected by the tendency for workers to "round" their reported wages.

2.3   Is the Extent of Nominal Rigidity Overstated?

2.3.1   Hourly-Rated versus Other Workers

All of the CPS data analyzed in the last section, and most of the PSID data, pertain to workers who report that they were paid by the hour. In the matched CPS samples, however, only about one-half of workers report that they are paid by the hour in both the beginning and end years.[18] This raises the question of whether measures of nominal rigidity based on hourly-rated workers are representative of the overall labor force.

To get some evidence on this issue, we examined changes in reported weekly earnings for individuals in the CPS samples who reported being non-hourly-rated in both years of our two-year panels.[19] The results of this analysis suggest that the incidence of rigid nominal wages is slightly *higher* for non-hourly-rated workers. For example, between 1979 and 1980, 7.4% of "always hourly-rated" workers with no change in industry or occupation had rigid nominal wages, versus 10.9% of "always non-hourly-rated" workers. Similarly, between 1987 and 1988 16.4% of "always hourly-rated" workers had rigid wages, versus 18.4% of "always non-hourly-rated" workers. There are some other differences between the distributions of real wage changes for hourly-rated and non-hourly-rated workers. Most noticeably, the dispersion in real wage changes for non-hourly-rated workers tends to be larger: the interquartile range of the change in real weekly pay for non-hourly-rated workers with the same industry and occupation is about 25–50% higher than the interquartile range of the change in real hourly pay for hourly-rated workers with the same industry and occupation. We suspect that the measurement errors in weekly pay for non-hourly-rated workers are larger than the errors in hourly pay for hourly-rated workers, in part because workers are asked to report their "usual" weekly pay rather than a "straight-time" earnings measure. In any case, there is no evidence that nominal wage rigidity is lower for non-hourly-rated workers, and for simplicity we therefore confine our attention to hourly-rated workers in the remainder of this paper.

2.3.2   Rounding of Wages and the Incidence of Measured Rigidities

One of the most prominent features of observed wage distributions is the tendency for workers to report "rounded" wage amounts, like $5.00 per hour, or $7.50 per hour. Among hourly-rated workers in our matched 1984–85 CPS file, for example, 34% reported an even dollar wage amount in 1984, and another 14% reported a wage rate ending in 0.50. If some or all of this phenomenon is due to systematic rounding (or "heaping") of data drawn from an underlying continuous distribution, then one explanation for measured nominal wage rigidity is that individuals with small nominal wage changes tend to report the same rounded wage amount in consecutive surveys. A simple tabulation of the probability of zero nominal wage growth by the initial level of wages reveals some support for this hypothesis. In the 1984–85 CPS file 24.1% of individuals who reported an even wage amount in 1984 had rigid nominal

---

18. The fraction is similar for workers who report the same industry and occupation in both years and are therefore classified as non–job changers.

19. In principle we can construct an hourly wage for non-hourly-rated workers by dividing usual weekly earnings by usual weekly hours. However, any measurement error in reported hours will lead to excessive volatility in imputed hourly wages.

wages between 1984 and 1985, versus a rigidity rate of only 9.2% for individuals who reported a wage amount not ending in either .00 or .50. In our matched CPS samples, individuals who reported an even dollar wage amount in the base year typically account for 55–60% of all those with rigid nominal wages.

The interpretation of these facts, however, depends crucially on the underlying explanation for spikes in the distribution of wages at dollar and fifty-cent intervals. If the *true* wage distribution contains spikes, and employees are more likely to report their true wage if it is an easily remembered amount like $5.00 or $7.50 per hour, then the measured rigidity rate for individuals who report an even wage may be a better estimate of the true rate of nominal rigidity than the overall rigidity rate for all wage earners. Some support for this hypothesis comes from the fact that the residual variance of a conventional wage equation is slightly *lower* when the model is fit to the subsample of workers who report a rounded wage amount than when the same model is fit to workers who report a wage that does not end in .00 or 50.[20] This evidence suggests that the noise in measured wages is lower for workers who report a rounded wage, contrary to the view that rounding is purely a result of measurement error.

To further explore this issue we used data from a January 1977 CPS validation study that collected self-reported wage information from workers and matching information from their employers (see Card 1996 for more information on this survey). Among hourly-rated workers paid above the minimum wage, the probability of a rounded wage (ending in either .00 or .50) is 30%— somewhat below the rate of 38% in our matched 1979–80 CPS sample.[21] The probability that the *employer* reports a rounded wage is lower (20%) but is far from negligible. Overall, 44% of employers and employees report exactly the same wage, with a significantly higher agreement rate (69%) conditional on the employer's reporting a rounded wage. Treating the employer reports as truth, these data imply that about one-half of the observed mass at rounded wage values is attributable to spikes in the true distribution of wages, with the other half attributable to rounding errors.[22]

To get an indication of the potential contribution of rounding behavior to measured rigidity rates, we decided to perform a simple simulation. In the

20. Specifically, we fit a model to the log hourly wage for hourly-rated workers in our pooled CPS files who report a wage ending in .00 or .50 and for those with other wages. The explanatory variables included education, a gender-specific cubic in experience, nonwhite and female dummies, and indicators for region and year. The residual standard error is slightly lower in the model for rounded wage observations than in the model for nonrounded observations. A similar finding holds by year.

21. The fraction of wages reported at even dollar or half-dollar amounts rose over the 1980s from 38% in 1979 to 48% in 1984 to 56% in 1992. We suspect that this trend may be due in part to inflation: at higher nominal wage levels, the percentage difference between "rounded" wage amounts is smaller, implying less "cost" to paying a "rounded" wage amount, and/or a smaller error in reporting a "rounded" amount.

22. Specifically, if 20% of employers report a rounded wage, and 69% of workers whose employer reports a rounded wage report the same wage, then 14% ($= 0.20 \times 0.69$) of workers report a "true" rounded wage.

simulation we assume that individual wage changes are generated from a continuous distribution, and that individuals have some probability of reporting either their true wage, a rounded wage, or their true wage plus a measurement error.[23] For plausible values of the parameters, the simulation implies that rounding generates a 4–5% rate of apparent nominal wage rigidity when the inflation rate is 5% and there is zero median wage growth. We believe this is an upper bound on the fraction of observed nominal rigidity that can be attributed to rounding behavior. If some of the observed rounding is due to spikes in the true distribution of wages at even wage amounts, or if the probability of reporting a rounded wage is less persistent over time than we have assumed, then the share of observed wage rigidity attributable to rounding is smaller.

An important feature of rounding behavior is its symmetry. Provided that individuals round their wages to the nearest even amount, rounding causes nominal wage changes *above and below* zero to be drawn toward zero. In this regard, rounding by employees is similar to "menu costs" that cause employers not to adjust wages if the optimal wage adjustment is small. By comparison, downward nominal rigidities exert an asymmetric effect on workers who would otherwise experience a nominal wage cut. In the next section we show how the symmetric effect of rounding or related phenomena can be used to empirically distinguish the contribution of downward rigidities to the total measured rigidity rate.

2.4   Measuring the Effect of Inflation on Wage Rigidities

2.4.1   Conceptual Framework

Suppose that in the absence of rigidities the distribution of real wage changes would be continuously distributed with some mean m. In the presence of rigidities, suppose that some individuals whose nominal wages would otherwise fall experience zero wage growth. This scenario is illustrated in figure 2.4A under the assumptions that $m = 0$, that the inflation rate π is 5%, and that one-half of individuals who would otherwise experience a negative real wage change are affected by downward rigidities. As illustrated by the figure, the net effect of downward nominal rigidity is to produce a *deficit* in the left-hand tail of the distribution of real wage changes (below $-\pi$) and a spike in the distribu-

---

23. In the simulation we assume that individual log wages are normally distributed according to a stationary autoregressive model, and that measured wages are generated as follows: with some probability (p_1) a worker reports the true wage; with some probability (p_2) the worker rounds the wage to the nearest even 50-cent amount; and with some probability $(1 - p_1 - p_2)$ the worker reports the true wage plus a (normally distributed) random measurement error. We calibrated the model by fixing the cross-sectional standard deviation of true log wages and the correlation of true log wages across years at 0.45 and 0.95, respectively. We set $p_1 = p_2 = 0.45$ and assumed that three-quarters of individuals who round their wage report in one year also round their report in the next year.

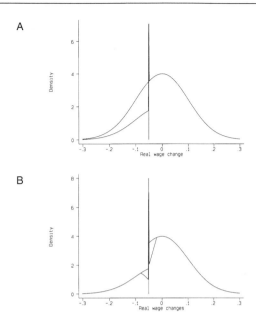

Fig. 2.4   Theoretical effects on the distribution of real wage changes. *A,* **downward nominal rigidities and,** *B,* **downward nominal rigidities and menu costs**

tion at $-\pi$.[24] It is easy to see that as the inflation rate falls (i.e., as $-\pi$ moves to the right) the effect of nominal rigidity becomes more pronounced.

A second source of nominal wage rigidity that we will attempt to separately identify is that due to menu costs or rounding in reported wage levels. For example, suppose that if the "optimal" nominal wage change is between $\pm x\%$, then there is some probability that the nominal wage will not change. Figure 2.4B illustrates this scenario when menu costs are present for wage changes of up to $\pm 2\%$, and the probability of nonadjustment declines symmetrically from 25% for a zero wage change to 0 for a 2% nominal wage change. To the extent that the density is not constant around $-\pi$, this assumption implies that menu costs induce *asymmetric* deficits in the observed distribution of real wage changes on either side of $-\pi$: if $-\pi$ lies in the left-hand tail of the distribution, there will be a larger menu-cost deficit to the right of $-\pi$ than to the left. If both downward rigidities and menu costs are present, we would expect to see a deficit in the distribution of real wage changes immediately to the left of $-\pi$, a somewhat larger deficit to the right of $-\pi$, and a spike at $-\pi$ that is larger

24. Note that if the effect of the rigidities is translated entirely into quantity effects (i.e., unemployment) there will be no spike. However, the deficit in the left-hand tail of the distribution of *observed* wage changes will exist regardless of this possibility.

than the "deficit" to the left of $-\pi$ (by the amount of the deficit to the right of $-\pi$). In principle, if the fraction of underlying wage changes that have been *shifted down* to zero can be estimated, then this fraction, suitably adjusted to take account of the different density on either side of the spike, can be subtracted from an estimate of the fraction of underlying wage changes that have been *shifted up* to zero to obtain an estimate of the net effect of downward rigidities.

2.4.2 Identifying a Counterfactual Wage-Change Distribution

The key issue in estimating the effect of nominal wage rigidities is the identification of a "counterfactual" distribution—a model for the distribution of real wage changes in the absence of downward wage rigidities and menu costs. The counterfactual that we adopt in this paper is based on the following three assumptions: (1) in the absence of rigidities, the distribution of wage changes would be symmetric; (2) the upper half of the distribution of observed wage changes is unaffected by rigidities; and (3) wage rigidities do not affect employment probabilities. Under these assumptions, the upper half of the distribution of observed wage changes can be used to infer what the lower half would have looked like in the absence of rigidities.

Although there is no *a priori* reason for imposing assumption 1, we believe that symmetry is a natural starting point for building a counterfactual distribution. Moreover, most conventional models of wage determination imply symmetry. For example, if real wage outcomes in consecutive periods are jointly normally distributed, or if the individual wage determination process is stationary, then symmetry holds.[25] An alternative approach, pursued by Kahn (1994), is to use the observed distribution of wage changes in other periods to infer the counterfactual in the absence of rigidities. An important objection to this alternative is that the *dispersion* of wage changes may be affected by inflation. Thus in this paper we rely on the symmetry assumption.

The second assumption, that wage changes above the median are unaffected by downward rigidities, may seem relatively innocuous. However, the presence of measurement errors in wages may lead downward nominal rigidities to exert some influence on the upper half of the observed wage-change distribution. Specifically, let Δw_t^* represent the true wage change of a given worker from period $t-1$ to t, and let

$$\Delta w_t = \Delta w_t^* + \Delta u_t$$

represent the measured wage change, where Δu_t is the measurement error in wage growth. Suppose that Δu_t is symmetric with median zero. Then if the distribution of true wage changes Δw_t^* is *asymmetric* (as implied by the down-

---

25. At least for workers in middle age, the assumption of stationarity may be appealing. If the process generating w_{it}, the real wage of individual i in period t, is stationary, then $w_{it} - w_{it-1}$ has the same distribution as $w_{it-1} - w_{it}$, implying that wage changes are symmetric.

ward rigidity hypothesis) the median of observed wage changes will not necessarily equal the median of Δw_i^*. Indeed, if Δw_i^* has the shape illustrated in figure 2.4a, then the median of observed wage changes will tend to exceed the median of Δw_i^*.[26] We return to this issue in more detail below.

The third assumption is perhaps the most problematic. Indeed, since much of the interest in downward nominal wage rigidity is driven by a concern over potential employment effects, the assumption that any employment effects may be ignored is troubling. One way to relax assumption 3 is to assume (3′) a fraction 2α of jobs that would otherwise be observed—all associated with nominal wage changes below the median—are lost due to nominal wage rigidities. In this case, a counterfactual distribution can be constructed by taking the observed distribution of wage changes beyond the $0.5 - \alpha$ quantile, and building a symmetric lower tail. For example, if 2% of continuing jobs are lost because of downward wage rigidities, then an appropriate counterfactual is the symmetric distribution constructed from the observed distribution to the right of the 49th percentile. In the analysis below, we also construct such a "49th percentile counterfactual" distribution and derive summary statistics from this, as a robustness check on the results from the "median" counterfactual.[27]

Formally, let $f(x)$ denote the probability density function of *observed* real wage changes in some period (for some given sample of workers). Let $\tilde{f}(x)$ denote the counterfactual density function. Then assumptions 1–3 or 1–3′ imply

$$\tilde{f}(x) = k_c \cdot f(x), \qquad x \geq c;$$
$$\tilde{f}(x) = k_c \cdot f(2c - x), \qquad x < c,$$

where k_c is a constant and c is the point of symmetry. Under assumption 3, c is equal to the median observed wage change, while under assumption 3′, c is equal to the $0.5 - \alpha$ quantile. Using the fact that $\tilde{f}(x)$ must integrate to 1, it is easy to see that $k_c = 0.5/(1 - F(c))$, where F is the distribution function associated with f. Note that if $c = m$ (the observed median) then $F(c) = 0.5$ and $k_c = 1$. Otherwise, if c is the $0.5 - \alpha$ quantile, then $k_c = 1/(1 + 2\alpha) \approx 1 - 2\alpha$.

2.4.3   Measuring the Effects of Rigidities

Given an observed distribution of real wage changes and a particular counterfactual distribution, it is possible to develop a variety of measures of the effect of nominal rigidities. We focus on two simple summary statistics: a mea-

26. Intuitively, measurement errors smear some of the true mass at $-\pi$, to the left and right of the spike. Any measurement errors larger than π, will therefore displace a nonzero mass to the right of the median of Δw_i^*.

27. An alternative is to construct the counterfactual distribution by imposing symmetry around the mode of the distribution of observed wage changes. This is equivalent to assuming that, in the absence of rigidities, the wage-change distribution would be symmetric with median equal to the mode. We tried this approach, but found that the resulting counterfactual distribution is extremely sensitive to the location of the mode. Also, in several years the mode is above the median, which would imply job gains, rather than job losses, from nominal rigidities.

sure of the fraction of people whose wages are affected by rigidities, and a measure of the net effect of rigidities on the average wage change.

Density Effects

In principle, nominal wage rigidities can affect workers whose wages would have fallen in the absence of rigidity, and people whose wages would have otherwise risen. Thus, we decompose the fraction of workers affected by rigidities into an estimate of the fraction whose wages were "held up," and an estimate of the fraction whose wages were "held down." The former is the cumulative density of the counterfactual distribution that has been "swept up" to the nominal wage rigidity spike (at $-\pi_t$):

$$(1) \qquad su_t = \int_{-\infty}^{-\pi_t^-} (\tilde{f}(x) - f(x))\, dx = \tilde{F}(-\pi_t^-) - F(-\pi_t^-),$$

where the upper limit of integration $(-\pi_t^-)$ excludes the mass point at $-\pi_t$, and $\tilde{F}(x)$ and $F(x)$ are the cumulative distribution functions corresponding to $\tilde{f}(x)$ and $f(x)$ respectively. The latter is the cumulative density of the counterfactual distribution that has been "swept back" to the nominal-wage rigidity spike:

$$(2) \qquad sb_t = \int_{-\pi_t^+}^{m_t} (\tilde{f}(x) - f(x))\, dx = (\tilde{F}(m_t) - \tilde{F}(-\pi_t^+)) \\ - (F(m_t) - F(-\pi_t^+)),$$

where m_t is the median real wage change in year t, and the lower limit of integration $(-\pi_t^+)$ excludes the mass point at $-\pi_t$. (Note that by assumption 2 above, we need only extend the upper limit of integration to the median.) The total fraction of individuals affected by rigidities is $su_t + sb_t$, which is equal to the mass at the spike point (suitably normalized, if the point of symmetry for the construction of the counterfactual density is not equal to the median).

If estimates of $F(x)$ and $\tilde{F}(x)$ are available, then su_t and sb_t can be evaluated directly.[28] In the absence of any menu costs or "rounding," su_t provides an esti-

---

28. Alternatively, using the definition of the counterfactual density, it is easy to show that

$$(1') \qquad su_t = k_c \cdot (1 - F(2c + \pi_t)) - F(-\pi_t^-),$$

where F is the distribution function of observed wage changes in year t, c is the point of symmetry for the counterfactual, and k_c is the constant defined earlier. This expression can be evaluated directly using the empirical distribution function for observed real wage changes. If c is set to the median real wage change in year $t(m_t)$, this expression simplifies to $su_t = (1 - F(2m_t + \pi_t)) - F(-\pi_t^-)$, and if $m_t = 0$ (which is roughly true for most of our sample years) then $su_t = (1 - F(\pi_t)) - F(-\pi_t^-)$, which represents a simple difference between the fraction of real wage changes *above* π_t and the fraction *below* $-\pi_t$. Similarly, the fraction of the density swept back can be written as

$$(2') \qquad sb_t = k_c \cdot (F(2c + \pi_t) - F(2c - m_t)) - (F(m_t) - F(-\pi_t^+)),$$

which, if the point of symmetry is set to the median, reduces to $sb_t = F(2m_t + \pi_t) - .5 - (.5 - F(-\pi_t^-))$, or to $sb_t = F(\pi_t) - .5 - (.5 - F(-\pi_t^+))$, if $m_t = 0$. This last expression is simply the fraction of observed wage changes between π_t and the median minus the fraction between the median and $-\pi_t$.

mate of the fraction of workers affected by downward wage rigidities. In the presence of menu costs or rounding, however, su_t will tend to overstate the effect of downward rigidities. Nevertheless, if menu costs affect an equal fraction of workers who otherwise would receive small nominal increases and decreases (as assumed in figure 2.4b), then the *net* sweep-up $su_t - sb_t$ provides a lower-bound estimate of the fraction of workers affected by downward nominal wage rigidity. To see why, notice that the counterfactual density to the right of $-\pi_t$ is bigger than the counterfactual density to the left. Thus if equal *fractions* of the counterfactual are affected by menu costs, the total density swept back to $-\pi_t$ by menu costs (measured by sb_t) will exceed the total density swept up to $-\pi_t$ by menu costs.

Wage Effects

In constructing a measure of the effect of nominal rigidities on average wage growth, we similarly distinguish between the effect for individuals whose wages are "held up" by rigidities and the effect for those whose wages are "held back." The effect on the former group is

$$
\begin{aligned}
wsu_t &= \int_{-\infty}^{-\pi_t^-} (\tilde{f}(x) - f(x))(-\pi_t - x)\, dx \\
&= -\pi_t su_t - E(\Delta w | \Delta w < -\pi_t; \tilde{f}) \times \tilde{F}(-\pi_t^-) \\
&\quad + E(\Delta w | \Delta w < -\pi_t; f) \times F(-\pi_t^-),
\end{aligned}
$$

(3)

which we refer to "wage sweep-up," while the effect on the latter group is

$$
\begin{aligned}
wsb_t &= -\int_{-\pi_t^+}^{m_t} (\tilde{f}(x) - f(x))(-\pi_t - x)\, dx \\
&= \pi_t sb_t + E(\Delta w | -\pi_t < \Delta w \le m_t; \tilde{f}) \times (\tilde{F}(m_t) - \tilde{F}(-\pi_t^+)) \\
&\quad - E(\Delta w | -\pi_t < \Delta w \le m_t; f) \times (F(m_t) - F(-\pi_t^+)),
\end{aligned}
$$

(4)

which we refer to as "wage sweep-back." Again, if estimates of the densities $f(w)$ and $\tilde{f}(x)$ are available, these expressions can be evaluated directly. Alternatively, they can be estimated using estimates of the fractions of individuals in various wage-change intervals, and the mean wage change within these intervals.[29]

---

29. Specifically, using the definition of the counterfactual density, it is straightforward to show that

(3')
$$
\begin{aligned}
wsu_t = k_c \cdot (1 - F(2c + \pi_t)) \cdot \{E(\Delta w | \Delta w \ge 2c + \pi_t) - \pi_t\} \\
- F(-\pi_t^-) \cdot \{-\pi - E(\Delta w | \Delta w \le -\pi_t)\},
\end{aligned}
$$

where the expectations are taken with respect to the actual distribution of wage changes. This expression can be evaluated using estimates of the fractions of real wage changes in the upper and lower tails of the observed wage-change distribution and estimates of the conditional mean wage changes in the two tails. A similar expression can be developed for wsb_t in terms of the fractions of wage changes in the intervals $[-\pi_t^+, c]$ and $[c, 2c + \pi_t]$, and the mean wage changes within these intervals.

Effects of Measurement Error

The nominal rigidity measures developed in equations 1–4 implicitly ignore any errors in reported wages. Random measurement errors will have several effects on the observed distribution of wage changes relative to the true underlying distribution. Most notably, the observed fraction of workers with rigid wages will be *lower* than the true fraction. In particular, assuming that the observed wage in period t w_t differs from the actual wage w_t^* by an error u_t, the observed wage change is

$$\Delta w_t = \Delta w_t^* + \Delta u_t.$$

If the distribution of true wage changes is continuous, apart from a spike at $-\pi_t$, only individuals with truly rigid wages who accurately report their wage change contribute to observed rigidity. The fraction of individuals with observed wage rigidity is therefore

$$P(\Delta w_t = 0) = R \times P(\Delta w_t^* = 0),$$

where $R = P(\Delta u_t = 0 | \Delta w^* = 0)$ is the probability of accurately reporting the true wage change, conditional on rigid wages. We are unaware of any direct estimates of R. However, evidence from the January 1977 CPS validation survey provides an indication of the magnitude of this probability. In that survey 44% of hourly-rated workers report exactly the same wage as their employers report. Treating the employers' reports as error free, this estimate suggests that R lies between 0.2 ($=0.44^2$) and 0.44, depending on the persistence in individuals' probabilities of making an error-free wage report.[30] If employers have about the same probability of making an erroneous wage report as employees, however, then this estimate suggests a range for R between 0.44 and 0.66 ($=0.44^{1/2}$), again depending on the persistence in the likelihood of making an error-free wage report. These estimates suggest that the observed fraction of rigid wages may understate the true rigidity rate by 30–80%.

A second implication of measurement error is that the observed distribution of wage changes will tend to show less evidence of menu costs than the true distribution. Specifically, suppose that with probability R individuals report their true wage change, and with probability $(1 - R)$ they report their true wage change plus a continuously distributed measurement error Δu_t. Then a fraction $(1 - R)$ of the true mass at $-\pi_t$ is transformed into a distribution of observed wage changes centered on $-\pi_t$ with the density function of Δu_t. Assuming that Δu_t has a "bell-shaped" distribution, this will add relatively more mass to the observed distribution just to the left and right of $-\pi_t$, partially "filling in" any deficit created by menu costs or rounding effects.

---

30. If the same individuals provide an error-free wage report in consecutive years, then the probability of an error-free wage change is 0.44. If the probability of an error-free wage report is independent over time, then the likelihood of an error-free change is 0.44^2.

A third implication of measurement error, mentioned above, is that nominal rigidities in the lower half of the wage-change distribution may spill over to the upper half, leading to a violation of the assumption that observed wage changes above the median are unaffected by rigidities. In particular, the addition of a symmetric measurement error to a right-skewed distribution of true wage changes, such as illustrated in figure 2.4A, will tend to lead to a measured median above the true median wage change.

Figure 2.5 displays the qualitative effects of measurement error on the observed distribution of wage changes. As illustrated in the figure, reporting errors attenuate the magnitude of the spike in the observed distribution at $-\pi_t$, while adding "shoulders" to either side of the spike. In the figure some of the displaced mass spills over above the median, causing an upward bias in the observed median relative to the true median.

To get some idea of the quantitative effect of measurement errors on the accuracy of our rigidity measures, we performed a series of simulations in which we added measurement errors to a distribution of true wage changes like the one in figure 2.4B and then formed estimates of *su, sb, wsu,* and *wsb.* A complete description of the simulations is presented in appendix B, with a table showing the actual and estimated levels of sweep-up (*su*), sweep-back (*sb*) and wage sweep-up (*wsu*). Although limited in scope, the simulations show that the addition of measurement error leads to *downward* biases in our estimates of downward rigidity effects. The estimates of wage sweep-up, for example, are downward biased by 10–30% under a plausible range of assumptions.

2.4.4   Kernel Density Estimates of the Actual and Counterfactual Distributions

As a preliminary step in describing the extent of nominal rigidities in our CPS and PSID samples, we used standard kernel estimation techniques to construct smoothed estimates of the densities of real wage changes, and corresponding estimates of the counterfactual densities. In contrast to simple histograms, which can display irregular "jumps," kernel density methods compute a weighted average of the density *near to* each point. In particular, the kernel estimator for the density at some value x is

$$\tilde{f}(x) = \frac{1}{nh} \sum_{i=1}^{n} K\left(\frac{x - x_i}{h}\right),$$

where n is the number of observations, h is a *bandwidth* parameter (sometimes called the *window width*), and $K(\cdot)$ is a kernel or weighting function, which integrates to 1 over the range of x.[31] The smoothed kernel estimates give a

31. Silverman (1986) provides a full treatment of the issues involved with density estimation. We estimate each of the densities of 250 equispaced points (x) in the range $(-0.35, 0.35)$ using an Epanechnikov kernel and a fixed bandwidth, $h = 0.005$. We also tried other bandwidths and found that the resulting distributions were qualitatively similar.

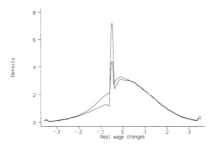

Fig. 2.5   Theoretical effect of measurement error on the distribution of real wage changes in the presence of menu costs and downward rigidities

clearer picture of the differences between the actual and counterfactual distributions of wage changes than can be obtained using simple histograms.

The actual and median-counterfactual densities for the CPS samples are shown in figure 2.6. As is true of the simple histograms in figure 2.1, the smoothed densities of the observed data show noticeable spikes at the point corresponding to rigid nominal wages (i.e., at minus the inflation rate), with a larger spike in years with lower inflation rates. A comparison of the actual and counterfactual distributions shows a deficit in the left tail of the actual distribution, and a small but typically noticeable deficit to the right of the spike point. These two characteristics are consistent with the stylized graph in figure 2.4B. The observed data seem to show both downward nominal rigidity effects *and* the presence of menu costs associated with small wage changes.

To better pinpoint the differences between the actual and counterfactual distributions, figure 2.7 presents graphs of the cumulative deviation between the two distributions at each point up to the median. For each wage change below the median, we compute the fraction of the actual distribution "missing" from the counterfactual distribution between that point and $-\pi_t$. Specifically, for each point below the spike (i.e., for each wage change $\Delta w < -\pi_t$), we estimate

$$G(\Delta w) = \frac{\displaystyle\int_{\Delta w}^{-\pi_t^-} (\tilde{f}(x) - f(x))\, dx}{\displaystyle\int_{\Delta w}^{-\pi_t^-} \tilde{f}(x)\, dx}.$$

Similarly, for each point between the spike and the median (i.e., for each wage change $-\pi_t < \Delta w < m_t$), we estimate

$$G(\Delta w) = \frac{\displaystyle\int_{-\pi_t^+}^{\Delta w} (\tilde{f}(x) - f(x))\, dx}{\displaystyle\int_{-\pi_t^+}^{\Delta w} \tilde{f}(x)\, dx}.$$

In practice, we set the limits of integration around the spike point to be $-\pi_t^- = -\pi_t - 0.0025$ and $-\pi_t^+ = -\pi_t + 0.0025$. If nominal rigidities prevent some individuals' real wages from falling faster than the inflation rate, then $G(\Delta w)$ will be positive for all $\Delta w < -\pi_t$. Indeed, in the simple case where a fixed fraction f of real wage declines bigger than $-\pi_t$ are prevented, $G(\Delta w)$ will equal f. Similarly, to the extent that menu costs prevent some individuals' nominal wages from rising, $G(\Delta w)$ will be positive for all $-\pi_t < \Delta w < m_t$.

In figure 2.7 we have graphed the estimated $G(\Delta w)$ functions for each year after renormalizing the real wage changes in a particular year relative to the spike point. That is, we graph $G(\Delta w + \pi_t)$, which is equivalent to graphing the deficits in the distributions of *nominal* wage changes. Inspection of the graphs suggests that in most years $G(\Delta w)$ is roughly constant for Δw in the left-hand tail of the distribution, and in the range from one-quarter to one-half; below, but near to, $-\pi_t$ the fraction displaced shows a sharp increase to one-half or more; and above $-\pi_t$, $G(\Delta w)$ falls off steadily from about one-half. These patterns suggest that a substantial fraction of wages are affected by downward nominal rigidity, and that, near to zero nominal change, menu costs may account for at least one-half and perhaps more of observed rigidity.

2.4.5   Estimates of the Effects of Nominal Rigidities

Tables 2.3 and 2.4 present estimates of the four summary measures of the effect of nominal wage rigidity $(su_t, sb_t, wsu_t, wsb_t)$ defined by equations 1–4, using our CPS samples of hourly-rated non–job changers. In implementing the formulas we restrict the upper and lower limit of integration for real wage changes to ± 0.3, in order to reduce the effect of any outliers in the extreme tails of the wage-change distributions. Table 2.3 contains estimates of the density displacement effects su_t and sb_t for two choices of the point of symmetry: the median real wage change, and the 49th percentile real wage change. Recall that the latter is appropriate under the assumption that 2% of potential wage change observations are missing because of employment responses to downward wage rigidity.

Consider first the estimated sweep-up effects (su_t) presented in columns 2 and 3. Under the median counterfactual, nominal wage rigidities are estimated to affect between 5.4 and 7.3% of hourly-rated non–job changers during the high-inflation years from 1979 to 1982, and between 9.7 and 13.5% of workers during the low-inflation period later in the sample. Using the 49th-percentile counterfactual the estimated effects are fairly similar: between 6.5 and 6.8% during the high-inflation years, and between 10.6 and 14.5% during the low-inflation years.

The estimated density sweep-back effects (sb_t) in columns 4 and 5 are generally much smaller than the sweep-up effects, although in some years sweep-back accounts for up to one-third of total nominal rigidity. If the sweep-back effects are interpreted as estimates of the effect of menu costs to the right of the spike, and if menu costs have a symmetric effect on negative and positive

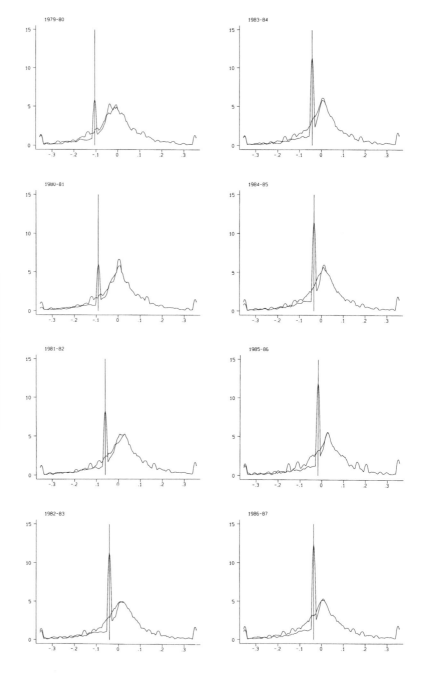

KERNEL DENSITY ESTIMATES

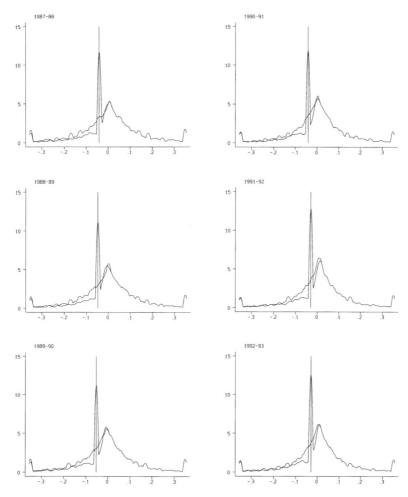

Fig. 2.6   Smoothed (kernel) estimates of actual and counterfactual densities of real wage changes, CPS samples from 1979–80 to 1992–93

wage changes, then the difference ($su_t - sb_t$) provides a *lower-bound* estimate of the fraction of people affected by downward nominal wage rigidities. In the mid-1980s this fraction is around 10–12%.

Simple regressions of our estimates of su_t on the inflation rate in year t yield statistically significant coefficients of -0.81 and -0.97 using the median and 49th-percentile counterfactuals respectively, with t-statistics of 4.1 and 4.9. Analogous regressions of the net sweep-up effects ($su_t - sb_t$) on the inflation rate yield smaller and less significant coefficients of -0.44 and -0.73, with t-statistics 1.3 and 2.2 These estimates suggest that higher inflation helps to reduce the effect of downward nominal rigidities. A 5 percentage-point increase in the inflation rate is associated with a 2.2 to 5.0 percentage-point reduction

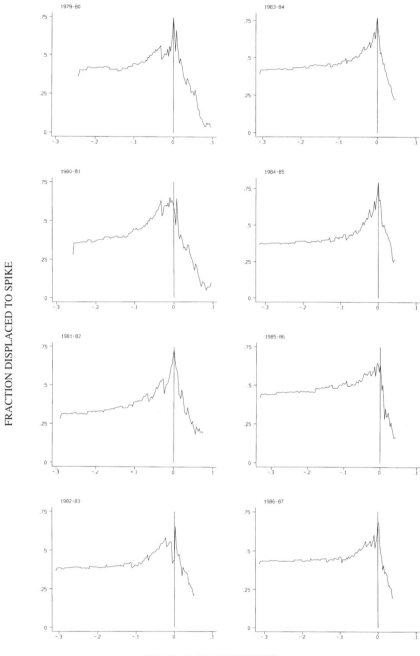

FRACTION DISPLACED TO SPIKE

NOMINAL WAGE CHANGE

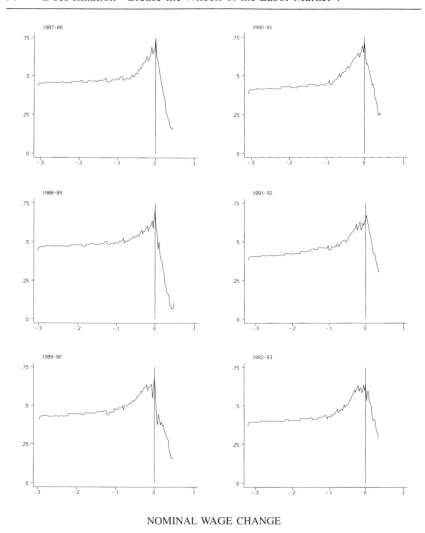

NOMINAL WAGE CHANGE

Fig. 2.7   Cumulative fraction of counterfactual density affected by rigidities, CPS samples from 1979–80 to 1992–93

in the fraction of nonmovers who are affected by downward nominal rigidity. As noted above, we suspect that this estimate is downward biased in magnitude to the extent that measured wage changes are incorrectly reported to the CPS.

Table 2.4 contains the estimated wage effects wsu_t and wsb_t associated with nominal rigidities. These vary over the sample period with larger effects in low-inflation years. Again, the estimates of wsu_t and wsb_t from the median and 49th-percentile counterfactuals are fairly similar. The estimates imply that nominal rigidities raised the mean real wages of non–job changers who would otherwise have suffered nominal wage declines by between 0.3 and 1.2%, with

Table 2.3   Estimated Fraction of Non-Job Changers Affected by Nominal
                   Wage Rigidities

| | | Density Swept-up[a] Counterfactual | | Density Swept-back[b] Counterfactual | |
| | Inflation Rate | Median | 49th Percentile | Median | 49th Percentile |
Year	(1)	(2)	(3)	(4)	(5)
1979–80	10.6	6.86	6.54	0.76	2.01
1980–81	9.1	6.20	5.92	2.02	2.88
1981–82	5.9	6.31	6.56	4.54	5.31
1982–83	4.1	9.98	11.60	4.79	4.17
1983–84	4.2	10.43	11.54	4.44	4.41
1984–85	3.5	10.84	11.24	4.49	4.92
1985–86	1.8	12.72	13.96	2.87	2.66
1986–87	3.6	13.45	13.49	2.66	3.63
1987–88	4.1	13.85	14.10	1.57	2.33
1988–89	4.7	13.04	14.09	1.82	1.77
1989–90	5.3	11.39	12.42	2.72	3.17
1990–91	4.1	10.79	12.09	4.89	4.59
1991–92	3.0	11.75	12.09	5.32	5.98
1992–93	2.9	11.10	12.13	5.45	5.43

Notes: Samples are based on matched CPS samples of hourly-rated workers who report the same industry and occupation code in consecutive years, and whose wages are not affected by the minimum wage in either year.

[a]Estimated percentage of workers who would have experienced a nominal wage cut in the absence of rigidities.

[b]Estimated percentage of workers who would have experienced a nominal wage increase in the absence of rigidities.

an average effect of about 1% in the low-inflation years of the mid-1980s. On the other hand, nominal rigidities do not seem to have had a large *negative* effect on people whose nominal wages otherwise would have risen. The maximum estimated wage sweep-back effect is 0.2%, and the estimates are typically less than 0.1%. On net, our estimates imply that nominal rigidities may have contributed to about 1% higher average growth for hourly-rated non–job changers in the mid-1980s, with smaller effects in the earlier and later years of our sample period.

One interesting question that the estimated sweep-up effects in tables 2.3 and 2.4 do *not* address is how far down in the lower tail of the counterfactual wage-change distribution are individuals with observed rigid wages drawn from. For example, one might argue that the institutional forces that generate downward rigidities have limited power to resist large wage cuts. In this case, most of the measured sweep-up in table 2.3 should arise from the interval of real wage changes just below $-\pi_r$.[32] Of course, if downward rigidities do pre-

32. This ignores measurement errors in wage changes. Given an observed wage change in the lower tail of the observed wage-change distribution, the best estimate of the true wage change is less negative.

Table 2.4   **Estimated Effect of Nominal Wage Rigidities on Average Real Wage Changes**

Year	Inflation Rate (1)	Wage Swept-Up Counterfactual[a]		Wage Swept-Back Counterfactual[b]	
		Median (2)	49th Percentile (3)	Median (4)	49th Percentile (5)
1979–80	10.6	0.54	0.51	0.00	0.03
1980–81	9.1	0.35	0.32	0.01	0.11
1981–82	5.9	0.25	0.30	0.16	0.16
1982–83	4.1	0.75	0.83	0.09	0.06
1983–84	4.2	0.81	0.82	0.06	0.09
1984–85	3.5	0.93	0.99	0.08	0.06
1985–86	1.8	0.87	0.95	0.03	0.03
1986–87	3.6	1.17	1.20	0.03	0.05
1987–88	4.1	1.13	1.20	0.00	0.01
1988–89	4.7	1.10	1.18	0.01	0.00
1989–90	5.3	0.93	0.96	0.00	0.05
1990–91	4.1	0.71	0.80	0.07	0.05
1991–92	3.0	0.71	0.74	0.08	0.09
1992–93	2.9	0.72	0.78	0.07	0.07

Notes: Samples are based on matched CPS samples of hourly-rated workers who report the same industry and occupation code in consecutive years, and whose wages are not affected by the minimum wage in either year.

[a]Estimated effect of nominal rigidities on average real wage change for workers who otherwise would have experienced a nominal wage cut, expressed in percentages.

[b]Estimated effect of nominal rigidities on average real wage change for workers who otherwise would have experienced a nominal wage increase, expressed in percentages. A positive entry means that rigidities reduced wages for this group.

vent large wage cuts, we might expect some wage-change observations to be missing from the lower tail of the distribution, consistent with our 49th-percentile counterfactual. Appendix tables 2A.3 and 2A.4 decompose the estimates of su_t and wsu_t into fractions attributable to nominal wage changes in three intervals: less than a 10% cut, from a 10 to 20% cut, and more than a 20% nominal cut. About 70% of the density swept up to the nominal rigidity spike is attributable to the interval of 0–10% nominal cuts. Another 20% is attributable to nominal cuts of 10 to 20% and only 10% is attributable to nominal cuts over 20%. The decomposition of wage sweep-up, however, is different, since wages swept up from farther in the tail contribute more to wsu_t. Indeed, roughly one-third of total estimated wage sweep-up is attributable to each of the three ranges.

The correlations of the estimated wage sweep-up (wsu_t) and net wage sweep-up ($wsu_t - wsb_t$) effects with the aggregate inflation rate are negative and significant. Regressions of wsu_t and ($wsu_t - wsb_t$) on the corresponding inflation rates over the fourteen-year sample period yield coefficient estimates between -0.057 and -0.079, with t-statistics between 1.8 and 2.5. These estimates imply that a rise in the inflation rate from 3% to 8% is associated with about 0.3% slower real average wage growth for non–job changers. We conclude that downward nominal wage rigidities exert a small but measurable effect on average wage growth, with a bigger effect in low-inflation years. Again, evidence from our simulations suggest that, if anything, these estimates may be downward biased in magnitude by the effects of reporting errors in the CPS wage data.

The conclusion that lower inflation rates increase the incidence of downward rigidity provides one possible insight into the "fact" that individuals seem to dislike inflation (see Shiller, chap. 1 in this volume). Our estimates suggest that a lower inflation rate acts like a higher "minimum wage" for the rate of growth of real wages. Indeed, the similarity between the histograms in figures 2.1 and 2.2 and histograms of real wage *levels* in the presence of a binding minimum wage is remarkable. The data in figure 2.7 suggest that between one-quarter and one-half of non–job changers who might have expected a nominal wage cut in the absence of any rigidities instead have rigid nominal wages. If workers have an implicit "guarantee" that their real wage will fall by no more than the inflation rate, their preference for a lower inflation rate is understandable.

2.5   Market-Level Evidence

While our analysis of individual wage data provides reasonably strong evidence that nominal rigidities affect the underlying distribution of real wage changes, much of the interest in nominal rigidities focuses at a higher level of aggregation. In this section we therefore examine the evidence that *state-level* average real wages fall more quickly in response to a given level of labor market slack in periods of high inflation than in periods of low inflation.

As a point of departure, consider a collection of workers indexed by i in some local labor market j. Let U_j represent a measure of slack in market j in some period (e.g., the difference between a market demand shock and a market supply shock). Suppose that, in the absence of rigidities,

$$(5) \qquad \Delta w_{ij} = b^* U_j + \varepsilon_{ij},$$

where Δw_{ij} is the real wage change for individual i in market j (over some specific time horizon) and ε_{ij} is a random term reflecting idiosyncratic factors. In the presence of downward nominal rigidities, suppose that a fraction f of nominal wage cuts required by equation 5 do not take place:

$$(6) \quad \Delta w_{ij} = b^* U_j + \varepsilon_{ij}, \qquad b^* U_j + \varepsilon_{ij} > -\pi$$
$$= I_{ij}(-\pi) + (1 - I_{ij}) \cdot (b^* U_j + \varepsilon_{ij}), \qquad b^* U_j + \varepsilon_{ij} < -\pi,$$

where I_{ij} is a random indicator variable with mean f.[33] Equation 6 implies that a regression of the average wage change observed in market j on the slack variable U_j has a coefficient that varies with the aggregate inflation rate:

33. Formally, equation 6 is a Tobit model with random censoring at $-\pi$.

(7) $$E(\Delta w_{ij}|U_j, \pi) = a(\pi) + b(\pi) \cdot U_j,$$

with a smaller coefficient $b(\pi)$, the lower the inflation rate and the higher the fraction f of individuals affected by downward rigidities. If the measure of labor market slack is the unemployment rate, then equation 7 implies that the "cross-sectional Phillips curve" is *flatter* in periods with low inflation than in periods with high inflation.

To test this prediction, we used individual microdata from the March CPS files from 1977 to 1992 to construct estimates of the average wage of workers in each state from 1976 to 1991. Specifically, we constructed two estimates of the average hourly wage for each state in each year: a simple average, and an adjusted average that accounts for differences in the observed characteristics of the workers in each state.[34] We then fit a variety of models of the form

(8) $$w_{jt} - w_{jt-1} = a_t + b_t \log U_{jt} + e_{jt},$$

where w_{jt} is the average wage index for state j in year t, a_t represents a year dummy, U_{jt} is the measured unemployment rate in the state in year t, and e_{jt} represents a residual. Finally, we analyzed the covariation between b_t (the slope coefficient in year t) and the inflation rates between years $t - 1$ and t.

Two aspects of the specification in equation 8 deserve comment. First, equation 8 describes the change in the average wage, while equation 7 describes the average individual-level wage change. In the absence of selection biases associated with nonrandom movements in and out of the labor market, this is not a problem, since with a fixed population $E(\Delta w_{ijt}) = E(w_{ijt}) - E(w_{ijt-1})$ (taking expectations over individuals in state j). While there is some evidence of a cyclical component in the gap between the average wage change for continuing workers and the change in average wages for all workers (see Solon, Barsky, and Parker 1994), this issue is somewhat less important in our application because an individual has to be unemployed (or out of the labor force) for an entire year in order not to have a wage in the March CPS data.

Second, although equation 8 is consistent with the original formulation of the Phillips curve, it is inconsistent with the formulation of the so-called wage curve recently popularized by Blanchflower and Oswald (1994). In particular, Blanchflower and Oswald argue that the wage *level* in a local labor market depends on the unemployment rate, while equation 8 implies that the rate of change of wages depends on the unemployment rate. A simple way to compare the two alternatives is to introduce the lagged unemployment rate into equation 8. If the correct model specifies the level of wages as a function of the level of unemployment, then the first difference of wages will depend on current and

---

34. To construct the adjusted average, we first estimated a wage-prediction equation for each year that included various observable characteristics (education, labor market experience, dummies for race, gender, Hispanic status) as well as dummies for each state of residence. We then used the coefficients to predict a wage for each individual, assuming that the individual lived in California. Finally, we constructed the average deviation of the observed wage from the predicted wage: this is our adjusted average (log) wage.

lagged unemployment with equal and opposite coefficients. If the correct model specifies the rate of growth of wages as a function of the unemployment rate, then lagged unemployment will have an insignificant effect on wage growth.[35]

Some evidence on this specific issue, and on the general performance of equation 8, is presented in appendix table 2A.5 where we summarize the results of estimating various versions of equation 8 *without allowing the coefficient b to vary across years*. In brief, the estimates suggest that wage growth is fairly responsive to local unemployment: a doubling of the unemployment typically reduces the rate of wage growth by 1.7–2.4% per year. Moreover, consistent with the specification of the conventional Phillips curve, but contrary to the wage-curve approach, lagged valued of local unemployment exert no significant effect on wage growth. These conclusions are robust to minor changes in specification, including the addition of dummies capturing permanent differences in wage growth across regions or states, the introduction of region times year effects capturing region-specific cycles, alternative weighting schemes, and the use of raw versus adjusted average wages for each state.

Using these findings, we proceeded to estimate a series of models that exclude lagged unemployment, but allow the coefficient on current unemployment to vary across years. Estimates of the critical coefficients b_t from five such specifications are reported in table 2.5. For reference, the top row in the table gives the estimates of the unemployment slopes from identical specifications when the slope b_t is constrained to be constant across years. The year-specific estimates of b_t are then tabulated, along with the estimated coefficients from simple ordinary least squares (OLS) regressions of the estimated b_ts on the inflation rate. Across the different specifications there is a tendency for unemployment to exert a bigger (more negative) effect on local wage determination in high inflation years. However, the correlation of b_t and π_t is weak: the biggest t-ratio (for the model in column 4) is around one.

The estimates in the bottom row of table 2.5 imply that a 5 percentage-point increase in inflation leads to an increase in the magnitude of the slope coefficient relating wage growth to local unemployment of between 0 and 0.012. To understand the implications of these estimates, suppose that $b_t = -0.034$ in an average year (as in column 2 of table 2.5). Then real wage growth is about 2.3 percentage points per year slower in a state with an 8% unemployment rate than in a state with a 4% unemployment rate. Raising the inflation rate by 5 percentage points would widen this gap by an additional 0 to 0.7 percentage

---

35. It is also possible to formulate a test based on a model for the level of wages. Specifically, the wage-curve hypothesis suggests that only the current unemployment rate affects the level of wages (controlling for state effects), while the Phillips-curve specification implies that lagged unemployment terms enter in the model with equal (negative) coefficients. Our findings from this approach are consistent with the results based on a model in first-differences.

Table 2.5   **Estimated Effects of State Unemployment on Real Wage Growth**

	Additional Control Variables Included in Models				
	Year	Year & Region	Year × Region	Year & State	Year × Region & State
Pooled slopes[a]	−0.025	−0.034	−0.025	−0.048	−0.056
	(0.005)	(0.006)	(0.007)	(0.007)	(0.012)
Year-specific slopes[b]					
1976–77	0.018	0.008	0.002	−0.004	−0.028
	(0.019)	(0.019)	(0.029)	(0.020)	(0.031)
1977–78	−0.020	−0.035	−0.027	−0.049	−0.057
	(0.020)	(0.020)	(0.031)	(0.021)	(0.034)
1978–79	0.001	−0.015	−0.005	−0.033	−0.040
	(0.020)	(0.021)	(0.030)	(0.022)	(0.033)
1979–80	−0.053	−0.068	−0.016	−0.088	−0.055
	(0.020)	(0.020)	(0.030)	(0.021)	(0.033)
1980–81	−0.042	−0.056	−0.034	−0.074	−0.067
	(0.018)	(0.018)	(0.026)	(0.019)	(0.028)
1981–82	−0.022	−0.037	−0.061	−0.056	−0.100
	(0.019)	(0.019)	(0.030)	(0.020)	(0.032)
1982–83	−0.047	−0.060	−0.057	−0.080	−0.087
	(0.018)	(0.019)	(0.026)	(0.020)	(0.028)
1983–84	−0.044	−0.058	−0.025	−0.076	−0.056
	(0.017)	(0.018)	(0.025)	(0.019)	(0.028)
1984–85	−0.018	−0.029	−0.040	−0.046	−0.071
	(0.019)	(0.019)	(0.029)	(0.020)	(0.031)
1985–86	−0.016	−0.024	0.018	−0.036	−0.011
	(0.016)	(0.017)	(0.030)	(0.017)	(0.033)
1986–87	−0.062	−0.066	−0.030	−0.077	−0.060
	(0.015)	(0.015)	(0.028)	(0.016)	(0.031)
1987–88	−0.004	−0.008	−0.023	−0.020	−0.050
	(0.015)	(0.016)	(0.025)	(0.016)	(0.028)
1988–89	−0.027	−0.033	−0.017	−0.050	−0.045
	(0.020)	(0.020)	(0.026)	(0.021)	(0.029)
1989–90	−0.030	−0.040	−0.069	−0.063	−0.099
	(0.025)	(0.025)	(0.028)	(0.027)	(0.031)
1990–91	0.019	0.006	0.010	−0.012	−0.017
	(0.023)	(0.023)	(0.027)	(0.024)	(0.029)
Effect of inflation rate	−0.097	−0.197	−0.041	−0.251	−0.146
on estimated slope[c]	(0.275)	(0.273)	(0.286)	(0.286)	(0.298)

Notes: Standard errors are in parentheses. Models are estimated on sample of 756 state times year observations. See note to table 2A.5.

[a]Estimated effect of unemployment on wage growth in model with constant coefficient.

[b]Estimated effects of unemployment on wage growth in model with year-specific coefficients.

[c]Estimated coefficient from OLS regression of year-specific unemployment effects on annual inflation rate (change in log CPI-U-X1).

points.[36] The upper range of this interval represents a sizeable increase in the "flexibility" of wages to local demand conditions between a low- and high-inflation regime. However, the imprecise nature of our estimates makes it impossible to distinguish such a possibility from the alternative that higher inflation has *no* effect on the rate of relative wage adjustment.

2.6 Conclusions

A traditional concern about very low inflation is that nominal wages are downward rigid. In this paper we have attempted to assemble two types of evidence on the extent of such rigidities: microlevel evidence based on the distribution of individual-specific wage changes; and market-level evidence based on the rate of adjustment of average real wages in a state to the state unemployment rates. Our microanalysis reveals three key insights. First, although many individuals experience (measured) nominal wage reductions from one year to the next, there is a substantial spike at zero in the distribution of nominal wage changes. Second, the magnitude of this spike is very highly correlated with inflation. In the high-inflation era of the late 1970s, 6–10% of workers with the same job reported exactly the same wage from one year to the next. In the low-inflation era of the mid-1980s, this fraction rose to over 15%. Third, informal and formal analyses suggest that most (but not all) of workers with rigid nominal wages would have had an even bigger decline in their real wage in the absence of rigidities. For the mid-1980s we estimate that downward nominal rigidities may have "held up" average real wages by 1% per year.

Our market-level analysis of real wage responses to local unemployment is less conclusive. As previous researchers have noted, real wages grow more quickly in local labor markets with low unemployment, and decline in local labor markets with high unemployment. In principle, the existence of downward nominal rigidities implies that the rate of adjustment to negative shocks will be faster, the higher the aggregate inflation rate. Empirically, however, we find only weak evidence of such an effect. Based on both types of evidence, we conclude that the overall impact of nominal wage rigidities is probably modest.

---

36. An increase in the unemployment rate from 4% to 8% is a 0.69 point change in the log unemployment rate. Multiplying this by the baseline coefficient estimate (-0.034) implies a 2.3 percentage-point reduction in the growth of log wages. The coefficients in the bottom row of table 2.5 imply that a 5 percentage-point increase in the inflation rate will raise the absolute magnitude of the unemployment coefficient by from 0.002 to 0.010, leading to a net unemployment coefficient of -0.036 to -0.044. In this case, the effect of doubling the unemployment rate is to slow the rate of growth of wages by from 2.5 to 3.0 percentage points per year.

Appendix A
Data Description and Sources

This appendix describes the construction of our matched CPS panels. We begin with the merged monthly "outgoing rotation group" files that pool the CPS sample observations in the two outgoing rotation groups (rotation groups 4 and 8) of each month of a given calendar year. The CPS sample design implies that households in rotation group 4 in a given month will be in rotation group 8 in the same month in the next year. For example, in the 1979 CPS sample there are 164,626 individuals age sixteen and older in rotation group 4, drawn from 80,557 uniquely identified households. All of these individuals were potentially reinterviewed in 1980. Since the CPS sample frame is based on physical addresses, rather than specific individuals or families, any family that moves between 1979 and 1980 is "replaced" in the sample by the family that moves into their old housing unit. Moreover, individuals who move out of a family are not tracked to their new address. Finally, since the CPS does not assign unique person identifiers to individuals within households, there is some slip-

Table 2A.1	Matched CPS Sample Selection		
Year	Total Number of Hourly-rated Workers in Matched CPS Sample	% with Same Industry & Occupation[a]	. . . And Unaffected by Minimum Wage[b]
1979–80	19,792	58.9	47.3
1980–81	22,362	59.8	48.1
1981–82	22,127	61.5	52.9
1982–83	21,768	32.8	28.5
1983–84	21,737	47.7	42.4
1984–85	10,491	57.0	51.2
1985–86	5,904	54.9	50.2
1986–87	23,187	56.1	51.5
1987–88	21,906	55.8	51.9
1988–89	21,751	55.2	52.0
1989–90	22,952	55.3	50.4
1990–91	23,365	56.0	48.9
1991–92	23,089	55.7	50.5
1992–93	22,847	56.3	52.2

[a]The industry and occupations are matched using detailed (two-digit) industry and occupation codes for all years except 1982–83, 1983–84, and 1988–89. Matching for the 1983–84 sample is based on three-digit 1980 census codes; for the 1982–83 sample, the industry is matched using the detailed (two-digit) codes which are comparable across years, while occupation was matched using an algorithm devised to convert 1970 census three-digit occupation codes to their 1980 census counterparts; and for the 1988–89 sample, occupation was matched using the detailed codes, and an algorithm was devised to match the detailed industry codes. The matching algorithms used for the 1982–83 and 1988–89 samples are available from the authors on request.

[b]Observations are assumed to be affected by minimum wage effects if *either* $w_{t-1} \leq \max(mw_{t-1}, mw_t)$, *or* $w_t \leq mw_t$.

Table 2A.2   PSID Sample Selection

Year	Total Number of Workers in 4-Year Panel	% Hourly-rated with Same Employer[a]
1976–77	1,965	41.2
1977–78	1,992	45.0
1978–79	2,214	41.3
1985–86	4,507	45.9
1986–87	4,447	45.0
1987–88	4,443	45.1

[a]Workers are treated as having changed employer if their reported tenure, in months, is less than the number of months since their previous interview. During 1976–79, tenure relates to time in the same *position*, while during 1985–88, tenure relates to time with the same employer.

Table 2A.3   Decomposition of Density Sweep-Up over the Range of Nominal Wage Changes

Year	Inflation Rate	Density Swept-up From[a]			
		All Negative Wage Changes	Wage Changes between -0.1 & 0	Wage Changes between -0.2 & -0.1	Wage Changes < -0.20
1979–80	10.6	6.86	5.11	1.34	0.42
1980–81	9.1	6.20	5.22	0.42	0.56
1981–82	5.9	6.31	5.55	0.53	0.23
1982–83	4.1	9.98	6.54	2.07	1.37
1983–84	4.2	10.43	7.27	2.21	0.94
1984–85	3.5	10.84	7.45	1.86	1.53
1985–86	1.8	12.72	9.41	2.16	1.15
1986–87	3.6	13.45	9.20	2.26	1.99
1987–88	4.1	13.85	9.38	3.04	1.42
1988–89	4.7	13.04	8.79	2.87	1.37
1989–90	5.3	11.39	8.02	2.26	1.12
1990–91	4.1	10.79	7.97	2.48	0.34
1991–92	3.0	11.75	8.74	2.15	0.87
1992–93	2.9	11.10	8.09	2.07	0.94

Note: Samples are based on matched CPS samples of hourly-rated workers who report the same industry and occupation code in consecutive years, and whose wages are not affected by the minimum wage in either year.

[a]Computed assuming "median" counterfactual wage-change distributions.

page in matching if an individual misreports a key characteristic (like race or age), or if a household contains two very similar people. These limitations imply that about 25–30% of individuals are unmatchable.

We matched individuals in rotation group 4 of year *t* with individuals in

Table 2A.4   **Decomposition of Wage Sweep-Up over the Range of Nominal Wage Changes**

		Density Swept-up From[a]			
Year	Inflation Rate	All Negative Wage Changes	Wage Changes between −0.1 & 0	Wage Changes between −0.2 & −0.1	Wage Changes < −0.20
1979–80	10.6	0.54	0.19	0.21	0.14
1980–81	9.1	0.35	0.17	0.06	0.12
1981–82	5.9	0.25	0.18	0.08	−0.01
1982–83	4.1	0.75	0.18	0.27	0.29
1983–84	4.2	0.81	0.27	0.31	0.24
1984–85	3.5	0.93	0.24	0.28	0.40
1985–86	1.8	0.87	0.39	0.30	0.18
1986–87	3.6	1.17	0.36	0.32	0.49
1987–88	4.1	1.13	0.33	0.44	0.36
1988–89	4.7	1.10	0.33	0.40	0.36
1989–90	5.3	0.93	0.28	0.32	0.33
1990–91	4.1	0.71	0.25	0.37	0.09
1991–92	3.0	0.71	0.26	0.25	0.19
1992–93	2.9	0.72	0.23	0.28	0.21

Note: Samples are based on matched CPS samples of hourly-rated workers who report the same industry and occupation code in consecutive years, and whose wages are not affected by the minimum wage in either year.

[a]Computed assuming "median" counterfactual wage-change distributions.

rotation group 8 in year $t + 1$ by household identity number, interview month, sex, race, ethnicity, and age. We allowed for errors in age of plus or minus one year in the matching algorithm (this gives about 6% more successful matches than a strict requirement that age increments by one). The overall match rates are between 70 and 75% in every year except 1984–85 and 1985–86. For example, 74.5% of the 164,626 individuals in rotation group 4 of the 1979 sample are successfully matched to a 1980 observation, and 74.4% of the 164,942 individuals in rotation group 4 of the 1992 sample are successfully matched to a 1993 observation. In July 1985 the CPS implemented a new sample frame: only individuals in the January–June 1985 CPS are matchable to observations in 1984, and only individuals in the October–December 1985 CPS are matchable to observations in 1986. These limitations lead to much lower match rates for 1984–85 (37.0% of all individuals in the 1984 sample) and 1985–86 (18.3% of all individuals in the 1985 sample).

Table 2A.5   **Estimated Models for the First-Difference of State-Average Log Wages, 1976–91**

| Dependent Variable | Estimated Coefficients of Log State Unemployment Rate | | | | Residual Standard Error | Other Controls Included |
	Current	Lag 1	Lag 2	Lag 3		
Adjusted log wage (weighted)	−0.025 (0.005)	—	—	—	0.042	year effects
Adjusted log wage (weighted)	−0.044 (0.011)	0.021 (0.011)	—	—	0.042	year effects
Adjusted log wage (weighted)	−0.038 (0.011)	−0.004 (0.016)	0.002 (0.015)	0.021 (0.011)	0.042	year effects
Adjusted log wage (weighted)	−0.034 (0.006)	—	—	—	0.042	year and region effects
Adjusted log wage (weighted)	−0.048 (0.011)	0.016 (0.011)	—	—	0.042	year and region effects
Adjusted log wage (weighted)	−0.025 (0.007)	—	—	—	0.040	year × region effects
Adjusted log wage (weighted)	−0.023 (0.014)	−0.003 (0.014)	—	—	0.040	year × region effects
Unadjusted log wage (weighted)	−0.029 (0.012)	−0.002 (0.012)	—	—	0.048	year and region effects
Adjusted log wage (unweighted)	−0.049 (0.012)	0.018 (0.012)	—	—	0.038	year and region effects

Notes: All models are fit to sample of 765 observations (51 states times 15 year-to-year changes). The dependent variable is the change from year $t − 1$ to year t in the state average wage, derived from March CPS data for all individuals who worked positive weeks and reported positive earnings (age 16–68). In all but one row, the state average wage is adjusted for the characteristics of workers in the state (using a year-specific wage prediction model). In all but one row, the estimates are obtained by weighted OLS, using as weights the relative number of workers in the state in 1976. Standard errors are in parentheses.

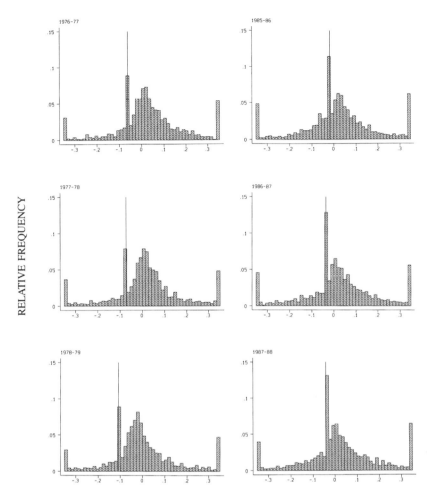

Fig. 2A.1 Histograms of real wage changes for all workers in PSID samples, 1976–79 and 1985–88

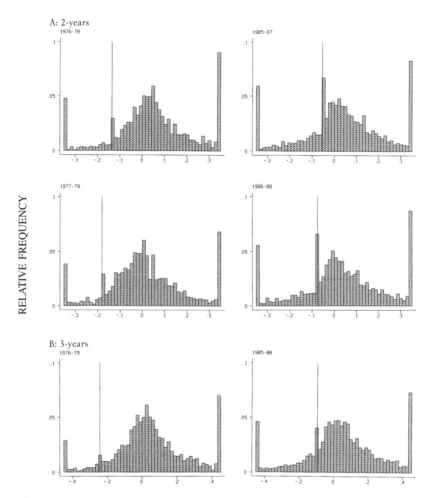

Fig. 2A.2   Histograms of real wage changes for all workers in PSID samples, over two-year and three-year horizons, 1976–79 and 1985–88

Appendix B
Simulations of the Effect of Measurement Error

This appendix describes the simulations we used to evaluate the effect of measurement error on our estimates of sweep-up, sweep-back, wage sweep-up, and wage sweep-back. The simulations all begin with an underlying distribution of real wage changes in the absence of any rigidities. We assume that this is a normal distribution with mean zero and standard deviation 0.12. The standard deviation of 0.12 is based on estimates of the dispersion in the upper half of the distribution of observed real wage changes in our CPS samples. To this underlying distribution we then add downward rigidities affecting a fraction of workers who would otherwise receive a nominal wage cut, and menu-cost rigidities affecting some individuals who would otherwise experience a "small" nominal wage change. Finally, we added a simple model of measurement error: with probability R the measurement error in the observed wage change is zero; with probability $(1 - R)$ the measurement error is drawn from a normal distribution with mean zero.

In all simulations we adjusted the standard deviation of the measurement error component so that the overall contribution of measurement errors to the variance of observed real wage changes is 20%. Most available evidence suggests that this is probably a lower bound on the share of observed wage changes attributable to reporting errors (see, e.g., McLaughlin 1994). However, even large changes in the fraction of the variance of observed wage changes attributable to measurement error have relatively little effect in our simulations, holding constant the probability of an accurately reported wage change (R).

We modeled the effect of menu costs as follows. For all observations that would otherwise obtain an absolute nominal wage change Δw of less than or equal to g, we assume that a fraction $0.5(1 - |\Delta w|/g)$ have rigid nominal wages. We set g to either 0.03 or 0.06.

In the simulation model the rate of measured wage rigidity at any inflation rate is determined by three factors: the fraction of workers affected by downward nominal rigidities (i.e., the fraction "swept up"); the fraction affected by menu costs; and the fraction of individuals who accurately report their true wage change (R). We developed three scenarios that combine these factors so as to generate observed rigidity rates of about 8–9% at 10% inflation and observed rigidity rates of 12–14% at 5% inflation. One of these combines a relatively high estimate of R (0.66) with a midrange estimate of the probability that a nominal wage cut is affected by downward rigidity (0.5) and a narrower range of menu costs ($\pm 3\%$). The second combines a higher rate of menu-cost rigidity with a more moderate estimate of R (0.50). The third assumes a very high probability of downward rigidity, conditional on a negative nominal wage change (0.7).

Table 2B.1   **Evaluation of Estimated Rigidity Effects in Presence of Measurement Errors**

Width of Interval Affected by Menu Costs	Probability of Downward Nominal Rigidity	Probability of No Error in Δw	Inflation Rate	Based on True Wage Changes, Fraction Affected by			Based on Observed Wage Changes				Ratio: Observed ÷ True wsu
				Menu Costs	Downward Rigidity	True wsu	Fraction Rigid	su	sb	wsu	
				Scenario 1							
±0.03	0.50	0.66	0.10	0.035	0.093	0.007	0.087	0.081	0.006	0.007	1.00
			0.05	0.046	0.157	0.013	0.136	0.123	0.013	0.010	0.77
			0.02	0.049	0.206	0.019	0.169	0.153	0.015	0.014	0.74
				Scenario 2							
±0.06	0.50	0.50	0.10	0.071	0.087	0.006	0.079	0.069	0.010	0.005	0.85
			0.05	0.091	0.147	0.013	0.119	0.100	0.018	0.009	0.69
			0.02	0.097	0.191	0.019	0.143	0.135	0.008	0.013	0.68
				Scenario 3							
±0.03	0.70	0.50	0.10	0.035	0.130	0.009	0.083	0.087	−0.003	0.007	0.78
			0.05	0.046	0.223	0.019	0.134	0.130	0.003	0.013	0.68
			0.02	0.049	0.290	0.027	0.168	0.154	0.013	0.016	0.59

Notes: Based on simulations of wage changes and rigidity effects. In all cases, the real wage change that would be observed in the absence of rigidities is assumed to be normally distributed with mean zero and standard deviation 0.12. Also, the ratio of the variance of the measurement error in wage changes to the total variance of observed wage changes is set to 0.20.

Table 2B.1 summarizes the true and observed nominal rigidity effects under each scenario at three different inflation rates (10%, 5%, and 2%). In scenario 1, which has a "high" value of R, the true fraction of workers affected by downward rigidity varies from 9 to 21%, and between 3.5 and 5% of workers are affected by menu costs. The true wage sweep-up effect is relatively modest, ranging from 0.7 to 1.9%. (The wage sweep-back effects are uniformly close to zero in all our simulations and are not shown.) Depending on the inflation rate, the observed density displacement and wage effects in this scenario are downward biased by 0–30%.

In scenario 2, which has a "high" fraction of workers affected by menu costs and/or rounding, the true sweep up effects are (virtually) the same as in scenario 1 and the measured effects are also similar. (The sweep-up effects are just slightly smaller in scenario 2 than scenario 1 because we first allow the effect of menu costs and then impose downward rigidities. With more rigidity attributable to menu costs, the net effect of downward rigidity is lessened.) Finally, in scenario 3, which has a "high" probability of downward rigidity for those who would otherwise experience wage cuts, the true sweep-up effects are slightly larger but the measured effects are about the same as in the other scenarios, implying slightly larger downward biases.

The last column of table 2B.1 shows the ratio of estimated wage sweep-up to true wage sweep-up. Note that estimated wage sweep-up is typically downward-biased by 20–30%, with a larger bias the lower the inflation rate.

References

Blanchflower, David G., and Andrew J. Oswald. 1994. *The Wage Curve*. Cambridge: MIT Press.

Brown, James N., and Audrey Light. 1992. Interpreting Panel Data on Job Tenure. *Journal of Labor Economics* 10:219–57.

Card, David. 1996. The Effect of Unions on the Structure of Wages: A Longitudinal Analysis. *Econometrica* 64 (July): 957–79.

DiNardo, John, Nicole M. Fortin, and Thomas Lemieux. 1996. Labor Market Institutions and the Distribution of Wages, 1973–1992: A Semi-Parametric Analysis. *Econometrica* 64 (September): 1001–44.

Kahn, Shulamit. 1994. Evidence of Nominal Wage Stickiness from Microdata. Boston University School of Management. Manuscript.

Krueger, Alan B., and Lawrence H. Summers. 1988. Efficiency Wages and the Inter-Industry Structure of Wages. *Econometrica* 56 (March): 259–93.

Lebow, David E., David J. Stockton, and William L. Wascher. 1995. Inflation, Nominal Wage Rigidity, and the Efficiency of Labor Markets. Board of Governors of the Federal Reserve System, Finance and Economics Discussion Paper 94–45. October.

McLaughlin, Kenneth J. 1994. Rigid Wages? *Journal of Monetary Economics* 34:383–414.

Silverman, B. W. 1986. *Density Estimation for Statistics and Data Analysis*. London: Chapman and Hall.

Solon, Gary, Robert Barsky, and Jonathan Parker. 1994. Measuring the Cyclicality of Real Wages: How Important Is Composition Bias? *Quarterly Journal of Economics* 109 (February): 1–26.
Tobin, James. 1972. Inflation and Unemployment. *American Economic Review* 62 (March): 1–18.

Comment   John Shea

Many economists believe that nominal labor market frictions cause excessive employment fluctuations. One often-mentioned type of nominal friction is downward nominal wage rigidity (DNWR), in which workers are either unwilling to accept reductions in nominal wages, or resent nominal wage cuts so much that firms optimally do not try to impose them. To see how DNWR can generate excessive employment volatility, consider figure 2C.1, which plots labor demand and supply curves relating employment (L) to the real wage (W). Under DNWR, workers will not work for less than last period's nominal wage, so labor supply becomes infinitely elastic at a real wage of $w(t-1)/(1+\pi)$, where π is this period's inflation rate and $w(t-1)$ is last period's real wage. Evidently, labor-demand shifts generate excessive employment volatility whenever labor demand intersects the flat portion of labor supply—that is, whenever the downward constraint on nominal wages binds.

Now consider figure 2C.2, which shows how DNWR interacts with inflation. When inflation is low, labor supply flattens at a high real wage, and excessive employment fluctuations are likely. When inflation is high, however, labor supply does not flatten until the real wage is low, and excessive employment fluctuations are less likely. This is the sense in which inflation "greases the wheels of the labor market" under DNWR—by making a wider range of real wage outcomes acceptable to workers, inflation can prevent excessive employment responses to negative labor-demand shocks.[1]

David Card and Dean Hyslop's paper uses two methods to assess the empirical significance of downward nominal wage rigidity for the United States. The first method examines the distribution of individual wage changes in U.S. microeconomic data. The second method examines the interaction between the inflation rate and the slope of the Phillips curve, using panel data for U.S. states. I will discuss each method in turn.

John Shea is associate professor of economics at the University of Maryland, College Park, and a faculty research fellow of the National Bureau of Economic Research.

1. This discussion ignores the question of why workers would accept declining real wages imposed by inflation but would not accept declining real wages imposed by nominal wage cuts. One possibility, of course, is that workers suffer from nominal illusion. Tobin (1972) suggests instead that workers care about relative wages in addition to absolute wages, and that workers rationally believe that inflation is more likely than nominal wage cuts to spread the pain across all workers equally.

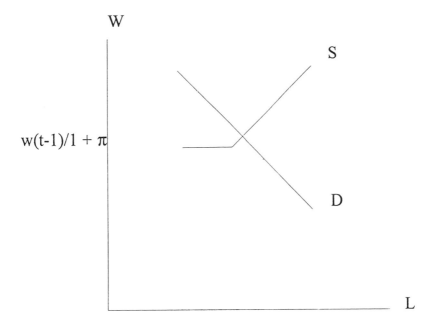

Fig. 2C.1   Downward nominal wage rigidity

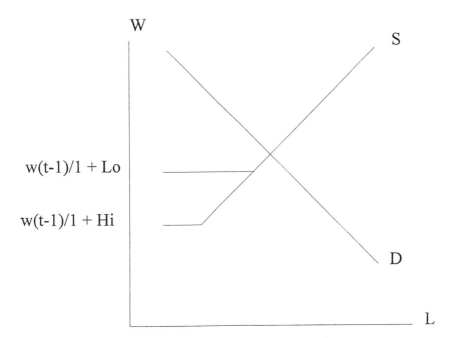

Fig. 2C.2   How inflation greases the wheels

Method One: Wage Distributions

If wages are downwardly rigid, then the distribution of workers' observed real wage changes should be skewed to the right, the more so the lower is the inflation rate. The first part of the paper tests this implication of DNWR by examining reported year-to-year real wage changes in the Current Population Survey (CPS) and the Panel Study of Income Dynamics (PSID).[2] The authors begin by constructing a counterfactual wage-change distribution that would hold in the absence of wage rigidity; this distribution is constructed by taking a mirror image of the upper half of the observed distribution. The authors then use the shortfall in the nominal-wage-cut region of the observed distribution relative to the counterfactual to estimate the fraction of workers whose real wages are propped up by DNWR (the "sweep up"), as well as the impact of DNWR on aggregate wage growth. The authors find that nominal wage cuts are not rare; the fraction of hourly-rated CPS workers reporting a nominal wage cut ranges from 11.6% in 1979–80 to 20.3% in 1992–93. Despite this, there is still some evidence of DNWR; averaging over the year-by-year results in table 2.3, the authors find that 10.6% of sample workers have their wages propped up in a typical year. As expected, DNWR binds more when inflation is low; the sweep up is 6.20% in 1980–81, but 13.85% in 1987–88. Overall, the authors find that the economic impact of DNWR is small; eliminating downward rigidity would have reduced real wage growth by only 0.78% per year between 1979 and 1993.

While Card and Hyslop's conclusions—downward rigidity exists, but it does not exert a very large impact on the labor market—accord with my priors, I have some concerns with the details of their methodology. In particular, there are three potential reasons why the authors' numbers might not reflect the true impact of DNWR on the U.S. economy.

First, Card and Hyslop's baseline sample is restricted to hourly workers who do not switch jobs from one year to the next. But hourly stayers make up only half of the working population.[3] Including job switchers and salaried workers would raise the authors' estimates of wage flexibility and reduce the estimated impact of DNWR. For instance, Lebow, Stockton, and Wascher (1995) examine the distribution of individual wage changes in the PSID. They find that 11.9% of hourly stayers experience nominal wage cuts in a typical year, compared to 19.3% of all workers, 17.8% of all stayers, and 24.8% of movers. They find that 9.7% of hourly wage stayers have their wages swept up in a typical year, compared to 7.4% of all workers, 6.8% of all stayers, and 5.1% of all movers. These figures suggest that the authors' sample-selection criteria cause them to overstate the average sweep-up by about 30% (9.7 divided by 7.4

2. Other recent studies examining the distribution of individual wage changes include McLaughlin 1994, Kahn 1995, and Lebow, Stockton, and Wascher 1995, the last of which is the closest to the present paper.
3. These figures are based on table 1 in Lebow, Stockton, and Wascher 1995.

equals 1.31).[4] The authors' sample may also overstate the sensitivity of sweep-up with respect to inflation; for instance, Lebow et al.'s regression of sweep-up on inflation yields a coefficient of -0.75 (with a t-statistic of -2.5) for hourly stayers, but only -0.35 (-1.2) for all stayers.

Second, the authors assume that the wage distribution would be symmetric absent DNWR. This assumption is obviously important to the quantitative results; if the counterfactual were assumed to be negatively skewed, for instance, the gap between the counterfactual and reality would be larger and the estimated impact of DNWR would be greater. To my knowledge, there is little evidence available on the shape of the distribution of microlevel shocks in the U.S. economy. Davis and Haltiwanger (1992), however, show the plant-level job destruction is much more cyclical than plant-level job creation—job destruction rises much more sharply in recessions than job creation rises in booms. This suggests that plant-level shocks may be negatively skewed, at least during recessions. On the other hand, the shock distribution and the wage distribution need not look alike. In particular, even if wages are flexible downward, bad microshocks would presumably in many cases lead to voluntary separations rather than wage cuts (McLaughlin 1991), which would counteract negative skewness in the shocks and could even create positive skewness in the wage distribution. Obviously, we need more evidence on the distribution of microlevel shocks and the determinants of voluntary separations before we can assess whether a symmetric counterfactual is plausible or not.

Third, Card and Hyslop's calculations assume that individuals' reported nominal wages are accurate. There is good reason to believe that individually reported nominal wages contain measurement error; for instance, the authors cite a January 1977 CPS survey in which employees and their employers agree on the wage only 44% of the time. As the authors show in appendix B, measurement error in the level of wages can cause their methodology to understate effects of DNWR considerably. One channel that the authors do not emphasize, but that seems important to me, is that measurement error might cause the data to vastly overstate the true fraction of workers receiving nominal wage cuts. I have heard several colleagues express disbelief at the notion that between 10 and 20% of hourly stayers experience nominal wage cuts from one year to the next. To see whether measurement error could explain such a result, I perform some calculations using a small sample of union workers from the PSID. In Shea (1995), I combine PSID information on individuals' industry, occupation, union affiliation, and county of residence with outside information about pattern bargaining, contract settlements, and the location of particular employers to match individual PSID household heads to the provisions of particular long-

---

4. In truth, Card and Hyslop's figures are probably not off by as much as 30%. The authors work primarily with CPS data, in which the distinction between movers and stayers is not as precise as in the PSID; thus, the authors' sample already includes some movers. Also, Card and Hyslop provide evidence contrary to the finding in Lebow, Stockton, and Wascher (1995) that salaries are more flexible than wages.

Table 2C.1   Percentage of Workers with Nominal Wage Cuts

Year	Sample Size	Contract	Reported
1981–82	79	0	11.4
1982–83	69	5.8	11.6
1983–84	55	1.8	25.5
1984–85	59	0	16.9
1985–86	57	0	35.1
1986–87	60	0	31.7

term union contracts. Here, I consider a subset of the sample from Shea (1995) for which hourly wages are reported at both t and $t + 1$, and for which reported tenure at time $t + 1$ is greater than twelve months. These restrictions leave 379 observations, ranging from 1981–82 through 1986–87.

Table 2C.1 reports statistics on nominal wage cuts for my sample, broken down by year. For each year, I report the number of observations, the percentage of observations whose published union settlements imposed nominal wage cuts, and the percentage of observations reporting nominal wage cuts in the PSID.[5] The figures are startling; overall, I find that only 1.3% of my sample observations have "true" nominal wage cuts according to their contracts, but that 21.1% of my sample report nominal wage cuts. Taken literally, these results suggest that measurement error could explain all of the evidence for downward nominal wage flexibility found in Card and Hyslop's sample. It is possible, of course, that contract information understates the incidence of "true" nominal wage cuts. For instance, contemporaneous accounts in the Bureau of Labor Statistics' *Current Wage Developments* indicate that some unionized trucking companies deviated from the trucking pattern bargain during the 1980s and imposed nominal wage cuts in the face of competition from nonunion companies. For robustness, I redid my experiment excluding truckers, and found that the gap between the reported and published incidence of nominal wage cuts was virtually unchanged (1.6 versus 21.0%). Another possibility is that my findings reflect the fact that senior union workers whose positions have been eliminated are typically allowed to "bump" less senior workers at the next highest pay rung, who in turn can move down a pay rung and bump even less senior workers, and so on.[6] I know of no data on the fraction of union workers who are bumped in a typical year. I would note, however, that the incidence of reported nominal wage cuts was lower during the 1982–83 recession than during the subsequent recovery, which seems inconsistent with

5. Hourly wages in the PSID are reported as of the time of interview. Since almost all PSID interviews occur during the spring, I compute "contract" wage changes over the interval April 1, year t through March 31, year $t + 1$. Contract wage changes are estimated using union settlement information published in various issues of the Bureau of Labor Statistics periodical *Current Wage Developments* and in the Bureau of National Affairs periodical *Government Employee Relations Reporter*. Contract wage changes include any changes imposed as a result of unexpected ex post contract renegotiations or reopenings.

6. I thank Chris Erickson and the authors for independently pointing out this possibility to me.

bumping being responsible for the bulk of reported nominal wage cuts in my sample. I also redid my experiment separating workers who report changing occupations from workers who do not; the incidence of reported nominal wage cuts among occupation switchers was only slightly higher (21.4%) than among occupation stayers (21.0%). Given that bumped workers should have a higher incidence of occupation switches than unbumped job stayers, this result again suggests that bumping is not very important in my sample.

My conclusion from this section is that it is difficult to say how important DNWR is to the labor market using the distribution of individual wage changes alone. We can adjust Card and Hyslop's sweep-up estimates to account for the exclusion of movers and salaried workers rather easily. But with existing data, it is hard to say how much we should adjust the authors' estimates for measurement error or for asymmetry in the counterfactual distribution.

Method Two: Phillips Curves

Given the problems with using individual wage distributions, the authors should be commended for formulating an alternative approach to estimating the impact of DNWR on the labor market. Recall from figures 2C.1 and 2C.2 that DNWR increases (decreases) the sensitivity of employment (wages) to labor-demand shocks, the more so the lower is the inflation rate. In the latter part of their paper, Card and Hyslop test this implication by looking for interactions between inflation and the slope of the Phillips curve in the United States. Since such interactions would probably be impossible to detect in aggregate data, the authors cleverly exploit cross-state variation in unemployment and wage growth to estimate separate Phillips curves year-by-year from 1976 through 1991. The authors find that higher state-level unemployment significantly reduces state-level wage growth in each year. They also find that the Phillips curve (plotted with unemployment on the horizontal axis) is steeper when inflation is high, consistent with DNWR, but that this interaction is imprecisely estimated and insignificantly different from zero.

I think the authors' approach has excellent potential as a tool for assessing the impact of downward nominal rigidity and other sorts of frictions on the labor market. I have two suggestions for making this tool sharper. First, the authors need more degrees of freedom. With fifty U.S. states, the authors have enough cross-section observations to estimate the year-by-year Phillips curve slopes reasonably precisely. However, with only sixteen years of data, the authors do not have enough slopes to estimate the interaction between inflation and the slope precisely. The authors could alleviate this problem either by getting more years of data for the United States, or by including other countries for which regional wage and employment information is available.[7]

---

7. Of course, expanding the data set would limit the extent to which the authors could correct wages for the skill composition of the workforce (as they currently do using the CPS). But this shouldn't be problematic if the skill distribution at the regional level does not vary much over the business cycle, an issue the authors could investigate directly with the CPS or the PSID.

Second, the authors need to pay careful attention to endogeneity issues. What the authors presumably want to estimate each year is the relative responsiveness of wages and unemployment to labor-demand shocks. An ordinary least squares regression of wage growth on unemployment will estimate the Phillips curve consistently only if all cross-state variation in unemployment is due to cross-state variation in the position of the labor-demand curve. It is easy to think of reasons why this condition would not hold. For instance, suppose that nominal wage growth is predetermined for union workers, but flexible for nonunion workers, and suppose that states differ in the extent of unionization. Now suppose the inflation rate changes unexpectedly. Real wages and unemployment would move in the same direction as firms moved along their labor-demand curves, causing the Phillips curve to shift, and this shift would be more pronounced in more heavily unionized states. In this example, then, unexpected inflation shocks would bias the estimated cross-section Phillips curve toward zero. Of course, what the authors are most interested in is not the slope of the Phillips curve, but rather the interaction of the slope with inflation. In this example, if the conditional variance of inflation is uncorrelated with the level of inflation, then the authors have nothing to fear. But if unexpected inflation shocks are more likely at higher levels of inflation, then high-inflation periods will also be periods in which the slope estimates are more biased toward zero, masking the interaction between inflation and the slope predicted by DNWR. To avoid such problems, the authors should estimate their Phillips curves instrumenting for state-level unemployment, using measures of state-level labor demand.[8]

Conclusion

Overall, I find Card and Hyslop's central conclusion—downward nominal rigidity has a positive but economically small impact on the labor market—sensible and well-founded. The reader should be cautioned, however, that the authors' results in no way prove that nominal rigidities are unimportant to labor market fluctuations. Downward nominal rigidities are only one type of nominal friction; even if downward rigidity is not important, generalized nominal wage stickiness or nominal illusion may still matter.

References

Blanchard, Olivier J., and Lawrence Katz. 1992. Regional Evolutions. *Brookings Papers on Economic Activity* 1:1–61.
Davis, Steven J., and John Haltiwanger, 1992. Gross Job Creation, Gross Job Destruction and Employment Reallocation. *Quarterly Journal of Economics* 107:819–63.

---

8. For example, the authors could capture the labor-demand-driven element of cross-state unemployment variation by computing a weighted average of disaggregated national-industry-level employment or output growth rates, using state-level industry-employment shares as weights, as in Blanchard and Katz 1992.

Kahn, Shulamit. 1995. Nominal Wage Stickiness: Evidence from Microdata. Boston University. Mimeo.

Lebow, David E., David J. Stockton, and William L. Wascher. 1995. Inflation, Nominal Wage Rigidity, and the Efficiency of Labor Markets. Board of Governors of the Federal Reserve System, Finance and Economics Discussion Paper 94–95, October.

McLaughlin, Kenneth. 1991. A Theory of Quits and Layoffs with Efficient Turnover. *Journal of Political Economy* 99:1–29.

———. 1994. Rigid Wages? *Journal of Monetary Economics* 34:383–414.

Shea, John. 1995. Union Contracts and the Life Cycle–Permanent Income Hypothesis. *American Economic Review* 85:186–200.

Tobin, James. 1972. Inflation and Unemployment. *American Economic Review* 62:1–18.

3 The Costs and Benefits of Going from Low Inflation to Price Stability

Martin Feldstein

3.1 Introduction

There is now widespread agreement in the economics profession that "high" rates of inflation have significant adverse consequences and that these adverse effects justify the sacrifices in employment and output that are generally needed to reduce inflation.[1] There is, however, much less professional support for the goal of "price stability" that central bankers advocate and that many governments and central banks are now seeking. The purpose of this paper is to examine the economic case for making the transition from low inflation to price stability.

Because measurement problems cause official inflation measures to overstate the rate of increase of buying a constant utility bundle of goods and services, price stability is generally taken to mean a measured inflation rate of about 2%.[2] The analysis in this paper therefore addresses the following question: If the true and fully anticipated rate of inflation (i.e., the measured rate of inflation minus 2 percentage points) has stabilized at 2%, is the gain from

Martin Feldstein is president of the National Bureau of Economic Research and the George F. Baker Professor of Economics at Harvard University.

The author is grateful to James Poterba and to the participants in the project and the conference for comments and suggestions and to Erzo Luttmer for research assistance and discussions.

1. See, e.g., Fischer (1981, 1994) and Fischer and Modigliani (1978). This has not always been so. Until the late 1970s, many economists in the United States argued that the cost of reducing the existing rate of inflation was too high and that the economy should learn to live with moderate rates of inflation. The high rate of inflation in the late 1970s and early 1980s together with the rapid disinflation during the early 1980s appears to have virtually eliminated professional support for that view.

2. This has been made explicit by the Federal Reserve and the Bundesbank, among other central banks.

reducing inflation to zero worth the sacrifice in output and employment that would be required to achieve it?[3]

To answer this question it is important to recognize that the cost of reducing inflation is a "one-time" loss of output and employment while the benefit of a lower inflation rate is permanent. The appropriate "cost benefit analysis" of reducing inflation is therefore a comparison of the one-time cost of reducing inflation with the present value of the permanent benefits of price stability.[4] The calculations presented in this paper show that the present value of the benefits of price stability exceed the costs of getting there. For the most plausible parameter values, the benefits of price stability exceed the costs of transition within six to nine years. For some parameter combinations, the relative gains are even larger. In every case, the present value of the benefits exceed the costs even when the benefits are discounted at the rate of return that individuals receive on a risky portfolio of common stocks.

This way of stating the problem makes it clear that it is not necessary to ask whether the benefit of price stability relative to a 2% inflation rate is "large" in some absolute sense (whatever that might mean) but only whether it is large enough to exceed the cost of transition. Similarly, the relevant policy decision does not depend on whether a higher rate of inflation reduces the rate of economic growth if it reduces the level of real income in each future year.[5]

Since the reduction in real income caused by inflation is proportional to national income, the annual benefit of having a lower rate of inflation grows over time (even though the rate of growth itself is unaffected). To see the implications of this, note that discounting an annual benefit equal to $x\%$ of GDP at a discount rate of d in an economy that grows at 2.5% a year (the rate of growth of U.S. real GDP from 1970 through 1994) yields a present value of $x/(d - 0.025)$.

Although a case could be made for discounting at a very low risk-free rate of return, to be more conservative I will use the return that individuals receive on a risky portfolio of corporate stocks. During the past quarter century, the real net-of-tax return that an individual investor received on an investment in the Standard and Poor's composite was 5.1%.[6] An annual benefit of x percent of GDP therefore has a present value of $x/(.051 - .025) = 38.5 x$. The evidence

3. Since it is the "true" rate of inflation that matters, I subtract 2 percentage points of inflation from the measured rate of inflation in all of the calculations presented in this paper.

4. There may of course be shocks in the future that raise or lower the inflation rate. I will not deal with this explicitly, focusing on the comparison of stable inflation at 2% versus price stability. Because the net benefit (i.e., the present value of the benefits of lower inflation minus the net cost of the change in inflation) is essentially constant in the range that we are considering, the appropriate response to such future inflation shocks is just a repetition of the basic problem discussed in this paper.

5. Barro (1995) presents evidence showing that there is no statistically significant relation between inflation and growth when the rate of inflation is under 10%.

6. Between 1970 and 1994, the Standard and Poor's index rose at a nominal rate of 6.4%. The average dividend yield was 4.0%. The rate of increase of the consumer price index was 5.7%, implying a "true" inflation rate of 3.7 percent. Assuming a 25% marginal rate of tax on dividends

discussed in section 3.2 implies that the likely cost of reducing inflation from 2% to zero is equal to between 4% and 6% of the initial GDP. Even using the upper limit of 6% implies that the benefits of disinflation outweigh the costs if the annual benefit of lower inflation exceeds $x^* = 6.0/38.5 = 0.16\%$ of GDP. The analysis in sections 3.3 through 3.6 implies that the annual benefit substantially exceeds this critical value, with the most plausible value of the annual gain being equal to about 1% of GDP, indicating that the gain from price stability would outweigh the costs of getting there from the current low level of inflation even if those gains were discounted at a very much higher rate.

The emphasis in my analysis is on the distortion in the process of household capital accumulation that occurs because of the interaction of inflation and tax rules[7] and on the consequence of that distortion for tax revenue. One important aspect of this is the negative effect of inflation on the real net return to saving. This distorts the allocation of lifetime consumption between early years and later years. Section 3.3 evaluates the deadweight loss that results from this distortion and from the associated effects on government revenue. Contrary to traditional welfare analysis, those revenue effects are important as soon as we recognize that any revenue gain from lower inflation permits a reduction in other distortionary taxes (and, similarly, any revenue loss from lower inflation requires an increase in some other distortionary tax).

The inflation-induced reduction in the net return to financial assets also induces increased investment in owner-occupied residential real estate. Section 3.4 evaluates the deadweight loss that results from this effect of higher inflation.

In both cases, even the small reduction of inflation from 2% to zero can have a substantial effect on economic welfare because inflation increases the tax-induced distortions that would exist even with price stability. The deadweight loss associated with the shift from zero inflation to a 2% inflation rate is therefore not the traditional "small triangle" that would result from distorting a first-best equilibrium but is the much larger "trapezoid" that results from increasing a large initial distortion.

These adverse effects of the tax-inflation interaction could in principle be eliminated by indexing the tax system or by shifting from our current system of corporate and personal income taxes to a tax based only on consumption or labor income. As a practical matter, however, such tax reforms are extremely unlikely. Section 3.8 discusses some of the difficulties of shifting to an indexed tax system in which capital income and expenses are measured in real terms. Although such a shift has been advocated for at least two decades, there has

---

and a 10% effective rate of tax on capital gains implies a real net return on the Standard and Poor's portfolio of 0.75 (4.0) + 0.90(6.4) − 3.7 = 5.1%.

7. In an earlier series of papers collected in Feldstein (1983), I examined the effect of the interaction of inflation and tax rules on tax liabilities, on equilibrium interest rates and asset prices, and on the accumulation of residential and nonresidential capital. None of those studies considered the welfare consequences of this interaction.

been no legislation along those lines. It is significant, moreover, that no industrial country has fully (or even substantially) indexed its tax laws. More generally, the annual gains from shifting to price stability that are identified in this paper exceed the costs of the transition within a very few years. Even if one could be sure that the tax-inflation distortions would be eliminated ten years from now, the present value gain from price stability until then would exceed the cost of the inflation reduction.

The inflation-induced distortion in the lifetime allocation of consumption and in the allocation of spending between housing and other forms of consumption are only two of the many ways in which inflation imposes a cost on the economy. The most studied of these is the distortion in the demand for money.[8] The interaction of inflation and tax rules also causes distortions in the mix of business investment,[9] in corporate finance,[10] and in the structure of individual portfolios.[11] Higher inflation rates may also imply more volatile inflation.[12]

Absolute price stability, as opposed to merely a lower rate of inflation, may bring a qualitatively different kind of benefit. A history of price stability may bring a "credibility bonus" in dealing with inflationary shocks. People who see persistent price-level stability expect that it will persist in the future and that the government will respond to shocks in a way that maintains the price level. In contrast, if people see that the price level does not remain stable, they may have less confidence in the government's ability or willingness to respond to inflation shocks in a way that maintains the initial inflation rate. If so, any given positive demand shock may lead to more inflation and may require a greater

8. Bailey (1956) quantified the welfare loss of the reduction in the use of non-interest-bearing money. This pioneering paper led to a very large literature of refinements and criticisms. Phelps (1973) argued that since seigniorage gains from inflation permit a reduction in other distortionary taxes some positive rate of inflation may be appropriate as part of an overall optimal tax structure. More precisely, it implies that the optimal rate of inflation would be greater than Milton Friedman's optimum (1969) of minus the marginal product of capital.

In Feldstein (1979), I evaluated the trade-off between the gains of reduced inflation and the costs of achieving that reduction in terms of the impact on the demand for money. That paper showed that a case can be made for a discount rate at which the permanent reduction in the "shoe-leather" costs of distorted money demand exceeds the temporary cost of achieving lower inflation.

None of these studies takes into account the taxation of capital income and the interaction of inflation and tax rules.

9. Because depreciation is not adjusted for inflation, an increase in the rate of inflation favors investment in inventories and short-lived equipment.

10. The mixture of debt and equity finance is affected by the fact that nominal interest rates are deducted by business borrowers. Although portfolio investors are taxed on nominal interest incomes, their tax rates are typically lower than the tax rates of the borrowers. Much corporate debt is also held by untaxed entities like pension funds.

11. The taxation of nominal interest and of nominal capital gains distorts the composition of household portfolios.

12. Although the relation between the level and volatility of inflation has been established in a number of studies, it is not clear if this applies at the low levels of inflation that are the subject of the current research.

output loss to reverse than would be true in an economy with a history of stable prices.

A stable price level is also a considerable convenience for anyone making financial decisions that involve future receipts and payments. While economists may be very comfortable with the process of converting nominal to real amounts, many people have a difficult time thinking about rates of change, real rates of interest, and so forth. Even among sophisticated institutional investors, it is remarkable how frequently projections of future returns are stated in nominal terms and based on past experience over periods with very different rates of inflation.

I will not attempt to evaluate all of these benefits of reducing inflation even though some of them may be as large as the improvements in the process of household capital accumulation that I do measure. The restricted set of benefits that I quantify substantially exceed (in present value at any plausible discount rate) the cost of getting to price stability from a low rate of inflation.

It would be wrong, however, to go from this calculation to the conclusion that the reduction in inflation increases net welfare without considering the possibility that there are also advantages of continuing a low rate of inflation rather than having price stability. The primary gain from inflation that has been identified in the literature is the seigniorage that the government enjoys from the higher rate of money creation. This seigniorage revenue reduces the need for other distortionary taxes and therefore eliminates the deadweight loss that such taxes would entail. In addition, the real cost of servicing the national debt varies inversely with the rate of inflation.[13] The value of these advantages of continuing the 2% inflation rate will be calculated explicitly in sections 3.5 and 3.6.[14]

Table 3.1 summarizes all of the welfare changes that are discussed in the remaining sections of the paper. The specific assumptions and parameters values will be discussed there. With the parameter values that seem most likely, the overall total effect of reducing inflation from 2% to zero, shown in the lower right corner of the table, is to reduce the annual deadweight loss by between 0.63 and 1.01% of GDP.

The costs of reducing inflation and the value of lower inflation both depend on the institutional features of the economy, including the functioning of the labor and capital markets as well as the tax rules. The current analysis applies specifically to the United States in recent years, but the method of analysis is clearly applicable to other countries and times.

---

13. A higher inflation rate reduces the real net cost of debt service because the equilibrium government bond rate rises point for point with inflation but the inflation premium is then subject to tax. The net nominal interest rate therefore rises less than point for point with inflation, and the real net rate declines.

14. There is also recent theoretical literature on the potential advantages of inflation in inducing search that improves resource allocation in imperfectly competitive markets (e.g., Benabou 1992). No attempt has been made to assess the possible magnitude of the benefit of this increased search.

Table 3.1 **The Net Welfare Effect of Reducing Inflation from 2% to Zero (changes as % of GDP)**

Source of Change	Direct Effect of Reduced Distortion		Welfare Effect of Revenue Change		Total Effect	
			$\lambda = 0.4$	$\lambda = 1.5$	$\lambda = 0.4$	$\lambda = 1.5$
Consumption timing	$\eta_{sr} = 0.4$	1.02	−0.10	−0.39	0.92	0.63
	$\eta_{sr} = 0$	0.73	−0.21	−0.78	0.52	−0.05
	$\eta_{sr} = 1.0$	1.44	0.05	0.20	1.49	1.64
Housing demand		0.10	0.12	0.45	0.22	0.55
Money demand		0.02	−0.05	−0.19	−0.03	−0.17
Debt service		NA	−0.10	−0.38	−0.10	−0.38
Totals	$\eta_{sr} = 0.4$	1.14	−0.13	−0.51	1.01	0.63
	$\eta_{sr} = 0$	0.85	−0.24	−0.90	0.66	−0.05
	$\eta_{sr} = 1.0$	1.56	0.02	0.08	1.58	1.64

Notes: A 2% inflation rate corresponds to a rise in the CPI at 4% a year. The welfare effects reported here are annual changes in welfare. *NA* = not applicable.

3.2   The Cost of Reducing Inflation

Although it can be argued that an unambiguous commitment to price stability would cause the inflation rate to decline with no loss of output, my reading of the experience of countries like Germany and New Zealand suggests that even a long tradition of a commitment to low inflation or a contractual obligation with strong potential penalties is insufficient to achieve a painless reduction of inflation. For the purpose of this paper, I will therefore assume that the cost of reducing inflation can be inferred from the parameters of a short-run Phillips curve based on the experience of the United States over the past two decades.

Laurence Ball (1995) provides a useful survey of previous empirical work in this area and new estimates of the cost of disinflation. More specifically, Ball estimates the cost of disinflation as the cumulative loss of GDP during the period when inflation is being reduced by raising the unemployment rate above the natural rate. He concludes that each percentage point reduction in the rate of inflation costs a cumulative output loss equal to between 2 and 3% of GDP. This implies that reducing inflation from 2% to zero has a one-time cost in the range of 4–6% of GDP.

This estimate makes no allowance for the offsetting value of leisure, home production, and job search among the unemployed. It also makes no allowance for the possible persistent ("hysteresis") effects of job loss that might be caused by a loss of job-specific human capital or, more generally, by an erosion of human capital during the period of unemployment.[15]

15. The relatively short duration of cyclical unemployment spells in the United States implies that raising the unemployment to reduce inflation is unlikely to have a significant adverse effect on human capital.

Rather than trying to make a more precise adjustment in the Ball measure of the cost of disinflation, I will assume the upper end of his range (6% of GDP) and ask whether the present value of the gain in having price stability rather than 2% inflation exceeds 6% of the initial GDP. The analysis in this paper implies that the answer to that question is yes and would probably be yes even if the cost were substantially higher.

3.3   Inflation and the Intertemporal Allocation of Consumption

Inflation reduces the real net of tax return to savers in many ways. At the corporate (or, more generally, the business) level, inflation reduces the value of depreciation allowances and therefore increases the effective tax rate. This lowers the rate of return that businesses can afford to pay for debt and equity capital. At the individual level, taxes levied on nominal capital gains and nominal interest also cause the effective tax rate to increase with the rate of inflation.

A reduction in the rate of return that individuals earn on their saving creates a welfare loss by distorting the allocation of consumption between the early years in life and the later years. Since the tax law creates such a distortion even when there is price stability, the extra distortion caused by inflation causes a first-order increased deadweight loss.

As I emphasized in an earlier paper (Feldstein 1978), the deadweight loss that results from capital income taxes depends on the resulting distortion in the timing of consumption and not on the change in saving per se. Even if there is no change in saving, a tax-inflation induced decline in the rate of return implies a reduction in future consumption and therefore a deadweight loss. In this section, I calculate the general magnitude of the reduction in this welfare loss that results from lowering the rate of inflation from 2% to zero.[16]

To analyze the deadweight loss that results from a distortion of consumption over the individual life cycle, I consider a simple two-period model of individual consumption. Individuals receive income when they are young. They save a portion, S, of that income and consume the rest. The savings are invested in a portfolio that earns a real net-of-tax return of r. At the end of T years, the individuals retire and consume $C = (1 + r)^T S$. In this framework, saving can be thought of as the expenditure (when young) to purchase retirement consumption at a price of $p = (1 + r)^{-T}$.

Even in the absence of inflation, the effect of the tax system is to reduce the rate of return on saving and therefore to increase the price of retirement consumption. As inflation increases, the price of retirement consumption increases further. Before looking at specific numerical values, I present graphically the welfare consequences of these changes in the price of retirement

---

16. Fischer (1981) used the framework of Feldstein (1978) to assess the deadweight loss caused by the effect of inflation on the return to savers. As the current analysis indicates, the problem is more complex than either Fischer or I recognized in those earlier studies.

consumption. Figure 3.1 shows the individual's compensated demand for retirement consumption C as a function of the price of retirement consumption at the time that saving decisions are made (p).

In the absence of both inflation and taxes, the real rate of return implies a price of p_0 and the individual chooses to save enough to generate retirement consumption of C_0. With no inflation, the existing structure of capital income taxes at the business and individual levels raises the price of retirement consumption to p_1 and reduces retirement consumption to C_1. This increase in the price of retirement consumption causes the individual to incur the deadweight loss (DWL) shown as the shaded area A, that is, the amount that the individual would have to be compensated for the rise in the price of retirement consumption in order to remain at the same initial utility level exceeds the revenue (REV) collected by the government by an amount equal to the area A. Raising the rate of inflation from zero to 2% increases the price of retirement consumption to p_2 and reduces retirement consumption to C_2. The deadweight loss now increases by the trapezoidal area $C + D = (p_1 - p_0)(C_1 - C_2) + 0.5 (p_2 - p_1)(C_1 - C_2)$.

The revenue effect of such tax changes are generally ignored in welfare analyses because it is assumed that any loss or gain in revenue can be offset by a lump-sum tax or transfer. More realistically, however, we must recognize that offsetting a revenue change due to a change in inflation involves distortionary taxes, and therefore each dollar or revenue gain or loss has an additional effect on overall welfare. The net welfare effect of reducing the inflation rate from 2% to zero is therefore the combination of the traditional welfare gain (the trapezoid $C + D$) and the welfare gain (loss) that results from an increase (decrease) in tax revenue. I begin by evaluating the traditional welfare

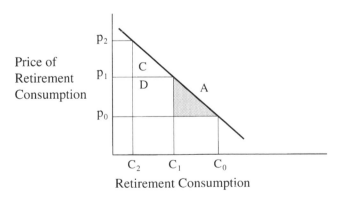

$$\Delta \text{DWL} = (p_1 - p_0)(C_1 - C_2) + 0.5 (p_2 - p_1)(C_1 - C_2)$$
$$\Delta \text{REV} = (p_1 - p_0)(C_1 - C_2) - (p_2 - p_1) C_2$$

Fig. 3.1   Retirement consumption

gain and then calculate the additional welfare effect of the changes in tax revenue.

3.3.1   The Welfare Gain from Reduced Intertemporal Distortion

The annual welfare gain from reduced intertemporal distortion is $(p_1 - p_0)(C_1 - C_2) + 0.5 (p_2 - p_1)(C_1 - C_2) = [(p_1 - p_0) + 0.5 (p_2 - p_1)](C_1 - C_2)$. The change in retirement consumption can be approximated as $C_1 - C_2 = (dC/dp)(p_1 - p_2) = C_2(p_2/C_2)(dC/dp)(p_1 - p_2)/p_2 = C_2\varepsilon_{Cp}[(p_1 - p_2)/p_2]$ where $\varepsilon_{Cp} < 0$ is the compensated elasticity of retirement consumption with respect to its price as evaluated at the observed initial inflation rate of 2%). Thus the gain from reduced intertemporal distortion is[17]

$$(1) \quad G_1 = [(p_1 - p_0) + 0.5 (p_2 - p_1)]C_2\varepsilon_{Cp}[(p_1 - p_2)/p_2]$$
$$= [(p_1 - p_0)/p_2 + 0.5 (p_2 - p_1)/p_2]p_2 C_2\varepsilon_{Cp}[(p_1 - p_2)/p_2].$$

Note that if there were no tax-induced distortion when the inflation rate is zero $(p_1 = p_0)$, G_1 would simplify to the traditional triangle formula for the deadweight loss of a price change from p_1 to p_2.

To move from equation 1 to observable magnitudes, note that the compensated elasticity ε_{Cp} can be written in terms of the corresponding uncompensated elasticity η_{Cp} and the propensity to save out of exogenous income σ as[18]

$$(2) \qquad\qquad \varepsilon_{Cp} = \eta_{Cp} + \sigma.$$

Moreover, since saving and retirement consumption are related by $S = pC$, the elasticity of retirement consumption with respect to its price and the elasticity of saving with respect to the price of retirement consumption are related by $\eta_{Cp} = \eta_{Sp} - 1$. Thus

$$(3) \qquad\qquad \varepsilon_{Cp} = \eta_{Sp} + \sigma - 1$$

and

$$(4) \qquad G_1 = [(p_1 - p_0)/p_2 + 0.5 (p_2 - p_1)/p_2][(p_2 - p_1)/p_2]$$
$$\times S_2 (1 - \eta_{Sp} - \sigma),$$

where $S_2 = p_2 C_2$, the gross saving of individuals at the early stage of the life cycle.

To evaluate equation 4 requires numerical estimates of the price of future consumption at different inflation rates and without any tax, as well as estimates of gross saving, of the saving elasticity, and of the propensity to save out of exogenous income.

17. This could be stated as the difference between the areas of the two deadweight loss triangles corresponding to prices p_1 and p_2, but the expression used here presents a better approximation.

18. This follows from the usual Slutsky decomposition: $dC/dp = \{dC/dp\}_{COMP} - C(dC/dy)$ where dC/dy is the increase in retirement consumption induced by an increase in exogenous income. Multiplying each term by p/C and noting that $p(dC/dy) = dpC/dy = dS/dy = \sigma$ yields equation 2.

Inflation Rates and the Price of Retirement Consumption

To calculate the price of retirement consumption, I assume the time interval between saving and consumption is thirty years; for example, the individual saves on average at age forty and then dissaves at age seventy. Thus $p = (1 + r)^{-30}$ where the value of r depends on the tax system and the rate of inflation. From 1960 through 1994, the pretax real return to capital in the U.S. nonfinancial corporate sector averaged 9.2%.[19] Ignoring general equilibrium effects and taking this as the measure of the discrete-time return per year that would prevail in the absence of taxes implies that the corresponding price of retirement consumption is $p_0 = (1.092)^{-(30)} = 0.071$.

Taxes paid by corporations to federal, state, and local governments equaled about 41% of the total pretax return during this period, leaving a real net return before personal taxes of 5.4% (Rippe 1995). I will take this yield difference as an indication of the combined effects of taxes and inflation at 2% (i.e., measured inflation at 4%) even though tax rules, tax rates, and inflation varied over this thirty-five-year interval.[20] The net of tax rate of return depends not only on the tax at the corporate level but also on the taxes that individuals pay on that after-corporate-tax return, including the taxes on interest income, dividends, and capital gains. The effective marginal tax rate depends on the form of the income and on the tax status of the individual. I will summarize all of this by assuming a marginal "individual" tax rate of 25%. This reduces the net return from 5.4 to 4.05%. The analysis of the gain from reducing the equilibrium rate of inflation is not sensitive to the precise level of this return or to the precise difference between it and 9.2% pretax return since our concern is with the effect of a difference in inflation rates on effective tax rates. Similarly, the precise level of the initial effective tax rate is not important to the current calculations since our concern is with the change in the effective tax rate that occurs as a result of the change in the equilibrium rate of inflation.[21] The price of retirement consumption that corresponds to this net return of 4.05% is $p_2 = (1.0405)^{-30} = 0.304$, where the subscript 2 on the price indicates that this represents the price at an inflation rate of 2%.

Reducing the equilibrium inflation rate from 2% to zero lowers the effective tax rate at both the corporate and individual levels. At the corporate level, changes in the equilibrium inflation rate alter the effective tax rate by changing the value of depreciation allowances and by changing the value of the deduction of interest payments. Because the depreciation schedule that is allowed

19. This 9.2% is the ratio of profits before all taxes (including property taxes as well as income taxes) plus real net interest payments to the replacement value of the capital stock. Feldstein, Poterba, and Dicks-Mireaux (1983) describe the method of calculation, and Rippe (1995) brings the calculation up to date. Excluding the property taxes would reduce this return by about 0.7 percentage points; see Poterba and Samwick (1995).

20. The average rate of measured inflation during this period was actually 4.7%, implying an average "true" inflation rate of 2.7%.

21. Some explicit sensitivity calculations are presented below.

for calculating taxable profits is defined in nominal terms, a higher rate of inflation reduces the present value of the depreciation and thereby increases the effective tax rate.[22] Auerbach (1978) showed that this relation can be approximated by a rule of thumb that increases taxable profits by 0.57 percentage points for each percentage point of inflation. With a marginal corporate-income-tax rate of 35%, a 2-percentage-point decline in inflation raises the net of tax return through this channel by $0.35(0.57)(0.02) = 0.0040$ or 0.40 percentage points.[23]

The interaction of the interest deduction and inflation moves the after-tax yield in the opposite direction. If each percentage point of inflation raises the nominal corporate borrowing rate by 1 percentage point,[24] the real pretax cost of borrowing is unchanged but the corporation gets an additional deduction in calculating taxable income. With a typical debt-capital ratio of 40% and a statutory corporate tax rate of 35%, a 2% decline in inflation raises the effective tax rate by $0.35(0.40)(0.02) = 0.0028$ or 0.28 percentage points.

The net effect of going from a 2% inflation rate to price stability is therefore to raise the rate of return after corporate taxes by 0.12 percentage points, from the 5.40% calculated above to 5.52%.[25]

Consider next how the lower inflation rate affects the taxes at the individual level. Applying the 25% tax rate to the 5.52% return net of the corporate tax implies a net yield of 4.14%, an increase of 0.09 percentage points in net yield to the individual because of the changes in taxation at the corporate level. In addition, because individual income taxes are levied on nominal interest payments and nominal capital gains, a reduction in the rate of inflation further reduces the effective tax rate and raises the real after-tax rate of return.

The portion of this relation that is associated with the taxation of nominal interest at the level of the individual can be approximated in a way that parallels the effect at the corporate level. If each percentage point of inflation raises

22. See Feldstein, Green, and Sheshinski (1978) for an analytic discussion of the effect of inflation on the value of depreciation allowances.

23. It might be argued that Congress changes depreciation rates in response to changes in inflation in order to keep the real present value of depreciation allowances unchanged. But although Congress did enact more rapid depreciation schedules in the early 1980s, the decline in inflation since that time has not been offset by lengthening depreciation schedules and has resulted in a reduction in the effective rate of corporate income taxes.

24. This famous Irving Fisher hypothesis of a constant real interest rate is far from inevitable in an economy with a complex nonneutral tax structure. For example, if the only nonneutrality were the ability of corporations to deduct nominal interest payments and all investment were financed by debt at the margin, the nominal interest rate would rise by $1/(1 - \tau)$ times the change in inflation, where τ is the statutory corporate tax rate. This effect is diminished, however, by the combination of historic cost depreciation, equity finance, international capital flows and the tax rules at the level of the individual. (See Feldstein 1983, 1995d; Hartman 1979). Despite the theoretical ambiguity, the evidence suggests that these various tax rules and investor behavior interact in practice in the United States to keep the real pretax rate of interest approximately unchanged when the rate of inflation changes; see Mishkin (1992).

25. Note that although the margin of uncertainty about the 5.5% exceeds the calculated change in return of 0.12%, the conclusions of the current analysis are not sensitive to the precise level of the initial 5.5% rate of return.

the nominal interest rate by 1 percentage point, the individual investors' real pretax return on debt is unchanged but the after-tax return falls by the product of the statutory marginal tax rate and the change in inflation. Assuming the same 40% debt share at the individual level as I assumed for the corporate capital stock[26] and a 25% weighted average individual marginal tax rate implies that a 2% decline in inflation lowers the effective tax rate by $0.25(0.40)(0.02) = 0.0020$ or 0.20 percentage points.

Although the effective tax rate on the dividend return to the equity portion of individual capital ownership is not affected by inflation (except, of course, at the corporate level), a higher rate of inflation increases the taxation of capital gains. Although capital gains are now taxed at the same rate as other investment income (up to a maximum capital gain rate of 28% at the federal level), the effective tax rate is lower because the tax is only levied when the stock is sold. As an approximation, I will therefore assume a 10% effective marginal tax rate on capital gains. In equilibrium, each percentage-point increase in the price level raises the nominal value of the capital stock by 1 percentage point. Since the nominal value of the liabilities remains unchanged, the nominal value of the equity rises by $1/(1 - b)$ percentage points where b is the debt-to-capital ratio. With $b = 0.4$ and an effective marginal tax on nominal capital gains of $\theta_g = 0.1$, a 2-percentage-point decline in the rate of inflation raises the real after-tax rate of return on equity by $\theta_g[1/(1 - b)]d\pi = 0.0033$ or 0.33 percentage points. However, since equity represents only 60% of the individual's portfolio, the lower effective capital gains tax raises the overall rate of return by only 60% of this 0.33 percentage points of 0.20 percentage points.[27]

Combining the debt and capital gains effects implies that reducing the inflation rate by 2 percentage points reduces the effective tax rate at the individual-investor level by the equivalent of 0.40 percentage points. The real net return to the individual saver is thus 4.54%, up 0.49 percentage points from the return when the inflation rate is 2 percentage points higher. The implied price of retirement consumption is $p_1 = (1.0454)^{-30} = 0.264$.

Substituting these values for the price of retirement consumption into equation 4 implies[28]

$$(5) \qquad\qquad G_1 = 0.092 \, S_2 \, (1 - \eta_{Sp} - \sigma).$$

26. This ignores individual investments in government debt. Bank deposits backed by noncorporate bank assets (e.g., home mortgages) can be ignored as being within the household sector.

27. The assumption that the share of debt in the individual's portfolio is the same as the share of debt in corporate capital causes the $1/(1 - b)$ term to drop out of the calculation. More generally, the effect of inflation on the individual's rate of return depends on the difference between the shares of debt in corporate capital and in the individual's portfolios.

28. To test the sensitivity of this result to the assumption about the pretax return and the effective corporate tax rate, I recalculated the retirement consumption prices using alternatives to the assumed values of 9.2% for the pretax return and 0.41 for the combined effective corporate tax rate. Raising the pretax rate of return from 9.2% to 10% only changed the deadweight loss value in equation 5 from 0.092 to 0.096; lowering the pretax rate of return from 9.2% to 8.4% lowered the deadweight loss value to 0.090. Increasing the effective corporate tax rate from 0.41 to 0.50 with

The Saving Rate and Saving Behavior

The value of S_2 in equation 5 represents the saving during preretirement years at the existing rate of inflation. This is, of course, different from the national income account measure of personal saving since personal saving is the difference between the saving of the younger savers and the dissaving of retired dissavers.

One strategy for approximating the value of S_2 is to use the relation between S_2 and the national income account measure of personal saving in an economy in steady-state growth. In the simple overlapping-generations model with saving proportional to income, saving grows at a rate of $n + g$, where n is the rate of population growth and g is the growth in per capita wages. This implies that the saving of the young savers is $(1 + n + g)^T$ times the dissaving of the older dissavers.[29]

Thus net personal saving (S_N) in the economy is related to the saving of the young (S_y) according to

(6) $$S_N = S_y - (1 + n + g)^{-T} S_y.$$

The value of S_2 that we need is conceptually equivalent to S_y. Real aggregate wage income grew in the United States at a rate of 2.6% between 1960 and 1994. Using $n + g = 0.026$ and $T = 30$ implies that $S_y = 1.86 \, S_N$. If we take personal saving to be approximately 5% of GDP, this implies that $S_2 = 0.09$ GDP.[30]

If the propensity to consume out of exogenous income (σ) is the same as the propensity to consume out of wage income, $\sigma = S_2/(\alpha \text{ * GDP})$, where α is the share of wages in GDP. With $\alpha = 0.75$, this simplies $\sigma = 0.12$.

The final term to be evaluated in order to calculate the welfare gain described in equation 5 is the elasticity of saving with respect to the price of retirement consumption. Since the price of retirement consumption is given by $p = (1 + r)^{-T}$, the uncompensated elasticity of savings with respect to the price of retirement consumption can be restated as an elasticity with respect to the real rate of return: $\eta_{Sr} = - rT \eta_{Sp} /(1 + r)$. Thus equation 5 becomes

(7) $$G_1 = 0.092 \, S_2 \, (1 + (1 + r) \, \eta_{Sr}/rT - \sigma).$$

Estimating the elasticity of saving with respect to the real net rate of return has proven to be very difficult because of the problems involved in measuring

---

a pretax return of 9.2 only shifted the deadweight loss value in equation 5 from 0.092 to 0.096. These calculations confirm that the effect of changing the equilibrium inflation rate is not sensitive to the precise values assumed for the pretax rate of return and the effective baseline tax rate.

29. Note that the spending of the older retirees includes both the dissaving of their earlier saving and the income that they have earned on their saving. Net personal saving is only the difference between the saving of the savers and the dissaving of the dissavers.

30. This framework can be extended to recognize that the length of the work period is roughly twice as long as the length of the retirement period without appreciably changing this result.

changes in expected real net-of-tax returns and in holding constant in the time-series data the other factors that affect savings. The large literature on this subject generally finds that a higher real rate of return either raises the saving rate or has no affect at all.[31] In their classic study of the welfare costs of U.S. taxes, Ballard, Shoven, and Whalley (1985) assumed a saving elasticity of $\eta_{Sr} = 0.40$. I will take this as the benchmark value for the current study. In this case, equation 7 implies (with $r = 0.04$)

$$(8) \quad G_1 = 0.092 \, S_2 \, (1 + (1 + r) \, \eta_{Sr}/rT - \sigma)$$
$$= 0.092 \, (0.09) \, (1 + 0.42/1.2 - 0.12) \, GDP = 0.0102 \, GDP.$$

The annual gain from reduced distortion of consumption is equal to 1.02% of GDP. This figure is shown in the first row of table 3.1.

To assess the sensitivity of this estimate to the value of η_{Sr}, I also examine two other values. The limiting case in which changes in real interest rates have no effect on saving, that is, that $\eta_{Sr} = 0$, implies[32]

$$(9) \quad G_1 = 0.092 \, S_2 \, (1 + (1 + r) \, \eta_{Sr}/rT - \sigma)$$
$$= 0.092 \, (0.09) \, (1 - .12) \, GDP = 0.0073 \, GDP,$$

that is, an annual welfare gain equal to 0.73 percentage points of GDP.

If we assume instead that $\eta_{Sr} = 1.0$, that is, that increasing the real rate of return from 4.0% to 4.5% (the estimated effect of dropping the inflation rate from 2% to zero) raises the saving rate 9% to 10.1%, the welfare gain is $G_1 = 0.0144 \, GDP$.

These calculations suggest that the traditional welfare effect on the timing of consumption of reducing the inflation rate from 2% to zero is probably bounded between 0.73% of GDP and 1.44% of GDP. These figures are shown in the second and third rows of table 3.1.

3.3.2   The Revenue Effects of a Lower Inflation Rate Causing a Lower Effective Tax on Investment Income

As I noted earlier, the traditional assumption in welfare calculations, and the one that is implicit in the calculation of section 3.3.1 is that any revenue effect can be offset by lump-sum taxes and transfer. When this is not true, as it clearly is not in the U.S. economy, an increase in tax revenue has a further welfare advantage because it permits reduction in other distortionary taxes while a loss of tax revenue implies a welfare cost of using other distortionary taxes to replace the lost revenue. In this section, I calculate the effect on tax revenue paid by the initial generation of having price stability rather than a 2% inflation rate and discuss the corresponding effect on economic welfare.

Reducing the equilibrium rate of inflation raises the real return to savers and

---

31. See among others Blinder (1975); Boskin (1978); Evans (1983); Feldstein (1995c); Hall (1987); Makin (1987); Mankiw (1978); and Wright (1969).

32. This is a limiting case in the sense that empirical estimates of η_{Sr} are almost always positive. In theory, of course, it is possible that $\eta_{Sr} < 0$.

therefore reduces the price of retirement consumption. The effect of this on government revenue depends on the change in retirement consumption implied by the compensated demand curve.[33] At the initial level of retirement consumption, reducing the price of future consumption from p_2 to p_1 reduces revenue (evaluated as of the initial time) by $(p_2 - p_1)C_2$. If the fall in the price of retirement consumption causes retirement consumption to increase from C_2 to C_1, the government collects additional revenue equal to $(p_1 - p_0)(C_1 - C_2)$. Even if $C_2 < C_1$, the overall net effect on revenue, $(p_1 - p_0)(C_1 - C_2) - (p_2 - p_1)C_2$, can in theory be either positive or negative.

In the present case, the change in revenue can be calculated as

$$
\begin{aligned}
(10) \quad d\ REV &= (p_1 - p_0)(C_1 - C_2) - (p_2 - p_1)C_2 \\
&= (p_1 - p_0)(dC/dp)(p_1 - p_2) - (p_2 - p_1)C_2 \\
&= (p_1 - p_0)(p_1 - p_2)(dC/dp)(p_2\ /\ C_2)(C_2\ /\ p_2) \\
&\quad - (p_2 - p_1)C_2 \\
&= (p_1 - p_0)(p_1 - p_2)\varepsilon_{Cp}(C_2\ /\ p_2) - (p_2 - p_1)C_2
\end{aligned}
$$

Replacing p_2C_2 by S_2 and recalling from equation 3 that $\varepsilon_{Cp} = \eta_{Sp} + \sigma - 1$ yields

$$
\begin{aligned}
(11) \quad d\ REV = S_2\ \{&[(p_1 - p_0)/p_2)][(p_2 - p_1)/p_2)] \\
&\times (1 - \eta_{Sp} - \sigma) - (p_2 - p_1)/p_2\}.
\end{aligned}
$$

Substituting the prices derived in the previous section ($p_0 = 0.071$; $p_1 = 0.264$; and $p_2 = 0.304$) implies

$$
\begin{aligned}
(12) \quad d\ REV &= S_2\ \{0.0836\ (1 - \eta_{Sp} - \sigma) - 0.1316\} \\
&= S_2\ \{0.0836\ (1 + (1 + r)\ \eta_{Sr}/rT - \sigma) - 0.1316\}.
\end{aligned}
$$

With $\sigma = 0.12$ (as derived in section 3.3.1), the benchmark case of $\eta_{Sr} = 0.4$ implies $dREV = -0.029\ S_2$ or, with $S_2 = 0.09\ GDP$ as derived above, $dREV = -0.0026\ GDP$.

The limiting case of $\eta_{Sr} = 0$ implies $dREV = -0.0052\ GDP$ while $\eta_{Sr} = 1.0$ implies $dREV = 0.0013\ GDP$.

Thus, depending on the uncompensated elasticity of saving with respect to the rate of interest, the revenue effect of shifting from 2% inflation to price stability can be either negative or positive.

3.3.3   The Welfare Gain from the Effects of Reduced Inflation on Consumption Timing

We can now combine the traditional welfare gain (G_1 of equations 8 and 9) with the welfare consequences of the revenue change ($dREV$ of equations 11

---

33. The compensated demand curve is used because, for taxpayers as a whole, other taxes are adjusted to keep total revenue constant. Although there is no exact compensation for each taxpayer, the compensated demand curve is much more nearly appropriate than the uncompensated demand curve.

and 12). If each dollar of revenue that must be raised from other taxes involves a deadweight loss of λ, the net welfare gain of shifting from 2% inflation to price stability is

(13a) $G_2 = [0.0102 - 0.0026\lambda]GDP$ if $\eta_{Sr} = 0.4$.

Similarly,

(13b) $G_2 = [0.0073 - 0.0052\lambda]GDP$ if $\eta_{Sr} = 0$.

and

(13c) $G_2 = [0.0144 + 0.0013\lambda]GDP$ if $\eta_{Sr} = 1.0$.

The value of λ depends on the change in taxes that is used to adjust to changes in revenue. Ballard, Shoven, and Whalley (1985) used a computable general equilibrium model to calculate the effect of increasing all taxes in the same proportion and concluded that the deadweight loss per dollar of revenue was between 30 cents and 55 cents, depending on parameter assumptions. I represent this range by $\lambda = 0.40$. Using this implies that the net welfare gain of reducing inflation from 2% to zero equals 0.92% of GDP in the benchmark case of $\eta_{Sr} = 0.4$. The welfare effect of reduced revenue (-0.10% of GDP) is shown in the second column of table 3.1 and the combined welfare effect of 0.92% of GDP is shown in column 4 of table 3.1.

In the other two limiting cases, the net welfare gain corresponding to $\lambda = 0.4$ is 0.52% of GDP with $\eta_{Sr} = 0$ and 1.49% of GDP with $\eta_{Sr} = 1.0$. These are shown in the second and third rows of column 4 of table 3.1.

The analysis of Ballard, Shoven, and Whalley (1985) estimates the deadweight loss of higher tax rates on the basis of the distortion in labor supply and saving. No account is taken of the effect of higher tax rates on tax avoidance through spending on deductible items or receiving income in nontaxable forms (fringe benefits, nicer working conditions, etc.). In a recent paper (Feldstein 1995a), I showed that these forms of tax avoidance as well as the traditional reduction of earned income can be included in the calculation of the deadweight loss of changes in income tax rates by using the compensated elasticity of taxable income with respect to the net of tax rate. Based on an analysis of the experience of high-income taxpayers before and after the 1986 tax rate reductions, I estimated that elasticity to be 1.04 (Feldstein 1995b). Using this elasticity in the National Bureau of Economic Research TAXSIM model, I then estimated that a 10% increase in all individual income tax rates would cause a deadweight loss of about $44 billion at 1994 income levels; since the corresponding revenue increase would be $21 billion, the implied value of λ is 2.06.

A subsequent study (Feldstein and Feenberg 1996) based on the 1993 tax rate increases suggests a somewhat smaller compensated elasticity of about 0.83 instead of the 1.04 value derived in the earlier study. Although this difference may reflect the fact that the 1993 study is based on the experience during the first year only, I will be conservative and assume a lower deadweight loss value of $\lambda = 1.5$.

With $\lambda = 1.5$, equations 13a through 13c imply a wider range of welfare gain estimates: reducing inflation from 2% to zero increases the annual level of welfare by 0.63% of GDP in the benchmark case of $\eta_{Sr} = 0.4$. With $\eta_{Sr} = 0$, the net effect is a very small loss of 0.05% of GDP, while with $\eta_{Sr} = 1.0$ the net effect is a substantial gain of 1.64% of GDP. These values are shown in column 5 of table 3.1.

These are of course just the annual effects of inflation on savers' intertemporal allocation of consumption. Before turning to the other effects of inflation, it is useful to say a brief word about nonsavers.

3.3.4 Nonsavers

A striking fact about American households is that a large fraction of households have no financial assets at all. Almost 20% of U.S. households with heads age fifty-five to sixty-four had no net financial assets at all in 1991 and 50% of such households had assets under $8,300; these figures exclude mortgage obligations from financial liabilities.

The absence of substantial saving does not imply that individuals are irrational or unconcerned with the need to finance retirement consumption. Since Social Security benefits replace more than two-thirds of after-tax income for a worker who has had median lifetime earnings and many employees can anticipate private pension payments in addition to Social Security, the absence of additional financial assets may be consistent with rational life-cycle behavior. For these individuals, zero saving represents a constrained optimum.[34]

In the presence of private pensions and Social Security, the shift from low inflation to price stability may cause some of these households to save and that increase in saving may increase their welfare and raise total tax revenue. Since the welfare gain calculated that I reported earlier in this section is proportional to the amount of saving by preretirement workers, it ignores the potential gain to current nonsavers.

Although the large number of nonsavers and their high aggregate income imply that this effect could be important, I have no way to judge how the increased rate of return would actually affect behavior. I therefore leave this out of the calculations, only noting that it implies that my estimate of the gain from lower inflation is to this extent undervalued.

---

34. The observed small financial balances of such individuals may be precautionary balances or merely transitory funds that will soon be spent. It would be desirable to refine the calculations of this section to recognize that some of the annual national income account savings are for precautionary purposes. Since there is no satisfactory closed-form expression relating the demand for precautionary saving to the rate of interest, I have not pursued that calculation further.

3.4   Inflationary Distortion of the Demand for Owner-Occupied Housing

Owner-occupied housing receives special treatment under the personal income tax.[35] Mortgage-interest payments and local property taxes are deducted, but no tax is imposed on the implicit "rental" return on the capital invested in the property. This treatment would induce too much consumption of housing services even in the absence of inflation.

Inflation reduces the cost of owner-occupied housing services in two ways. The one that has been the focus of the literature on this subject (e.g., Rosen 1985) is the increased deduction of the nominal mortgage-interest payments. Since the real rate remains unchanged while the tax deduction increases, the subsidy increases and the net cost of housing services declines. In addition, inflation increases the demand for owner-occupied housing by reducing the return on investments in the debt and equity of corporations.

Reducing the rate of inflation therefore reduces the deadweight loss that results from excessive demand for housing services. In addition, a lower inflation rate reduces the loss of tax revenue; if raising revenue involves a deadweight loss, this reduction in the loss of tax revenue to the housing subsidy provides an additional welfare gain.

3.4.1   The Welfare Gain from Reduced Distortion of Housing Consumption

In the absence of taxes, the implied rental cost of housing per dollar of housing capital (R_0) reflects the opportunity cost of the resources:

$$(14) \qquad R_0 = \rho + m + \delta,$$

where ρ is the real return on capital in the nonhousing sector, m is the cost of maintenance per dollar of housing capital, and δ is the rate of depreciation. With $\rho = 0.092$ (the average pretax real rate of return on capital in the nonfinancial corporate sector between 1960 and 1994), $m = 0.02$, and $\delta = 0.02$,[36] $R_0 = 0.132$; the rental cost of owner-occupied housing would be 13.2 cents per dollar of housing capital.

Consider in contrast the corresponding implied rental cost per dollar of housing capital under the existing tax rules for a couple who itemize their tax return:

$$(15) \qquad RI = \mu(1-\theta)i_m + (1 - \mu)(r_n + \pi)$$
$$+ (1 - \theta)\tau_p + m + \delta - \pi,$$

where RI indicates that it is the rental cost of an itemizer; μ is the ratio of the mortgage to the value of the house; θ is the marginal income tax rate; i_m is the

---

35. This section benefits from the analysis in Poterba (1984, 1992) but differs from the framework used there in a number of ways.

36. These values of m and δ are from Poterba (1992).

interest rate paid on the mortgage; r_n is the real net rate of return available on portfolio investments; τ_p is the rate of property tax;[37] m and δ are as defined above; and π is the rate of inflation (assumed to be the same for goods in general and for house prices). This equation says the annual cost of owning a dollar's worth of housing is the sum of the net-of-tax mortgage-interest payments $\mu[(1 - \theta)i_m]$ plus the opportunity cost of the equity invested in the house $((1 - \mu)(r_n + \pi))$ plus the local property tax reduced by the value of the corresponding tax deduction $((1 - \theta)\tau_p)$ plus the maintenance (m) and depreciation (δ) less the inflationary gain on the property (π).

In 1991, the year for which other data on housing used in this section were derived, the rate on conventional mortgages was $i_m = 0.072$ and the rate of inflation was $\pi = 0.01$.[38] The assumption that $di_m/d\pi = 1$ implies that i_m would be 0.082 at an inflation rate of $\pi = 0.02$.[39] Section 3.3 derived a value of $r_n = 0.0405$ for the real net return on a portfolio of debt and equity securities when $\pi = 0.02$. With a typical mortgage-to-value ratio among itemizers of $\mu = 0.5$,[40] a marginal tax rate of $\theta = 0.25$, a property tax rate of $\tau_p = 0.025$, $m = 0.02$, and $\delta = 0.02$, the rental cost per dollar of housing capital for an itemizer when the inflation rate is 2% is $RI_2 = 0.0998$. Thus the combination of the tax rules and a 2% inflation rate reduces the rental cost from 13.2 cents per dollar of housing capital to 9.98 cents per dollar of housing capital.

Consider now the effect of a decrease in the rate of inflation on this implicit rental cost of owner-occupied housing:

(16) $dRI/d\pi = \mu(1 - \theta)\ di_m/d\pi + (1 - \mu)\ d(r_n + \pi)/d\pi - 1.$

Section 3.3 showed that if each percentage-point increase in the rate of inflation raises the rate of interest by 1 percentage point, the real net rate of return on a portfolio of corporate equity and debt decreases from $r_n = 0.0454$ at $\pi = 0$ to $r_n = 0.0405$ at $\pi = 0.02$, that is, $dr_n/d\pi = -0.245$ and $d(r_n + \pi) / d\pi = 0.755$. Thus, with $\theta = 0.25$, $dRI/d\pi = 0.75\ \mu + 0.755\ (1 - \mu) - 1$. For an itemizing homeowner with a mortgage-to-value ratio of $\mu = 0.5$, $dRI/d\pi = -0.25$. Since $RI_2 = 0.0998$ at 2% inflation, $dRI/d\pi = -0.25$ implies that $RI_1 = 0.1048$ at zero inflation. The lower rate of inflation implies a higher rental cost per unit of housing capital and therefore a smaller distortion.

Before calculating the deadweight loss effects of the reduced inflation, it is

---

37. Following Poterba (1992), I assume that $\tau_p = 0.025$.

38. The CPI rose by 3.1% from December 1990 to December 1991, implying a "true" inflation rate of 1.1%. While previous rates were higher, subsequent inflation rates have been lower.

39. The assumption that $di/d\ \pi = 1$ is the same assumption made in section 3.3. See note 24 above for the reason that I use this approximation.

40. The relevant μ ratio is not that on new mortgages or on the overall stock of all mortgages but on the stock of mortgages of itemizing taxpayers. The Balance Sheets for the U.S. Economy indicate that the ratio of home-mortgage debt to the value of owner-occupied real estate has increased to 43% in 1994. I use a higher value to reflect the fact that not all homeowners are itemizers and that those who do itemize are likely to have higher mortgage-to-value ratios. The results of this section are not sensitive to the precise level of this parameter.

necessary to derive the corresponding expressions for homeowners who do not itemize their deductions. For such nonitemizers mortgage-interest payments and the property tax payments are no longer tax deductible, implying that[41]

(17) $RN = \mu i_m + (1 - \mu)(r_n + \pi) + \tau_n + m + \delta - \pi.$

The parametric assumptions made for itemizers, modified only by assuming a lower mortgage-to-value ratio among nonitemizers of $\mu = 0.2$, implies $RN_2 = 0.1098$ and $RN_1 = 0.1137$. Both values are higher than the corresponding values for itemizers, but both imply substantial distortions that are reduced when the rate of inflation declines from 2% to zero.

Figure 3.2 shows the nature of the welfare gain from reducing inflation for taxpayers who itemize. The figure presents the compensated demand curve relating the quantity of housing capital demanded to the rental cost of such housing. With no taxes, $R_0 = 0.132$ and the amount of housing demanded is H_0. The combination of the existing tax rules at zero inflation reduces the rental cost to $R_1 = 0.1048$ and increases housing demand to H_1. Since the real pretax cost of providing housing capital is R_0, the tax-inflation combination implies a deadweight loss shown by area A, that is, the area between the cost of providing the additional housing and the demand curve. A rise in inflation to 2% reduces the rental cost of housing further to $RI_2 = 0.0998$ and increases the demand for housing to H_2. The additional deadweight loss is the area C + D between the real pretax cost of providing the increased housing and the value to the users as represented by the demand curve.

Thus, the reduction in the deadweight loss that results from reducing the distortion to housing demand when the inflation rate declines from 2% to zero is

(18) $G_3 = (R_0 - R_1)(H_2 - H_1) + 0.5(R_1 - R_2)(H_2 - H_1).$

With a linear approximation,

(19)
$$G_3 = (R_0 - R_1)(dH/dR)(R_2 - R_1) + 0.5(R_1 - R_2)(dh/dR)$$
$$\times (R_2 - R_1)$$
$$= -(R_2/H_2)(dH/dR)\{[(R_0 - R_1)/R_2][(R_1 - R_2)/R_2] + 0.5(R_1 - R_2)^2 R_2^{-2}\}R_2 H_2.$$

Writing $\varepsilon_{HR} = -(R_2/H_2)(dH/dR)$ for the absolute value of the compensated elasticity of housing demand with respect to the rental price (at the observed values of observed values of R_2 and H_2) and substituting the rental values for an itemizing taxpayer yields

(20) $GI_3 = \varepsilon_{HR}\{(0.273)(0.050) + 0.5(0.050)^2\} RI_2 HI_2$
         $= 0.0149 \varepsilon_{HR} RI_2 HI_2.$

---

41. This formulation assumes that taxpayers who do not itemize mortgage deductions do not itemize at all and therefore do not deduct property tax payments. Some taxpayers may in fact itemize property tax deductions even though they no longer have a mortgage.

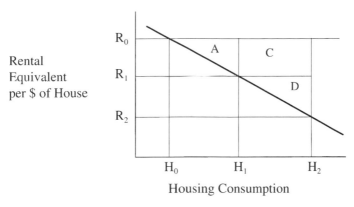

Fig. 3.2   **Homeownership investments**

A similar calculation for nonitemizing homeowners yields

(21) $GN_3 = 0.0065\varepsilon_{HR}RN_2HN_2.$

Combining these two on the assumption that the compensated elasticities of demand are the same for itemizers and nonitemizers gives the total welfare gain from the reduced distortion of housing demand that results from reducing equilibrium inflation from 2% to zero:

(22) $G_3 = \varepsilon_{HR}[0.0149RI_2HI_2 + 0.0065RN_2HN_2].$

Since the calculations of the rental rates take into account the mortgage-to-value ratios, the relevant measures of HI_2 and HN_2 are the total market values of the owner-occupied housing of itemizers and nonitemizers. In 1991, there were 60 million owner-occupied housing units and 25 million taxpayers who itemized mortgage deductions.[42] Since the total 1991 value of owner-occupied real estate of $6,440 billion includes more than just single-family homes (e.g., two-family homes and farms), I take the value of owner-occupied homes (including the owner-occupiers' portion of two-family homes) to be $6,000 billion. The Internal Revenue Service reported that the tax revenue reductions in 1991 due to mortgage deductions were $42 billion, implying approximately $160 billion of mortgage deductions and therefore about $2,000 billion of mortgages. The mortgage-to-value ratio among itemizers of $m/v = 0.5$ implies that the market value of housing owned by itemizers is $HI_2 = \$4,000$ billion. This implies that the value of housing owned by nonitemizers is $HN_2 = \$2,000$ billion.

Substituting these estimates into equation 22 (with $RI_2 = 0.0998$ and $RN_2 = 0.1098$) implies that

42. The difference between these two figures reflects the fact that many homeowners do not itemize mortgage deductions (because they have such small mortgages that they benefit more from using the standard deduction or have no mortgage at all) and that many homeowners own more than one residence.

(23) $G_3 = \$7.4\varepsilon_{HR}$ billion.

Using Rosen's estimate (1985) of $\varepsilon_{HR} = 0.8$ implies that this gain from reducing the inflation rate is \$5.9 billion at 1991 levels. Since the 1991 GDP was \$5,723 billion, this gain is 0.10% of GDP.

3.4.2 The Revenue Effects of Lower Inflation on the Subsidy to Owner-Occupied Housing

The G_3 gain is based on the traditional assumption that changes in tax revenue do not affect economic welfare because they can be offset by other lump-sum taxes and transfers. The more realistic assumption that increases in tax revenue permit reductions in other distortionary taxes implies that it is important to calculate also the reduced tax subsidy of housing that results from a lower rate of inflation.

The magnitude of the revenue change depends on the extent to which the reduction in inflation shifts capital from owner-occupied housing to the business sector. To estimate this, I use the compensated elasticity of housing with respect to the rental value,[43] $\varepsilon_{HR} = 0.8$. The 5% increase in the rental price of owner-occupied housing for itemizers from $RI_2 = 0.0998$ at $\pi = 0.02$ to $RI_1 = 0.1048$ at zero inflation implies a 4% decline in the equilibrium stock of owner-occupied housing, from \$4,000 billion to \$3,840 billion (at 1991 levels). Similarly, for nonitemizers, the 3.6% increase in the rental price from $RN_2 = 0.1098$ at $\pi = 0.02$ to $RN_1 = 0.1137$ at zero inflation implies a 2.9% decline in their equilibrium stock of owner-occupied housing, from \$2,000 billion to \$1,942 billion (at 1991 levels).

Consider first the reduced subsidy on the \$3,840 billion of remaining housing stock owned by itemizing taxpayers. Maintaining the assumption of a mortgage-to-value ratio of $\mu = 0.5$ implies total mortgages of \$1,920 billion on this housing capital. The 2-percentage-point decline in the rate of inflation reduces mortgage-interest payments by \$38.4 billion and, assuming a 25% marginal tax rate, increases tax revenue by \$9.6 billion.

The shift of capital from owner-occupied housing to the business sector affects revenue in three ways. First, the itemizers lose the mortgage deduction and property tax deduction on the \$160 billion of reduced housing capital. The reduced capital corresponds to mortgages of \$80 billion and, at the initial inflation rate of 2%, of mortgage interest deductions of 8.2% of this \$80 billion, or \$6.6 billion. The reduced stock of owner-occupied housing also reduces property tax deductions by 2.5% of \$160 billion of forgone housing, or \$4 billion. Combining these two reductions in itemized deductions (\$10.6 billion) and applying a marginal tax rate of 25% implies a revenue gain of \$2.6 billion.

Second, the increased capital in the business sector (\$160 billion from itemizers plus \$58 billion from nonitemizers) earns a pretax return of 9.2% but

---

43. I use the compensated elasticity because other taxes are adjusted to keep total revenue constant. See note 33.

provides a net-of-tax yield to investors of only 4.54% when the inflation rate is zero. The difference is the tax collections of 4.66% on the additional $218 billion of business capital, or $10.2 billion of additional revenue.

Third, the reduced housing capital causes a loss of property tax revenue equal to 2.5% of the $218 billion reduction in housing capital, or $5.4 billion.

Combining these three effects on revenue implies a net revenue gain of $16.9 billion, or 0.30% of GDP (at 1991 levels).

3.4.3 The Welfare Gain from the Housing-Sector Effects of Reduced Equilibrium Inflation

The total welfare gain from the effects of lower equilibrium inflation on the housing sector is the sum of (1) the traditional welfare gain from the reduced distortion to housing consumption, 0.10% of GDP; and (2) the welfare consequences of the $16.9 billion revenue gain, a revenue gain of 0.30% of GDP. If each dollar of revenue raised from other taxes involves a deadweight loss of λ, this total welfare gain of shifting from 4% inflation to 2% inflation is

$$(24) \qquad\qquad G_4 = [0.0010 + .0030\lambda] \; GDP.$$

The conservative Ballard, Shoven, and Whalley (1985) estimate of $\lambda = 0.4$ implies that the total welfare gain of reducing inflation from 2% to zero is 0.22 % of GDP. With the value of $\lambda = 1.5$ implied by the behavioral estimates for the effect of an across-the-board increase in all personal income tax rates, the total welfare gain of reducing inflation from 2% to zero is 0.55% of GDP. These figures are shown in row 4 of table 3.1.

Before combining this with the gain from the change in the taxation of savings and comparing the sum to the cost of reducing inflation, I turn to two other ways in which a lower equilibrium rate of inflation affects economic welfare through the government's budget constraint.

3.5 Seigniorage and the Distortion of Money Demand

An increase in inflation raises the cost of holding non-interest-bearing money balances and therefore reduces the demand for such balances below the optimal level. Although the resulting deadweight loss of inflation has been the primary focus of the literature on the welfare effects of inflation since Bailey's pioneering paper (1956), the effect on money demand of reducing the inflation rate from 2% to zero is small relative to the other effects that have been discussed in this paper.[44]

This section follows the framework of sections 3.3 and 3.4 by looking first

---

44. Although the annual effect is extremely small, it is a perpetual effect. As I argued in Feldstein (1979), in a growing economy a perpetual gain of even a very small fraction of GDP may outweigh the cost of reducing inflation if the appropriate discount rate is low enough relative to the rate of aggregate economic growth. In the context of the current paper, however, the welfare effect of the reduction in money demand is very small relative to the welfare effects that occur because of the interaction of inflation and the tax laws.

at the distortion of demand for money and then at the revenue consequences of the inflation "tax" on the holding of money balances.

3.5.1   The Welfare Effects of Distorting the Demand for Money

As Milton Friedman (1969) has noted, since there is no real cost to increasing the quantity of money, the optimal inflation rate is such that it completely eliminates the cost to the individual of holding money balances, that is, the inflation rate should be such that the nominal interest rate is zero. In an economy with no taxes on capital income, the optimal inflation rate would therefore be the negative of the real rate of return on capital: $\pi^* = -\rho$. More generally, if we recognize the existence of taxes, the optimal inflation rate is such that the nominal after-tax return on alternative financial assets is zero.

Recall that at $\pi = 0.02$ the real net return on the debt-equity portfolio is $r_n = 0.0405$ and that $dr_n/d\pi = -0.245$. The optimal inflation rate in this context is such that $r_n + \pi = 0.$[45] Figure 3.3 illustrates the reduction in the deadweight loss that results if the inflation rate is reduced from $\pi = 0.02$ to 0, thereby reducing the opportunity costs of holding money balances from $r_n + \pi = 0.0605$ to the value of r_n at $\pi = 0$, that is, $r_n = 0.0454$. Since the opportunity cost of supplying money is zero, the welfare gain from reducing inflation is the area $C + D$ between the money demand curve and the zero opportunity-cost line:

$$G_5 = 0.0454\,(M_1 - M_2) + 0.5\,(0.0605 - 0.0454)\,(M_1 - M_2)$$
$$(25) \quad = 0.0530\,(M_1 - M_2)$$
$$= -0.0530\,[d\,M/d(r_n + \pi)]\,(0.0151)$$
$$= 0.00080\varepsilon_M M(r_n + \pi)^{-1},$$

where ε_M is the elasticity of money demand with respect to the nominal opportunity cost of holding money balances, and $r_n + \pi = 0.0605$.

Since the demand deposit component of M_1 is now generally interest-bearing, non-interest-bearing money is now essentially currency plus bank reserves. In 1994, currency plus reserves were 6.1% of GDP. Thus, $M = 0.061$ GDP. There is a wide range of estimates of the elasticity of money demand, corresponding to different definitions of money and different economic conditions. An estimate of $\varepsilon_M = 0.2$ may be appropriate in the current context, with money defined as currency plus bank reserves.[46] With these assumptions, $G_5 =$

---

45. If $dr_n/d\pi$ remains constant, the optimal rate of inflation is $\pi^* = -0.060$. Although this assumption of linearity may not be appropriate over the entire range, the basic property that $r_n > \pi^* > -\rho$ is likely to remain valid in a more exact calculation, reflecting the interaction between taxes and inflation.

46. In Feldstein (1979), I assumed an elasticity of one-third for non-interest-bearing M_1 deposits. I use the lower value now to reflect the fact that the non-interest-bearing money is now just currency plus bank reserves. These are likely to be less interest sensitive than the demand-deposit component of M_1. The assumption that $\varepsilon_M = 0.2$ when the opportunity cost of holding money balances is approximately 0.06 implies that a 1 percentage point increase in $r_n + \pi$ reduces M by approximately $.2\,(0.01)/0.06 = 0.033$, a semielasticity of 3.3. Since the Cagan estimates (1953) of this semielasticity ranged from $F = 3$ to $F = 10$, the selection of $\varepsilon_M = 0.2$ in the current context may be quite conservative.

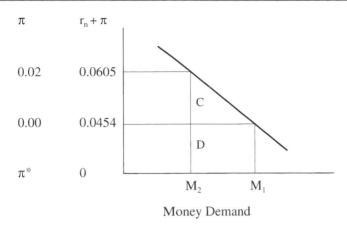

Fig. 3.3   Money demand and seigniorage

0.00016 *GDP.* Thus even when Friedman's standard for the optimal money supply is used, the deadweight loss due to the distorted demand for money balances is only 0.0002 *GDP.*

3.5.2   The Revenue Effects of Reduced Money Demand

The decline in inflation affects government revenue in three ways. First, the reduction in the inflation "tax" on money balances results in a loss of seigniorage and therefore an associated welfare loss of raising revenue by other distortionary taxes (Phelps 1973). In equilibrium, inflation at rate π implies revenue equal to πM. Increasing the inflation rate raises the seigniorage revenue by

$$\text{(26)} \quad \begin{aligned} d(Seigniorage)/d\pi &= M + \pi(dM/d\pi) \\ &= M + \pi\,[dM/d(r_n + \pi)][d(r_n + \pi)/d\pi] \\ &= M\,\{1 - \varepsilon_M\,[d(r_n + \pi)/d\pi]\pi(r_n + \pi)^{-1}\}. \end{aligned}$$

With $M = 0.061$ *GDP*, $\varepsilon_M = 0.2$, $d(r_n + \pi)/d\pi = 0.755$, $\pi = 0.02$, and $r_n + \pi = 0.0605$, equation 26 implies that $d(Seigniorage)/d\pi = 0.058$ *GDP*. A decrease of inflation from $\pi = 0.02$ to $\pi = 0$ causes a loss of seigniorage of 0.116% of GDP.

The corresponding welfare loss is $0.116\lambda\%$ of GDP. With $\lambda = 0.4$, the welfare cost of the lost seigniorage is 0.046% of GDP. With $\lambda = 1.5$, the welfare cost of the lost seigniorage is 0.174% of GDP.

The second revenue effect is the revenue loss that results from shifting capital to money balances from other productive assets.[47] The decrease in business capital is equal to the increase in the money stock, $M_1 - M_2 = [dM/d(r_n + \pi)](0.0151) = 0.0151\,\varepsilon_M M(r_n + \pi)^{-1} = 0.30\%$ of GDP. When these assets are invested in business capital, they earn a real pretax return of 9.2% but a net-of-tax return of only 4.54%. The difference is the corporate and personal

---

47. This is analogous to the revenue gain associated with the shift of assets from housing into business capital discussed in section 3.4.

tax payments of 4.66%. Applying this to the incremental capital of 0.30% of GDP implies a revenue loss of $0.0466(0.30) = 0.014\%$ of GDP. The welfare gain from this extra revenue is $0.014\lambda\%$ of GDP. With $\lambda = 0.4$, the welfare loss from this source is 0.006% of GDP, while with $\lambda = 1.5$ the loss is 0.021% of GDP.

The final revenue effect of the change in the demand for money is the result of the government's ability to substitute the increased money balance of $M_1 - M_2$ for interest-bearing government debt. Although this is a one-time substitution, it reduces the government debt service permanently by $r_{ng}(M_1 - M_2)$, where r_{ng} is the real interest rate paid by the government on its outstanding debt net of the tax that it collects on those interest payments. A conservative estimate of r_{ng}, based on the observed 1994 ratio of interest payments to national debt of 0.061, an assumed tax rate of 0.25, and a 1994 inflation rate of 2.7% is $r_{ng} = 0.75(0.061) - 0.027 = 0.018$. The reduced debt service cost in perpetuity is thus $0.018(M_1 - M_2) = 0.000054\ GDP$. The corresponding welfare gains are 0.002% of GDP at $\lambda = 0.4$ and 0.008% of GDP at $\lambda = 1.5$.

Combining these three effects yields a net welfare loss due to decreased revenue of 0.05% of GDP if $\lambda = 0.4$ and of 0.19% of GDP if $\lambda = 1.5$.

Although all of the effects that depend on the demand for money are small, the welfare loss from reduced seigniorage revenue is much larger than the welfare gain from the reduced distortion of money demand and the shift of assets to tax-paying business investments. When considering this small reduction in inflation, the Phelps revenue effect dominates the Bailey money-demand effect.

3.6   Debt Service and the Government Budget Constraint

The final effect of reduced inflation that I will consider is the higher real cost of servicing the national debt that results from a reduction in the rate of inflation. This higher debt service cost occurs because inflation leaves the real pretax interest rate on government debt unchanged while the inflation premium is subject to tax at the personal level. A lower inflation rate therefore does not change the pretax cost of debt service but reduces the tax revenue on the government debt payments. This in turn requires a higher level of other distortionary taxes.[48]

To assess the effect of inflation on the net cost of debt service, note that the increase in the outstanding stock of government debt (B) can be written as

$$(27) \qquad \Delta B = (r_g + \pi)\, B + G - T - \theta_i\, (r_g + \pi)\, B,$$

where $(r_g + \pi)$ is the nominal pretax interest rate of government debt and θ_i is the effective rate of tax on such interest payments. Thus, $(r_g + \pi)B$ is the gross

---

48. Note that the effect of inflation on business tax revenue (through the tax-inflation interaction on depreciation and corporate debt) has been counted in the above discussion of taxes and saving. This ignores the role of retained earnings and the effect of changes in the mixture of corporate investment on the overall tax revenue.

interest payment on the government debt, and $(1 - \theta_i)(r_g + \pi)B$ is the net interest on that debt. G is all other government spending, and T is all tax revenue other than the revenue collected from taxing the interest on government debt.

In equilibrium, the stock of government debt must grow at the same rate as nominal GDP, that is, $\Delta B = B(n + g + \pi)$, where n is the rate of growth of population and g is the rate of growth per capita output. Combining this equilibrium condition with equation 27 implies

$$(28) \quad T/GDP = G/GDP + [(1 - \theta_i)\, r_g - n - g - \theta_i \pi]\, B/GDP.$$

Thus, $d(T/GDP)/d\pi = -\theta_i\,(B/GDP)$.

Reducing the inflation rate from 2% to zero increases the real cost of debt service (i.e., increases the level of taxes required to maintain the existing debt/ GDP ratio) by $0.02\,\theta_i B$. With $\theta_i = 0.25$ and the current debt-to-GDP ratio of $B/GDP = 0.5$, the 2-percentage-point reduction would reduce tax revenue by 0.25% of GDP and would therefore reduce welfare by $0.25\lambda\%$ of GDP. The welfare cost of increased net debt service is therefore between 0.10% of GDP and 0.38% of GDP, depending on the value of λ. These figures are shown in row 6 of table 3.1.

3.7   The Net Effect of Lower Inflation on Economic Welfare

I can now bring together the several effects of reduced inflation that have been identified and evaluated in sections 3.3 through 3.6 and compare them with the one-time output losses required to achieve that inflation reduction that were discussed in section 3.2.

Table 3.1 summarizes the four effects, distinguishing the direct effects of reduced distortion and the indirect effects that occur through the change in revenue. Separate values are given for the alternative savings demand elasticities ($\eta_{Sr} = 0.4$, $\eta_{Sr} = 0$, and $\eta_{Sr} = 1.0$) and for the alternative estimates of the deadweight loss per dollar of revenue raised through alternative distorting taxes ($\lambda = 0.4$ and $\lambda = 1.5$).

These relatively large gains from reduced inflation reflect primarily the fact that the existing system of capital taxation imposes large deadweight losses even in the absence of inflation and that these deadweight losses are exacerbated by inflation.

Reducing these distortions by lowering the rate of inflation produces annual welfare gains of 1.14% of GDP in the benchmark saving case where there is a very small positive relation between saving and the real net rate of interest ($\eta_{Sr} = 0.4$). The deadweight loss distortions in the other two cases, shown at the bottom of column 1, are 0.85% of GDP and 1.56% of GDP.

The additional welfare effects of changes in revenue, summarized at the bottom of columns 3 and 4) can be either negative or positive but on balance are smaller than the direct effects of reduced distortion. In the benchmark case of $\eta_{sr} = 0.4$, the total revenue effects reduce welfare, but the reductions are relatively small (between -0.13 at $\lambda = 0.4$ and -0.51 at $\lambda = 1.5$).

The total welfare effect of reducing inflation from 2% to zero is therefore a gain in the benchmark saving case of between 0.63% of GDP a year and 1.01% of GDP a year. A higher saving response increases the net gain, while a lower saving response reduces it.

If the cost of reducing the inflation rate from 2% to zero is a one-time cumulative loss of 6% of GDP, as Ball's analysis (1994) discussed in section 3.2 implies, the estimated gains in the benchmark case would offset this cost within six to eight years. If savings are more responsive, the gain from price stability would offset the cost even more quickly. Only if saving is completely interest-inelastic and revenue raising has a high deadweight loss does the estimated total effect imply that the welfare gains would take more than a decade to exceed the lost GDP that is required to achieve price stability. Even in this case, the present value of the annual benefits of eliminating inflation exceeds 10% of the initial GDP if the growing benefit stream is discounted by the historic real return on the Standard and Poor's portfolio.

3.8   The Limits of Indexing

Since the gains from reduced inflation that are evaluated in this paper reflect the interaction of taxes and inflation, it is natural to ask whether the same gains might not be achieved without a loss of output by indexing the tax system. While this would in theory be possible, I present here some of the reasons why that is not a practical alternative to reducing inflation.

It should be noted from the outset that there is a long history of proposals to index the tax system, motivated not only by the desire to reduce the deadweight losses of the type discussed in this paper but also because a tax system that bases taxes on nominal capital income and expenses is regarded as inherently unfair. Individuals pay capital gains taxes even if they have real losses. The effective tax rate on interest income may exceed 100% even if the statutory rate is only 25%. Allowing only nominal depreciation on plant and equipment can be substantially reduce the return on business investment during times of relatively high inflation. All of these issues received heightened public and professional attention in the late 1970s and early 1980s when U.S. inflation rates exceed 10%.

Despite public and professional support for indexing and proposals by the Reagan administration to introduce such indexing, the taxation of capital income remains unindexed.[49] The United States is not alone in not indexing the taxation of capital income. In no major industrial country are taxes levied only

---

49. Although tax brackets are adjusted for the rise in the price level, this does nothing to remedy the mismeasurement of capital income and expenses.

on real income and deductions allowed only for real expenses.[50] The reasons are partly technical, partly administrative, and partly, as in Germany, a matter of political conviction.

Consider first the technical "legal" problems of designing rules about what should be indexed and what should not. In principle, the problem is easy. Interest income should be taxed only after subtracting the product of the inflation rate and the principle of the fixed-income asset. Thus, a bond with a market price of $100 that pays interest of $7 in a year in which the price level rose by 4% would create taxable income of only $3.[51] In contrast, the dividend income on a stock should be taxed in full because the value of the underlying equity is not fixed in nominal terms and should in principle rise with the general price level. When the stock is sold, a capital gain would be taxed only to the extent that the nominal value of the asset rises by more than the increase in the price level.

But the world consists of more than such "plain vanilla" bonds and stocks. Consider a convertible bond. If the price of the stock is high enough relative to the conversion price and the bond can currently be converted, the bond has all of the "inflation protection" attributes of the stock (as well as the extra protection of a fixed-interest obligation). How should such a convertible bond be taxed? If the "bond" is trading in the market like a stock, it might seem reasonable to tax it like a stock and not allow any inflation adjustment even though the annual payments are called "interest" payments. Failure to do so might encourage companies to issue short-term convertible bonds below the conversion price. But a general rule that convertible bonds should be taxed like equity would not be appropriate for a bond that has a conversion price far above the actual price of the stock and is therefore trading like a bond.

To take another simple but realistic example, consider commercial mortgages in which the interest and principle are linked to the rents in the building or, in the case of stores, to the gross nominal receipts of the store. What if the mortgage pays the higher of some fixed nominal amounts and the rent-linked amount? Should these mortgage payments be treated like debt or equity? How should they be treated for the borrower?

Any rule that tries to draw a line between debt and equity for the purpose of inflation adjustment will create powerful incentives to create tax-advantaged

---

50. Some countries have indexed some part of their tax laws. In the United Kingdom, capital gains are taxed on an inflation-adjusted basis and only above a substantial annual exclusion. Mexico has probably gone further than any other country in the Organization for Economic Cooperation and Development in adopting the indexation principles first outlined by the Carter Commission in Canada in the 1960s, but even Mexico has not provided full indexation. The Canadians never adopted the indexation proposals of the Carter Commission.

51. Even in this simple case there is a problem if the nominal price of the bond fluctuates during the year. Does one use the beginning or the end or the average value? If some "reasonable" but arbitrary compromise like using the beginning-of-year value is used, will sophisticated investors trade such bonds to get unfair (and distorting) real net-of-tax interest rates?

securities. The ability to create derivative securities tailored to the tax law makes this problem even worse because it would allow investors to have and to trade the tax-advantaged features of securities without having other attributes that they do not want. In the case of the index-linked mortgage, it would be possible to strip out the excess, if any, of the index-linked portion over the fixed-income portion. How should that derivative security be taxed?

In addition to the technical legal problems, there are purely administrative problems. Consider for example the problem of inflation-adjusting interest receipts on securities held for only part of a year. In principle, the solution is easy. But consider the administrative problem for an individual who transfers money frequently into and out of a saving account or checking account.

Again, any simplification or rough approximation would provide an incentive for sophisticated investors to move large sums of money to take advantage of the opportunity to borrow and lend under different tax rules. These problems of microtiming may not matter much when the inflation rate is low, but any tax rule should be applicable in higher-inflation-rate environments.

Consider next the special problem of indexing capital gains. This has been a frequent proposal in the Congress over the past two decades and has received bipartisan support because of the widely perceived unfairness of taxing nominal "profits" when the real gains on those transactions are negative. The basic idea would be to increase the "cost" for the purpose of calculating taxable gain by the ratio of the price level at the time of sale to the price level at the time that the asset was purchased. If this adjustment is permitted to create taxable losses when the rise in the nominal value of the security is less than the rise in the price level, it is likely that the capital gains tax would cease to collect any revenue at all. Since individuals can decide when to realize gains and losses, it is very likely that individuals holding a widely diversified portfolio could always find enough stocks with real losses to offset the real taxable gains on those stocks that they choose to sell.[52] To avoid this result, indexation proposals in the Congress would not allow individuals to take a loss when the nominal value of the asset has not fallen. If such legislation were to pass, it would create the incentive to produce new conglomerate securities that preserved as much as possible of this tax advantage. The indexing rule would substitute one distortion for another.[53]

Consider finally the tax treatment of owner-occupied housing. It would in principle be possible to limit the mortgage deduction only to the real compo-

52. Recall that under current law assets held until death are not subject to a capital gains tax in the hands of either the decedent or the heir; the "cost" of the asset is "stepped up" to the market value at the time of the owner's death and subsequent gains are calculated only relative to the value at that time.

53. It is, of course, easy to suggest that these problems could be remedied by more fundamental reforms of the taxation of capital gains. It would take this paper too far afield to discuss some of the reasons why proposals like accrual taxation of gains are not practical solutions.

nent of the mortgage payment.[54] That would of course create incentives for individuals who can do so to borrow in other more tax-favored ways. But even apart from that, it is clear from the analysis of section 3.4 that limiting the mortgage deduction alone does very little to reduce the distortion and the revenue loss associated with the current tax treatment of owner-occupied housing. As the analysis there showed, reducing the inflation rate from 2% to zero would produce a substantial welfare gain even for those who do not currently itemize their mortgage deductions at all.

In addition to these technical and administrative problems, there is a more fundamental concern that an indexed tax system might lead to less public support for anti-inflationary policies. If the tax indexing serves only to reduce but not to eliminate the adverse effects of inflation but leads to policies that produce a higher rate of inflation, the net effect of indexing on economic welfare may be negative.[55]

3.9 Conclusion

The calculations in this paper imply that the interaction of existing tax rules and inflation cause a significant welfare loss even at a low rate of inflation. More specifically, the analysis implies that shifting the equilibrium rate of inflation from 2% to zero would cause a perpetual welfare gain equal to about 1% of GDP a year. The deadweight loss of 2% inflation is so large because inflation exacerbates the distortions that would be caused by existing capital income taxes, even with price stability.

To assess the desirability of achieving price stability, the gain from eliminating this loss has to be compared to the one-time cost of disinflation. Shifting from 2% inflation to price stability is estimated to have a cost equal to about 5% of GDP. Since the 1% of GDP annual welfare gain from price stability continues forever and grows at the same rate as GDP (i.e., at about 2.5% a year), the present value of the welfare gain is very large. Discounting the annual gains at the rate that investors require for risky equity investments (i.e., at the 5.1% real net-of-tax rate of return on Standard and Poor's portfolio from 1969 to 1994) implies a present value gain equal to more than 35% of the initial level of GDP. The benefit of achieving price stability therefore substantially exceeds its cost.

This welfare gain could in principle also be achieved by eliminating all capital-income taxes or by indexing capital-income taxes so that taxes are

54. I should emphasize "in principle" because any attempt to limit mortgage deductions meets with overwhelming political objections. In a nation of 60 million homeowners, even those who do not currently have mortgages worry rightly that limiting the mortgage deduction would reduce the value of their largest asset.

55. This is the argument developed in Fischer and Summers (1989). It is the logic that underlies the German constitutional prohibition against any kind of indexing.

based only on real income and real expenses. The paper has discussed the technical and administrative difficulties that are likely to keep such indexing from being adopted. Although some of the current proposals for tax reform would eliminate capital-income taxation, their prospects are very uncertain. The magnitude of the annual gain from reducing inflation is so large that the expected present value of the gain from disinflating from 2% inflation to price stability would be positive even if there were a 50% change that capital-income taxes would be completely eliminated after ten years.

The analysis in this paper does not discuss the distributional consequences of the disinflation or of the reduced inflation. Some readers may believe that the output loss caused by the disinflation should be weighted more heavily than the gain from low inflation because the output loss falls disproportionately on lower-income individuals and does so in the form of the large individual losses associated with unemployment. It would, however, take very large weights to overcome the difference between the 5% of GDP output loss of disinflation and the 35 + % of GDP present-value gain from lower inflation.

The analysis in this paper could be extended in several ways. The paper presents estimates of the annual steady-state gain from lower inflation. To get a more accurate calculation of the present value, it would be desirable to study the time path of those gains. A more complete measure of the effects of inflation on saving and on the timing of consumption would extend the analysis to precautionary saving and to institutional saving in pensions and insurance. It would also be desirable to look at the deadweight losses and revenue effects of the impact of inflation on business investment.

Although the current research has shown that shifting from low inflation to price stability is likely to raise economic welfare, the paper has not derived the optimal rate of inflation. The large literature on that subject, starting with the contributions of Friedman (1969) and Phelps (1973), has focused on the distortion to money demand and the resulting seigniorage gain. As the present paper shows, those effects are much smaller than the effects caused by the interaction of inflation and capital taxation. A future paper will report the implications of the current analysis for the optimal rate of inflation.

References

Auerbach, Alan. 1978. Appendix: The Effect of Inflation on the Tax Value of Depreciation. In Martin Feldstein, Jerry Green, and Eytan Sheshinki, Inflation and Taxes in a Growing Economy with Debt and Equity Finance, *Journal of Political Economy,* part 2 (April): S68–69.
Bailey, Martin. 1956. The Welfare Cost of Inflationary Finance. *Journal of Political Economy* 64, 93–110.
Ball, Laurence. 1994. What Determines the Sacrifice Ratio? In *Monetary Policy,* ed. N. Gregory Mankiw. Chicago: University of Chicago Press.

Ballard, Charles, John Shoven, and John Whalley. 1985. General Equilibrium Computations of the Marginal Welfare Cost of Taxes in the United States. *American Economic Review* 75 (March): 128–38.

Barro, Robert. 1995. Inflation and Economic Growth. NBER Working Paper no. 5326. Cambridge, MA: National Bureau of Economic Research, October.

Benabou, Roland. 1992. Inflation and Efficiency in Search Markets. *Review of Economic Studies,* no. 2: 299–329.

Blinder, Alan. 1975. Distribution Effects and the Aggregate Consumption Function. *Journal of Political Economy* 83, no. 3: 447–75.

Boskin, Michael. 1978. Taxation, Saving, and the Rate of Interest. *Journal of Political Economy* 86, no. 2, part 2 (April): S3–27.

Cagan, Phillip. 1953. The Monetary Dynamics of Hyperinflation. In *Studies in the Quantity Theory of Money,* ed. Milton Friedman. Chicago: University of Chicago Press.

Evans, O. 1983. Tax Policy, the Interest Elasticity of Saving, and Capital Accumulation. *American Economic Review* 83 (June): 398–410.

Feldstein, Martin. 1978. The Welfare Cost of Capital Income Taxation. *Journal of Political Economy* 86, no. 2, part 2 (April): S29–51.

———. 1979. The Welfare Cost of Permanent Inflation and Optimal Short-Run Economic Policy. *Journal of Political Economy* 87, no. 4: 749–68.

———. 1983. *Inflation, Tax Rules, and Capital Formation.* Chicago: University of Chicago Press.

———. 1995a. The Effect of Marginal Tax Rates on Taxable Income: A Panel Study of the 1986 Tax Reform Act. *Journal of Political Economy* 103, no. 3:551–72.

———. 1995b. Fiscal Policies, Capital Formation, and Capitalism. *European Economic Review* 39:399–420.

———. 1995c. Tax Avoidance and the Deadweight Loss of the Income Tax. NBER Working Paper no. 5055. Cambridge, MA: National Bureau of Economic Research.

———. 1995d. Tax Policy and International Capital Flows. *Weltwirtschaftsliches Archiv* 4:675–97.

Feldstein, Martin, and Daniel Feenberg. 1996. The Effect of Increased Tax Rates on Taxable Income and Economic Efficiency: A Preliminary Analysis of the 1993 Tax Rate Increases. NBER Working Paper no. 5370. Cambridge, MA: National Bureau of Economic Research.

Feldstein, Martin, Jerry Green, and Eytan Sheshinski. 1978. Inflation and Taxes in a Growing Economy with Debt and Equity Finance. *Journal of Political Economy,* part 2 (April): S53–70.

Feldstein, Martin, James Poterba, and Louis Dicks-Mireaux. 1983. The Effective Tax Rate and the Pretax Rate of Return. *Journal of Public Economics* 21, no. 2: 129–58.

Fischer, Stanley. 1981. Towards an Understanding of the Costs of Inflation, 2. In *The Costs and Consequences of Inflation,* ed. K. Brunner and A. Meltzer. Carnegie-Rochester Conference Series on Public Policy, vol. 15. Amsterdam: North Holland.

Fischer, Stanley. 1994. Modern Central Banking. In F. Capie, G. Goodhart, S. Fischer, and N. Schnadt, *The Future of Central Banking.* Cambridge: Cambridge University Press.

Fischer, Stanley, and Franco Modigliani. 1978. Toward an Understanding of the Real Effects and Costs of Inflation. *Weltwirtschaftliches Archiv* 114:810–33.

Fischer, Stanley, and Lawrence Summers. 1989. Should Governments Learn to Live with Inflation. *American Economic Review* 83, no. 1: 312–13.

Friedman, Milton. 1969. The Optimum Quantity of Money. In *The Optimum Quantity of Money and Other Essays.* Chicago: Aldine.

Hall, Robert. 1987. Intertemporal Substitution in Consumption. *Journal of Political Economy* 96, no. 2 (April): 339–57.

Hartman, David. 1979. Taxation and the Effects of Inflation on the Real Capital Stock in an Open Economy. *International Economic Review* 20, no. 2: 417–25.

Makin, John. 1987. *Saving, Pension Contributions, and Real Interest Rates.* American Enterprise Institute.

Mankiw, N. Gregory. 1978. Consumer Spending and the After-Tax Real Interest Rate. In *The Effects of Taxation on Capital Accumulation,* ed. Martin Feldstein. Chicago: University of Chicago Press.

Mishkin, Frederic. 1992. Is the Fischer Effect for Real? *Journal of Monetary Economics* 30:195–215.

Phelps, Edmund. 1973. Inflation in the Theory of Public Finance. *Swedish Journal of Economics* 75:67–82.

Poterba, James. 1984. Tax Subsidies to Owner Occupied Housing: An Asset Market Approach. *Quarterly Journal of Economics* 99:729–45.

———. 1992. Taxation and Housing: Old Questions, New Answers. *American Economic Review* 82, no. 2: 237–42.

Poterba, James, and Andrew Samwick. 1995. Stock Ownership Patterns, Stock Market Fluctuations, and Consumption. *Brookings Papers on Economic Activity* 2:295–357.

Rippe, Richard. 1995. Further Gains in Corporate Profitability. *Economic Outlook Monthly* (Prudential Securities, Inc.), August.

Rosen, Harvey. 1985. Housing Subsidies: Effects on Housing Decisions, Efficiency, and Equity. In *Handbook of Public Economics,* ed. Martin Feldstein and A. Auerbach, vol. 1. Amsterdam: North Holland.

Wright, Charles. 1969. Saving and the Rate of Interest. In *The Taxation of Income from Capital,* ed. M. J. Bailey. Washington DC: Brookings Institution.

Comment   Andrew B. Abel

Martin Feldstein has presented a fresh and interesting analysis of the costs and benefits of moving from a low rate of inflation to a zero rate of inflation. This analysis emphasizes fiscal channels—both direct and indirect. The direct fiscal channels are familiar to readers of the literature on inflation and taxation that Feldstein pioneered almost two decades ago, though the calculations and the context presented here are new. These effects arise because the tax code in the United States is not neutral with respect to inflation—in particular the taxation of capital income is sensitive to the rate of inflation. The indirect fiscal channels arise through the government's budget constraint, which requires that any changes in seigniorage associated with a reduction in inflation be offset by changes in other taxes and/or government expenditures.

In order to judge the desirability of moving to price stability, one needs to compare the costs and benefits of eliminating inflation. The potential cost of eliminating inflation is the temporary increase in unemployment that might

Andrew B. Abel is the Robert Morris Professor of Banking in the finance department of the Wharton School of the University of Pennsylvania and is a research associate of the National Bureau of Economic Research.

The author thanks Lutz Hendricks for checking the calculations in this comment.

accompany a reduction in the rate of inflation. Feldstein uses the results of a survey by Ball (1994) to conclude that reducing the rate of inflation from 2% per year to zero would impose a one-time cost of 4–6% of GDP. The calculation of the benefits of reducing inflation occupies the bulk of the paper. Reducing the rate of inflation reduces various distortions, and Feldstein calculates that the benefit of having zero inflation rather than 2% inflation is about 1% of GDP per year. Because the benefits of reduced distortions accrue forever (and they are proportional to GDP, which is growing), Feldstein concludes that the present value of the permanent flow of benefits (using any reasonable discount rate) exceeds the one-time unemployment cost of eliminating inflation.

Like Feldstein's paper, this comment focuses on the calculation of the benefits of eliminating inflation, though I follow a different analytic strategy. I will use a variant of the Sidrauski (1967) model to compute the welfare effects of eliminating inflation. The major features of Feldstein's analysis can be incorporated by the following three modifications of the Sidrauski model. First, the model includes two types of capital that are to be interpreted as housing capital and nonhousing capital. Second, the model includes a government budget constraint that integrates monetary and fiscal policy. This budget constraint captures the effects of various distortionary taxes and takes account of the fact emphasized by Feldstein that distortionary tax rates will need to be changed to offset any change in seigniorage when inflation is eliminated. Third, labor supply is endogenized so that taxes on labor income are distortionary. In the standard version of the Sidrauski model with exogenous labor supply, taxes on labor income do not distort labor supply and would fail to capture some of the effects arising through distortionary taxation that are important in Feldstein's calculations.

An Extension of the Sidrauski Model

Consider a closed economy with N_t identical consumers in period t. The population grows at rate n so that $1 + n \equiv N_t/N_{t-1}$. There are two types of capital: nonhousing capital (type 1) and housing capital (type 2). Let $K_{i,t}$ be the aggregate capital stock of type i ($i = 1,2$) at the beginning of period t, L_t be the aggregate labor input in period t, p_t be the price of goods in terms of money, M_t be the aggregate nominal money supply at the beginning of period t, and B_t be the aggregate nominal stock of government bonds at the beginning of period t. It is convenient to focus on the real per capita values of these variables: $k_{i,t} \equiv K_{i,t}/N_t$, $\ell_t \equiv L_t/N_t$, $m_t \equiv M_t/(p_t N_t)$, and $b_t \equiv B_t/(p_t N_t)$.

The Consumer's Problem

Asset accumulation of an individual consumer is described by

$$(1)\; c_t + (1 + n)(k_{1,t+1} + k_{2,t+1}) + (1 + n)\pi_{t+1}m_{t+1} + (1 + n)\pi_{t+1}b_{t+1} =$$
$$(1 - \tau_w)w_t\ell_t + R_{1,t}k_{1,t} + R_{2,t}k_{2,t} + (1 + i_t^b)b_t + m_t.$$

The right-hand side of equation 1 represents the consumer's real disposable resources in period t which consists of (1) after-tax wage income, where w_t is the real wage rate and τ_w is the tax rate on wages; (2) the value of capital held at the beginning of period t plus any earnings on the capital, where $R_{i,t}$ represents the after-tax gross return (i.e., principal plus income, after tax) on capital of type i; (3) the value of government bonds held at the beginning of period t plus after-tax interest earnings on the bonds, where i_t^b is the after-tax interest rate on bonds; and (4) the real value of money balances held at the beginning of period t. The left-hand side of equation 1 represents the consumer's spending in period t, which consists of (1) consumption c_t; (2) capital to carry into period $t + 1$; (3) real money balances to carry into period $t + 1$, where $\pi_{t+1} \equiv p_{t+1}/p_t$ is the gross rate of inflation; and (4) bonds to carry into period $t + 1$.

The utility function of the consumer is

$$(2) \qquad \sum_{t=0}^{\infty} \beta^t u(c_t, m_t, \ell_t) \equiv \sum_{t=0}^{\infty} \beta^t \left(\frac{c_t^{1-\rho}}{1 - \rho} + \phi \frac{m_t^{1-\delta}}{1 - \delta} - \psi \frac{\ell_t^{1+\eta}}{1 + \eta} \right),$$

where ρ, δ, η, ϕ, and ψ are positive constants. The consumer chooses consumption, each type of capital, real money balances, bonds, and labor supply to maximize utility in equation 2 subject to the budget constraint in equation 1. Letting $\beta^t \lambda_t$ be the Lagrange multiplier on the constraint in equation 1, the first-order conditions are

(3a) $\qquad (c_t): c_t^{-\rho} = \lambda_t;$

(3b) $\qquad (k_{i,t}): \beta \lambda_t R_{i,t} = \lambda_{t-1}(1 + n), \quad i = 1,2;$

(3c) $\qquad (m_t): \beta \phi m_t^{-\delta} + \beta \lambda_t = \lambda_{t-1}(1 + n)\pi_t;$

(3d) $\qquad (b_t): \beta \lambda_t (1 + i_t^b) = \lambda_{t-1}(1 + n)\pi_t;$

(3e) $\qquad (\ell_t): -\psi \ell_t^{\eta} + \lambda_t (1 - \tau_w)w_t = 0.$

I will focus on the steady state in which all of the time-subscripted variables in equation (3) are constant. Solving these equations yields the following steady-state relations:

(4a) $$R_i = \frac{1 + n}{\beta}, \quad i = 1,2;$$

(4b) $$1 + i^b = \frac{1 + n}{\beta} \pi;$$

(4c) $$\frac{\phi m^{-\delta}}{c^{-\rho}} = i^b;$$

(4d) $$\frac{\psi \ell^{\eta}}{c^{-\rho}} = (1 - \tau_w)w.$$

In the steady state, the after-tax real gross return on all nonmonetary assets is $(1 + n)/\beta$. According to equation 4a, the after-tax real return on both types of capital is $(1 + n)/\beta$.[1] The after-tax real return on bonds is $(1 + i^b)/\pi$, which, according to equation 4b, is also equal to $(1 + n)/\beta$. Money offers a lower pecuniary rate of return than bonds (if $i^b > 0$), but consumers willingly hold money because money offers a nonpecuniary return $\phi m^{-\delta}$. The optimal holding of money is reflected in equation 4c. Finally, equation 4d shows that the consumer supplies labor to the point that the disutility of working an additional unit is just offset by the additional utility made possible by earning additional after-tax wage income.

The Production Function

The production function is a Cobb-Douglas function of labor and each type of capital. Under the assumption of constant returns to scale, the production function can be written (omitting time subscripts) in intensive form as

$$(5) \qquad y = A k_1^{\alpha_1} k_2^{\alpha_2} \ell^{1 - \alpha_1 - \alpha_2},$$

where $y \equiv Y/N$ is output per capita, and the factor shares α_1, α_2, and $1 - \alpha_1 - \alpha_2$ are all positive. In a competitive economy, factors are paid the value of their marginal product. Thus the wage rate equals the marginal product of labor,

$$(6) \qquad w = (1 - \alpha_1 - \alpha_2)y/\ell.$$

The marginal product of type i capital is $\alpha_i y/k_i$. Thus, assuming that capital does not depreciate, the after-tax gross rate of return on type i capital is

$$(7) \qquad R_i = (1 - \tau_i)\alpha_i \frac{y}{k_i} + 1,$$

where τ_i is the tax rate on the (net) return to capital of type i.

Government Budget Constraint

Monetary and fiscal policy are integrated by the government budget constraint. In the steady state the government budget constraint is

$$(8) \qquad \tau_w(1 - \alpha_1 - \alpha_2)y + \tau_1 \alpha_1 y$$
$$+ \tau_2 \alpha_2 y + [(1 + n)\pi - 1]m = g + [1 + i^b - (1 + n)\pi]b.$$

The four terms on the left-hand side of equation 8 are the sources of government revenue: wage tax revenue, tax on income accruing to k_1, tax on income accruing to k_2, and seigniorage revenue. The right-hand side of equation 8 contains two types of government spending: real purchases of goods and services in the amount of g per capita; and interest payments on government debt, net of taxes on interest and rollover of debt. Now divide both sides of equation 8 by y, and use equation 4b to obtain

---

1. The rate of return on each type of capital is determined endogenously by equation 7 below. In the absence of any taxes, the condition that the gross rate of return on capital equals $(1 + n)/\beta$ is simply the Modified Golden Rule.

(9) $$\tau_w (1 - \alpha_1 - \alpha_2) + \tau_1\alpha_1 + \tau_2\alpha_2 + [(1 + n)\pi - 1]\frac{m}{y}$$

$$= \frac{g}{y} + (\beta^{-1} - 1)(1 + n)\pi \frac{b}{y}.$$

The government chooses the values of inflation π, the tax rates on capital τ_1 and τ_2, the ratio of government purchases to output g/y, and the ratio of government bonds to output b/y. The tax rate on wages τ_w is determined endogenously by equation 9.

Steady-State Equilibrium

The steady state is characterized by equations 4–7 and 9 and the goods market clearing condition

(10) $$c + n (k_1 + k_2) = \left(1 - \frac{g}{y}\right)y.$$

It can be shown that the steady-state values of k_1, k_2, c, m, and ℓ are given by

(11a) $$k_1 = \left[\left(\frac{1 + n}{\beta} - 1\right)^{-1}(1 - \tau_1)\alpha_1 AB^{\alpha_2}\right]^{\frac{1}{1-\alpha_1-\alpha_2}} \ell,$$

where $B \equiv \dfrac{(1 - \tau_2)\alpha_2}{(1 - \tau_1)\alpha_1};$

(11b) $$k_2 = Bk_1;$$

(11c) $$c = \left(1 - \frac{g}{y}\right) AB^{\alpha_2} k_1^{\alpha_1 + \alpha_2} \ell^{1-\alpha_1-\alpha_2} - nk_1 (1 + B);$$

(11d) $$m = \left[\frac{1}{\phi}\left(\frac{1 + n}{\beta}\pi - 1\right)c^{-\rho}\right]^{-\frac{1}{\delta}};$$

(11e) $$\ell = \left[\frac{1}{\psi}(1 - \tau_w)(1 - \alpha_1 - \alpha_2)\frac{y}{\ell}c^{-\rho}\right]^{\frac{1}{\eta}}.$$

Calibration of the Model

The population growth rate n is set equal to 0.01. The values of other parameters and variables used in the initial calibration of the model are presented in table 3C.1. Of the six preference parameters, four are set exogenously. The time-preference discount factor β is 0.95, which implies a rate of time preference of about 5% per year. Calibration studies typically choose values of ρ greater than one but generally not much larger than five, though there are examples of much larger values of ρ in the asset pricing literature. Here I choose

Table 3C.1   **Initial Calibration of the Model**

Variable	Value	Source
Preference parameters		
β	0.95	exogenous
ρ	4	exogenous
η	10	exogenous
δ	5	exogenous
ϕ	0.001651	chosen to match m below
ψ	7.71×10^{-12}	chosen to make $\ell = 1$
Production parameters		
A	388.1744	chosen to match y below
α_1	0.233	exogenous
α_2	0.067	exogenous
Government policy variables		
g/y	0.2	exogenous
b/y	0.5	exogenous
π	1.02	exogenous
τ_1	0.5598	exogenous (from Feldstein)
τ_2	-0.2061	exogenous (from Feldstein)
τ_w	0.1550	residual: government budget constraint
Empirical aggregates to be matched		
y	6,011	net national product
m	390	monetary base

$\rho = 4$. The value of η is even less well established. Here I set $\eta = 10$. The interest elasticity of money demand equals $-1/\delta$. Estimates of this elasticity are very small, so I choose $\delta = 5$, which implies an interest elasticity of money demand equal to -0.2, as in Feldstein's calculations. The value of ϕ is chosen so that the model produces a value of $m = 390$, which is the 1994 value of monetary base in the United States measured in billions of dollars. The value of ψ is chosen so that the model produces a value of $\ell = 1$ in its initial calibration.

The values of α_1 and α_2 that appear in the production function are chosen so that $k_2/k_1 = 0.79$, which is the ratio of residential capital to the sum of equipment and structures.[2] Using the fact that $k_2/k_1 = ((1 - \tau_2)\alpha_2)/((1 - \tau_1)\alpha_1)$, constraining $\alpha_1 + \alpha_2$ to equal 0.3, and using the values of τ_1 and τ_2 based on Feldstein's calculations (see table 3C.2), yields $\alpha_1 = 0.233$ and $\alpha_2 = 0.067$. The total factor productivity parameter A is chosen so that y matches the value of actual output. The assumption that capital does not depreciate can be interpreted to mean that all depreciation is a reduction in output, and thus the production function can be viewed as a function that yields net national product (NNP) rather than gross national product. Thus, the value of y that is matched is 6,011, which is the 1994 value of NNP measured in billions of dollars.

2. This ratio is calculated using 1991 data from "Summary of Fixed Reproducible Tangible Wealth Series 1925–91," table 1, in U.S. Department of Commerce 1992, 29.

Table 3C.2   **Tax Rates**

Rate of Return Nonhousing Capital			
$R_1 - 1$	0.0920	Δ_1	−0.0533
$(1 - \tau_1^{\pi=1.02})(R_1 - 1)$	0.0405	$\tau_1^{\pi=1.02}$	0.5598
$(1 - \tau_1^{\pi=1})(R_1 - 1)$	0.0454	$\tau_1^{\pi=1}$	0.5065

Rental Cost of Housing			
Itemizers			
r	0.1320	Δ_2	0.0379
$(1 + \tau_2^{\pi=1.02})r$	0.0998	$\tau_2^{\pi=1.02}$	−0.2439
$(1 + \tau_2^{\pi=1})r$	0.1048	$\tau_2^{\pi=1}$	−0.2061
Nonitemizers			
r	0.1320	Δ_2	0.0295
$(1 + \tau_2^{\pi=1.02})r$	0.1098	$\tau_2^{\pi=1.02}$	−0.1682
$(1 + \tau_2^{\pi=1})r$	0.1137	$\tau_2^{\pi=1}$	−0.1386
Average of itemizers and nonitemizers			
r	0.1320	Δ_2	0.0337
$(1 + \tau_2^{\pi=1.02})r$	0.1048	$\tau_2^{\pi=1.02}$	−0.2061
$(1 + \tau_2^{\pi=1})r$	0.1093	$\tau_2^{\pi=1}$	−0.1723

Of the six variables representing government policy, three are chosen to match the data directly: the ratio of government purchases to output, g/y, is set equal to 0.2; the ratio of government debt to output, b/y, is set equal to 0.5; and the gross rate of inflation, π, is set equal to 1.02 per year. The tax rates on the two types of capital are based on the calculations in Feldstein, as displayed in table 3C.2. Consider, for example, nonhousing capital. As shown in table 3C.2, the pretax rate of return, $R_1 - 1$, on this capital is 9.2% per year, and the after-tax rate of return is 4.05% per year when the rate of inflation is 2% per year. (These rates of return are computed by Feldstein.) Thus, the tax rate on non-housing capital when inflation is 2% is $\tau_1^{\pi=1.02} = 0.5598$. Feldstein calculates that at zero inflation the after-tax rate of return on nonhousing capital is 4.54%, so that the tax rate on type 1 capital is $\tau_1^{\pi=1} = 0.5065$. Thus, the change in the tax rate that results directly from a reduction in inflation is $\Delta_1 = -0.0533$. For housing capital I use the average of the values reported by Feldstein for item-izers and nonitemizers. The tax rate on wage income, τ_w, is a residual that makes the government's steady-state budget constraint in equation 9 hold.

Effect of Eliminating Inflation

As emphasized by Feldstein, the effective tax rates on both types of capital depend on the rate of inflation. Therefore, the elimination of inflation changes these effective tax rates. Let Δ_i be the direct effect on the tax rate τ_i of reducing the rate of inflation to zero (i.e., setting $\pi = 1$). In addition, there are indirect effects on the tax rates that are needed to satisfy the government's budget constraint. The new set of tax rates, incorporating both the direct effect of inflation (including the possibility of a direct effect, Δ_w, of inflation on the labor income tax rate) and the indirect effect of the government's budget constraint, are

$$(12a) \qquad\qquad \tau_w = (\tau_w^0 + \Delta_w)\theta,$$
$$(12b) \qquad\qquad \tau_1 = (\tau_1^0 + \Delta_1)\theta,$$

and

$$(12c) \qquad\qquad \tau_2 = (\tau_2^0 + \Delta_2)\theta,$$

where the superscript 0 denotes the initial values of the tax rates, and θ is the amount by which all three tax rates must be multiplied in order to satisfy the government's steady-state budget constraint. The direct effects, Δ_i, are exogenous but the indirect effect, captured by θ, is endogenous.[3]

To illustrate the welfare effects of eliminating inflation, I compare the initial equilibrium in which the steady-state value of the triplet (c,m,ℓ) equals $(c^0,m^0,1)$ and the new steady-state equilibrium in which the triplet equals $(c^{new}, m^{new}, \ell^{new})$. To express the change in welfare in terms of a change in consumption, define c^* to be the level of consumption, combined with the initial values of real money balances and labor, that yields the same level of utility in the steady state as the zero-inflation steady-state equilibrium. That is,

$$(13) \qquad\qquad u(c^*, m^0, 1) \equiv u(c^{new}, m^{new}, \ell^{new}).$$

Using the utility function specified in equation 2, the definition of c^* in equation 13 can be rewritten as

$$(14) \quad c^* = \left((1 - \rho) \left[u(c^{new}, m^{new}, \ell^{new}) - \phi \frac{(m^0)^{1-\delta}}{1 - \delta} + \frac{\psi}{1 + \eta} \right] \right)^{\frac{1}{1 - \rho}}.$$

I use $(c^* - c^0)/c^0$ as a measure of the benefit of eliminating inflation, and I compare it to Feldstein's measure of the benefit of eliminating inflation, which is expressed as a fraction of GDP.

Table 3C.3 presents the effects of reducing the inflation rate from 2% per year ($\pi = 1.02$) to zero ($\pi = 1$). Column 1 ignores the direct effect of inflation on the effective tax rates on the two types of capital, and takes account only of the indirect effects on tax rates arising as a result of the change in seigniorage revenue when inflation is reduced. This channel corresponds most closely to Feldstein's "money demand" channel, and the calculated benefit, $(c^* - c^0)/c^0$, is in the middle of the range of benefits found by Feldstein and reported in the last row of numbers in table 3C.3. Column 2 focuses on the direct effect of inflation on the effective tax rate on nonhousing capital, which corresponds most closely to Feldstein's "consumption timing" channel. Column 3 focuses

---

3. In all policies examined here, the values of g/y and b/y are held constant.

Table 3C.3   **Effects of Policy Changes**

	(1)	(2)	(3)	(4)
	Government Policy Variables: Exogenous			
Δ_w	0	0	0	0
Δ_1	0	−0.0533	0	−0.0533
Δ_2	0	0	0.0337	0.0337
π	1	1.02	1.02	1
	Government Policy Variables: Endogenous			
θ	1.0033	1.0584	0.9901	1.0507
τ_w	0.1555	0.1641	0.1535	0.1629
τ_1	0.5616	0.5361	0.5542	0.5322
τ_2	−0.2068	−0.2181	−0.1707	−0.1811
	Steady-State Effects (%)			
Change in				
k_1	−0.53	6.88	1.37	7.77
k_2	−0.06	2.43	−2.83	−0.69
y	−0.11	1.42	0.11	1.40
c	−0.10	1.29	0.13	1.31
m	5.89	1.03	0.11	7.08
ℓ	0.02	−0.43	−0.02	−0.43
$(c^* − c^0)/c^0$	**−0.08**	**1.64**	**0.15**	**1.69**
Benefit as % of	(−0.17, −0.03)	(0.63, 0.92)[a]	(0.22, 0.55)	(0.63, 1.01)[a]
GDP (from		(−0.05, 1.64)		(−0.05, 1.64)
Feldstein)				

[a]This range corresponds to parameter values that Feldstein considers most likely. The wider range below is based on a broader set of parameter values used by Feldstein.

on the direct effect of inflation on the effective tax rate on housing capital, which corresponds most closely to Feldstein's "housing demand" channel. The final column of table 3C.3 considers all three effects together.[4]

Considering the differences in analytic strategies, the results that I obtained using the Sidrauski model are strikingly close to those reported by Feldstein. Both sets of results have the following four features: First, the benefits arising through the money-demand channel are slightly negative but tiny. Second, the benefits arising through the housing-demand channel are positive but relatively small. Third, the largest benefits arise as a result of reducing the distortions in the effective tax rate on nonhousing capital. Fourth, taking account of all three

4. Feldstein also calculates effects operating through a "debt service" channel, but in the Sidrauski model presented here, the steady-state after-tax real interest rate on debt is invariant to the inflation rate, so the debt-service channel is inoperative.

Table 3C.4   **Robustness of Results**

	$(c^* - c^0)/c^0$			
	$\pi = 1$ $\Delta_1 = 0$ $\Delta_2 = 0$	$\pi = 1.02$ $\Delta_1 = -0.0533$ $\Delta_2 = 0$	$\pi = 1.02$ $\Delta_1 = 0$ $\Delta_2 = 0.0337$	$\pi = 1$ $\Delta_1 = -0.0533$ $\Delta_2 = 0.0337$
Baseline	**-0.08**	**1.64**	**0.15**	**1.69**
$\beta = 0.99$	-0.14	1.19	0.24	1.30
$\beta = 0.9$	0.01	1.91	0.10	2.00
$\rho = 10$	-0.08	1.59	0.14	1.65
$\rho = 2$	-0.09	1.68	0.15	1.73
$\eta = 100$	-0.09	1.72	0.15	1.78
$\eta = 1$	-0.08	1.46	0.14	1.52
$\delta = 20$	-0.12	1.63	0.15	1.65
$\delta = 2$	-0.02	1.65	0.15	1.78
$\alpha_1 + \alpha_2 = 0.4$[a]	-0.15	1.50	0.41	1.77
$\alpha_1 + \alpha_2 = 0.2$[a]	-0.04	1.33	0.02	1.30
$n = 0$	-0.10	1.75	0.13	1.77
$n = 0.02$	-0.08	1.55	0.17	1.63

[a]a_1/a_2 is same as in baseline.

effects, the annual benefit of eliminating inflation is about 1% of GDP per year (Feldstein) or about 1.7% of consumption per year (table 3C.3), which is slightly higher.

Table 3C.4 explores the sensitivity of the results to changes in various parameters. The baseline row of numbers repeats the values of $(c^* - c^0)/c^0$ from the four columns of table 3C.3. In each of the other rows, one parameter at a time is changed from its baseline value, and the four values of $(c^* - c^0)/c^0$ are reported. In view of the large changes in parameter values examined, the results of the model are very robust. Of course, a more complete sensitivity analysis would change the values of more than one parameter at a time, but such an analysis is beyond the scope of this comment.

The results of tables 3C.3 and 3C.4 lend strong support to Feldstein's conclusion that the annual benefit of reducing the inflation rate from 2% to zero is on the order of 1% of GDP. This support is especially strong in light of the fact that Feldstein and I used different analytic strategies to compute the benefits of reducing inflation.

As discussed by Feldstein, for plausible discount rates, the calculated benefit of eliminating inflation has a present value that exceeds 6% of GDP, which is taken as a measure of the cost of eliminating inflation. This comparison of benefits and costs leads to the conclusion that welfare would be increased by reducing inflation to zero, though one might place more confidence in this conclusion if the benefits and costs of reducing inflation were computed together within a single model.

References

Ball, Laurence. 1994. What Determines the Sacrifice Ratio? In *Monetary Policy,* ed. N. Gregory Mankiw. Chicago: University of Chicago Press.

Sidrauski, Miguel. 1967. Rational Choice and Patterns of Growth in a Monetary Economy. *American Economic Review* 57:534–44.

U.S. Department of Commerce. 1992. *Survey of Current Business.* October.

4   Disinflation and the NAIRU

Laurence Ball

4.1   Introduction

Average unemployment in the countries of the Organization for Economic Cooperation and Development (OECD) stood at 3.1% in 1970. It rose to 5.7% in 1980 and 8.1% in 1994. The rise in unemployment was especially severe in the European Community, where 1994 unemployment averaged 11.5%. Although these movements had a cyclical component, there was also a large rise in the long-run trend, as captured by the non-accelerating-inflation rate of unemployment–the NAIRU. OECD estimates of the NAIRU rose for most countries in both the 1970s and 1980s (OECD 1994).

A large literature has sought to explain the rise in unemployment. In recent years, most explanations have focused on imperfections in the labor market arising from labor unions and from government interventions such as unemployment insurance and firing restrictions. Often, economists argue that these imperfections have interacted negatively with changing economic conditions. On the back cover of its 1994 *Jobs Study,* the OECD summarizes its views: "[M]uch unemployment is the unfortunate result of societies' failure to adapt to a world of rapid change and intensified global competition. Rules and regulations, practices and policies, and institutions designed for an earlier era have resulted in labour markets that are too inflexible for today's world." Krugman (1994) is more specific about the key economic changes. Summarizing "the conventional wisdom," he focuses on the decline in the equilibrium relative

Laurence Ball is professor of economics at Johns Hopkins University and a research associate of the National Bureau of Economic Research.

The author is grateful to Jorgen Elmeskov and Marco Doudeyns of the Organization for Economic Cooperation and Development for providing data, and to Christopher Ruebeck and Tao Wang for research assistance. Helpful suggestions were provided by Olivier Blanchard, Jorgen Elmeskov, the editors, conference participants, and seminar participants at Columbia, the Kansas City Fed., and the Massachusetts Institute of Technology.

wages of low-skill workers (arising, perhaps, from skill-biased technical change). In Krugman's view, labor market distortions create a floor on real wages, and unemployment rises when equilibrium wages fall below the floor.

This paper argues that the conventional wisdom misses a central cause of the rise in unemployment: macroeconomic policy. In particular, I focus on the decade of the 1980s and argue that the main cause of rising unemployment was the tight monetary policy that most OECD countries pursued to reduce inflation. My evidence comes from a cross-country comparison: countries with larger decreases in inflation and longer disinflationary periods had larger increases in the NAIRU. My principal measure of the NAIRU is the one constructed by Elmeskov (1993) and used in *The OECD Jobs Study*.

In the "natural rate" theories of Friedman (1968) and Phelps (1968), the NAIRU is determined by labor market imperfections and is independent of monetary policy. My argument is inconsistent with traditional natural-rate models. My findings fit easily, however, with "hysteresis" theories (Blanchard and Summers 1986). In these theories, a disinflation causes a cyclical rise in unemployment, which in turn causes a rise in the NAIRU. My results suggest that hysteresis is highly relevant for explaining recent experience.

This paper also examines the role of labor market imperfections in the rise of the NAIRU. I consider various measures of these distortions, and find that their cross-country correlations with the change in the NAIRU are low. However, one labor market variable—the duration of unemployment benefits—has a large effect on the size of the NAIRU increase resulting from disinflation. That is, much of the rise in unemployment is explained by the *interaction* between benefit duration and changes in inflation. Once again, my results support hysteresis theories, which attribute the persistence of unemployment changes to labor market distortions. More specifically, the results about unemployment benefits support hysteresis models based on decreasing job search by the unemployed.

The remainder of this paper contains six sections. Section 4.2 describes how I measure changes in the NAIRU. Sections 4.3–4.5 investigate the cross-country relations among changes in the NAIRU, the size and speed of disinflation, and labor market distortions. Section 4.6 considers robustness, and section 4.7 discusses the results.

4.2   The NAIRU in the 1980s

4.2.1   Measuring the NAIRU

The concept of the NAIRU is based on an accelerationist Phillips curve:

$$(1) \qquad\qquad \pi - \pi_{-1} = a(U - U^*),$$

where U is unemployment, π and π_{-1} are current and lagged inflation, a is a negative constant, and I ignore supply shocks. U^* is the NAIRU—the level of unemployment consistent with stable inflation. In the Friedman-Phelps model,

U^* is determined by microeconomic features of labor markets. In hysteresis models, U^* is also influenced by the path of actual unemployment, and hence by macroeconomic policy.

In calculating the NAIRU, I follow Elmeskov (1993), whose approach is also used in *The OECD Jobs Study*. Elmeskov estimates the unemployment rate consistent with stable *wage* inflation (he calls his variable the NAIWRU rather than the NAIRU). There is no clear reason for focusing on wage inflation or on price inflation, and so I follow Elmeskov for simplicity. To estimate the NAIRU in a given year, Elmeskov compares unemployment and the change in wage inflation in that year and the previous one. Assuming a Phillips curve, equation 1, the two observations determine the NAIRU, U^*. For some countries, Elmeskov makes ad hoc adjustments to the NAIRU series to eliminate outliers. Finally, he smooths the series mildly: he applies the Hodrick-Prescott filter with a parameter of 25. This smoothing reduces the influence of supply shocks and other transitory shifts in the Phillips curve.[1]

Elmeskov's NAIRU series for several countries are plotted in figure 4.1, along with actual unemployment. Generally, the series appear close to what one would draw by hand if attempting to capture the long-term trend in unemployment. Elmeskov finds that his NAIRU series are similar to two other "natural-rate" series he calculates, one based on the relation between unemployment and vacancies and the other based on capacity utilization.

Elmeskov's procedure is not perfect, of course. The appropriate approach to estimating the NAIRU is controversial. In section 4.6, I consider biases that might arise if Elmeskov's procedure does not completely eliminate the cyclical component of unemployment. I also consider an alternative measure of the NAIRU based on a univariate smoothing of the unemployment series.

4.2.2 The Sample

I seek to explain the change in the NAIRU from 1980 to 1990. I chose this period because the most important macroeconomic shocks were shifts in demand, especially monetary tightenings aimed at reducing inflation and supporting currencies. One can find reasonable proxies for the tightness of policy in different countries, such as the total fall in inflation. Accounting for unemployment movements during the 1970s is more difficult: one has to measure the severity of supply shocks in different countries.

I end the analysis in 1990 because it is difficult to estimate the NAIRU in more recent years. It is not yet clear, for example, whether the large increases in unemployment in Sweden and Finland are changes in the NAIRU or deviations from the NAIRU. At a technical level, Elmeskov's procedure relies on the Hodrick-Prescott filter, which is imprecise near the endpoints of series.

---

1. To understand Elmeskov's procedure, note that equation 1 implies $\pi_{-1} - \pi_{-2} = a(U_{-1} - U^*)$. Given two years' data on inflation changes and unemployment, this equation and (1) are two equations in two unknowns, a and U^*. The solution for U^* is Elmeskov's initial estimate of the NAIRU.

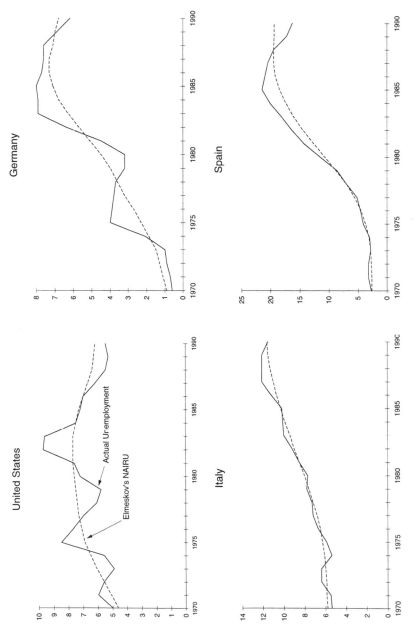

Fig. 4.1 The NAIRU, 1970–90

Elmeskov calculates NAIRU series for twenty-one OECD countries. Of these countries, I examine the twenty with moderate inflation; I exclude Turkey, where inflation was 110% in 1980. My sample of countries is identical to the main sample that Layard, Nickell, and Jackman examine in their 1991 book on unemployment. For each country, I use an updated NAIRU series that Elmeskov has calculated using data in the December 1994 *Economic Outlook* of the OECD. For two countries, the Netherlands and Ireland, I adjust the series based on revisions in unemployment data in the June 1995 *Economic Outlook*.[2]

In Table 4.1, the first column reports the change in the NAIRU from 1980 to 1990. The NAIRU rose in all countries except the United States, Portugal, and Belgium; Ireland and Spain have the largest increases by a wide margin. The unweighted average increase across countries is 2.1 percentage points.

4.3   The Effects of Disinflation

4.3.1   The Policy Variables

I examine two variables concerning disinflation. The first is the total fall in inflation from 1980 to 1990. This variable measures the overall tightness of monetary policy during the decade. In hysteresis models, a larger disinflation produces a larger cyclical rise in unemployment, which in turn produces a larger rise in the NAIRU. I measure inflation with the year-over-year change in consumer prices, as reported in the June 1995 *Economic Outlook*. The fall in inflation from 1980 to 1990 is reported in the second column of table 4.1.

The other variable measures the *length* of disinflation. For each country, I determine the longest disinflation during the 1980s, defined as the greatest number of consecutive years in which inflation fell or was constant. This variable shows whether a given fall in inflation occurred quickly or slowly.

There are two reasons that the speed of disinflation may affect the change in the NAIRU. First, it may affect the size of the cyclical downturn caused by disinflation. Ball (1994) finds that slower disinflations produce larger cyclical output losses. Second, a given amount of cyclical unemployment may have a larger effect on the NAIRU if it is spread over time. This is true in some hysteresis models. It is true, for example, if the unemployed take more than one period to become "outsiders" in wage bargaining (Lindbeck and Snower 1989), or if only long-term unemployment reduces workers' job search (Pissarides 1994). All these effects suggest that a longer disinflation produces a larger rise in the NAIRU.

The third column of table 4.1 reports the length of disinflation in each coun-

2. For the Netherlands and Ireland, I compute an initial NAIRU series for both the December 1994 data and the June 1995 data, using the approach in note 1. I add the difference between the two series to Elmeskov's final NAIRU series. This procedure assumes that the data revision does not affect the difference between the initial NAIRU and the final (smoothed) NAIRU.

Table 4.1   The Sample

	Change in NAIRU 1980–90 (%)	Decrease in Inflation 1980–90 (%)	Longest Disinflation (years)	Duration of Unemployment Benefit (years)[a]
Australia	1.1	2.9	2	4
Austria	1.4	3.0	3	4
Belgium	−0.5	3.3	4	4
Canada	0.6	5.4	4	0.5
Denmark	2.5	9.7	6	2.5
Finland	0.5	5.5	5	4
France	3.7	10.2	6	3.75
Germany	2.3	2.8	5	4
Ireland	9.3	15.0	7	4
Italy	3.6	15.1	7	0.5
Japan	0.3	4.7	3	0.5
Netherlands	2.7	4.0	3	4
New Zealand	4.6	11.0	2	4
Norway	2.3	6.8	4	1.5
Portugal	−1.4	3.2	3	0.5
Spain	8.7	8.9	8	3.5
Sweden	0.4	3.2	4	1.2
Switzerland	0.9	−1.4	3	1
United Kingdom	1.1	8.5	3	4
United States	−1.4	8.1	3	0.5

[a]Indefinite benefits are coded as four years.

try. After experimentation with functional forms, I used the square of this variable in the regressions below.[3]

4.3.2 Results

Table 4.2 reports regressions of the change in the NAIRU on the fall in inflation, on the square of disinflation length, and on both of these variables. Figure 4.2 plots the two bivariate relations.[4]

In each of the simple regressions, the independent variable explains a substantial fraction of the variation in the change in the NAIRU. For the fall in inflation, the t-statistic is 3.5 and the $\bar{R}^2$ is 0.37. For length squared, the t-

3. Inflation in Spain was 8.8% in both 1985 and 1986. The Spanish disinflation would be three years shorter if I required inflation to fall in all years rather than fall or stay constant. On the other hand, I count only years of disinflation after 1980. If I measured the longest disinflation that overlaps with the 1980s, the Spanish disinflation would be three years *longer*. This adjustment would not affect any other country.

4. In the reported regressions, I assume that errors are uncorrelated across countries, and use ordinary least squares (OLS). I have also considered a specification in which errors are correlated for countries in the same region. Regions are defined as North America, the EC, non-EC Europe, the Antipodes, and Japan. The estimated within-region correlation is close to zero. Consequently, two-step generalized least squares (GLS) estimates accounting for this correlation are close to OLS estimates.

Table 4.2   **Disinflation and the Change in the NAIRU**

	Dependent Variable: Change in NAIRU from 1980 to 1990		
Constant	−0.593	−0.444	−1.033
	(0.935)	(0.700)	(0.801)
Inflation decrease	0.420		0.183
	(0.121)		(0.131)
Length squared		0.123	0.095
		(0.026)	(0.033)
$\bar{R}^2$	0.367	0.528	0.552

Note: Standard errors are in parentheses.

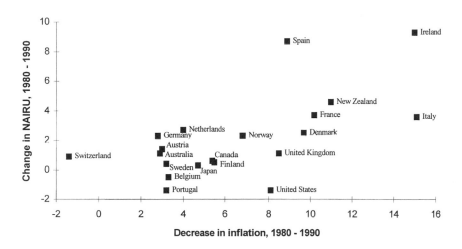

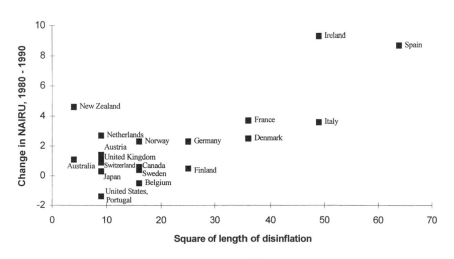

Fig. 4.2   Disinflation and the change in the NAIRU

statistic is 4.7 and the $\bar{R}^2$ is 0.53. The scatter plots confirm the positive relationships between the change in the NAIRU and the right-side variables.[5]

The correlation between the fall in inflation and length squared is 0.63. It is difficult to separate the effects of these variables with twenty observations, but the data suggest that length squared has greater explanatory power. In the multiple regression, the t-statistic is 2.9 for length squared and only 1.4 for the fall in inflation, although standard confidence intervals include large effects for both variables. The $\bar{R}^2$ for the multiple regression is 0.55, only slightly higher than the $\bar{R}^2$ with length squared alone.

The size and speed of disinflation explain an important part of changes in the NAIRU during the 1980s. Yet large residuals remain. As one example, Ireland and Italy had inflation changes of 15.0 and 15.1%, respectively, and both had longest disinflations of eight years. These figures put Ireland and Italy near the high end for both variables. Despite these similar disinflation experiences, the NAIRU rose 9.3% in Ireland and only 3.6% in Italy. Something besides macropolicy must explain such differences.

4.4   The Effects of Labor Market Variables

Most discussions of unemployment focus on imperfections in labor markets. Observers blame unemployment on the power of labor unions and on government policies such as unemployment insurance and firing restrictions. Layard, Nickell, and Jackman (1991) show that measures of labor market distortions explain much of the cross-country variation in unemployment levels in the mid-1980s. It is harder, however, to explain *changes* in unemployment during the 1980s. Most labor market distortions remained constant during the decade or decreased, as some countries weakened firing restrictions and reduced unemployment benefits (OECD 1990; Blank 1994). These changes go in the wrong direction for explaining why unemployment rose.

Nonetheless, authors such as Krugman and the OECD emphasize labor market distortions in explaining the 1980s. They argue that preexisting distortions contributed to rising unemployment through interactions with market forces such as greater wage dispersion. If OECD countries experienced similar economic changes, this view suggests that unemployment rose more in countries with more distorted labor markets. Many authors use this idea to explain why unemployment has risen in Europe but not the United States, where markets are more flexible. Motivated by this view, I explore the relation between the change in the NAIRU and labor market distortions in my twenty countries.

My principal measures of labor market distortions are the six variables that Layard et al. emphasize. Two of the variables concern unemployment insurance: the replacement ratio and the duration of benefits. Three concern wage

---

5. When the change in the NAIRU is regressed on the length of disinflation rather than length squared, the t-statistic is 3.8 and $\bar{R}^2$ is 0.42.

Table 4.3   **Labor Market Variables and the Change in the NAIRU**

		Dependent Variable: Change in NAIRU from 1980 to 1990		
Variable	Benefit duration	Replacement ratio	Coverage of collective bargaining	Employer coordination
$\bar{R}^2$	0.125	−0.053	0.039	0.050
Variable	Union coordination	Expenditure on labor market programs	All six variables	
$\bar{R}^2$	−0.048	−0.017	0.064	

bargaining: the percentage of workers covered by collective agreements, and the coordination among workers and among employers. The final variable is government spending to help the unemployed find jobs. Layard et al. report these variables as of the mid-1980s. To check robustness, I also examine a set of six variables drawn from *The OECD Jobs Study* (1994). These include four variables similar to Layard et al.'s, and two others: an index of legal employment protection, and the tax wedge between labor costs and workers' incomes.

I run simple regressions of the change in the NAIRU on each of the six Layard et al. variables, and a regression on all six at once. Most of the results are negative. In the multiple regression, the *p* value for the hypothesis that all coefficients are zero is 0.36. In five of the six simple regressions, the *t*-statistic is less than 1.5; the $\bar{R}^2$, reported in table 4.3, range from −0.05 to 0.05. The only variable close to significant is the duration of unemployment benefits: it yields a *t*-statistic of 1.9 and an $\bar{R}^2$ of 0.12. Figure 4.3 plots the change in the NAIRU against the duration of benefits; it suggests a mild positive relationship, but a number of countries have long durations and small changes in the NAIRU. (Following Layard et al., I count indefinite unemployment benefits as a duration of four years.)

Regressions using the six *Jobs Study* variables yield even more negative results. No variable approaches significance, and the $\bar{R}^2$ are all below 0.01. (The *Jobs Study* variables do not include the duration of unemployment benefits.)

As discussed above, *changes* in labor market distortions are not a promising explanation for the overall rise in OECD unemployment, because most changes go in the wrong direction. Nonetheless, changes in distortions could help explain cross-country differences in unemployment changes; for example, some authors argue that Thatcher's reforms dampened the rise in British unemployment. There is less cross-country data on changes in distortions than on levels, but the OECD has constructed three variables for both 1980 and 1990, or for nearby years. The variables are union density, the benefit replacement rate, and the tax wedge. (As stressed by Phelps [1994], the tax wedge is one distortion that worsened for most countries during the 1980s.) I regress the change in the NAIRU on the change in each labor market variable over the 1980s. Once again, the results are negative: all coefficients are insignificant.

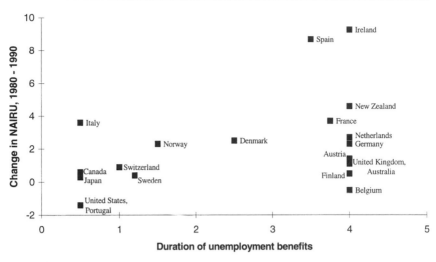

Fig. 4.3   Benefit duration and the change in the NAIRU

Thus an extensive search has failed to find any labor market variable that explains nearly as much of the rise in the NAIRU as the size and length of disinflation.

4.5   Interactions between Disinflation and Labor Market Variables

In hysteresis models, increases in unemployment are triggered by cyclical factors such as demand contractions. But labor market imperfections are the reason that cyclical unemployment leads to a rise in the NAIRU. Thus the models suggest an interaction between disinflation and labor market variables. A given disinflation has a larger effect on the NAIRU in countries with more distorted labor markets.

In exploring this idea, I mainly consider the interaction between disinflation and the duration of unemployment benefits. Recall that the duration of benefits is the only labor market variable with any direct relation to the change in the NAIRU. It also proves to be the variable that interacts most strongly with disinflation.

Figure 4.4 plots the change in the NAIRU against two interaction variables: the fall in inflation times benefit duration ($(\Delta\pi)\times(ben)$), and length squared times benefit duration ($(L^2\times(ben))$). Table 4.4 reports regressions of the change in the NAIRU on various combinations of the interactions and the individual variables from which they are constructed. The interactions are very important. Simple regressions yield $\bar{R}^2$ of 0.55 for $(\Delta\pi)\times(ben)$ and 0.59 for $(L^2)\times(ben)$. When both interactions are included, the $\bar{R}^2$ is 0.67. When $(\Delta\pi)\times(ben)$ is included in the regression, the separate $(\Delta\pi)$ and (ben) coefficients are insignificant. The data do, however, suggest a direct effect of L^2: it helps explain the change in the NAIRU even controlling for $(L^2)\times(ben)$.

The last column of table 4.4 presents a particularly successful combination

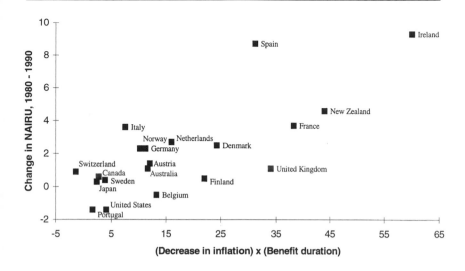

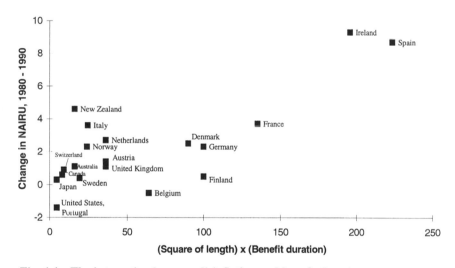

Fig. 4.4   The interaction between disinflation and benefit duration

of variables: L^2 and $(\Delta\pi)\times(ben)$. The t-statistics for these variables are 4.0 and 4.2, and the $\overline{R}^2$ is 0.75. Figure 4.5 shows the close relationship between the fitted and actual values of the change in the NAIRU. With twenty observations, I cannot draw firm conclusions about which specification is best. (A priori, there is no obvious reason that L^2 affects unemployment directly while $(\Delta\pi)$ interacts with (ben).) Nonetheless, a broad conclusion is robust: the explanatory power of macropolicy variables increases greatly when we account for interactions with benefit duration.

I have also explored the interactions between disinflation and the other labor

Table 4.4   **Interactions between Disinflation and Labor Market Variables**

	Dependent Variable: Change in NAIRU from 1980 to 1990					
Constant	−0.142	0.165	−0.493	−1.451	−0.367	−1.217
	(0.627)	(0.550)	(1.428)	(1.258)	(0.545)	(0.537)
(Inflation decrease) ×	0.131		0.112		0.072	0.092
(benefit duration)	(0.026)		(0.065)		(0.031)	(0.022)
(Length squared) ×		0.034		0.008	0.022	
(benefit duration)		(0.006)		(0.018)	(0.008)	
Inflation decrease			0.131			
			(0.188)			
Length squared				0.093		0.084
				(0.057)		(0.021)
Benefit duration				−0.069	0.450	
				(0.506)	(0.410)	
$\bar{R}^2$		0.552	0.590	0.529	0.605	0.669	0.754

Note: Standard errors are in parentheses.

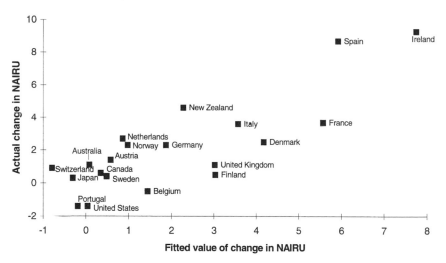

Fig. 4.5   Fitted and actual values of the change in the NAIRU. Independent variables: (decrease in inflation) × (benefit duration) and square of length

market variables that Layard et al. measure. In most cases, these interactions do not help explain changes in the NAIRU once we control for the direct effects of disinflation. One exception is the interaction between the fall in inflation and the coverage of collective bargaining. However, even this variable adds little once we control for the interaction between disinflation and benefit duration.[6]

It makes sense that the duration of unemployment benefits is the variable that interacts most strongly with disinflation. In some hysteresis theories,

6. A simple regression of the change in the NAIRU on the inflation change/union coverage interaction yields an $\bar{R}^2$ of 0.46. However, adding this variable to the last column in table 4.4 reduces $\bar{R}^2$.

workers who lose their jobs become accustomed to an unemployed lifestyle, stop searching for work, and become detached from the labor force. This effect is likely to be strongest where unemployment benefits are long-lived, making it easier to become satisfied with unemployment. My results support hysteresis theories based on these ideas.

Recall that another of the Layard et al. variables is the replacement rate for unemployment insurance. This is one of the variables that does *not* magnify the long-run effects of disinflation. As long as benefits are cut off quickly, they can be generous while they last without promoting hysteresis.

4.6 Robustness

4.6.1 An Alternative Unemployment Variable

The results so far depend on a particular approach to measuring the NAIRU, the one devised by Elmeskov. Do the results hinge on this choice, or do they hold for other reasonable approaches? Elmeskov estimates the NAIRU with data on unemployment and inflation. An alternative approach (e.g., Mankiw 1994) is simply to smooth the univariate unemployment series. Following this approach, I used the Hodrick-Prescott filter to derive a trend-unemployment series for each country. (I set the HP parameter to 100, a conventional value for annual data.) I then redid my regressions with the change in the HP-filtered variable from 1980 to 1990 as the dependent variable.[7]

Table 4.5 presents a sample of the results. They are qualitatively the same as when Elmeskov's procedure is used to measure the NAIRU. The coefficients and $\overline{R}^2$ are smaller than before, but only moderately; for example, $\overline{R}^2$ drops from 0.75 to 0.62 in the equation with L^2 and $(\Delta\pi) \times (ben)$. The lower $\overline{R}^2$ may reflect greater measurement error, since the HP-filter uses less information to estimate the NAIRU than does Elmeskov. In any case, my basic message does not depend on Elmeskov's procedure.

4.6.2 A Change in Timing

Any measure of the NAIRU is imperfect. In general, measurement error in the dependent variable does not cause bias in my regressions. Problems may arise, however, if the error is correlated with cyclical unemployment—if cyclical fluctuations are not completely filtered out of the NAIRU. Since disinflation causes cyclical unemployment, a cyclical component in the error could bias my estimates of the effects of disinflation. This problem might arise with either Elmeskov's NAIRU variable or the HP variable.[8]

---

7. I use OECD standardized unemployment series for countries where they exist, and local unemployment series for other countries. Unemployment data from 1975 to 1994 are used to construct the filtered series.

8. There is, however, no clear reason that the bias goes in a particular direction. If the measured NAIRU contains a cyclical component, the errors in the regressions are correlated with the difference in cyclical unemployment between 1980 and 1990. This causes an upward bias in the disin-

Table 4.5   **Disinflation and the Change in Detrended Unemployment**

Dependent Variable: Change in HP-filtered Unemployment from 1980 to 1990

Constant	0.115	0.115	0.329	0.558	0.161	−0.464
	(0.811)	(0.614)	(0.551)	(0.490)	(0.508)	(0.534)
Inflation decrease	0.294					
	(0.105)					
Length squared		0.091				0.061
		(0.023)				(0.021)
(Inflation decrease) ×			0.097		0.054	0.069
(benefit duration)			(0.023)		(0.029)	(0.022)
(Length squared) ×				0.026	0.016	
(benefit duration)				(0.006)	(0.007)	
$\bar{R}^2$	0.264	0.438	0.465	0.496	0.556	0.625

Note: Standard errors are in parentheses.

To address this problem, I perform versions of my basic regressions with a change in the timing. In these regressions, the dependent variable is the change in the NAIRU from 1976 to 1994, not the change from 1980 to 1990. The independent variables are unchanged: they still measure the size and speed of disinflation during the 1980s. If disinflation raises unemployment permanently, disinflation during the 1980s should affect the change in the NAIRU from 1976 to 1994. And with this dependent variable, cyclical unemployment causes less of a problem. If the measured NAIRU contains a cyclical component, the errors in the regressions are correlated with cyclical unemployment in 1976 and in 1994. The errors are uncorrelated with disinflation during the 1980s as long as cyclical fluctuations die out within four years. Under this assumption, there is no bias.[9]

Table 4.6 presents regressions with the 1976–94 change in Elmeskov's NAIRU as the dependent variable. The coefficients are similar to those when the dependent variable covers 1980–90. The fall in inflation contributes less to $\bar{R}^2$, but length squared contributes just as much. Indeed, a simple regression on $(L^2) \times (ben)$ produces an $\bar{R}^2$ of 0.72. A likely explanation is that, for most countries, the longest disinflation between 1976 and 1994 is the same as the longest disinflation between 1980 and 1990. Consequently, the difference in timing between the left-side and right-side variables makes little difference when the latter is length squared. Changes in inflation differ considerably across the two periods, and so the difference in timing adds noise to the regression.

In any case, the results again suggest that my findings are robust.

flation coefficient if countries with larger disinflations had greater cyclical unemployment in 1990 than in 1980. It is not obvious whether this condition holds.

9. Elmeskov's NAIRU series does not extend back to 1976 for Belgium, Finland, or Ireland. For these countries, I use another of Elmeskov's natural-rate series, the one based on capacity utilization, to proxy for the NAIRU in 1976.

Table 4.6   Disinflation 1980–1990 and the Change in the NAIRU 1976–1994

	Dependent Variable: Change in NAIRU from 1976 to 1994					
Constant	2.803	1.655	2.380	2.169	1.914	0.821
	(1.506)	(0.969)	(0.973)	(0.620)	(0.689)	(0.882)
Inflation decrease	0.352					
	(0.195)					
Length squared		0.164				0.121
		(0.036)				(0.035)
(Inflation decrease) ×			0.155		0.035	0.099
(benefit duration)			(0.041)		(0.040)	(0.036)
(Length squared) ×				0.051	0.045	
(benefit duration)				(0.007)	(0.010)	
$\bar{R}^2$	0.106	0.507	0.413	0.716	0.712	0.640

Note: Standard errors are in parentheses.

4.6.3 Reverse Causality?

Does the correlation between disinflation and changes in the NAIRU reflect a causal relationship? Several readers have suggested a noncausal explanation. In their story, shocks or unwise policies produced both NAIRU increases during the 1980s and high inflation at the start of the 1980s. Countries with the largest NAIRU increases also experienced the highest inflation. And high initial inflation led to large disinflations, since most countries sought low inflation during the 1980s.

My discussant, Olivier Blanchard, has suggested a test of this idea. The size of disinflation is the difference between initial and final inflation—the levels of inflation in 1980 and 1990. Shocks that cause rises in the NAIRU might also cause high initial inflation, but they do not cause low final inflation. That is, there is no apparent reason that countries with large NAIRU increases would push inflation down to especially low levels. We can therefore learn about causality by including initial and final inflation separately in the regressions, relaxing the assumption that only their difference matters. A significant coefficient on final inflation suggests that causality runs from disinflation to the NAIRU.

Table 4.7 presents the results of this test. Both initial and final inflation have significant effects on the change in the NAIRU. One cannot reject the hypothesis that these variables have coefficients of the same absolute size, as assumed before. The point estimate is larger for the final-inflation coefficient, which goes in the wrong direction for the reverse-causality story. Similar results arise when I separate the (inflation change) × (benefit duration) interaction into (initial inflation) × (benefit duration) and (final inflation) × (benefit duration). Thus the data support a causal effect of disinflation on the NAIRU.[10]

10. Blanchard has suggested a specific version of the reverse-causality story that goes as follows. Problems in labor markets caused a rise in the NAIRU that was spread over the 1970s

Table 4.7   **The Effects of Initial and Final Inflation**

Dependent Variable: Change in NAIRU from 1980 to 1990			
Constant	0.566	0.373	−1.035
	(1.422)	(0.715)	(0.689)
Inflation in 1980	0.404		
	(0.121)		
Inflation in 1990	−0.596		
	(0.203)		
(Inflation in 1980) ×		0.153	0.099
(benefit duration)		(0.030)	(0.028)
(Inflation in 1990) ×		−0.222	−0.118
(benefit duration)		(0.071)	(0.063)
Length squared			0.080
			(0.023)
$\bar{R}^2$	0.373	0.574	0.742

Note: Standard errors are in parentheses.

4.7   Discussion

This paper argues that disinflations were a major cause of the rise in OECD unemployment during the 1980s. I show that measures of the NAIRU rose more in countries with larger and longer disinflations. I also find that disinflation had a greater effect on the NAIRU in countries with long-lived unemployment benefits. These results support hysteresis theories based on decreasing job search by the unemployed.

To conclude the paper, I examine several well-known country experiences in light of my results. I then discuss policy implications.

4.7.1   Country Experiences

The United States versus Europe. Many discussions of OECD unemployment emphasize differences between the United States and Europe. During the 1980s, inflation fell as much in the United States as in many European countries, but the NAIRU did not rise in the United States. My results suggest two explanations for the U.S. case. First, unemployment benefits last only half a year, a much shorter period than in most European countries. Consequently,

---

and 1980s. The rise in the 1970s caused inflation to rise, because policymakers resisted rising unemployment with expansionary policy. In the 1980s, policymakers reversed course and disinflated. Countries with more severe labor market problems experienced larger rises in the NAIRU in both the 1970s and 1980s, and larger disinflations.

In this story, the ultimate cause of disinflation was the rise in the NAIRU between 1970 and 1980. Therefore, following a suggestion by John Shea, I have added this variable to the regressions. Once again, my basic results are robust: the new variable is never significant, and there is little change in the other coefficients. These results reflect the weak relationship between changes in the NAIRU across decades: a simple regression of the change in the 1980s on the change in the 1970s yields an $\bar{R}^2$ of 0.05.

there is little hysteresis in the United States, and the cyclical downturn caused by disinflation did not raise the NAIRU. Second, the U.S. disinflation was short. The Volcker disinflation was accomplished in three years, from 1980 to 1983; many European disinflations started at the same time but lasted several years longer.

Portugal versus Spain. A number of authors, notably Blanchard and Jimeno (1995), have puzzled over the different experiences of Portugal and Spain. Their economies are similar in many ways, yet Spain experienced a large rise in the NAIRU during the 1980s while Portugal's NAIRU fell. Here, my results point to three explanations. First, Portugal's fall in inflation during the 1980s was much smaller than Spain's. (This partly reflects an increase in Portugal's inflation in the late 1980s after an earlier disinflation.) Second, in 1985 the duration of unemployment benefits was half a year in Portugal and 3.5 years in Spain. And finally, Portugal's disinflation lasted three years, while Spain's lasted eight years. (If one extends the data before 1980, Spain's disinflation lasted eleven years, from 1977 to 1988. No other country experienced a disinflation longer than seven years.)[11]

Ireland versus Italy. As discussed earlier, Ireland and Italy had almost identical disinflations, but the NAIRU rose much more in Ireland. My results suggest a simple explanation: the difference in unemployment benefits. Benefits last indefinitely in Ireland, but only six months in Italy.

This comparison puts the Italian case in an unusual light. The NAIRU rose 3.6% in Italy, less than in Ireland but more than in most other countries. The rise in Italian unemployment is often blamed on rigid labor markets; in particular, Italy tops the OECD in most measures of legal employment protection (OECD 1994). My results suggest that the rise in Italian unemployment was *low* considering the large, slow disinflation. And this is explained by labor market *flexibility* along the key dimension of unemployment benefits. Firing restrictions do not appear important for explaining unemployment changes.

Belgium. Belgium demonstrates that long-lived unemployment benefits are not sufficient for a rise in the NAIRU. Belgium has indefinite benefits, but its NAIRU fell during the 1980s. The main explanation is that disinflation was mild: inflation fell only 3.3% (compared, for example, to 10% in France and 15% in Italy). Disinflation was also moderately quick (four years). Disinflation

---

11. A confusing feature of the Portugese experience is that unemployment benefits have become more generous over time. Currently, most parameters of benefits, including duration, are similar in Portugal and Spain. This similarity led Blanchard and Jimeno to deemphasize benefits as a source of unemployment differences. But Portugese benefits were much less generous during the mid-1980s, when disinflation occurred. Stingy benefits during disinflation prevented the cyclical rise in unemployment from affecting the NAIRU.

was mild in Belgium because inflation was low to start with: it was only 6.7% in 1980.

4.7.2   Policy

My results imply that disinflation is very costly, especially in countries with long-lived unemployment benefits. Disinflation raises unemployment not only in the short run, but also in the long run. Previous studies, including Ball (1994), underestimate the costs of disinflation because they assume only transitory losses. Unless we know that living with inflation is very costly, it may be unwise to reduce inflation.

On the other hand, if policymakers choose to disinflate, they should do so aggressively. Both this paper and Ball (1994) find that disinflation is less costly if it is quick. This paper also finds that the costs are smaller if workers are denied long-term unemployment benefits. Efforts to soften the impact of disinflation—whether through gradualism or through support for the unemployed—are counterproductive.

In many countries, policymakers disinflated during the 1980s and left a legacy of high unemployment. Can we now reduce unemployment? My findings do not answer this question. Limits on unemployment benefits prevent increases in the NAIRU if adopted *before* disinflation, but it is not clear that cutting benefits would be helpful today. Such a policy might force the unemployed back to work, but it might not. If the unemployed are detached from the labor market and their human capital is gone, cutting benefits might only increase poverty. So far, no country has reduced benefits enough to test these ideas.

My results suggest another idea for fighting unemployment: expansion of aggregate demand. If tight monetary policy has raised the NAIRU, perhaps loose policy can reduce it — and perhaps a risk of higher inflation is an acceptable price. On the other hand, it is not clear that the effects of tight and loose policy are symmetric. A demand expansion would cause a cyclical fall in unemployment, but would this reverse the hysteresis process, with workers becoming reattached to the labor force? We do not know the answer, because countries have not tried demand expansions to reduce the NAIRU.

References

Ball, Laurence. 1994. What Determines the Sacrifice Ratio? In *Monetary Policy,* ed. N. Gregory Mankiw. Chicago: University of Chicago Press.

Blanchard, Olivier J., and Juan F. Jimeno. 1995. Structural Unemployment: Spain versus Portugal. *American Economic Review* 85 (May): 212–18.

Blanchard, Olivier J., and Lawrence H. Summers. 1986. Hysteresis and the European Unemployment Problem. *NBER Macroeconomics Annual* 1:15–78.

Blank, Rebecca. 1994. Does a Larger Social Safety Net Mean Less Economic Flexibility? In *Working under Different Rules,* ed. Richard B. Freeman. New York: Russell Sage Foundation.

Elmeskov, Jorgen. 1993. High and Persistent Unemployment: Assessment of the Problem and Its Causes. OECD Economics Department Working Paper no. 132, Paris.

Friedman, Milton. 1968. The Role of Monetary Policy. *American Economic Review* 58:1–17.

Krugman, Paul. 1994. Past and Prospective Causes of High Unemployment. In *Reducing Unemployment: Current Issues and Policy Options.* Kansas City, MO: Federal Reserve Bank of Kansas City.

Layard, Richard, Stephen Nickell, and Richard Jackman. 1991. *Unemployment: Macroeconomic Performance and the Labor Market.* New York: Oxford University Press.

Lindbeck, Assar, and Dennis J. Snower. 1989. *The Insider-Outsider Theory of Employment and Unemployment.* Cambridge: MIT Press.

Mankiw, N. Gregory. 1994. *Macroeconomics.* 2d edition. New York: Worth.

Organization for Economic Cooperation and Development. 1990. *Labour Market Policies for the 1990s.* Paris: Organization for Economic Cooperation and Development.

———. 1994. *The OECD Jobs Study.* Paris: Organization for Economic Cooperation and Development.

Phelps, Edmund S. 1968. Money-Wage Dynamics and Labor-Market Equilibrium. *Journal of Political Economy* 76:678–711.

———. 1994. *Structural Slumps: The Modern Equilibrium Theory of Unemployment, Interest, and Assets.* Cambridge: Harvard University Press.

Pissarides, Christopher A. 1994. Commentary. In *Reducing Unemployment: Current Issues and Policy Options.* Kansas City, MO: Federal Reserve Bank of Kansas City.

Comment   Olivier J. Blanchard

In his paper, Laurence Ball develops five propositions:

1. Traditional explanations for the increase in the natural rate in Europe—that is, explanations based on shifts in exogenous factors from the form of bargaining, to taxes, to labor-market rigidities—are empirical failures.

2. There is, however, a strong empirical relation in the data. It is between the natural rate and disinflation: countries that have had larger disinflations have experienced a larger increase in their natural unemployment rate.

3. Furthermore, for a given disinflation, the increase in the natural unemployment rate has been larger in countries that had more generous (in the sense of longer-lasting) unemployment benefits.

4. The last two relations are causal: disinflation is the main cause of the increase in the natural rate. And the more generous benefits have been, the stronger has been the effect of disinflation on the natural rate.

5. This is strong evidence in favor of hysteresis theories, which emphasize the effects of the evolution of the actual unemployment rate on the natural rate.

Olivier J. Blanchard is the Class of 1941 Professor of Economics at the Massachusetts Institute of Technology and a research associate of the National Bureau of Economic Research.

Given my past work on European unemployment, it will come as no surprise that I like and believe Ball's conclusions. Indeed, my reaction when I read the paper is that I should have run these regressions long ago. I blame myself for not doing it, and I thank Ball for performing the task. I am, however, the discussant of this paper, and my role should be to play devil's advocate. Are the facts really that clear-cut? If so, does causality really run from disinflation to the natural rate? And, if so, do hysteresis theories provide a convincing explanation? My answers are largely yes, probably yes, and unfortunately not yet.

Are Traditional Explanations of the Increase in the Natural Rate Such Obvious Empirical Failures?

There is no question that the current official rhetoric that attributes the rise in the natural rate to labor and goods market rigidities has run far ahead of the evidence. The worst culprit here may be *The OECD Jobs Study* (OECD 1994). The study has two parts. The first is composed of two long "annexes," part 1 and part 2, which do a remarkable job of presenting and analyzing the available micro- and macro-evidence on all relevant aspects of labor markets, from the role of reallocation and relative shifts in demand, to the role of wage setting, to the role of unemployment-benefit systems, to the role of taxes, and so on. The second is the official report itself, which could have been (and may well have been) written independently of the two annexes, and singles out labor market flexibility as the key to achieving lower unemployment. The contrast between the carefully argued conclusions of the annex and the simple message of the official report is simply jarring.

It is also true that formal econometric panel studies of OECD countries have had limited success in explaining either the increase in the natural rate over time or cross-country differences in current unemployment rates. The evidence is reviewed in a recent paper by P. N. Junankar and Jakob Madsen (1995). Junankar and Madsen estimate unemployment equations for a panel of twenty-two OECD countries for the years 1960–85 and examine the fit of four different specifications based on four influential theories, by Bruno and Sachs in the 1970s, by Layard and Nickell in the early 1980s, by McCallum and by Phelps more recently. They show the very limited success of these regressions, in terms of fit, subsample stability, and so on. More importantly, they show that, in the postsample years 1986–91, a second-order autoregressive process for the unemployment rate, with country effects, has substantially lower mean square error than all four structural specifications.

The state of the art in such unemployment regressions may be a recent paper by Jackman, Layard, and Nickell (1996), written for a recent OECD conference. The results of estimation of their basic specification for two time periods and twenty countries are reproduced in the first column of table 4C.1. To get a sense of what these results imply, I give the values and the contributions of the explanatory variables for two countries, Spain and Portugal, and show how the estimated equation explains the difference between unemployment rates

Table 4C.1   **Unemployment Rate Regressions from Jackman, Layard, and Nickell (1996)**

Unemployment Rate Equals	Spain		Portugal	
	Value	Contribution	Value	Contribution
−0.22 × constant		−0.2		−0.2
+0.11* × replacement rate	80	8.8	60	6.6
+0.35 × benefit duration	3.5	1.2	0.5	1.7
−0.09 × active labor policy	3.2	−0.3	5.9	−0.5
+4.14* × union coverage	3	12.3	3	12.3
−2.80* × union coordination	2	−5.6	2	−5.6
−2.82* × employer coordination	1	−2.8	2	−5.6
+0.10 × employment protection	19	1.9	18	1.8
−0.64 × change in inflation	−1.24	0.8	−2.74	1.7
+0.54 × dummy 1989–94				
Implied unemployment rate 1983–88		16.1		12.2
Actual unemployment rate 1983–88		19.6		7.6

Source: Jackman, Layard, and Nickell 1996, tables 2 and 3.

Notes: The dependent variable is the average unemployment rate for 1983–88 and for 1989–94, for twenty OECD countries. There are thus forty observations. $\bar{R}^2 = 0.74$. Many of the variables on the right-hand side are ranking indices. The "change in inflation" is the average annual change in inflation during the corresponding six-year period, and is there to capture the difference between the actual unemployment rate and the natural unemployment rate.

*t-statistic above 2.

in the two countries. (I see Spain and Portugal as providing an acid test of any theory of unemployment [Blanchard and Jimeno 1995]: Spain has the highest unemployment rate in the OECD, Portugal one of the lowest.)

At first glance, the regression does a good job of fitting cross-country differences. $\bar{R}^2$ is 0.74. The regression also appears to explain the movement of unemployment over time, at last since the mid-1980s: the time dummy for the second period, 1989–94, is neither large nor significant. The statistical and economically significant variables are the generosity of the unemployment-benefit system (in contrast to Ball's results, however, the variable that is significant is the replacement rate, not the duration of benefits), and the structure of bargaining (union and employer coordination). Labor market rigidities (employment protection) play only a marginal role. Tax rates, which figured preeminently in earlier studies, are altogether absent. Note also the absence of variables such as the minimum wage, or proxies for the intensity of reallocation and structural change, which figure so much in current discussions.

But the limits of this regression are also clear. This specification is surely unable to explain the increase in unemployment from the early 1970s to the mid-1980s, the most important puzzle to be explained: most of the explanatory variables have moved the wrong way. And the application to Spain versus Portugal gives reason to doubt that robust structural relations have been uncovered. The regression predicts a difference in unemployment rates of only 4%, in contrast to an actual difference of 12%. Most of the difference is accountable to a difference of 1 in the "employer coordination" index (which ranges from 1 to 3), obviously a difficult variable to measure.

To summarize, I agree with Ball. Economists have been largely unsuccessful at isolating robust relations between the increase in unemployment over time and shifts in exogenous factors. It is surely justifiable to look for other mechanisms.

Has Disinflation Caused the Increase in the Natural Rate?

In contrast, the facts on disinflation and the change in the unemployment rate emphasized in the paper are, I believe, very robust. The main issue is whether correlation should be interpreted as causality. When I discussed the paper at the conference, my comments focused primarily on this issue. I suggested the following alternative interpretation of the data:

- In contrast to Ball's interpretation, the increase in the natural rate has been due to exogenous factors in all countries.
- Countries that had the largest increase in the natural rate in the 1970s also had the largest increase in the 1980s.
- Countries were slow to allow the actual rate to adjust to the new, higher, natural rate. Thus countries that had the largest increase in the natural rate in the 1970s also had the highest rate of inflation at the end of the 1970s.
- All countries now have low inflation. Thus countries that had the highest rate of inflation at the end of the 1970s have had the largest disinflation.
- It follows that countries that have had the largest disinflation are also the countries where the natural unemployment rate increased the most in the 1980s. But the relation is spurious. Or put another way, the increase in the natural rate is what has caused the size of the inflation, and thus the size of the disinflation, not the other way around.

This story may be challenged on various grounds. But it is a logically impeccable alternative to Ball's interpretation. Can the two alternative interpretations be told apart? At the conference, I suggested one way in which this might be done. Decompose disinflation as inflation in 1990 minus inflation in 1980, and allow the two inflation terms to enter with separate coefficients. Under Ball's hypothesis that disinflation matters, the two terms should come in with coefficients equal but of opposite sign. Under the alternative hypothesis, only inflation in 1980 should matter, not how low governments decided to push inflation down at the end of the 1980s.

I was not optimistic that this would work. Ball has carried it out, and the results are reported in table 4.7. It works like a charm: the coefficients are nearly equal and of opposite sign. I cannot think of alternative stories for reverse causality.

Can Hysteresis Theories Explain the Results?

Do hysteresis theories provide a satisfactory explanation for Ball's results? At some general level, yes. Hysteresis theories of unemployment were developed precisely to explain why disinflation and high actual unemployment can lead, at least for some time, to an increase in the natural rate of unemployment.

Let me briefly review these theories. Most give a central role to long-term unemployment: high prolonged unemployment leads to a high proportion of long-term unemployed.

This affects labor supply. The long-term unemployed adapt to unemployment. Some give up looking for work, because they find the probability of getting work too small to justify intensive search. They find ways of surviving, often by relying on the other earners in the family. They return home. In short, they adjust—not happily, but they adjust—to unemployment. And, although they might be formally looking for work, and therefore be classified as unemployed, many no longer effectively are, and, therefore, they put very little pressure on wages. This leads to a higher natural rate of unemployment.

On the labor-demand side, firms look at the long-term unemployed as less employable than the short-term unemployed. From the point of view of firms, this may not be a major decision. In a depressed labor market, vacancies generate many applications, and firms need simple ways of ranking applicants. One simple way, once they have accounted for the objective characteristics of applicants, is to rank them according to the length of time that they have been out of work. Other things equal, someone who has been out of work for a longer time is likely to be less employable than somebody who has not, either because of intrinsic characteristics that the market has recognized, or just because work habits have deteriorated and this person might be harder to train. As a result, firms tend to hire the short-term unemployed first and the long-term unemployed next.

This is tough on the long-term unemployed, but it also has implications for wage determination and for the natural rate. It implies that for those who are still employed, labor market prospects are substantially better than the aggregate unemployment number would suggest: they know that, if they were to lose their job, they would actually be ahead of a number of people in the labor market, namely the long-term unemployed. To the extent that firms have a policy of hiring first people who have been out of work for a short time, their prospects as an employed worker are actually much better than the prospects of the typical unemployed worker, who has been unemployed for a longer period of time. As a result, the pressure of unemployment on wages is low. Put another way, the natural rate of unemployment may become quite high.

These factors point to a more general and more diffuse effect at work here, namely that society, in its many dimensions, also adapts to higher persistent unemployment. When unemployment and the proportion of long-term unemployed becomes high, society is compelled, mostly through the political process, to make life bearable for those who are long-term unemployed. Through unemployment benefits, safety nets, real or pseudo-training programs, governments basically make sure that people do not starve. This is the normal response both from a normative and a positive point of view to high unemployment. Nevertheless, it has very much the same effect as the factors I discussed earlier, namely that, by making unemployment more bearable, it increases the natural rate of unemployment.

Are these channels plausible? Yes. Can they explain the magnitudes of the results found in the paper, the apparently large effects of disinflation on the natural rate? The honest answer is, we do not know. We have some formal models, some pieces of empirical evidence. But whether these channels can explain large and long-lasting effects of disinflation on unemployment is far from established.

In my last point, stimulated by one of the results in the paper, I explore one aspect of these models at more length.

Hysteresis and the Speed of Disinflation

Ball finds that short disinflations have less of an effect on the natural rate. He argues that this is what one would expect from hysteresis theories. A long, drawn-out recession, he argues, will lead to more long-term unemployment, to more discouraged and unemployable workers, and thus to a larger increase in the natural rate. If you have to disinflate, he concludes, it is therefore better to make it short: this will have less effect on the natural rate.

The argument is appealing. But it is not right. The shorter the recession, the deeper it is, and the higher the proportion of long-term unemployed. A short but deep recession may in fact lead to more discouraged workers, and more of an increase in the natural rate.

To make progress, consider the following simple model:

- Assume that disinflation requires n point years of excess active unemployment (i.e., counting only those unemployed who are searching). Let the length of disinflation be x years, at n/x point years of excess unemployment. Our focus is on the effects of alternative values of x.
- Assume that variations in unemployment are achieved by equal and opposite variations in hires and layoffs. Thus an increase in unemployment of 1 is achieved by hires being lower and layoffs being higher for a year, each by 0.5.
- Let U_0, U_1 denote short (less than one year) and long-term unemployment. Let e_0, e_1 denote the exit rates to employment from U_0 and U_1, respectively.
- Let the long-term unemployed differ from the short-term unemployed in two ways. First, let their intensity of search relative to the short-term unemployed be equal to $\beta \leq 1$. Second, let the drop-out rate for the long-term unemployed be equal to γ.

Table 4C.2   **Cumulative Stock of Dropouts at the End of the Disinflation, as a Function of the Size and Length of Disinflation, and the Intensity of Search β**

	Large Disinflation (20 point years)		Small Disinflation (10 point years)	
	Slow (10 years)	Fast (2 years)	Slow (10 years)	Fast (2 years)
β = 1.0	1.44	2.13	0.40	0.75
β = 0.5	3.47	2.79	1.62	1.55

Let l_t and h_t be the valves of layoffs and hires required to achieve the desired path of unemployment. Under the assumptions above, the equations of motion for $U_{0,t}$ and $U_{1,t}$ are given by

(1) $$U_{0,t} = l_t$$

and

(2) $$U_{1,t} = (1 - e_{0,t-1})U_{0,t-1} + U_{1,t-1}(1 - \gamma)(1 - e_{1,t-1}).$$

Short-term unemployment is equal to layoffs. The number of long-term unemployed is equal to those short-term unemployed who did not get a job, plus those long-term unemployed who did not get a job and did not drop out.

The exit rates from short- and long-term unemployment are in turn given by:

(3) $$e_{0,t} = \frac{h_t}{U_{0,t} + \beta U_{1,t}}$$

and

(4) $$e_{1,t} = \frac{\beta h_t}{U_{0,t} + \beta U_{1,t}},$$

where the number of unemployed is adjusted for their search intensity.

Let me measure the increase in the natural rate as the cumulative sum of workers who give up searching as a result of the disinflation. (Thus, I am assuming that they will still be counted as unemployed in official statistics, although they are in fact not searching anymore.) Denote this sum by S_t.

Table 4C.2 reports the value of S when disinflation ends. It does it for a large and a small disinflation (the proportion of long-term unemployment is nonlinear in the level of unemployment, so that the size of disinflation matters). In each case, it looks at both a slow (ten years) and a fast (two years) disinflation, and does it for two values of the relative search intensity of the long-term unemployed, $\beta = 1.0$ and $\beta = 0.5$. The steady-state flows of layoffs and hires are assumed to be equal to six so that the steady-state values of U_0 and U_1 are equal to six and zero, respectively.

The results make clear that the larger the disinflation, the larger the increase in *S*. But they show that the effect of length is ambiguous. When $\beta = 1.0$, then short and deep recessions lead to a larger increase in the natural rate. When $\beta = 0.5$, long and shallow recessions, which allow the stock of long-term unemployment to build up, lead to a larger increase in the natural rate.

Thus, if there is hysteresis, should central banks go for short and strong disinflations? The answer from the table is ambiguous. It could be fun to examine this issue at more length, and the model above may provide a starting point.

References

Blanchard, Olivier, and Juan Jimeno. 1995. Structural unemployment: Spain versus Portugal. *American Economic Review* 85: 212–18.

Jackman, R., R. Layard, and S. Nickell. 1996. Combating unemployment: Is flexibility enough? Paper presented at the OECD conference, *Interactions between Structural Reform, Macroeconomic Policies, and Economic Performance,* Paris. January.

Junankar, P. N., and Jakob Madsen. 1995. Unemployment in the OECD: Models, myths, and mysteries. Working paper 278, Australian National University.

Organization for Economic Cooperation and Development. 1994. *The OECD Jobs Study.* Paris: Organization for Economic Cooperation and Development.

II Improving the Conduct of Monetary Policy

5   How Precise Are Estimates of the Natural Rate of Unemployment?

Douglas Staiger, James H. Stock, and Mark W. Watson

5.1   Introduction

Debates on monetary policy in the United States often focus on the level of unemployment and, in particular, on whether the unemployment rate is approaching its natural rate. This is commonly taken to be the rate of unemployment at which inflation remains constant, the NAIRU (non-accelerating-inflation-rate of unemployment). Unfortunately, the NAIRU is not directly observable, and so some combinations of economic and statistical reasoning must be used to estimate it from observable data. The task of measuring the NAIRU is further complicated by the general recognition that, plausibly, the NAIRU has changed over the postwar period, perhaps as a consequence of changes in labor markets.

Although there is a long history of construction of empirical estimates of the NAIRU, measures of the precision of these estimates are strikingly absent

Douglas Staiger is assistant professor of public policy at the Kennedy School of Government at Harvard University and a faculty research fellow of the National Bureau of Economic Research. James H. Stock is professor of political economy at the Kennedy School of Government at Harvard University and a research associate of the National Bureau of Economic Research. Mark W. Watson is professor of economics and public affairs in the Department of Economics and the Woodrow Wilson School at Princeton University and a research associate of the National Bureau of Economic Research.

The authors have benefited from discussions with and/or comments from Francis Bator, Robert Gordon, Robert King, Spencer Krane, Alan Krueger, John M Roberts, Christina Romer, David Romer, Geoffrey Tootell, David Wilcox, Stuart Weiner, colleagues at the National Bureau of Economic Research and the Kennedy School of Government, and numerous seminar participants. The authors thank Dean Croushore and the Research Department of the Federal Reserve Bank of Philadelphia for providing the inflation survey forecast data. An earlier draft of this paper was circulated under the title "Measuring the Natural Rate of Unemployment." The research was supported in part by National Science Foundation grant no. SBR-9409629.

from this literature; the only published estimates of standard errors of the NAIRU of which we are aware are the recent limited results reported by Fuhrer (1995) and King, Stock, and Watson (1995). In this paper, we therefore undertake a systematic investigation of the precision of estimates of the NAIRU. This is done using both conventional models, in which the NAIRU is treated as constant over the sample period, and models that explicitly allow the NAIRU to change over time. As a by-product, we obtain formal evidence on whether the NAIRU has changed over the postwar period, and if so by how much. We also investigate whether these changes in the NAIRU are linked to labor market variables, such as demographic measures, which are suggested by search models of unemployment as plausible theoretical determinants of the natural rate.

To answer these questions, we consider two classes of models that implicitly or explicitly define the NAIRU. In the first class, the NAIRU is defined so that a stable Phillips-type relation exists between unexpected inflation and the deviation of unemployment from the NAIRU. A variant of this approach introduces labor market variables as determinants of the NAIRU within the Phillips curve framework. These models for the NAIRU include those in the recent empirical literature (Congressional Budget Office 1994; Weiner 1993; Tootell 1994; Fuhrer 1995; Eisner 1995; King, Stock, and Watson 1995; Gordon 1997), along with other candidates. In the second class, the NAIRU is defined solely in terms of the univariate behavior of unemployment, with the assumption that over time unemployment returns to its natural rate.

Our main finding is that the natural rate is measured quite imprecisely. For example, we find that a typical estimate of the NAIRU in 1990 is 6.2%, with a 95% confidence interval for the NAIRU in 1990 being 5.1% to 7.7% (this is the "Gaussian" confidence interval for the quarterly specification with a constant NAIRU, reported in section 5.2). This confidence interval incorporates uncertainty about the parameters, given a particular model of the NAIRU; because different models yield different point estimates and different confidence intervals, if one informally incorporates uncertainty over models then the imprecision with which the NAIRU is measured is arguably larger still. We find this substantial imprecision whether the natural rate is measured as a constant, as an unobserved random walk, or as a slowly changing function of time (implemented here alternatively as a cubic spline in time or as a constant with discrete jumps or breaks). This finding of imprecision is also robust to using alternative series for unemployment and inflation, to including additional supply-shift variables in the Phillips curve (following Gordon 1992, 1990), to using monthly or quarterly data, to using labor market variables to model the NAIRU, and to using various measures for expected inflation.

Because we find this imprecision for the models that are conventional in the literature for the measurement of the NAIRU (as well as for the unconventional models that we consider), these results raise serious questions about the role that estimates of the NAIRU should play in discussions of monetary policy.

The paper is organized as follows. Section 5.2 lays out our main findings in the context of a Phillips relation estimated with monthly data, with various specifications for the NAIRU. Section 5.3 provides details on the econometric methodology and describes additional statistical and economic models for the NAIRU. In the statistical models, the NAIRU is determined implicitly by the time-series properties of the macroeconomic variables; in the economic models, labor market variables are investigated as possible empirical determinants of the NAIRU. Section 5.4 discusses some further econometric issues associated with computation of the confidence intervals, and includes a Monte Carlo comparison of two alternative approaches to the construction of confidence intervals in this problem. A full set of empirical results are given in section 5.5. Section 5.6 concludes.[1]

5.2   The Phillips Relation and Conventional Estimates of the NAIRU

The leading framework for estimating the NAIRU arises from defining it to be the value of unemployment that is consistent with a stable expectations–augmented Phillips relation. Ignoring lagged effects for the moment, the expectations-augmented Phillips relation considered is

(1) $$\pi_t - \pi_t^e = \beta(u_{t-1} - \bar{u}) + \gamma X_t + v_t,$$

where u_t is the unemployment rate, π_t is the rate of inflation, π_t^e is expected inflation, $\bar{u}$ is the NAIRU, and v_t is an error term. The additional regressors X_t in equation 1 are included in some of the empirical specifications. These regressors are intended to control for supply shocks, in particular the Nixon-era price controls and shocks to the prices of food and energy, which some have argued would shift the intercept of the Phillips curve (cf. Gordon 1990).

Empirical implementation of equation 1 requires a series for inflationary expectations. Following Gordon (1990), the Congressional Budget Office (1994), Weiner (1993), Tootell (1994), Fuhrer (1995), and Eisner (1995), in this section we restrict attention to the "random walk" model for inflationary expectations, that is, $\pi_t^e = \pi_{t-1}$, so $\pi_t - \pi_t^e = \Delta\pi_t$; alternative measures of expected inflation are examined in section 5.5. (Note that, when lags of $\pi_t - \pi_t^e$ are included on the right-hand side of equation 1, this is equivalent to specifying the Phillips relation in the levels of inflation and imposing the restriction that the sum of the coefficients on the lags add to one.) Equation 1 becomes

(2) $$\Delta\pi_t = \beta(u_{t-1} - \bar{u}) + \gamma X_t + v_t.$$

Empirical evidence on the expectations-augmented Phillips curve (equation 2), excluding supply shocks, is presented in figure 5.1, in which the year-to-

---

1. Subsequent to the writing of this paper, we performed similar calculations on updated data, including models with other measures of inflation including various measures of core inflation. These are reported in Staiger, Stock, and Watson (1997). The qualitative conclusions reported in this chapter do not change, although the specific numerical values differ.

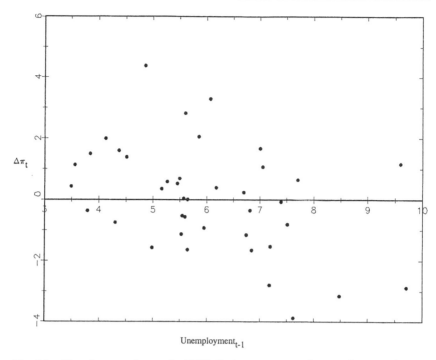

Fig. 5.1   Year-to-year change in CPI inflation versus total unemployment in the previous year, annual data for the United States, 1955–94

year change in CPI inflation is plotted against the lag of the annual unemployment rate, for annual U.S. data from 1955 to 1994. Two key features are apparent from this figure. First, there is clear evidence of a negative relation: lower unemployment is associated with higher inflation. At least at this level of aggregation, the figure suggests that this relation holds in a more or less linear way throughout the range in which unemployment and inflation have fluctuated over the past four decades. Thus unemployment is a valuable predictor of changes in future inflation. Second, there appears to be considerable ambiguity about the precise value of the NAIRU, which in this bivariate relation would be the point at which a line drawn through these observations intersects the unemployment axis. Over these four decades, a value of unemployment in the range of five to seven is roughly equally likely to have been associated with a subsequent increase in inflation as with a subsequent decrease. For example, in the thirteen years in which unemployment was between 5 and 6%, eight years subsequently had an increase in inflation, while in the six years in which unemployment was between 6 and 7%, three years saw a subsequent increase in inflation; these percentages, 61% and 50%, respectively, are qualitatively close and do not differ at any conventional level of statistical significance.

Although this graphical analysis suggests that the NAIRU will be difficult to measure precisely, this approach omits important subtleties, such as the effects of additional lags and supply shocks. Importantly, it does not provide rigorous statements of statistical precision. To address these concerns, it is conventional to perform regression analysis of the Phillips relation. The model (equation 1) neglects lagged effects and plausible serial correlation in the error term, which might arise, for example, from serially correlated measurements error in inflation. Accordingly, in this section we consider regression estimates of

(3) $\Delta\pi_t = \beta(L)(u_{t-1} - \bar{u}) + \delta(L)\Delta\pi_{t-1} + \gamma(L)X_t + \varepsilon_t,$

where L is the lag operator, $\beta(L)$, $\delta(L)$, and $\gamma(L)$ are lag polynomials, and ε_t is a serially uncorrelated error term.

Table 5.1 reports estimated Phillips relations of the form 3, using data on the CPI and total unemployment for the United States, 1955–94. The regressions include two variables controlling for supply shocks. NIXON is a step function taken from Gordon (1990), designed to capture effects of imposing and eliminating Nixon-era price controls. PFE_CPI is a measure of the contribution of food and energy supply shocks constructed according to King and Watson (1994, note 18), specifically, the difference between food and energy inflation and overall CPI inflation; here it is deviated from its mean over the regression period so that by construction it has zero net effect on the measurement of the NAIRU, and it enters the specifications with one quarter's worth of lags. Each regression in table 5.1 includes one year's worth of lags of unemployment and changes in inflation. The first three regressions were performed on monthly data, and the final regression is based on quarterly data.

These regressions are consistent with others in the literature. The sum of coefficients on lagged unemployment are negative and statistically significant. The additional lags of unemployment and the change in inflation both enter significantly, and the variable for the food and energy supply shock is significant (although NIXON is not).

When the NAIRU is treated as constant over the sample, as it is in regression a in table 5.1, it can be estimated directly from the coefficients of the unrestricted regression including an intercept. Specifically, because $\beta(L)(u_{t-1} - \bar{u}) = \beta(L)u_{t-1} - \beta(1)\bar{u}$, where $\beta(1) = \sum_{i=1}^{p}\beta_i$ (where p is the order of the lag polynomial $\beta(L)$), $\bar{u}$ can be estimated as $\hat{\bar{u}} = -\hat{\mu}/\hat{\beta}(1)$, where $\hat{\mu}$ is the estimated intercept from the unrestricted regression

(4) $\Delta\pi_t = \mu + \beta(L)u_{t-1} + \delta(L)\Delta\pi_{t-1} + \gamma(L)X_t + \varepsilon_t,$
$$\mu = -\beta(1)\bar{u}.$$

For specification a in table 5.1, this yields an estimate of the NAIRU of 6.20%, a value within the range of plausible values based on the discussion of figure 5.1.

The fact that the NAIRU is computed as a nonlinear function of the regres-

Table 5.1   Estimated Models of the NAIRU

	(a)	(b)	(c)	(d)
Frequency	monthly	monthly	monthly	quarterly
	55:1–94:12	55:1–94:12	55:1–94:12	55:I–94:IV
Number of lags $(u_t, \Delta\pi_t)$	(12, 12)	(12, 12)	(12, 12)	(4, 4)
NAIRU model	constant	spline, 3	2 breaks,	constant
		knots	estimated at	
			73:8 and	
			80:4	
$\beta(1)$	−.217	−.413	−.384	−.242
(standard error)	(.085)	(.136)	(.127)	(.085)
p-values of F-tests of				
Lags of unemployment	<.001	<.001	<.001	<.001
Lags of inflation	<.001	<.001	<.001	<.001
PFE_CPI	.002	.003	.003	.002
NIXON	>.1	>.1	>.1	>.1
$\bar{R}^2$	.431	.429	.443	.391
Estimates of NAIRU and 95% confidence intervals				
1970:1	6.20	5.36	5.12	6.20
	(4.74, 8.31)	(4.10, 8.05)	(4.07, 6.34)	(5.05, 7.70)
	[5.16, 7.24]	[4.26, 6.46]	[4.24, 6.00]	[5.28, 7.12]
1980:1	6.20	7.32	8.81	6.20
	(4.74, 8.31)	(5.29, 8.77)	(7.22, 12.80)	(5.05, 7.70)
	[5.16, 7.24]	[6.16, 8.48]	[6.85, 10.77]	[5.28, 7.12]
1990:1	6.20	6.22	6.18	6.20
	(4.74, 8.31)	(4 17, 8.91)	(4.25, 7.19)	(5.05, 7.70)
	[5.16, 7.24]	[4.87, 7.57]	[5.16, 7.20]	[5.28, 7.12]

Notes: NAIRU is estimated from the regression

$$\Delta\pi_t = \beta(L)(u_{t-1} - \bar{u}) + \delta(L)\Delta\pi_{t-1} + \gamma(L)X_t + \varepsilon_t$$

using the CPI inflation rate and the Total Civilian Unemployment rate. Gaussian confidence intervals for the NAIRU are reported in parentheses. Delta-method confidence intervals (based on a heteroskedasticity-robust covariance matrix) are reported in brackets. In all specifications, one quarter's worth of lags (and no contemporaneous value) of PFE_CPI was included, and NIXON enters contemporaneously. The spline and break models and the construction of the associated confidence intervals are described in section 5.3.

sion coefficients introduces a bit of a complication into the computation of a confidence interval for the NAIRU. However, such a confidence interval is readily constructed by considering the related problem of testing the hypothesis that the NAIRU takes on a specific value, say $\bar{u}_0$. Suppose that the null hypothesis is correct, and further suppose that the errors ε_t are independent identically distributed (iid) normal and that the regressors in equation 4 are strictly exogenous. Because under the null hypothesis $\bar{u} = \bar{u}_0$ the intercept in 4 is nonzero, an exact test of the null hypothesis against the two-sided alternative can be obtained by comparing the sum of squared residuals under the null $(SSR(\bar{u}_0))$ computed from equation 3, with $u_t - \bar{u}_0$ as a regressor, to the un-

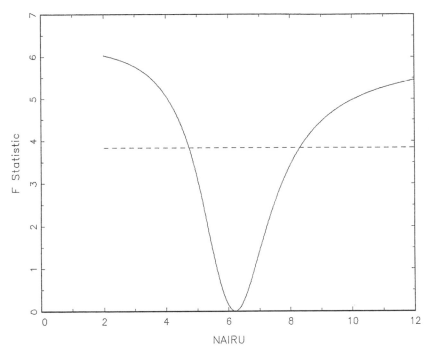

Fig. 5.2   *F*-statistic testing of the hypothesis $\bar{u} = \bar{u}_0$, with $\bar{u}_0$ plotted on the horizontal axis, for specification a in table 5.1

restricted sum of squared residuals from equation 4 ($SSR(\hat{\bar{u}})$), using the *F*-statistic,

(5) $$F_{\bar{u}_0} = [SSR(\bar{u}_0) - SSR(\hat{\bar{u}})]/[SSR(\hat{\bar{u}})/d.f.],$$

where *d.f.* is degrees of freedom in the unrestricted specification (equation 4). Under the stated assumptions, this statistic has an exact $F_{1,d.f.}$ distribution.

Figure 5.2 plots $F_{\bar{u}_0}$ against $\bar{u}_0$ for various values of $\bar{u}_0$, along with the 5% critical value. For example, for $\bar{u}_0 = 7$, the *F*-statistic is not significant, so the hypothesis that the NAIRU is 7% cannot be rejected using this specification. On the other hand, the hypothesis that the NAIRU is 10% can be rejected at the 5% level.

The duality between confidence intervals and hypothesis testing permits us to use figure 5.2 to construct a 95% confidence interval for $\bar{u}$. A 95% confidence set for $\bar{u}$ is the set of values of $\bar{u}$ that, when treated as the null, cannot be rejected at the 5% level. Thus, a 95% confidence interval is the set of $\bar{u}$ for which $F_{\bar{u}_0}$ is less than the 5% critical value. Under the classical assumptions of exogenous regressors and Gaussian errors, the hypothesis test based on $F_{\bar{u}_0}$ is exact (its finite sample rejection rate under the null is exactly the specified significance level). Because of these properties, we will refer to confidence intervals constructed using this approach as "Gaussian."[2]

For figure 5.2, this approach yields a 95% confidence interval of (4.7%, 8.3%) for the NAIRU in 1990. The confidence interval is wide, but this is perhaps unsurprising in light of the wide range of plausible estimates of the NAIRU in figure 5.1. Indeed, there is striking agreement between the plausible range based on informal inspection of figure 5.1 and the interval estimated using the formal techniques embodied in figure 5.2. Although there is a statistically significant negative relationship between unemployment and future changes in inflation, the observed data do not fall tightly along this relationship, and the data simply do not contain enough information to provide precise estimates of the point around which this relationship is centered, the NAIRU.

Another approach to the construction of confidence intervals is to use the so-called delta method, which involves making a first-order Taylor series approximation to the nonlinear function $-\hat{\mu}/\hat{\beta}(1)$ and then using the formula for the asymptotic variance of this linearized function. In section 5.4, we compare the Gaussian confidence intervals and the delta-method confidence intervals in a Monte Carlo experiment, with a design based on a typical empirical Phillips relation. We find that the Gaussian intervals both have better finite-sample coverage rates(that is, their coverage rates are closer to the desired 95%) and have better finite-sample accuracy. For this reason, we place primary weight on the Gaussian intervals. However, because the delta method is the usual textbook approach for constructing asymptotic standard errors, for completeness in table 5.1 we also present delta-method confidence intervals (in brackets). Generally speaking, the delta-method confidence intervals are tighter than the Gaussian confidence intervals. For example, in specification a, the spread of the Gaussian interval is 3.6 percentage points, while the spread of the delta-method interval is 2.1 percentage points. Based on the Monte Carlo results, a plausible explanation for these shorter intervals is that their finite-sample coverage rates are less than the purported 95%. Indeed, 90% Gaussian confidence intervals for the specifications in table 5.1 are similar to the 95% delta-method intervals. For example, the 90% Gaussian interval for table 5.1 column a is (5.14, 7.57), while the 95% delta-method interval is (5.16, 7.24). Despite the differences between the Gaussian and delta-method confidence intervals, the main qualitative conclusion, that the confidence intervals are quite wide, obtains using either approach.

Quite plausibly, the NAIRU has not been constant over time, and specifications b and c in table 5.1 investigate two models for a time-varying NAIRU. In specification b, NAIRU is modeled using a cubic spline with three knot points, while in specification c it is allowed to take on three constant values over the

---

2. Our Gaussian intervals are the regression extension of Fieller's method (1954) for computing exact confidence intervals for the ratio of the means of two jointly normal random variables. We thank Tom Rothenberg for pointing out this reference to us.

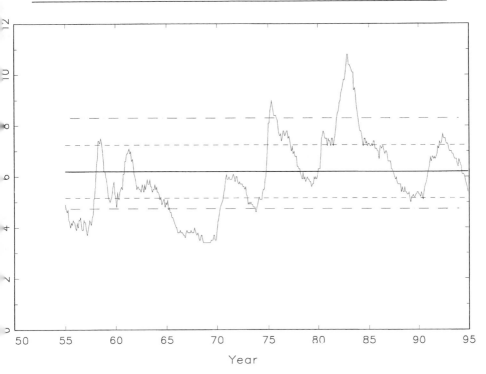

Fig. 5.3   Constant estimate of NAIRU, 95% Gaussian confidence interval (*long dashes*), delta-method confidence interval (*short dashes*), and unemployment

Notes: $\pi_t^e = \pi_{t-1}$, monthly, January 1955–December 1994 (table 5.1, model a).

sample, that is, to be a constant with two break points. (The econometric details of these specifications and the computation of associated confidence intervals for the NAIRU are discussed in section 5.3.) Interestingly, the point estimate of the NAIRU for 90:1 based on these three approaches is quite similar, approximately 6.2 percentage points. Although the confidence intervals differ, they all provide the same qualitative conclusion that the NAIRU is imprecisely estimated. The tightest of the three Gaussian confidence intervals for 90:1 is based on the two-break model and is (4.3, 7.2), a spread of 2.9 percentage points of unemployment.

The unemployment rate, the estimated NAIRU, and the 95% confidence interval for the NAIRU are plotted in figures 5.3, 5.4, and 5.5 for specifications a, b, and c in table 5.1. Although the point estimates and confidence intervals produced by the spline and break models differ for some dates, the two sets of estimates are generally similar and yield the same qualitative conclusions. Both models estimate the NAIRU to have been higher during the late 1970s and early 1980s than before or after, and suggest that the NAIRU in the 1990s is slightly higher than it was in the 1960s. Throughout the historical period, the NAIRU is imprecisely estimated using either model, although the precision

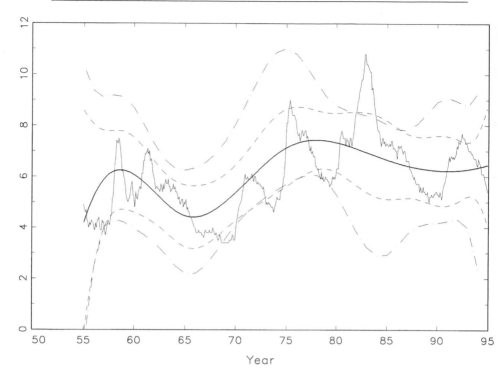

Fig. 5.4   Spline estimate of NAIRU, 95% Gaussian confidence interval (*long dashes*), delta-method confidence interval (*short dashes*), and unemployment
Notes: $\pi_t^e = \pi_{t-1}$, monthly, January 1955–December 1994 (table 5.1, model b).

during the 1960s appears to be somewhat better than the precision during later periods.

Recent work using Canadian data has demonstrated that point estimates of the NAIRU (or, similarly, potential output) can be sensitive to seemingly modest changes in specification of the estimating equations (Setterfield, Gordon, and Osberg 1992; van Norden 1995). Therefore, a critical question is whether the main conclusion of this analysis, that the NAIRU is imprecisely estimated, is sensitive to changes in the specifications in table 5.1.

One such alternative specification is given in column d in table 5.1, which reports the constant NAIRU model estimated using quarterly data. In general, the monthly and quarterly models are quite similar, and the estimated NAIRU is 6.20 in both models. The Gaussian confidence intervals are somewhat tighter for the quarterly model, with a spread of 2.6 percentage points of unemployment compared with 3.1 percentage points for the monthly model. Looking ahead to the empirical results in section 5.5, this somewhat lower spread is perhaps more typical of the confidence intervals that obtain from other specifications. As was the case using monthly data, the main qualitative conclusion from this quarterly specification is that the NAIRU is imprecisely estimated.

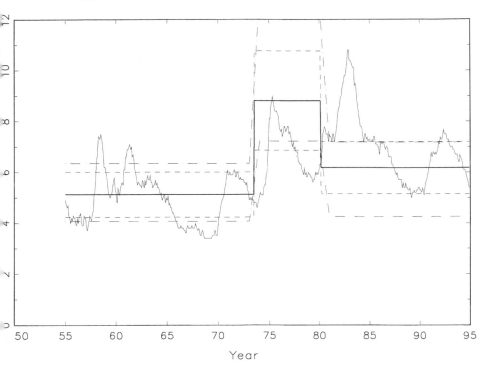

**Fig. 5.5   Two-break estimate of NAIRU, 95% Gaussian confidence interval
(*long dashes*), delta-method confidence interval (*short dashes*), and
unemployment**
Notes: $\pi_t^e = \pi_{t-1}$, monthly, January 1955–December 1994 (table 5.1, model c).

The main task of the remainder of this paper is to investigate more thoroughly the robustness of the conclusion that the NAIRU is imprecisely measured, by examining alternative specifications. These include alternative measures of inflation and unemployment, alternative supply-shock variables, different frequencies of observation, the use of other measures of inflationary expectations (including survey measures of expected inflation), and other statistical and economic models for the NAIRU. Before presenting those results, however, we first discuss econometric issues involved in these extensions.

5.3   Alternative Models and Econometric Issues

This section provides more precise descriptions of the various models of the NAIRU considered in the empirical analysis and the associated econometric issues. In addition to models based on Phillips-type relations, we also consider models based on univariate properties of the unemployment rate.

5.3.1   Estimates of the NAIRU Based on the Phillips Curve

The first set of models is based on the generalized Phillips relation,

$$
(6) \qquad \pi_t - \pi_t^e = \beta(L)(u_{t-1} - \bar{u}_{t-1}) \\
+ \delta(L)(\pi_{t-1} - \pi_{t-1}^e) + \gamma(L)X_t + \varepsilon_t.
$$

To estimate equation 6, an auxiliary model or data source is needed to construct a proxy of inflationary expectations. In addition, statistical and/or economic assumptions are needed to identify the NAIRU when it is permitted to vary over time; these assumptions are discussed in subsequent subsections.

Three alternative approaches are used to model inflationary expectations:

$$
(7a) \qquad \pi_t^e = \mu + \alpha\pi_{t-1} \qquad \text{("AR(1) expectations"),}
$$
$$
(7b) \qquad \pi_t^e = \mu + \alpha(L)\pi_{t-1} \qquad \text{("Recursive } AR(p) \text{ expectations"),}
$$

and

$$
(7c) \qquad \pi_t^e = \text{consensus or median forecast survey,}
$$

where AR denotes autoregressive and the survey forecasts refer to real-time forecasts as collected by contemporaneous surveys of economists and forecasters. Two surveys of forecasters are used, the Survey of Professional Forecasters (SPF) now maintained by the Federal Reserve Bank of Philadelphia (previously collected as the American Statistical Association and National Bureau of Economic Research [ASA-NBER] survey), and the Livingston survey, also now maintained by the Federal Reserve Bank of Philadelphia.

The premise of the $AR(1)$ expectations model is that inflation is a highly persistent series: a unit root in the monthly consumer price index (CPI) cannot be rejected at the 10% level using the augmented Dickey-Fuller (1979) test. Thus inflationary expectations might plausibly be set to capture the long-run movements in inflation. Because the unit root cannot be rejected, a simple approach is to set $\alpha = 1$. However, other values for the largest autoregressive root cannot be rejected, and in the empirical implementation we consider the end points of a 90% equal-tailed confidence interval for the largest autoregressive root in inflation and the value of the median-unbiased estimator of this largest root following the method of Stock (1991). Three methods of determining μ are used: setting $\mu = 0$; estimating μ over the full sample for fixed α; and estimating μ recursively for fixed α to simulate real-time expectations formation.

The recursive $AR(p)$ expectations are formed by first estimating a pth order autoregression for inflation and using the predicted values as π_{t-1}^e. This is implemented by recursive least squares estimation of the $AR(p)$, which simulates the real-time forecasts that would be produced under the autoregressive assumption.

The SPF forecast is the median value of forecasts from a panel of professional forecasters, which were originally collected in real time as a joint project of the ASA and the NBER. These data are available quarterly from the first quarter of 1968 for the GNP (subsequently GDP) deflator and constitute a true real-time forecast of inflation. The data used here are the forecast of GDP inflation over the quarter following the survey date. The SPF/ASA-NBER survey is described in more detail in Zarnowitz and Braun (1993).

The Livingston survey forecast is the mean from a semiannual forecast of the CPI. The specific forecast series used here is the mean forecast of the inflation rate over the six months following the survey date.

5.3.2   Statistical Models of the NAIRU

Four alternative statistical models for the NAIRU are investigated.

(8a) $\bar{u}_t = \bar{u}$ for all t ("Constant NAIRU")

(8b) $\bar{u}_t = \phi'S_t$ ("Spline NAIRU")

(8c) $\bar{u}_t = \bar{u}_i$ if $t_{i-1} < t \le t_i,$ $i = 1, \ldots, I$ ("Break NAIRU")

(8d) $\bar{u}_t = \bar{u}_{t-1} + \eta_t, \; \eta_t \; IID \; N(0, \lambda\sigma_\varepsilon^2),$ $E\eta_t\varepsilon_\tau = 0,$
        all t, τ ("TVP NAIRU"),

where *TVP* means time-varying parameter.

The constant NAIRU model assumes that the NAIRU does not change over the sample period. The remaining models permit the NAIRU to vary over time. These models use no additional economic variables to identify the NAIRU (models that do this are introduced in the next section), and so additional statistical assumptions are required to determine the NAIRU. The spline, break, and TVP models represent different sets of statistical assumptions with a similar motivation, specifically, that the NAIRU potentially varies over time, but that this variation is smooth and in particular these movements are unrelated to the errors ε_t in the Phillips relation (equation 3).

In the spline model, the NAIRU is approximated by a cubic spline in time, written as $\phi'S_t$, where S_t is a vector of deterministic functions of time. (Including the constant, the dimension of S_t is the number of knots plus 4.) The knot points of the spline are determined so that each spline segment is equidistant up to integer constraints. Accordingly, equation 6 can be rewritten

(9) $$\pi_t - \pi_t^e = -\beta(1)\bar{\phi}'S_{t-1} + \beta(L)u_{t-1} + \gamma(L)X_t$$
        $$+ \; \delta(L)(\pi_{t-1} - \pi_{t-1}^e) - \beta^*(L)\bar{\phi}'\Delta S_{t-1} + \varepsilon_t,$$

where $\beta^*(L) = \sum_{i=1}^p \beta_i^* L^i$, with $\beta_i^* = -\sum_{j=i+1}^p \beta_j$, and where $\beta(L)$ and $\gamma(L)$ are defined above. If the NAIRU changes slowly, then the term $\beta^*(L)\bar{\phi}'\Delta S_{t-1}$ will be small ($\beta^*(L)$ has finite order), and so to avoid nonlinear optimization over the parameters, it is convenient to treat this term as negligible. This approximation yields the estimation equation

(10) $$\pi_t - \pi_t^e = \phi'S_{t-1} + \beta(L)u_{t-1}$$
        $$+ \; \gamma(L)X_t + \delta(L)(\pi_{t-1} - \pi_{t-1}^e) + \varepsilon_t,$$

where $\phi = -\beta(1)\overline{\phi}$. Equation 10 is estimated by ordinary least squares (OLS), and NAIRU is estimated as $-\hat{\phi}'S_t/\hat{\beta}(1)$.

In the break model, the NAIRU is treated as taking on one of several discrete values, depending on the date. Given the break dates $\{t_i\}$, the estimation of the break model is similar to that of the spline model. Let $B_t = (B_{1t}, \ldots, B_{lt})$ be a set of dummy variables, where $B_{it}=1$ if $t_{i-1} < t \le t_i$ and $B_{it}=0$ otherwise. Then under the break model, the NAIRU can be written as $\overline{u}_t = \lambda'B_t$, where λ is an I-vector of unknown coefficients. Given the break dates $\{t_i\}$, the coefficients are estimated using the specification 10 with $\phi'S_{t-1}$ replaced by $\lambda'B_{t-1}$ (so $\lambda = -\beta(1)\lambda$). The breaks $\{t_i\}$ may either be fixed a priori or estimated. In specifications in which they are fixed, we choose the breaks to divide the sample equally. In specifications in which they are estimated, they are chosen to minimize the sum of squared residuals from the regression 10 with $\lambda'B_{t-1}$ replacing $\phi'S_{t-1}$, subject to the restriction that no break occur within a fraction τ of another break or the start or end of the regression period. In the empirical work, τ is set to 7%, corresponding to approximately three years in our full data set. When there is more than one break, the computation of the exact minimizer of this sum of squares becomes burdensome, so we adopt a sequential estimation algorithm in which one break is estimated, then this break date is fixed and a second break is estimated and so forth. Recently, Bai (1995) has shown that this algorithm yields consistent estimators of the break dates.

The TVP model is of the type proposed by Cooley and Prescott (1973a, 1973b, 1976), Rosenberg (1972, 1973), and Sarris (1973), although here the time variation is restricted to a single parameter, whereas in the standard TVP model all coefficients are permitted to vary over time. Estimation of the TVP model parameters and the NAIRU proceeds by maximum likelihood using the Kalman filter. (A related exercise is contained in Kuttner [1994], where the TVP framework is used to estimate potential output.) Standard errors of coefficients in the TVP model are computed assuming that $(u_t - \overline{u}_t, \pi_t - \pi_t^e)$ are jointly stationary, the same assumption as for the spline model. The standard errors reported for the NAIRU are the square root of the sum of the Kalman smoother estimate of the variance of the state and the delta-method estimate of the variance of the estimate of the state (Ansley and Kohn 1986). Gordon (1997) estimates the NAIRU using the TVP model in specifications similar to those examined here, but does not provide confidence intervals for those estimates.

5.3.3 Models of the NAIRU Based on Theories of the Labor Market

An alternative to these statistical models is to model the NAIRU as a function of observable labor market variables. Search models of the labor market have proved useful in explaining the cyclical components of unemployment and provide a reasonable basis for the existence of a short-run Phillips curve (see, for example, Bertola and Caballero 1993; Blanchard and Diamond 1989, 1990; Davis and Haltiwanger 1992; and Layard, Nickell, and Jackman 1991).

While most of the work with search models focuses on understanding cyclical variation, these models also provide a conceptual framework for modeling the NAIRU, which can be viewed as the model's steady-state unemployment rate.

For our purposes, the key theoretical and empirical insight of the recent search literature is that cyclical variation in unemployment is largely driven by variation in inflow rates (job destruction) while longer-term trends in unemployment are largely driven by changes in exit hazards from unemployment (or equivalently, unemployment duration). Thus, unemployment exit hazards and the underlying factors that theoretically should influence these hazards may provide useful information for explaining the NAIRU.

We calculate the fraction of those recently unemployed who remain unemployed (one minus the exit hazard) as the number of persons unemployed five to fourteen weeks in a given month divided by the number of new entrants into unemployment over the prior two months. To proxy for changes in search intensity and reservation wages among the unemployed, we calculate the fraction of the civilian labor force that is teen, female, and nonwhite. We also consider three institutional features of the labor market that have been hypothesized to affect search intensity and reservation wages: the nominal minimum wage, the unemployment insurance replacement rate (e.g., the ratio of average weekly benefits to average weekly wage), and the percentage of the civilian labor force that are union members.

This leads to modeling the NAIRU as

$$(11) \qquad \bar{u}_t = \Psi(L)Z_t \qquad \text{(``Labor Market NAIRU''),}$$

where Z_t is a vector of labor market variables. With the assumption that the variance of ΔZ_t is small, the derivation of equation 10 applies here as well, with Z_t replacing S_t. Under the assumption that Z_t is uncorrelated with ε_t in a suitably redefined version of 10, then $\Psi(L)$ can be estimated by OLS.

5.3.4 Estimates of the NAIRU Based Solely on Unemployment

If expectations of inflation are unbiased and if the supply-shock variables X_t have mean zero or are absent, then the mean unemployment rate will equal the NAIRU. Alternatively, one can simply posit without reference to a Phillips curve that, over medium to long horizons, the unemployment rate reverts to its natural rate. In either case, the implication is that univariate data on unemployment can be used to extract an estimate of the NAIRU as a local mean of the series. For example, this view is implicit in estimates of the NAIRU based on linear interpolation of the unemployment rate between comparable points of the business cycle.

Our empirical implementation of the univariate approach starts with the autoregressive model, $u_t - \bar{u}_t = \beta(L)(u_{t-1} - \bar{u}_{t-1}) + \varepsilon_t$, where $\bar{u}_t$ follows one of the models 8a–8c. For the spline model 8b, applying the derivation of equation 10 to the univariate model then yields

$$\text{(12)} \qquad u_t = \phi' S_{t-1} + \beta(L) u_{t-1} + \varepsilon_t,$$

where $\phi = -(1+\beta(1))\bar\phi$. Estimation of equation 12 is by OLS, and the NAIRU is estimated as $-\hat\phi' S_{t-1}/(1+\hat\beta(1))$. Estimation of the constant NAIRU model is a special case with $S_{t-1} = 1$. Estimation of the break model proceeds by replacing $\phi' S_{t-1}$ with $\lambda' B_{t-1}$, as described following equation 10, with the modification that here $\lambda = -(1+\beta(1))\bar\lambda$.

5.4   Confidence Intervals for the NAIRU: Econometric Issues

We briefly digress to discuss additional issues in the computation of confidence intervals based on the models of the NAIRU other than the TVP model. The approach described in section 5.2 for computing confidence intervals must be modified when the NAIRU is allowed to vary over time. To be concrete, consider the spline NAIRU model 10, rewritten as

$$\text{(13)} \qquad \pi_t - \pi_t^e = \beta(1)(u_{t-1} - \bar\phi' S_{t-1}) + \beta^*(L)\Delta u_{t-1} \\ + \gamma(L)X_t + \delta(L)(\pi_{t-1} - \pi_{t-1}^e) + \varepsilon_t,$$

where $\beta_j^* = -\sum_{i=j+1}^p \beta_i$. Suppose interest is in testing the null hypothesis relating to NAIRU at a fixed time $\tau - 1$, $\bar u_{\tau-1} = \bar u_{\tau-1,0}$. Without loss of generality, suppose that the constant appears as the first spline regressor, so that $S_{t-1} = (1, S_{2,t-1})$, where $S_{2,t-1}$ denotes the additional spline regressors. Then the space spanned by regressors $\{S_t\}$ is equivalent to the space spanned by $\{\tilde S_t\}$, where $\tilde S_{t-1} = (1, S_{2,t-1} - S_{2,\tau-1})$, so in particular there is a unique $\tilde\phi$ such that $\tilde\phi' \tilde S_{t-1} = \bar\phi' S_{t-1}$. Let $\tilde\phi$ be partitioned as $(\tilde\phi_1, \tilde\phi_2)$ conformably with $\tilde S_{t-1}$. By construction, $\tilde S_{\tau-1} = (1, 0)$, so $\bar u_{\tau-1} = \tilde\phi' \tilde S_{\tau-1} = \tilde\phi_1$. Then equation 13 can be rewritten

$$\text{(14)} \qquad \pi_t - \pi_t^e = \beta(1)(u_{t-1} - \bar u_{\tau-1}) + \phi_2' \tilde S_{2,t-1} + \beta^*(L)\Delta u_{t-1} \\ + \gamma(L)X_t + \delta(L)(\pi_{t-1} - \pi_{t-1}^e) + \varepsilon_t,$$

where $\phi_2 = -\beta(1)\tilde\phi_2$

Because the hypothesis $\bar u_{\tau-1} = \bar u_{\tau-1,0}$ imposes no restrictions on $\tilde\phi_2$, $\beta(1)$, or the other coefficients, equation 14 can be used to construct an F-statistic testing $\bar u_{\tau-1} = \bar u_{\tau-1,0}$ by comparing the restricted sum of squared residuals from 14 to the unrestricted sum of squared residuals, obtained by estimating 14 including an intercept. Evidently, confidence intervals for $\bar u_{\tau-1}$ can be constructed by inverting this test statistic, as discussed in section 5.2.

This procedure requires constructing separate regressors $\{\tilde S_t\}$ for each date of interest. However, the special structure of the linear transformation used to construct $\{\tilde S_t\}$ and standard regression matrix algebra deliver expressions that make this computationally efficient.

As mentioned in section 5.2, under the classical assumptions of exogenous regressors and Gaussian errors, the Gaussian confidence intervals have exact coverage rates. In the application at hand, however, the errors are presumably not normally distributed, and the regressors, while predetermined, are not strictly exogenous (for example, they include lagged dependent variables). Thus the formal justification for using these confidence intervals here relies on the asymptotic rather than the finite sample theory.

An alternative, more conventional approach is to compute confidence intervals based on the delta method, which is an asymptotic normal approximation. However $\hat{u} = -\hat{\mu}/\hat{\beta}(1)$ is the ratio of random variables, and such ratios are well known to have skewed and heavy-tailed distributions in finite samples. To the extent that the estimated coefficients have a distribution that is well approximated as jointly normal, then this ratio will have a doubly noncentral Cauchy distribution with dependent numerator and denominator. When $\beta(1)$ is imprecisely estimated, normality can provide a poor approximation to the distribution of this ratio. In this event, confidence intervals computed using the delta method may have coverage rates that are substantially different than the nominal asymptotic coverage rate.

The Gaussian and delta-method tests of the hypothesis $\bar{u}_t = \bar{u}_{t,0}$ have the same local asymptotic power against the alternative $\bar{u}_t = \bar{u}_{t,0} + d / \sqrt{T}$, where d is a constant. Which test to use for the construction of confidence intervals therefore depends on their finite sample properties. With fixed regressors and iid normal errors, the Gaussian test is uniformly most powerful invariant. However, the regressors include lagged endogenous variables, and the errors are plausibly nonnormally distributed, at least because of truncation error in the estimation of inflation. Thus, while the finite sample theory supporting the Gaussian intervals and the questionable nature of the first-order linearization that underlies the delta-method intervals both point toward preferring the Gaussian test, the exact distribution theory does not strictly apply in this application. Consequently, neither the asymptotic nor the exact finite sample theory provides a formal basis for selecting between the two intervals.

We therefore performed a Monte Carlo experiment to compare the finite sample coverage rates and accuracy for the two confidence intervals, which is equivalent to comparing the size and power of the tests upon which the confidence intervals are based. The design is empirically based and is intended to be representative of, if simpler than, the empirical models considered here. A first-order vector autoregression in u_t and $\Delta\pi_t$ (total unemployment and the CPI) was estimated using eighty biannual observations from the first half of 1955 to the second half of 1994. In both equations, u_{t-1} enters significantly using the standard t-test at the 5% significance level, but the coefficient π_{t-1} is insignificant at the 10% level. To simplify the experiment, we therefore imposed these two zero restrictions. Upon reestimation under these restrictions, we obtained

(15a) $$u_t = .566 + .906u_{t-1} + \varepsilon_{1t}$$

and

(15b) $$\Delta\pi_t = \mu + \beta(1)u_{t-1} + \varepsilon_{2t},$$

where $(\hat{\mu}, \hat{\beta}(1)) = (1.608, -0.260)$.

The data for the Monte Carlo experiment were generated according to equation 15 for various values of $(\mu, \beta(1))$. Two methods were used to generate the pseudorandom errors. In the first, the bivariate errors from the 1955–94 regression were randomly sampled with replacement and used to generate the artificial draws. When μ and $\beta(1)$ take on the values estimated using the 1955–94 regression, this corresponds to the bootstrap. In the second $\{\varepsilon_t\}$ was drawn from an iid bivariate normal with covariance matrix set to the sample covariance matrix of the restricted VAR residuals.

The values of (μ, β) for which the performance of the procedures is investigated are the point estimates for the biannual 1955–94 sample, (1.608, -0.260), which correspond to an estimate of the NAIRU of 6.18, and three selected values that lie on the boundary of the usual 80% confidence ellipse for (μ, β) estimated from these eighty observations, specifically, (0.261, -0.026), (0.394, -0.070), and (2.202, -0.404), which correspond to values of the NAIRU of 10.04, 5.63, and 5.45.

Monte Carlo coverage rates of the two procedures are summarized in appendix table 5A.1. The Monte Carlo coverage rate of the Gaussian interval is generally close to its nominal confidence level. In contrast, the coverage rate of the 95% delta-method confidence interval ranges from 64% to 99%, depending on μ and $\beta(1)$. Generally speaking, the deviations from normality of the delta-method t-statistic are, unsurprisingly, greatest when $\beta(1)$ is smallest in absolute value. Evidently the coverage rate of the delta-method confidence interval is poorly controlled over empirically relevant portions of the parameter space.

In finite samples, one of the intervals might be tighter in some sense than the other, and if the delta-method intervals were substantially tighter in finite samples, then some researchers might prefer the delta-method intervals to the Gaussian intervals despite the poor coverage rates in some regions of the parameter space. We therefore investigated the tightness of the confidence intervals, or more precisely, their accuracy. The accuracy of a confidence interval is one minus its probability of covering the true parameter, so it suffices to compare the power of tests upon which the delta-method and Gaussian confidence intervals are based. Because the tests do not have the same rejection rates under the null, we compare size-adjusted as well as size-unadjusted (raw) powers of the tests. The size-unadjusted power is computed using asymptotic critical values; the size-adjusted power is computed using the finite-sample critical value for which, for this data-generating process, the test has rejection rate 5% under the null. The power was assessed by holding $\beta(1)$ constant at -0.26 and varying $\bar{u}$ (equivalently, μ). The results are summarized in appendix table 5A.2. In brief, for alternatives near the null, the delta-method and Gaussian tests have comparable size-adjusted power. However, for more distant alternatives, the Gaussian test has substantially greater power than the delta-method test.

In summary, in this experiment the Gaussian intervals were found to have

Table 5.2   Selected Estimates of the NAIRU and β(1) for Alternative Models of π^e and the NAIRU

Differences from Base Case	Formation of π^e	# of Lags $(U, \pi-\pi^e)$	Determinants of NAIRU	$\beta(1)$[a]	Selected Estimates of NAIRU (Gaussian 95% confidence interval)[b]			F-Test of Constant NAIRU[c]
					1970:1	1980:1	1990:1	
None	$\pi^e_t = \pi_{t-1}$	(12,12)	constant	−0.217 (0.085)	6.20 (4.74, 8.31) [0.53]	6.20 (4.74, 8.31) [0.53]	6.20 (4.74, 8.31) [0.53]	NA
None	recursive AR(12) forecast	(12,12)	constant	−0.241 (0.093)	6.41 (5.30, 8.50) [0.50]	6.41 (5.30, 8.50) [0.50]	6.41 (5.30, 8.50) [0.50]	NA
None	$\pi^e_t = \pi_{t-1}$	(12,12)	spline, 3 knots	−0.413 (0.136)	5.36 (4.10, 8.05) [0.56]	7.32 (5.29, 8.77) [0.59]	6.22 (4.17, 8.91) [0.69]	0.96 (0.455)
None	recursive AR(12) forecast	(12,12)	spline, 3 knots	−0.751 (0.160)	5.76 (5.08, 6.82) [0.34]	7.74 (7.07, 8.47) [0.32]	5.93 (4.98, 6.91) [0.37]	3.87 (0.001)
None	$\pi^e_t = \pi_{t-1}$	(12,12)	2 breaks, estimated	−0.384 (0.127)	5.12 (4.07, 6.34) [0.45]	8.81 (7.22, 12.80) [1.00]	6.18 (4.25, 7.19) [0.52]	3.66
None	recursive AR(12) forecast	(12,12)	2 breaks, estimated	−0.324 (0.104)	8.40 (6.90, 13.90) [1.01]	8.40 (6.90, 13.90) [1.01]	6.02 (3.40, 7.23) [0.59]	8.90
53:01–94:12 no supply shocks	$\pi^e_t = \pi_{t-1}$	(12,12)	TVP (λ = .05)	−0.195 (0.103)	6.15 (NA) [0.72]	6.33 (NA) [0.68]	6.18 (NA) [0.73]	NA

(continued)

Table 5.2 (continued)

Differences from Base Case	Formation of π^e	# of Lags $(U, \pi - \pi^e)$	Determinants of NAIRU	$\beta(1)$[a]	Selected Estimates of NAIRU (Gaussian 95% confidence interval)[b]			F-Test of Constant NAIRU[c]
					1970:1	1980:1	1990:1	
53:01–94:12 no supply shocks	$\pi^e_t = \pi_{t-1}$	(12,12)	TVP ($\lambda = .15$)	−0.148 (0.120)	6.30 (NA) [1.27]	7.12 (NA) [1.14]	6.03 (NA) [1.20]	NA
53:01–94:12 no supply shocks	recursive AR(12) forecast	(12,12)	TVP ($\lambda = .05$)	−0.237 (0.125)	6.57 (NA) [0.66]	6.75 (NA) [0.60]	6.48 (NA) [0.65]	NA
53:01–94:12 no supply shocks	recursive AR(12) forecast	(12,12)	TVP ($\lambda = .15$)	−0.288 (0.156)	6.94 (NA) [0.94]	7.79 (NA) [0.82]	6.14 (NA) [0.82]	NA
55:01–93:12	$\pi^e_t = \pi_{t-1}$	(12,12)	labor-market variables	−0.889 (0.260)	4.96 (3.24, 5.49) [0.34]	6.93 (5.63, 8.02) [0.45]	5.43 (4.08, 6.46) [0.50]	1.44 (0.186)
55:01–93:12	recursive AR(12) forecast	(12,12)	labor-market variables	−0.973 (0.267)	5.52 (4.06, 6.41) [0.40]	7.33 (6.28, 8.45) [0.44]	5.46 (4.26, 6.38) [0.45]	3.61 (0.001)

Note: Base case is monthly (January 1955–December 1994), π from All-Items Urban CPI, All-Worker Unemployment.
[a]Standard errors are in parentheses.
[b]Standard errors in brackets are for delta method.
[c]P-values are in parentheses.

both less distortions in coverage rates and greater accuracy than the delta-method confidence intervals. For this reason, when interpreting the empirical results, we place primary emphasis on the Gaussian intervals.

5.5   Empirical Results for the Postwar United States

This section examines a variety of alternative specifications of the Phillips curve in an attempt to assess the robustness of the main finding in section 5.2, the imprecision of estimates of the NAIRU. As in section 5.2, the base specifications use monthly data for the United States, and regressions are run over the period January 1955–December 1994, with earlier observations as initial conditions. Unless explicitly stated otherwise, all regressions control for the Nixon price controls and one quarter's worth of lags of shocks to food and energy prices (PFE_CPI). Throughout, inflation is measured as period-to-period growth at an annual rate.

Results for several baseline monthly models, using the all-items CPI for urban consumers and the total unemployment rate, are presented in table 5.2. The table provides results from each of the five models of the NAIRU given in equations 8 and 11. The first column provides information on any changes from the base specification. The second column describes the model for inflation expectations; in table 5.2, estimates are reported for models in which inflationary expectations are equal to lagged inflation or, alternatively, equal to a recursive AR(12) forecast. The third column gives the number of lags of inflation and unemployment used in the models (twelve of each for these baseline specifications), and the next column describes the NAIRU specification. The final five columns of the table summarize the estimation results. The column labeled $\beta(1)$ shows the estimated sum of coefficients for the lags of unemployment entering the Phillips relation. The next three columns present estimates of the NAIRU in January 1970, January 1980, and January 1990 with 95% Gaussian confidence intervals and delta-method standard errors. The final column of the table presents the F-statistic testing the null hypothesis that the NAIRU is constant. (This was computed for the spline, break, and labor market models only. Evidence on time variation in the TVP model is discussed below.)

The confidence intervals in table 5.2 are comparable to those discussed in section 5.2. For example, the tightest estimate of the NAIRU in January 1990 among the models reported in table 5.2 is 5.93 with a 95% Gaussian confidence interval of (4.98, 6.91). In this case, the NAIRU is modeled as a cubic spline and inflationary expectations come from a recursive AR(12) forecast. The NAIRU estimates are fairly similar across the specifications, and the point estimates across the different specifications fall within each confidence interval in the table. The models that allow for a time-varying NAIRU generally suggest that the NAIRU was approximately 1–2 percentage points higher in 1980 than it was in 1970 or 1990. However, due to the imprecision in estimating the NAIRU, typically only the models with recursive AR(12) forecasts of inflation reject the null of a constant NAIRU. (*P*-values for the *F*-tests are not reported for the break model with estimated breaks because the statistics do not have standard *F* distributions under the null of no breaks.)

An important factor contributing to the imprecision in the estimates of the NAIRU is that $\beta(1)$ is generally estimated to be small. If $\beta(1)=0$, then unemployment enters the Phillips relation only in first differences; the level of the unemployment rate does not enter the equation. In this case, the NAIRU is not identified from the Phillips relations. Although the hypothesis that $\beta(1)=0$ can be rejected at conventional levels for most of the models reported in table 5.2, the rejection is not overwhelming for many of the specifications. In other words, the estimates for most specifications are consistent with small values of $\beta(1)$, which would lead to imprecise estimates of the NAIRU. It is noteworthy that the specifications with the largest estimates of $\beta(1)$ also report the smallest confidence intervals for the NAIRU. This is a general property of the alternative specifications reported in the subsequent tables.

We investigate the robustness of the estimates to alternative inflation and unemployment series in table 5.3. In this table, we consider models using inflation computed using the CPI excluding food and energy, and the unemployment rate for prime-aged males (age 25–54), or alternatively, the married-male unemployment rate. For simplicity, only results for constant NAIRU and spline NAIRU models are reported, and models in which inflationary expectations are either $\pi_t^e=\pi_{t-1}$ or are derived from a recursive AR(12) forecast. Once again, the most striking fact seen in these specifications is the large confidence intervals for all estimates of the NAIRU. In fact, the basic findings do not appear to be particularly sensitive to the choice of the inflation or unemployment series—except, of course, the NAIRU is estimated to be lower in models using prime aged-male and especially married-male unemployment. As in table 5.2, models using the recursive AR(12) inflation forecast tend to estimate the largest values of $\beta(1)$ and the tightest confidence intervals for the NAIRU.

The sensitivity of the estimates to the specification of inflationary expectations is investigated in table 5.4. Again, only constant NAIRU and spline NAIRU models are considered. The various specifications report alternative methods of forming inflationary expectations. In forming AR(1) expectations, we used a median unbiased estimate of 0.984 for the largest autoregressive root of inflation, and the endpoints of the 90% confidence interval of (0.965, 1.003). In addition, table 5.4 also reports estimates based on levels of inflation and estimates based on the univariate (unemployment-only) approach of section 5.3.4. As in the earlier tables, there is a striking similarity in the estimates and standard errors across models. For example, the univariate estimates of the NAIRU based only on unemployment are not very different (and no more precise) than the Phillips curve estimates with spline NAIRU from table 5.2. Similarly, the NAIRU results are not much affected by alternative methods of forming inflationary expectations. The one exception is when the model is estimated in levels of inflation, rather than deviations from expectations. How-

Table 5.3   Sensitivity of Estimates of the NAIRU and β(1) to Use of Alternative Data Series for π and U

Differences from Base Case	Formation of π^e	# of Lags $(U, \pi-\pi^e)$	Determinants of NAIRU	$\beta(1)$[a]	Selected Estimates of NAIRU (Gaussian 95% confidence interval)			F-Test of Constant NAIRU[b]
					1970:1	1980:1	1990:1	
Male 25–54 unemployed	$\pi^e_t = \pi_{t-1}$	(12,12)	constant	−0.188 (0.076)	4.50 (2.53, 7.74)	4.50 (2.53, 7.74)	4.50 (2.53, 7.74)	NA
Male 25–54 unemployed	$\pi^e_t = \pi_{t-1}$	(12,12)	spline, 3 knots	−0.388 (0.133)	3.02 (1.60, 5.94)	5.14 (2.94, 6.84)	5.32 (3.12, 8.62)	0.84 (0.536)
Male 25–54 unemployed	recursive AR(12) forecast	(12,12)	spline, 3 knots	−0.609 (0.154)	3.58 (2.75, 5.13)	5.52 (4.64, 6.52)	4.97 (3.72, 6.29)	1.85 (0.088)
Married male unemployed 57:01–94:12	$\pi^e_t = \pi_{t-1}$	(12,12)	constant	−0.268 (0.107)	3.62 (2.20, 5.15)	3.62 (2.20, 5.15)	3.62 (2.20, 5.15)	NA
Married male unemployed 57:01–94:12	$\pi^e_t = \pi_{t-1}$	(12,12)	spline, 3 knots	−0.472 (0.165)	2.52 (1.27, 5.18)	4.26 (2.46, 5.61)	4.00 (2.16, 6.57)	0.63 (0.706)
Married male unemployed 57:01–94:12	recursive AR(12) forecast	(12,12)	spline, 3 knots	−0.643 (0.185)	3.47 (2.58, 6.01)	4.39 (3.43, 5.32)	3.73 (2.43, 5.06)	0.92 (0.481)
CPI less food/energy 62:01–94:12	$\pi^e_t = \pi_{t-1}$	(12,12)	constant	−0.195 (0.084)	6.17 (4.22, 8.17)	6.17 (4.22, 8.17)	6.17 (4.22, 8.17)	NA
CPI less food/energy 62:01–94:12	$\pi^e_t = \pi_{t-1}$	(12,12)	spline, 3 knots	−0.429 (0.137)	5.08 (3.69, 7.58)	7.73 (6.23, 9.40)	6.31 (4.67, 8.49)	1.58 (0.151)
CPI less food/energy 62:01–94:12	recursive AR(12) forecast	(12,12)	spline, 3 knots	−0.545 (0.148)	4.69 (3.53, 6.07)	8.63 (7.70, 10.47)	5.88 (4.50, 7.18)	4.30 (0.000)

(*continued*)

Table 5.3 (continued)

Differences from Base Case	Formation of π^e	# of Lags $(U, \pi-\pi^e)$	Determinants of NAIRU	$\beta(1)$[a]	Selected Estimates of NAIRU (Gaussian 95% confidence interval)			F-Test of Constant NAIRU[b]
					1970:1	1980:1	1990:1	
CPI less food/energy male 25–54 unemployed 62:01–94:12	$\pi^e_t = \pi_{t-1}$	(12,12)	constant	−0.169 (0.072)	4.41 (1.90, 7.30)	4.41 (1.90, 7.30)	4.41 (1.90, 7.30)	NA
CPI less food/energy male 25–54 unemployed 62:01–94:12	$\pi^e_t = \pi_{t-1}$	(12,12)	spline, 3 knots	−0.357 (0.128)	2.81 (0.89, 6.26)	5.53 (3.69, 8.51)	5.45 (3.38, 8.88)	1.20 (0.305)
CPI less food/energy male 25–54 unemployed 62:01–94:12	recursive AR(12) forecast	(12,12)	spline, 3 knots	−0.417 (0.137)	2.44 (0.59, 4.48)	6.58 (5.34, 10.77)	4.91 (2.75, 6.99)	2.70 (0.014)
CPI less food/energy married male unemployed 62:01–94:12	$\pi^e_t = \pi_{t-1}$	(12,12)	constant	−0.293 (0.106)	3.54 (2.47, 4.56)	3.54 (2.47, 4.56)	3.54 (2.47, 4.56)	NA
CPI less food/energy married male unemployed 62:01–94:12	$\pi^e_t = \pi_{t-1}$	(12,12)	spline, 3 knots	−0.535 (0.155)	2.52 (1.38, 4.06)	4.41 (3.30, 5.69)	4.00 (2.76, 5.61)	1.19 (0.312)
CPI less food/energy married male unemployed 62:01–94:12	recursive AR(12) forecast	(12,12)	spline, 3 knots	−0.590 (0.164)	2.25 (1.09, 3.46)	5.19 (4.31, 7.07)	3.65 (2.33, 4.91)	2.87 (0.010)

Note: Base case is monthly (January 1955–December 1994), π from All-Items Urban CPI, All-Worker Unemployment.

[a]Standard errors are in parentheses.

[b]P-values are in parentheses.

Table 5.4   Sensitivity of Estimates of the NAIRU and $\beta(1)$ to Use of Alternative Models of π^e

Differences from Base Case	Formation of π^e	# of Lags $(U, \pi-\pi^e)$	Determinants of NAIRU	$\beta(1)$[a]	Selected Estimates of NAIRU (Gaussian 95% confidence interval)			F-Test of Constant NAIRU[b]
					1970:1	1980:1	1990:1	
Full-sample demeaning of $\pi-\pi^e$	$\pi_t^e = \pi_{t-1}$	(12,12)	constant	−0.217 (0.085)	6.08 (4.46, 7.95)	6.08 (4.46, 7.95)	6.08 (4.46, 7.95)	NA
Full-sample demeaning of $\pi-\pi^e$	$\pi_t^e = \pi_{t-1}$	(12,12)	spline, 3 knots	−0.413 (0.136)	5.29 (4.01, 7.86)	7.25 (5.12, 8.65)	6.15 (4.05, 8.75)	0.96 (0.455)
None	full-sample AR(12) forecast	(12,12)	constant	−0.134 (0.086)	6.06 (0.91, 11.22)	6.06 (0.91, 11.22)	6.06 (0.91, 11.22)	NA
None	full-sample AR(12) forecast	(12,12)	spline, 3 knots	−0.745 (0.151)	5.16 (4.48, 5.95)	8.09 (7.45, 8.93)	5.87 (4.90, 6.84;	5.76 (0.000)
Recursive demeaning of $\pi-\pi^e$	$\pi_t^e = \pi_{t-1}$	(12,12)	constant	−0.190 (0.085)	5.55 (1.76, 7.19)	5.55 (1.76, 7.19)	5.55 (1.76, 7.19)	NA
Recursive demeaning of $\pi-\pi^e$	$\pi_t^e = \pi_{t-1}$	(12,12)	spline, 3 knots	−0.372 (0.135)	5.10 (3.46, 8.23)	6.90 (2.92, 8.32)	6.12 (3.42, 9.51)	0.75 (0.613)
Recursive demeaning of $\pi-\pi^e$	$\pi_t^e = 0.965*\pi_{t-1}$	(12,12)	constant	−0.192 (0.086)	6.73 (5.36, 10.81)	6.73 (5.36, 10.81)	6.73 (5.36, 10.81)	NA
Recursive demeaning of $\pi-\pi^e$	$\pi_t^e = 0.965*\pi_{t-1}$	(12,12)	spline, 3 knots	−0.636 (0.141)	5.75 (4.96, 7.05)	8.27 (7.53, 9.39)	5.81 (4.63, 6.96)	4.42 (0.000)

(continued)

Table 5.4   (continued)

Differences from Base Case	Formation of π^e	# of Lags $(U, \pi - \pi^e)$	Determinants of NAIRU	$\beta(1)^a$	Selected Estimates of NAIRU (Gaussian 95% confidence interval)			F-Test of Constant NAIRU^b
					1970:1	1980:1	1990:1	
Recursive demeaning of $\pi - \pi^e$	$\pi_t^e = 0.984*\pi_{t-1}$	(12,12)	constant	−0.198 (0.085)	6.17 (4.25, 9.07)	6.17 (4.25, 9.07)	6.17 (4.25, 9.07)	NA
Recursive demeaning of $\pi - \pi^e$	$\pi_t^e = 0.984*\pi_{t-1}$	(12,12)	spline, 3 knots	−0.501 (0.138)	5.49 (4.50, 7.30)	7.72 (6.60, 8.99)	5.93 (4.31, 7.58)	2.11 (0.051)
Recursive demeaning of $\pi - \pi^e$	$\pi_t^e = 1.003*\pi_{t-1}$	(12,12)	constant	−0.186 (0.085)	5.41 (1.43, 6.95)	5.41 (1.43, 6.95)	5.41 (1.43, 6.95)	NA
Recursive demeaning of $\pi - \pi^e$	$\pi_t^e = 1.003*\pi_{t-1}$	(12,12)	spline, 3 knots	−0.347 (0.135)	4.99 (2.93, 8.76)	6.67 (2.13, 8.15)	6.18 (2.96, 10.78)	0.60 (0.729)
π in levels	NA	(12,12)	constant	−0.203 (0.086)	6.42 (3.88, 13.43)	6.42 (3.88, 13.43)	6.42 (3.88, 13.43)	NA
π in levels	NA	(12,12)	spline, 3 knots	−0.882 (0.180)	7.01 (6.04, 8.28)	10.78 (9.40, 12.54)	7.60 (6.68, 8.83)	3.76 (0.001)
Univariate model	NA	(12,NA)	constant	−0.017 (0.006)	6.06 (4.72, 7.53)	6.06 (4.72, 7.53)	6.06 (4.72, 7.53)	NA
Univariate model	NA	(12,NA)	spline, 3 knots	−0.045 (0.011)	4.78 (3.95, 5.64)	7.63 (6.78, 8.48)	6.15 (5.04, 7.42)	2.46 (0.024)

Note: Base case is monthly (January 1955–December 1994), π from All-Items Urban CPI, All-Worker Unemployment.

^{a}Standard errors are in parentheses.

^{b}P-values are in parentheses.

ever, the spline estimates of the NAIRU with inflation in levels are implausibly large: nearly 11% in January 1980 and well over 7% in January 1990. The estimates from this specification are, we suspect, biased by the near unit root in inflation.

The sensitivity of the results to the choice of lag length is investigated in table 5.5. The first three rows present models that include contemporaneous unemployment in three baseline specifications. For these baseline specifications, we also report alternative estimates when lags are chosen by the Bayesian information criterion (BIC). The results are not sensitive to these changes. It is worth nothing that the lag lengths selected by BIC are generally shorter than a year, occasionally much shorter.

Table 5.6 investigates the sensitivity of the results to a variety of other specification changes. As in tables 5.3 and 5.5, we focus on baseline specifications for the NAIRU and inflationary expectations. The first eight rows of the table report results for models with more and less flexible specifications of spline NAIRU and break NAIRU. The next three rows report models that do not control for supply shocks. The final three rows report results for models that use the log of the unemployment rate in place of unemployment in levels (although NAIRU is reported in levels in the table). This final alteration permits considering a log-linear Phillips relation. Comparing these results to those of table 5.2, it is apparent that the results are not particularly sensitive to any of these specification changes. For example, the specifications in table 5.6 that use spline NAIRU and recursive AR(12) forecasts of inflation give estimates and confidence intervals for the NAIRU that are all quite similar to each other and also to the comparable results in table 5.2

One possibility is that the imprecision in the NAIRU estimates are a consequence of using noisy monthly data, and that the estimates will be more precise when temporally aggregated data are used. Table 5.7 therefore reports selected models using quarterly data, and documents that the lack of precision in the NAIRU estimates is not a consequence of using monthly data. The first eight specifications in table 5.7 correspond to baseline specifications reported in table 5.2 using monthly data, and the estimates of the NAIRU and its confidence interval are little changed (although confidence intervals are slightly smaller using quarterly data). The next three specifications present models using inflation constructed from the GDP deflator (which is not available at the monthly level). These models yield similar estimates of the NAIRU but confidence intervals that are noticeably larger. The final three specifications use inflation constructed from the fixed-weight personal consumption expenditure (PCE) deflator (one of the series used by the Congressional Budget Office [1994] and by Eisner [1995] in their estimation of the NAIRU). These specifications also yield results that are quite similar to the baseline models.

Table 5.8 investigates the sensitivity of the estimates to specifying inflationary expectations as ether Livingston or SPF forecasts. Models using the Livingston forecast are estimated using semiannual observations that conform

Table 5.5   Sensitivity of Estimates of the NAIRU and $\beta(1)$ to Contemporaneous Unemployment and BIC Lag Choice

Differences from Base Case	Formation of π^e	# of Lags $(U, \pi - \pi^e)$	Determinants of NAIRU	$\beta(1)^a$	Selected Estimates of NAIRU (Gaussian 95% confidence interval)			F-Test of Constant NAIRU^b
					1970:1	1980:1	1990:1	
Include contemporaneous U	$\pi^e_t = \pi_{t-1}$	(12,12)	constant	−0.220 (0.086)	6.20 (4.76, 8.26)	6.20 (4.76, 8.26)	6.20 (4.76, 8.26)	NA
Include contemporaneous U	$\pi^e_t = \pi_{t-1}$	(12,12)	spline, 3 knots	−0.431 (0.138)	5.34 (4.14, 7.77)	7.33 (5.47, 8.69)	6.22 (4.30, 8.70)	1.03 (0.405)
Include contemporaneous U	recursive AR(12) forecast	(12,12)	spline, 3 knots	−0.766 (0.160)	5.75 (5.09, 6.78)	7.74 (7.08, 8.45)	5.94 (5.01, 6.89)	3.93 (0.001)
Lags chosen by BIC	$\pi^e_t = \pi_{t-1}$	(5,8)	constant	−0.203 (0.089)	6.17 (4.52, 8.35)	6.17 (4.52, 8.35)	6.17 (4.52, 8.35)	NA
Lags chosen by BIC	$\pi^e_t = \pi_{t-1}$	(5,8)	spline, 3 knots	−0.365 (0.123)	5.28 (3.81, 7.90)	7.31 (5.09, 8.93)	6.25 (3.95, 9.17)	0.75 (0.612)
Lags chosen by BIC	recursive AR(12) forecast	(2,1)	spline, 3 knots	−0.508 (0.130)	5.64 (4.69, 7.18)	7.71 (6.65, 8.81)	5.91 (4.41, 7.39)	1.75 (0.107)

Note: Base case is monthly (January 1955–December 1994), π from All-Items Urban CPI, All-Worker Unemployment

^{a}Standard errors are in parentheses.

$^b P$-values are in parentheses.

Table 5.6   **Sensitivity of Estimates of the NAIRU and β(1) to Other Changes in Specification**

Differences from Base Case	Formation of π^e	# of Lags $(U, \pi - \pi^e)$	Determinants of NAIRU	$\beta(1)$[a]	Selected Estimates of NAIRU (Gaussian 95% confidence interval)			F-Test of Constant NAIRU[b]
					1970:1	1980:1	1990:1	
None	$\pi_t^e = \pi_{t-1}$	(12,12)	spline, 4 knots	−0.409 (0.135)	5.20 (3.62, 8.65)	7.65 (5.40, 9.59)	6.30 (4.13, 9.07)	0.89 (0.511)
None	recursive AR(12) forecast	(12,12)	spline, 4 knots	−0.725 (0.157)	5.83 (4.95, 7.27)	7.85 (6.99, 8.73)	6.01 (4.99, 7.04)	3.53 (0.001)
None	$\pi_t^e = \pi_{t-1}$	(12,12)	3 breaks, estimated	−0.334 (0.124)	5.13 (3.80, 6.76)	9.23 (7.38, 16.29)	6.67 (4.72, 8.42)	3.33
None	recursive AR(12) forecast	(12,12)	3 breaks, estimated	−0.561 (0.150)	5.90 (4.76, 7.73)	8.83 (7.69, 10.92)	6.36 (5.38, 7.03)	6.89
None	$\pi_t^e = \pi_{t-1}$	(12,12)	4 breaks, estimated	−0.441 (0.148)	5.08 (4.17, 6.12)	8.64 (7.25, 12.22)	6.04 (4.44, 7.43)	2.72
None	recursive AR(12) forecast	(12,12)	4 breaks, estimated	−0.506 (0.148)	7.52 (5.67, 11.93)	9.40 (8.05, 12.61)	6.24 (4.99, 6.98)	6.50
None	$\pi_t^e = \pi_{t-1}$	(12,12)	2 breaks, fixed	−0.236 (0.099)	7.09 (5.26, 12.73)	7.09 (5.26, 12.73)	6.02 (0.78, 7.92)	1.02 (0.361)

(continued)

Table 5.6 (continued)

Differences from Base Case	Formation of π^e	# of Lags (U, $\pi-\pi^e$)	Determinants of NAIRU	$\beta(1)^a$	Selected Estimates of NAIRU (Gaussian) 95% confidence interval			F-Test of Constant NAIRU^b
					1970:1	1980:1	1990:1	
None	recursive AR(12) forecast	(12,12)	2 breaks, fixed	−0.341 (0.110)	7.69 (6.41, 11.22)	7.69 (6.41, 11.22)	6.20 (3.94, 7.45)	5.11 (0.006)
No supply shocks	$\pi^e_t = \pi_{t-1}$	(12,12)	constant	−0.235 (0.087)	6.17 (4.87, 7.86)	6.17 (4.87, 7.86)	6.17 (4.87, 7.86)	NA
No supply shocks	$\pi^e_t = \pi_{t-1}$	(12,12)	spline, 3 knots	−0.401 (0.140)	5.62 (4.37, 9.34)	7.28 (4.94, 8.81)	6.20 (3.96, 9.17)	1.07 (0.377)
No supply shocks	recursive AR(12) forecast	(12,12)	spline, 3 knots	−0.733 (0.161)	5.93 (5.21, 7.19)	7.72 (7.01, 8.49)	5.92 (4.91, 6.94)	3.95 (0.001)
Log unemployment	$\pi^e_t = \pi_{t-1}$	(12,12)	constant	−1.151 (0.490)	6.05 (4.35, 10.80)	6.05 (4.35, 10.80)	6.05 (4.35, 10.80)	NA
Log unemployment	$\pi^e_t = \pi_{t-1}$	(12,12)	spline, 3 knots	−2.338 (0.797)	5.10 (4.06, 8.67)	7.17 (4.85, 9.39)	6.23 (4.31, 10.70)	1.01 (0.419)
Log unemployment	recursive AR(12) forecast	(12,12)	spline, 3 knots	−4.913 (0.930)	5.42 (4.90, 6.30)	7.69 (6.96, 8.58)	5.93 (5.16, 6.82)	4.44 (0.000)

Note: Base case is monthly (January 1955–December 1994), π from All-Items Urban CPI, All-Worker Unemployment.

^{a}Standard errors are in parentheses.

^{b}P-values are in parentheses.

Table 5.7   **Selected Estimates of the NAIRU and β(1) Using Quarterly Data**

Differences from Base Case	Formation of π^e	# of Lags $(U, \pi - \pi^e)$	Determinants of NAIRU	$\beta(1)^a$	Selected Estimates of NAIRU (Gaussian 95% confidence interval) 1970:1	1980:1	1990:1	F-Test of Constant NAIRU[b]
None	$\pi_t^e = \pi_{t-1}$	(4,4)	constant	-0.242 (0.085)	6.20 (5.05, 7.70)	6.20 (5.05, 7.70)	6.20 (5.05, 7.70)	NA
None	recursive AR(4) forecast	(4,4)	constant	-0.244 (0.088)	6.35 (5.23, 8.17)	6.35 (5.23, 8.17)	6.35 (5.23, 8.17)	NA
None	$\pi_t^e = \pi_{t-1}$	(4,4)	spline, 3 knots	-0.448 (0.143)	5.51 (4.38, 7.66)	7.26 (5.54, 8.47)	6.15 (4.42, 8.29)	1.23 (0.293)
None	recursive AR(4) forecast	(4,4)	spline, 3 knots	-0.769 (0.161)	5.91 (5.20, 6.84)	7.78 (7.15, 8.47)	5.83 (4.96, 6.74)	5.94 (0.000)
None	$\pi_t^e = \pi_{t-1}$	(4,4)	2 breaks, estimated	-0.431 (0.117)	5.18 (4.37, 6.15)	8.34 (7.10, 10.83)	6.15 (4.72, 7.00)	7.59
None	recursive AR(4) forecast	(4,4)	2 breaks, estimated	-0.308 (0.099)	8.58 (7.02, 14.49)	5.84 (<-10, 10.19)	5.84 (2.91, 7.05)	10.46
Quarterly 55:I–93:IV	$\pi_t^e = \pi_{t-1}$	(4,4)	labor market variables	-0.691 (0.312)	4.91 (2.91, 7.00)	7.06 (5.26, 9.65)	5.85 (4.66, 8.97)	1.06 (0.389)
Quarterly 55:I–93:IV	recursive AR(4) forecast	(4,4)	labor market variables	-0.821 (0.326)	5.76 (4.22, 8.62)	7.63 (6.31, 10.12)	5.96 (4.83, 7.99)	3.79 (0.001)

(*continued*)

Table 5.7 (continued)

Differences from Base Case	Formation of π^e	# of Lags $(U, \pi-\pi^e)^a$	Determinants of NAIRU	$\beta(1)^a$	Selected Estimates of NAIRU (Gaussian 95% confidence interval)			F-Test of Constant NAIRU^b
					1970:1	1980:1	1990:1	
GDP deflator	$\pi^e_t = \pi_{t-1}$	(4,4)	constant	−0.168 (0.093)	5.97 (1.90, 10.03)	5.97 (1.90, 10.03)	5.97 (1.90, 10.03)	NA
GDP deflator	$\pi^e_t = \pi_{t-1}$	(4,4)	spline, 3 knots	−0.195 (0.145)	6.40 (−5.06, 17.85)	6.65 (−1.08, 14.37)	5.83 (0.08, 11.59)	0.20 (0.977)
GDP deflator	recursive AR(4) forecast	(4,4)	spline, 3 knots	−0.503 (0.183)	6.62 (5.53, 10.70)	7.50 (6.07, 8.75)	5.62 (3.58, 7.24)	2.86 (0.012)
Fixed-weight PCE deflator	$\pi^e_t = \pi_{t-1}$	(4,4)	constant	−0.213 (0.066)	6.21 (5.12, 7.63)	6.21 (5.12, 7.63)	6.21 (5.12, 7.63)	NA
Fixed-weight PCE deflator	$\pi^e_t = \pi_{t-1}$	(4,4)	spline, 3 knots	−0.374 (0.122)	5.57 (4.44, 7.97)	7.39 (5.68, 8.67)	5.92 (3.98, 7.96)	1.35 (0.241)
Fixed-weight PCE deflator	recursive AR(4) forecast	(4,4)	spline, 3 knots	−0.622 (0.142)	5.85 (5.11, 6.81)	7.87 (7.22, 8.63)	5.92 (5.01, 6.91)	4.14 (0.001)

Note: Base case is quarterly (first quarter 1955 to fourth quarter 1994), π from All-Items Urban CPI, All-Worker Unemployment.

^{a}Standard errors are in parentheses.

^{b}*P*-values are in parentheses.

Table 5.8   Sensitivity of Estimates of the NAIRU and β(1) to Alternative Models of πᵉ, Quarterly Data

Differences from Base Case	Formation of πᵉ	# of Lags $(U, \pi - \pi^e)$	Determinants of NAIRU	β(1)ᵃ	Selected Estimates of NAIRU (Gaussian 95% confidence interval)			F-Test of Constant NAIRUᵇ
					1970:1	1980:1	1990:1	
GDP deflator 71:I–94:IV	SPF forecast	(4,4)	constant	−0.223 (0.123)	NA	7.20 (3.87, 10.53)	7.20 (3.87, 10.53)	NA
GDP deflator 71:I–94:IV	SPF forecast	(4,4)	spline, 2 knots	−0.836 (0.178)	NA	8.00 (7.41, 8.86)	6.16 (5.50, 6.92)	3.99 (0.003)
GDP deflator 73:I–94:IV	SPF forecast	(2,2)	constant	−0.309 (0.122)	NA	7.20 (6.04, 9.17)	7.20 (6.04, 9.17)	NA
GDP deflator 73:I–94:IV lags chosen by BIC	SPF forecast	(2,1)	spline, 2 knots	−0.562 (0.118)	NA	7.92 (7.07, 9.10)	6.21 (5.30, 7.23)	4.52 (0.001)
Semiannual	Livingston forecast	(2,2)	constant	−0.284 (0.153)	7.07 (5.27, 12.27)	7.07 (5.27, 12.27)	7.07 (5.27, 12.27)	NA
Semiannual	Livingston forecast	(2,2)	spline, 3 knots	−0.782 (0.232)	7.07 (5.75, 9.69)	7.97 (7.00, 9.45)	6.06 (4.58, 7.76)	2.77 (0.018)
Semiannual lags chosen by BIC	Livingston forecast	(2,1)	constant	−0.308 (0.142)	7.11 (5.82, 11.95)	7.11 (5.82, 11.95)	7.11 (5.82, 11.95)	NA
Semiannual lags chosen by BIC	Livingston forecast	(2,1)	spline, 3 knots	−0.716 (0.227)	7.06 (5.69, 10.11)	7.94 (6.89, 9.57)	6.09 (4.46, 7.94)	2.70 (0.021)

Note: Base case is quarterly (first quarter 1955 to fourth quarter 1994), π from All-Items Urban CPI, All-Worker Unemployment.

ᵃStandard errors are in parentheses.

ᵇP-values are in parentheses.

with the timing of the Livingston forecasts (taken in June and December), while models using the SPF forecasts use the GDP deflator and limit the sample to first quarter 1971 to fourth quarter 1994 (or in some cases first quarter 1973 to fourth quarter 1994) because the SPF forecasts began only in fourth quarter 1968. For each forecast, we present both constant NAIRU and spline NAIRU models for baseline specifications (with one year of lags) and models in which lags are chosen by BIC. The estimates of the NAIRU over the entire sample for both these series are notably higher than for other methods of expectations formation. This is a consequence of the survey participants' underestimating inflation on average over the history of the surveys. Otherwise the estimates are generally similar to earlier tables. The exception is the rather tight confidence intervals based on the SPF forecast in the spline model with one year of lags.

Table 5.9 further investigates the performance of models of the NAIRU based on labor market variables. For our base specifications, we report results when the NAIRU is modeled using various subsets of the labor market variables discussed in section 5.3.3. It is apparent that no combination of these labor market variables yields precise estimates of the NAIRU. The most precise Gaussian confidence interval for the NAIRU in January 1990 is (4.26, 6.38), which is for a specification that uses all of the labor market variables. In the models using monthly data, the only determinant of the NAIRU that is individually significant is the unemployment exit hazard, and it has the expected negative relationship with the NAIRU. In the models using quarterly data, the only determinant of the NAIRU that is individually significant is the fraction of the labor force in their teens. A larger fraction of teens is associated with a higher NAIRU, as would be expected. As a group, the demographic variables tend to be the most significant predictors of the NAIRU, primarily in models with recursive forecasts of inflation. On balance, the labor market variables appear to enter the model as expected, but fail to provide estimates of the NAIRU any more precise than do the statistical models.

The one set of specifications in which it is possible to obtain tight confidence intervals is that which includes long lags of inflation. Several such specifications are reported in table 5.10. To facilitate a comparison with delta-method standard errors reported by Fuhrer (1995) and King, Stock, and Watson (1995), in this table the delta-method standard error is reported in brackets. The first specification is essentially the specification in Fuhrer (1995) and Tootell (1994) (they use only one quarterly lag of unemployment); the delta-method standard error of 0.37 in table 5.10 is similar to the delta-method standard error reported by Fuhrer (1995) of 0.33. (The specifications in table 5.10 are for quarterly data, but tight confidence intervals can also be obtained using thirty-six lags of $\Delta\pi_t$ with monthly data.) However, the more reliable Gaussian confidence intervals remain relatively large. Furthermore, the Akaike information criterion (AIC) and BIC choose the substantially shorter lags (2, 3), for which the delta-method standard error is 0.84. Moreover, a conventional F-test of the

Table 5.9   Sensitivity of Estimates of the NAIRU and $\beta(1)$ to Alternative Labor Market Models of the NAIRU

Difference from Base Case	Formation of π^e	# of Lags $(U, \pi - \pi^e)$	Determinants of NAIRU	$\beta(1)^a$	Selected Estimates of NAIRU (Gaussian 95% confidence interval) 1970:1	1980:1	1990:1	F-Test of Constant NAIRU[b]
55:01–93:12	$\pi_t^e = \pi_{t-1}$	(12,12)	demographics, institutions, exit hazard	−0.889 (0.260)	4.96 (3.24, 5.49)	6.93 (5.63, 8.02)	5.43 (4.08, 6.46)	1.44 (0.186)
55:01–93:12	recursive AR(12) forecast	(12,12)	demographics, institutions, exit hazard	−0.973 (0.267)	5.52 (4.06, 6.41)	7.33 (6.28, 8.45)	5.46 (4.26, 6.38)	3.61 (0.001)
55:01–93:12	$\pi_t^e = \pi_{t-1}$	(12,12)	demographics, institutions	−0.435 (0.175)	5.44 (3.47, 9.00)	7.68 (4.51, 10.29)	6.35 (3.41–9.24)	0.49 (0.815)
55:01–93:12	recursive AR(12) forecast	(12,12)	demographics, institutions	−0.611 (0.195)	6.22 (5.16, 8.66)	8.10 (6.75, 9.81)	6.03 (4.34, 7.48)	2.84 (0.010)
55:01–93:12	$\pi_t^e = \pi_{t-1}$	(12,12)	demographics	−0.264 (0.101)	6.30 (3.67, 10.20)	6.91 (4.96, 10.36)	6.43 (2.48, 9.13)	0.44 (0.725)
55:01–93:12	recursive AR(12) forecast	(12,12)	demographics	−0.426 (0.112)	6.91 (5.76, 8.90)	7.72 (6.81, 9.60)	6.36 (4.74, 7.66)	4.62 (0.003)
55:01–93:12	$\pi_t^e = \pi_{t-1}$	(12,12)	exit hazard	−0.456 (0.183)	5.15 (3.27, 7.52)	6.08 (5.34, 7.00)	5.53 (4.68, 7.09)	2.62 (0.106)

(continued)

Table 5.9 (continued)

Difference from Base Case	Formation of π^e	# of Lags $(U, \pi - \pi^e)$	Determinants of NAIRU	$\beta(1)$[a]	Selected Estimates of NAIRU (Gaussian 95% confidence interval) 1970:1	1980:1	1990:1	F-Test of Constant NAIRU[b]
55:01–93:12	recursive AR(12) forecast	(12,12)	exit hazard	−0.350 (0.181)	5.67 (3.53, 10.39)	6.28 (5.45, 8.64)	5.92 (4.87, 9.53)	0.630 (0.428)
Quarterly 55:I–93:IV	$\pi^e_t = \pi_{t-1}$	(4,4)	demographics, institutions, exit hazard	−0.691 (0.312)	4.91 (2.91, 7.00)	7.06 (5.26, 9.65)	5.85 (4.66, 8.97)	1.06 (0.389)
Quarterly 55:I–93:IV	recursive AR(4) forecast	(4,4)	demographics, institutions exit hazard	−0.821 (0.326)	5.76 (4.22, 8.62)	7.63 (6.31, 10.12)	5.96 (4.83, 7.99)	3.79 (0.001)
Quarterly 55:I–93:IV	$\pi^e_t = \pi_{t-1}$	(4,4)	demographics, institutions	−0.417 (0.171)	4.93 (2.71, 7.69)	7.34 (4.84, 10.22)	6.60 (4.72, 9.92)	1.04 (0.400)
Quarterly 55:I–93:IV	recursive AR(4) forecast	(4,4)	demographics, institutions	−0.619 (0.187)	6.07 (5.10, 8.09)	7.99 (6.92, 9.64)	6.38 (4.97, 7.93)	4.30 (0.001)
Quarterly 55:I–93:IV	$\pi^e_t = \pi_{t-1}$	(4,4)	exit hazard	−0.334 (0.192)	5.73 (3.56, 9.63)	6.26 (5.15, 8.37)	5.93 (4.97, 8.79)	0.38 (0.536)
Quarterly 55:I–93:IV	recursive AR(4) forecast	(4,4)	exit hazard	−0.143 (0.188)	7.89 (−17.13, 32.91)	6.52 (0.93, 12.10)	7.37 (−9.35, 24.08)	0.44 (0.510)

Note: Base case is monthly (January 1955–December 1994), π from All-Items Urban CPI, All-Worker Unemployment.

[a]Standard errors are in parentheses.

[b]P-values are in parentheses.

Table 5.10   Sensitivity of Estimates of the NAIRU and β(1) to Long Lags

Differences from Base Case	Formation of πᵉ	# of Lags $(U, \pi - \pi^e)$	Determinants of NAIRU	$\beta(1)$[a]	Selected Estimates of NAIRU (Gaussian 95% confidence interval)[b]			F-Test of Constant NAIRU[c]
					1970:1	1980:1	1990:1	
None	$\pi^e_t = \pi_{t-1}$	(2,12)	constant	−0.295 (0.123)	6.01 (4.76, 7.20) [0.37]	6.01 (4.76, 7.20) [0.37]	6.01 (4.76, 7.20) [0.37]	NA
Lags chosen by BIC (same as AIC)	$\pi^e_t = \pi_{t-1}$	(2,3)	constant	−0.136 (0.084)	6.00 (0.95, 11.05) [0.84]	6.00 (0.95, 11.05) [0.84]	6.00 (0.95, 11.05) [0.84]	NA
None	$\pi^e_t = \pi_{t-1}$	(2,12)	spline, 3 knots	−0.451 (0.179)	6.53 (5.31, 10.99) [0.74]	6.68 (3.45, 7.92) [0.56]	5.93 (3.65, 8.21) [0.38]	1.06 (0.389)
Lags chosen by BIC (same as AIC)	$\pi^e_t = \pi_{t-1}$	(2,3)	spline, 3 knots	−0.084 (0.124)	9.35 (−35.06, 53.76) [7.40]	5.25 (−20.69, 31.18) [4.32]	5.71 (−7.36, 18.79) [2.18]	0.31 (0.930)
None	recursive AR(4) forecast	(2,12)	constant	−0.200 (0.102)	6.16 (2.84, 9.49) [0.55]	6.16 (2.84, 9.49) [0.55]	6.16 (2.84, 9.49) [0.55]	NA
Lags chosen by AIC	recursive AR(4) forecast	(2,3)	constant	−0.208 (0.097)	6.15 (4.33, 8.69) [0.54]	6.15 (4.33, 8.69) [0.54]	6.15 (4.33, 8.69) [0.54]	NA
Lags chosen by BIC	recursive AR(4) forecast	(2,1)	constant	−0.257 (0.086)	6.11 (5.01, 7.33) [0.44]	6.11 (5.01, 7.33) [0.44]	6.11 (5.01, 7.33) [0.44]	NA
None	recursive AR(4) forecast	(2,12)	spline, 3 knots	−0.657 (0.202)	6.90 (5.92, 9.30) [0.58]	7.58 (6.78, 8.53) [0.32]	5.61 (4.31, 6.71) [0.26]	3.60 (0.002)
Lags chosen by AIC	recursive AR(4) forecast	(3,6)	spline, 3 knots	−0.760 (0.203)	6.42 (5.67, 7.79) [0.45]	7.56 (6.87, 8.26) [0.28]	5.67 (4.68, 6.59) [0.23]	4.94 (0.000)

(continued)

Table 5.10 (continued)

Differences from Base Case	Formation of π^e	# of Lags $(U,\ \pi-\pi^e)$	Determinants of NAIRU	$\beta(1)$[a]	Selected Estimates of NAIRU (Gaussian 95% confidence interval)[b]				F-Test of Constant NAIRU[c]
					1970:1	1980:1	1990:1		
Lags chosen by BIC	recursive AR(4) forecast	(2,1)	spline, 3 knots	−0.350 (0.119)	7.28 (5.72, 13.53) [1.13]	7.43 (5.44, 9.22) [0.65]	5.53 (2.62, 7.81) [0.53]		2.74 (0.015)
73:I–94:IV	SPF forecast	(2,8)	constant	−0.160 (0.117)	NA	6.92 (2.75, 11.09) [0.70]	6.92 (2.75, 11.09) [0.70]		NA
Lags chosen by AIC 73:I–94:IV	SPF forecast	(3,4)	constant	−0.217 (0.115)	NA	7.05 (3.90, 10.21) [0.53]	7.05 (3.90, 10.21) [0.53]		NA
Lags chosen by BIC 73:I–94:IV	SPF forecast	(2,2)	constant	−0.309 (0.122)	NA	7.20 (6.04, 9.17) [0.38]	7.20 (6.04, 9.17) [0.38]		NA
73:I–94:IV	SPF forecast	(2, 8)	spline, 2 knots	−1.067 (0.202)	NA	8.45 (7.98, 9.17) [0.24]	6.23 (5.74, 6.69) [0.13]		8.60 (0.000)
Lags chosen by AIC 73:I–94:IV	SPF forecast	(3, 8)	spline, 2 knots	−1.196 (0.204)	NA	8.37 (7.98, 8.99) [0.22]	6.19 (5.77, 6.59) [0.13]		8.34 (0.000)
Lags chosen by BIC 73:I–94:IV	SPF forecast	(2,1)	spline 2 knots	−0.562 (0.118)	NA	7.92 (7.07, 9.10) [0.40]	6.21 (5.30, 7.23) [0.28]		4.52 (0.00.)

Note: Base case is quarterly (first quarter 1955 to fourth quarter 1994), π from All-Items Urban CPI, All-Worker Unemployment

[a]Standard errors are in parentheses.

[b]Standard errors in brackets are for delta method.

[c]*P*-values are in parentheses.

significance of the additional nine lags of inflation in the first specification has a p-value of .49. Thus the statistical support for the long-lag specification appears to us to be thin.

Similar or tighter confidence intervals obtain when three years of lags are used with the spine NAIRU models. For example, when π_t^e is constructed by recursive AR(4) for the spline model, the delta-method standard error for the NAIRU in the first quarter of 1990 is less than 0.3, although once again the Gaussian confidence interval remains relatively large. However, the additional lags in the (2,12) and AIC specifications are statistically insignificant at the 5% level, relative to the BIC-chosen lags of (2,1), for which the delta-method standard error is 0.53.

The tightest confidence intervals occur for long-lag specifications using the SPF forecast for π_t^e. (Because these models are estimated over a shorter time span, the maximum number of lags is set to two years for the AIC and BIC specifications with the SPF forecast.) The AIC specification with spline NAIRU has a delta-method standard error of 0.13 in the first quarter of 1990, and the Gaussian confidence interval is similarly tight. Unlike the other long-lag specifications, these additional lags are significant at the 5% (but not at the 1%) significance level, relative to the BIC-chosen lags. Note that the point estimate of $\beta(1)$ in these long-lag specifications with SPF inflation expectations is substantially larger than for the other specifications. In our view, the apparently tight estimates for the NAIRU in these specifications reflect overfitting the model, given the relatively short time span.

Our main conclusion from these long-lag results is that, for selected combinations of unemployment series and inflationary expectations, it is possible to estimate apparently tight confidence intervals for the NAIRU when long lags of inflation and a flexible NAIRU model are used. However, the additional lags necessary to obtain these tight intervals are not selected by the BIC and indeed are not statistically significant, with a single exception. The statistical evidence for using these long lags is therefore lacking, and the associated tight intervals therefore are plausibly statistical artifacts that are a consequence of overfitting.

Time series of estimates of the NAIRU and associated (pointwise) confidence intervals are presented in figures 5.6–5.10 for selected alternative specifications. The TVP estimate of the NAIRU and its confidence interval are plotted in figure 5.6 for the case $\lambda = .15$, with inflationary expectations formed as $\pi_t^e = \pi_{t-1}$. For the TVP model, the highest value of the likelihood occurs at $\lambda = 0$, corresponding to a constant NAIRU. However, this estimation problem is similar to the problem of estimating a moving average root when the root is close to one, and the maximum likelihood estimator (MLE) can have a mass point at zero when the true value is small but nonzero.

Figures 5.3–5.10 provide an opportunity to compare the delta-method and Gaussian confidence intervals. The delta-method confidence intervals are typically tighter. Generally, however, the two sets of confidence intervals have sim-

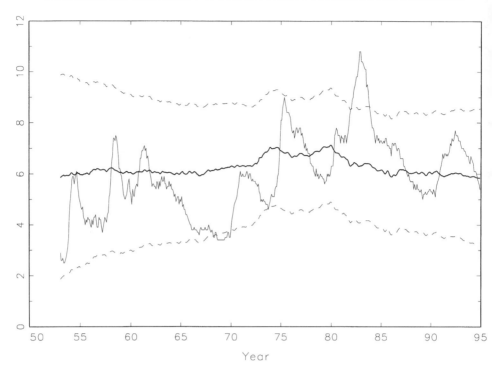

Fig. 5.6   TVP estimate of NAIRU (*thick line*), 95% delta-method confidence interval (*dashes*), and unemployment rate (*thin line*)

Notes: $\lambda = 0.15$, $\pi_t^e = \pi_{t-1}$, monthly, January 1953–December 1944.

ilar qualitative features. In many cases, the confidence intervals contain most observed values of unemployment. An exception to this is the confidence intervals based on the Livingston and SPF forecast. For example, according to the Livingston estimates, unemployment was outside the 95% confidence band, and indeed far (over 2 percentage points) below the point estimate of the NAIRU, for most of the fifteen years from 1965 to 1980 fig. 5.10). Mechanically, the explanation for this is that during this period the Livingston forecast systematically underpredicted inflation. This consistent misestimation of even the average level of inflation raises questions about the reliability of this forecast as a basis for the NAIRU calculations. In particular, this casts further doubt on the relatively precise estimates found in table 5.10 using the SPF survey.

These results confirm the finding in table 5.1 that the NAIRU is measured quite imprecisely. This conclusion is insensitive to model specification. It is not solely a consequence of the NAIRU being nearly unidentified when $\beta(1)$ is near zero, because comparable confidence intervals obtain when the NAIRU is estimated using the univariate unemployment model. Because of the nonlinearity of the estimator of the NAIRU, delta-method confidence intervals may

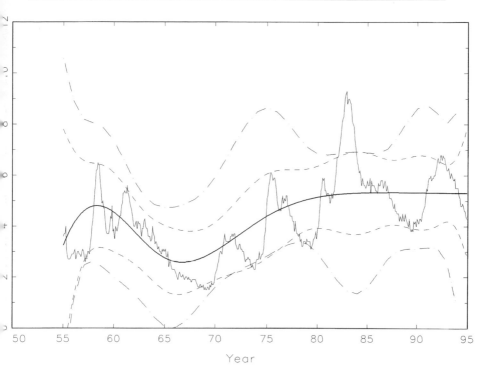

Fig. 5.7   Spline estimate of NAIRU, 95% Gaussian confidence interval (*long dashes*), delta-method confidence interval (*short dashes*), and unemployment
Notes: $\pi_t^e = \pi_{t-1}$, monthly, January 1955–December 1994, (12,12) lags, CPI, prime age male unemployment.

have poor coverage rates, and we have therefore relied on Gaussian confidence intervals instead. Although the empirical Gaussian confidence intervals are typically wider than delta-method confidence intervals, as can be seen from the figures, the general conclusions are little changed by using delta-method intervals instead.

5.6   Discussion and Conclusions

There are at least three different types of uncertainty that produce imprecision of the estimates of the NAIRU. The first is the uncertainty arising from not knowing the parameters of the model at hand. All the confidence intervals presented in this paper incorporate this source of imprecision, and the Monte Carlo results in section 5.4 suggest that the Gaussian confidence intervals provide reliable and accurate measures of this imprecision.

A second source of uncertainty arises from the possibly stochastic nature of the NAIRU, and only the TVP confidence intervals include this additional source. Consider for example the break model of the NAIRU. In the implemen-

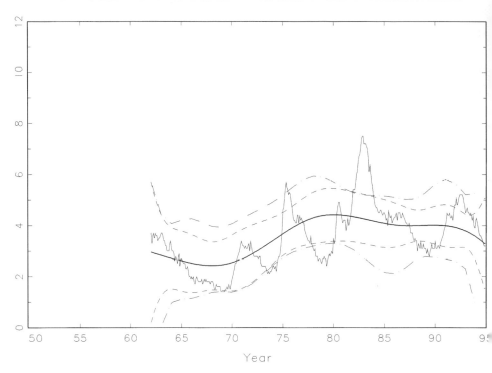

Fig. 5.8   **Spline estimate of NAIRU, 95% Gaussian confidence interval (*long dashes*), delta-method confidence interval (*short dashes*), and unemployment**
Notes: $\pi_t^e = \pi_{t-1}$, monthly, January 1962–December 1994, (12,12) lags, CPI excluding food and energy, married-male unemployment.

tation here, the breaks are treated as occurring nonrandomly and, once they have occurred, are treated as if they are known with certainty. An extension of this model, which is arguably more plausible on *a priori* grounds, would be that the NAIRU switches stochastically among several regimes, and that at a given date it is unknown which regime the NAIRU is in. While the point estimates of the NAIRU in this regime-switching model might not be particularly different from those for the deterministic break model, the confidence intervals presumably would be, because the stochastic-regime model intervals would incorporate the additional uncertainty of not knowing the current regime. The TVP model incorporates this additional source of uncertainty because the NAIRU is explicitly treated as unobserved and following a stochastic path. From our perspective, it is desirable to incorporate both sources of uncertainty in construction of confidence intervals. However, incorporating the second source of uncertainty increases the computational burden dramatically, so it would have been impractical to estimate the large number of models reported here using an explicitly stochastic model of the NAIRU. As a consequence, the confidence intervals for the NAIRU for the spline and break models arguably

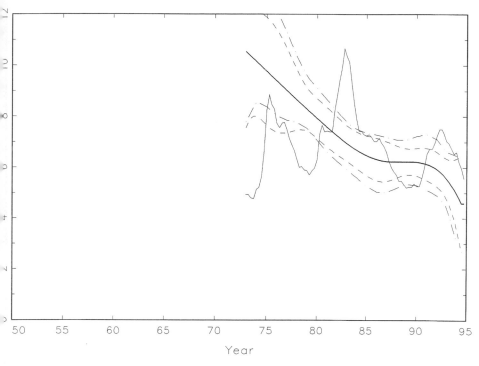

Fig. 5.9   Spline estimate of NAIRU, 95% Gaussian confidence interval (*long dashes*), delta-method confidence interval (*short dashes*), and unemployment

Notes: π_t^e = Survey of Professional Forecasters, quarterly, first quarter 1973–fourth quarter 1994, BIC lags, GDP deflator, total unemployment.

understate the actual imprecision that arises from unpredictable movements in the NAIRU itself.

A third source of uncertainty arises from the choice of specification (in textbook terminology, not knowing which of the models is "true"). To the extent that imprecision of estimates of the NAIRU has been mentioned in the literature, it has tended to be this type of uncertainty, as quantified by a range of point estimates from alternative, arguably equally plausible specifications. None of the confidence intervals presented in this paper formally incorporate this uncertainty. However, a comparison of the point estimates and confidence intervals in tables 5.3–5.10 for plausible alternative specifications indicates that informally incorporating this additional source further increases the uncertainty surrounding the actual value of the NAIRU.

A central conclusion from this analysis is that a wide range of values of the NAIRU are consistent with the empirical evidence. However, the unemployment rate and changes in the unemployment rate are useful predictors of future changes in inflation. While these two results might seem contradictory, they need not be; in principal, changes in unemployment could be strongly related

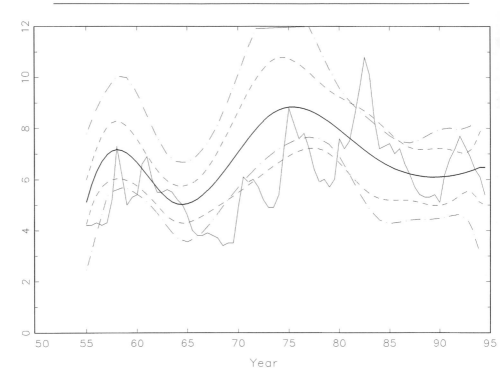

Fig. 5.10   Spline estimate of NAIRU, 95% Gaussian confidence interval (*long dashes*), delta-method confidence interval (*short dashes*), and unemployment
Notes: π_t^e = Livingston survey, semiannual, first half 1955–second half 1994, BIC lags, CPI, total unemployment.

to future changes of inflation, but the level of unemployment could enter with a negligibly small coefficient. In most of the specifications here, this slope, $\beta(1)$, is small (in the range -0.25 to -0.45) and imprecisely measured, although it is statistically significantly different from zero. This corresponds to the lesson from figure 5.1 that the value of unemployment corresponding to a stable rate of inflation is imprecisely measured, even though an increase in unemployment will on average be associated with a decline in future rates of inflation.

It should be cautioned that the conclusion of imprecision relates to conventional methods of estimating the NAIRU and to several time-varying extensions. Although we have examined a large range of specifications and found this conclusion robust, future research might produce new, more precise methods of estimating the NAIRU.

An obvious next step is the analysis of monetary policy rules in light of these findings. We do not undertake a thorough investigation here but offer some initial thoughts on the matter. Recent work on monetary policy in the presence of measurement error (for example Kuttner 1992; Cecchetti 1995) is consistent with placing less weight on poorly measured targets. In this spirit, a trigger strategy, in which monetary policy takes a neutral stance until unemployment hits the natural rate and then responds vigorously, is unlikely to produce the desired outcomes because the trigger point (the natural rate) is poorly estimated. Clearly, under a trigger strategy it matters whether the NAIRU is five or seven percentage points. In contrast, a rule in which monetary policy responds not to the level of the unemployment rate but to recent changes in unemployment without reference to the NAIRU (and perhaps to a measure of the deviation of inflation from a target rate of inflation) is immune to the imprecision of measurement that is highlighted in this paper. An interesting question is the construction of formal policy rules that account for the imprecision of estimation of the NAIRU.

Appendix
Results of Monte Carlo Experiment Comparing Delta-Method and Gaussian Confidence Intervals

Table 5A.1   **Finite Sample Coverage Rates of Delta-Method and Gaussian Confidence Intervals**

| | | Quantiles of Delta-Method t-Statistic | | | Monte Carlo Coverage Rages | | | |
| | | | | | Delta Method | | Gaussian | |
$\beta(1)$	$\bar{u}$	0.10	0.50	0.90	90%	95%	90%	95%
A. Errors Drawn from the Empirical Distribution								
−0.26	6.18	−0.92	−0.01	0.82	0.98	0.99	0.89	0.94
−0.03	10.04	−4.96	−1.21	0.03	0.58	0.64	0.89	0.94
−0.07	5.63	−0.55	0.09	1.04	0.96	0.98	0.88	0.94
−0.40	5.45	−0.92	−0.04	1.16	0.96	0.98	0.88	0.94
B. Gaussian Errors								
−0.26	6.18	−0.92	0.00	0.84	0.98	0.99	0.88	0.94
−0.03	10.04	−4.75	−1.19	0.03	0.59	0.64	0.89	0.94
−0.07	5.63	−0.56	0.09	1.01	0.96	0.98	0.09	0.94
−0.40	5.45	−0.90	−0.05	1.13	0.96	0.99	0.89	0.94

Notes: Data generated using a restricted VAR(1) as described in the text. Based on 10,000 Monte Carlo replications, with eighty observations (plus sixty startup draws).

Table 5A.2   **Finite-Sample Power of Delta-Method and Gaussian Confidence Tests, Probability of Rejecting the Null Hypothesis $\bar{u}_H$ 6.18**

	Size Unadjusted (asymptotic critical values)				Size Adjusted (adjusted critical values)			
	Delta Method		Gaussian		Delta Method		Gaussian	
$\bar{u}$	10%	5%	10%	5%	10%	5%	10%	5%
2.00	0.56	0.46	1.00	0.99	0.74	0.66	1.00	0.99
3.00	0.55	0.43	0.98	0.97	0.73	0.65	0.98	0.97
4.00	0.47	0.34	0.90	0.84	0.70	0.60	0.89	0.83
5.00	0.22	0.13	0.53	0.41	0.48	0.35	0.50	0.38
6.00	0.03	0.01	0.12	0.07	0.12	0.06	0.11	0.06
6.18	0.02	0.01	0.11	0.06	0.10	0.05	0.10	0.05
7.00	0.08	0.04	0.35	0.24	0.28	0.16	0.32	0.21
8.00	0.32	0.19	0.84	0.75	0.62	0.48	0.82	0.73
9.00	0.47	0.33	0.98	0.97	0.71	0.61	0.98	0.96
10.00	0.51	0.39	1.00	0.99	0.72	0.63	1.00	0.99

Notes: Data generated using a restricted VAR(1) with $\beta(1) = -0.26$, as described in the text. The column headers 10% and 5% refer to the nominal level of the test (this is 100% minus the nominal confidence level of the associated confidence interval). The size-unadjusted results are the rejection rates computed using the asymptotic critical value from the χ_1^2 distribution. The size-adjusted results are computed using the finite-sample critical value taken from the Monte Carlo distribution of the test statistic computed under the null $\bar{u} = 6.18$. Based on 10,000 Monte Carlo replications, with eighty observations (plus sixty startup draws).

References

Ansley, Craig F., and Robert Kohn. 1986. Prediction Mean Squared Error for State Space Models with Estimated Parameters. *Biometrika* 73:467–73.

Bai, Jushan. 1995. Estimating Multiple Breaks One at a Time. Department of Economics, MIT. Manuscript.

Bertola, Giuseppe, and Ricardo Caballero. 1993. Cross Sectional Efficiency and Labor Hoarding in a Matching Model of Unemployment. NBER Working Paper no. 4472. Cambridge, MA: National Bureau of Economic Research.

Blanchard, Olivier, and Peter Diamond. 1989. The Beveridge Curve. *Brookings Paper on Economic Activity* 1:1–60.

———. 1990. The Cyclical Behavior of the Gross Flows of U.S. Workers. *Brookings Papers on Economic Activity* 2:85–143.

Cecchetti, S. 1995. Inflation Indicators and Inflation Policy. *NBER Macroeconomics Annual* 1995: 189–219.

Congressional Budget Office. 1994. Reestimating the NAIRU. In *The Economic and Budget Outlook*. Washington, DC: Government Printing Office, August.

Cooley, T. F., and E. C. Prescott. 1973a. An Adaptive Regression Model. *International Economic Review* 14:364–71.

——. 1973b. Tests of an Adaptive Regression Model. *Review of Economics and Statistics* 55:248–56.

——. 1976. Estimation in the Presence of Stochastic Parameter Variation. *Econometrica* 44:167–84.

Davis, Steve, and John Haltiwanger. 1992. Gross Job Creation, Gross Job Destruction, and Employment Reallocation. *Quarterly Journal of Economics* 107:819–64.

Dickey, D. A., and W. A. Fuller. 1979. Distribution of the Estimators for Autoregressive Time Series with a Unit Root. *Journal of the American Statistical Association* 74:427–31.

Eisner, Robert. 1995. A New View of the NAIRU. Northwestern University, July. Manuscript.

Fieller, E. C. 1954. Some Problems in Interval Estimation. *Journal of the Royal Statistical Society,* Ser. B, 16:175–85.

Fuhrer, Jeffrey C. 1995. The Phillips Curve Is Alive and Well. *New England Economic Review of the Federal Reserve Bank of Boston,* March–April, 41–56.

Gordon, Robert J. 1982. Price Inertia and Ineffectiveness in the United States. *Journal of Political Economy* 90:1087–1117.

——. 1990. What Is New-Keynesian Economics? *Journal of Economic Literature* 28:1115–71.

——. 1997. The Time-Varying NAIRU and Its Implications for Economic Policy. *Journal of Economic Perspectives.* In press.

King, Robert G., James H. Stock, and Mark W. Watson. 1995. Temporal Instability of the Unemployment-Inflation Relationship. *Economic Perspectives of the Federal Reserve Bank of Chicago,* May–June, 2–12.

King, Robert G., and Mark W. Watson. 1994. The Postwar U.S. Phillips Curve: A Revisionist Econometric History. *Carnegie-Rochester Conference Series on Public Policy.* 41 (December): 157–219.

Kuttner, K. N. 1992. Monetary Policy with Uncertain Estimates of Potential Output. *Economic Perspectives* (Federal Reserve Bank of Chicago) 16 (January–February):2–15.

——. 1994. Estimating Potential Output as a Latent Variable. *Journal of Business and Economic Statistics.* 12:361–68.

Layard, Richard, Stephen Nickell, and Richard Jackman. 1991. *Unemployment: Macroeconomic Performance and the Labor Market.* New York: Oxford University Press.

Rosenberg, B. 1972. The Estimation of Stationary Stochastic Regression Parameters Re-Examined. *Journal of the American Statistical Association* 67:650–54.

——. 1973. The Analysis of a Cross-Section of Time Series by Stochastically Convergent Parameter Regression. *Annals of Economic and Social Measurement* 2:461–84.

Sarris, A. H. 1973. A Bayesian Approach to Estimation of Time Varying Regression Coefficients. *Annals of Economic and Social Measurement* 2:501–23.

Setterfield, M. A., D. V. Gordon, and L. Osberg. 1992. Searching for a Will o' the Wisp: An Empirical Study of the NAIRU in Canada. *European Economic Review* 36:119–36.

Staiger, Douglas, James H. Stock, and Mark W. Watson. 1997. The NAIRU, Unemployment, and Monetary Policy. *Journal of Economic Perspectives*, in press.

Stock, James H. 1991. Confidence Intervals for the Largest Autoregressive Root in U.S. Economic Time Series. *Journal of Monetary Economics* 28:435–60.

Tootell, Geoffrey M. B. 1994. Restructuring, the NAIRU, and the Phillips Curve. *New England Economic Review of the Federal Reserve Bank of Boston,* September–October, 31–44.

van Norden, Simon. 1995. Why Is It So Hard to Measure the Current Output Gap? International Department, Bank of Canada. Manuscript.

Weiner, Stuart E. 1993. New Estimates of the Natural Rate of Unemployment. *Economic Review of the Federal Reserve Bank of Kansas,* fourth quarter, 53–69.
Zarnowitz, Victor, and Phillip Braun. 1993. Twenty-two Years of the NBER-ASA Quarterly Economic Outlook Surveys: Aspects and Comparisons of Forecasting Performance. In *Business Cycles, Indicators, and Forecasting,* ed. James H. Stock and Mark W. Watson, 11–84. Chicago: University of Chicago Press.

Comment   Alan B. Krueger

The twin facts that the U.S. unemployment rate has been below 6%—which many economists and macro textbooks consider the natural rate of unemployment—for over fourteen straight months, while the inflation rate has remained comfortably below 3% with little sign of acceleration for three years, have set off a debate on whether the natural rate has declined. This paper moves this debate forward, about as far forward as the time-series data would permit.

The paper raises an important question: How well can we measure the natural rate? Surprisingly, hardly any paper in the previous literature has estimated the standard error of the natural rate. To fill this void, Staiger, Stock, and Watson estimate a wide variety of models that are common in the literature—indeed, the total number of parameters they estimate exceeds the total number of monthly observations in their sample. Because the natural rate in an inflation-unemployment Phillips curve is a nonlinear function of the estimated parameters, calculating the standard error of the natural rate is not entirely straightforward. Staiger, Stock, and Watson use two methods for calculating the standard error and confidence interval for the natural rate: the delta method and a "Gaussian" procedure. Their Monte Carlo results tend to favor the Gaussian method, which tends to yield larger confidence intervals. It is unusual to find a paper that devotes more attention to the standard errors of the estimates than to the estimates themselves; it is even more unusual to be interested in a paper for precisely that reason.

Their findings are sobering. For two reasons, the data are incapable of distinguishing between a wide range of estimates of the natural rate. First, a variety of plausible models yield widely differing estimates of the natural rate at a point in time (e.g., models with varying assumptions about expectations, or models that include varying explanatory variables). For example, the point estimates of the natural rate in table 5.2 range from 5.4 to 6.4% in 1990. Second, as the authors stress, the standard errors of the estimated natural rates are quite large—a typical 95% confidence interval runs from 5 to 8%. Staiger, Stock, and Watson conclude that this range is too wide to make monetary policy on without explicitly taking into account measurement error. This conclusion is

Alan B. Krueger is the Bendheim Professor of Economics and Public Affairs at Princeton University and a research associate of the National Bureau of Economic Research.

almost too timid. Based on their findings, I think an alternative title for this paper could be "We Don't Know What the Natural Rate Is, and Neither Do You." Even with forty-two years of monthly time-series observations, the data just do not provide precise estimates.

A natural follow-up question to ask is, How long will it be until we have a precise estimate of the natural rate? For example, how many more months of data are required to bring the standard error down to an acceptable level, say 0.25? Assuming the model is covariance stationary, this would require roughly four times as many observations as are currently available. By my calculation, it will be another 126 years before the 95% confidence interval is within plus or minus 0.5%. That is a long time to wait.

I don't see any reason to quarrel with the basic conclusion of the paper— that the natural rate is imprecisely estimated. Instead, I make some comments on the literature, and on the possible implications of Staiger, Stock, and Watson's findings.

Specific Comments on Estimation

Given the difficulty of precisely estimating the natural rate, I wonder if the focus of this literature should shift more toward $\beta(1)$—the effect of a change in the unemployment rate on inflation. As the paper points out, all estimates of $\beta(1)$ that it finds are negative. This strongly suggests that the Phillips curve slopes down. But I'm a little surprised that in at least some of their specifications Staiger, Stock, and Watson (and the previous literature) do not allow $\beta(1)$ to change over time. Some structural changes in the labor market would affect the slope as well as the intercept of the Phillips curve. For example, an increase (or decrease) in labor's share will mean that a given wage change will translate into a larger (smaller) price change.

An important issue concerns the interpretation of the natural rate in the "labor market models." The literature tends to derive the natural rate as the ratio of the intercept to the slope coefficient on the unemployment rate (ignoring lags), whether or not labor market variables are included as regressors in the regression. An alternative approach would be to add the labor market variables times their coefficients to the intercept, at a specified level of the labor market variables. For example, the natural rate might have fallen because the union rate has declined. In the alternative approach, the current union rate times the coefficient on the union rate could be added to the intercept, and then divided by the coefficient on the unemployment rate, to derive the current natural rate. It is of interest to policymakers to know what the natural rate is at the *current* level of unionization, not at some fixed level.

Another issue that affects Phillips curve estimates involves the redesign of the Current Population Survey (CPS), which is used to measure the unemployment rate. In January 1994, the Bureau of Labor Statistics (BLS) introduced a major redesign of the CPS. The redesign was widely expected to influence the measured unemployment rate. As it turns out, I think this is not a critical issue for the present paper for two reasons, which are interesting in their own right. First, the CPS redesign took place in January 1994, so it only affects one year's worth of data in the analysis. Second, and more important, in contrast to their initial research, the latest BLS research indicates that the CPS redesign has had very little effect on measured unemployment, probably increasing the official unemployment rate by 0.1 to 0.2 percentage points.

The BLS conducted a separate "parallel" survey that asked the new questionnaire in the eighteen months preceding the start of the redesign (see Polivka 1996). The parallel survey showed that the unemployment rate was 0.6 points higher than the standard CPS. However, this is not the end of the story. The BLS continued the parallel survey after the redesign was implemented, now giving the parallel sample the old CPS questionnaire. As figure 5C.1 shows, to everyone's surprise the parallel sample continued to have a higher unemployment rate even after the questionnaires were switched in January 1994, about 0.4 points higher. What is going on? The parallel sample was not selected in the same way as the CPS sample; it was based on an unused sample for a crime survey. The samples do not seem to be representative of the same populations. The redesign increases the measured unemployment rate by at least 0.1% because new 1990 census weights (which adjusted for the census undercount) were used in the redesigned CPS, and the unemployment rate is 0.1% higher with the 1990 weights than when it is calculated with the 1980 weights.

A more important measurement issue may concern the dependent variable, the inflation rate. As is now well known, there is widespread suspicion that the consumer price index (CPI) overstates inflation. One obvious problem concerns substitution bias. The CPI is a Laspeyres index with weights that change about once a decade. Some have argued that the further we get from the base year, the greater the "substitution" bias in the CPI. One way to adjust for this would be to include a variable that measures the number of months away from the latest base weight adjustment. More difficult problems are caused by quality adjustment, outlet substitution, and new products.

Alternative Estimation Approaches

More fundamentally, given the seemingly inherent limitations with the aggregate time-series approach, I wonder if a conclusion of this paper should be that macroeconomists should try a different approach. Here I have two suggestions. First, why not estimate the Phillips curve with state-level data? Regional labor markets face different economic shocks, and provide more experiences on which to base estimates of the natural rate than the aggregate economy. The implicit state-level GDP deflators could be used to measure state price changes, or wage growth could be used as the dependent variable instead of price growth, as Phillips originally proposed. A state-level analysis raises additional questions, such as whether the labor market is a national market, and are state-level residuals spatially correlated. But this approach has the obvious

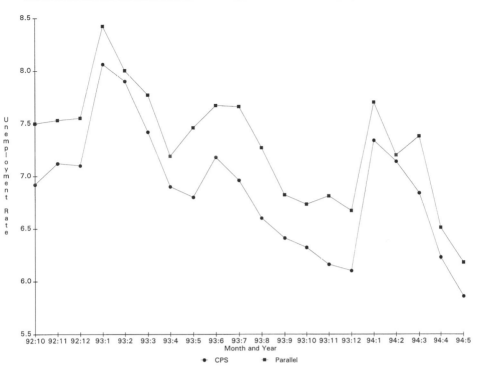

Fig. 5C.1   New and old unemployment rate
Source: Polivka 1996.

advantage of providing more data, which is a critical limitation of the aggregate time-series approach.

Second, why not examine structural changes in the labor market more directly? What I have in mind here is work on changes in the determinants of vacancies, unemployment spells, labor's share, and so forth. This indirect evidence can shed some light on whether the aggregate Phillips curve has changed.

Since I doubt any one at the conference will be around in 126 years, I feel safe in predicting that we will never know the natural rate with reasonable certainty if the literature continues to rely exclusively on aggregate time-series data. I further would conjecture that, if the research proceeds based on the aggregate time-series data alone, the natural rate will never be known with reasonable certainty because of changes in the data and model selection issues. In other words, 126 years from now I would predict that economists will still be debating the magnitude of the natural rate—to the extent they are still interested in this question—and the range of estimates will still be pretty wide.

In sum, Staiger, Stock, and Watson have done a commendable job exploring the precision of time-series estimates of the natural rate. Their findings suggest that we know much less about the exact magnitude of the natural rate than is commonly believed. After reading the paper, one must wonder whether there are other areas in economics where policymakers and economists also think they know what they know with too much precision.

Reference

Polivka, Anne E. 1996. Data Watch: Effects of the Redesigned Current Population Survey. *Journal of Economic Perspectives* 10:169–80.

6   America's Peacetime Inflation: The 1970s

J. Bradford De Long

> In a world organized in accordance with Keynes' specifications, there would be a constant race between the printing press and the business agents of the trade unions, with the problem of unemployment largely solved if the printing press could maintain a constant lead.
>
> Jacob Viner, "Mr. Keynes on the Causes of Unemployment"

6.1   Introduction

Examine the price level in the United States over the past century. Wars see prices rise sharply, by more than 15% per year at the peaks of wartime and postwar decontrol inflation. The National Industrial Recovery Act and the abandonment of the gold standard at the nadir of the Great Depression generated a year of nearly 10% inflation. But aside from wars and Great Depressions, at other times inflation is almost always less than 5% and usually 2–3% per year—save for the decade of the 1970s.

The 1970s are America's only peacetime outburst of inflation. The sustained elevation of inflation for a decade has no parallel in the past century (fig. 6.1). The 1970s was the only era in which business enterprise and financing transactions were also "speculation[s] on the future of monetary policy" (Simons 1947) and concern about inflation was an important factor in nearly all business decisions.

J. Bradford De Long is associate professor of economics at the University of California, Berkeley, an Alfred P. Sloan Foundation research fellow, and a research associate of the National Bureau of Economic Research.

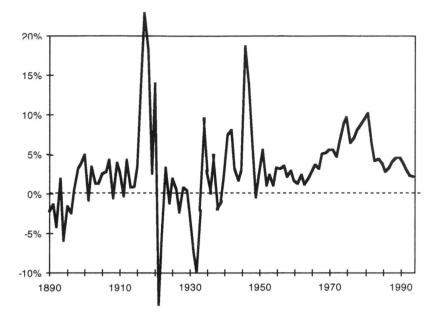

Fig. 6.1   Annual inflation (GDP deflator), 1890–1995

The cumulative impact of the decade of 5–10% inflation was large, as figure 6.2 shows. Since 1896, there has been a steady upward drift in the price level. Superimposed on this drift are rapid jumps as a result of World War I and the removal of World War II's price controls, and a sharp decline during the slide into the Great Depression. On this scale, the inflation of the 1970s was as large an increase in the price level relative to drift as either of this century's major wars. And the inflation of the 1970s was *broad-based*: as figure 6.3 shows, the qualitative pattern is similar no matter which particular price index is examined.

Economists' instincts are that uncertainty about current prices, future prices, and the real meaning of nominal trade-offs between the present and the future; distortions introduced by the failure of government finance to be inflation-neutral; windfall redistributions; and the focusing of attention not on preferences, factors of production, and technologies but on predicting the future evolution of nominal magnitudes *must* degrade the functioning of the price system and reduce the effectiveness of the market economy at providing consumer utility. The cumulative jump in the price level as a result of the inflation of the 1970s may have been very expensive to the United States in terms of the associated reduction in human welfare.[1]

1. For a discussion of the failure of public finance to be inflation-neutral, see Feldstein (1982). For an argument that the real costs of inflation just might be quite high, see Rudebusch and Wilcox (1994). For an argument that the reductions in consumption and the increases in risk occasioned by inflation of the magnitude seen in the United States in the 1970s are relatively low (and thus

Price Level (1896 = 100)

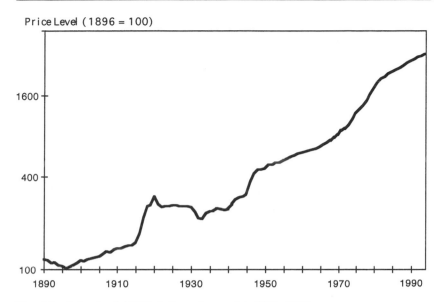

Fig. 6.2   Price level (GDP deflator, log scale), 1890–1995

Why did the United States—and, to a greater or lesser extent, the rest of the industrial world—have such a burst of inflation in the 1970s?

At the surface level, the United States had a burst of inflation in the 1970s because no one—until Paul Volcker took office as chairman of the Federal Reserve—in a position to make anti-inflation policy placed a sufficiently high priority on stopping inflation. Other goals took precedence: people wanted to solve the energy crisis, or maintain a high-pressure economy, or make certain that the current recession did not get any worse. As a result, policymakers throughout the 1970s were willing to run some risk of nondeclining or increasing inflation in order to achieve other goals. After the fact, most such policymakers believed that they had misjudged the risks, that they would have achieved more of their goals if they had spent more of their political capital and institutional capability trying to control inflation earlier.

At a somewhat deeper level, the United States had a burst of inflation in the 1970s because economic policymakers during the 1960s dealt their successors a very bad hand. Lyndon Johnson, Arthur Okun, and William McChesney Martin left Richard Nixon, Paul McCracken, and Arthur Burns nothing but painful dilemmas with no attractive choices. And bad luck coupled with bad cards made the lack of success at inflation control in the 1970s worse than anyone had imagined ex ante.

---

implicitly that the heavy cost paid to reduce moderate inflation did not increase the general welfare), see Blinder (1987). For an argument that people *feel* that the costs of inflation are very high—and perhaps that high inflation enters *directly* into the utility function with a negative sign—see Shiller, chap. 1 in this volume.

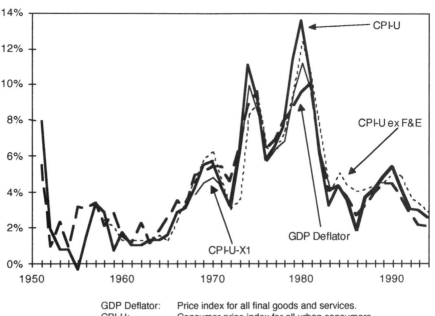

GDP Deflator: Price index for all final goods and services.
CPI-U: Consumer price index for all urban consumers.
CPI-U-X1:   Consumer price index for all urban consumers with revised
                   rental-equivalent housing price component for the 1970s.
CPI-U-ex F&E: Consumer price index for all urban consumers omitting volatile food
                   and energy prices.

Fig. 6.3   Inflation in the United States, 1951–94

At a still deeper level, the United States had a burst of inflation in the 1970s that was not ended until the early 1980s because no one had a mandate to do what was necessary in the 1970s to push inflation below 4%, and keep it there. Had 1970s Federal Reserve chairman Arthur Burns tried, he might well have ended the Federal Reserve Board as an institution, or transformed it out of all recognition. It took the entire decade for the Federal Reserve as an institution to gain the power and freedom of action necessary to control inflation.

And at the deepest level, the truest cause of the inflation of the 1970s was the shadow cast by the Great Depression. The Great Depression made it impossible—for a while—for almost anyone to believe that the business cycle was a fluctuation *around* rather than a shortfall *below* some sustainable level of production and employment. An economy would have to have some "frictional" unemployment, perhaps 1% of the labor force or so, to serve the "inventory" function of providing a stock of workers looking for jobs to match the stock of vacant jobs looking for workers. An economy might have some "structural" unemployment. But there was no good theory suggesting that either of these would necessarily be a significant fraction of the labor force. Everything else was "cyclical" unemployment: presumably curable by the expansionary policies that economists would now prescribe in retrospect for the Great Depression.

The shadow cast by the Great Depression had the least impact on economic policy in the 1950s, when Eisenhower administration officials who were concerned about rising unemployment held the balance point between unreconstructed Keynesians on the one hand and those who still believed in the possibility of rolling back the New Deal on the other. But even Eisenhower-era Council of Economic Advisors (CEA) chairman Arthur Burns believed as strongly as anyone that changing economic institutions and economic policies had tamed the business cycle. And critics of Eisenhower-era policies were successful at *all* levels—among professional economists, among literate commentators, and in the voting booths—when they argued that a decade like the 1950s that showed above-par economic performance still fell far short of what the American economy could accomplish, and that it was important to "get the economy moving again."

Sooner or later in post-World War II America, random variation would have led the economy to fall off of the tightrope of full employment and low inflation on the overexpansionary side. Although there was nothing foreordained or inevitable about the particular way in which America found itself with strong excess aggregate demand at the end of the 1960s, it was foreordained and inevitable that eventually some combination of shocks would produce a macroeconomy with strong excess demand. And once that happened—given the shadow cast by the Great Depression—there was no institution with enough authority, power, and will to quickly bring inflation back down again.

It took the decade of the 1970s to persuade economists, and policymakers, that "frictional" and "structural" unemployment were far more than 1–2% of the labor force (although we still lack fully satisfactory explanations for why this should be the case). It took the decade of the 1970s to convince economists and policymakers that the *political* costs of even high single-digit inflation were very high. Once these two lessons of the 1970s had been learned, the center of American political opinion was willing to grant the Federal Reserve the mandate to do whatever was necessary to contain inflation. But until these lessons had been learned, it is hard to see how the U.S. government could have pursued an alternative policy of sustained disinflation in response to whatever shocks had happened to create chronic excess demand.

It is in this sense that the inflation of the 1970s was an accident waiting to happen: the memory of the Great Depression meant that the United States was highly likely to suffer an inflation like that of the 1970s in the post–World War II period—maybe not as long, and maybe not in that particular decade, but nevertheless an inflation of recognizably the same *genus*.

Section 6.2 briefly sketches the background against which the decisions that led to the inflation of the 1970s were made. It examines the legacy left for economists and policymakers by John Maynard Keynes. It considers the shadow cast by the Great Depression that created a climate in which few were willing to endorse any sacrifice of this year's higher employment for next year's lower inflation. It discusses whether economists' visions had any significant impact on economic policy. And it summarizes how the boom of the 1960s left the United States with the relatively high and apparently persistent rate of increase in nominal wages that, in combination with oil price shocks and the productivity slowdown, fueled the inflation of the 1970s.

Section 6.3 narrates how a relatively conservative administration as far as economic policy was concerned, the Nixon administration, wound up committed to a policy of inflation reduction through wage and price controls rather than through monetary and fiscal restraint. One powerful contributing factor was Nixon's sensitivity to what he saw as the adverse political consequences of slow growth for his own reelection. A second was the natural desire to postpone hard choices and to hope that good luck would make painful dilemmas go away. A third was that Federal Reserve chairman Arthur Burns had little confidence in the ability of higher unemployment to put downward pressure on inflation.

Section 6.4 considers the impact of the supply shocks of the 1970s on inflation. Section 6.5 discusses the slow and painful process by which a relative consensus to reduce inflation through monetary restraint emerged. Section 6.6 summarizes the paper.

6.2   The Background

> Involuntary unemployment is the most dramatic sign and disheartening consequence of underutilization of productive capacity. . . . We cannot afford to settle for *any* prescribed level of unemployment.
>
> John F. Kennedy (emphasis added)

6.2.1   The Legacy of Keynes?

Begin with the conclusion to Samuelson and Solow (1960), "Analytical Aspects of Anti-Inflation Policy" (emphasis added):

> We come out with guesses like the following:
>   . . . In order to achieve the *nonperfectionist's* goal of high enough output to give us no more than 3 percent unemployment, the price index might have to rise by as much as 4 to 5 percent per year. That much price rise would seem to be the necessary cost of high employment and production in the years immediately ahead.
>   All this is shown in our . . . Phillips curve [fig. 6.4]. . . . The point A, corresponding to price stability, is seen to involve about 5.5 percent unemployment; whereas the point B, corresponding to 3 percent unemployment, is seen to involve a price rise of about 4.5 percent per annum. We rather

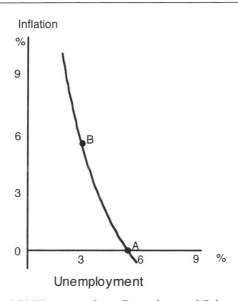

Fig. 6.4   Estimated Phillips curve from Samuelson and Solow (1960)
Note: Original caption reads: "Modified Phillips Curve for U.S. This shows the menu of choices between different degrees of unemployment and price stability, as roughly estimated from the last twenty-five years of American data."

expect that the tug of war of politics will end us up in the next few years somewhere in between.

The authors are the best of the post-World War II American economics profession. Yet when we read these paragraphs and examine the associated figure, "Modified Phillips Curve for U.S.," we wince.

Ignore the fact that the curve plotted between points *A* and *B* is not "as roughly estimated from [the] last twenty-five years of American data." When Samuelson and Solow wrote, they were barely out of the age where "computer" was a job description rather than a machine; they lacked the batteries of statistical procedures, diagnostics, and sensitivity analyses that we use as a matter of course; and they did present the raw scatter of unemployment and wage growth (in which it is hard to see any Phillips curve). The regression for the twenty-five years before 1960 of American wage growth on unemployment has no slope to the regression at all.[2]

Ignore the suppression of the magnitude of sampling variability and of uncertainty in the estimated parameters—even though it had been nearly a decade since Milton Friedman (1953) had made an extremely powerful argument

2. It *is* possible—by throwing out the Depression years (during which wages and prices rose, even with unemployment in double digits), throwing out the years of World War II price controls, and adding the 1920s into the sample—to estimate a curve relatively close to Samuelson and Solow's "menu of choices between different degrees of unemployment and price stability" with a *t*-statistic more than two. But you have to work hard to find such a Phillips curve.

Wage Growth - 2.5%

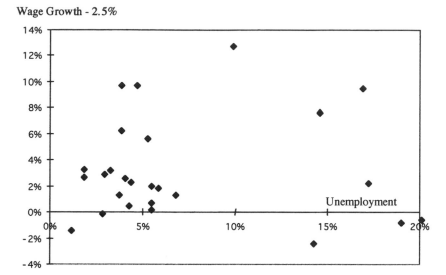

Fig. 6.5   Unemployment and wage growth minus 2.5% per year, 1935–60

that successful stabilization policy requires that you *know* the structure of the economy with substantial precision: using erratic instruments in response to noisy signals of the state of the system is likely to add variance and to make matters worse.

What makes us wince the most is the description of 3% unemployment—a goal outside the historical operating range of the peacetime economy—as a "nonperfectionist's goal."[3]

Samuelson and Solow were not exceptional. As late as April 1969, ex-CEA chair Arthur Okun (1970) was calling for a long-term "4 percent rate of unemployment and a 2 percent rate of annual price increase" as possibly "compatible" with what he called "an optimistic-realistic view" of the structure of the American economy, and certainly as a target worth aiming at—even though the post-World War II United States had been southwest of Okun's target in only one year (fig. 6.6).

Thus economists in the 1960s were at least flirting with hubris by categorizing as "nonperfectionist" policy goals that required shifting the economy beyond and holding it indefinitely outside of its peacetime operating range.

One standard explanation of the source of this *hubris* is that it was part of the legacy left by John Maynard Keynes (1936). Jacob Viner's review (1936)

---

3. The American economy had not seen unemployment less than or equal to 3% save in wartime: 1943–45 and 1952–53. Lebergott (1964) had estimated unemployment in 1926 at less than 3%. But his concept of unemployment is the shortfall of measured employment relative to a "normal" cyclically insensitive labor force. It is not comparable to post-World War II data and, as Romer (1986) has argued, incorrectly extrapolates employment patterns from manufacturing to other sectors of the economy.

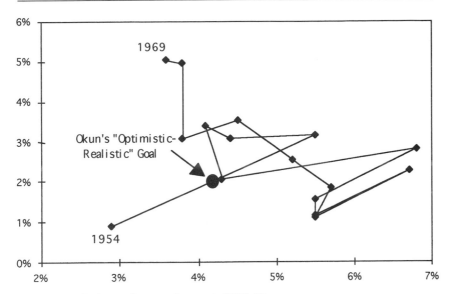

Fig. 6.6   Inflation and unemployment, 1954–69

had forecast that, "in a world organized in accordance with Keynes' specifications, there would be a constant race between the printing press and the business agents of the trade unions, with the problem of unemployment largely solved if the printing press could maintain a constant lead."[4] The policies undertaken—on the recommendation of Keynesians—in the 1960s, and the inflation that followed, lend plausibility to this interpretation.

6.2.2   The Shadow of the Great Depression

But it may be more accurate to see the views of Okun (1970) and of Samuelson and Solow (1960) as a consequence of the very long shadow cast by the Great Depression. The Great Depression had broken any link that might have been drawn between the average level of unemployment over any time period, and the desirable, attainable, or sustainable level of unemployment. With the memory of the Great Depression still fairly fresh, it was extremely difficult to argue that the normal workings of the business cycle led to fluctuations around any sort of equilibrium position.

There was "frictional" unemployment—workers looking for jobs and jobs looking for workers before the appropriate matches had been made—which served as a kind of "inventory" of labor for the economy. There could be "structural" unemployment—people with low skills in isolated regions where it was not worth any firm's while to employ them at wages they would accept—which could not be tackled by demand-management tools.

Everything else was "cyclical" unemployment: a smaller case of the same

---

4. Viner also called Keynes's book one "likely to have more influence than it deserves."

disease as the unemployment of the Great Depression, which could presumably be cured by the standard expansionary policy means that economists believed would have cured the Great Depression if they had been tried at the time.

The Great Depression had taught everyone the lesson that business cycles were shortfalls below, and not fluctuations around, sustainable levels of production and employment. As of the start of the 1960s, there was no good theory to explain why "frictional" and "structural" unemployment should even together add up to any significant fraction of the labor force.[5] Thus anyone—it did not have to be John Maynard Keynes—developing a macroeconomics in a context in which the Great Depression was the dominant empirical datum would find that the path of least resistance led to expansionary policy recommendations: Depression-level unemployment certainly did not serve any useful economic or social function; the bulk of observed post–World War II unemployment looked like Depression-era unemployment; therefore policy should be expansionary.

6.2.3   Did Economists' Optimism Matter?

Did economists' overoptimism matter? Did it make a difference that they were talking at the beginning of the 1960s of 3% unemployment as a "nonperfectionist" goal, and were arguing at the end of the 1960s that 4% unemployment and 2% inflation was likely to be a sustainable posture for the American economy over the long run?

During periods of Republican political dominance, perhaps not: the 1950s saw not gap closing but rather stabilization policies of the kind that Herbert Stein had pushed for from the Committee on Economic Development (CED), as Eisenhower's economic advisers balanced between Keynesians to the left and residual Hooverites to the right. But during periods of Democratic political dominance, economists' overoptimism almost certainly did matter.

The core of the Democratic political coalition saw every level of unemployment as "too high." And economists' professional opinions about what was and was not feasible, given the policy tools at the U.S. government's disposal, were in a sense the only possible brake on the natural expansionary policies that would have been pursued in any case by the post–World War II Democratic Party.

Perhaps economic advisers would have proven irrelevant in any case. If the profession had been less heavily concentrated toward the Keynesian end of the spectrum, and if Walter Heller and James Tobin had possessed views on macroeconomic policy like those of Arthur Burns and Herbert Stein, perhaps President Kennedy's economic advisers would have had other names.

It may be that for every conceivable policy there is an economist who can wear a suit and pronounce the policy sound and optimal, and that to a large

---

5. Indeed, as of the middle of the 1990s there is still relatively little to account for cross-country and cross-era differences in "natural" rates of unemployment.

degree presidents and senators get the economic advice that they ask for. It may be that a less optimistic group of advisers drawn from the academic economics community would have had no more effect on macroeconomic policy in the 1960s than advisers from the academic economics community had on fiscal policy at the beginning of the 1980s, when they pointed out that revenue projections seemed, as Martin Feldstein (1994) politely put it, "inconsistent with the Federal Reserve's very tight monetary policy."

Perhaps the United States was likely to see a spurt of inflation in the 1960s even had Republican political dominance continued throughout the decade. It may be that even a Republican president and a Republican Congress would have exhibited the same unwillingness to use fiscal and monetary tools to slow economic growth during the buildup of American forces in Vietnam.

But sooner or later, the turning of the political wheel would bring a left-of-center party to effective power in the United States. And when that happened everything—the memory of the Great Depression, the elements of that party's core political coalition, the theories of economists in the mainstream of the profession—would push for policies of significant expansion.

If 4% unemployment had turned out to be the natural rate, the cry would have arisen for a reduction in unemployment to 2%. It is well within the bounds of possibility that the United States might have avoided a burst of inflation in the late 1960s and early 1970s. But then it would have been vulnerable to an analogous burst of inflation in the late 1970s, or in the early 1980s. And if inflation had been avoided through the early 1980s, analogous policy missteps might well have generated inflation in the late 1980s. The "monetary constitution" of the United States at the end of the 1960s made something like the 1970s, at some time, a very likely probability. And I do not see how the "monetary constitution" could have shifted to anything like its present state in the absence of an object lesson, like the experience of the 1970s.

6.2.4   The Situation at the End of the 1960s

By the beginning of 1969, the United States had already finished its experiment: was it possible to have unemployment rates of 4% or below without accelerating inflation? The answer was reasonably clear: no. Average nonfarm nominal wage growth, which had fluctuated around or below 4% per year between the end of the Korean War and the mid-1960s, was more than 6% during calendar 1968.

A gap of 1.5 percentage points per year between wage and price inflation had prevailed on average in the post–Korean War 1950s and the late 1960s. Given such a differential, from the perspective of the end of the 1960s a reduction in inflation from 5% per year or more down to 2–3% required some significant deceleration of nominal wage growth.

Comparing patterns of wage and price inflation highlights an ambiguity in the character of inflation in the 1970s. In prices, as measured by the GDP deflator, the major jump in inflation occurred after 1968: from 5% in 1968 to

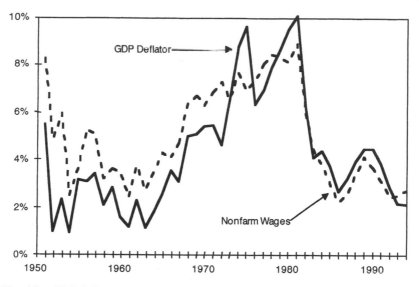

Fig. 6.7   GDP deflator and nonfarm wage inflation, 1950–94

the peak of just over 10% in 1981 (fig. 6.7). In wages, the major jump had already occurred by 1968: rates of increase in nominal hourly wages were already 6.5% per year, and rose to a peak of little more than 8% per year at the end of the 1970s. The difference springs, arithmetically, from the productivity slowdown (which erased the gap between core nominal wage inflation and core nominal price inflation) and the supply shocks of the 1970s (which pushed inflation temporarily above its "core" magnitude).

The magnitude of the inflation-control problem changed between the late 1960s, when the problem became apparent, and the end of the 1970s, when Federal Reserve chairman Paul Volcker embarked on the policies that produced the Volcker disinflation and the recession of 1982–83. But the qualitative nature of the problem did not change. By the end of the 1970s, average nominal wage growth was some 8% per year rather than 6% per year, and the wedge between nominal wage and nominal price growth had vanished as a result of the productivity slowdown. Thus Paul Volcker and his Open Market Committee at the end of the 1970s faced the problem of how to slow the rate of nominal wage growth, and thus the rate of core inflation, by some 5 percentage points per year or so. Arthur Burns and his Open Market Committee at the beginning of the 1970s faced the problem of how to slow the rate of nominal wage growth, and thus the rate of core inflation, by 2 percentage points per year or so.

Such a permanent deceleration in nominal wage growth might have been accomplished by shifting inflationary expectations downward directly (so that a lower rate of nominal wage increase would have been associated with the same rate of increase in real wages), or by triggering a recession sufficiently deep and sufficiently long that fear of future excess supply in the labor market would restrain demand for rapid wage increases.

6.3   Nixon's Mistake

> I know there's the myth of the autonomous Fed . . . [short laugh] and when you go up for confirmation some Senator may ask you about your friendship with the President. Appearances are going to be important, so you can call Ehrlichman to get messages to me, and he'll call you.
>
> Richard Nixon to Arthur Burns

Could such a deceleration have been accomplished at the end of the 1960s? At a technical level, of course it could have. Consider inflation in the five largest industrial economies, the G-5 (fig. 6.8). Before the breakdown of the Bretton Woods fixed exchange-rate system, the price levels in these five countries were loosely linked together. But the Bretton Woods system broke down at the beginning of the 1970s, and thereafter domestic political economy predominated as inflation rates and price levels fanned out both above and below their pre-1970 track.

West Germany was the first economy to undertake a "disinflation." The peak of German inflation in the 1970s came in 1971: thereafter the *Bundesbank* pursued policies that accommodated little of supply shocks or other upward pressures on inflation. The mid-1970s cyclical peak in inflation was lower than the 1970–71 peak; the early-1980s cyclical peak in West German inflation is invisible.

Japan began its disinflation in the mid-1970s, in spite of the enormous impact of the 1973 oil price rise on the balance of payments and the domestic economy of that oil-import-dependent country. The other three of the G-5— Great Britain, France, and the United States—waited until later to begin their disinflations. France's last year of double-digit inflation was 1980. Britain's last year of double-digit inflation was 1981. Certainly there were no "technical" obstacles to making the burst of moderate inflation the United States experienced in the late 1960s a quickly reversed anomaly.

6.3.1   Six Crises

There were, however, political obstacles. The first of them was that the newly elected president, Richard Nixon, was extremely wary of economic policies that promised to fight inflation by increasing unemployment. He attributed his defeat in the 1960 presidential election to the unwillingness of Eisenhower and his economic advisers to stimulate production and employment at

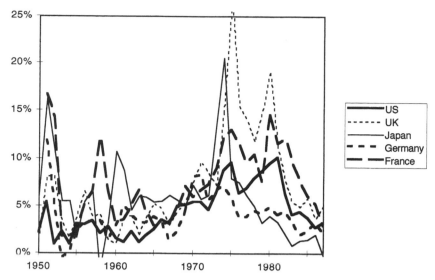

Fig. 6.8   Inflation in the G-5 economies, 1950–94

the risk of triggering increasing inflation. We know that Nixon blamed his defeat on a failure of Eisenhower to act as naive political-business-cycle theory suggests because Nixon (1962) says so:

> Two other developments occurred before the convention, however, which were to have far more effect on the election outcome. . . .
>
> Early in March [1960], Dr. Arthur E. Burns . . . called me. . . . [He] expressed great concern about the way the economy was then acting. . . . Burns' conclusion was that unless some decisive government action were taken, and taken soon, we were heading for another economic dip which would hit its low point in October, just before the elections. He urged strongly that everything possible be done to avert this development . . . by loosening up on credit and . . . increasing spending for national security. The next time I saw the President, I discussed Burns' proposals with him, and he in turn put the subject on the agenda for the next cabinet meeting.
>
> The matter was thoroughly discussed by the Cabinet. . . . [S]everal of the Administration's economic experts who attended the meeting did not share his bearish prognosis. . . . [T]here was strong sentiment against using the spending and credit powers of the Federal Government to affect the economy, unless and until conditions clearly indicated a major recession in prospect.
>
> In supporting Burns' point of view, I must admit that I was more sensitive politically than some of the others around the cabinet table. I knew from bitter experience how, in both 1954 and 1958, slumps which hit bottom early in October contributed to substantial Republican losses in the House and Senate. . . .
>
> Unfortunately, Arthur Burns turned out to be a good prophet. The bottom of the 1960 dip did come in October. . . . In October . . . the jobless roles

increased by 452,000. All the speeches, television broadcasts, and precinct work in the world could not counteract that one hard fact.

Richard Nixon's statement that he and Arthur Burns were forceful advocates of trying to fine-tune economic policy to avoid a preelection recession in 1960 has led many to search diligently for evidence that they sacrificed economic health for political advantage in 1971–72 (see, for example, Tufte 1978). In fact, things were considerably more complicated: Democratic as well as Republican politicians were pressing Arthur Burns for faster money growth in late 1971.

Nevertheless, Nixon's past had made him extremely sensitive to—and eager to avoid—policies that his Democratic political adversaries could and would characterize as the sacrifice of the economic welfare of working Americans for the benefit of Republican Wall Street bondholders.

6.3.2 Wishing for Favorable Parameter Values

Thus Herbert Stein (1984) describes how he and his colleagues at the Nixon-era CEA, Paul McCracken and Hendrik Houthakker, were "surprised and unhappy" when they learned that President Nixon had authorized labor secretary George Shultz to tell the AFL-CIO that the Nixon administration would "control inflation without a rise of unemployment." Afterwards, Stein concluded that he should have paid more attention to the subtext of his first meeting with Nixon, in December 1968: "He asked me what I thought would be our main economic problems, and I started, tritely, with inflation. He agreed but immediately warned me that we must not raise unemployment. I didn't at the time realize how deep this feeling was or how serious its implications would be" (135). How were economic advisers to deal with a situation in which they found the Phelps-Friedman argument—that reducing unemployment would require a period during which inflation would have to be above its natural rate—convincing, yet in which their political superiors did not authorize such a policy?

McCracken, Stein, and Nixon's other economic advisers did so by minimizing the cognitive dissonance: they reassured themselves that the rise of unemployment would not have to be large: "The inflation rate was about 5 percent at the beginning of 1969. It did not have to be reduced very far. Unemployment was only 3.3 percent. There seemed considerable room for an increase of unemployment without reaching a level that anyone could consider unusually high" (Stein 1984, 150). They were hoping that parameters values would turn out to be favorable, and thus that the Nixon administration could avoid painful dilemmas. The relative optimism of the Nixon CEA as to the likely success of "gradualism"—tighten monetary and fiscal policy until the unemployment rate rose just high enough to put downward pressure on inflation, and keep unemployment there until inflation was no longer perceived as a problem—fits oddly with the lack of quantitative knowledge about the relationship between inflation and unemployment at the time.

Even today, after three decades during which price and unemployment gyrations have given us all the identifying variance we could possible wish, and during which the "accelerationist" Phillips curves of the style that Robert Gordon and others started estimating very early in the 1970s have stayed remarkably stable, we do not know enough about the structure of the economy to reliably plan a "gradualist" policy of inflation reduction. Straightforward simple estimates of the non-accelerating-inflation rate of unemployment (NAIRU) today that take no account of possible drift in parameters over the past forty years or of uncertainty about the "correct" specification tend to produce a one-sigma confidence interval for the NAIRU that runs from 5 to 7.5%: one chance in six that the "true" NAIRU is less than 5% unemployment, and one chance in six that the "true" NAIRU is greater than 7.5% in which case we are likely to see a very unpleasant inflation surprise in the next few years.

I think that the power, formal correctness, and elegance of the Lucas critique has put into shadow the limits of macroeconomic knowledge *even assuming that the policy and institutional regime is unchanged.* There is a sense in which Milton Friedman (1968) gave the wrong presidential address to the American Economic Association: he should have repeated his message of 1953, "The Effects of Full-Employment Policy on Economic Stability," and argued that uncertainty about parameters makes "fine-tuning"—and its cousin, "gradualism"—next to impossible.

6.3.3   "Progress toward Economic Stability"

A third obstacle to a policy of disinflation in the early 1970s was that the newly installed chairman of the Federal Reserve Board, Arthur Burns, did not believe that he could use monetary policy to control inflation.

In 1959, Arthur Burns had given his presidential address to the American Economic Association, "Progress toward Economic Stability." Burns spent the bulk of his time detailing how automatic stabilizers and monetary policy based on a better sense of the workings of the banking system had made episodes like the Great Depression extremely unlikely in the future.

Toward the end of his speech, Burns (1960, 18) spoke of an unresolved problem created by the progress toward economic stability that he saw: "a future of secular inflation."

During the postwar recessions the average level of prices in wholesale and consumer markets has declined little or not at all. The advances in prices that customarily occur during periods of business expansion have therefore become cumulative. It is true that in the last few years the federal government has made some progress in dealing with inflation. Nevertheless, wages and prices rose appreciably even during the recent recession, the general public has been speculating on a larger scale in common stocks, long-term interest rates have risen very sharply since mid-1958, and the yield on stocks relative to bonds has become abnormally low. All these appear to be symptoms of a continuation of inflationary expectations or pressures.

Before World War II such inflationary expectations and pressures would have been erased by a severe recession, and by the pressure put on workers' wages and manufacturers' prices by falling aggregate demand. But Burns could see no way in which such pressures could be generated in an environment in which workers and firms rationally expected demand to remain high and recessions to be short.

Burns' skepticism about the value of monetary policy as a means of controlling inflation in the post–World War II era cannot but have been reinforced by the pressure for avoiding any significant rise in unemployment coming from his long-time ally, patron, and friend, President Nixon: "'I know there's the myth of the autonomous Fed . . .' Nixon barked a short laugh. ". . . and when you go up for confirmation some Senator may ask you about your friendship with the President. Appearances are going to be important, so you can call Ehrlichman to get messages to me, and he'll call you'" (Ehrlichman 1982, 248–49). The date was October 23, 1969. The speaker was Richard Nixon. The listener was Arthur Burns. Nixon had just announced his intention to nominate Burns to replace William McChesney Martin as chairman of the Federal Reserve. Nixon was thinking, You see to it, Arthur: no recession. We can speculate what Arthur Burns was thinking: just how independent was this central bank?[6]

Making Arthur Burns and the Federal Reserve sensitive to White House concerns was a subject of conversation in Nixon's White House in 1970 and 1971. "What shall I say to Arthur?" Nixon would ask. "Ask him if he shares the President's objective of full employment by mid-1972," George Shultz suggested. Paul McCracken added, "If he says yes, say that the Fed's monetary path can't and won't bring us to that outcome" (Ehrlichman 1982, 251). Such pressures must have made Burns sensitive to White House concerns, and may be the source of an axiom in the Federal Reserve's institutional memory that the Federal Reserve is better off having fewer rather than more direct contacts with the White House staff.

But Arthur Burns, once ensconced at the Federal Reserve, could take care of himself. He was at least a match for Ehrlichman at bureaucratic intrigue. There is admiration in Ehrlichman's recounting of one of Burns's responses to a "stern admonition" from Nixon. Ehrlichman wrote that he found "Arthur [Burns]'s response . . . so artfully ambiguous that I wrote it down: 'You know the idea . . . the idea that I would ever let a conflict arise between what I think is right and my loyalty to Dick Nixon is outrageous.'" Thus Ehrlichman could tell a senior Federal Reserve official that "every morning when you look in the mirror, I want you to think 'what am I going to do today to increase the money supply.'" But Burns and his Open Market Committee would set monetary policy.

---

6. John Ehrlichman, the source of the conversation, was in the room. But this picture is only as reliable as Ehrlichman's memory and perceptions.

We know that Arthur Burns placed little weight on being what Nixon called "a team player" because he began contradicting administration policy almost from the day he moved into the chairman's office. As a critic of Kennedy-Johnson policy and as a counselor to the president in the first year of the Nixon administration, Burns had been opposed to wage-price guideposts. But things looked different from the Federal Reserve: on May 18, 1970, Burns called for Nixon to adopt an "incomes policy" to "shorten the period between suppression of excess demand and restoration of price stability" (Stein 1984, 155).

Paul McCracken, especially, was irritated because he thought that Burns had "proposed [an incomes policy] without anything in mind but the phrase" (Wells 1994, 61), but such a proposal is consistent with Burns's vision. *If* the president who appointed you does not want a deep recession, and *if* you do not believe that even a deep recession would generate significant downward pressure on prices—for in post–World War II circumstances who would believe *ex ante* that a recession would be deep or *ex post* that it would be long?—then you need some kind of incomes policy. That President Nixon is opposed to an incomes policy and is upset with your advocacy of it would be irrelevant, because the alternatives to an incomes policy are things that the president would dislike even more.

Thus there is a very real sense in which monetary policy did not contain inflation in the early 1970s because it was not tried. And it was not tried because the chairman of the Federal Reserve did not believe that it would work at an acceptable cost. Even the threatening breakdown of the fixed exchange rate system, which Burns "feared . . . with a passion," would not induce him to tighten sufficiently to risk a more-than-moderate recession. Paul Volcker reports an "interesting discussion with Arthur Burns" over lunch at the American embassy in Paris, at which "the Chairman of the Federal Reserve Board made one last appeal" to retain a system of fixed exchange rates (see Volcker and Gyohten 1992, 113). Volcker reports that "to me, it simply seemed too late, and with some exasperation I said to him 'Arthur, if you want a par value system, you better go home right away and tighten money.' With a great sigh, he replied, 'I would even do that.'"

In economists' models, an important feature leading to higher-than-optimal inflation is the "time inconsistency" of economic policy (see Kydland and Prescott 1977). It may be optimal for this year's central bank to build anti-inflation credibility, but it is also optimal for next year's central bank to exploit that credibility through higher-than-anticipated inflation and thus higher-than-anticipated output and employment growth. Private-sector investors and firms sophisticated enough to look ahead to future stages of the economic-policy game tree thus make it impossible for a central bank to build anti-inflation credibility through restrictive policies in the first place. In economists' models, at least, a powerful factor keeping this year's central bank from embarking on the first steps of a long-run, consistent anti-inflation policy is its realization that no one outside the bank will find its actions and commitments credible (Chari, Christiano, and Eichenbaum 1995).

While the theoretical logic is impeccable and powerful, I have found no sign in Federal Reserve deliberations in the 1970s that time-inconsistency issues— either that future central bankers would not carry out the policies to which earlier central bankers had tried to commit them, or that the private sector would fail to believe long-run commitments to a low-inflation policy—played any role in policy formation. Moreover, there have been *none* of the institutional changes thought likely to diminish the severity of time-inconsistency problems since the 1970s, yet inflation has abated. And there were no significant institutional changes between the low-inflation 1950s and the high-inflation 1970s. Time-inconsistency issues may well exert a constant background pressure toward higher inflation, but it is difficult to argue that shifts in the economy's vulnerability to such problems has played much of a role in the variation of post–World War II inflation rates.

6.3.4   The Nixon Price-Control Program

Herbert Stein (1984), especially, attributes to Arthur Burns a key role in the Nixon administration's eventual adoption of a wage-price freeze in late 1971. The context was one of a CEA averse to *all* forms of incomes policy, from guideposts on up, as "wicked in themselves and steps on the slippery slope . . . to controls" (143); of a president who "did not like 'incomes policies' and knew they did not fit with his basic ideological position"(143); and of an opposition party that had a "great interest in pointing out that there was another, less painful, route to price stability [than gradualism and recession], which Mr. Nixon was too ideological to follow" (155). And Burns's intervention on the procontrols side so that "every editorial writer who wanted to recommend some kind of incomes policy could say that 'even' Arthur Burns was in favor of it" (156) led Stein to liken

> the administration . . . [to] a Russian family fleeing over the snow in a horse-drawn troika pursued by wolves. Every once in a while they threw a baby out to slow down the wolves, hoping thereby to gain enough time for most of the family to reach safety. Every once in a while the administration would make another step in the direction of incomes policies, hoping to appease the critics while the [gradualist] demand management policy would work. In the end, of course, the strategy failed and the administration made the final concession on August 15, 1971, when price and wage controls were adopted. (157)

Rockoff (1984) finds nothing good in the 1971–74 experience with controls. The controls did not calm inflationary expectations. Instead, they appear to have created them—with a general expectation that prices would rebound once the controls were lifted. The controls imposed the standard microeconomic, compliance, and administrative costs on the American economy. Perhaps most serious, the fact that wage and price controls were still in effect in the fall of 1973, when the price of oil jumped, created a substantial divergence between the cost of energy to U.S. users and the world price of energy, which slowed down the process of adjustment. Energy price controls remained, until eliminated as one of the good deeds of the Reagan administration in the early 1980s.

The Nixon controls program had an odd impact on monetary policy. The "Phase II" program consisted of a Cost of Living Council supervising a presidentially appointed Price Commission and a "tripartite" labor-management-public Pay Board. But in addition there was a Committee on Interest and Dividends (CID): the day after Nixon announced his controls program, the chairman of the House Banking Committee, Wright Patman, argued that "if controls are needed on the wages of workers and the prices of businessmen, then surely the prices—interest rates—charged by banks also need to be controlled" (Wells 1994, 113). Burns took the chairmanship of the CID, presumably in fear that the alternative chairman might be someone dangerous and in hope that the mere establishment of the CID would quiet populist critics of interest rate hikes.

Burns's hopes proved misguided. At one point—caught between the likes of Wright Patman demanding that the CID keep interest rates from rising and his own desire to curb money growth—Burns presided over a "dual prime rate," by which banks were forced to charge borrowers of less than a third of a million *below* the prevailing prime interest rate. "What an ugly tree has grown from your seeds," said Richard Nixon to Arthur Burns, contemplating the workings of the CID (Wells 1994, 113).

And perhaps the controls led to overoptimism, and hence to looser monetary and fiscal policy than would have otherwise been put in place, because of their apparent initial success. If so, the Nixon administration suffered less from such overoptimism than did its critics. Stein (1984, 411) cites Walter Heller, testifying before the Joint Economic Committee on July 27, 1972, that Nixon administration policy was too contractionary: "As I say, now that we are again on the [economic] move the voice of overcautious conservatism is raised again at the other [White House] end of Pennsylvania Avenue. Reach for the [monetary] brakes, slash the [fiscal] budget, seek an end to wage-price restraints."

And private-sector forecasters agreed.[7] One of the striking features of the inflation of the 1970s was that increases in inflation were almost always unanticipated. Figure 6.9 plots the average forecast for the forthcoming calendar year, made as late in the year as possible, from the survey of professional forecasters alongside actual December-to-December GDP deflator inflation. In every single year in the 1970s, the consensus forecast made late in the previous year *understated* the actual value of inflation.

---

7. Romer and Romer (1995) report the similar overoptimism—although smaller in magnitude—in the Federal Reserve staff *Green Book* forecasts of the inflation outlook in the 1970s.

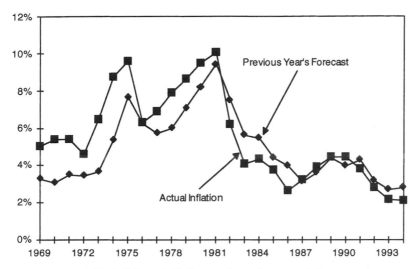

Fig. 6.9   Actual GDP deflator inflation, and previous year's forecast

Moreover, in every year inflation was expected to fall. Anyone seeking to be reassured about the future course of inflation had to do nothing more than glance at the consensus of private-sector economic forecasters to be told that the economy was on the right track, and that inflation next year would be lower than it had been this year. Mistakes in judgment made by economists and government policymakers were also shared by private-sector forecasters, and by those who paid to receive their forecasts. Perhaps the policies adopted truly were prudent and optimal given the consensus understanding of the structure of the economy held by both public- and private-sector decision makers. But this consensus understanding was flawed.

6.4   Supply Shocks and Asymmetric Price Adjustment

Blinder (1982) is among many who have argued that double-digit inflation in the 1970s had a single cause: supply shocks that sharply increased the nominal prices of a few categories of goods, principally energy and secondarily food, mortgage rates, and the "bounce-back" of prices upon elimination of the Nixon controls program. Such shocks were arithmetically responsible for, in Blinder's words, "the dramatic acceleration of inflation between 1972 and 1974? . . . The equally dramatic deceleration of inflation between 1974 and 1976. . . . [And] while the rate of inflation . . . rose about eight percentage points between 1977 and early 1980, the 'baseline' . . . rate may have risen by as little as three" (264).

Arithmetic decompositions of the rise in inflation into upward jumps in the prices of special commodities were never convincing to those working in the monetarist tradition. As Milton Friedman (1975, cited in Ball and Mankiw

1995, 161–62) asked: "The special conditions that drove up the price of oil and food required purchasers to spend more on them, leaving them less to spend on other items. Did that not force other prices to go down, or to rise less rapidly than otherwise? Why should the *average* level of prices be affected significantly by changes in the price of some things relative to others?"

Ball and Mankiw (1995) have recently argued that the missing link in Blinder's argument can be provided by menu-cost models.[8] Supply shocks entail large increases in the prices of goods in a few concentrated sectors. They reduce nominal demand for products in each unaffected sector by a little bit—and so reduce the optimal nominal price in each unaffected sector by a small amount. Small administrative or information processing costs might plausibly prevent full adjustment in many of the unaffected sectors, leaving an upward bias in the overall price level. Concentrated shocks that are (1) significantly larger than the average variance of shocks but (2) not so large as to require relative price movements that overwhelm administrative and information processing costs in *all* sectors appear to have the best chance of generating large upward boosts in inflation.

Ball and Mankiw (1995) argue that their indices of the asymmetry of relative price changes are better indices of supply shocks than are the standard direct measures of the supply shocks themselves. Certainly the swings in prices relative to measures of "core" inflation like the average rate of nominal wage growth are substantial, and match the dates of the Organization of Petroleum Exporting Countries (OPEC) price increase announcements and of the acceleration of food price inflation in 1972–73.

6.4.1 Did Supply Shocks Have Persistent Effects?

The story as told by Blinder (1982) is that in the wake of the supply shocks of the 1970s makers of economic policy faced a very difficult choice. Should they refuse to accommodate the upward one-time jump in prices of the supply shock, thus restraining inflation at the cost of a depression? Or should they accommodate, watch increases in inflation get built into the pattern of wage expectations and settlements, and end the episode having avoided a deep recession at the price of a permanent jump in the rate of inflation?

At least one strand of the conventional wisdom holds that such overaccommodation in response to supply shocks was responsible for a good deal of the rise in inflation during the 1970s: policies that expanded the money supply to avoid a still deeper oil shock–driven recession succeeded in transforming what was a temporary burst of inflation into a permanent jump in the level of inflation by building it into the expected rate of change of the wage base. Yet the year-over-year plots of annual nominal wage growth lend little support to this view (fig. 6.10).

Economywide nominal wage growth rises slowly, smoothly, and steadily

---

8. See Mankiw 1985; Akerlof and Yellen 1985; Ball, Mankiw, and Romer 1988; and Gordon 1990; along with many others.

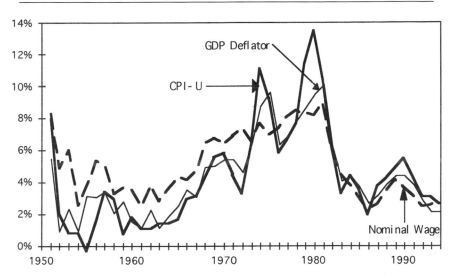

Fig. 6.10   Consumer price, GDP deflator, and nonfarm wage inflation, 1950–94

from its late-1960s plateau to its early 1980s peak without noticeable jumps surrounding supply shocks. The bursts of inflation in 1972–74 and 1978–80 are very visible in price inflation, yet are invisible in the track of average nonfarm wage growth.

Perhaps the supply shocks of the 1970s had so little apparent effect on the rate of growth of nominal wages because they were not fully accommodated, but were instead accompanied by serious recessions. Perhaps an alternative world in which the Federal Reserve sought to fully accommodate the increases in nominal spending and avoid a supply-shock recession entirely would have generated significant acceleration in wage increases. This seems likely: certainly in the absence of such supply shocks a recession as deep as that of 1974–75 could reasonably have been expected to cause a considerable slowdown in nominal wage growth.

But the combination of supply-shock inflation and supply-shock recession, taken together, appears to have had little permanent impact on the nominal wage dynamics of the U.S. economy in *either* the mid- or the late 1970s. Before the supply shocks hit, wage inflation was slowly trending upward. After the supply shocks had passed, price inflation quickly returned to levels consistent with wage and productivity growth, and wage inflation was slowly trending upward.

Thus it is hard to sustain the argument that the root of the U.S. inflation problem in the 1970s was the interaction of one-shot upward supply shocks with a backward-looking wage-price mechanism that incorporated past changes in prices into future changes in wages. As Blinder (1982, 264) put it, attempts to diminish the size of the recession that followed such a shock would lead "inflation from the special factor [to] get built into the baseline. . . . This . . . interaction between special factors and the baseline rate . . . helps us under-

stand why baseline inflation [rose from] . . . perhaps 1–2% in the early 1960s
. . . to perhaps 4–5% by the early 1970s and to perhaps 9–10% by 1980."

The alternative narrative that I would prefer goes roughly as follows: the
baseline inflation rate was some 5% per year in the early 1970s *before* there
were any supply shocks; the baseline inflation rate was pushed up by perhaps
2 percentage points as a result of the collapse in productivity growth; the baseline inflation rate appeared to be 8 or 9% per year by 1980. Supply shocks may
well have tended to push baseline inflation up, but the supply-shock recessions—which no one anticipated—put approximately equal and opposite
amounts of downward pressure on baseline inflation.

There is, arithmetically, little to be accounted for by the feedback of supply-
shock-induced price increases onto the wage-setting process—unless you hold
a strong belief that nominal wage growth would have significantly *decelerated*
in the 1970s in the absence of supply shocks.

6.4.2   Linkage

Were the supply shocks of the 1970s the result of bad luck or bad policy?

One of the many theories floating around the Nixon administration is that
Secretary of State Henry Kissinger sought the tripling of world oil prices as a
way of subsidizing the shah of Iran. In the aftermath of the Vietnam War, Kissinger did not believe that the United States would ever project its own military
power into regions like the Persian Gulf, yet also believed that the gulf area
needed to be protected against Soviet or Soviet-client military threat. The policy adopted was to arm the shah: in Kissinger's words, "we adopted a policy
which provides, in effect, that we will accede to any of the Shah's requests for
arms purchases from us" (Isaacson 1992, 503). But in order to buy U.S. weap-
ons, the shah needed U.S. dollars. The tripling of world oil prices in late 1973
provided the shah with ample U.S. dollars; former Treasury Secretary William
Simon believes that the linkage was not accidental; Nixon's ambassador to
Saudi Arabia claimed that Kissinger refused Saudi requests to pressure Iran
not to push for major price increases at 1973 OPEC meetings.

The judgment of Kissinger biographer Walter Isaacson (1992)—a judgment
that it is easy to share after working for the government, or for any large organization—is that conspiracy assumes more rationality and foresight than a government possesses.[9]

6.5   Toward Volcker's Disinflation

6.5.1   Humphrey-Hawkins

The recession of 1974–75 made it politically dangerous to be an advocate
of restrictive monetary policy to reduce inflation. Near the trough of the reces-

9. Nevertheless the Nixon administration showed little interest in making a rollback of the 1973
oil price increase a principal aim of its foreign policy. When Treasury Secretary William Simon

sion, Hubert Humphrey and Augustus Hawkins sought to require that the government reduce unemployment to 3% *within four years after passage,* that it offer employment to all who wished at the same "prevailing wage" that Davis-Bacon mandated be paid on government construction projects, and (in its House version) that individuals have the right to sue in federal court for their Humphrey-Hawkins jobs if the federal government had not provided them.

In early 1976, the *National Journal* assessed the Humphrey-Hawkins bill's chances of passage as quite good—though principally as veto bait to create an issue for Democrats to campaign against Gerald Ford, rather than as a desirable policy.

Arthur Burns tried to avoid getting sucked into this lose-lose situation: "Humphrey-Hawkins . . . continues the old game of setting a target for the unemployment rate. You set one figure. I set another figure. If your figure is low, you are a friend of mankind; if mine is high, I am a servant of Wall Street. . . . I think that is not a profitable game" (Wells 1994, 199). And Humphrey-Hawkins eventually did generate significant opposition from within the Democratic coalition. Labor would not support the bill unless Humphrey-Hawkins jobs paid the prevailing wage (fearing the consequences for unionized public employment if the "prevailing wage" clause was dropped); legislators who feared criticism from economists' judgment that Humphrey-Hawkins was likely to be inflationary would not support the bill unless the "prevailing wage" clause was removed (see Weir 1992).

The bill that finally passed and was signed in 1977 set a target of reducing unemployment to 4% by 1983, elevated price stability to a goal equal in importance to full employment, set a goal of zero inflation by 1988, called for the reduction of federal spending to the lowest level consistent with national needs, and required the Federal Reserve chairman to testify twice a year. It did nothing at all—save commit the Federal Reserve chairman to a twice-a-year round of congressional testimony.

6.5.2 Jimmy Carter

Nevertheless, the existence of Humphrey-Hawkins, and the consequent commitment of first the Carter administration and then Carter's selection as Arthur Burns's successor, G. William Miller, to returning the economy to full employment had unpleasant consequences. To a small degree it was a matter of bad luck: senior Carter economic officials have talked of the year "when our forecasts of real GNP growth were dead on—only the productivity slowdown meant that the end-of-year unemployment rate was a full percentage point below where we had forecast." To a larger degree it was the result of the lack of interest and focus in the Carter White House on inflation, in spite of efforts by

---

sought to use the shah's fear of the Soviet Union and dependence on American military advisers for training as levers for a rollback on the price of oil, Kissinger proved "reluctant to use leverage and linkage—usually the paired arrows of his diplomatic quiver—to put pressure on the shah" (Isaacson 1992, 50).

economists like Charles Schultze to warn that inflation was likely to suddenly become a severe surprise problem in 1979 and 1980—unless a strategy for dealing with it was evolved earlier.

Inflation did become a severe surprise political problem in 1979, generating the only episode in history in which a CEA chairman (Charles Schultze) and a treasury secretary (Michael Blumenthal) waged a campaign of leak and innuendo to try to get the Federal Reserve chairman (G. William Miller) to *tighten* monetary policy (Kettl 1986). Almost invariably the pressure from the White House to the Federal Reserve is exerted in the opposite direction.

Few if any people are willing to say a good word about G. William Miller's tenure as chairman of the Federal Reserve. He lasted sixteen months, and then replaced Michael Blumenthal as secretary of the treasury. Stuart Eizenstat— President Carter's assistant for domestic policy—always claimed that Miller's departure from the Federal Reserve was an accident.

> The President "accepts" the resignation of [Treasury Secretary] Blumenthal. Blumenthal is known as a voice against inflation, and this adds to the confusion. So we were without a Treasury Secretary. So the President makes calls. Reg Jones of General Electric, Irv Shapiro of Du Pont, David Rockefeller of Chase Manhattan—all are asked and turn it down. This becomes a grave situation. The idea surfaces—I'm not sure where—that Bill Miller take the job. Bill takes it. That then creates a hole at the Fed. and that makes the financial markets even more nervous. (Grieder 1987, 20–21)

Could the Volcker disinflation have been undertaken earlier? Had Gerald Ford won reelection in 1976 and reappointed Arthur Burns, would we now speak of the Burns disinflation? Or would the same political pressure that had driven Nixon into wage and price controls have driven a second Ford administration into overestimation of the available room for economic expansion? Herbert Stein (1984, 215), at least, is skeptical: "We do not know whether a Ford administration . . . kept in office . . . would have persisted" in a course that would have kept inflation declining, "but we do know that the basis for the persistence of such a course had not been laid." And he attributes the failures of the Carter administration and the Carter-era Federal Reserve at inflation control "not . . . chiefly a reflection of the personalities involved . . . [but] a response to the prevailing attitude in the country about the goals of monetary policy." In Stein's opinion, the Federal Reserve did not as of the mid-1970s have a mandate to do whatever turned out to be necessary to curb inflation.

G. William Miller's successor as chairman of the Federal Reserve Board was Paul Volcker.

6.6 Conclusion

6.6.1 The Truest Cause

If the particular chain of events that caused the inflation of the 1970s had been avoided, another crisis in a later year would have begun a similar inflation:

the most important factor was not the particular misstep of policy but the background situation that made it highly probable that sooner or later *a* misstep would generate an inflation like that of the 1970s. Perfect macroeconomic management—successful walking of the fine line between too-low employment and accelerating inflation—in the 1960s would not have eliminated the burst of inflation seen in the 1970s. The burst would have come differently, probably later. Perhaps it would have been larger, perhaps it would have been smaller.

But sooner or later politicians and economists working in a 1960s-style Keynesian framework would have tried to squeeze a little too much production and employment out of the economy, wound up with the average annual rate of nominal wage growth ratcheted upward from 3–6% or more per year, and faced the same dilemmas and painful choices faced at the start of the 1970s.

Thus the "truest cause" was not President Johnson's reluctance to raise taxes to offset the costs of the Vietnam War, but a situation in which attempting to drive unemployment down to and keep it at 3% was regarded as a "nonperfectionist goal" by economists and politicians alike. Indeed, given the limited influence of economists over economic policy, it was probably sufficient for the inflation of the 1970s that politicians remembered the Great Depression, and took the reduction of unemployment to its minimum as a major goal of economic policy.

6.6.2   Could the 1970s Inflation Have Been Curbed Earlier?

There were no technical factors that would have prevented an earlier, rapid curb of the inflation of the 1970s. But there were political factors that would have prevented a quick reversal of the runup in core inflation that occurred in the late 1960s. At the start of the 1970s, the Federal Reserve lacked a mandate to fight inflation by inducing a significant recession. No one then had a mandate to fight inflation by allowing the unemployment rate to rise. Indeed, there was close to a mandate to do the reverse—to throw overboard any institutional arrangements, like the Bretton Woods international monetary system, as soon as they showed any sign of requiring that internal economic management be subordinated to external balance.

This lack of a mandate showed itself in many places, in many aspects. In the absence of such a mandate, the Federal Reserve's "independence" not just from the executive branch, but from the rest of the government in total, was purely theoretical. It is difficult to imagine *any* chairman of the Board of Governors pursuing anti-inflation policy to the limits necessary to achieve significant containment, and thus risking the survival of the institution, in the circumstances of the early 1970s.

A mandate to fight inflation by inducing a significant recession was probably not in place by the end of 1976. The original drafts of Humphrey-Hawkins contained language that "if the President determines that the [Federal Reserve] Board's policies are inconsistent with . . . this Act, the President shall make recommendations . . . to insure closer conformity" (Weir 1992, 194).

A mandate was barely in place by the end of 1978, when we saw—and this is perhaps the only time we will ever see it—a CEA chair and a secretary of the treasury wage a bureaucratic war-by-leak in an attempt to induce the Federal Reserve to *tighten* monetary policy.

A mandate to fight inflation by inducing a significant recession was in place by 1979, as a result of a combination of perceptions and fears about the cost of inflation, worry about what the "transformation of every business venture into a speculation on monetary policy" was doing to the underlying prosperity of the American economy, and fear that the structure of expectations was about to become unanchored and that permanent double-digit inflation was about to become a possibility.

But the process by which the Federal Reserve obtained its information mandate to fight inflation by inducing significant recession was slow and informal. Part of its terms of existence require that it never be made explicit. It is difficult to imagine its coming into being—and thus the Federal Reserve's "independence" being transformed from a quirk of bureaucratic organization into a real and powerful feature of America's political economy—without some lesson like that taught by the history of the 1970s.

Today many observers would say that the costs of the Volcker disinflation of the early 1980s were certainly worth paying, comparing the U.S. economy today with relatively stable prices and relatively moderate unemployment with what they estimate to have been the likely consequence of business as usual: inflation slowly creeping upward from near 10 toward 20% per year over the 1980s, and higher unemployment as well as inflation deranged the functioning of the price mechanism. In the United States today, inflation is low, and the reduction of inflation to low single-digit levels has been accomplished without the seemingly permanent transformation of "cyclical" into "structural" unemployment seen in so many countries of Europe.

Nevertheless, other observers believe that there ought to have been a better way: perhaps inflation could have been brought under control more cheaply by a successful incomes policy made up of a government-business-labor compact to restrain nominal wage growth (which certainly would have been in the AFL-CIO's interest, as it is harder to think of anything worse for that organization's long-term strength than the 1980s as they actually happened). Perhaps inflation could have been brought under control more cheaply by a Federal Reserve that did a better job of communicating its expectations and targets; but note that the dispute over whether "gradualism" (in the sense of the British Tory Party's medium-term financial strategy; see Taylor 1980, 1992) or "cold-turkey" (see Sargent 1982) was the most cost-effective way of reducing inflation has not been resolved; it is hard to fault those who made economic policy decisions when even those economists with ample hindsight do not speak with one voice.

References

Akerlof, George, and Janet Yellen. 1985. A Near-Rational Model of the Business Cycle, with Wage and Price Inertia. *Quarterly Journal of Economics* 100:823–38.

Ball, Laurence, and N. Gregory Mankiw. 1995. Relative Price Changes as Aggregate Supply Shocks. *Quarterly Journal of Economics* 110: 161–93.

Ball, Laurence, N. Gregory Mankiw, and David Romer. 1988. The New Keynesian Economics and the Output-Inflation Trade-off. *Brookings Papers on Economic Activity* no. 1: 1–65.

———. 1982. The Anatomy of Double-Digit Inflation. In *Inflation: Causes and Effects,* ed. Robert E. Hall. Chicago: University of Chicago Press.

———. 1987. *Hard Heads, Soft Hearts: Tough-Minded Economics for a Just Society.* Reading, MA: Addison-Wesley.

Burns, Arthur F. 1960. Progress toward Economic Stability. *American Economic Review* 50, no. 1: 1–19.

Chari, V. V., Lawrence Christiano, and Martin Eichenbaum. 1995. Expectational Traps and Discretion. Conference paper, Federal Reserve Bank of San Francisco.

Ehrlichman, John. 1982. *Witness to Power: The Nixon Years.* New York: Simon and Schuster.

Feldstein, Martin. 1982. Inflation, Capital Taxation, and Monetary Policy. In *Inflation: Causes and Effects,* ed. Robert E. Hall. Chicago: University of Chicago Press.

———. 1994. American Economic Policy in the 1980s: A Personal View. In *American Economic Policy in the 1980s,* ed. Martin Feldstein. Chicago: University of Chicago Press.

Friedman, Milton. 1953. The Effects of Full-Employment Policy on Economic Stability: A Formal Analysis. In *Essays on Positive Economics.* Chicago: University of Chicago Press.

———. 1968. The Role of Monetary Policy. *American Economic Review* 58, no. 1: 1–17.

———. 1975. Perspectives on Inflation. *Newsweek,* June 24, 1975, 73.

Gordon, Robert. 1990. What is New-Keynesian Economics? *Journal of Economic Literature* 28: 1115–71.

Grieder, William. 1987. *Secrets of the Temple: How the Federal Reserve Runs the Country.* New York: Simon and Schuster.

Isaacson, Walter. 1992. *Kissinger.* New York: Simon and Schuster.

Kettl, Donald. 1986. *Leadership at the Fed.* New Haven, CT: Yale University Press.

Keynes, John Maynard. 1936. *The General Theory of Employment, Interest, and Money.* London: Macmillan.

Kydland, Finn, and Edward Prescott. 1977. Rules Rather Than Discretion: The Inconsistency of Optimal Plans. *Journal of Political Economy* 85: 473–91.

Lebergott, Stanley. 1964. *Manpower and Economic Growth: The American Record since 1800.* New York: McGraw-Hill.

Mankiw, N. Gregory. 1985. Small Menu Costs and Large Business Cycles: A Macroeconomic Model of Monopoly. *Quarterly Journal of Economics* 100: 529–37.

Nixon, Richard. 1962. *Six Crises.* Garden City, NY: Doubleday.

Okun, Arthur. 1970. *The Political Economy of Prosperity.* Washington, DC: Brookings Institution.

Rockoff, Hugh. 1984. *Drastic Measures: A History of Wage and Price Controls in the United States.* New York: Cambridge University Press.

Romer, Christina. 1986. Spurious Volatility in Historical Unemployment Data. *Journal of Political Economy* 94 February: 1–37.

Romer, Christina, and David Romer. 1995. Federal Reserve Private Information and the Behavior of Interest Rates. University of California, September. Manuscript.

Rudebusch, Glenn, and David Wilcox. 1994. Productivity and Inflation: Evidence and Interpretations. San Francisco: Federal Reserve Bank of San Francisco. Photocopy.

Samuelson, Paul A., and Robert M. Solow. 1960. Analytical Aspects of Anti-Inflation Policy. *American Economic Review* 50 (May): 185–97.

Sargent, Thomas. 1982. The Ends of Four Big Inflations. In *Inflation: Causes and Effects,* ed. Robert E. Hall. Chicago: University of Chicago Press.

Simons, Henry. 1947. Rules versus Authorities in Monetary Policy. In *A Positive Program for Laissez-Faire and Other Essays.* Chicago: University of Chicago Press.

Stein, Herbert. 1984. *Presidential Economics.* New York: Simon and Schuster.

Taylor, John. 1980. Aggregate Dynamics and Staggered Contracts. *Journal of Political Economy* 88: 1–23.

———. 1992. The Great Inflation, the Great Disinflation, and Policies for Future Price Stability. In *Inflation, Disinflation, and Monetary Policy,* ed. Adrian Blundell-Wignal. Sidney, Australia: Ambassador Press.

Tufte, Edward. 1978. *Political Control of the Economy.* Princeton: Princeton University Press.

Viner, Jacob. 1936. Mr. Keynes on the Causes of Unemployment: A Review of John Maynard Keynes, *The General Theory of Employment Interest and Money. Quarterly Journal of Economics* 51, no. 1: 147–67.

Volcker, Paul, and Toyoo Gyohten. 1992. *Changing Fortunes: The World's Money and the Threat to American Leadership.* Ed. Lawrence Malkin. New York: Random House.

Weir, Margaret. 1992. *Politics and Jobs.* Princeton: Princeton University Press.

Wells, Wyatt C. 1994. *Economist in an Uncertain World: Arthur F. Burns and the Federal Reserve, 1970–1978.* New York: Columbia University Press.

Comment   John B. Taylor

Bradford De Long's paper is a wonderful read. It starts with a convincing demonstration of the historical significance of the 1970s inflation (the great inflation), documenting its long duration, its multinational dimension, and its probable lasting effect on the future course of economic policy and history. As the 1970s fade into the past—already today's college freshmen have no direct memory of this period—it is valuable merely to record these events and the lessons to be drawn from them. Monetary theory—more so than any other branch of economics—needs this type of history to supplement our understanding of how policy affects the economy. The paper brings this history alive with juicy quotes from both the economists and the politicians who made economic policy during this period.

De Long not only documents the history of the great inflation, he examines its causes. He concludes, and I agree, that the "price shocks" of the 1970s were not the cause of the inflation; in fact, the inflation was already under way before 1972 when the oil price shocks began. To this I would add that the oil price

John B. Taylor is professor of economics at Stanford University.

shocks of the late 1970s had very small inflationary effects in Japan after a much less accommodative monetary policy was put in place.

De Long also apparently rejects modern time-inconsistency arguments as an explanation of the great inflation. The rejection is implicit because he completely omits any discussion of the subject. Surprisingly, he does not even mention the well-known time-inconsistency work of Barro and Gordon (1983) or Kydland and Prescott (1977), which may be the most frequently cited reason why monetary policy led to excessively high inflation. Is De Long correct in dismissing this argument out of hand?

In fact, the time-inconsistency model does have the potential to explain the great inflation, as argued by Parkin (1993). In the basic Kydland-Prescott model of the inflation/unemployment trade-off, the "suboptimal" consistent policy (or what Barro and Gordon call the discretion policy) is assumed to be the long-run equilibrium inflation rate and unemployment rate. There is an important theorem about this suboptimal equilibrium: the higher the natural rate of unemployment is, the higher the equilibrium inflation rate is.

Parkin uses this theorem to explain the 1970s inflation in the United States by noting that the natural rate of unemployment rose in the 1970s, as the young postwar baby-boom generation entered the workforce, and declined in the 1980s as the baby-boom generation aged. Hence, the time-inconsistency model implies that the equilibrium inflation rate should have risen in the 1970s and fallen in the 1980s, just as the actual inflation rate rose and fell. I have questioned the Parkin explanation (Taylor 1993b) on the grounds that the time-inconsistency model is not persuasive as a positive economic theory in the case of the inflation-unemployment trade-off, because people would see the suboptimality of the equilibrium and attempt to fix it with laws or other social arrangements. But even if one finds the time-inconsistency model persuasive in this case, the Parkin explanation fails another important test; in particular, it does not explain why inflation also rose and then fell in Europe where the natural rate of unemployment kept rising throughout the 1980s. Hence, as my brief summary indicates, De Long is probably right to reject time inconsistency as an explanation of the great inflation.

De Long argues that the main reason for the great inflation—the "truest" cause—was the memory of the Great Depression itself and the deep fear people had of a return to high unemployment. In other words, he argues, policymakers and the public were willing to let inflation rise because, having recently experienced the high unemployment of the 1930s, they worried that maintaining price stability would lead to greater unemployment.

I have doubts about De Long's explanation. If the experience of the Great Depression caused Americans and their political leaders to sacrifice the goal of price stability in the late 1960s and 1970s, then why did monetary policy leave the price level so nearly stable during the 1950s and early 1960s—a period much closer to the Great Depression and nearly as long? We should have seen the inflation rate rise much earlier. The timing is off in De Long's story. True, as De Long argues, the great inflation may just have been an accident waiting to happen, but I think there are more explicit factors that must have played a role.

In my view the development by economists and the adoption by policymakers of new macroeconomic ideas in the 1960s (the New Economics) deserves much of the credit, or blame, for the great inflation. The ideas were intellectually exciting, carefully explained, and widely disseminated; and the timing was just about perfect to explain the events.

First was the idea that there was a long-run Phillips curve, which appeared in the *Economic Report of the President* (for example, 1969, 95) and many textbooks, and which was widely discussed by the media. This idea indicated that the cost of an overheated economy would simply be higher inflation, rather than accelerating inflation.

Second was the view that the "full-employment unemployment rate" (what we would now call the natural rate) was 4%, and perhaps even lower. Although there was little evidence for this low figure at the time, it was put forth by many economists, including the Council of Economic Advisers (CEA), and it became widely accepted and difficult to change. As late as 1976 when a different CEA revised the estimate to 4.9%, they were widely criticized by politicians and the public for doing so (*Economic Report of the President* 1977). I recall that when Alan Greenspan and Burt Malkiel testified before the Joint Economic Committee about their CEA's upward revision, they were lambasted by Senator Hubert Humphrey. That their estimate did not quite hit 5% may be indicative of their concern about confronting too directly the persistent and strongly held views about the 4% estimate held outside of economists' circles.

This low estimate of the natural rate and the notion of a long-run Phillips curve trade-off led politicians to a certain fearlessness about using monetary policy to overstimulate the economy. For example, President Johnson was driven by his desire to put "easy money" people on the Federal Reserve Board. According to Joseph Califano in the "Guns and Butter" chapter of his *Triumph and Tragedy of Lyndon Johnson* (1991, 109), Federal Reserve Board chairman Martin "was threatening to resign if Johnson put another liberal on the Board." Califano then goes on to explain how, nevertheless, Johnson managed to find yet another Federal Reserve Board candidate, who the president was convinced had good "easy money" credentials, and then make this appointment to the board despite Martin's strong misgivings.

A counter to this argument about the influence of the long-run Phillips curve is that as early as 1968 Milton Friedman and Edmund Phelps were explaining that there was no such thing as a Phillips curve; excessive monetary expansion which temporarily brought unemployment below the natural rate would lead to *accelerating* inflation. However, at least in its early years, the Friedman-Phelps accelerationist model appears to have had little practical influence in leading to greater price stability. What the accelerationist model did, in my view, was transform analysis based on the old-fashioned Phillips-curve model, which had already led to higher inflation, into an analysis showing that the costs of disinflation were so great that we should either not reduce inflation or we should do so incredibly gradually. For example, as late as 1978, in a *Brookings Papers on Economic Activity* issue entitled "Innovative Policies to Slow Inflation," George Perry (1978) showed that it would require 10% of GDP to reduce inflation by 1%. Pessimistic estimates such as these undoubtedly affected policymakers' thinking.

In the 1974 White House *Economists Conference on Inflation* with President Ford, virtually all the distinguished economists bemoaned the extraordinarily high costs of inflation reduction. Because of these costs Paul Samuelson and Walter Heller emphasized that perhaps inflation was not much of a problem. As Walter Heller stated at the conference, "in bringing inflation to its knees, we will put the economy flat on its back" (128). And Samuelson argued eloquently that we do not need a Winston Churchill-like "blood, sweat, and tears" program to reduce inflation (71). Among the economists at the conference only Milton Friedman argued unequivocally for inflation reduction: the "strength [of the U.S. economy] is currently being eroded by the disease of inflation. If that disease is not checked it will take a heavy toll including, in my opinion, the very likely destruction of our personal, political and economic freedoms. . . . I heartily applaud, also, the expressed determination of the Federal Reserve to slow monetary growth . . . despite the cries of anguish about this table and elsewhere about tight money, the slowing has so far lasted two or three months so we cannot yet be sure the Fed has really departed from the ever more inflationary path it has been following for the past decade" (122–23).

But Milton Friedman was the exception. The more common view among economists throughout the 1970s was that it was hardly worth the high costs to reduce inflation, and this view was based on the expectations-augmented Phillips curve, not simply the original Phillips curve.

In my view, the introduction of rational expectations as a model of the expectations term in the Phillips curve was ultimately influential in changing views both about the costs of reducing inflation and the costs of inflation itself. Thomas Sargent and Neil Wallace's striking estimate (1975) that the costs of disinflation were essentially zero for a credible policy certainly got people to think about alternative views. My own estimate made in the late 1970s (which incorporated both sticky prices and rational expectations) found that the disinflation costs were 60% smaller than George Perry had reported (see Taylor 1993a).

But whatever its source, the realization that the costs of disinflation might be smaller than the most dire warnings coupled with the clear dislike by the general public of inflation ultimately led to the end of the great inflation orchestrated by Paul Volcker at the Fed. Jimmy Carter and his advisers get credit for appointing Volcker to the Fed, and Ronald Reagan and his advisers get credit for helping to maintain the Fed's disinflation resolve through the early 1980s.

Ronald Reagan's explicit support for the Fed's price-stability goals in 1982 even when unemployment was high and the midterm elections approached (see Martin Feldstein's retrospective [1994]), contrasts sharply with Lyndon Johnson's attitude toward inflation in the late 1960s as reported by Joseph Califano. Hence, the fifteen-year cycle of macroeconomic opinion corresponds closely with changes of opinion of the top national economic policymakers as well as with the timing of the rise and fall of the inflation rate, that is, with both the great inflation and the great disinflation.

In my view, these changing economic theories and opinions about inflation are the ultimate cause of the changes in actual inflation. At the least this view provides a more complete explanation of the timing of the event than the "accident waiting to happen" view put forth in De Long's excellent history of the times.

References

Barro, Robert, and David B. Gordon. 1983. Rules, Discretion, and Reputation in a Model of Monetary Policy. *Journal of Monetary Economics* 12 (July): 101–21.

Califano, Joseph A., Jr. 1991. *The Triumph and Tragedy of Lyndon Johnson.* New York: Simon and Schuster.

Economic Report of the President. 1969. Washington, DC: Government Printing Office.

Economic Report of the President. 1977. Washington, DC: Government Printing Office.

Economists Conference on Inflation. 1974. Report Volume 1. Washington, DC. September 5.

Feldstein, Martin. 1994. American Economic Policy in the 1980s: A Personal View. In *American Economic Policy in the 1980s,* ed. Martin Feldstein, 1–79. Chicago: University of Chicago Press.

Kydland, Finn, and Edward Prescott. 1977. Rules Rather Than Discretion: The Inconsistency of Optimal Plans. *Journal of Political Economy* 85 (June): 473–92.

Parkin, Michael. 1993. Inflation in North America. In *Price Stabilization in the 1990s,* ed. Kumiharu Shigehara, 47–83. London: Macmillan.

Perry, George. 1978. Slowing the Wage-Price Spiral: The Macroeconomic View. *Brookings Papers on Economic Activity* 2 (1978): 259–99.

Sargent, Thomas, and Neil Wallace. 1975. "Rational" Expectations, the Optimal Monetary Instrument, and the Optimal Money Supply Rule. *Journal of Political Economy* 83: 241–54.

Taylor, John B. 1993a. *Macroeconomic Policy in a World Economy.* New York: Norton.

———. 1993b. Price Stabilization in the 1980s: An Overview. In *Price Stabilization in the 1990s,* ed. Kumiharu Shigehara, 1–6. London: Macmillan.

7   Do "Shortages" Cause Inflation?

Owen Lamont

7.1 Introduction

Policymakers and the media frequently state that inflation is in some way caused or preceded by shortages. For example, consider the following report on testimony by Federal Reserve Board chairman Alan Greenspan: "'At some point you really do run into restraints. . . . And the way you know that is that deliveries on materials begin to slow down, shortages begin to pop up, and you have all sorts of collateral indications that the system is running into shortages.' . . . The worry of Mr. Greenspan and other economists is that such tightness, if it persists, will eventually bring on inflation pressures" (*Wall Street Journal,* April 6, 1995, 2). This paper tests the hypothesis that shortages in goods and service markets cause inflation.

To test this hypothesis, one needs both a definition of the word "cause," and a measure of shortages. For causality I use Granger causality, so that I test whether observing shortages can assist in forecasting future inflation, given past inflation.

A measure of shortages is more problematic, since shortages by definition cannot be observed from price and quantity. One way to empirically estimate shortages is through the methods in Quandt (1988) and Fair and Jaffee (1972),

Owen Lamont is assistant professor of finance at the University of Chicago Graduate School of Business and a faculty research fellow of the National Bureau of Economic Research.

The author thanks Ben Bernanke, Olivier Blanchard, Kenneth Kuttner, Christina Romer, David Romer, Matthew Shapiro, Jeremy Stein, and participants at the University of Michigan Macroeconomics Seminar, the NBER Monetary Economics summer conference, and the Islamorada conference for helpful comments. The author also thanks Steve Cecchetti and John Driscoll for providing data, and Amy C. Ko, Kevin Grundy, and Sydney Ludvigson for research assistance.

which involve estimating a latent variable model using structural demand-and-supply equations. Another is to look at the "collateral indications" alluded to by Greenspan, which include vendor delivery speeds and measures of unfilled orders.

I attempt instead a frontal attack on the problem of observing shortages. I construct a new measure of shortages, namely the frequency with which the word "shortage" (or variants thereof) appears on the front page of the *Wall Street Journal* (*WSJ*) or the *New York Times* (*NYT*), two national daily newspapers. The basic idea is that, unlike the econometrician, the *WSJ* and *NYT* are able to observe and report on shortages that affect the national economy.

I proceed as follows. Section 7.2 very briefly reviews the intellectual pedigree of the idea of connection between inflation and shortages. Section 7.3 describes the method used to create the measure of shortages, and describes its univariate properties. Section 7.4 tests whether the shortage measure is statistically related to inflation, using a variety of specifications and types of data. I find that, using this measure, shortages are strongly positively correlated with, and strongly Granger-cause, monthly inflation. It appears that this measure of shortages captures information not found in other traditional measures of tightness and other variables and specifications designed to predict inflation. Section 7.5 concludes.

7.2   Shortages and Inflation: Theory

The connection between shortages and inflation has both theoretical history and some current interest.

An equilibrium price vector clears all markets. If for some reason prices do not immediately adjust to changes in demand or supply, markets do not clear: there are shortages or surpluses of goods. Textbook expositions of general equilibrium theory in the absence of a Walrasian auctioneer, for example Varian (1984), discuss the possibility that prices adjust according to a *tâtonnement* process: $dp/dt = G(z(p))$, where p is the price vector, $z(p)$ is a vector of excess demand, and G is some sign-preserving function of excess demand.

Macroeconomists are also interested in the possibility of sticky prices (e.g., Ball and Mankiw 1994b; Blanchard and Kiyotaki 1987; Blinder 1991; Mankiw 1985). If prices don't adjust, either quantities adjust or markets don't clear. Most recent work on the microfoundations of sticky prices has focused on the first possibility, that quantities adjust. For example, the models in Mankiw (1985) and Blanchard and Kiyotaki (1987) have firms who increase quantities and leave nominal prices fixed when faced with an increase in the money supply. The second possibility, that markets don't instantaneously clear, has received increasingly less attention as New Keynesian microfoundations for sticky prices have replaced older fixed-price assumptions. Blanchard and Fischer (1989) report that interest in disequilibrium dynamics peaked in the late 1970s.

For shortages to occur, it is necessary but not sufficient that prices be sticky; quantities must also be sticky. The traditional aim of sticky-price models has been to show that nominal variables, such as money, can have real effects. But if quantities are sticky, it is no longer clear that nominal money has real effects. It presumably depends whether quantities or prices adjust faster to disequilibria.

7.3 Data Construction

The data were constructed using the Nexis database of newspaper article abstracts for the *WSJ* and the *NYT*. The Nexis database had two main drawbacks. First, over the relevant time period it contained only abstracts, not the full text of articles. For an article to be included in the sample, "shortage" had to appear in either the abstract or the subject classification.[1] Second, the time period is fairly limited; the *WSJ* abstracts run from May 1973 to December 1994, while the *NYT* abstracts run from January 1969 to December 1994.[2]

Between May 1973 and December 1994, the word "shortage" appeared in 2,582 abstracted articles in the *WSJ*.[3] I limited my study to articles that appear on the front page of the newspaper, leaving 509 articles. Some of these articles reported on shortages in other countries (chiefly in the Soviet bloc and in third-world countries), and a very small portion reported on noneconomic shortages.[4] After removing articles that were not about shortages in the U.S. economy, a baseline sample of 433 articles remained.[5] I then created a monthly time series by counting the number of articles that occurred each month.[6] The *NYT* sample was derived similarly.

Table 7.1 shows summary statistics for both newspapers. Figure 7.1 shows the shortages measure derived from the *WSJ*.[7] It is immediately obvious from figure 7.1 that shortages were largely a phenomenon of the 1970s. Both the level of shortages and the variation fall markedly after 1980.

1. It appears as though the abstracts grew somewhat more verbose over time.
2. Unlike the *WSJ*, the *NYT* was inconsistently coded over this period. Abstracts were not available after 1980. Subjects were not available prior to 1973. Therefore, the *NYT* series is based on abstracts from 1969–73 and on subjects 1973–94. It did not appear that the slight change in series definition in January 1973 was a significant discontinuity, based on the overlap period of 1973–80.
3. More precisely, I searched for the eight-character string "shortage" so that the word "shortages" would also be found.
4. In general, the screening procedure erred on the side of inclusiveness. For example, shortages of blood, organs, and priests were all included. An example of article about noneconomic shortages was an article about hypoglycemia, described as a shortage of sugar in the blood.
5. Articles were judgmentally deleted if they were primarily about shortages in other countries (or, more rarely, about noneconomic shortages). These declines were clear-cut in articles about the Soviet Union, but somewhat arbitrary in dealing with articles about "world-wide shortages" and the Organization of Petroleum Exporting Countries.
6. I made the data monthly because standard measures of inflation are available at the monthly level. In principle, however, the times series could be daily (or, moving to electronic media such as the Dow Jones news tape, even hourly).
7. The complete data set is printed in the appendix.

Table 7.1   Summary Statistics: Monthly Shortages, *WSJ* and *NYT*

	WSJ	*NYT*
Sample	73:5–94:12	69:1–94:12
Number of months	260	312
Mean	1.67	2.36
Maximum	19	48
Minimum	0	0
Standard deviation	2.63	5.68
Autocorrelation	0.70	0.75

Note: "Monthly shortages" is the number of articles containing the word "shortage" or "shortages" per month.

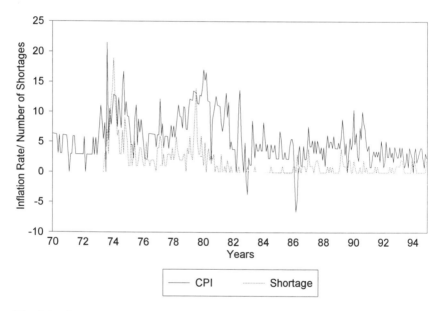

Fig. 7.1   Consumer price index inflation and *WSJ* shortages

The *WSJ* and *NYT* shortage series both appear to be stationary, since an augmented Dickey-Fuller test rejected the null hypothesis that there is a unit root.[8] There appeared to be no seasonal component in either shortage series.

The *WSJ* is ex ante likely to be a more accurate measure of shortages for two reasons. First, as a business journal, it seems more likely to cover economically important shortages. Second, the *NYT* covers metropolitan news of the New

8. Using twelve monthly lags and a constant term, the *t*-statistic was −4.65 < −2.89 for the *WSJ* and −4.11 < −2.89 for the *NYT*.

York area, so that it is a more noisy measure of national shortages.[9] Therefore, in what follows, I shall focus primarily on the *WSJ* results.

The method used to construct the shortage measure did not require that the article stated that shortages existed; it merely counted the appearance of the word, whether used hypothetically, in past or future tense, positively or negatively, and so forth.

I attempted to systematically classify *WSJ* shortages by product. About 40% of the *WSJ* shortages were energy related, 25% were labor related, and 7% were food related. Many of the shortages in the 1970s were petroleum related. The highest value of the *WSJ* shortage measure was nineteen in January 1974. Of these nineteen articles, eighteen were about shortages of energy and other petroleum-related products (the nonenergy article was about a shortage of paper). The next highest was July 1979, with fourteen articles. Of these fourteen, eleven were about shortages of energy and petroleum products (the other three were about shortages of shepherds, shortages of groceries due to a truckers' strike, and shortage of conversion equipment to convert from oil to gas heat). In the 1980s, in contrast, more of the shortages were related to labor. Of the four articles in March 1989, all were about shortages of workers (with one article on a shortage of produce workers, one on a shortage of service workers, and two on a shortage of nurses).

Attempts to gather other text-based measures of excess demand were not successful, since related words appeared far less frequently than the 1.67 monthly appearances of "shortage" in the *WSJ*. Synonyms for "shortage" that might indicate positive excess demand seemed rare; for example, the word "bottleneck" appeared a grand total of 3 times (or 0.01 times per month) in the *WSJ*.

Antonyms for "shortage" that might indicate negative excess demand were also relatively rare in the *WSJ*. In an economic context for the United States, "surplus" appeared only 0.29 times per month and "glut" appeared only 0.15 times per month. The vast majority of the "surplus" articles referred to a trade surplus or a budget surplus. I conclude from this that either surpluses and gluts of goods and services do not often occur in the U.S. economy, or the *WSJ* does not find them newsworthy. If gluts do not occur but shortages do, it may indicate that price adjustment is asymmetric.[10]

---

9. This is especially the case in the latter half of the sample, when there are very few nationally important shortages. Prior to 1982 the *NYT* and *WSJ* series are highly correlated; after 1982 they are essentially uncorrelated. For example, all of the five shortages in August 1985 *NYT* relate to local shortages in New York City.

10. See Ball and Mankiw (1994a) for one reason that price adjustment might be asymmetric. Note, however, that Ball and Mankiw's asymmetry cannot explain this pattern: they find with trend inflation, prices should be sticky downward, so we would expect to see gluts, not shortages.

7.4 Results

I examined two properties of the shortage measures. First, I tested whether shortages are contemporaneously correlated with inflation. Second, I examined whether shortages have predictive power for future inflation. In both cases I examined different subperiods, different levels of time aggregation, and different alternative models. Where possible, I tried to test the properties of the shortage measure in the context of previous empirical research on inflation.

7.4.1 Contemporaneous Correlation

Table 7.2 reports the coefficients and t-statistics from regressions of inflation on the shortage measure from the same period. The regressions also included lagged inflation, and a time trend. The results show that inflation is very strongly positively correlated with the shortage measure, at the monthly, quarterly, and annual level.

The coefficients from table 7.2 show the effect of an increase of one article per month on the inflation rate in percentage. So the first entry on the first line shows that if the *WSJ* increases the front-page appearance of the word "shortage" by one article per month, we would expect to see annualized consumer price index (CPI) inflation rise by about 0.32 percentage points.

The last row in table 7.2 puts the shortage measure into a simple empirical

Table 7.2   **Contemporaneous Correlation of Shortages and Inflation**

	WSJ Shortages		*NYT* Shortages	
	CPI	PPI	CPI	PPI
Monthly data	73:5–94:12		69:1–94:12	
	0.32	0.82	0.09	0.13
	(3.95)	(5.00)	(3.15)	(2.18)
Quarterly data	73:II–94:IV		69:I–94:IV	
	0.39	0.88	0.14	0.21
	(3.08)	(3.65)	(3.01)	(2.36)
Annual data	1973–94		1969–94	
	1.02	1.69	0.60	0.94
	(4.41)	(5.32)	(5.13)	(5.57)
Ball and Mankiw specification[a]				
		1973–89		1969–89
		0.95		0.50
		(4.35)		(3.71)

Notes: The table reports the coefficient and t-statistics (in parentheses) on the contemporaneous value of the shortage measure. All regressions include a constant term and one year of lagged dependent variables, but no lags of shortages; all regressions except the Ball-Mankiw specification include a time trend. The dependent variable is $100(\ln(P_t) - \ln(P_{t-1}))$ and is annualized.

[a]Current shortages put into the specification of Ball and Mankiw (1994a), table 4, column 2, which includes lagged annual inflation and ASYM10 (a measure of the asymmetry of price changes) on the right-hand side.

specification from Ball and Mankiw (1995), which includes as a regressor ASYM10, their measure of the asymmetry of relative price changes. The annual shortage measure survives the inclusion of Ball and Mankiw's variable.

7.4.2   Causality Tests

Table 7.3 reports Granger causality tests from shortages to CPI and producer price index (PPI) inflation. Panel A shows standard bivariate regressions and tests whether, given lagged inflation, lagged shortages help predict inflation. The results show that, beyond the shadow of a doubt, shortages Granger-cause inflation at a monthly frequency. At quarterly frequencies, the results are more ambiguous; shortages are significant in two out of four cases (and are near significant once). Finally, using annual data, last year's shortages appear to be mostly useless in forecasting this year's inflation, although we have at most twenty-five observations with which to test this hypothesis.

Panels B and C further explore the forecasting ability of shortages at the monthly level, using additional right-hand-side variables identified by previous researchers.[11] The table reports the p-value testing the proposition that shortages have predictive power for inflation in an equation that also includes these other control variables.

Panel B uses specifications from Bernanke (1990), who used interest rate variables to predict inflation. The first line shows the p-value for shortages in an equation that also includes lags of four different interest rate variables, including the federal funds rate (which captures the stance of monetary policy) and the slope of the yield curve (which captures inflationary expectations).[12] The second line shows the p-value from an equation including only the federal funds rate, which Bernanke found to be the single best predictor of inflation. Shortages are significant in seven out of these eight regressions, and near significant in the last; therefore shortages contain information about future inflation not present in interest rates.

Panel C uses specifications from Rotemberg, Driscoll, and Poterba (1991), who used various monetary aggregates, including the monetary base, M2, and their own proposed currency equivalent, CE-3. Shortages are significant eleven out of twelve times, so that it appears shortages contain information about monthly inflation that is not present in monetary aggregates in this period.

The main conclusion from table 7.3, then, is that shortages Granger-cause inflation at a monthly frequency, even conditional on other proposed predictors of inflation.

As shown in figure 7.1, shortages were dramatically less evident in the second half of the sample. The 1970s included two oil shocks and were a time of

---

11. I note that both Bernanke (1990) and Rotemberg, Driscoll, and Poterba (1991) used CPI inflation and did not investigate PPI inflation, so that their specifications might be more relevant for the CPI.

12. Fama (1990) and Mishkin (1990) also explore the use of the term structure to predict inflation.

Table 7.3   Granger Causality Tests

RHS Variable:	*WSJ* Shortages		*NYT* Shortages	
LHS Variable:	CPI	PPI	CPI	PPI
A. Bivariate Regressions[a]				
Monthly data	74:5–94:12		70:1–94:12	
	0.003	0.004	0.02	0.001
Quarterly data	74:II–94:IV		70:I–94:IV	
	0.20	0.001	0.07	0.01
Annual data	1974–94		1970–94	
	0.19	0.07	0.59	0.63
B. Bernanke Specification				
Monthly data	73:11–94:12		69:7–94:12	
4-RHS variables[b]	0.08	0.03	0.02	0.001
Fed funds only[c]	0.001	0.0001	0.01	0.0001
C. Rotemberg, Driscoll, and Poterba Specification[d]				
Monthly data	74:5–94:12		70:1–94:12	
MBASE	0.02	0.01	0.03	0.004
M2	0.001	0.01	0.01	0.0003
CE-3 (74:5–89:7)	0.01	0.11	0.01	0.001

Notes: the *p*-value tests the hypothesis that lagged shortages do not help predict inflation. All regressions include a constant term, trend, and lagged dependent variables.

[a]Each regression includes one year's worth of lagged dependent variables and lagged shortage variable.

[b]Following Bernanke (1990), table 5, model size 4, includes six-month lags of the federal funds rate, the six-month commercial paper rate, the spread between the long corporate bond rate and the ten-year treasury bond rate, and the spread between the federal funds rate and the ten-year treasury bond rate.

[c]Following Bernanke (1990), model size 1, includes six-month lags of the federal funds rate.

[d]Following Rotemberg, Driscoll, and Poterba (1991), table 6, includes twelve monthly lags of all variables. CE-3 is a version of Rotemberg et al.'s proposed monetary aggregate.

regulation of energy prices by the U.S. government. The disastrous experiment with price controls (1971–74) under the Nixon administration also occurred in this period, and led to widespread shortages (see Gordon 1984 for details).

One concern is, therefore, that the results in table 7.3 are driven either by the energy price shocks of the 1970s or by the Nixon price controls. I look next at these two issues.

7.4.3   Commodity Prices and Inflation

Since many of the shortages of the 1970s appear to have been oil related, it is important to test whether "shortages" just capture the "shortages" of oil. Table 7.4 explores the question of commodity price shocks and shortages. Is the shortage measure just a proxy for oil prices, or for the fact that oil prices in the United States were regulated during this period?

Panel A attempts to control for energy and food commodity price shocks by including lagged measures of commodity price shocks on the right-hand side,

Table 7.4   Controlling for Commodity Shocks Using Commodity Prices and Other Measures of Inflation

RHS Variable:	WSJ Shortages	
LHS Variable:	CPI	PPI
A. Controlling for Commodity Prices on RHS[a]		
	74:5–94:12	
PPI food, PPI fuel	0.01	0.01
	75:2–94:3	
Refiners' cost	0.01	0.06
	75:1–94:3	
Imported/domestic refiners' cost	0.02	0.16
B. Inflation Excluding Energy and Food on LHS[b]		
		76:2–94:12
PPI excluding energy		0.02
		74:5–94:12
PPI excluding energy and food		0.00
	74:5–94:12	
CPI excluding energy and food	0.00001	
C. Inflation Excluding Energy and Food, Controlling for Imported/Domestic Refiners' Cost on LHS[c]		
		76:2–94:3
PPI excluding energy		0.05
		75:1–94:3
PPI excluding energy and food		0.01
	75:1–94:3	
CPI excluding energy and food	0.00002	
D. Nonenergy Shortages on RHS[d]		
	74:5–94:12	
	0.05	0.08
E. Median CPI on LHS[e]		
	74:5–92:12	
CPI (mean)	0.004	
Median CPI	0.08	
Deviation (mean − median)	0.05	

Note: All regressions are monthly data as in table 7.3, panel A.

[a]Includes on the right-hand side lags of both PPI Fuel and PPI Food inflation, lags of the inflation rate of the refiner cost of imported oil, or lags of the ratio of the refiner cost of imported pertroleum to the refiner cost of domestic petroleum.

[b]Includes as left-hand-side variables different PPI and CPI inflation rates as calculated by the Bureau of Labor Statistics.

[c]Identical to panel B except that it includes lags of the imported/domestic refiner cost ratio as right-hand-side variables.

[d]Identical to table 7.3, panel A, except that it uses *WSJ* shortages excluding shortages of energy-related items.

[e]Median CPI as calculated by Bryan and Cecchetti (1994). "Deviation" is the mean CPI inflation rate minus the median CPI inflation rate.

in addition to the shortage measure. The first row uses inflation rates for the PPI Food and PPI Fuel indices. These two indices are also used by Ball and Mankiw (1995) to control for commodity price shocks in their study of PPI inflation. The second row uses the inflation rate for the refiners' cost of imported petroleum. The third row uses the ratio of the refiners' cost of imported petroleum to the refiners' cost of domestic petroleum; this is a measure of the regulation-induced price distortion in U.S. oil markets.[13] If the shortage measure is merely a proxy for regulation-induced price distortion, we might expect the shortage measure to lose its explanatory power in the presence of this variable.

The shortage measure remains significant in four out of these six regressions, and near significant in a fifth. The shortage measure fares worse using the imported/domestic petroleum cost ratio, but here as elsewhere it still significantly Granger-causes CPI inflation. In summary, panel A shows that for monthly inflation the shortage measure contains information about future inflation that is not present in commodity price inflation, at least for CPI inflation. Shortages are not just a proxy for oil prices.

Panel B uses, as dependent variables, measures of so-called core inflation, which exclude the effects of food and energy prices.[14] The results clearly show that the shortage measure contains information about the course of future core inflation at the monthly level. At very high levels of significance the shortage measure Granger-causes inflation excluding food and energy.

Of course, panel B is not proof that the shortages are not a proxy for oil shocks, since presumably oil prices also lead core inflation. Therefore panel C uses core inflation as a dependent variable and the imported/domestic petroleum cost ratio as a control variable. The shortage measure passes this particular test with flying colors. In fact, excluding food and energy from the PPI *improves* the significance of shortages (after controlling for the imported/domestic petroleum cost ratio).

Another way to disentangle the effects of the energy-related shortages of the 1970s is to remeasure the shortage variable itself. Panel D uses as an explanatory variable "nonenergy" *WSJ* shortages, defined as with all shortages excluding those related to petroleum, gasoline, natural gas, and other energy-related materials (which total about 40% of the observations). Nonenergy shortages are significant in explaining CPI inflation, and marginal in explaining PPI inflation.

Bryan and Cecchetti (1994) have found that the weighted median inflation rate is a good measure of (their definition of) core inflation, in that median inflation is more closely related to money growth and is a good predictor of future inflation. Panel E documents the relationship between the shortage mea-

---

13. I thank Matthew Shapiro for suggesting this variable.
14. These indices are calculated for the Bureau of Labor Statistics, and are seasonally adjusted except for the PPI excluding fuel and food.

sure and Bryan and Cecchetti's median CPI inflation series. Shortages are more closely related to mean inflation than to median inflation; consequently, shortages are positively correlated with (and significantly Granger-cause) inflation's deviation from median. This result is consistent with the idea that shortages are a transitory, high-frequency phenomena.

7.4.4   Subsample Stability

If the empirical significance of the shortage measure is limited to the decade of the 1970s, then it will be hard to conclude that shortages are a generally important phenomenon, since we know price controls lead to shortages. Thus the stability of the relationship between shortages and inflation is of particular interest. Table 7.5 addresses two questions. First, is the inflation-shortage connection purely a product of the Nixon price controls? Second, is the inflation-shortage connection limited to the 1970s, when energy prices were regulated? This second question is another way of addressing the issues in table 7.4.

Table 7.5 examines the stability of the relationship between *WSJ* shortages and inflation in different subsamples. I examine Granger causality and contemporaneous correlations. For comparison, the last column reports Granger-causality tests for inflation over the same subperiods for the growth rate of the M2 monetary aggregate.

First, is the explanatory power of the shortage measure driven by the Nixon price controls? On this narrow question we have a definite answer from table 7.5. Limiting the sample to January 1976 to December 1994 (well after the Nixon price controls, which ended in 1974) does not affect the overall results. Shortages strongly Granger-cause inflation in the post-Nixon period.[15]

On the wider question of the 1970s, panel A shows that lagged shortages have predictive power for CPI and PPI inflation in the first half of the sample (1974–82) but not in the second (1983–1994). Like M2, the shortage measure is by this reckoning not a robust predictor of inflation in this period.[16]

The importance of these oil-shock years is a common finding in empirical work on inflation, as is the general nonrobustness of time-series relationships in recent macroeconomics. As noted by Fischer (1981), for example, much of the relationship between relative price variability and inflation comes from energy and food price changes in these years.[17] Bernanke (1990) finds that the forecasting power of interest rates for inflation has also deteriorated significantly since 1980.

Panel B reports contemporaneous correlations between inflation and short-

---

15. I thank David Romer for suggesting this subsample.

16. Using the monetary base instead of M2 produces similar results: the monetary base has predictive power in only half the sample. The difference is that the monetary base has power in the first half of the sample but not in the second.

17. Debelle and Lamont (1997), however, offer some evidence that, cross-sectionally in U.S. cities, the relationship between inflation and relative price variability is not dependent on these years.

Table 7.5   **Subsample Stability**

RHS Variable:	WSJ Shortages			M2 (Log-Differenced)[a]		
LHS Variable:	CPI	PPI	Wages	CPI	PPI	Wages
A. Monthly Granger-Causality Tests						
74:5–82:12	0.04	0.01	0.05	0.91	0.14	0.92
83:1–94:12	0.68	0.38	0.01	0.01	0.64	0.46
76:1–94:12	0.03	0.01	0.0004	0.30	0.91	0.30
B. Contemporaneous Correlation						
73:5–82:12	0.27	0.82	−0.05			
	(2.23)	(4.04)	(0.36)			
83:1–94:12	0.45	1.11	−0.34			
	(2.04)	(2.01)	(1.22)			
76:1–94:12	0.32	0.59	0.11			
	(3.01)	(2.85)	(0.80)			

Notes: See notes to tables 7.2 and 7.3. *t*-statistics are in parentheses.
[a]Subsample stability for log-differenced M2, for comparison only.

ages, and gives us some additional evidence on the stability of the shortages-inflation connection. Unlike lagged shortages, current shortages maintain their statistical significance over both halves of the sample, and the correlations are roughly the same over the two periods.

Since many of the shortages of the 1980s were labor shortages, table 7.5 also reports on analogous subsample stability statistics for a different type of inflation measure: the rate of change of manufacturing workers' hourly earnings. Panel A shows that, unlike CPI and PPI inflation, wage inflation is Granger-caused by shortages in both subperiods. Panel B shows that, unlike CPI and PPI inflation, there appears to be no contemporaneous correlation between monthly shortages and monthly wage inflation (for the whole sample, the coefficient is 0.01). In sum, the connection between wage inflation and shortages is highly stable over time.

Why does the predictive ability of shortages break down in panel A? As is visually obvious from figure 7.1, there is marked shortage of "shortages" in the 1990s. It is likely to be difficult to estimate the effect of "shortages" using a time period in which there was very little variation in the explanatory variable. Unlike M2, we have a good idea why the predictive ability of lagged shortages breaks down: because there very few shortages in the second half of the sample.

One way to summarize the relationship's subsample stability is to estimate a vector autoregression (VAR) over the two subsamples. Figure 7.2 shows impulse response functions from VARs estimated separately over the pre-1982 and post-1982 period.[18] The figure shows the dynamic response of the annu-

18. This VAR included on the right-hand side a constant term and twelve monthly lags of both WSJ shortages and the annualized monthly PPI inflation rate. The shortage measure was ordered

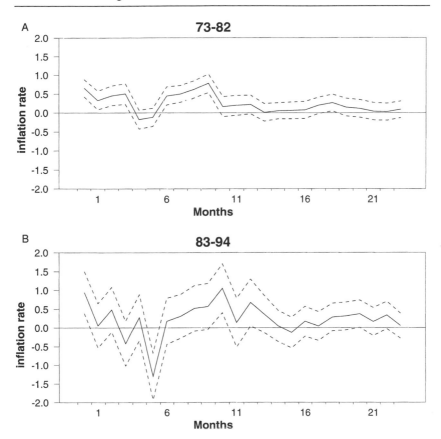

Fig. 7.2 **Response of producer price index inflation to *WSJ* shortages, 1973–82 and 1982–94**

alized PPI inflation rate in an innovation in the *WSJ* shortages measure of one additional article per month. The figure also shows one-standard-error bands, constructed using standard Monte Carlo simulation.

As one would expect from panel B, in both subperiods the publication of one additional article results in a contemporaneous increase in (annualized) PPI inflation of about 1 percentage point. This increase is somewhat lower than 1 before 1982, and somewhat higher than 1 after 1982. As one would expect from panel A, the response of inflation to shortages is positive and more than two standard errors from zero prior to 1982. After 1982, the response of inflation is larger but is less than two standard errors from zero.

Figure 7.2 certainly does not present a ringing endorsement of a positive correlation between shortages and future inflation in the post-1982 period. On

first in the VAR system. Annualized PPI inflation is defined as 1,200 times the difference in the log of the PPI index.

the other hand, the shape of the impulse response functions is broadly similar over the two periods, although the magnitude of the response is more erratic in the later period. Figure 7.2 also shows that standard error bands are much wider in the later period, so that one cannot reject the hypothesis that shortages and future inflation are positively correlated after 1982.[19]

The bottom line from table 7.5 and figure 7.2 is that the evidence is ambiguous. One cannot reject the hypothesis that there is no relationship between inflation and lagged shortages after 1982, but one also cannot reject the hypothesis that the relationship is stable over the two periods. Contemporaneously, CPI and PPI inflation and shortages are always positively and significantly correlated.

7.4.5   Is "Shortage" Just a Synonym for "Inflation"?

One possible problem with the shortage measure constructed here is that it depends on the precise use of language by journalists. Business reporters might simply use the word "shortage" when they really mean inflation (or perhaps shifts in the supply schedule). For example, the following was one of the data points: "buying could push some industries closer to capacity limits, lead to shortages, and force prices up further" (*WSJ*, February 17, 1977, 1). This sentence describes purely hypothetical shortages, and is consistent with a world where shortages never occur in actuality.

If "shortage" is just another word for "inflation," then the shortage measure constructed here might have predictive power because it captures the inflationary expectations of business reporters. To test this hypothesis, I measured the appearance of "inflation" in the same way that I measured "shortage." Table 7.6 reports the results.

Taken in isolation, the word "inflation" has little predictive power. What happens when the regression includes both lagged "inflation" and lagged "shortage"? Conditional on monthly "shortage," monthly "inflation" does not have predictive power for inflation at conventional significance levels. Conditional on monthly "inflation," monthly "shortage" does have significant predictive power for inflation.[20] I therefore conclude from table 7.6 that "shortage" is not merely a synonym for inflation. When a *WSJ* reporter uses the word "shortage," he or she does something that is statistically distinguishable from using the word "inflation."

---

19. The analogous impulse response functions for CPI inflation look less similar to each other. However, it is still true that both periods have impulse response functions with positive contemporaneous effects of a shock and fairly wide standard-error bands. One certainly can't reject that the correlation between shortages and future CPI inflation is positive in the post-1982 period.
20. Similar results hold for the *NYT* series. An earlier version of this paper used the *NYT* data on "inflation" and "shortage" in the period January 1970–June 1980 and found that, conditional on monthly "shortage," monthly "inflation" does not have predictive power for inflation at conventional significance levels.

Table 7.6   **"Shortage" versus "Inflation" Granger-Causality Tests**

	WSJ	
LHS Variable:	CPI	PPI
	74:5–94:12	
"Inflation" only[a]	0.48	0.08
"Inflation" and "Shortage"	74:5–94:12	
"Inflation"[b]	0.57	0.47
"Shortage"[c]	0.01	0.05

Notes: The *p*-value tests the hypothesis that lagged shortages do not help predict inflation. All regressions include a constant term, trend, and twelve months of lagged dependent variables.

[a]Tests the hypothesis that twelve lags of the number of "inflation" articles do not help predict actual inflation.

[b]Tests the hypothesis that twelve lags of the number of "inflation" articles do not help predict actual inflation, given lagged "shortage" and lagged inflation.

[c]Tests the hypothesis that lagged "shortage" does not predict actual inflation given lagged "inflation" and lagged inflation.

7.4.6   Other Measures of Tightness/Shortages

Table 7.7 compares the shortage measure with other traditional measures of tightness in the U.S. economy. If the shortage measure used here really does measure economically important shortages, it should be positively correlated with other measures of tightness and negatively correlated with other measures of slack. If on the other hand, it is so correlated with these other measures that it contains no additional information, then we would conclude that the shortage measure is not a useful contribution to economic analysis.

Capacity utilization and industrial production are perhaps the most widely used measures of tightness, and are explicitly used by the Fed to predict inflation.[21] Unfilled orders and the National Association of Purchasing Managers' vendor performance index are also popular measures.[22] The *WSJ* article cited in section 7.1 discusses the merits of, and the Fed's fondness for, the vendor performance index as an indicator of inflationary pressures. Inventory-sales ratios are included to measure possible stockouts of goods. Overtime hours, the help-wanted advertising index, and the unemployment rate are standard measures of labor market tightness; the regression with the unemployment rate might be interpreted as a Phillips curve.[23] Finally, the Commerce Department's leading indicators index is included as a summary of economic conditions.

Table 7.7 tests both the predictive relationship between shortages and these

21. A long tradition uses capacity utilization to explain inflation; see Gordon (1989) for references. Shapiro (1989) finds, however, that capacity utilization is not helpful in explaining cross-sectional price changes.

22. Shapiro (1989) discusses both these measures.

23. I thank Olivier Blanchard for suggesting the help-wanted index.

Table 7.7   **Other Measures of Tightness/Slack, Monthly PPI Inflation**

	Correlation[a]	Granger Causality[b]		PPI Inflation[c]	
		S to C	C to S	S to π	C to π
Capacity utilization					
WSJ	0.38	0.0003	0.06	0.07	0.001
NYT	0.27	0.0000004	0.14	0.01	0.19
Industrial production (log differenced)					
WSJ	−0.19	0.00004	0.31	0.004	0.12
NYT	−0.16	0.00	0.79	0.001	0.04
Unfilled orders, durable manufactured goods (log differenced)					
WSJ	0.35	0.01	0.18	0.03	0.19
NYT	0.22	0.01	0.01	0.02	0.05
Vendor performance index (slower deliveries)					
WSJ	0.40	0.06	0.04	0.08	0.69
NYT	0.36	0.0004	0.0002	0.03	0.54
Inventory-sales ratios, manufacturing and trade					
WSJ	−0.33	0.02	0.29	0.03	0.02
NYT	−0.20	0.08	0.12	0.01	0.002
Manufacturing workers overtime					
WSJ	−0.05	0.02	0.02	0.07	0.04
NYT	0.004	0.00001	0.01	0.06	0.08
Unemployment rate					
WSJ	−0.31	0.04	0.25	0.09	0.49
NYT	−0.21	0.0002	0.30	0.004	0.47
Help-wanted index (log)					
WSJ	0.04	0.002	0.57	0.01	0.07
NYT	0.06	0.002	0.16	0.002	0.12
Leading indicators index (log differenced)					
WSJ	−0.24	0.0001	0.84	0.01	0.75
NYT	−0.23	0.000001	0.85	0.001	0.38

Notes: Estimation period is May 1974–December 1994 for *WSJ* and January 1970–December 1994 for *NYT*. *S* is shortage measure, *C* is candidate alternative measure for tightness. Every regression includes a time trend, and twelve months' lags of all variables.

[a]The correlation coefficient of the shortage measure, *S*, with the candidate measure, *C*.

[b]Tests whether *S* Granger-causes *C* and whether *C* Granger-causes *S*.

[c]Tests whether *S* or *C* Granger-cause PPI inflation, in a regression with both lagged *S* and lagged *C*.

measures, and whether shortages have predictive power for inflation that is not contained in these measures. The first column displays the correlation coefficient of shortages with the candidate measure of tightness.[24] As expected, shortages are positively correlated with other measures of tightness, such as capacity utilization, unfilled orders, and the slowness of vendors' deliveries. Shortages are negatively correlated with indicators of slack such as the unemployment rate and the inventory-sales ratio.

24. This is the standard correlation coefficient, as opposed to the regression coefficient reported in table 7.2.

The next two columns test whether shortages Granger-cause these candidate measures, and whether these candidate measures Granger-cause shortages. In five out of eighteen cases the candidate measures of tightness Granger-cause the shortage measure. In contrast, shortages have predictive power for the candidate measure in sixteen out of eighteen cases at the 5% level and in every case at the 10% level. Interestingly, shortages appear to be an excellent predictor of output-related series such as employment and industrial production. I leave for future research a full examination of the relationship between shortages and output.

The last two columns report on the predictive power of shortages and the candidate variables, in the presence of each other, for PPI inflation. Conditional on the lagged candidate variable, lagged shortages have predictive power at the 5% level in thirteen out of eighteen cases and at the 10% level in all cases. In contrast, the candidate variables have a spotty record (six are significant at the 5% level and eight are significant at the 10% level).

In terms of consistent Granger causality, inventory-sales ratios have the best record, since they Granger-cause inflation in the presence of either the *WSJ* or the *NYT* shortages. In this case, shortages are also significant at the 5% level. Shortages fare worse in the presence of overtime hours; here the *p*-values are 0.07 for the *WSJ* and 0.06 for the *NYT*.

I conclude from table 7.7 that the shortage measure contains information about inflation not present in other measures of tightness in the economy. It appears to fairly robust to the inclusion of these other measures, and is always significant at the 10% level.

7.5 Conclusion

The methodology used here shares some of the features of the "narrative" approach of Romer and Romer (1989), since both involve examining textual evidence. Compared with the "narrative" approach, however, the approach used here is more quantitative and requires less judgment from the empiricist. It might be called the "quantitative textual" approach. Although this approach is new to macroeconomics, it is often used in other disciplines that analyze texts.

This methodology has produced a variable that appears to be strongly related to high-frequency movements in inflation. At the very least, then, this paper introduces a potentially useful new variable for forecasting inflation at the monthly level. On the other hand, this variable appears to be less useful in forecasting long-term inflation. Of course, I have considered only twenty-one years of *WSJ* data here, so making long-term evaluations is difficult. One possible avenue for future research would be collecting more data, since in principle the time series could go back as far as the *WSJ* itself.

Since there is little evidence that shortages can predict long-term inflation, and since there have so far been very few "shortages" in the 1990s, the usefulness of the shortage measure for monetary policymaking appears limited (although the quotation at the beginning of this paper suggests that the Fed seriously worries about shortages). On the other hand, should the appearance of the word "shortage" on the front page of the *WSJ* suddenly increase in coming months, it would appear prudent for forecasters and policymakers to take this into account.

We all know from personal experience that markets do not literally clear perfectly and instantaneously. Prices do not always equilibrate supply and demand; this fact explains the existence of such economic phenomena as restaurant reservations, waiting lists, queues, and stockouts. Whether disequilibrium is empirically important to macroeconomics is another question. The evidence presented here suggests that disequilibrium is an observable part of the dynamic adjustment of prices to macroeconomic shocks, since the shortage measure contains information that is not present in other variables.

Appendix

Table 7A.1   Monthly Data Shortage Measure

	NYT Monthly Shortage												WSJ Monthly Shortage											
	1	2	3	4	5	6	7	8	9	10	11	12	1	2	3	4	5	6	7	8	9	10	11	12
1969	1	3	2	0	1	3	2	6	6	3	1	7												
1970	4	3	1	4	1	2	7	6	5	2	3	2												
1971	3	3	4	1	2	1	5	2	0	0	5	3												
1972	4	3	1	1	1	2	1	2	0	1	4	4												
1973	1	0	4	1	1	3	7	7	0	2	23	48	19	12	10	6	0	3	3	7	3	8	12	14
1974	30	47	20	5	4	4	1	1	7	7	5	10	1	1	5	1	7	3	3	7	3	9	7	5
1975	4	3	0	1	0	3	2	1	2	1	0	1	1	1	5	2	3	5	1	1	2	4	4	2
1976	0	3	1	0	1	0	0	0	3	1	0	2	1	1	5	2	2	1	2	2	2	1	0	4
1977	24	20	5	2	3	0	3	0	1	2	4	2	4	6	5	1	3	1	2	3	3	3	2	4
1978	5	7	3	1	3	1	0	1	0	0	2	0	2	3	6	4	3	2	2	2	3	3	0	4
1979	1	6	7	6	25	32	34	9	4	0	2	0	3	6	3	2	5	10	14	5	3	3	6	3
1980	2	2	2	1	2	0	0	0	0	1	0	0	1	5	0	3	4	2	3	2	3	0	1	1
1981	4	4	0	1	2	0	2	3	0	0	2	0	0	0	3	0	1	0	0	1	1	0	1	0
1982	0	0	0	0	0	0	0	0	0	1	0	0	0	0	0	0	0	1	0	0	0	0	0	0
1983	0	0	0	1	0	2	0	0	0	0	0	0	0	0	0	0	0	0	1	0	0	0	0	0
1984	0	1	2	0	0	3	1	5	3	1	0	1	0	0	0	3	0	0	0	1	1	1	0	0
1985	0	0	0	4	0	1	4	0	0	1	0	0	0	1	1	1	0	1	2	2	1	0	0	1
1986	2	2	1	1	0	1	2	0	1	0	1	0	4	0	1	1	0	1	2	2	1	0	0	1
1987	0	1	0	0	1	1	2	0	0	0	0	1	0	0	0	1	0	0	0	1	0	0	0	0
1988	0	2	0	0	1	0	3	1	0	1	0	3	0	1	4	2	1	1	1	0	0	2	0	0
1989	1	0	2	2	1	0	1	0	2	1	0	0	2	1	0	0	0	1	0	1	2	2	0	0
1990	0	1	1	0	1	0	0	2	2	0	0	2	0	0	0	0	0	1	0	0	2	0	1	0
1991	1	0	0	0	0	0	0	0	0	0	1	0	0	0	0	0	0	0	0	0	0	0	0	0
1992	0	0	1	0	0	0	0	0	1	0	0	1	1	0	2	0	0	0	0	1	0	0	1	1
1993	1	0	0	0	3	0	1	0	0	1	0	0	1	1	1	2	1	0	0	0	0	0	0	2
1994	2	2	1	1	3	0	0	0	0	0	1	1	1	2	1	0	0	0	0	0	0	0	0	2

References

Ball, Laurence, and N. Gregory Mankiw. 1994a. Asymmetric Price Adjustment and Economic Fluctuations." *Economic Journal* 104 (March): 247–61.

———. 1994b. A Sticky Price Manifesto. *Carnegie-Rochester Conference Series on Public Policy* 41:127–51.

———. 1995. Relative Price Changes as Aggregate Supply Shocks. *Quarterly Journal of Economics* 110 (February): 161–93.

Bernanke, Ben S. 1990. On the Predictive Power of Interest Rates and Interest Rate Spreads. *New England Economic Review* (November–December): 51–68.

Blanchard, Olivier J., and Stanley Fischer. 1989. *Lectures on Macroeconomics.* Cambridge: MIT Press.

Blanchard, Olivier J., and Nobuhiro Kiyotaki. 1987. Monopolistic Competition and the Effects of Aggregate Demand. *American Economic Review* 77 (September): 647–66.

Blinder, Alan S. 1991. Why Are Prices Sticky? Preliminary Results from an Interview Study. *American Economic Review* 81 (May): 89–96.

Bryan, Michael F., and Stephen G. Cecchetti. 1994. Measuring Core Inflation. In *Monetary Policy,* ed. N. Gregory Mankiw, 195–219. Chicago: University of Chicago Press.

Debelle, Guy L., and Owen Lamont. 1997. Relative Price Variability and Inflation: Evidence from US Cities. *Journal of Political Economy,* forthcoming.

Fair, Ray C., and Dwight M. Jaffee. 1972. Methods of Estimation for Markets in Disequilibrium. *Econometrica* 4 (May): 497–514.

Fama, Eugene F. 1990. Term Structure Forecasts of Interest Rates, Inflation, and Real Returns. *Journal of Monetary Economics* 25: 59–76.

Fischer, Stanley. 1981. Relative Shocks, Relative Price Variability, and Inflation. *Brookings Papers on Economic Activity,* no. 2: 381–431.

Gordon, Robert J. 1984. *Macroeconomics.* 3d ed. Boston: Little, Brown and Co.

———. 1989. Assessing the Federal Reserve's Measures of Capacity and Utilization: Comment. *Brookings Papers on Economic Activity,* no. 2: 226–35.

Mankiw, N. Gregory. 1985. Small Menu Costs and Large Business Cycles: A Macroeconomic Model of Monopoly. *Quarterly Journal of Economics* 100 (May): 529–37.

Mishkin, Frederick S. 1990. The Information in the Longer Maturity Term Structure about Future Inflation. *Quarterly Journal of Economics* 105 (August): 815–28.

Quandt, Richard. 1988. *The Econometrics of Disequilibrium.* Cambridge, MA: Basil Blackwell.

Romer, Christina D., and David H. Romer. 1989. Does Monetary Policy Matter? A New Test in the Spirit of Friedman and Schwartz. *NBER Macroeconomics Annual* 4:121–69.

Rotemberg, Julio J., John C. Driscoll, and James M. Poterba. 1991. Money, Output, and Prices: Evidence from a New Monetary Aggregate. NBER Working Paper no. 3824. Cambridge, MA: National Bureau of Economic Research.

Shapiro, Matthew D. 1989. Assessing the Federal Reserve's Measures of Capacity and Utilization. *Brookings Papers on Economic Activity,* no. 2: 181–225.

Varian, Hal R. 1984. *Microeconomic Analysis.* 2d ed. New York: Norton.

Comment   Matthew D. Shapiro

Owen Lamont has assembled a new data set in the best spirit of social science. He has identified a question: Do shortages or disequilibrium conditions cause inflation? He observes: data on prices and quantities do not provide a direct measure of disequilibrium. He therefore seeks new data. Specifically, he systematically collects a new data set designed to provide a direct measure of the phenomena in question. His data on shortages—as well as his paper calling attention to their role in an important period of economics history—are likely to stimulate further analysis. The paper is valuable in calling attention to the topic of shortages. And its original data set should stimulate further research.

We should applaud the effort to create and analyze new and unconventional data. Too often, economists limit themselves to conventional measures that are readily available in databases. Lamont's effort, and that of Robert Shiller in this volume, to use textual searches as a source of data is an interesting approach that is worthy of further study. There is presumably research on how to do such searches optimally. Economists using these techniques should avail themselves of such research.

My discussion concerns Lamont's analysis of this time series of shortages. First, I discuss the historical setting and economic institutions in which these shortages arose. I then turn to the statistical analysis of the effect of Lamont's index of shortages on the price level.

Let me begin the historical discussion with some personal history. The time: June 1979. I am driving to Washington, DC, after graduating from college to start working as a junior staffer at President Carter's Council of Economic Advisers. I am driving my first car (yes, it was my father's Oldsmobile) and am considering the class-day address of John Kenneth Galbraith. It was as if his speech were made directly to me. Galbraith had exhorted the class to government service. I thought the principles he had articulated in the address would be useful as I strolled the corridors of government.

But I was about to get a much more visceral lesson in economic policy. I was greeted in Washington by two-hour waits for gasoline at the Georgetown Amoco station. I had to cancel a Fourth of July rafting trip because it was clear I would not be able to get gasoline for the return trip. Perhaps I should have been reading Galbraith's *Theory of Price Control*. Although President Nixon's price controls had largely been phased out several years earlier, price controls for petroleum products remained in place. When the second Organization of Petroleum Exporting Countries (OPEC) price shock occurred, these controls led to a large gap between the domestic and world price of oil. The shortages that I so woefully experienced were caused by the price controls.

There was a complicated system of "entitlements" allocating the cheaper,

Matthew D. Shapiro is professor of economics at the University of Michigan and a research associate of the National Bureau of Economic Research.

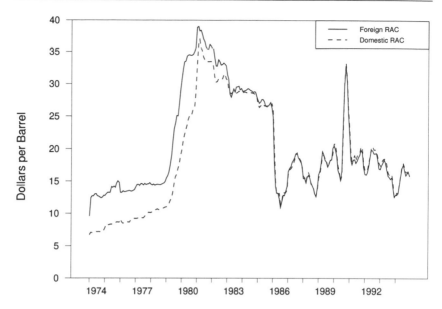

Fig. 7C.1   Refiners' acquisition cost

domestically produced oil to U.S. refineries. Owing to this regulation of supply, there are data on the price refiners paid for oil. Figure 7C.1 shows refiners'
acquisition cost (RAC) for a barrel of foreign and domestically produced crude
oil. Figure 7C.2 shows the difference between the prices. The difference widened sharply after the first OPEC shock, narrowed, and then widened dramatically after the second OPEC shock. The prices converged following President
Carter's phased deregulation of oil prices in 1980.

The key result of Lamont's paper—that newspaper mentions of "shortage"
are correlated with inflation—can be explained by the interaction of the oil
price shocks and the price controls. The oil price shocks created upward pressure on the price level. The partial price controls caused rationing and queues:
it was hard to buy gasoline, but when it was purchased, the price was higher.

Figure 7C.3 shows the *Wall Street Journal* index of shortages versus the
difference of the foreign and domestic RAC from figure 7C.2. The two spikes
in the shortages come at the beginning of the two OPEC episodes. Newspapers
cover events when they first occur. Coverage diminishes for ongoing events.
Hence, the shortage index has spikes and is a leading indicator. Yet it is clear
that most of the leverage of the shortages series is associated with the widening
of the wedge between foreign and domestic RAC.

Lamont is aware of the possibility that "shortage" is a proxy for "oil shock."
He presents two types of statistical evidence to support the hypothesis of the
incremental explanatory power of shortages. First, he checks directly for incremental explanatory power by estimating equations for predicting inflation with
both the shortages and other variables. Second, he looks for the effect of short-

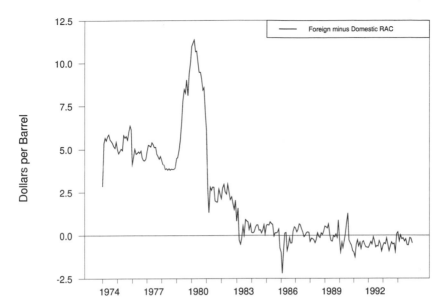

Fig. 7C.2   Difference between foreign and domestic refiners' acquisition cost

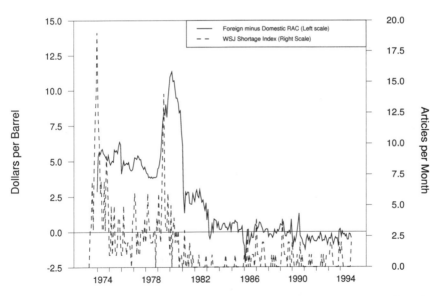

Fig. 7C.3   "Shortages" versus difference between foreign and domestic refiners' acquisition cost

ages in the sample period excluding the OPEC shocks. My reading of the statistical evidence is that the correlation of shortage and inflation is strictly a phenomenon of the oil shocks.

In table 7.4 Lamont examines whether the predictive power for inflation of shortages remains statistically significant when other variables are also included in the regression. The statistical significance of shortages drops when RAC or the wedge between the foreign and domestic RAC is included in the regression. In particular, if inflation is measured by the PPI, shortages are no longer statistically significant when the RAC is included (panel A). Moreover, the nonpetroleum shortages have only marginally significant predictive power for inflation (panel D).

Lamont checks for subsample stability in table 7.5 and figure 7.2. The aim is to establish whether inflation is predicted by shortages when the economy is not afflicted by the oil shocks. The first panel of table 7.5 gives the statistical significance of the forecastability of inflation by the index of shortages. There is essentially no predictive power of shortages for inflation in the 1983–94 sample. This finding is consistent with the hypothesis that the shortage index is merely a proxy of the oil price shocks. It predicts inflation only in the 1970s. There is, however, a significant contemporaneous correlation between price increase and shortages (table 7.5, panel B). This correlation could lead to dynamic response of inflation to a shortage through the lags in the inflation process. Lamont's figure 7.2 reports such dynamic responses. There is a significant response of inflation to shortages in the first subsample—the period of the oil shocks. But in the second subsample, the impact is small and insignificant. Indeed, after about half a year, the impact on the price level of shortages is zero (the positive impulse responses of inflation are followed by negative ones).

Interestingly, the Granger test of shortages for wages rejects no causality in the second subsample. But the contemporaneous correlation has the wrong sign. This wrong sign is likely also a feature of the dynamic response of wages to shortage. Given that most mentions of shortage in the 1980s refer to the labor market, this wrong sign is particularly problematic for the claim that shortages have a generic role in explaining U.S. inflation.

In summary, though Lamont's paper makes a substantial contribution by calling attention to the role of oil shortages in the 1970s, it fails to show that shortages have any generic role in the U.S. inflation process. What the paper does suggest, however, is another channel for the stagflationary supply shocks of the 1970s. Partial price controls allowed some of the world oil price increase to affect the overall price level, but they also had the effect of reducing output by the rationing and queues they created.

III   The Contribution of
        Monetary Institutions

8   Institutions for
Monetary Stability

Christina D. Romer and David H. Romer

8.1 Introduction

A generation ago, economists who believed that the performance of monetary policy could be improved focused their criticisms and proposals on the specifics of how policy was conducted. Friedman (1960) and other monetarists, for example, argued that monetary policy mistakes would be greatly reduced if the Federal Reserve adopted such policies as money targeting and 100% reserve requirements.

Since that time, there has been growing empirical and theoretical evidence that the specifics of policy are highly dependent on institutional arrangements. On the empirical side, characteristics of central banks such as their legal independence, the average tenure of their governors, and the objectives enshrined in their charters have been found to have strong associations with average inflation rates (see, for example, Alesina 1988; Grilli, Masciandaro, and Tabellini 1991; Cukierman, Webb, and Neyapti 1992). On the theoretical side, it has been shown that policymakers' ability to commit to their actions, the government's ability to delegate control over policy, and contracts between the government and policymakers can affect average money growth and many other

Christina D. Romer is professor of economics at the University of California, Berkeley, and a research associate of the National Bureau of Economic Research. David H. Romer is professor of economics at the University of California, Berkeley, and a research associate of the National Bureau of Economic Research.

The authors thank Laurence Ball, Guy Debelle, Jeffrey Frankel, Benjamin Friedman, Donald Kohn, Maurice Obstfeld, Dani Rodrik, Lars Svensson, and Carl Walsh for helpful comments, and the National Science Foundation for financial support.

features of policy (see, for example, Kydland and Prescott 1977; Rogoff 1985; Walsh 1995b; Persson and Tabellini 1993).

This evidence suggests that efforts to improve the performance of policy should focus not on the specifics of policy, but on institutions. This paper is therefore concerned with the design of institutions to produce desirable monetary policy. We seek to identify the governmental structures that would overcome the obstacles to good monetary policy both today and in the future.

The first step in this analysis is to identify the sources of monetary policy mistakes in the past: only by knowing what the obstacles to good policy have been can we think sensibly about what institutions could make policy better. In section 8.2, we argue that dynamic inconsistency has been overemphasized as a source of monetary policy failures. While there surely is an incentive for policymakers to inflate once expectations are set, this is not the crucial obstacle to desirable policy that many have assumed.[1] Instead, we suggest that limited knowledge about how the economy operates and the effects of policy has been a much more pervasive obstacle to good policy. We use a series of examples of monetary policy failures in the United States and abroad to show that limited knowledge on the part of economists, monetary policymakers, and elected leaders and voters has been a frequent source of monetary policy mistakes.

Sections 8.3 and 8.4 consider the design of monetary institutions in light of this analysis. Section 8.3 considers what institutional features are likely to address the individual problems we identify. As one might expect, the solutions to one problem may exacerbate another. For example, a binding rule concerning the ultimate objectives of policy or the specifics of how policy is to be conducted is an obvious way to deal with the problem of dynamic inconsistency. But such a legislated rule may be highly undesirable if expert knowledge about how the economy operates is limited. Similarly, long terms for monetary policymakers may lessen the problems caused by uninformed politicians and voters, but they make it hard to remove policymakers who turn out to be incompetent.

In section 8.4, we discuss one combination of institutions, selected from the menu of possibilities presented in section 8.3, that is likely to produce desirable outcomes in the face of the whole array of problems. Some components of this institutional arrangement are completely standard. For example, it includes a highly independent central bank as a way of both overcoming dynamic inconsistency and of allowing policy to be determined by specialists who are likely to be particularly well informed about monetary policy issues.[2] Other features of the arrangement, however, are less conventional. For example, it

---

1. Previous studies of the design of monetary institutions by Rogoff (1985), Lohmann (1992), Walsh (1995b), Persson and Tabellini (1993), and Debelle and Fischer (1994) all presume that the central problem that needs to be solved is inflationary bias arising from dynamic inconsistency.

2. Walsh (1995b) and Debelle and Fischer (1994) mention the potential value of having monetary policy conducted by specialists, but do not develop this idea.

includes complete goal and instrument independence for the central bank so that advances in economic understanding can be incorporated rapidly into decision making. It also includes a two-tier system, where politicians choose a board of trustees for the central bank and the board of trustees chooses the actual policymakers. If the trustees have long terms of office, this system creates a delay in the government's control over the central bank that is likely to largely eliminate political pressure on policymakers. At the same time, this system makes it possible to have short terms of office for the actual policymakers, and thus allows incompetent policymakers to be removed quickly.

Section 8.5 discusses the recent monetary reforms in industrialized countries and the proposed design of the European Central Bank in light of our analysis of the causes and remedies for monetary policy mistakes. Most of these reforms consist of shifts within the existing institutions to policies that make price stability the central goal of policy. We argue that these changes do not address the underlying problems that gave rise to excessive inflation and other policy failures in the past, and that they therefore do little to reduce the likelihood of policy failures in the future. But we find that the reforms in New Zealand and in proposals for the European Central Bank do alter monetary institutions in ways that are likely to lead to substantial improvements in policy.

8.2 Sources of Monetary Policy Failures

In order to determine which policy institutions are likely to produce desirable outcomes, it is important to understand the reasons that policy can go astray. This section therefore describes the most important potential sources of problems in monetary policy. We identify four major sources of problems.

8.2.1 Dynamic Inconsistency

The first, and best-known, potential source of suboptimal monetary policy is the dynamic inconsistency of low-inflation policy. Dynamic inconsistency arises when expectations are forward-looking and the socially optimal level of output exceeds the equilibrium level. In this situation, the rate of money growth that is optimal after expectations are determined is greater than the rate that is optimal ex ante. As a result, rational policymakers who wish to maximize social welfare have an incentive to be overly expansionary.

Dynamic inconsistency may be an important source of high inflation. For example, the fact that inflation is lower in countries with central banks that are more independent is consistent with the view that dynamic inconsistency leads to excessive inflation. Similarly, Romer (1993) and Lane (1994) show that, because the real exchange depreciation that is caused by unanticipated monetary expansion is more harmful in more open economies, theories based on dynamic inconsistency predict that inflation should be lower in more open economies. Both studies find that this prediction is confirmed by the data.

8.2.2   The Limits of Available Knowledge

Dynamic inconsistency, however, may not be the central source of imperfect monetary policy that many assume. A second potential source of problems is that expert knowledge at any time of the workings of the economy and the effects of policy is imperfect. The best that policymakers can do is to act on the basis of the evidence that is available when they make a decision. Subsequent improvements in knowledge may reveal, however, that different policies would have been preferable under the circumstances.

There are many important examples of problems in monetary policy that appear to have been caused at least partly by the limitations of the best available knowledge. Freedman (1993) and De Long (chap. 6 in this volume), for example, argue that such incomplete knowledge was an important source of the high inflation rates of the 1970s. The evidence available at the time suggested that there was (or at least that there might be) a permanent output-inflation trade-off. In addition, the costs of moderate inflation appeared small. As a result, when policymakers were confronted with negative supply shocks, increases in the natural rate of unemployment, and the productivity growth slowdown, they rationally believed that the benefits of accommodating these shocks exceeded the costs. It seems unlikely that they would have made the same choices if they had known then, as we know today, that there is not a permanent trade-off and that the costs of moderate inflation are in fact substantial. If this analysis is correct, it implies that one important reason for the overly expansionary policies of the 1970s was not dynamic inconsistency, but limited expert knowledge.

Friedman and Schwartz's (1963) description of U.S. monetary policy after World War I provides a very different example of the effects of imperfect understanding. According to Friedman and Schwartz, little was known at that time about the lags in the effects of monetary policy. As a result, when the Federal Reserve's initial shifts toward tighter policy in November 1919 did not have an immediate impact on the economy, policymakers responded with additional rounds of tightening in January and June 1920 (Friedman and Schwartz 1963, 229–39). The result was a major downturn in the economy that was largely unintended.

The issues of optimal inflation and the benefits of stabilization provide more timely examples of the potential importance of limited knowledge. There has not been any comprehensive quantitative analysis of the potential costs and benefits of alternative rates of inflation. For example, it is only very recently that the first thorough attempt has been made to quantify the impact of inflation on welfare through its impact on saving and the composition of the capital stock (Feldstein, chap. 3 in this volume); there are only a handful of studies of the issue of whether moderate inflation improves microeconomic efficiency by permitting downward adjustments in real wages without nominal wage cuts (McLaughlin 1994; Kahn 1994; Card and Hyslop, chap. 2 in this volume); and empirical work on the link between inflation and long-run growth has barely advanced beyond the examination of simple correlations (Fischer 1991, 1993; Rudebusch and Wilcox 1994; Barro 1995).

As a result, policymakers have no choice but to operate on the basis of intuition and fragments of evidence. Estimates of the optimal inflation rate range from moderate deflation, to zero, to moderate inflation, and policymakers in different countries appear to have different estimates. It is likely that once we have a fuller understanding of the costs and benefits of inflation, we will be able to determine that some or all of these estimates were inaccurate, and we may find that in many cases there would have been large gains from aiming for different inflation rates.

Similarly, defensible views about the benefits of using policy to stabilize the economy range from the position that the benefits are trivial to the view that they are enormous. If stabilization policy only reduces the variance of output around its mean, its likely benefits are small (Lucas 1987; Atkeson and Phelan 1994). But if the aggregate supply curve is significantly nonlinear, then stabilization policy can fill in the troughs in output with only small offsetting reductions in the peaks, and can thus raise average output considerably (De Long and Summers 1988). Likewise, if stability has an important effect on investment, then stabilization policy can have a substantial impact on long-run growth (Meltzer 1988).

Since we have little clear evidence on nonlinearities in aggregate supply or the importance of macroeconomic stability to investment, we do not know whether the benefits of stabilization are large or small. Thus again policymakers must make their judgments on the basis of highly imperfect evidence, and again there is a substantial chance that advances in knowledge will eventually cause them to change those judgments.

8.2.3 Policymakers' Limited Knowledge

A third potential source of imperfect policy is incomplete understanding on the part of policymakers. Even if good information about the workings of the economy and the effects of policy is available, the individuals who determine policy may not have that information. There is no reason to expect knowledge of matters that are relevant to monetary policy to be instantly disseminated to everyone in the economy: since there are costs to acquiring even knowledge that is in the public domain, individuals' understanding of monetary policy issues is likely to be heterogeneous. For citizens whose only influence over monetary policy is through voting, for example, the benefits of acquiring accurate information about policy are negligible. Thus it would be surprising if they had a state-of-the-art understanding of the relevant issues, and it would not be surprising if they were unaware of important pieces of knowledge. At the other extreme, individuals who specialize in conducting policy are likely to have strong incentives to acquire relevant information. Even among these individuals, however, understanding is likely to vary: such factors as their experience, their instrinsic abilities, and the rewards that they face for conducting policy successfully are likely to influence their knowledge. Finally, since elected leaders are likely to have less control over monetary policy than those directly in charge of policy, and since they have less time to devote to monetary policy, their understanding of the relevant issues is likely to fall between that of voters and that of monetary policymakers.

U.S. monetary policy in the Great Depression provides the most famous example of a policy failure that may have been due to policymakers' lack of awareness of the best available evidence about the workings of the economy and the effects of policy. In Friedman and Schwartz's view, the failure of policy to respond to the banking panics and the depression was largely the result of the death of Benjamin Strong and the shift of power from the Federal Reserve Bank of New York to the Board of Governors in Washington. According to Friedman and Schwartz (1963, chap. 7), the governors knew relatively little about the importance of monetary policy in stemming the panics and in combating the depression— not because such knowledge was unavailable, but because they had little experience or expertise in such matters. It was this lack of knowledge on the part of policymakers that led the Federal Reserve to stand idly by as the U.S. economy collapsed in the early 1930s.

The modern experiences of less-developed countries provide many examples of policy failures that appear to have been caused by policymakers' incomplete understanding of existing knowledge. Even among those who make monetary policy, knowledge of such basic matters as the importance of money growth to inflation is not universal. For example, Simonsen (1988) argues that the underlying source of the failure of Brazil's Cruzado plan in 1986 was that policymakers believed that Brazilian inflation was entirely inertial, and that it could therefore be eliminated by incomes policies alone. As he puts it: "The big mistake of the government was to confound necessary with sufficient conditions and to diagnose inflation as a purely inertial problem. Demand inflation took its revenge" (262). The necessity of lowering aggregate demand growth in order to reduce inflation is sufficiently well documented that it is unlikely that more knowledgeable policymakers would have made the same mistake. Nor is Simonsen's diagnosis controversial: Cardoso (1988, 288), Macedo (1988, 296), and Ortiz (1988, 300) all concur with his analysis.

Russian monetary policy under Viktor Gerashchenko in 1992–93 provides another example of a policy failure that appears to have been due to policymakers' lack of understanding of existing knowledge about the sources of inflation. As many observers have described, Gerashchenko believed that the underlying source of Russian inflation in this period was inadequate supply, and that low money balances were an important constraint on supply. He therefore believed that rapid expansion of the money stock through credits to former state enterprises would reduce inflation (see Sachs 1994, for example). The result was massive inflation.

8.2.4 Elected Leaders' and Voters' Limited Knowledge

The final potential source of problems in monetary policy is that, even if the individuals who set policy share the best available knowledge about the economy, they may answer to individuals who do not. This problem can take two general forms. The first is that elected leaders' understanding of the economy may be limited. De Long (chap. 6 in this volume), for example, argues that, regardless of whether Federal Reserve officials understood the dangers of expansionary policies in the late 1960s and early 1970s, the presidents and their political advisers did not. Thus an underlying source of the expansionary policies in that period, in his view, was elected leaders' imperfect understanding of the economy.

A more common example of the potential harms of elected leaders' imperfect knowledge is the widespread tendency of newly elected leaders from liberal parties—Carter and Clinton in the United States in 1977 and 1993, Mitterrand in France in 1981, and many others—to pressure monetary policymakers to pursue expansionary policies early in their terms. These policies are not plausibly explained as resulting from optimizing economic or political calculations: more often than not, the resulting inflation requires moves to tighter policies later in the leader's term, often with highly unfavorable political consequences. Instead, they appear to result from a desire to improve economic conditions (either for political benefit or out of genuine concern for social welfare), coupled with imperfect knowledge of the long-run consequences of expansionary policy.

The macroeconomic policies of "populist" Latin American leaders described by Dornbusch and Edwards (1990, 1991) are more extreme instances of this type of policy failure. Peru's economic policies under Alan Garcia from 1985 to 1990 provide the clearest example. Garcia and his advisers believed that inflation resulted from such factors as oligopoly, limited credit availability, and exchange rate depreciation. Indeed, they believed that expansion of aggregate demand, by allowing firms to exploit returns to scale, would reduce inflation. They therefore pursued policies of rapid monetary and fiscal expansion coupled with price controls (Dornbusch and Edwards 1990; Lago 1991). The results were disastrous.

The second, and possibly more important, way in which monetary policymakers may be influenced by incompletely informed individuals is that elected leaders must in turn answer to voters, whose understanding is likely to be quite limited. There are many different ways in which voters' imperfect understanding can cause problems in monetary policy. For example, like many politicians, voters are likely to understand the short-run benefits of monetary expansion, but may fail to realize the long-run inflationary consequences. As a result, voters generally favor expansionary policy. Citizens, and the journalists from whom they receive most of their information, seem to view reductions in interest rates as obviously good and increases in interest rates as typically bad. This view leads to pressure on monetary policymakers for expansion.[3]

A related example of how imperfect knowledge on the part of voters may lead to poor monetary policy is the political business cycle. Since voters do not know precisely how the economy operates and have little incentive to find out, they may evaluate leaders on the basis of unemployment and inflation at the ends of their terms. This gives leaders an incentive to advocate monetary policies that produce recessions early in their terms (and hence lower inflation), and rapid growth as election day approaches. Nordhaus (1975) shows that this effect of voters' limited knowledge is indeed present to some extent in the United States and other industrial democracies.

Voters' imperfect information can also give rise to fiscal pressures on monetary policy. Persistent budget deficits, coupled with limits on the government's ability to borrow, are an important source of high inflation in many less-developed countries. One possible explanation of this reliance on money finance is that the public has only a limited understanding of the links between deficit spending and inflation. The harms of reduced deficits, such as higher taxes, reduced government employment, and higher prices of subsidized goods, are readily apparent and thus likely to be well understood. But, as Buchanan and Wagner (1977) argue, the benefit of reduced deficits—namely, lower inflation—is not as clearly linked to fiscal policy, and thus may be systematically underestimated.

8.3 Possible Institutional Remedies for Policy Failures

Having described the most important sources of problems in monetary policy, we now turn to the issue of how to design the institutions of monetary policy to deal with these problems. Our argument proceeds in two steps. In this section, we investigate what institutional features can address each problem individually. Then, in section 8.4, we discuss the question of what combination of institutions would be likely to produce desirable outcomes in the face of all of the problems.

8.3.1   Dynamic Inconsistency

The most straightforward solution to the problems created by the dynamic inconsistency of low-inflation policy is for policy to be made according to a binding rule. Under such a rule, policy cannot depart from what is announced ex ante. Thus there is no barrier to following a low-inflation policy.

---

3. The fact that limited knowledge on the part of politicians and voters leads to pressure for expansion may help explain the widespread acceptance of dynamic inconsistency as the crucial problem of monetary policy. Dynamic inconsistency provides an elegant explanation for the tendency toward overexpansion that we often observe. But it may not in fact be the main source of this tendency: the pressure for expansion typically comes from outside the central bank rather than from within, and the pressure appears to stem more from limited knowledge of the long-run consequences of expansionary policy than from optimizing calculations.

Arrangements that make it costly but not impossible to deviate from an announced policy can also allow policymakers to achieve lower inflation than they can under complete discretion. The costs can take the form of monetary penalties, loss of prestige, or removal of policymakers from their positions. For example, there are generally believed to be costs to governments of breaking agreements to keep their exchange rates fixed. Such agreements can therefore help countries maintain low inflation. Similarly, directly penalizing policymakers for pursuing expansionary policies can also counteract the inflationary bias created by dynamic inconsistency (Walsh 1995b; Persson and Tabellini 1993).

Empirically, we often observe countries achieving low inflation without any of these types of arrangements. And, as Taylor (1983) observes, many governments overcome dynamic inconsistency problems in other settings, such as patent law and capital taxation, without such measures. In the case of monetary policy, there are three leading explanations of these successes. The first is that they stem from the delegation of policy to individuals who place more weight on achieving low inflation than is warranted by its effect on social welfare (Rogoff 1985). The second is that they arise because policymakers' horizons are longer than a single period. With longer horizons, policymakers have incentives to establish reputations as being anti-inflationary (for example, Barro and Gordon 1983; Backus and Driffill 1985). The final possibility is that forward-looking expectations are relatively unimportant to the output-inflation trade-off. For example, as we describe below, New Zealand took major steps in the late 1980s to make credible commitments to reducing inflation. But Debelle (1996) finds that these efforts had little impact on the output costs of the subsequent disinflation. In the extreme case where there is no forward-looking element to the behavior of inflation, low-inflation policy is not dynamically inconsistent, and thus no measures are needed to deal with dynamic inconsistency. In sum, if dynamic inconsistency is a problem at all, there appear to be several ways of overcoming it.

8.3.2   The Limits of Available Knowledge

The fact that the best available knowledge about the economy and policy is limited clearly cannot be fully solved. But there are at least two ways of allowing improvements in knowledge to be reflected as rapidly as possible in policy. The first, which we discuss below, is to put policy under the control of individuals with a state-of-the-art understanding of the relevant issues. Such experts are likely to incorporate advances in knowledge into monetary policymaking faster than less-informed individuals.

The second way of dealing with limited knowledge is to give policymakers the ability to use their state-of-the-art understanding. That is, one important way of dealing with the fact that our knowledge is growing is the opposite of the first solution to the dynamic inconsistency problem: policy should be made according to discretion. If the best available evidence at a given time about policy is incorporated into a binding rule, the conduct of policy cannot reflect improvements in knowledge. If monetary policymakers had adopted a rule in the 1920s, for example, it might have been one of procyclical policy to provide an "elastic currency"; in the 1950s or 1960s, it might have been one of rapid feedback aimed at stabilization and at maintaining low unemployment; and in the 1970s, it might have been one of steady growth of M1 or M2. In light of what has been learned since those times, it seems likely that any one of those rules would have had large costs. And as we emphasize above, there is little reason to believe that we now have a firm understanding of the best policy rule.

Our imperfect knowledge concerns not just the specifics of how policy should be conducted to achieve a given set of objectives, but also what those objectives should be. For example, as described above, there have been major advances is recent decades in our understanding of the appropriateness of low unemployment as a goal for monetary policy, and there is still great uncertainty about such fundamental issues as the optimal rate of inflation and the benefits of stabilization. Thus, for discretion to address the problem of limited knowledge, the discretion must concern both the implementation and the objectives of policy. That is, our analysis implies that—in contrast to the presumption of such authors as Fischer (1995)—policymakers should have not only instrument independence, but goal independence as well.

8.3.3 Policymakers' Limited Knowledge

The natural solution to the problem that policymakers' knowledge may not be at the frontier of our understanding is to delegate policymaking to experts. When knowledge is heterogeneous, policy should be made by well-informed individuals with the discretion to use their knowledge. The natural way to do this is to delegate control of policy to an independent central bank.

This argument for central bank independence is very different from the argument implied by dynamic inconsistency. In that case, the purpose of central bank independence is to delegate policy to individuals who do not share prevailing views about social welfare. Here, in contrast, the purpose is to delegate policy to individuals who are particularly adept at evaluating and maximizing social welfare.

In addition, concern about policymakers' knowledge and skills provides an argument for short terms of office for policymakers and for allowing for their reappointment. Policymakers' knowledge and skills are heterogeneous, and their conduct of policy is likely to reveal considerable information about them along these dimensions. If policymakers can be evaluated frequently and dismissed if they are not performing well, then it is possible to take advantage of this information. Thus it will be possible to raise policymakers' average skill level.

8.3.4 Elected Leaders' and Voters' Limited Knowledge

The problems created by the facts that policymakers must answer to elected officials, who must in turn answer to the public, may be the hardest to solve.

Policymakers must ultimately be responsible to the public; if not, there would be nothing to prevent them from pursuing objectives completely unrelated to social welfare. Yet if elected leaders or voters have systematic misunderstandings of policy, it is hard to see how to prevent those misunderstandings from being reflected in policy.

The key to resolving this difficulty is that many important cases of imperfect understanding stem from the fact that the costs and benefits of restrained money growth occur at different horizons. The costs of a recession to achieve price stability are immediate, but the benefits of the resulting increased capital formation and higher standard of living are spread over the indefinite future. The pain of eliminating a money-financed budget deficit through higher taxes, lower government employment, and higher prices of previously subsidized goods is felt quickly, while again the advantages of greater stability and growth accrue only slowly.

This discrepancy in the timing of the costs and benefits of low money growth suggests two institutional features that may help overcome the problems created by elected leaders' and the public's limited knowledge. The first is to make policymakers' terms relatively long. Specifically, their terms should be long enough that a substantial fraction of the benefits of any moves toward low money growth are apparent by the ends of their terms. Consider, for example, policymakers faced with high inflation. If their terms are short, they will know that, if they embark on a policy of disinflation, the economy will probably be suffering through a recession when their terms end. If their terms are long, on the other hand, they will know that inflation may be low and unemployment normal by the time they are eligible for reappointment.

The second way to address these problems is to create delays in elected leaders' influence over policy. Specifically, if there are long enough lags that elected leaders cannot determine the policies that will be undertaken during their terms, they have no incentive to try to influence policy to exploit the public's misunderstandings. For example, leaders who cannot influence policy until after they are up for reelection have no way of catering to the public's desire for low interest rates during their terms, or of pursuing a traditional political-business-cycle policy.

Long terms of office for policymakers are one way to create delays in elected leaders' control over policy: if policymakers' terms are considerably longer than elected leaders', then policy during a leader's term will be determined mainly by individuals appointed by his or her predecessors. Even with long terms of office, however, an elected leader who can appoint a policymaker has an immediate influence over policy. For example, if the term of the head of the central bank ends shortly before an election, the elected leader may have an incentive to appoint someone who will pursue expansionary policy.

A more effective way to create delays in elected leaders' influence over policy is therefore through a two-level system where the leaders appoint members of a board of trustees of the central bank, which in turn selects the ultimate policymakers. If the trustees' terms are long enough that an elected leader cannot appoint a majority of members of the board during his or her term, then the elected leader has essentially no ability to bring about expansionary policy before he or she is up for reelection.

The appointment of the presidents of the regional Federal Reserve banks in the United States has elements of this type of two-level system: the appointment of the bank presidents must be approved by the Board of Governors, whose members are in turn appointed by the president and confirmed by Congress. Our analysis predicts that policymakers appointed indirectly will favor less expansionary policies than ones appointed directly. This prediction is confirmed by the behavior of the bank presidents and governors: the bank presidents have a systematic tendency to favor less expansionary policies than the governors (Belden 1989).

8.4   Combining the Possible Remedies

The analysis in the previous section does not provide clear guidance concerning what set of institutions is likely to produce desirable overall outcomes. Several of the institutional features we discuss, such as binding rules and long terms of office for policymakers, are helpful with regard to some problems but counterproductive with regard to others. This section therefore considers how the different features could be combined.

8.4.1   A Possible Combination

A possible combination of institutions that could substantially address all of the problems we have discussed is one with the following key features:

* an independent central bank with discretion concerning both the ultimate goals and the specific operation of policy;
* a two-level structure where policymakers are appointed by a board of trustees, who are in turn appointed by elected leaders;
* reasonably long terms of office for the trustees and reasonably short terms for the policymakers, with the policymakers but not the trustees eligible for reappointment;
* provision for the dismissal of policymakers before the ends of their terms by supermajority vote of the trustees.

8.4.2   Benefits

This package of institutions has several benefits. Most importantly, these institutions have features that would address the various problems that arise from misunderstandings of the operation of the economy and the effects of policy. By giving policymakers discretion, they allow advances in knowledge to be quickly incorporated into the conduct of policy. By delegating policy to an independent central bank, they provide for the conduct of policy by specialists. By allowing for the reappointment of policymakers, making their terms relatively short, and allowing the board of trustees to remove policymakers by supermajority vote, they allow the trustees to retain high-skill policymakers and dismiss low-skill ones. And, as described in section 8.3, both the two-level structure and the relatively long terms of office for the trustees help to overcome the problems created by the public's and elected leaders' imperfect understanding.[4]

In addition, these institutions allow the dynamic inconsistency problem to be overcome either through reputation or through the appointment of conservative trustees or policymakers. Specifically, the policymakers have an incentive to establish reputations for following low-inflation policies, and the trustees have an incentive to establish reputations for rewarding policymakers who follow such policies. Alternatively, elected leaders can appoint trustees who attach unusual importance to keeping inflation low, or the trustees can appoint such individuals as policymakers.

A further advantage of the two-level structure is that it places the choice of whether to select conservative individuals as policymakers in the hands of the trustees rather than of elected leaders. The optimal degree of conservatism for policymakers depends on such considerations as the relative importance of keeping inflation low and responding optimally to shocks (Rogoff 1985), the costs and benefits of surprise inflation, and the extent to which reputational forces overcome the dynamic inconsistency problem. The trustees are likely to have much more knowledge about these issues than are elected leaders.

Finally, the two-level structure provides for the delegation of policy to specialists, while keeping ultimate control over monetary policy in the hands of elected leaders (and thus of the public). In the current system in the United States, some of the ultimate control over policy is exercised by directors of the regional reserve banks, two-thirds of whom are appointed by the member banks in the districts. In addition to introducing the obvious problem of regulated firms helping to select their regulators, this feature of the current system appears antidemocratic; indeed, its constitutionality has been challenged. The two-level structure, in contrast, achieves independence and delegation to specialists without placing any of the underlying control over policy in the hands of anyone other than the public.

---

4. Most of the independence of policy from the public and elected leaders under the two-level structure stems from the trustees' independence from elected leaders, rather from policymakers' independence from the trustees. A formal analysis of the optimal way to create independence would show that the optimal structure depends on the relative difficulties of finding individuals who are skilled at conducting policy and finding individuals who are skilled at evaluating policymakers. If, for example, it is difficult to evaluate policymakers but a good evaluator can confidently identify a large pool of skilled policymakers, then the optimal way to create independence is to make policymakers highly independent of the trustees and to allow for frequent reevaluation of the trustees. Our implicit assumption is that the reverse holds—that is, that it is easier to identify skilled evaluators than skilled policymakers.

8.4.3   The Specifics of the Two-Tier System

The purpose of the two-level system is to provide policymakers with substantial independence from elected leaders while allowing for their relatively rapid removal if they are not conducting policy well. To accomplish these goals, it is important that the system be structured so that the trustees do not take control of the day-to-day conduct of policy. This can be accomplished by limiting the frequency of the board's meetings and by giving it no powers other than the appointment, reappointment, and dismissal of the ultimate policymakers. For example, the members of the ultimate policymaking body could be appointed to staggered two-year terms. The board of trustees could then meet every six months, with its authority limited to the consideration of the reappointment of policymakers, the appointment of new policymakers, and (if need be) the early dismissal of policymakers whose terms have not expired.

Because the trustees' meetings would be infrequent, serving as a trustee would be much less than a full-time job. There is a wide range of activities from which trustees could be drawn. Since the trustees would not determine the specifics of policy, there is no reason that the board could not include individuals who are involved in financial markets (as long as the policymaking body was not making regulatory decisions concerning their firms). Other types of individuals who could naturally serve as trustees include academics, members of think tanks, former members of the policymaking body, former members of the executive and legislative branches with expertise concerning monetary policy, and industrial and labor leaders. As in other arenas, having individuals from a variety of backgrounds would be a safeguard against the appointment of policymakers with extreme or idiosyncratic views. Finally, since the responsibilities of the ultimate policymakers under this proposal are similar to what they are under conventional systems of direct appointment, moving to a two-level system does not require any major changes in the types of individuals appointed as ultimate policymakers.

The structures of the Reserve Banks of Australia and New Zealand show that having a part-time board of trustees is practicable. Both banks have part-time boards of directors. In Australia, the board consists of academics and business and labor leaders; in New Zealand, it consists of academics and members of the business, agricultural, and financial communities. Conflicts of interest are prevented by prohibiting bank employees from serving on the boards, and by providing for board members' recusal or dismissal in the event of other conflicts of interest. In New Zealand, as we describe in section 8.5, the board plays a role similar to the one we envision for the board of trustees: it helps to choose the governor and monitors his or her performance. In Australia, in contrast, the board is technically responsible for all aspects of monetary policy, though in practice it generally defers to the governor. Nonetheless, the arrangements in both countries demonstrate the feasibility of a part-time board.

8.4.4   Alternative Structures

If a two-level structure for appointing policymakers is infeasible for some reason, then there would be large advantages to lengthening policymakers' terms. If policymakers have short terms and are directly appointed by elected leaders, there would be substantial risk of inflationary bias arising from dynamic inconsistency, of elected leaders manipulating policy to exploit the public's misunderstandings, and of shifts to low-inflation policy being aborted before their benefits were apparent. Longer terms would reduce all of these problems. But having elected leaders directly appoint policymakers to long terms would eliminate the possibility of quickly removing policymakers whose skills prove to be low. It would also give elected leaders more control over policy during their terms, and it would leave the choice of the degree of conservatism of policymakers to elected leaders rather than to a board of trustees. For these reasons, a two-level system is likely to produce more desirable outcomes than the direct appointment of policymakers to long terms.

A more fundamental alternative to the two-tier structure is one that makes policy follow a binding rule or that specifies the ultimate goals of policy. If the only source of problems in policy were dynamic inconsistency, such an arrangement might be preferable to the set of institutions we have been discussing. If it is possible to identify the optimal policy rule, for example, then committing to that rule is optimal.

As described above, such a rule is not necessary to overcoming dynamic inconsistency: countries often achieve low inflation without any arrangement along these lines. Moreover, the set of institutions we discuss allows reputation and delegation to overcome dynamic inconsistency. Thus the potential advantages of binding rules and prespecified goals over the combination of an independent central bank and a two-tier structure are small.

More importantly, commitment to a binding rule is likely to be less successful in addressing problems other than dynamic inconsistency. We do not in fact know the optimal policy rule. The issue is not just that it is impossible to identify every possible type of shock in advance. The more fundamental problem is that, as described above, there is great uncertainty about such basic issues as the optimal inflation rate and the relative importance of keeping inflation on target versus smoothing fluctuations in output. Thus trying to specify a binding rule for policy, or even what policymakers' ultimate goals should be, may have large costs.

Specifying a rule but allowing it to be changed easily will not solve the problems caused by limited knowledge. Since the elected officials responsible for setting and modifying such a rule would be likely to have limited expertise concerning monetary policy, this system would not allow advances in the best available knowledge to be reflected quickly in policymaking, and it could force policymakers to follow policies that are highly suboptimal. At the same time, if a policy rule can be easily changed, it is of little value in dealing with the dynamic inconsistency problem. Similarly, having a vague goal or rule, such as a requirement that monetary policy be conducted so as to promote social welfare, would be essentially the same as granting the central bank complete goal independence.

Finally, two features could easily be added to the combination of institutions we have been discussing. First, one could penalize policymakers for deviating from low-inflation policies, as proposed by Walsh (1995b) and Persson and Tabellini (1993). But, just as determining the optimal degree of conservatism for policymakers is difficult, so too is determining the optimal penalty for inflationary policies. The optimal penalty depends on such factors as the importance that policymakers attach to their own compensation or prestige relative to social welfare, and the extent to which reputation already overcomes dynamic inconsistency. If reputational forces and the selection of conservative policymakers would already largely eliminate inflationary bias, then adding penalties for inflation could result in inefficiently low inflation.

Second, Debelle and Fischer (1994) and others argue for the importance of increasing policymakers' accountability by requiring them, for example, to periodically state the goals of policy, explain how the conduct of policy is designed to achieve those goals, and justify any departures from the previously announced path of policy. Again, it would be straightforward to add such requirements to the combination of institutions we have been discussing. The potential benefits of these requirements appear to be small, however. To the extent that they help policymakers build support for their policies, increase their credibility, and reduce uncertainty, then policymakers have an incentive to take these steps without a formal requirement. And policymaking is sufficiently complicated that such a requirement would not be a substantial impediment to policymakers who wanted to pursue goals other than maximizing social welfare.

8.5   Recent and Proposed Monetary Reforms

This section analyzes the most important recent monetary reforms in industrialized countries in light of the preceding discussion. We also analyze the proposed design of the European Central Bank.

8.5.1   Policy Changes

The most common type of recent monetary reform in industrialized countries is a shift to a low-inflation policy within existing institutional arrangements. Changes to policies that made low inflation or price stability the primary or the sole objective of policy were made in New Zealand in 1984, Canada in 1988, the United Kingdom in 1992, and Sweden and Finland in

1993. In every case, the change was followed by a large reduction in inflation, and a large rise in unemployment.[5]

These policy shifts have two implications for our analysis. First, they provide clear evidence of the importance of advances in knowledge for the conduct of policy. Since these changes occurred without any changes in institutions, they cannot be due to changes in the incentives that policymakers face. Nor, since they occurred in so many countries, can they be attributed to such factors as random fluctuations in policymakers' tastes. Rather, the changes appear to be due to the growing evidence of the absence of a long-run output-inflation trade-off, of the costs of moderate inflation, and of the limitations of stabilization policy.

Second, these shifts are further evidence that policy can avoid inflationary bias without binding rules or legislated goals. In all of these countries, policymakers reduced inflation substantially under existing institutional arrangements. This again suggests that dynamic inconsistency was not the source of these countries' high inflation rates. And since policymakers would have the ability to make low inflation their main objective under the institutional framework discussed in section 8.4, this suggests that these arrangements would be sufficient to avoid excessive inflation.[6]

At the same time, our analysis has an important implication for these policy reforms. Policy was overly inflationary in these countries for extended periods. Given what we now know about the costs of expansionary policies, this particular mistake is unlikely to be repeated. And by making low inflation the central goal of policy, the reforms in these countries provide additional insurance against the reoccurrence of this mistake, and make a specific judgment about how much weight policy should put on keeping inflation low.

But these reforms do not address the underlying problems that led to the policy failures: they do nothing to give specialists greater control over policy, or to raise those specialists' average skill levels. As a result, although they reduce the likelihood of repetition of a particular failure of policy, they do nothing to reduce the likelihood of other failures. Suppose that evidence appears that a major change in policy is warranted—evidence, for example, that there are substantial benefits of moderate deflation, or of trying to aggressively stabilize the economy while keeping average inflation low. The recent policy reforms do nothing that will cause such evidence to be reflected in the conduct

---

5. Of course, policymakers in almost all countries have put more emphasis on low inflation over the past fifteen years. We focus on the clearest shifts in the goals of policy.

6. One could argue that the fact that these countries have been able to reduce inflation only through high unemployment indicates that their policies were not fully credible, and that binding low-inflation rules would produce a more favorable unemployment-inflation trade-off. But since all of these shifts in the announced goals of policy were followed by large declines in actual inflation, the idea that the policies—particularly the later ones—did not have substantial credibility is implausible. Thus a more reasonable interpretation of the fact that the disinflations had substantial output costs is that inflation has an important inertial component, and thus that any use of monetary policy to disinflate requires a period of high unemployment.

of policy any more rapidly than was the evidence about the costs of inflation. Indeed, by emphasizing our current beliefs about desirable policy, the reforms could slow the response to evidence that changes in policy are warranted.

8.5.2   Institutional Reforms in New Zealand and France

The two industrialized countries that have significantly altered their monetary institutions in recent years are New Zealand and France. The Reserve Bank Act of 1989 altered New Zealand's monetary institutions in several ways (see Dawe 1990; Lloyd 1992; Fischer 1993; Dowd and Baker 1994; Walsh 1995a). First, it greatly increased the independence of the Reserve Bank and gave it much greater control over monetary policy. Second, it made price stability the sole objective of policy. Third, it provided for periodic Policy Targets Agreements between the bank and the government on a definition of price stability and a timetable for achieving it. The governor of the bank may be dismissed if the goals set out in the agreement are not met, unless the failure is due to changes in indirect taxes, terms-of-trade shocks, or a natural disaster. Fourth, the act requires the governor to issue a monetary policy statement at least every six months that discusses how policy is being conducted and how that conduct relates to the Policy Targets Agreement and the goal of price stability. Fifth, it clearly delineates the roles of the governor of the Reserve Bank and the bank's board of directors. The governor is solely responsible for the conduct of policy and for achieving the objectives in the Policy Targets Agreement; the board of directors has only a monitoring role.

Finally, the act changes the procedures for appointing the governor and the directors. The directors are appointed by the minister of finance to five-year terms, and can be reappointed. The governor, in contrast, is chosen by the minister of finance from a list of candidates submitted by the board of directors. Like the directors, he or she has a five-year term and can be reappointed.

These institutional reforms have much in common with the combination of institutions we discuss in section 8.4. Policy is conducted by a highly independent central bank with considerable discretion over the implementation of policy. The fact that the government must choose the governor of the Reserve Bank from a list drawn up by the directors sets up a two-level system. While not identical to the arrangement described in the previous section, the New Zealand two-tier system does mean that the government has only limited control in the short run over who is in charge of policy. Furthermore, it makes it possible to have the governor subject to dismissal without compromising the independence of the central bank. Because of these features, we would expect the reforms to produce desirable policy.

The one major feature of New Zealand's reforms that differs from the framework described in section 8.4 is the emphasis on price stability. As suggested above, this emphasis appears unnecessary: the institutional framework gives the governor enough independence and flexibility to pursue price stability if that is the most appropriate goal of policy, and does not have any features that would incline him or her not to do so in such situations. Indeed, Dowd and Baker (1994) find that the main shifts in monetary policy and expected inflation in New Zealand came in 1984, with a shift in the conduct of policy under the old institutions, rather than in 1989. In addition, as we have emphasized, the focus on price stability has a drawback: if evidence appears that this is not the best goal of policy, policymakers will be unable to respond rapidly.

France overhauled its monetary institutions in 1993 (Banque de France 1993). As in New Zealand, the changes in France gave the central bank much more independence and control over policy, made price stability the central goal of policy, and required the bank to make periodic reports on its conduct of policy. The reforms gave authority over monetary policy to a monetary policy council consisting of a governor, two deputy governors, and six other members. The governor and deputy governors are appointed by the government to six-year terms that can only be renewed once. The other members are appointed by the government to nonrenewable nine-year terms.

The overwhelming advantage of these reforms is that they grant control over policy to an independent central bank. This will almost surely produce more desirable outcomes than having policy determined by the government. The reforms, however, do little beyond increasing the central bank's independence. The emphasis on price stability, as we have argued, is probably unnecessary and potentially counterproductive. And the reforms do not have any features that allow low-skill policymakers to be dismissed rapidly or that prevent the government from appointing individuals who would overstimulate the economy prior to elections. In short, the French reforms appear to be driven by a single-minded focus on central bank independence and price stability, and not by a thorough rethinking of the sources of problems in monetary policy and of the measures that would overcome them.

8.5.3   The European Central Bank

The proposed European Central Bank (ECB) provides another important example of radical changes in monetary institutions. As agreed to in the 1991 Maastricht Treaty, the ECB would largely eliminate the monetary policy functions of the various national central banks. As a result, the institutional features of the ECB are likely to be a crucial determinant of monetary stability in a united Europe.[7]

One important feature of the ECB is that it is highly independent. The six-member Executive Board is chosen by "common accord" of the governments forming the monetary union, based on the recommendation of the European Council. The members of the board are appointed for nonrenewable eight-year

---

7. Kenen (1992), Giovannini (1993), and Thygesen (1993) provide useful descriptions of the key features of the ECB.

terms, and cannot be dismissed arbitrarily. Monetary policy is decided by the Governing Council, which consists of the heads of all the national central banks and the members of the Executive Board. To ensure the independence of the national central bank governors, all of their terms must be at least five years, though they can be renewable.

The independence of the Governing Council is ensured in other ways. First, because the ECB is set up by treaty, it is inherently very hard to change its institutional structure. This is in contrast to the Federal Reserve, whose independence can be changed at any time by a simple act of Congress. Second, independence is assured by a series of articles that prohibit both the European Community and the national governments from trying to influence the Governing Council of the ECB, and that impose strict limits on the monetary financing of official entities.

While the independence of the ECB is clearly consistent with the institutional arrangement we discuss in section 8.4, its organizational structure differs in an important way from that framework. The political appointees to the Governing Council make monetary policy directly, rather than merely choosing the policymakers. As a consequence, the policymakers must have long, nonrenewable terms to ensure their independence. This has the effect that policymakers who prove incompetent cannot be removed and those who prove adept cannot be reappointed.

Another important feature of the ECB is its degree of goal and instrument independence. The Statute of the European System of Central Banks (ESCB) states that the "primary objective" of the ECB is to maintain price stability. Many other goals are also mentioned, such as balanced development, a high level of employment, and social cohesion. However, the statute explicitly states that these goals may be considered only if they do not conflict with the goal of price stability.

As discussed above, explicit goals may be problematic because knowledge about the desirability of various objectives may improve over time. For this reason, the ECB's explicit goal may be less than ideal. On the other hand, it is not clear how binding this stated goal will actually be. The ESCB statute contains no definition of price stability, no procedures for setting targets or transition plans, no punishments for failure to achieve price stability, and few requirements for explaining undesirable inflation outcomes. As a result, it is quite likely that the goal will not be binding. Indeed, Thygesen (1993, 18) suggests that many fear that the ECB will be more inflationary than the current system, which is dominated by the conservative Bundesbank. Therefore, it is possible that the ECB has a nearly ideal level of goal independence.

The ECB also has essentially complete instrument independence. The Maastricht Treaty delegates the implementation of monetary policy entirely to the Executive Board of the ECB. This institutional feature is consistent with the view that it is undesirable to tie the monetary authority to particular targets or instruments when knowledge is limited.

8.6 Conclusion

The central argument of this paper is that, in designing the institutions of monetary policy, it is not enough to consider the incentives that the institutions create for fully informed, optimizing individuals. It is also important to consider the limitations of knowledge. Specifically, it is important to account for the facts that knowledge is likely to continue growing, that policymakers' skills are heterogeneous, and that elected leaders' and voters' knowledge is likely to be especially limited.

These considerations suggest that, in order to reduce monetary policy mistakes, the institutions of monetary policy should be designed to give control over policy to specialists with discretion about both the ultimate goals of policy and the specifics of policy operations. They also suggest that the policy institutions should allow for frequent evaluation of policymakers' performance, while insulating them from political pressures. One way to do this is to make policymakers responsible to a board of trustees, and to give the trustees considerable independence from elected leaders and the public.

A natural question is whether limitations in knowledge are important to other policy issues. For example, it is widely believed that many countries' budget deficits are excessive. Efforts to explain a tendency toward excessive deficits on the basis of strategic considerations with fully informed individuals have had only limited success. For example, Persson and Svensson (1989) and Tabellini and Alesina (1990) find that strategic interactions between political parties with differing views lead to excessive deficits only when certain parties are in power, or only when preferences exhibit features that are not particularly natural. Given the limitations of these theories, and given the evidence we have presented about the sources of failures in monetary policy, the possibility that excessive deficits stem from limited knowledge deserves serious consideration.

More generally, our analysis suggests that the potential effects of limited knowledge should be an important consideration in the design of any policy institutions. We leave it to future research to determine what undesirable outcomes have arisen from limited knowledge in other policy settings and how other policy institutions could be designed to avoid those outcomes.

References

Alesina, Alberto. 1988. Macroeconomics and Politics. *NBER Macroeconomics Annual* 3:13–52.

Atkeson, Andrew, and Christopher Phelan. 1994. Reconsidering the Costs of Business Cycles with Incomplete Markets. *NBER Macroeconomics Annual* 9:187–207.

Backus, David, and John Driffill. 1985. Inflation and Reputation. *American Economic Review* 75 (June): 530–38.

Banque de France. 1993. *Annual Report.* Paris: Imprimerie Nationale.
Barro, Robert J., 1995. Inflation and Economic Growth. NBER Working Paper no. 5326. Cambridge, MA: National Bureau of Economic Research, October.
Barro, Robert J., and David B. Gordon. 1983. Rules, Discretion, and Reputation in a Model of Monetary Policy. *Journal of Monetary Economics* 12 (July): 101–21.
Belden, Susan. 1989. Policy Preferences of FOMC Members as Revealed by Dissenting Votes. *Journal of Money, Credit, and Banking* 21 (November): 432–41.
Buchanan, James M., and Richard E. Wagner. 1977. *Democracy in Deficit: The Political Legacy of Lord Keynes.* New York: Academic Press.
Cardoso, Eliana A. 1988. Comment. In *Inflation Stabilization: The Experience of Israel, Argentina, Brazil, Bolivia, and Mexico,* ed. Michael Bruno, Guido Di Tella, Rudiger Dornbusch, and Stanley Fischer, 287–94. Cambridge: MIT Press.
Cukierman, Alex, Steven B. Webb, and Bilin Neyapti. 1992. Measuring the Independence of Central Banks and Its Effect on Policy Outcomes. *World Bank Economic Review* 6 (September): 353–98.
Dawe, Stephen. 1990. Reserve Bank of New Zealand Act 1989. *Bulletin* (Reserve Bank of New Zealand) 53 (March): 29–36.
Debelle, Guy. 1996. The Ends of Three Small Inflations: Australia, New Zealand, and Canada. *Canadian Public Policy* 22 (March): 56–78.
Debelle, Guy, and Stanley Fischer. 1994. How Independent Should a Central Bank Be? In *Goals, Guidelines, and Constraints Facing Monetary Policymakers,* ed. Jeffrey C. Fuhrer, 195–221. Federal Reserve Bank of Boston Conference Series, no. 38. Boston: Federal Reserve Bank of Boston.
De Long, J. Bradford, and Lawrence H. Summers. 1988. How Does Macroeconomic Policy Affect Output? *Brookings Papers on Economic Activity,* no. 2:433–80.
Dornbusch, Rudiger, and Sebastian Edwards. 1990. Macroeconomic Populism. *Journal of Development Economics* 32 (April): 247–77.
———, eds. 1991. *The Macroeconomics of Populism in Latin America.* Chicago: University of Chicago Press.
Dowd, Kevin, and Simon Baker. 1994. The New Zealand Monetary Policy Experiment: A Preliminary Assessment. *World Economy* 17 (November): 855–67.
Fischer, Andreas M. 1993. Inflation Targeting: The New Zealand and Canadian Cases. *Cato Journal* 13 (spring-summer): 1–27.
Fischer, Stanley. 1991. Growth, Macroeconomics, and Development. *NBER Macroeconomics Annual* 6:329–64.
———. 1993. The Role of Macroeconomic Factors in Growth. *Journal of Monetary Economics* 32 (December): 485–512.
———. 1995. The Unending Search for Monetary Salvation. *NBER Macroeconomics Annual* 10:275–86.
Freedman, Charles. 1993. Designing Institutions for Monetary Stability: A Comment. *Carnegie-Rochester Conference Series on Public Policy* 39 (December): 85–94.
Friedman, Milton. 1960. *A Program for Monetary Stability.* New York: Fordham University Press.
Friedman, Milton, and Anna J. Schwartz. 1963. *A Monetary History of the United States, 1867–1960.* Princeton: Princeton University Press.
Giovannini, Alberto. 1993. Central Banking in a Monetary Union: Reflections on the Proposed Statute of the European Central Bank. *Carnegie-Rochester Conference Series on Public Policy* 38 (June): 191–229.
Grilli, Vittorio, Donato Masciandaro, and Guido Tabellini. 1991. Political and Monetary Institutions and Public Financial Policies in the Industrial Countries. *Economic Policy* 13 (October): 341–92.
Kahn, Shulamit. 1994. Evidence of Nominal Wage Stickiness from Microdata. Boston University School of Management. Manuscript.

Kenen, Peter B. 1992. *EMU after Maastricht.* Washington, DC: Group of Thirty.

Kydland, Finn E., and Edward C. Prescott. 1977. Rules Rather Than Discretion: The Inconsistency of Optimal Plans. *Journal of Political Economy* 85 (June): 473–92.

Lago, Ricardo. 1991. The Illusion of Pursuing Redistribution through Macropolicy: Peru's Heterodox Experience, 1985–1990. In *The Macroeconomics of Populism in Latin America,* ed. Rudiger Dornbusch and Sebastian Edwards, 263–323. Chicago: University of Chicago Press.

Lane, Philip R. 1994. Openness, Inflation, and Exchange Rate Regimes. Harvard University. December. Manuscript.

Lloyd, Michele. 1992. The New Zealand Approach to Central Bank Autonomy. *Bulletin* (Reserve Bank of New Zealand) 55 (September): 203–20.

Lohmann, Suzanne. 1992. Optimal Commitment in Monetary Policy: Credibility versus Flexibility. *American Economic Review* 82 (March): 273–86.

Lucas, Robert E., Jr. 1987. *Models of Business Cycles.* Oxford: Basil Blackwell.

Macedo, Roberto. 1988. Comment. In *Inflation Stabilization: The Experience of Israel, Argentina, Brazil, Bolivia, and Mexico,* ed. Michael Bruno, Guido Di Tella, Rudiger Dornbusch, and Stanley Fischer, 294–98. Cambridge: MIT Press.

McLaughlin, Kenneth J. 1994. Rigid Wages? *Journal of Monetary Economics* 34 (December): 383–414.

Meltzer, Allan. 1988. *Keynes's Monetary Theory: A Different Interpretation.* Cambridge: Cambridge University Press.

Nordhaus, William D. 1975. The Political Business Cycle. *Review of Economic Studies* 42 (April): 169–90.

Ortiz, Guillermo. 1988. Comment. In *Inflation Stabilization: The Experience of Israel, Argentina, Brazil, Bolivia, and Mexico,* ed. Michael Bruno, Guido Di Tella, Rudiger Dornbusch, and Stanley Fischer, 298–302. Cambridge: MIT Press.

Persson, Torsten, and Lars E. O. Svensson. 1989. Why a Stubborn Conservative Would Run a Deficit: Policy with Time-Inconsistent Preferences. *Quarterly Journal of Economics* 104 (May): 325–45.

Persson, Torsten, and Guido Tabellini. 1993. Designing Institutions for Monetary Stability. *Carnegie-Rochester Conference Series on Public Policy* 39 (December): 53–84.

Rogoff, Kenneth. 1985. The Optimal Degree of Commitment to an Intermediate Monetary Target. *Quarterly Journal of Economics* 100 (November): 1169–89.

Romer, David. 1993. Openness and Inflation: Theory and Evidence. *Quarterly Journal of Economics* 108 (November): 869–903.

Rudebusch, Glenn D., and David W. Wilcox. 1994. Productivity and Inflation: Evidence and Interpretations. Federal Reserve Board. May. Typescript.

Sachs, Jeffrey D. 1994. Prospects for Monetary Stabilization in Russia. In *Economic Transformation in Russia,* ed. A. Aslund, 34–58. London: Pinter Publishers.

Simonsen, Mario Henrique. 1988. Price Stabilization and Incomes Policies: Theory and the Brazilian Case Study. In *Inflation Stabilization: The Experience of Israel, Argentina, Brazil, Bolivia, and Mexico,* ed. Michael Bruno, Guido Di Tella, Rudiger Dornbusch, and Stanley Fischer, 259–86. Cambridge: MIT Press.

Tabellini, Guido, and Alberto Alesina. 1990. Voting on the Budget Deficit. *American Economic Review* 80 (March): 37–49.

Taylor, John B. 1983. Comments. *Journal of Monetary Economics* 12 (July): 123–25.

Thygesen, Niels. 1993. EMU: A Solid Framework from Maastricht. In *The Monetary Future of Europe.* London: Centre for Economic Policy Research.

Walsh, Carl E. 1995a. Is New Zealand's Reserve Bank Act of 1989 an Optimal Central Bank Contract? *Journal of Money, Credit, and Banking* 27 (November): 1179–91.

———. 1995b. Optimal Contracts for Central Bankers. *American Economic Review* 85 (March): 150–67.

Comment   Benjamin M. Friedman

One of the more positive developments in economic thinking within recent years has been the renewed realization that institutions matter. Not so long ago, a seeming preponderance of economists earnestly maintained that, even if some poor benighted economy had oddly neglected to put in place its frictionless markets, Walrasian auctioneer, and full set of Arrow-Debreu contingency claims, it was nonetheless inappropriate if not outright impolite to take such a harmless oversight into account in analyzing that economy's systematic behavior. By contrast, today there is renewed attention to the economic implications of a wide variety of institutional arrangements, including elements of market structure, legal and regulatory restrictions, business practice, and organizational structure at both the business and government levels. Christina Romer and David Romer's paper follows the path established by this newer literature, and it is the more valuable for doing so.

To begin at the beginning, however, the paper's title is misleading. By calling it "Institutions for Monetary Stability," Romer and Romer clearly seek a resonance with Milton Friedman's 1960 classic, *A Program for Monetary Stability,* to which they indeed refer at the very outset. But in Friedman's case, there was a clear reason for identifying "monetary stability" as the objective of the program he was proposing. His main recommendation, listed as number one in the book's concluding summary, was that the Federal Reserve System not only "produce a 4% per year rate of growth in the total of currency held by the public and adjusted deposits in commercial banks" but also "keep the rate of growth as steady as it can week by week and month by month" (100). Now there's monetary stability! By contrast, Romer and Romer explicitly reject a money growth rule. Indeed, they argue forcefully against any kind of policy rule at all for the central bank, and even against specifying a particular goal, like stable prices, as the central bank's objective. What does their paper have to do with "monetary stability"?

As I shall indicate in due course, this misplaced appeal to "monetary stability" is more than just a matter of title semantics. But there is other ground to cover first.

Romer and Romer's proposals for the design of central banking institutions revolve around three principles. First, actual policy decisions should rest in the hands of knowledgeable specialists. Second, higher government authorities should specify neither the goals that these policymakers are to pursue nor the precise methods by which they are to do so. (In other words, the policymakers should enjoy both "goal independence" and "instrument independence.") Third, there should be institutional buffers between central bank policymakers and publicly elected government officials.

Benjamin M. Friedman is the William Joseph Maier Professor of Political Economy at Harvard University.

It is easy to quibble around the edges of each of these ideas as Romer and Romer actually apply them. For example, there are many distinguished "specialists" to whom I would not entrust monetary policy—not because they know too little, but because they know so much and because so much of what they know is wrong. Similarly, I do not think Romer and Romer make a convincing case that their specific suggestion for a layer of "trustees" that would stand between the politicians and the central bankers would be a substantive improvement. The Federal Reserve System's current structure, with evenly staggered fourteen-year terms for seven governors, already embodies the two features that Romer and Romer highlight, namely, long terms for policymakers and "mechanisms that create delays in elected leaders' influence over policy." I also suspect that conflicts of interest would be a far greater problem for their proposed system's part-time "trustees" than the cursory attention paid to this issue here suggests. But dwelling on these details distracts attention from the more important issues raised in the paper.

The more compelling question to address concerns the economic motivation underlying these organizational principles and others that the recent burgeoning literature on this subject has put forth. The motivation that this literature has emphasized more than any other is the familiar dynamic inconsistency argument, and Romer and Romer too cite this idea as one element of their own reason for proposing institutional change. They sensibly opt to address this issue by relying on reputation and delegation, rather than precommitted rules of policy behavior, so as to preserve the well-known advantages of discretion in circumstances in which knowledge is imperfect and what may appear to be true at one time—for example, that prices and any particular measure of money move closely together—is often demonstrably false not long thereafter. Indeed, their paper nicely articulates just the reasons why many knowledgeable people have long favored discretionary policy over fixed rules in the first place. (Romer and Romer represent the key issue as the evolution of knowledge, as if the underlying behavior in question remained invariant, while I would prefer to put the problem also in terms of changing behavior; but this may well be just a question of semantics. Either way, I certainly agree on the advantages of discretion as opposed to fixed rules of central bank behavior.)

A particularly welcome aspect of Romer and Romer's treatment of this issue is their recognition that, for purposes of practical policymaking, dynamic consistency is probably not the major problem that the existing literature makes it out to be. Notwithstanding the appeal of the logical argument at an abstract level, there is no persuasive evidence that dynamic inconsistency is in practice a major cause of bad central bank policy or poor economic performance in the United States or in economies that resemble the U.S. economy. Fifteen years ago, when economists first advanced this idea, persistently high rates of inflation were a major issue in most industrialized countries. The dynamic inconsistency model, pointing to institutional arrangements that allowed discretionary policy together with incentives to misuse that discretion in admittedly well-meaning but nevertheless short-sighted ways, seemed to offer an explanation. But during the last fifteen years most industrialized countries have succeeded in dramatically reducing their inflation—and, importantly, in most cases they have done so under institutional arrangements no different from that which they had before.

The one apparently hard fact that the relevant literature has highlighted in the attempt to bolster the case that dynamic inconsistency is actually a serious problem is that countries with more-independent central banks have enjoyed lower average inflation rates. But as Romer and Romer are careful to note, this fact "is consistent with" empirical importance of dynamic inconsistency; it does not show dynamic inconsistency to be empirically important. Further, a related proposition that, if true, would provide evidence that the correlation between central bank independence and low inflation were indeed a consequence of dynamic inconsistency fails when tested. In particular, the logic of the dynamic inconsistency argument implies that more-independent central banks should have greater "credibility" and on that account enjoy a smaller "sacrifice ratio" whenever they do need to disinflate. As Adam Posen (1995) and others have shown, however, the evidence does not support this proposition. For example, Posen has shown for a sample including the seventeen principal OECD economies that there is no evidence that the costs of disinflation are lower in countries with independent central banks, even when cross-country differences in wage contracting behavior are taken into account.

Although Romer and Romer usefully downplay the importance of dynamic inconsistency as a motivation for the changes that they propose, their discussion of "the widespread tendency of newly elected leaders *from liberal parties* ... to pressure monetary policymakers to pursue expansionary policies" (emphasis added) nevertheless perpetuates the kind of half-truths that have somehow evolved into stylized facts in this particular literature. The specific reference to Democratic presidents Carter and Clinton is, of course, correct. But why have the authors neglected similar pressure from President Bush, which even assumed the high profile of the president's televised State of the Union address? It is true that President Reagan never personally called for more expansionary monetary policy, at least not in public, but forceful public statements along such lines were a regular staple of the "first" Reagan Treasury Department (that is, when Donald Regan was secretary of the treasury). The authors have also apparently forgotten that the U.S. president who provided the single more famous example within recent decades of pressuring the Federal Reserve to pursue expansionary policies was Richard Nixon. These three presidents were Republicans. Finally, the authors' reference in this context to French president Mitterrand (a socialist) is again correct. But why recall Mitterrand's statements while ignoring last year's quite public disagreement, along just these lines, between newly elected President Chirac (a Gaullist) and Banque de France governor Trichet? One ultimately suspects that this line of research may have a broader agenda than merely analyzing monetary policy institutions.

To return to the paper's main line of argument, what are the implications, for Romer and Romer's suggestions for institutional change, of the fact that the story of monetary policy during the last decade and a half—in the United States as well as many other countries—has been one of such apparent success? Not that Romer and Romer's suggestions are necessarily bad ideas. Only that neither they themselves nor the extensive literature to which they appeal has provided much empirical motivation for them. Perhaps discretionary policymaking, carried out within the existing institutional framework, already does the job pretty well.

In light of this conclusion, and especially of Romer and Romer's useful emphasis on the more general benefits of discretionary policymaking, it is important to address explicitly the question, discretion to what end? Perhaps the sharpest difference between what Romer and Romer suggest here and the prevailing consensus view on such matters is their call for "goal independence" as well as "instrument independence." For all the familiar reasons highlighted in the voluminous literature of rules versus discretion, the prevailing consensus today largely favors instrument independence over any kind of dictated rule like what Milton Friedman proposed decades ago. (Today even advocates of responsive feedback rules, like John Taylor, mostly argue that such relationships would be useful as presumptive baselines, not as hard rules.) I certainly favor discretion in this sense, as apparently do Romer and Romer. By contrast, I believe the prevailing consensus does expect the central bank to pursue goals established by higher government authority.

One part of Romer and Romer's argument for goal independence is parallel to the usual argument for instrument independence. Economic circumstances change, as does our knowledge of economic behavior and of the consequences of central bank actions. Constraining policymakers to pursue a specific set of goals—especially a narrowly specified set of goals—risks directing the generals to concentrate on fighting the last war. Although Romer and Romer do not explicitly mention this example, a bill currently pending in the U.S. Senate under the sponsorship of the chairman of the Joint Economic Committee and the cosponsorship of the Senate majority leader (S. 1226) is a good illustration of what they have in mind. This bill would establish "long-run price stability" as the Federal Reserve's one basic policy objective. (It would allow policymakers to take account of the short-run implications of monetary policy actions for employment and output, but only within an overriding requirement of long-run price stability; hence any tolerated price increases—associated, for example, with adverse supply shocks—would presumably have to be offset by absolute price declines later on.) Compared to such a narrow alternative, I too would favor leaving the goals unspecified.

After reading their paper, however, I think Romer and Romer favor goal independence at least in part for another reason: a discomfort, when it comes to matters of monetary policy, with the political process that constitutes the apex of governmental authority in a democracy. As the authors choose to state the issue, "The . . . possibly more important way in which monetary policymakers may be influenced by incompletely informed individuals is that elected leaders must in turn answer to voters, whose understanding is likely to be quite limited." Indeed, "the problems created by the fact that policymakers must answer to elected officials, who must in turn answer to the public, may be the hardest to solve." *Eurekoun!* The Romers have discovered democracy.

This, I believe, is the relevance of their misleading title. By focusing attention on the substantively irrelevant but vaguely reassuring concept of "monetary stability," Romer and Romer sidestep saying what is the intended purpose of their suggestions for changing our central bank institutions. Is it price stability? Or superior economic growth? Or more stable economic growth? Or a smoothly functioning financial system? Is it all of these? They do not say. And they do not want any governmental authority higher than the central bank to say either.

To be sure, as the pending Senate bill illustrates, there are sets of central banking goal instructions that are probably worse than having none at all. But having none at all results in a logical circularity that risks potentially imposing just the kind of limitation Romer and Romer seek to avoid: Suppose our central bankers are instructed only to use the instruments at their disposal to do as much good for the American people as they can, however they conceive it. The central bank's goals are then implicitly defined by whatever can be achieved with the instruments at hand today. So far, so good. But how could anyone, under this arrangement, cogently evaluate a potential change in the central bank's set of instruments? Contemplating the introduction of a new instrument, or a change in the authorized use of an existing one, is possible only when there are agreed objectives that have a status independent of the instruments themselves.

More important, we do live in a democracy and we are fortunate that we do. Yes, "elected leaders' understanding of the economy may be limited." And yes, "elected leaders must in turn answer to voters, whose understanding is likely to be quite limited." For just these reasons, delegating central bank policymaking to appointed officials and giving those appointees substantial independence makes sense, just as it makes sense to place administration of the legal system in the hands of a substantially independent judiciary. But conceiving of central banking along the lines of a Platonic republic, with knowledgeable "specialists" as the philosopher-kings, is not the answer. The central bank's philosopher-kings should at least pursue objectives established by the ultimate source of their authority. The democratic process, with all its faults, is that source.

References

Friedman, Milton. 1960. *A program for monetary stability.* New York: Fordham University Press.

Posen, Adam. 1995. Central bank independence and disinflationary credibility: A missing link. Federal Reserve Bank of New York Staff Report no. 1. May.

9   Why Does Inflation Differ across Countries?

Marta Campillo and Jeffrey A. Miron

9.1   Introduction

The inflation performance of economies is interesting to academic economists, policymakers, politicians, and the electorate. Economists are in broad agreement about how policy actions affect inflation rates, and they share much common ground about the factors that policy should consider in choosing an economy's inflation rate.

Perhaps surprisingly, given the relative consensus about what determines inflation and about how inflation rates should be set, inflation differs substantially across countries. Figure 9.1 graphs the inflation rate by country for the 1973–94 period. The highest average inflation rate in the sample is 127% (Brazil) and the lowest is 2% (Central African Republic). Even excluding what might be considered special cases, inflation rates differ markedly. If these differences reflect differences in the factors that determine desired inflation, given the constraints each economy faces, then the differences provide support both for economic models of inflation and for the notion that policymakers choose inflation in a reasonably intelligent fashion. If the differences in inflation cannot be at least approximately attributed to factors that should explain these differences, then either economists' models or policymakers' actions, or both, are lacking.

This paper attempts to explain the differences in inflation performance across countries. Some earlier research has examined this topic, but it has considered only a few of the factors that might be empirically important determi-

Marta Campillo is a graduate student in economics at Boston University. Jeffrey A. Miron is professor of economics at Boston University and a research associate of the National Bureau of Economic Research.

Comments from Maury Obstfeld, Christina Romer, David Romer, Greg Mankiw, and seminar participants at Harvard, Brown, Yale, Colgate, and Hamilton are appreciated. Adam Posen kindly provided his data on financial opposition to inflation.

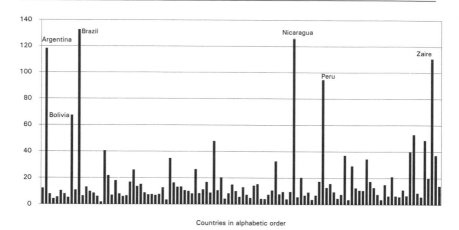

Countries in alphabetic order

Fig. 9.1   Average annual inflation rates, 1973–94, 110 countries

nants of inflation rates. In particular, existing research has focused on institutional characteristics like central bank independence (Grilli, Masciandaro, and Tabellini 1991; Cukierman, Webb, and Neyapti 1992), on the degree of openness (Romer 1993; Lane 1995), and on financial-sector opposition to inflation (Posen 1993, 1995). These factors are potentially important determinants of inflation, and existing evidence supports a role for each. Nevertheless, a priori reasoning suggests a number of additional factors that should matter as well.

We analyze the degree to which prior inflation experience, optimal tax considerations, and time-consistency issues other than central bank independence, as well as the factors considered in the existing literature, are important determinants of inflation rates across countries. The basic approach, as in earlier papers, is cross-country regressions of average inflation rates on country characteristics. The innovation of this paper is simply to include a broader range of country characteristics on the right-hand side.

The paper provides several interesting conclusions relative to the existing literature. First, institutional arrangements play almost no role in determining inflation outcomes, once other factors are held constant. Thus, central bank independence and the nature of exchange rate arrangements are not empirically important determinants of inflation rates. Second, time-consistency issues other than central bank independence play a more significant role in determining inflation rates: openness, political stability, and proxies for government policy distortions are all related to inflation in the direction suggested by time-consistency considerations, usually in a robust manner. Third, optimal tax considerations are an important determinant of differences in inflation performance: countries with greater expenditure needs make greater use of the inflation tax, and countries that face greater difficulty in collecting noninflation taxes make heavier use of the inflation tax. Fourth, financial-sector opposition to inflation does not explain much of the cross-country variation in inflation.

Finally, prior inflation experience—possibly through its effect on the taste for inflation, possibly because it proxies unmeasured but persistent determinants of current inflation—plays a nonnegligible role in determining inflation performance. All of these conclusions are subject to significant caveats, which we discuss in section 9.4.

9.2 Review of the Literature and Discussion of Additional Issues

This section summarizes briefly the earlier empirical work on the determinants of average inflation rates and then discusses the additional factors that we consider in our analysis.

9.2.1 Review of the Literature

The framework that has guided the literature to date consists of time-consistency models of inflation, especially Kydland and Prescott (1977) and Barro and Gordon (1983). In these models, the absence of credible commitment devices means central banks choose higher than optimal inflation rates, even though they share the private sector's preferences for inflation relative to output. This class of models suggests that institutional features of a central bank, as well as other political and institutional features of an economy, might have important effects on inflation outcomes. For example, central banks whose governors are appointed for long terms might be better insulated from political pressures to inflate, implying a relatively low inflation rate. More generally, this line of reasoning suggests that low inflation should be associated with the degree to which central banks are insulated from political pressure, a condition usually referred to as central bank independence (CBI).

A number of authors examine the relation between average inflation and proxies for CBI. Grilli, Masciandaro, and Tabellini (1991), for example, construct one indicator of political independence and another of economic independence for a sample of high-income countries. They regress cross-country differences in inflation rates on both indicators and a dummy variable for participation in the European Monetary System (EMS). The indicators of CBI always have the expected negative sign, while the estimated coefficient of the EMS dummy is not significantly different from zero. Alesina and Summers (1993) report a similar result using closely related indices and samples. Cukierman, Webb, and Neyapti (1992), using a more sophisticated index of independence, also document a negative relation between inflation and CBI for high-income countries, but they show that the relation has the wrong sign for middle- and low-income countries.

The failure of CBI to correlate negatively with inflation in developing countries is just one problem with this literature. A second is that the relation between CBI and inflation is not necessarily causal, a point emphasized by Posen (1993, 1995). He argues that CBI is not universally desired because of the distributive consequences of alternative monetary policies. Given these consequences, CBI is unlikely to be self-enforcing, so the preferences for price stability embodied by CBI require political support. If CBI does not embody such preferences, it will not affect inflation, and if such preferences were already supported, independence is unnecessary.

Posen argues that a major source of political opposition to inflation derives from the financial sector. Moreover, national differences in both the financial sector's distaste for inflation and its ability to express that distaste are likely to play a major role in determining both inflation and CBI. Posen creates a variable called financial opposition to inflation (FOI) that is designed to measure these two effects. The index is a significant predictor of CBI and also of average inflation rates. Moreover, CBI does not predict averages rates of inflation once Posen controls for FOI. The commonly presumed ability of CBI to lower inflation, independent of the central bank's political context, is not supported by his analysis.

Posen's results apply both to the countries in the Organization for Economic Cooperation and Development (OECD) and to a broader sample consisting of low-to-moderate-inflation countries. Posen suggests that the relationship should not hold for high or hyperinflation countries, since the financial sectors of such countries have long since given up opposing inflation. To survive in hyperinflations, banking and other financial firms adapt to their monetary environment, and once adapted they have much less incentive to oppose inflation. With its main protector absent, an independent central bank cannot pursue a sustained counter-inflationary policy, so CBI will not affect inflation in this case. According to this view, the pattern of which countries' inflation levels correlate negatively with CBI is explained by the incentives facing the financial sector.

Another issue that arises in interpreting the results of the CBI literature is whether other aspects of a country's political structure are important determinants of its ability to precommit. Cukierman, Edwards, and Tabellini (1992) note that, controlling for the stage of development and the structure of the economy, more unstable and polarized countries are likely to collect a larger fraction of their revenues from the inflation tax, at least partially because such countries are likely to have difficulty in maintaining a time-consistent policy. They provide evidence, based on various measures of political stability, that inflation is higher and CBI lower the greater is the degree of political instability.[1]

The literature summarized so far examines the political and institutional constraints on the central bank's ability to choose low inflation. A different line of work examines the central bank's incentive to choose low inflation, political and institutional constraints held constant. Romer (1993) argues that unantici-

---

1. Grilli and Milesi-Ferretti (1995) also provide evidence that political factors play an important role in determining inflation outcomes. The primary focus of their paper, however, is not inflation but the effects and determinants of capital controls. Moreover, their empirical specification differs substantially from the one we consider below, so we do not examine further the particular issues addressed in their paper.

pated monetary expansion causes real exchange rate depreciation, and since the harms of real depreciation are greater in more open economies, the benefits of surprise inflation are a decreasing function of the degree of openness. This implies that, in the absence of binding precommitment, monetary authorities in more open economies will on average expand less, and the result will be lower average rates of inflation.

The empirical evidence indicates that average rates of inflation are significantly lower in more open economies. These results are stronger in countries that are less politically stable and have less independent central banks. This is consistent with the idea that the openness-inflation relationship arises from the dynamic inconsistency of discretionary policy, since one would expect such countries to have had less success in overcoming the dynamic inconsistency problem. The link between openness and inflation holds across virtually all types of countries with the exception of the most highly developed countries. In this small group of countries, average inflation rates are low and essentially unrelated to openness. Again the results are consistent with the view that these countries have largely overcome the dynamic inconsistency of optimal monetary policy.

Lane (1995) argues that Romer's explanation of the influence of openness on inflation is a limited one, because it applies only to countries large enough to affect the structure of international relative prices. He claims the openness-inflation relation is rather due to imperfect competition and nominal price rigidity in the nontraded sector. The idea is that a surprise monetary expansion, given predetermined prices in the nontraded sector, increases production of nontradables. This expansion is socially beneficial because of the inefficient monopolistic underproduction in the nontraded sector in the equilibrium before the shock. The more open an economy, the smaller is the share of nontradables in consumption and the less important the correction of the distortion in that sector. Assuming the existence of a government that cares about social welfare, this generates an inverse relationship between openness and the incentive to unleash a surprise inflation, even for a country too small to affect its terms of trade.

Lane shows that the inverse relationship between openness and inflation is strengthened when country size is held constant; that is, independent of the size of the country, openness negatively impacts inflation, consistent with the small-country explanation of the relationship advanced in his paper. The result is robust to the inclusion of additional control variables such as per capita income, measures of CBI, and political stability. Moreover, controlling for country size makes the result strong and robust in the high-income countries, the one sample in which Romer did not find a strong result.

Overall, therefore, the existing literature suggests that CBI is associated with lower inflation in rich countries, that this relation derives significantly from political constraints flowing from the financial sector, and that openness is negatively associated with inflation, possibly through a number of mechanisms.

9.2.2   Additional Factors to Consider

Our analysis considers three main issues in addition to those addressed in the existing literature.

The first is whether differences in inflation across countries reflect differences in the distaste for inflation. Such differences might arise for a number of reasons. Countries that experienced high inflation in the past might be more aware of the negative consequences of high inflation and therefore be more opposed to repeated episodes; this explanation is frequently offered to explain Germany's low inflation rate. Similarly, countries that experienced variable inflation in the past might be relatively inflation averse, either because the electorate does not readily distinguish between means and variances or because high inflation is indeed more likely to be variable (Ball and Cecchetti 1990).

Inflation aversion might also differ across countries at a given point in time because of existing institutional and legal structures. For example, a country with an indexed tax system might be less opposed to inflation, other things equal, than one without such indexation. Other factors along these lines include the degree of wage indexation and the prevalence of long-term contracts. Each of the factors is endogenous with respect to inflation over a sufficiently long period of time, but since these arrangements take time to change, they might be regarded as approximately predetermined at any point in time.

Still another factor that might determine a given country's aversion to inflation is its industrial structure. In particular, the financial sectors of economies have traditionally been active opponents of inflation (Posen 1995), so countries with relatively large and politically influential financial sectors might tend to experience low inflation.

A second set of issues we introduce consists of optimal tax considerations. A considerable literature examines whether the behavior of inflation over time, and especially its relation to other taxes, is consistent with the principles of optimal taxation (e.g., Mankiw 1987; Poterba and Rotemberg 1990; Grilli, Masciandaro, and Tabellini 1991). With the exception of Mankiw's results for the United States, this exercise has generated relatively little support for the hypothesis that inflation rates change from year to year because the optimal inflation tax changes from year to year.

The analysis here considers a cruder question, which is whether differences in average inflation rates across countries are consistent with optimal tax considerations. On the one hand, optimal tax considerations suggest that countries with higher expenditures (relative to output) should have higher levels of all taxes, including the inflation rate. On the other hand, these considerations imply that, holding expenditures constant, inflation should be higher in countries where the demand for money is relatively inelastic. Differences in this elasticity might occur because of differences in the sophistication of the banking system, since highly developed banking systems provide good substitutes for money and therefore more elastic money demand. Alternatively, differences might occur because of differences in the size of the underground economy, since illegal activity will tend to be conducted with currency rather than with demand deposits or other substitutes.

The third new issue we address concerns aspects of the time-consistency problem other than CBI. Models like those of Barro and Gordon (1983) indicate that the incentive to create surprise inflation exists only if the rate of output targeted by a central bank differs from the rate of output consistent with nonaccelerating inflation (the "natural" rate). The central bank might target a rate higher than the natural rate if it believes the natural rate is below the social optimum. Thus, the rate of inflation should be increasing in the difference between the natural rate of output and the socially optimal rate, and several observable factors might produce such a difference. Unemployment insurance, minimum wage laws, and other labor market policies are likely to reduce the efficiency of the labor market and thereby lower the natural rate of output. Other sources of distortion include excessive levels of government purchases.

9.3   Empirical Specification and Results

We examine the determinants of country-level inflation rates as measured by the consumer price index (CPI) for the period 1973–94.[2] Our basic specification differs slightly from earlier papers, especially Romer (1993) and Lane (1995); they consider a shorter sample period (1973–89), use the log rather than the level of inflation as the dependent variable, and measure inflation using the GDP/GNP deflator. As demonstrated below, none of these differences makes a significant difference to the results. We employ the CPI because this measure of prices is available for the broadest sample of countries and for the longest sample periods.

The basic sample we consider consists of the sixty-two countries for which Cukierman, Webb, and Neyapti provide their measure of CBI. We restrict the basic sample in this way for two reasons. First, the role of CBI has been regarded as central in much of the previous research on cross-country variation in inflation, so it seems important to include this variable in our initial examinations. Second, many of the other variables we consider are unavailable for a number of countries outside this list of sixty-two, so restricting the sample in this way sacrifices relatively few observations in any event.

Figure 9.2 plots inflation for this sample of sixty-two countries. Although we have dropped a number of observations in going from the longer to the shorter list of countries, most of the really high inflation countries remain. Thus, we have not inadvertently excluded all the interesting variation in the key variable.

In addition to considering our basic sample, we examine a number of subsamples. To determine whether our results derive mainly from the influence of

2. Specifically, the dependent variable is $(1/21) \ln(CPI_{1994}/CPI_{1973})$.

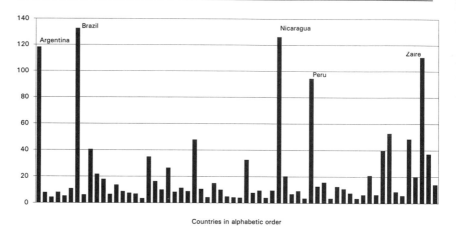

Fig. 9.2   **Average annual inflation rates, 1973–94, 62 countries**

a few extreme observations, we consider samples that omit countries with average inflation in excess of 100% per year or in excess of 50% per year. To determine whether the results apply mainly to developed or less-developed economies, we split the basic sample into the eighteen high-income countries versus
all the remaining countries.[3]

The estimation technique is ordinary least squares, with standard errors estimated by the White (1980) procedure. Data are from the International Financial Statistics of the International Monetary Fund, except as noted.[4]

Tables 9.1 and 9.2 present summary statistics—means, standard deviations,
and cross correlations—for the variable considered in the analysis below.[5]

9.3.1   Preliminaries

We begin by reproducing the key results from the previous literature using
our data set. Although these results are not new in any interesting sense, they
allow us to conclude that the new variables we introduce, rather than some
difference in specification, are responsible for any differences in results.

Table 9.3 reviews the results on CBI. Panel A displays the univariate regression of inflation on CWN's measure of CBI.[6] In the eighteen high-income

3. The eighteen high-income countries are the same as in Romer (1993): Australia, Austria,
Belgium, Canada, Denmark, Finland, France, Germany, Iceland, Japan, Luxembourg, the Netherlands, New Zealand, Norway, Sweden, Switzerland, the United Kingdom, and the United States.
4. When we calculate the mean of a variable over a period of time, we do not always have
observations for all the years in the specified period. In cases where the number of missing observations is large, we drop the country from that regression. In cases where it is small, we calculate
the mean based on the available subsample.
5. The results for the samples that exclude high-inflation countries are similar in most respects
to those for the full sample.
6. In our main regressions, we use the CWN index that is based only on the legal and institutional structure of the central bank and its operating procedures (Cukierman, Webb, and Neyapti
1992, table 2, 362). We use this index, rather than one that partially reflects the performance of
the economy, since we believe it is more plausibly taken as predetermined relative to inflation

Table 9.1   **Means and Standard Deviations**

	Whole Sample		High-Income Countries		Less-Developed Countries	
	Mean	Standard Deviation	Mean	Standard Deviation	Mean	Standard Deviation
Average inflation, 1974–94	17.07	23.25	7.19	5.12	22.80	27.66
Average inflation, 1948–72	6.56	9.57	4.11	1.66	7.99	11.80
Central bank independence	0.34	0.12	0.37	0.16	0.33	0.09
Political instability	0.15	0.23	0.01	0.05	0.23	0.25
Imports/GDP, 1973–94	33.05	20.95	33.99	19.14	32.50	22.23
Log income, 1980	17.68	1.76	18.39	1.80	17.27	1.63
Log income per capita, 1980	8.16	1.08	9.13	0.12	7.60	0.98
Exchange rate regime, 1974	1.04	0.76	1.33	0.97	0.87	0.56
Debt/GDP (%), 1975	27.87	24.20	20.73	13.66	32.03	27.97
Quality of the data[a]	4.57	1.58	5.89	0.32	3.81	1.51

[a]Summers and Heston 1988.

countries, the relation is negative and robust, consistent with the predictions of standard time-consistency models. In the low-to-moderate-income sample, however, or in the entire sample for which CBI exists, the relation is positive, albeit insignificantly. This is not simply the influence of a few extreme countries; exclusion of the very high inflation rate observations still leaves a positive relation.

Panel B adds Barro's measure (1991) of political instability (the number of coups and revolutions) to the regression, while panel C adds the log of income per capita in 1980, and panel D adds both. In some cases, these additional variables enter significantly, and we discuss their interpretation below. None of these modifications changes the basic story documented in panel A, however. Thus, our data set suggests that same basic conclusions about CBI documented earlier: the predicted negative relation holds in high-income countries but not generally.

In table 9.4, we review the Romer (1993) and Lane (1995) results on openness. Panel A reproduces the basic result in Romer, which is that openness is negatively associated with inflation. The relation holds for the overall sample, for the less-developed countries, and for the sample that excludes countries with high or very high inflation. The relation does not hold for the high-income countries, as noted in Romer. Panel B adds the log level of income in 1980, as suggested by Lane. This modification always leads to a larger absolute value of the coefficient and a smaller standard error; in particular, the relation becomes significant in the high-income countries (although the magnitude of the effect is still relatively small). Panel C adds CBI, political instability, and per capita

---

performance. We demonstrate in our robustness checks that this choice has little effect on the results.

Table 9.2   **Correlation Matrices**

	Inf7494	Inf4872	CBI	Political Inst.	Imports	GDP	GDP/Capita	Exch. Rate	Debt	Q
					Whole Sample					
Average inflation, 1974–94	1									
Average inflation, 1948–72	0.37	1								
	(2.74)									
Central bank independence	0.08	−0.11	1							
	(0.58)	(−0.76)								
Political instability	0.55	0.23	0.08	1						
	(4.53)	(1.62)	(0.57)							
Imports/GDP, 1973–94	−0.24	−0.20	0.07	−0.34	1					
	(−1.67)	(−1.41)	(0.51)	(−2.47)						
Log income, 1980	−0.17	0.02	0.04	−0.08	−0.52	1				
	(−1.16)	(0.16)	(0.25)	(−0.53)	(−4.21)					
Log income per capita, 1980	−0.32	−0.20	0.14	−0.64	0.26	0.34	1			
	(−2.31)	(−1.42)	(0.96)	(−5.69)	(1.85)	(2.52)				
Exchange rate regime, 1974	−0.04	0.03	−0.02	−0.20	0.19	−0.30	0.15	1		
	(−0.25)	(0.19)	(−0.15)	(−1.39)	(1.30)	(−2.14)	(1.05)			
Debt/GDP (%), 1975	0.18	−0.03	−0.08	−0.10	0.28	−0.11	−0.03	−0.14	1	
	(1.29)	(−0.20)	(−0.59)	(−0.71)	(1.99)	(−0.79)	(−0.20)	(−0.98)		
Quality of the data[a]	−0.40	−0.19	0.15	−0.50	0.21	0.39	0.81	0.19	0.01	1
	(−2.98)	(−1.34)	(1.03)	(−3.96)	(1.51)	(2.93)	(9.47)	(1.30)	(0.09)	

High-Income Countries

Average inflation, 1974–94	1									
Average inflation, 1948–72	0.76 (4.76)	1								
Central bank independence	−0.23 (−0.96)	−0.27 (−1.13)	1							
Political instability	−0.01 (−0.03)	−0.15 (−0.60)	0.05 (0.20)	1						
Imports/GDP, 1973–94	−0.07 (−0.28)	−0.21 (−0.87)	−0.09 (−0.36)	−0.11 (−0.45)	1					
Log income, 1980	−0.54 (−2.57)	−0.44 (−1.94)	0.12 (0.50)	0.30 (1.25)	−0.63 (−3.22)	1				
Log income per capita, 1980	−0.12 (−0.49)	−0.40 (−1.73)	0.26 (1.09)	−0.23 (−0.97)	0.15 (0.59)	0.12 (0.50)	1			
Exchange rate regime, 1974	0.19 (0.76)	0.24 (0.97)	−0.03 (−0.11)	−0.25 (−1.05)	0.47 (2.15)	−0.63 (−3.23)	−0.24 (−1.00)	1		
Debt/GDP (%), 1975	0.11 (0.45)	−0.14 (−0.43)	−0.40 (−1.77)	0.43 (1.92)	−0.03 (−0.13)	0.14 (0.55)	−0.30 (−1.25)	−0.10 (−0.42)	1	
Quality of the data[a]	−0.55 (−2.66)	−0.34 (−1.44)	−0.27 (−1.11)	0.11 (0.46)	−0.02 (−0.09)	0.43 (1.89)	−0.12 (−0.47)	0.12 (0.50)	0.18 (0.73)	1

(*continued*)

Table 9.2 (continued)

	Less-Developed Countries									
	Inf7494	Inf4872	CBI	Political Inst.	Imports	GDP	GDP/Capita	Exch. Rate	Debt	Q
Average inflation, 1974–94	1									
Average inflation, 1948–72	0.32	1								
	(1.85)									
Central bank independence	0.30	−0.10	1							
	(1.70)	(−0.53)								
Political instability	0.49	0.16	0.31	1						
	(3.00)	(0.89)	(1.74)							
Imports/GDP, 1973–94	−0.28	−0.22	0.22	−0.43	1					
	(−1.57)	(−1.23)	(1.21)	(−2.57)						
Log income, 1980	−0.03	0.16	−0.18	0.07	−0.53	1				
	(−0.18)	(0.86)	(−0.98)	(0.38)	(−3.39)					
Log income per capita, 1980	−0.14	−0.09	0.02	−0.50	0.38	0.24	1			
	(−0.75)	(−0.49)	(0.12)	(−3.08)	(2.24)	(1.31)				
Exchange rate regime, 1974	0.07	0.12	−0.16	−0.07	−0.04	−0.24	−0.09	1		
	(0.39)	(0.65)	(−0.85)	(−0.39)	(−0.21)	(−1.30)	(−0.51)			
Debt/GDP (%), 1975	0.12	−0.08	0.11	−0.29	0.38	−0.11	0.20	−0.09	1	
	(0.67)	(−0.42)	(0.61)	(−1.61)	(2.22)	(−0.58)	(1.12)	(−0.48)		
Quality of the data[a]	−0.25	−0.08	0.15	−0.30	0.31	0.29	0.67	−0.03	0.22	1
	(−1.43)	(−0.45)	(0.84)	(−1.71)	(1.73)	(1.65)	(4.92)	(−0.16)	(1.21)	

Note: *t*-statistics are in parentheses.

[a]Summers and Heston 1988.

Table 9.3   Cross-sectional Regressions

	Whole Sample	High Income	Other Countries	$\pi \leq 100$	$\pi \leq 50$
Dependent Variable = Average Inflation Rate, 1973–94					
		Panel A			
Constant	15.87	9.92	7.57	11.24	12.23
	(1.48)	(4.81)	(0.41)	(2.42)	(3.11)
Central bank independence	18.88	−7.37	61.33	12.63	3.95
	(0.62)	(−2.24)	(1.16)	(0.85)	(0.36)
R^2	0.005	0.05	0.03	0.008	0.001
N	62	18	44	58	56
		Panel B			
Constant	9.17	9.92	3.94	8.52	11.08
	(0.86)	(4.66)	(0.21)	(1.78)	(2.69)
Central bank independence	10.30	−7.38	41.30	11.59	3.77
	(0.39)	(−2.29)	(0.83)	(0.87)	(0.36)
Political instability	61.44	0.36	48.71	22.51	9.54
	(2.82)	(0.04)	(1.93)	(1.80)	(1.13)
R^2	0.18	0.05	0.12	0.07	0.02
N	62	18	44	58	56
		Panel C			
Constant	70.13	34.55	16.79	43.81	32.56
	(2.77)	(1.38)	(0.43)	(3.29)	(3.19)
Central bank independence	22.90	−6.82	61.15	16.35	6.58
	(0.80)	(−2.04)	(1.16)	(1.20)	(0.65)
Log income per capita, 1980	−6.97	−2.71	−1.21	−4.21	−2.62
	(−2.21)	(−0.98)	(−0.22)	(−2.62)	(−2.19)
R^2	0.06	0.05	0.03	0.08	0.05
N	62	18	44	58	56
		Panel D			
Constant	6.40	35.98	−35.45	33.22	33.21
	(0.20)	(1.31)	(−0.94)	(2.03)	(2.43)
Central bank independence	9.96	−6.76	37.79	14.80	6.66
	(0.37)	(−2.12)	(0.75)	(1.18)	(0.69)
Political instability	62.51	−1.53	59.12	10.53	−0.66
	(2.34)	(−0.17)	(2.37)	(0.74)	(−0.06)
Log income per capita, 1980	0.33	−2.87	5.10	−3.01	−2.70
	(0.09)	(−0.96)	(0.98)	(−1.73)	(−1.86)
R^2	0.18	0.05	0.14	0.09	0.05
N	62	18	44	58	56

Note: White (1980) *t*-statistics are in parentheses.

Table 9.4   **Cross-sectional Regressions**

Dependent Variable = Average Inflation Rate, 1973–94

	Whole Sample	High Income	Less Developed	$\pi \leq 100$	$\pi \leq 50$
		Panel A			
Constant	36.74	7.83	46.67	23.24	18.25
	(4.49)	(6.14)	(4.66)	(5.23)	(6.56)
Imports/GDP, 1973–94	−0.43	−0.01	−0.55	−0.22	−0.13
	(−2.61)	(−0.87)	(−2.74)	(−2.58)	(−2.24)
R^2	0.07	0.004	0.10	0.07	0.05
N	62	18	44	58	56
		Panel B			
Constant	137.80	63.79	103.43	95.38	71.73
	(3.21)	(2.87)	(1.62)	(4.55)	(4.29)
Imports/GDP, 1973–94	−0.66	−0.18	−0.67	−0.38	−0.26
	(−3.71)	(−2.78)	(−3.37)	(−3.50)	(−3.39)
Log income, 1980	−5.35	−2.74	−3.09	−3.82	−2.80
	(−2.38)	(−2.56)	(−0.86)	(−3.91)	(−3.43)
R^2	0.15	0.56	0.12	0.20	0.18
N	62	18	44	58	56
		Panel C			
Constant	76.97	−29.75	41.26	83.46	70.54
	(2.15)	(−0.56)	(0.85)	(4.05)	(3.61)
Imports/GDP, 1973–94	−0.51	−0.22	−0.78	−0.38	−0.27
	(−3.18)	(−3.18)	(−3.03)	(−3.15)	(−3.03)
Log income, 1980	−5.42	−3.30	−6.09	−4.12	−3.01
	(−2.35)	(−3.13)	(−1.88)	(−3.34)	(−2.90)
Central bank independence	8.46	−8.02	43.44	13.57	6.34
	(0.35)	(−2.00)	(1.07)	(1.15)	(0.69)
Political instability	56.90	35.06	42.94	9.12	−0.62
	(2.24)	(3.38)	(1.76)	(0.70)	(−0.06)
Log income per capita, 1980	5.67	11.78	12.33	1.40	0.40
	(1.43)	(1.64)	(2.06)	(0.69)	(0.24)
R^2	0.24	0.70	0.24	0.22	0.19
N	62	18	44	58	56

Note: White (1980) *t*-statistics are in parentheses.

income to the specification; the results on openness remain robust. Thus, our data set also reproduces the basic results about openness.

9.3.2 Basic New Results

We now turn to examining the additional issues raised in section 9.2. We first provide a base case regression and then consider robustness checks.

The basic regression contains the following variables: CBI, political instability, openness, the log level of output, the log level of output per capita, an exchange-rate-regime dummy (explained below), the average inflation rate during the 1948–72 period, the level of government debt relative to output in 1975, and the grade assigned by Summers and Heston (1988) to the quality of their national accounts data for each country. Several comments about this specification are in order.

The average inflation rate from the presample period is included as a possible measure of the taste for inflation. According to one view, high past inflation implies lower current inflation because countries learn about the costs of inflation and then reform. This implies a negative coefficient. According to a different view, high past inflation leads the economy to invest in technologies for avoiding inflation's negative effects, which subsequently reduces the costs of inflation. Under this interpretation, the coefficient should be positive. Alternatively, past inflation might measure persistent aspects of the factors that determine inflation but are unmeasured or poorly measured in our regressions, which again implies a positive coefficient.

We include political instability to proxy a number of possible effects. The most commonly discussed is that more instability makes it difficult for policymakers to commit to low inflation. In addition, countries with political instability probably tend to have larger amounts of underground activity, which raises the optimal inflation rax. Similarly, countries with political instability tend to run inefficient economic programs, which suggests their natural and socially optimal rates of output or unemployment diverge. Nothing in our regressions allows us to sort out these effects, but in each case the expected sign on the coefficient is positive.

We include debt relative to output in 1975 as a measure of the need for tax revenue.[7] This variable will not capture all differences in expenditure paths, but the effect of a high initial level of debt on desired tax collections is unambiguously positive, and this variable is less obviously endogenous with respect to inflation than other possible measures. We show below that other measures, such as expenditure relative to output, produce similar results.

We include the log of income per capita in 1980 to capture several possible effects. A higher level of income per capita is likely to be accompanied by a more sophisticated tax system and a more developed financial system, both of which imply lower optimal inflation tax and thus a negative coefficient. On the other hand, high-income countries might be better at innovating technologies for reducing the costs of inflation, so their inflation aversion might be lower. This implies a positive coefficient.

We include the Summers and Heston quality-of-data score to control for the level of the inflation tax relative to other taxes. For example, countries with large informal sectors, which are typically untaxed, are also likely to have

---

7. Since we measure inflation over the period 1973–94, it might be preferable to use debt over output in 1973 or 1974. We could not construct this variable for a sufficient number of countries, however.

poor-quality data. The Summers-Heston score is higher for countries with better-quality data, so the coefficient should be negative if the reasoning offered here is correct. This variable might also be correlated with factors that make the socially optimal rate of output or unemployment diverge from the natural rate; again, the expected coefficient is negative.

We include a dummy variable for the kind of exchange rate regime, as in many previous papers, as a further check on the role on the time-consistency considerations. In particular, countries that have agreed to peg their currencies, especially when those agreements involve many countries, may face political costs of excessive inflation and therefore find it relatively easy to maintain a consistent policy. The variable we construct takes a value of 2 for countries that were in multilateral exchange rate systems in 1974, 1 for countries that were in unilateral exchange rate systems, and 0 for countries that allowed their currencies to float. Thus, a higher value of the variable implies, other things equal, a greater commitment to low inflation, so the coefficient should be negative according to the time-consistency hypothesis.

We note that our measure of the exchange rate regime is possibly a poor proxy for any effects of the exchange rate mechanism on inflation. By using data for 1974, we are failing to capture any effects that might have resulted from decisions about the exchange rate regime later in the sample. It is important to avoid using a variable that measures the exchange rate regime during the middle of the sample, however, because such a variable is likely endogenous with respect to inflation. A country might maintain a pegged exchange rate over much or all of a particular sample period *because* it has solved the time-consistency problem, even if the decision to peg has no marginal effect on its ability to maintain low inflation. Even the variable we construct is problematic, since countries with an underlying distaste for inflation might choose multilateral exchange rate systems consistently, knowing they will have the discipline to live within the implied constraints. The beginning-of-sample measure should be "less endogenous," however, and we attempt to control for the differences in inflation aversion separately.

This specification omits two key variables. First, we have no direct measure of the discrepancy between the natural rate of output and the socially optimal rate of output. Political instability and quality of the data might capture this effect to some degree, and we attempt more direct measurement below. These attempts are problematic, however, so we omit them from the basic specification. Second, we do not include FOI since it exists only for a narrow sample. Additional results below suggest this omission is not critical.

Table 9.5 presents the main results. CBI enters with the wrong sign in all samples except the high-income sample, and even in this case the coefficient is nowhere near significant. Thus, CBI appears even less reliably related to inflation than indicated by the more parsimonious regressions in table 9.3. The dummy for the exchange rate regime enters with the wrong sign, although not significantly.

Table 9.5 **Cross-sectional Regressions**

Dependent Variable = Average Inflation Rate, 1973–94					
	Whole Sample	High Income	Less Developed	$\pi \leq 100$	$\pi \leq 50$
Constant	−12.78	−92.31	−29.91	16.61	16.61
	(−0.28)	(−1.29)	(−0.51)	(0.94)	(0.94)
Average inflation, 1948–72	0.59	1.83	0.59	0.25	0.25
	(1.31)	(3.63)	(1.41)	(1.58)	(1.58)
Central bank independence	20.63	−3.45	80.11	10.34	10.34
	(1.32)	(−0.71)	(2.47)	(1.15)	(1.15)
Political instability	60.55	21.51	49.81	7.46	7.46
	(2.64)	(2.38)	(2.17)	(0.80)	(0.80)
Imports/GDP, 1973–94	−0.37	−0.08	−0.55	−0.30	−0.30
	(−3.71)	(−2.38)	(−2.69)	(−5.33)	(−5.33)
Log income, 1980	−3.87	−1.12	−4.14	−2.49	−2.49
	(−2.52)	(−3.00)	(−1.75)	(−2.74)	(−2.74)
Log income per capita, 1980	12.75	15.13	14.07	7.53	7.53
	(2.13)	(1.96)	(2.06)	(3.65)	(3.65)
Exchange rate regime, 1974	2.58	0.77	5.50	0.78	0.78
	(1.32)	(0.94)	(1.69)	(0.55)	(0.55)
Debt/GDP (%), 1975	0.35	0.11	0.37	0.23	0.23
	(4.98)	(3.48)	(3.57)	(4.25)	(4.25)
Quality of the data[a]	−5.68	−4.29	−6.33	−5.28	−5.28
	(−2.29)	(−1.86)	(−2.61)	(−3.65)	(−3.65)
R^2	0.58	0.87	0.58	0.55	0.55
N	49	18	31	47	47

Note: White (1980) t-statistics are in parentheses.
[a]Summers and Heston 1988.

Political instability enters positively, which is consistent with each of several possible mechanisms, but the result is not overwhelmingly consistent across samples. The magnitude of the estimated effect, however, is large. A one standard-deviation-higher level of political instability is associated with almost a 14.0% higher rate of inflation in the full sample and with a more than 12.0% higher inflation rate in the low-to-moderate-income sample. The estimated effect is essentially zero in the high-income sample, perhaps unsurprisingly.

Past inflation experience is consistently positively associated with current inflation, although the strength of the relation is modest outside the high-income countries. The estimated coefficient in the entire sample is about 0.6, which means 1 percentage-point higher value of prior inflation is associated with more than half a percentage point higher value of current inflation. The estimated effect is more than three times greater in the high-income sample.

The relative strength and magnitude of this relation in the high-income countries might simply indicate that we have failed to capture some determinant of inflation that is especially persistent in the high-income countries. A more interesting possibility is that high inflation induces investments in technologies for avoiding the costs of inflation. Once these are developed, they are not costly to use, so they reduce future aversion to inflation. The creation or adoption of such technologies might be easier in high-income countries (e.g., they have better-developed financial markets), which would explain the comparative strength of this effect in the high-income countries. The positive relation documented certainly fails to indicate that countries with bad past inflation performances learn from their mistakes and therefore choose lower inflation in the future, other factors held constant.

Openness and the level of income enter both negatively and significantly, although the magnitudes of the estimated effects and their statistical significance fall relative to the more parsimonious regressions in table 9.4. Thus, earlier results appear to have produced estimates of these effects on the high side, but the basic message is robust to controlling for a number of factors not considered in earlier papers. Moreover, the magnitude of the estimated openness effect is still substantial. For the whole sample, the coefficient estimates indicate that a one-standard-deviation-lower import share is associated with an almost 8.0% higher inflation rate. In the high-income sample the estimated effect is only about 1.5%, while in low-to-moderate-income sample it is over 12.0%.

The two variables proxying optimal tax considerations enter consistently with the correct sign and are quite robust: an initially high level of government debt is associated with high future inflation, and countries with lousy data, which we interpret to be countries where collecting revenue via noninflation taxes is difficult, make relatively greater reliance on the inflation tax. These results do not determine whether the inflation tax (and other taxes) are set at exactly the right level given past and future expenditures, nor whether the inflation tax is set exactly right relative to other taxes; in this sense the tests being carried out are far weaker than in the optimal tax literature on the time path of inflation. Nevertheless, the results are consistent with the view that inflation is being used roughly as it should be from an optimal tax perspective.

The magnitudes of these two effects are also substantial. A one-standard-deviation-higher level of the debt-to-income ratio is associated with a more than 8.0% higher inflation rate in the full sample and with a more than 1.5% higher inflation rate in the high-income sample. A one-standard-deviation-higher data-quality score is associated with almost a 9.0% lower rate of inflation using the full sample estimates and with a more than 1.0% lower inflation rate using the high-income sample estimates.

The final result is that, holding constant all the factors discussed, the level of income per capita is consistently positively related to inflation, usually in a robust manner. This outcome suggests the second of the two interpretations offered above, namely, that richer countries adapt to inflation more easily, so their distaste for inflation is lower. The magnitude of the relation is again large: a one-standard-deviation-higher level of income per capita is associated with approximately a 14.0% higher inflation rate using the full-sample estimates and with an almost 2.0% higher inflation rate using the high-income-sample estimates.

To summarize, the results in table 9.5 suggest that institutional characteristics of an economy, particularly CBI and exchange rate arrangements, are unimportant determinants of inflation. Time-consistency issues play a substantial role through the openness mechanism, and possibly through political instability, and optimal tax considerations are critical as well. We now examine whether these conclusions stand up to more rigorous scrutiny.

9.3.3 Robustness Checks

As a first check on the robustness of the results presented above, it is useful to examine the simple correlations between the variables shown in table 9.2. The key fact is that the main results discussed above are present and reasonably robust just in the simple correlations. CBI is positively correlated with inflation in the full sample but negatively correlated in the high-income sample. The exchange rate variable is essentially uncorrelated with inflation in both samples. In most other cases, the signs on the simple correlations are the same as in the multiple regression, and these correlations are often statistically significant.[8] The main exception is income per capita. The simple correlation with inflation is negative, but the estimated regression coefficients are always positive. The explanation appears to be that income per capita is positively correlated with a number of other variables, especially the quality-of-data variable.

The next set of checks considers other measures of the taste for inflation. One possibility is that high inflation plays an important role in shaping the tastes for inflation only when past inflation is extreme in some manner. As one check on this possibility, we include the standard deviation of past inflation as an explanatory variable in addition to the mean of past inflation. In all cases, this variable enters negatively, with a t-statistic between 1.0 and 1.5, and the other coefficients are not strongly affected. Thus, this specification provides mild evidence that countries reform in response to past mistakes.[9]

A third set of checks concerns our measure of the need for tax revenue. Instead of using the initial level of government debt relative to output, we include the average level of government expenditure relative to output over the 1973–94 period. The results from this specification are consistent with those in table 9.5; expenditure over output always enters positively, although the statistical significance is not overwhelming. When we include both expenditure over output and initial debt relative to output, debt enters positively and robustly while expenditure tends to enter positively but not significantly.

We have also considered a number of alternatives to the Summers-Heston quality-of-data variable as an indicator of countries' ability to raise noninfla-

---

8. The calculations of the t-statistics follow Bickel and Doksum 1977, 220–21.
9. All the additional results summarized in this section are available on request from the authors.

tion tax revenue. These include the share of agriculture in GDP, the infant mortality rate, and the high school enrollment rate. None of these variables enters in a robust manner, but the coefficients on all the remaining variables are not particularly sensitive to treatment of this issue.

We have not pursued one further approach to examining this effect, which would consist of estimating the interest elasticity of money demand for each country and including that as a regressor. Such a variable is problematic for our purposes since the estimated elasticity in a particular country in a given time period is likely a function of that country's inflation rate. This problem is small if the estimated elasticities are approximately equal to the underlying structural parameter, but this condition seems unlikely to hold in practice. The elasticities might be relatively free of this bias if they were estimated for sample periods that do not overlap with our inflation rate sample period, but we do not have the necessary data for the appropriate time periods for a sufficiently large sample of countries.

Our fifth set of robustness checks attempts to measure more directly the gap between the socially optimal rate of output/unemployment and the non-inflation-accelerating rate of output/unemployment. One natural measure of this gap is the average level of unemployment, assuming the socially optimal but unobserved rates of output/unemployment are not systematically related to policies that create divergences between the two rates. Unfortunately, data on unemployment tend to be inconsistent, both over time and across countries, so we can construct this variable for a relatively limited set of countries. In this set, the variable enters negatively, contrary to the implications of the time-consistency models, but the relation is weak. In the high-income countries, the estimated relation is positive, although again weak.

As a second way to measure the degree to which policymakers other than the central bank have given the central bank an incentive to raise output, we add the level of government consumption relative to output, with and without the square of this variable. Assuming such consumption increases economic efficiency up to a point but decreases it thereafter, the expected effect on inflation is positive according to the time-consistency models. In both specifications, however, we fail to find a significant effect, and the sign of the estimated effect is sometimes negative.

An issue related to our estimated standard errors is that some observations might be correlated cross-sectionally, perhaps through common involvement in a given exchange rate mechanism or perhaps because geographic proximity produces common susceptibility to certain kinds of shocks. As a crude attempt to address this issue, we reestimated the basic specification including dummy variables for geographic regions.[10] This modification has almost no effect on the results in the full sample. It does lead to significant changes in the high-

---

10. We included dummies for Africa, Asia, Europe, North and Central America, and South America, and omitted Oceania.

income sample, but these should be discounted since they are based on a regression with only three degrees of freedom.

The fact that we employ a different measure of CBI than in the papers by Romer and Lane raises the question of whether this decision plays a role in the results. We have also estimated the basic specification with the measure used by Romer and Lane, which includes information on actual rates of turnover in central bank governor. This modification has no substantive effect on the results.

One hypothesis we have not examined above is that supply shocks produce inflation differentially across countries. We consider this hypothesis by adding oil imports as a share of output to the basic regression. This variable enters positively in all samples, and the relation is strong (*t*-statistic of 2.8) for the high-income sample. The remaining coefficients are not affected to any substantial degree by the addition of this variable. Thus, our evidence does suggest that supply shocks play a nonnegligible role, especially in the high-income countries.

The final issue we address is Posen's measure of FOI. This variable exists for only a subset of countries (roughly, those with inflation rates below 30% during the 1960–89 period), so we cannot add it to all of our specifications. When we add it to our basic regression estimated on Posen's low-to-moderate inflation sample, however, it enters insignificantly and with a much smaller coefficient than in his results. This is probably not because our additional variables knock it out. Instead, it appears that FOI is only moderately related to inflation even in Posen's data for the 1970s and 1980s; much of the strength in his results derives from the data for the 1960s.

As a final result, it is useful to consider one further specification. In this regression, we drop CBI, since it does not appear to play an important role and since it is the variable that limits our sample most significantly. This specification provides results for a sample of sixty-eight countries that is almost identical to that for the narrower sample for which CBI exists. Thus, the basic relations documented above appear to exist more broadly.

9.4 Conclusions

The results presented in this paper must be taken with a certain number of grains of salt. Even in the best case, we do not have an enormous number of observations, and in many cases this problem is severe. Many of the proxies we employ are crude, to say the least, and some are potentially endogenous with respect to inflation. The earlier papers in this literature are subject to more or less the same critiques, but caution is nevertheless in order.

Subject to these caveats, our results shed new light on the cross-country determinants of inflation. The more modest conclusions concern the two main hypotheses examined in earlier papers. These papers suggested that CBI is not a substantial causal factor in inflation performance, but our results make this conclusion inescapable. Conversely, earlier papers made a strong case that openness causes low inflation, and our results help eliminate any residual doubt.

The more interesting results in the paper concern the new issues addressed. We find some evidence that prior inflation experience plays a nonneglible role in inflation performance. The most interesting interpretation is that high inflation produces investments in inflation-avoiding technologies, which then reduce the costs of inflation. The fact that higher income tends to predict higher inflation is consistent with this interpretation. We recognize, however, that other interpretations are possible.

We also find consistent evidence that optimal tax considerations do matter in determining inflation rates. This is perhaps not surprising, since this result is implied by a broad class of models and has been documented in the cases of particular countries. But the result has not previously been demonstrated to hold as widely as found here, and we show both that the overall need for revenue matters and that inflation is adjusted relative to other taxes in the right direction, given the need for revenue.

Our overall summary of these results is that institutional arrangements do not by themselves seem to be of much help in achieving low inflation. Economic fundamentals, such as openness, political instability, and tax policy, seem to play a much larger role. This does not mean policymakers should ignore institutions or that institutions play no role; our work might simply have little power to demonstrate the importance of institutions or to isolate the critical aspects of institutional arrangements. Nevertheless, our results suggest that quick fixes—increasing the tenure of the central bank governor—do not make a big difference unless the underlying conditions for low inflation are present. Creating those conditions is undoubtedly difficult, but it also appears to be essential.

References

Alesina, Alberto, and Lawrence H. Summers. 1993. Central Bank Independence and Macroeconomic Performance: Some Comparative Evidence. *Journal of Money, Credit, and Banking* (May): 151–62.

Ball, Laurence, and Stephen G. Cecchitti. 1990. Inflation Uncertainty at Long and Short Horizons. *Brookings Papers on Economic Activity* 1:215–54.

Barro, Robert J. 1991. Economic Growth in a Cross Section of Countries. *Quarterly Journal of Economics* 106:407–43.

Barro, Robert J., and David B. Gordon. 1983. A Positive Theory of Monetary Policy in a Natural Rate Model. *Journal of Political Economy* 91:589–610.

Bickel, Peter J., and Kjell A. Doksum. 1977. *Mathematical Statistics: Basic Ideas and Selected Topics.* Oakland, CA: Holden-Day.

Cukierman, Alex, Sebastian Edwards, and Guido Tabellini. 1992. Seigniorage and Political Instability. *American Economic Review* 82:537–55.

Cukierman, Alex, Steven B. Webb, and Bilin Neyapti. 1992. Measuring the Independence of Central Banks and Its Effect on Policy Outcomes. *World Bank Economic Review* 6, no. 3: 353–98.

Grilli, Vittorio, Donato Masciandaro, and Guido Tabellini. 1991. Political and Monetary Institutions and Public Financial Policies in the Industrial Countries. *Economic Policy* 13:341–92.

Grilli, Vittorio, and Gian Maria Milesi-Ferretti. 1995. Economic Effects and Structural Determinants of Capital Controls. *IMF Staff Papers* 42, no. 3: 517–51.

Kydland, Finn E., and Edward C. Prescott. 1977. Rules Rather Than Discretion: The Inconsistency of Optimal Plans. *Journal of Political Economy* 85 (June): 473–92.

Lane, Philip. 1995. Inflation in Open Economies. Columbia University. Manuscript.

Mankiw, N. Gregory. 1987. The Optimal Collection of Seigniorage: Theory and Evidence. *Journal of Monetary Economics* 20, no. 2: 327–41.

Posen, Adam S. 1993. Why Central Bank Independence Does Not Cause Low Inflation: The Politics behind the Institutional Fix. Federal Reserve Bank of New York. Manuscript.

———. 1995. Declarations Are Not Enough: Financial Sector Sources of Central Bank Independence. *NBER Macroeconomics Annual* 10:251–74.

Poterba, James, and Julio Rotemberg. 1990. Inflation and Taxation with Optimizing Governments. *Journal of Money, Credit, and Banking* 22:1–18.

Romer, David. 1993. Openness and Inflation: Theory and Evidence. *Quarterly Journal of Economics* 107, no. 4: 869–903.

Summers, Robert, and Alan Heston. 1988. A New Set of International Comparisons of Real Product and Price Levels Estimates for 130 Countries, 1950–1985. *Review of Income and Wealth* 34:1–25.

White, Halbert. 1980. A Heteroskedasticity-Consistent Covariance Matrix Estimator and a Direct Test for Heteroskedasticity. *Econometrica* 48:817–38.

Comment   Maurice Obstfeld

This careful and important paper by Marta Campillo and Jeffrey Miron is the latest to caution against a premature causal interpretation of simple correlations between long-term inflation performance and various measures of central bank independence (CBI). In this spirit, Posen (1995) has argued that CBI and low inflation are both explicable by the effectiveness of the financial community's opposition to inflation. The Campillo-Miron study, which systematically assesses an array of potential determinants of inflation for a broad cross-section of countries, suggests that Posen's empirical results are largely germane to the 1960s. Like Posen, the present authors see little evidence that CBI per se contributes to low inflation. Here the factors most robustly and unconditionally correlated with favorable inflation outcomes appear to be low public debt, economic openness, political stability, and quality of aggregate data. Higher past

Maurice Obstfeld is the Class of 1958 Professor of Economics at the University of California, Berkeley, and a research associate of the National Bureau of Economic Research.

Research support was provided by the National Science Foundation, the Ford Foundation, and the Center for German and European Studies at the University of California, Berkeley.

inflation and higher per capita income appear to aggravate inflation, for reasons that remain unclear.

The authors acknowledge the difficulty of interpreting empirical correlations in the presence of pervasive endogeneity. To address the problem they carry out numerous sensitivity checks, and in their main results often use explanatory variables measured at or close to the start of their sample period, 1973–94. In some cases this choice probably dooms them to finding insignificance.

For example, it is hard to believe that much information about the preferred exchange rate regime is contained in the 1974 observation, drawn from the transitional year between the final Bretton Woods collapse and the International Monetary Fund's formal decision to live without universally fixed exchange rates. On the other hand, the authors are right in their reluctance to use later data. Most satisfactory would be to include as regressors the potential determinants of the exchange rate regime. One of the most important of these, openness, is included and does appear to have a strong negative impact on inflation. One way to assess the channels through which openness discourages inflation would be to study its effect on exchange-rate-regime choice through cross-section regression.

Use of initial (1975) public debt–GDP ratios also appears problematic at first glance, but turns out to be revealing. As figure 9C.1 shows, many industrial countries have experienced sharp increases in debt-GDP ratios since the early 1970s. (The same statement is true of developing countries.) How much information, then, would one expect to find in data two decades old? Perhaps surprisingly, the answer is, a lot. Figure 9C.2 shows the striking positive correlation between fifteen industrial countries' debt-GDP ratios in 1975 and in 1991. Least-squares regression yields

$$\frac{Debt_{91}}{GDP_{91}} = \underset{(0.07)}{0.21} + \underset{(0.23)}{1.19} \frac{Debt_{75}}{GDP_{75}}, \quad R^2 = 0.67$$

(with standard errors in parentheses). Interestingly, the high-debt industrial countries of the early 1970s also tended to be the high-debt countries of the early 1990s.

Campillo and Miron interpret the significance of their public-debt variable as evidence of optimal inflation choice, along the lines of Phelps's extension (1973) of Ramsey taxation to include taxation of money balances. They view their openness, political instability, and data-quality variables as being more directly related to potential dynamic inconsistency in monetary policy, a factor fundamental to the normative case for an independent central bank. However, public debt itself, if denominated in domestic currency, as it generally is, can also be a powerful source of additional inflation credibility problems. I will illustrate the reason at some length, as the point has an important bearing on the lessons to be drawn from this paper's results.

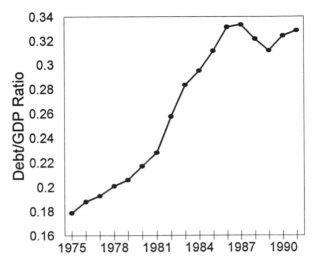

Fig. 9C.1   Growth in debt, fifteen OECD countries (GDP-weighted average)

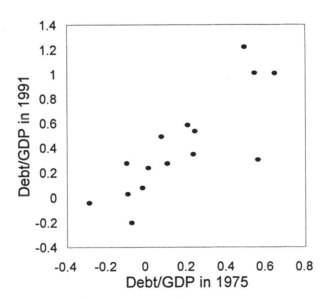

Fig. 9C.2   Debt ratios, fifteen OECD countries

Consider the following rudimentary model. (See also Calvo 1989.) The government inherits a nominal debt D_0 contracted at a nominal interest rate of i_0, which it must pay off entirely through taxes τ on nominal output Py and through money creation $M - M_0$, where M_0 is the previous period's nominal money stock. After this repayment, the economy comes to an end. The resulting government budget constraint is

$$(1 + i_0)D_0 = P\tau y + M - M_0.$$

The demand for money in any period is given by the quantity equation $M = kPy$ (notwithstanding the impending end of the economy). If P_0 denotes the previous period's price level and the inflation rate π is defined as a tax rate on nominal claims,

$$\pi = \frac{P - P_0}{P},$$

then the preceding budget constraint can be reformulated as

(1) $$\tau y + \pi k y - (1 + i_0)(1 - \pi)\frac{D_0}{P_0} = 0.$$

Plainly inflation taxes not only real balances ky, but also the real value of the scheduled nominal debt repayment $(1 + i_0)D_0$.

Now consider the optimal level of inflation when the government chooses τ and π according to a Phelpsian optimal tax rule. The government minimizes the loss function

$$\mathcal{L} = \frac{1}{2}\tau^2 + \frac{a}{2}\pi^2,$$

where a measures relative inflation aversion, subject to budget constraint 1. Define the inherited real debt, $d_0 = D_0/P_0$. The first-order condition for an optimal tax package is

$$\pi = \frac{\tau}{a}[k + (1 + i_0)\frac{d_0}{y}],$$

which, in combination with constraint 1, yields the government's preferred ex post inflation choice:

(2) $$\pi = \frac{(1 + i_0)d_0[ky + (1 + i_0)d_0]}{ay^2 + [ky + (1 + i_0)d_0]^2}.$$

It is easy to see that inflation is an increasing function of the inherited real debt burden, $(1 + i_0)d_0$.

The responsiveness of inflation to past debts allows dynamic inconsistency to creep in. If there were no possibility of devaluing the debt ex post through surprise inflation—imagine that all government debt were indexed—then the first-order condition for taxes would be $\pi = \tau k/a$ and, assuming the same past real debt d_0, optimal inflation would be

$$\pi = \frac{(1 + r)d_0(ky)}{ay^2 + (ky)^2},$$

where r is the (exogenous) real interest rate. But if there is nominal debt, the government will set inflation higher than this level in equilibrium (as one can show). How high will equilibrium inflation be? Given rational expectations on the part of bondholders, the past nominal interest rate i_0 fully reflects anticipated future inflation:

$$1 + i_0 = \frac{1 + r}{1 - \pi}.$$

An equilibrium inflation rate (there may be more than one) is found by substituting this expression into equation 2 and solving for π. Equilibrium inflation is higher than it would be with indexed debt because, in equilibrium, inflation is anticipated and thus fails to reduce the government's real interest obligation.

In analogy with the Kydland-Prescott and Barro-Gordon accounts of high-employment monetary policy, inflation expectations raise nominal interest rates and the debt burden, prompting an accommodating monetary response that ultimately is checked by a rising marginal cost of inflation. Not only is inflation higher than it would be with indexed government debt, so are conventional distorting taxes, which also rise to bear part of the increased real debt burden. Thus, the presence of nominal debt creates a classic dynamic inconsistency problem that magnifies the conventional optimal-tax effect of government debt on inflation.

If the Campillo-Miron results on debt levels reflect dynamic inconsistency, rather than a more benign optimal balancing of marginal distortions in a setting of credible policies, then the normative case for CBI certainly is strengthened. Indeed, one potent argument for CBI is that it imposes fiscal discipline by closing off the easy options of money financing and debt devaluation. Thus, an independent central bank may discourage both government debt issue and the ultimate resort to inflationary finance. A world in which CBI affected inflation primarily through this fiscal-discipline channel could yield regression results much like those the authors report. It would be interesting to know if, cross-sectionally, CBI has any impact on fiscal prudence. For industrial countries, casual empiricism indicates a negative answer.

The remarkable positive correlation of debt ratios over time (figure 9C.2) suggests to me instead that political fragmentation and polarization, of the type Roubini and Sachs (1989) link to public deficits, may also help explain long-run inflation performance. Indeed, this is also the main point of Cukierman, Edwards, and Tabellini (1992). Consistent with this view, Posen's financial opposition to inflation measure (1995) includes information on characteristics of the political scene.

The array of unanswered questions does not detract from Campillo and Miron's contribution in investigating a broad range of explanations for inflation within a unified empirical framework. While they rightly view their interpretations as tentative, the patterns they have uncovered provide important starting points for future research. An obvious focus would be the potential casual mechanisms that the authors discuss. Future research should also exploit the dynamic properties of the data, as in the related study by Grilli and Milesi-Ferretti (1995). One puzzle that might be addressed using time-series data is the following: If public debt, through whatever mechanism, is such an important determinant of inflation, why have inflation rates in the industrial world come down since the early 1980s despite the continuing increase in the average public debt–GDP ratio? And if greater CBI has contributed to this development, can that contribution endure in the absence of parallel fiscal reform?

References

Calvo, Guillermo A. 1989. Controlling Inflation: The Problem of Non-Indexed Debt. In *Debt, Adjustment and Recovery: Latin America's Prospect for Growth and Development,* ed. S. Edwards and F. Larrain, 156–75. New York: Blackwell.

Cukierman, Alex, Sebastian Edwards, and Guido Tabellini. 1992. Seigniorage and Political Instability. *American Economic Review* 82:537–55.

Grilli, Vittorio, and Gian Maria Milesi-Ferretti. 1995. Economic Effects and Structural Determinants of Capital Controls. *IMF Staff Papers* 42:517–51.

Phelps, Edmund S. 1973. Inflation in the Theory of Public Finance. *Swedish Journal of Economics* 75:67–82.

Posen, Adam S. 1995. Declarations Are Not Enough: Financial Sector Sources of Central Bank Independence. *NBER Macroeconomics Annual* 10:251–74.

Roubini, Nouriel, and Jeffrey D. Sachs. 1989. Political and Economic Determinants of Budget Deficits in the Industrial Democracies. *European Economic Review* 33:903–38.

10   How the Bundesbank Conducts Monetary Policy

Richard Clarida and Mark Gertler

10.1   Introduction

Over the last decade there has been a growing belief among economists and policymakers that the primary objective of monetary policy should be to control inflation. Two kinds of arguments are cited. First, experience suggests that fine-tuning the economy is not a realistic option and that inflation is difficult to lower. By taking preemptive steps to avoid high inflation, a central bank can reduce the likelihood of having to engineer a costly disinflation. Second, a central bank that establishes a clear commitment to controlling inflation may be able to maintain low inflation for far less cost than if it did not have this reputation.

In this context German monetary policy is of great interest. From the breakup of Bretton Woods in 1973 until the year prior to reunification, 1989, average annual inflation in West Germany was lower than in any other Organization for Economic Cooperation and Development (OECD) country. Based in large part on this historical performance, the Deutsche Bundesbank is known for its commitment to fighting inflation, perhaps more than any other central bank. The institutions of German monetary policy, further, appear specifically geared toward controlling inflation. Each year since 1974 the Bundesbank has set targets for both inflation and monetary growth.

Richard Clarida is professor of economics at Columbia University and a research associate of the National Bureau of Economic Research. Mark Gertler is professor of economics at New York University and a research associate of the National Bureau of Economic Research.

Thanks for helpful comments to Rudi Dornbusch, Willy Friedman, Jeff Fuhrer, Jordi Gali, Dale Henderson, Otmar Issing, Christy Romer, Dave Romer, Chris Sims, Mike Woodford, and seminar participants at the Federal Reserve Board, Boston University, the Federal Reserve Bank of Boston, Yale University, the University of Miami, the Bundesbank, the Massachusetts Institute of Technology, and the Federal Reserve Bank of Philadelphia. Special thanks to Eunkyung Kwon for tireless research assistance. Thanks also to Rosanna Maddalena. Gertler acknowledges support from the National Science Foundation and the C. V. Starr Center.

This paper provides a broad-based description of German monetary policy. The goal is to learn about the mechanics of maintaining low inflation, and about the net benefits and costs of doing so. In the end we provide a description of how the Bundesbank conducts monetary policy that is based on both a reading of the historical evidence and a formal statistical analysis of the Bundesbank's policy rule.

What makes the general problem of evaluating Bundesbank policy challenging is that for much of the last fifteen years the performance of the real economy has been mixed. Unraveling the precise role of monetary policy in this performance is a complex issue, one that our analysis cannot fully resolve. By closely studying the record of monetary policy, however, we try to shed light on the matter.

Section 10.2 describes the institutions of German monetary policy. Here we outline the system of inflation and monetary targeting. As is commonly understood by close observers of the Bundesbank, the targets are meant as guidelines. In no sense do they define a strict policy rule. In terms of operating procedures, the Bundesbank chooses a path for short-term interest rates to meet its policy objectives, similar in spirit to the Federal Reserve Board.

Section 10.3 reviews the history of Bundesbank policy since the breakup of Bretton Woods. Here our objective is to obtain narrative evidence on how the Bundesbank operates in practice. As one might expect, we find that the Bundesbank is aggressive in managing short-term interest rates to dampen inflationary pressures, the exception being the period between the two major oil shocks, 1975 to early 1979. On the other hand, it clearly factors in the performance of the real economy in setting rates, though perhaps not explicitly. For example, it often cites exchange rate considerations to pursue what closely resembles a countercyclical policy. We also find, as have others, that curtailing inflation is not a costless process for the Bundesbank, despite its reputation.

Sections 10.4 and 10.5 supplement the narrative evidence with a formal statistical analysis of Bundesbank policy. Specifically, we attempt to identify a policy reaction function that characterizes how the Bundesbank sets the short-term interest rate. In general, estimating a policy reaction function involves a number of formidable identification issues, as we discuss. We take a two-step approach. We first obtain a reaction function by estimating a structural vector autoregression (VAR). This approach permits us to formally characterize how the Bundesbank adjusts short-term rates in response to different disturbances to the economy, using only a minimal set of identifying assumptions. As we show, the results are highly consistent with the narrative evidence. The disadvantage of this approach is that the reaction function is difficult to summarize intuitively because it is based on the entire information set in the VAR.

Section 10.5 presents the second step. We place additional structure on the model to obtain a more conventional-looking reaction function based on inflation and output objectives. We estimate a reaction function for the German short-term rate that is close in general form to the one developed by Taylor (1993) to characterize how the Federal Reserve Board has set the funds rate during the Greenspan era. In particular the central bank adjusts the short-term interest rate in response to the gaps between inflation and output and their respective targets. One key difference from Taylor is that under our rule the central bank is forward-looking in the sense that it responds to expected future inflation as opposed to lagged inflation. To form these expectations, our rule uses the information about the economy that is contained in the VAR model. Another key difference is that we allow for an asymmetric policy response to inflation; that is, we allow for the possibility that the Bundesbank may tighten more aggressively when expected inflation is above target than it eases when expected inflation is below target.

Overall, the estimated reaction function does a reasonably good job of characterizing the path of the German short-term rate over the post–Bretton Woods era. In addition the Bundesbank does appear to respond asymmetrically to the inflation gap. Finally, as we show, our modified "Taylor" rule provides a useful benchmark to gauge the position of policy at different critical junctures of the economy. Taken all together, our results suggest that Bundesbank policy since 1973 may be characterized as being reasonably similar to Federal Reserve policy under Alan Greenspan.

Section 10.6 offers concluding remarks.

10.2 Institutions of Bundesbank Policy

As is commonly presumed, the overriding objective of German monetary policy is to control inflation. The institutional design supports this goal in two main ways. First, formal legislation explicitly restricts political influence. Second, each year the Bundesbank clearly articulates an inflation objective and then establishes a target for the growth of a key monetary aggregate, based on this objective.

At the same time it is important to recognize that the system allows for flexibility. The monetary and inflation targets, for example, are only guidelines and not legal mandates. Events in the real economy can (and often do, as we will see) induce the Bundesbank to deviate from these guidelines, though not without some kind of official explanation.

With these general observations in mind, we proceed to characterize the institutional design of Bundesbank policy. Section 10.2.1 describes the organization and jurisdiction of the German central bank. Section 10.2.2 discusses the practice of monetary and inflation targeting. Section 10.2.3 describes the operating procedures for conducting monetary policy. Here we argue that, despite the focus on monetary aggregates, short-term interest rates provide a better overall indication of the thrust of policy than do the aggregates. In this respect there are some strong similarities with U.S. monetary policy.

10.2.1   Central Bank Design and Jurisdiction

Much as the experience of the Great Depression shaped the development of monetary and financial institutions in the United States, memories of the hyperinflation influenced the design of the German central bank. Article 3 of the Deutsche Bundesbank Act of 1957 empowers the German central bank to regulate the amount of currency and credit in circulation with the aim of safeguarding the currency. To ensure that this goal is feasible, legal mandates free monetary policy from the demands of fiscal policy. To avoid the mistakes of the hyperinflation, article 20 of the act prohibits the central bank from financing government deficits. Decisions on the course of monetary policy are made by a council that is independent of the federal government. Article 12 of the act makes this independence explicit.[1]

The formal body that sets monetary policy is the Central Bank Council, which closely resembles the federal Open Market Committee. It consists of the Bundesbank Board (analogous to the Federal Reserve Board) and the presidents of the German *Land* central banks (analogous to the presidents of the regional reserve banks). The Bundesbank Board consists of a president, vice president, and up to six other board members. The federal government nominates the board members, while the state governments nominate the presidents of the *Land* central banks. Terms are for eight years. Except for the constraint of mandatory retirement, council members typically are invited to serve a second term. The long terms are justified as a means to insulate the governing body from political pressures.

From the perspective of political independence, any differences between the institutional setup of the Bundesbank and the Federal Reserve are not dramatic. Grilli, Masciandaro, and Tabellini (1991) assign the German central bank a slightly higher independence rating than its U.S. counterpart because the Bundesbank president is guaranteed a longer term than is the Federal Reserve Board chair (eight years versus four years.)

Finally, the Bundesbank's jurisdiction is not completely independent of the federal government. The latter has discretion over exchange rate agreements. At least in practice, however, the government cannot force the Bundesbank to maintain agreements that threaten domestic price stability. Before Germany entered the European Monetary System (EMS), for example, the Bundesbank won a provision from the federal government that it could deviate from the exchange agreement if it was deemed necessary to do so in order to maintain low inflation (Neumann and Von Hagen 1993). In effect this meant that the Bundesbank assumed a clear leadership role in the EMS. At least for a period

---

1. Article 12 encourages the Bundesbank to cooperate with the economic objectives of the federal government, but not to the extent that doing so may conflict with the overriding goal of price stability. The article explicitly forbids the federal government to formally participate in monetary policy decisions.

of time, this was a suitable arrangement for the other countries involved. Because of its reputation the Bundesbank served as an informal nominal anchor. On numerous occasions other central banks simply followed the response of German interest rates to exogenous shocks.[2]

10.2.2   Monetary and Inflation Targeting

The Bundesbank is widely known for its practice of setting monetary targets. Perhaps its most distinctive feature, though, is its simultaneous practice of setting inflation targets. Inflation targeting is slowly increasing in popularity among central banks, and is currently a popular subject of academic discussion. It is perhaps not widely appreciated, however, that always underlying Germany's announced monetary target is an explicitly stated goal for inflation.[3] This contrasts with the United States, for example, where in the past monetary targets have been set without any explicit public rationalization.

Also not widely appreciated is the flexibility built into the policy rule. There is no blind commitment to hitting the monetary targets.[4] The view is that the monetary policy will be judged on its inflation scorecard, and it will not be penalized for missing monetary targets if inflation is under control. In addition there has not been a unilateral focus on inflation. As we show later, on a number of occasions, the Bundesbank has tolerated deviations from the targets in order to pursue what may be construed as a countercyclical policy.[5]

The Targeting Procedure

The practice of targeting began in 1975, after the breakup of Bretton Woods. The Bundesbank felt the need to maintain some kind of explicit nominal anchor to guide policy in the post–Bretton Woods era. The procedure works as follows: Each year the Bundesbank first establishes a goal for inflation. A target growth rate for a designated monetary aggregate is then established that is meant to be consistent with the inflation goal. In particular the money-growth

2. Uctum (1995), among others, provides some formal evidence for the Bundesbank's leadership role in the EMS. The paper identifies a clear causal relationship between German short-term interest rates and the short-term interest rates of other countries.

3. Bundesbank officials are resistant to equating their selection of an inflation goal with inflation targeting. They maintain that the ultimate target is price stability. Any deviation of the inflation goal from price stability is due to what they term "unavoidable" factors.

4. The notion that the targets serve as guidelines rather than as rigid mandates is a prominent theme in many studies of Bundesbank behavior. See, for example, Bernanke and Mishkin (1992); Kahn and Jacobson (1989); Trehan (1988); Von Hagen (1994). In addition, Bundesbank officials themselves are rather open about the flexibility inherent in the system. For example, to quote, Otmar Issing (1995, 5), the current head of the Bundesbank's research department, "Even in Germany, where a high degree of stability of financial relationships was observed, the central bank has never seen fit to transfer monetary targeting to an 'autopilot,' as it were."

5. Even in its official publications, the Bundesbank makes clear that circumstances may justify deviating from the targets. It states that, while the monetary targets "include a recognizable steadying element, they are not meant to preclude any reaction to the developments of economic activity, exchange rates, costs, and prices" (Deutsche Bundesbank 1989, 99).

target is backed out of a conventional quantity-theory equation that links money, velocity, prices, and output. As inputs into the equation, the Bundesbank uses the target rate of inflation and estimates of the trend growth of velocity and the trend growth of capacity output. The motive for using estimates of trend as opposed to near-term output and velocity growth in the calculation is to avoid trying to fine-tune inflation.[6] Instead, the objective is to maintain a low long-run average inflation rate. By clearly signaling its intent to gear policy toward achieving this long-term inflation goal, the Bundesbank seeks to influence private-sector wage and price adjustments.[7]

Originally, a fixed money target was announced. After two years, however, this was changed to a fixed range. The move to the range reflects the reality that the monetary aggregate is difficult to tightly regulate and that both output and velocity may deviate considerably from trend in the short run. Additional flexibility is provided by a midyear review of targets, which allows changing the targets in light of new information. The Bundesbank has made use of this option only once, however, during 1991, in the early stages of reunification. Finally, the targets are fixed for a fourth-quarter-to-fourth-quarter growth rate of a variable. Originally, they were from December to December, but the monthly pinpointing introduced too much transitory noise.

How does the Bundesbank set its inflation target? The official goal is to keep inflation from rising above its "unavoidable" level. Using this criteria, the Bundesbank has set a goal of 2% annual inflation for each year since 1986 (see table 10.1). The Bundesbank refrains from reducing the target to 0% because the official price index may overstate the true inflation rate since it tends to undercompensate for improvements in the quality of goods. Fixing the target at 2% ensures that measurement error in the price index will not inadvertently induce the Bundesbank to tighten (Issing 1995).

In the past the Bundesbank has also taken into account stabilization considerations in fixing the target inflation rate, at least implicitly. In the initial year of targeting, 1975, it set the inflation goal at 4.5%. This objective was picked with the aim of gradually reducing inflation over time. At the time, Germany (like the United States) was experiencing stagflation, due to the oil shocks of 1973 and 1974. The target was reduced to 2% gradually over time. The fact

---

6. Indeed, Bundesbank officials state explicitly that the central bank does not try to fine-tune either inflation or money growth in the short term. To quote Issing (1995, 8) again: "in the short term the relationship between the money stock and the overall domestic price level is obscured by a host of influencing factors. Any attempt at keeping the money stock on the desired growth path at all times would therefore inevitably spark off considerable interest rate and exchange rate fluctuations, provoke shocks to the trend of economic activity and hence cause unnecessary economic costs in the shape of adjustment on the part of economic agents. Accordingly, the Bundesbank has time and again pointed to the medium term nature of its strategy which is aimed at cyclical stabilization."

7. In particular the Bundesbank states that an important purpose of the targeting procedure is to "make the aims of monetary policy clearer to labor and management, whose cooperation is essential if inflation is to be brought under control without detrimental effects to employment" (Deutsche Bundesbank 1989, 97).

Table 10.1   **History of Money-Growth Targets and Unavoidable Inflation**

Year	Money Growth		Inflation	
	Target	Actual	Target	Actual
1975	8	10	4.5	5.6
1976	8	9	4.5	3.7
1977	8	9	3.5	3.3
1978	8	11	3.0	2.6
1979	6–9	6	3.0	5.4
1980	5–8	5	4.0	5.3
1981	4–7	4	3.8	6.7
1982	4–7	7	3.5	4.5
1983	4–7	7	3.5	2.6
1984	4–6	5	3.0	2.0
1985	3–5	4.5	2.5	1.6
1986	3.5–5.5	8	2.5	−1.0
1987	3–6	8	2.0	1.0
1988	3–6	6.7	2.0	1.9
1989	5	4.6	2.0	3.0
1990	4–6	5.6	2.0	2.7
1991	4–6	5.2	2.0	4.2
1992	3.5–5.5	9.4	2.0	3.7
1993	4.5–6.5	7.4	2.0	3.7

Sources: Kole and Meade 1994; Von Hagen 1994.

Notes: From 1975 to 1984 the Bundesbank announced a rate of "unavoidable" inflation as its input to the determination of money-growth targets. From 1985 to 1993 the objective was the rate of inflation consistent with "price stability."

that the target was not set lower initially suggests that, while controlling inflation may be its primary goal, the Bundesbank is not willing to do it at any cost.[8]

As further evidence of the Bundesbank's pragmatism, the previous year's performance of inflation relative to its target does not directly affect the current target choice. The targets are simply rebenchmarked, implying that the Bundesbank accommodates any overshooting in the previous year. It thus does not try to target a path for the price level. We return to this point in section 10.3, during the historical review of monetary policy.

Choice of a Monetary Aggregate

What determines the monetary aggregate that the Bundesbank targets? The desired aggregate must satisfy two conventional criteria. First, it should be reasonably controllable. Second, it should obey a relatively predictable relationship with nominal GDP. These criteria quickly eliminate narrow money

8. The Bundesbank officially acknowledges that the need for a gradualist approach to reducing inflation influenced its targeting decisions. It states that in setting the targets "it took account of the fact that price increases which have already entered the decisions of economic agents cannot be eliminated immediately, but only by degrees" (Deutsche Bundesbank 1989, 97).

aggregates like M1. Substitution between demand deposits and near-money substitutes (e.g., time and savings deposits) make this aggregate difficult to regulate. It also induces large fluctuations in M1 that are unrelated to the course of economic activity.

The Bundesbank originally settled on a construct it termed central bank money (CBM). The idea underlying the construct was to develop an aggregate that was a weighted average of all existing monetary instruments, where the weights reflect the relative "moneyness" of each instrument. The elements of CBM are, roughly speaking, the sum of currency held outside the banking system and the components of the broad aggregate M3 (which corresponds to M2 for the United States) weighted by the respective reserve requirement that existed in 1974. Thus, CBM is roughly the monetary base minus excess reserves. It differs by not including reserves against foreign deposits and by using the 1974 reserve requirements as opposed to the current ones. The rationale for using reserve requirements to weight the aggregates was that reserve requirements reasonably reflected the relative liquidity of each bank deposit liability.

In 1988 the Bundesbank switched to targeting the broader money aggregate M3. Strong currency growth in 1987 (due possibly to low interest rates) led to a rapid expansion of CBM. The Bundesbank felt that the broader aggregate was less susceptible than CBM to gyrations stemming from currency substitution (Trehan 1988). The decision to change the target aggregate is one of a number of pieces of evidence that the Bundesbank does not conduct policy on automatic pilot. New market developments can influence policy.

A number of studies have demonstrated that the relation between M3 and nominal GDP has been fairly stable over time (e.g., Trehan 1988). Some papers have argued that the early stages of reunification have not disrupted this relationship (e.g., Von Hagen 1994; Kole and Meade 1994). Very recently, however, there has been considerable financial innovation, patterned after what has occurred in the United States over the last five to ten years.[9] There is some possibility that this development may introduce the same kind of instability in M3 that the United States has experienced with its M2 aggregate. If this does occur, we should not be surprised to see a new target aggregate emerge.

10.2.3   Operating Procedures

Despite the public focus on monetary aggregates, the daily management of policy is concerned with the setting of short-term market interest rates. Like many other central banks, the Bundesbank translates its main policy goals (e.g., controlling inflation) into near-term interest rate objectives. It in turn supplies bank reserves to meet these objectives. Even in its official publications, the Bundesbank states (in its own oblique way) that, in the short run,

---

9. For a description of how recent financial innovation is affecting the monetary aggregates in Germany, see *German Economic Commentary* (Goldman Sachs), no. 42 (1994).

moderating market interest rate fluctuations takes precedence over meeting monetary targets.[10] In section 10.4 we present formal evidence that supports this contention.

Until the mid-1980s the Bundesbank manipulated short-term market interest rates (and bank reserves) via discount window lending to commercial banks. It made available two types of credit: discount and Lombard. Banks could receive discount credit at a preferred rate, up to a fixed quota. To meet short-term liquidity needs beyond the quota limit, they could obtain Lombard credit at a premium rate. Under normal circumstances Lombard credit was generally available in elastic supply. In periods of tightening, though, limits could also be placed on the use of this credit.

Both the discount and Lombard rates are posted rates. The market rate that discount window lending most directly affects is the rate in the interbank market for reserves, known as the day-to-day rate or the call money rate. As in the United States, reserve management policy is geared toward influencing the interbank rate.[11] Short-term variation in this rate therefore reflects the intention of monetary policy. As figure 10.1 indicates, the day-to-day rate tends to fluctuate in the band fixed by the discount and Lombard rates.

Since 1985 the Bundesbank has supplied banks with reserves mainly via repurchase agreements, which are essentially collateralized loans with a maturity of two to four weeks. Lombard credit has largely dried up. Nonetheless, the Bundesbank still posts a Lombard rate, mainly as a way to signal its intentions. Reserve management continues to directly influence the day-to-day rate, which still tends to fluctuate between the discount and Lombard rates, as figure 10.1 illustrates. Further, the day-to-day rate also tends to move closely with the rate on repurchase agreements, known as the repo rate. Despite the midstream change in operating procedures, therefore, it is still reasonable to view the day-to-day rate as the Bundesbank's policy instrument for the full post–Bretton Woods era.

10.3 A Narrative Description of Bundesbank Policy

In this section we provide a selective review of Bundesbank policy during the post–Bretton Woods era.[12] Our goal is to obtain narrative evidence on how the Bundesbank operates in practice.

It is useful to divide the review into four episodes: (1) 1973–78, the period

10. For example, the Bundesbank states that, because commercial banks' demand for reserves is "virtually inelastic" in the short run, it "has no choice but to meet the credit institutions' need for central bank balances in the short run. At times it may even have to provide more central bank balances than are strictly compatible with the growth in the money stock" (Deutsche Bundesbank 1989, 105).

11. Bernanke and Blinder (1992) propose treating the funds rate as the operating instrument for U.S. monetary policy. Bernanke and Mihov (1995) present evidence in support of this approach.

12. For additional information on the history of postwar Bundesbank policy, see Tsatsaronis (1993).

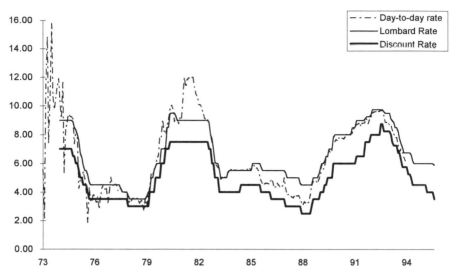

Fig. 10.1   German short-term interest rates

immediately after Bretton Woods was abandoned and after the first major oil shock occurred; (2) 1979–83, when the second major oil shock occurred and the United States tightened monetary policy; (3) 1983–89, the era of stagnation and late recovery in West Germany; (4) 1990–93, the early years of reunification. After a brief discussion of each episode, we summarize the key lessons about the conduct of Bundesbank policy.

To aid the discussion, we refer (often implicitly) to figure 10.2, which plots consumer price index (CPI) inflation, the growth rate of industrial production, and the day-to-day rate, all for West Germany. To provide a benchmark, the figure also plots the analogous variables for the U.S. economy. In addition figure 10.3 plots the behavior of both the real D-mark/dollar exchange rate, and the trade weighted exchange rate.

10.3.1   1973–1978

Shortly after it was freed from its obligations under Bretton Woods in early 1973, the Bundesbank raised short-term interest rates dramatically in order to curtail steadily rising inflation. On a number of occasions during this period it publicly announced a commitment to maintaining a tight monetary policy until inflation was under control (Tsatsaronis 1993). Unfortunately, later in the year came the first major oil shock. Thus, despite a restrictive policy through most of 1973, inflation climbed above 7% by the end of 1974. Though below the nearly double-digit level reached in the United States, this rate was clearly high by West German standards.

The Bundesbank continued to signal its intent to combat inflation. By the end of 1974, it had the system of inflation and monetary targeting intact. It announced a target rate of inflation for 1975 of 4.5% and a target rate of mone-

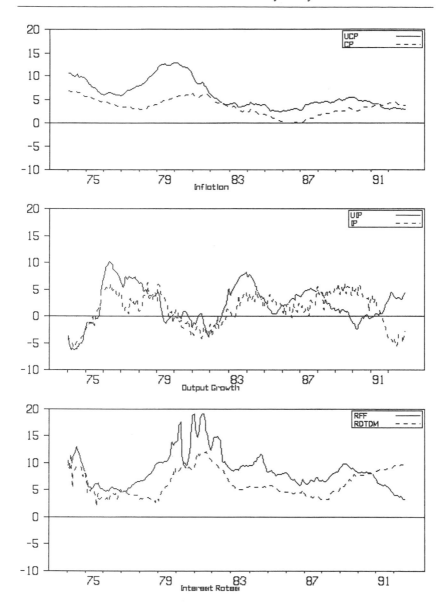

Fig. 10.2   Inflation, output growth, and interest rates: *UCPI,* **U.S. consumer price index;** *CPI,* **German CPI;** *UIP,* **U.S. industrial production;** *IP,* **German industrial production;** *RFF,* **federal funds rate;** *RDTDM,* **day-to-day interest rate**

tary growth of 8%. While these goals were ambitious, they nonetheless reflected a gradualist approach to reining in inflation.

As in the United States, the combined force of the oil shocks and a restrictive monetary policy forced the economy into a deep recession. The severe downturn induced the Bundesbank to ease, along with the Federal Reserve Board.

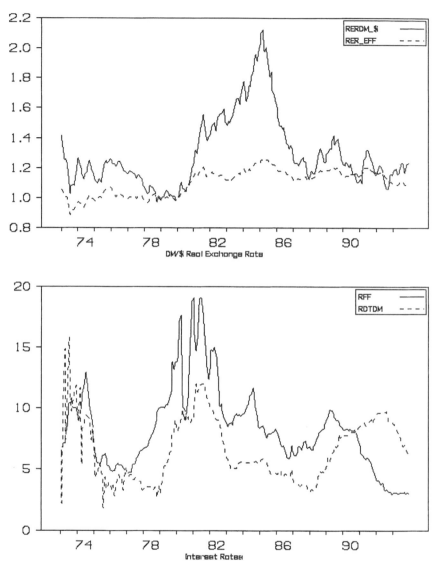

Fig. 10.3   Exchange rates and interest rates: *RERDM$,* **D-Mark/dollar exchange rate;** *RER EFF,* **trade-weighted exchange rate;** *RFF,* **federal funds rate;** *RDTDM,* **day-to-day interest rate**

It permitted both inflation and money growth to overshoot their targets by 1.1 and 2 percentage points, respectively. In particular it reduced short-term rates and kept them low through most of the rest of the decade. While ex post real short-term rates were above the negative rates being recorded in the United States, they were nonetheless clearly below the trend for the era.

After a brief expansion period, growth began to slacken in 1978. At this time the Bundesbank cited an appreciating mark to justify continued easing. In effect the Bundesbank was easing rates to stimulate a softening real economy. While it is not always so forthcoming, it has acknowledged that concern for the real economy influenced its behavior during this period.[13]

10.3.2   1979–1983

Just prior to 1979, macroeconomic conditions in West Germany were more favorable than in the United States. Output growth was roughly similar. While the inflation rate was still stubbornly high by West German standards, it was well below the U.S. inflation rate. Fortunes were reversed, however, in the eight years after.

The first oil shock and the subsequent shift in U.S. monetary policy ushered in a return to tight money. The Bundesbank was committed to avoiding (what it viewed as) its earlier mistake of largely accommodating the increases in oil prices during 1973 and 1974 (Tsatsaronis 1993). In addition the sharp rise in U.S. interest rates precipitated a sharp and steady depreciation of the mark relative to the dollar that lasted until 1985.

The Bundesbank responded to these events by raising the day-to-day rate from about 3% in 1979 to about 12% in the first quarter of 1981. In terms of basis points, this increase was similar in magnitude to the rise in the U.S. funds over same period. Ex post real rates rose sharply, as they did in the United States.

Again, its pragmatic side showed through: the Bundesbank raised the target rate of inflation from 3% in 1979 to 4% in 1980. And it still permitted inflation to overshoot its target by 1.3%. The weakening of the real economy at the time was again apparently a factor in the Bundesbank's decision making. For the next two years it continued the gradualist policy, tolerating above-target inflation in order to avoid further weakening a recessionary economy.

From the period of peak inflation to the beginning of 1983, the contraction in real activity in West Germany was of similar magnitude to that in the United States. On the other hand, the drop in inflation over the same time interval was far more dramatic in the United States. At the start of the period the U.S. inflation rate was nearly double that in West Germany. By the end it was roughly equal. These facts correspond closely to Ball's observation (1994) that the sacrifice ratio in Germany actually exceeds its counterpart for the United States.

Many have found this outcome surprising. Underlying this view is the belief that the Bundesbank's reputation for fighting inflation should have made the transition to lower inflation less painful in this country relative to other countries at the time. This in turn raises the possibility that the practical gains from establishing credibility in fighting inflation may not be substantial. Fully re-

---

13. The Bundesbank states that when the D-mark appreciated "excessively" in 1978 (and also in 1986–87), it felt "forced to pursue a more expansionary monetary policy and allow interest rate reductions . . . which led to an overshooting of the monetary target. Otherwise the appreciation shock would have too much for the economy, while inflationary pressures were being moderated by the appreciation" (Deutsche Bundesbank 1989, 103).

solving this issue is well beyond the scope of this paper, though we return to the matter later.

For now we simply note two considerations. First, the sacrifice ratio could be highly nonlinear in practice, something for which the Ball calculation does not allow. One could imagine why trying to move an economy from 6% to 2% inflation might result in greater short-run output loss than, say, trying to move it from 10% to 6%. This nonlinear relationship could resolve at least some of the differences in the U.S. and West German experience.

Second, and somewhat related, at the beginning of 1979 the public perception of the Bundesbank's commitment to reduce inflation below 5–6% may have been more ambiguous than it is today. As we have discussed, the Bundesbank pursued a relatively lax monetary policy in the roughly four years prior to the shift to tightening. Again, we turn to this issue later.

10.3.3   1983–1989

While the U.S. economy staged a strong recovery following the 1981–82 recession, the same was not true of the West German economy. Growth was slightly below trend in 1983 and only slightly above trend in 1984 and 1985. The unemployment rate continued to rise steadily, reaching 9.3% in 1985. On the other hand, a product of the weak economy was receding inflation. Inflation was below target from 1983 to 1985. During this period the Bundesbank returned short-term nominal rates to slightly above pre-1979 levels. Lower inflation, however, implied significantly higher real interest rates than during the late 1970s. As we show in section 10.5, real rates during this period hovered slightly around and above long-run equilibrium.

Why the West German economy (along with the rest of the European economy) performed poorly over this period is a complex issue, another that is well beyond the paper's scope. It is plausible that high real interest rates were a factor. Real rates were similarly high in the United States at this time. The United States, however, had shifted to an expansionary fiscal policy. The same kind of fiscal stimulus was not present in West Germany.

Another often-cited possibility is that the German economy was experiencing structural labor market problems at this time (e.g., Kahn and Jacobson 1989). This would imply that the stagnant economy was due mainly to supply-side problems, that is, declines in capacity output. It is true that real wages grew rapidly from 1973 through 1989. The period 1982–85, though, does not appear to have been a period of rapid wage growth. While we do not claim to resolve the issue, later we examine more carefully the behavior of output relative to capacity and real interest rates over this period.

In mid-1984 the United States began a systematic reduction of the funds rate in an effort, among other things, to reduce the value of the dollar. In early 1985 the mark began a steady appreciation against the dollar that lasted through early 1988. In response to the appreciating mark, the real economy weakened. Output growth declined over 1986 and 1987. Inflation fell below the 2% target.

The weak economy prompted the Bundesbank to once again demonstrate its flexibility in both actions and language. Citing an appreciating mark, the Bundesbank eased short-term interest rates. Real short-term rates fell, though not to the levels of the mid- to late 1970s. Following the easing, output growth picked up in 1989. A strong recovery finally materialized.

10.3.4 1990–1993

The robust output growth in West Germany that began in 1989 continued through reunification in 1990, and into 1991. The unemployment rate fell over this period, for the first time in a decade.

Reunification of course introduced new complexities for monetary management. At the time, though, the Bundesbank had two particular concerns. First, the robust expansion led inflation to accelerate above target in 1991. Second, the one-for-one currency exchange with East Germany led to a whopping 13% increase in the M3 aggregate within a single month. The jump complicated the problem of monetary targeting. Of greater concern to the Bundesbank was the possible consequence for inflation, especially given the large implicit subsidy in the currency swap.

Fear of renewed inflation induced the Bundesbank to aggressively tighten. It raised short-term nominal rates above 9%. Real rates rose to the high levels of the early 1980s. For the first time since Bretton Woods, both nominal and real rates in Germany were higher than in the United States. One casualty of the tightening was the EMS. The EMS collapsed in September 1992 due in large part to the unwillingness of other members, especially the United Kingdom, to keep their interest rates in line with the soaring German rates. The tightening also had predictable effects on the Germany economy. Due at least in part to monetary policy, output plummeted. West German industrial production dropped 15% from January 1992 through September 1993. And the unemployment rate rose nearly 3 percentage points over this same period.

The recessionary economy prompted the Bundesbank to ease rates. The easing, however, was modest. While both nominal and real rates declined, the level of the real rate remained high relative to earlier periods of downturns. We return to this issue in section 10.5.

10.3.5 Bundesbank Policy in Practice: Summary of the Narrative Evidence

The Bundesbank aggressively raises short-term interest rates in response to perceived inflationary pressures. An exception was the period 1975–78, when it maintained subnormal short-term real interest rates while inflation was above the desired trend, much as the United States was doing at the same time. There is some suggestion, even in official Bundesbank publications, that the experience with stagflation during this period explains why the Bundesbank has been more vigilant about controlling inflation in the years since then. The German experience suggests that, once inflation starts to persist above trend, it is difficult to bring down costlessly, even for a central bank with the reputation of the Bundesbank. Again, there is a clear parallel with the U.S. experience.

In its actions, if not its public pronouncements, the Bundesbank also clearly takes into account the performance of the real economy. While it desires to control inflation, it will not do so at any cost. Conversely, a soft economy with an appreciating D-mark normally induces the Bundesbank to ease. A case can be made, though, that in recent years the easings have been more modest relative to the overall condition of the economy.

What role does targeting play in the day-to-day formulation of policy? The targets do not define a rigid rule for money growth. In the period 1975–93 the Bundesbank failed to meet its money-growth target in 9 of 19 possible instances. Rather, as the Bundesbank has made clear on numerous occasions, the targets are to be viewed as guidelines. They provide the policy decision with a clear reference point. The Bundesbank is free to deviate from this reference point. But it is expected to explain the circumstances that lead it to do so. In this way the targets place discipline on the policymaking process.

The pattern of deviations from the inflation and money-growth targets are in our view symptomatic of the implicit stabilization component in the Bundesbank policy rule. The top panel of figure 10.4 plots the target price level (in logarithms) implied by the sequence of target inflation rates, relative to the actual price level. The middle panel does the same for the money supply. Note that during the high inflation of the late 1970s and early 1980s the Bundesbank persistently accommodated overshooting of the price target by simply rebenchmarking the path for the target price each year. That is, it made no attempt to target a long-term path for the price level, presumably because it feared the consequences for the real economy.

The bottom panel plots the percentage deviation of each variable from its target. Note that between 1979 and 1989 the two series are almost mirror images of one another. This strong negative relationship between the price-level and money-stock deviations also reveals an element of stabilization within the policy rule. Generally speaking, when the price level significantly overshoots its target, the Bundesbank pursues a contractionary policy that tends to push the money supply below target. As we have been emphasizing, the Bundesbank's toleration of this overshooting is evidence of a stabilization concern. In a way, the simultaneous undershooting of the money-growth target provides it with a formal justification not to tighten further.

Conversely, in periods where the price level is significantly under target, the Bundesbank often pushes money growth above target. The undershooting of the price target presumably gives it leeway to ease monetary policy. In these situations, as we have discussed, it usually cites an overvalued D-mark to rationalize its aims.

10.4   Identifying the Bundesbank's Policy Reaction Function: A Structural VAR Approach

In section 10.3 we developed a set of informal conclusions about the nature of Bundesbank policy. In this section and the next we probe the issues further

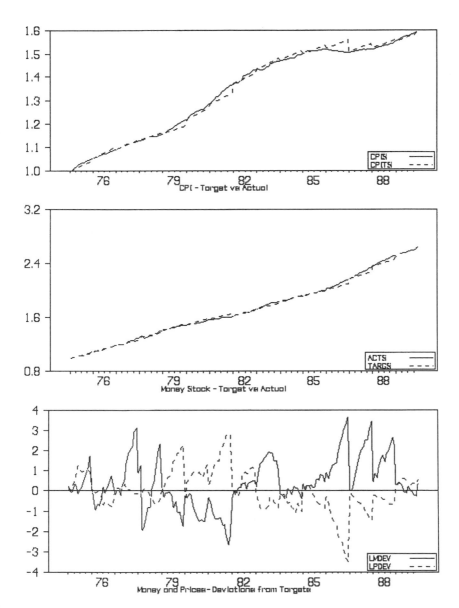

Fig. 10.4 **Bundesbank money and price targets:** *CPI%,* **consumer price index (January 1975 = 1) percentage (log);** *CPIT%,* **CPI target (January 1975 = 1) percentage (log);** *ACTS,* **actual money supply (log; January 1975 = 1);** *TARGS,* **target money supply (log; January 1975 = 1);** *LMDEV,* **percentage of money-stock deviation;** *LPDEV,* **percentage of price-level deviation**

by estimating policy reaction functions. Based on the previous discussion, we take as the Bundesbank's policy instrument the day-to-day interest rate. Our goal then is to identify an empirical relationship that is useful for characterizing how the Bundesbank adjusts the short-term rate over time.

In general, identifying a reaction function for central bank policy involves confronting two basic complex issues. First, one has to take a stand on the set of information to which the central bank responds. The central bank may have a primary goal of stabilizing inflation and output, for example. But it may (and in general does) take account of a far broader set of information than simply inflation and output. Additional information may be useful for forecasting future inflation and future output. Good examples are exchange rates and commodity prices. Also, the central bank may make use of intermediate targets such as the exchange rate or the money supply, either because it cannot directly observe current inflation and current output or because it desires some kind of commitment device. Indeed, the discussion in section 10.3 suggests that both the money supply and exchange rates are factored into Bundesbank policy decisions in an important way.

Second, there is a problem of simultaneity between the policy instrument and the information set. The Bundesbank may adjust short-term interest rates in light of news about exchanges rates, for example. But, certainly, the change in the short-term rate will feed back into the behavior of the exchange rate.

We take a two-pronged approach to the identification problem. The first prong, which we pursue in this section, is to estimate a policy reaction function for the day-to-day rate that is derived from a structural VAR model of the German macroeconomy.[14] With this reaction function we can characterize in a fairly general way how the Bundesbank adjusts policy in response to disturbances, such as supply shocks, changes in U.S. monetary policy, exogenous exchange rate shifts, and so on. The benefit of this approach is that we can address the identification issues by employing relatively few a priori restrictions (at least relative to other approaches). The cost is that because the estimated reaction function includes all the variables in the VAR it is difficult to interpret. Therefore, in section 10.5 we move on to the second prong, which involves imposing additional structure on the basic empirical model developed in this section.

10.4.1   Using a Structural VAR to Identify Policy Rules

The General Identification Strategy

Let y_t be a vector of macroeconomic variables and e_t be an associated vector of structural disturbances. The elements of e_t are mutually orthogonal iid disturbances. They are structural shocks in the sense that they are the primitive

---

14. For some useful descriptions of the structural VAR methodology, see Blanchard 1989; Gali 1992; Sims and Zha 1994; Kim and Roubini 1995; Bernanke and Mihov 1995.

exogenous disturbances to the economy. A very general representation of a macroeconomic framework that determines y_t is

$$(1) \qquad\qquad y_t = Cy_t + \sum_{i=1}^{\infty} A_i y_{t-1} + e_t,$$

where C and A_i are conformable square coefficient matrices, and where the diagonal elements of C are equal to zero. Equation 1 simply states that within this macroeconomy each variable may depend on its own lagged values plus the current and lagged values of all the other variables in the system. The feedback policy rule we are interested in identifying is the equation for the element of y_t that is the central bank policy instrument.

The logic of the structural VAR approach is to place a priori restrictions on the contemporaneous interactions among the macroeconomic variables in order to identify the coefficient matrix C. Once estimates of C are available, then it is possible to identify the dynamic impact of the structural shocks on the elements of y_t without placing any further restrictions on the data.[15] For the element of y_t that is the policy instrument, the exercise leads to a policy reaction function.

Subtract from each side of equation 1 $E_{t-1}\{y_t\}$, the expected value of y_t implied by the model, conditional on information at $t - 1$. Then define $y_t \equiv y_t - E_{t-1}\{y_t\}$ as the forecast error to obtain (dropping time subscripts for convenience):

$$(2) \qquad\qquad u = Cu + e.$$

In practice u is calculated as the forecast error of the reduced-form (i.e., VAR) representation of equation 1 (see note 15). Comparison of equations 1 and 2 indicates the restrictions on the contemporaneous interactions among the variables boil down to restrictions on the contemporaneous interactions between the reduced-form innovations. The identifying assumptions, therefore, take the form of restrictions on C (e.g., exclusion restrictions) based on assumptions about causality among the elements of u.[16]

Nonpolicy versus Policy Variables

To organize the identifying assumptions, it is useful to divide elements of y into nonpolicy and policy variables. For the purpose of studying monetary policy, we take as a policy variable any variable that the central bank may influ-

---

15. To see this, note that the reduced form of equation 1 is $y_t = \sum_{i=1}^{\infty} B_i y_{t-i} + u_t$, where $B_i = (I - C)^{-1}A_i$ and $u_t = (I - C)^{-1}e_t$. Since the lagged values of y_t are orthogonal to the vector of reduced-form disturbances u_t, estimates of the B_i may be readily obtained using least squares. Knowing both C and the B_i then makes it possible to trace the impact of a shock to any element of e_t on the path of any element in y_t.

16. Roughly speaking, a necessary condition for identification is that the number of restrictions on C (beyond the zero restrictions on all the diagonal elements of C) be at least as large as the number of parameters in C to be estimated.

ence within the current period (e.g., within the current month). This definition thus includes not only the central bank's direct policy instrument (e.g., the day-to-day interest rate), but also observable "jump" variables such as the exchange rate, over which it exerts indirect influence within the period. Due to the within-period simultaneity, the central bank is effectively choosing values of all the variables that move contemporaneously. Presumably, when the central bank adjusts the short-term interest rate, for example, it takes into account the implied contemporaneous reaction of the exchange rate.

The dual implication of our classification scheme is that nonpolicy variables respond only with a lag to movements in the policy variables. Output may react over time to a shift in interest rates, for example, but due to adjustment costs and so on, it does not respond instantaneously. From the standpoint of identification, innovations in the nonpolicy variables are exogenous to the innovations in the policy variables.[17] To identify the equation for the policy instrument, therefore, we need to worry only about addressing the possible contemporaneous simultaneity among the policy variables (e.g., how the day-to-day rate responds to the exchange rate and vice versa).

10.4.2   The Empirical Model

Variables

We use eight variables to describe the German macroeconomy. Five are non-policy variables. Of these, three are meant to characterize the state of the German economy: industrial production (ip), retail sales (ret), and the consumer price level (p). The two others reflect important external factors that influence the German economy: real commodity prices (cp) (meant to capture supply shocks) and the U.S. federal funds rate (ff).

The three Bundesbank policy variables are the day-to-day (i.e., short-term) interest rate (rs); the real money supply (m) (specifically the broad money aggregate M3 divided by the price level), and the real D-mark/dollar exchange rate (er). We treat the short-term interest rate as the Bundesbank's policy instrument, for reasons discussed in section 10.2.3.

---

17. In particular the contemporaneous exogeneity of the nonpolicy variables implies a set of useful exclusion restrictions on the coefficient matrix C in equation 2. Let u^x be the vector of reduced-form disturbances to the elements of y that are nonpolicy variables and let u^{pol} be the vector of reduced-form disturbances to the policy variables. Then equation 2 may be disaggregated as follows:

$$\begin{bmatrix} u^x \\ u^{pol} \end{bmatrix} = \begin{bmatrix} C^{xx} & 0 \\ C^{px} & C^{pp} \end{bmatrix} \begin{bmatrix} u^x \\ u^{pol} \end{bmatrix} + \begin{bmatrix} e^x \\ e^{pol} \end{bmatrix},$$

where the diagonal elements of the submatrices C^{xx} and C^{pp} are all equal to zero. The recursive structure implies we can separate the problem of identifying the equations for nonpolicy variables from that of doing the same for the policy innovations. It also implies that we can use the nonpolicy innovations as instruments in the policy-innovation equations. We will make use of both of these implications.

The real money supply and real exchange rate fit our policy-variable classification, since the Bundesbank can quickly influence these variables (via its
choice of the short-term interest rate), and because its choice of interest rates
presumably is influenced by these variables.[18] We use the D-mark/dollar rate
since our reading of the narrative evidence suggests that it is this exchange rate
that has had the the most influence over Bundesbank policy.

Identifying Assumptions

Our identifying assumptions about the contemporaneous interactions among
the reduced-form innovations are as follows:

- Among the five nonpolicy variables, there is a recursive causal relationship,
  ordered as follows: commodity prices, industrial production, retail sales, the
  price level, and the funds rate.
- The reduced-form money and interest rate innovations (i.e., the money-
  demand and money-supply innovations) are given by

(3) $$u^m = \alpha_1 u^{ip} + \alpha_2 u^{rs} + e^m$$

(money demand), and

(4) $$u^{rs} = \beta_1 u^{cp} + \beta_2 u^m + \beta_3 u^{er} + e^{rs}$$

(money supply).

- The exchange rate innovation (u^{er}) may be influenced by any of the other
  seven innovations in the system (i.e., we place no restrictions on the exchange
  rate equation).

In general our main results are robust to different orderings among the nonpolicy variables. Nonetheless, some specific considerations motivated the particular sequence we picked. Over our sample, oil price shocks primarily drove
movements in real-world commodity prices. Since oil shocks contain a large
idiosyncratic component (due to the Organization of Petroleum Exporting
Countries [OPEC], etc.), it seems reasonable to order commodity prices first
in the system. Also, since movements in the U.S. funds rate are unlikely to
affect German output and prices within the period, it seems reasonable to order
this variable last among the nonpolicy variables. We place retail sales after
production, based on the view that production adjusts to movements in demand
with a lag.

Equation 4 reveals our assumptions about the contemporaneous information
that the Bundesbank uses to adjust the short-term rate. This equation is key.
We make two assumptions. First, any contemporaneous information the Bundesbank employs in its decision making must actually be available within the

---

18. Kim and Roubini (1995) also develop a structural VAR model with a nonrecursive relationship between the interest rate and the exchange rate.

period of its decision. Since news about industrial production, retail sales, and consumer prices become available only with a lag, we exclude innovations in these variables from the Bundesbank's information set. On the other hand, we let the Bundesbank adjust the interest rate to contemporaneous innovations in commodity prices, the money supply, and the exchange rate, since these variables are directly observed within the period. The second assumption, following Kim and Roubini (1995), is that within the period the Bundesbank only cares about the implications of news in the U.S. funds rate for the D-mark/dollar rate. Thus, the innovation in the funds rate does not enter the reaction function independently of the exchange rate.

The only other relation we restrict is money demand. Equation 3 relates the demand for real money balances to real output and the nominal interest rate, in keeping with standard convention.

Intuitively, the identification scheme works as follows: Excluding certain nonpolicy variable innovations from the money-supply equation 4 permits using these innovations as instruments for the two endogenous right-hand-side variables, specifically the exchange rate and money-supply innovations. Our decision criterion (which was based on assumptions about the timing of data release) led us to exclude more nonpolicy variables than was necessary to achieve identification. The results, however, do not rely on overidentification. We also consider a just identified version of the model and show that the results are essentially unchanged.

Sample Period and Estimation

Since our key identifying restrictions are based on assumptions about timing (e.g., variable X affects variable Y only with a lag), we use monthly data, the shortest frequency available. The sample period is August 1974 to September 1993. We begin shortly after the dismantling of Bretton Woods and continue through the early stages of reunification. To ensure that our results are not influenced by structural changes stemming from reunification, we also consider the sample period August 1974 to December 1989. In general we find that the results do not change over the two different samples.

We estimate the eight variable VARs, entering all variables in log-difference form except the two interest rates, which are in levels. In addition we impose two cointegrating relationships: between retails sales and industrial production, and between real money balances and industrial production.[19] In each case, cointegration tests justified imposing these long-run restrictions. Finally, in the VAR we include six lags of each variable, but we stagger the lags as follows: 1, 2, 3, 6, 9, 12. Convention dictates using twelve lags with monthly

---

19. We include a time trend in the cointegrating vector for real money balances and industrial production. We use the error-correction form rather than the standard log level representation because in the next section we need to make use of the model's forecasts of long-run equilibrium. Because the error correction imposes long-run restrictions among variables, it is better suited for making long-run forecasts.

data to avoid problems of seasonality. However, because the sample period is short relative to the number of variables and because we also want to use the model to make long-horizon forecasts in the next section, we opted for a more parsimonious parameterization.

10.4.3 Results

We are interested in assessing how the Bundesbank adjusts the short-term interest rate to disturbances to the economy, particularly in light of the narrative evidence developed in section 10.3. We first report evidence on how the Bundesbank adjusts the day-to-day rates to within-period news. We then analyze the response of the interest rate over time to various shocks to the economy. In this way we are able to characterize policy reaction function for the Bundesbank.

Policy Response to Contemporaneous News

Table 10.2 reports estimates of money-supply equation 4, which relates the innovation in the interest rate to the innovations in commodity prices, the money supply, and the exchange rate. The point estimates are as one would expect. The Bundesbank lets the short-term rate rise in response to news of increases in inflationary pressures, manifested in either a rise in commodity prices, a rise in the money supply, or a depreciation of the exchange rate. None of the news variables is statistically significant, however. This suggests that the Bundesbank does not try to tightly meet monetary or exchange rate targets within the month. It also suggests that it is mainly lagged rather than current information that is fed into the Bundesbank's policy rule. Within a given month the Bundesbank tends to maintain a desired short-term rate, given the information available at the start of the period.

As a check that our identification scheme is reasonable, we also report the estimates of the two other equations that enter the policy block, the money-demand and exchange rate relations. In both cases the outcomes are quite sensible. Money demand has a significant negative interest elasticity. An innovation in the funds rate causes the exchange rate to depreciate significantly, while an innovation in the German short-term rate does the reverse. Finally, a just-identified version of the model yields very similar coefficient estimates for all three equations.

Dynamic Policy Response to Various Shocks

We next assess how the Bundesbank adjusts the short-term rate over time to disturbances to the economy. To do so, we report the response to each of the eight structural shocks of a subset of four core variables that characterize the overall state of the economy and policy: industrial production, inflation, the short-term interest rate, and the real exchange rate. In addition we report the response of the variable that is shocked. Figures 10.5 and 10.6 show the results, the mean responses of the variables and their 95% confidence intervals.

Table 10.2   **Structural VAR Estimates**

	Overidentified Model				

$$u^m = 0.024u^{ip} - 0.003u^{rs} + e^m$$
$$\quad\quad (0.021) \quad\quad (0.001)$$

$$u^{rs} = 0.459u^{cp} + 12.39u^m + 4.25u^{er} + e^{rs}$$
$$\quad\quad (0.727) \quad\quad (13.51) \quad\quad (5.75)$$

$$u^{er} = 0.09u^{ip} - 0.03u^{ip} - 0.03u^{ret} - 0.50u^p - 0.01u^{rs}$$
$$\quad\quad (0.12) \quad\quad (0.04) \quad\quad (0.09) \quad\quad (1.01) \quad\quad (0.003)$$
$$\quad + 0.008u^{ff} - 0.423u^m + e^{er}$$
$$\quad\quad\;\; (0.002) \quad\quad (0.39)$$

	Exactly Identified Model				

$$u^m = 0.032u^{ip} - 0.003u^{rs} + \ldots + e^m$$
$$\quad\quad (0.019) \quad\quad (0.001)$$

$$u^{rs} = 0.427u^{cp} + 11.45u^m + 4.04u^{er} + \ldots + e^{rs}$$
$$\quad\quad (0.756) \quad\quad (13.95) \quad\quad (5.75)$$

$$u^{er} = 0.09u^{ip} - 0.03u^{cp} - 0.03u^{ret} - 0.45u^p - 0.01u^{rs}$$
$$\quad\quad (0.12) \quad\quad (0.04) \quad\quad (0.09) \quad\quad (1.01) \quad\quad (0.004)$$
$$\quad + 0.008u^{ff} - 0.392u^m + e^{er}$$
$$\quad\quad\;\; (0.003) \quad\quad (0.39)$$

Notes: The sample is August 1974–September 1993. Estimation is by instrumental variables. For the u^m equation, the instruments are u^{cp}, u^{ip}, u^{ret}, u^p, u^{ff}, and e^{rs}. For the u^{rs} equation the instruments are u^{cp}, u^{ip}, u^{ret}, u^p, and u^{ff}. For the u^{er} equation, the instruments are u^{cp}, u^{ip}, u^{ret}, u^p, u^{ff}, e^{rs}, and e^m.

The results are very consistent with the narrative evidence, in two main ways. First, the Bundesbank aggressively adjusts short-term rates to control inflationary pressures. Second, it responds to exchange rate movements in a clearly countercyclical fashion.

Consider the effects of a commodity price shock, as portrayed in figure 10.5. The outcome looks very much like the consequence of a supply shock, as one would hope. Output declines while inflation rises. The Bundesbank sharply increases the short-term rate, to a point where it produces a sustained significant rise in the real rate. As the figure shows, the Bundesbank similarly adjusts the short-term rate to curtail inflationary pressures in response to output, retail sales, and inflation shocks.

The countercyclical response to the exchange rate may be seen two different ways. First, figure 10.6 shows that a depreciation of the exchange rate produces a sharp sustained rise in both nominal and real short-term rates. The rise in rates in turn generates a decline in output. After rising initially in response to the exchange rate depreciation, inflation rate drops quickly back to trend as the economy weakens. It follows, of course, that an exchange rate appreciation does just the opposite: there is an easing of rates and an eventual expansion, consistent with the narrative evidence. Second, the short-term rate also rises as

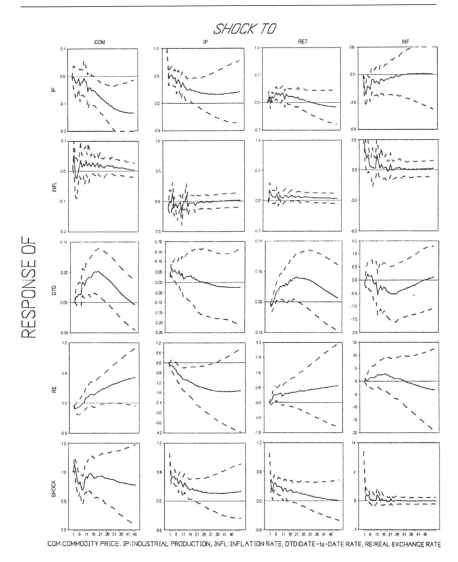

Fig. 10.5   Impulse responses to shocks: *COM*, commodity price; *IP*, industrial production; *RET*, retail sales; *INFL*, inflation rate; *RE*, real exchange rate; *DTD*, day-to-day rate

the currency depreciates in response to an increase in the funds rate, as figure 10.6 indicates.[20]

The response of the economy to a money-demand shock provides support

20. The response of the D-mark dollar rate to the funds rate shock is consistent with Eichenbaum and Evans (1995).

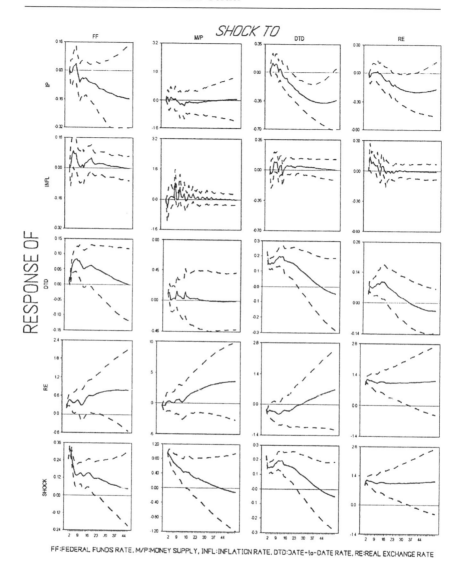

Fig. 10.6 Impulse responses to shocks: *FF*, federal funds rate; *M/P*, money supply; *DTD*, day-to-day rate; *RE*, real exchange rate; *INFL*, inflation rate; *IP*, industrial production

for the view that the Bundesbank treats the short-term interest rate as its policy instrument. Under strict money targeting, money-demand shocks should induce interest rate fluctuations that in turn affect the real economy. Figure 10.6, on the other hand, suggests that the Bundesbank accommodates money-demand shocks. Shocks to money demand have no significant affect on interest rates or on any other variables, except for real money balances.

Impact of a Day-to-Day Rate Shock

Finally, we examine the impact of an orthogonalized innovation in the short-term rate. This is the issue on which the structural VAR literature has tended to focus attention.[21] We interpret this kind of exercise not as an attempt to determine whether unsystematic policy shocks are important driving forces in the economy (we doubt that they are), but rather as a (less than ideal) way to show that policy movements matter to the economy.[22] The reduced-form policy-response exercises that we have just conducted do not permit us to sort out how much of the impact on output and inflation was due to the policy reaction, for example, and how much was due to the initial shock (e.g., the rise in commodity prices). By examining the effect of orthogonalized policy shocks, we gain a limited feel for the role of policy.

Figure 10.6 shows that, as one would expect, the unanticipated rise in the short-term rate reduces output and, at least in the very short run, causes the exchange rate to appreciate. There is, however, no significant impact on inflation. The point estimates go in the wrong direction, but they are small and insignificant. Two interpretations are possible. First, since the policy shock produces only a modest temporary rise in short rates, it does not induce a sufficient tightening to bring down inflation. Second, the policy shock may not be perfectly identified; there may be some news about inflation that the Bundesbank uses but is not summarized in the information set of the model. It is likely that some combination of these two factors is at work.

10.4.4 Sources of Variation in the Policy Instrument

In section 10.4.3 we analyzed how the Bundesbank adjusts short-term nominal and real rates in response to different kinds of primitive disturbances to the economy. Now we ask what kinds of disturbances are important to the variation in rates. That is, to what kinds of disturbances has the Bundesbank responded primarily, particularly during critical junctures for the economy?

Variance Decomposition

Table 10.3 presents a simple variance decomposition of the nominal rate, as implied by the structural VAR. Since there are eight structural disturbances in the model, there are eight potential sources of variation. As the table indicates, aside from the "own disturbance" to the German short-term rate, four kinds of shocks are important: the exchange rate, the funds rate, commodity prices, and retail sales. Consistent with the narrative evidence, the exchange rate and the funds rate shocks appear to have particularly strong influence on the Bundes-

21. For some recent examples, see Sims and Zha 1994; Christiano, Eichenbaum, and Evans 1995; and Bernanke and Mihov 1995.
22. We find, as does Kim (1994), that monetary shocks are not an important source of output variation in Germany. This does not mean, however, that monetary policy is unimportant. Variance decomposition exercises are silent on the importance of the policy feedback rule.

Table 10.3   **Variance Decomposition for the Nominal Interest Rate**

Horizon (months)	Fraction of Forecast Error Variance due to							
	e^{cp}	e^{ip}	e^{ret}	e^{p}	e^{ff}	e^{m}	e^{rs}	e^{er}
6	0.01	0.04	0.03	0.01	0.16	0.01	0.57	0.16
12	0.06	0.03	0.08	0.01	0.15	0.01	0.50	0.17
24	0.11	0.02	0.18	0.01	0.13	0.01	0.42	0.13
48	0.12	0.02	0.22	0.01	0.13	0.01	0.38	0.12

bank behavior in the short run, together accounting for about a third of the overall variation in the short-term rate over a six-month horizon. At twelve- and twenty-four-month horizons, the commodity and retail sales shocks rise in relative importance. Overall, the four shocks account for about half the variation in the short-term rate over twelve months and about 60% over twenty-four months.

Historical Decomposition

How do the four shocks account for the observed temporal pattern of German short-term rates? Figure 10.7 presents a historical decomposition of the variation in the nominal rate. The top panel shows the cumulative error in the forecast of the nominal rate as the sample period unwinds. This measure indicates how the short-term rate adjusted over time to shocks taking place during the sample. The two periods of unforecastable declines in the short-term rate are the late 1970s and the late 1980s. These correspond to the periods of policy easing cited in the narrative evidence. Similarly, the two periods are unforecastable increases are the early 1980s and the early 1990s, periods where the informal evidence suggests policy tightness.

In the panels below we plot the contribution to the cumulative forecast error by each of the four main sources (other than the own disturbance) of variation in the short-term rate. Again, there is a reasonable correspondence between the narrative and statistical evidence. Unexpected appreciations of the mark help account for the unexpected rates declines in 1978–79 and 1986–87. The rise in rates in the early 1980s is associated with a rise in real commodity prices, a depreciation of the currency, and a rise in the funds rate, much as the narrative evidence suggests. In particular these three factors appear to account for about two-thirds of the rate increase that occurred at this time.

Finally, there are some direct signs that the real economy influences Bundesbank behavior. Unexpected declines in retail sales, along with an unexpected appreciation of the mark, contributed to the decline in rates during the mid- to late 1980s. Conversely, following this period, interest rates surged in large part as a consequence of an unexpected sharp rise in retail sales, in conjunction with an unexpected currency depreciation.

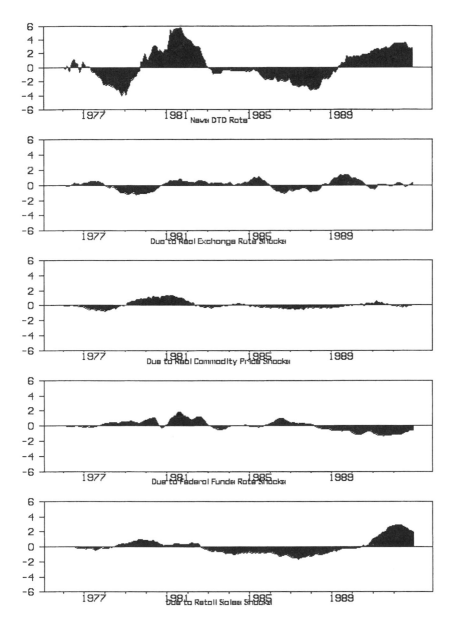

Fig. 10.7   Historical decomposition of day-to-day rate

10.5   Adding Structure: A Policy Reaction Function Based on Inflation and Output Objectives

From the structural VAR we are able to ascertain how different primitive disturbances to the economy influence the Bundesbank's choice for the time path of short-term interest rates. However, the policy reaction function we obtain from this exercise—the identified VAR equation for the day-to-day interest rate—is difficult to compactly summarize. We learn, for example, how the Bundesbank has responded to movements in the D-mark. But we do not directly learn why. Was inflation the primary consideration? Or was concern about output also a factor?

In this section we estimate a compact and intuitive reaction function for the day-to-day rate. We do so by imposing additional structure on the reaction function obtained from the identified VAR. We assume that the Bundesbank cares about stabilizing both inflation and output. In addition we allow for the possibility that the Bundesbank is forward-looking in the sense that it adjusts policy in response to anticipation of future inflation as opposed to simply past inflation. Further, we take into account that in setting interest rates the Bundesbank may not know the current values of inflation and output (which is consistent with what we assumed in section 10.4).

To form beliefs about expected inflation and output relative to their respective targets, the Bundesbank (we assume) filters the current and lagged information about the economy, as captured by our eight variable VARs. Thus, for example, we allow for movements in exchange rates to influence the day-to-day rate, as the reduced-form evidence suggests. But we restrict these movements to enter the policy reaction function based on the information they contain about expected inflation and output (relative to capacity). In the end we obtain a simple policy reaction function that relates the movement in short-term rates to two "gap" variables that reflect the position of inflation and output. As we show, this reaction function provides a very useful yardstick to interpret the course of Bundesbank monetary policy.

10.5.1   A Day-to-Day Rate Reaction Function

Let rs_t be the nominal day-to-day rate and rs_t^0 be the Bundesbank's target for this rate. Let rrs_t denote the real day-to-day rate. Let π_{t-j}^k be the rate of inflation from period $t - j$ to $t - j + k$: equivalently, $\pi_{t-j}^k = p_{t-j+k} - p_{t-j}$, where, as before, p_t is the logarithm of the price level. Also, as before, ip_t is the logarithm of output. Finally, let an asterisk denote the steady-state trend value of a variable. We assume that the following two equations characterize the day-to-day rate reaction function:

$$(5)\quad rs_t^0 = E_t\{\pi_{t-j}^k\} + rrs^* + \gamma^p[E_t\{\pi_{t-j}^k\} - \pi^{*k}] + \gamma^{ip}[E_t\{ip_t - ip_t^*\}]$$

and

$$(6) \qquad rs_t = \lambda rs_t^0 + (1 - \lambda)[\sum_{i=1}^{k} w_i rs_{t-1}] + \varepsilon_t,$$

with $\sum_{i=1}^{k} w_i = 1$ and where the expectation operator $E_t\{\quad\}$ is conditioned on the central bank's information set at t.[23] As we noted in section 10.4, the Bundesbank observes certain variables, such as industrial production and consumer prices, with a one-month lag.

Equation 5 is a slight variation of the type of reaction function that Taylor (1993) used to characterize the behavior of the Federal Reserve Board under Alan Greenspan.[24] Underlying the rule is the notion that monetary policy is neutral in the long run: the central bank cannot influence the long-run equilibrium values either of the real interest rate, rrs^*, or of output, ip_t^*. Due to nominal rigidities, however, the central bank does have leverage over the short-term real interest rate, and can thus influence the course of real activity in the short run.

The feedback rule has a general kind of lean-against-the-wind form. Roughly speaking, it has the central bank raise the short-term real interest rate as either inflation or output rise relative to long-run trend. Trend inflation is the steady-state inflation rate that the central bank is willing to accept, as is implicit in its policy rule. That is, it is the rate of inflation that the central bank is willing to accommodate when output is at its trend capacity value. It is thus a choice variable for the central bank. Trend output is the value of output that would arise if the economy were currently in long-run equilibrium, and is thus beyond the control of the central bank.

We assume further, according to equation 6, that each month the Bundesbank sets the actual day-to-day rate equal to a convex combination of the target rate and a weighted average of lagged rates. We allow for partial adjustment because institutional factors in policymaking likely preclude the Bundesbank from always reaching its target at the same frequency of our data. For example, the effective decision-making interval may be longer than the monthly interval we use. In practice we find that the adjustment period is usually very fast (as we show later).

An important difference between our specification and Taylor's is that we allow for the possibility that the central bank is forward-looking in its concern for inflation, whereas Taylor instead assumes that the central bank responds to inflation over the past year. In particular we consider three formulations of the inflation gap variable: two that are forward-looking and one that corresponds to Taylor.

Case 1 (forward-looking, one-year horizon):

23. We assume further that the Bundesbank responds only to movements in anticipated inflation that are exogenous with respect to movements in the current short-term rate. In the estimation we take account of this assumption explicitly by using instrumental variables. For this reason our rule is not subject to the instrument instability problem discussed in Woodford (1994). In addition we allow for partial adjustment of the interest rate, which is also a stabilizing factor.

24. Taylor does not formally estimate his model. He does demonstrate, however, that his informal method of choosing parameters seems to work quite well for the Greenspan period.

$$E_t\{\pi_{t-j}^k\} - \pi^{*k} = E_t\{\pi_t^{12}\} - \pi^{*12}$$

Case 2 (forward-looking, infinite horizon):

$$E_t\{\pi_{t-j}^k\} - \pi^{*k} = \lim_{k \to \infty} E_t\{\pi_t^k\} - \pi^{*k} = E_t\{p_t^* - p_t\}$$

Case 3 (backward-looking, Taylor):

$$E_t\{\pi_{t-j}^k\} - \pi^{*k} = E_t\{\pi_{t-12}^{12}\} - \pi^{*12}$$

Case 1 is the mirror image of the Taylor specification: the central bank looks one year forward at inflation, as opposed to one year back. Because the one-year horizon is somewhat arbitrary, in case 2 we have the central bank respond to expected total cumulative excess inflation. We define the latter as the expected percentage of change in the price level relative to trend indefinitely into the future. This measure corresponds exactly to the percentage of difference between the current trend and spot price levels. Intuitively, if the price level is 5% below trend (i.e., $p_t^* - p_t = 5\%$), then the spot price level is expected to grow 5% faster than trend before reverting to long-run equilibrium.[25]

Finally, for comparison purposes, in case 3 we consider the backward-looking measure that Taylor used. The expectation operator appears in this case only because we allow for the possibility that the central bank may not observe the current price level. (In equation 5 we similarly allow for the possibility that it does not observe current output.)

We proceed by first computing the long-run equilibrium variables and the gap variables that enter the policy reaction function. We use our estimated structural VAR to obtain values of these variables for each calendar month. In addition to obtaining inputs for the reaction function, we also extract information that is helpful for judging the position of the economy and monetary policy, as we discuss below.

10.5.2   Long-Run Equilibria and Short-Run Deviations: A Historical Decomposition of the Data

To identify the long-run equilibrium and the inflation and output gap variables, we return to the eight variable VARs of the German economy. We obtain the steady-state value for any (stationary) variable in the VAR simply by finding the k-step-ahead forecast of the respective variable, for k large.

Long-Run Equilibrium Interest Rates and Inflation

Figure 10.8 reports estimates of the long-run equilibrium values of the nominal interest rate, inflation, and the real interest rate. In each panel is the time

---

25. We emphasize that stabilizing the gap $p_t^* - p_t$ does not correspond to stabilizing the price level around a deterministic trend. The empirical model of section 10.4 on which we base the analysis presumes a stochastic trend rather than a deterministic trend for the price level, owing to the presence of a unit root in the price level. The unit-root assumption (which is consistent with the data) reflects the fact that the Bundesbank accommodates changes in the price level, as the narrative evidence suggests (see section 10.3).

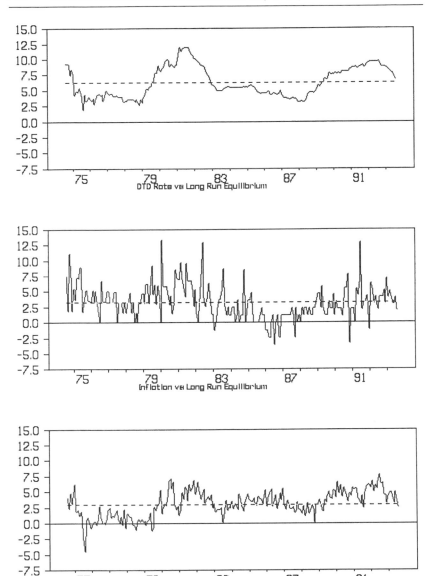

Fig. 10.8   Interest rates and inflation

series of the current value of the respective variable. To construct a time series for the real interest rate, we used the observed nominal rate minus the inflation forecast generated by the VAR. We computed steady-state values of 6.28 for the nominal rate, 3.2 for inflation, and 3.1 for the real rate (simply the difference between the two). In each instance the estimates are close to the sample mean (and are quite sensible).

As we emphasized earlier, the steady-state inflation rate provides a measure of the long-run dimension of monetary policy. Since this number is a product of the steady-state money growth rate that the policy rule generates, it is ultimately a choice variable of the Bundesbank. In this respect we confirm the obvious: the Bundesbank policy rule is geared toward maintaining a long-run equilibrium inflation rate.

The behavior of the real interest rate can potentially tell us something about monetary policy in the short run. Given that the monetary policy may influence the short-run but not the long-run real rate, we may interpret a rise in the real rate above its long-run equilibrium as one piece of evidence of a tightening of Bundesbank policy. This spread alone does not provide sufficient information to judge whether policy is tight or loose; the answer, of course, also depends on the overall condition of the economy. Nonetheless, knowledge of where real rates stand relative to the long run is an important reference point.

The bottom panel of figure 10.8 provides us with a sharper perspective on the path of policy than that in our previous analysis. Real interest rates were very low relative to the long-run equilibrium during the mid- to late 1970s, which is consistent with the narrative evidence that the Bundesbank eased during this period.[26] Conversely, real rates were well above the steady state during the two main periods of tightening, the early 1980s and the early 1990s. Despite economic stagnation during most of the 1980s, real rates were either above or not far below long-run equilibrium.[27]

Inflation and Output Gaps

We next compute the inflation and output gap variables. The top panel of figure 10.9 presents the two forward-looking measures of the inflation gap: (1) the anticipated percentage of change in the price level relative to trend over a one-year horizon and (2) the same over the infinite horizon. In each case we use the VAR model of section 10.4 to compute anticipated excess inflation.[28] Interestingly, the two measures are highly correlated, with the latter typically being about twice the size of the former. That is, if the percentage of change

---

26. One possibility is that the shift in the real interest rate from the 1970s to the 1980s could also reflect a permanent change in the long-run equilibrium. However, our empirical analysis indicates that the real rate is stationary over that period, which appears to rule out this possibility. Also, the notion that the real rate contains a unit root is unappealing as a matter of theory.

27. We account for the influence of high real interest rates during this time by allowing the U.S. interest rate (which enters our VAR) to influence the forecast of the gap variables for inflation and output that enter the equation for the target interest rate (equation 5).

28. As we argue in the text, the expected percentage of change in the price level over the infinite horizon is simply the difference between the trend log price level p_t^* and the current log price level p_t. To obtain p_t^*, we first find the long-horizon forecast of the price level. We then use the estimate of the steady-state inflation rate to determine the portion of the long-horizon forecast that is due to the long-run drift in the price level. To obtain p_t^*, we simply remove the estimated drift from the long-horizon forecast. Thus p_t^* is the estimate of where the German price level would be at time t had been no shocks pushing it away from the long-run equilibrium. Formally, p_t^* is the Beveridge-Nelson permanent component of the price level, as derived from the forecast of our eight variable VARs.

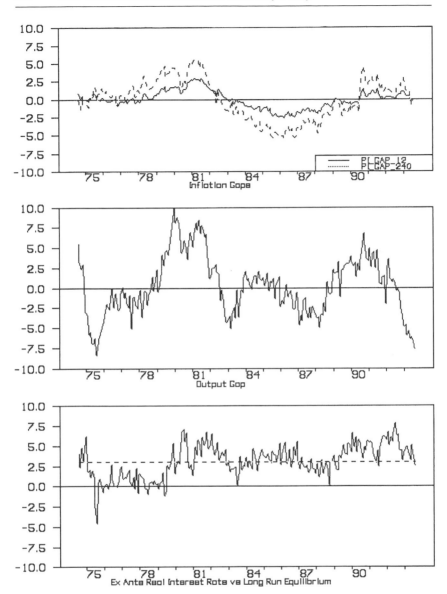

Fig. 10.9   Inflation gaps, output gap, and real interest rates: *PI GAP 12*, price-level gap for one year; *PI GAP 240*, infinite horizon price-level gap

in the price level is expected to be 1% above trend for the next year, then it is likely to be a total of 2% above trend over the indefinite future.

The middle panel of figure 10.9 presents our measure of the gap between output and its long-run equilibrium, $ip_t - ip_t^*$. To compute long-run equilibrium output, we allow for the possibility that the trend drift in output is stochastic due to the presence of a unit root. The unit root will arise, for example, if (as we might expect) shocks to the level of technology have a permanent component.[29]

Finally, the bottom panel of figure 10.9 plots the real interest rate (taken from figure 10.8). The two main periods of monetary tightening in the sample, the late 1970/early 1980s and the late 1980/early 1990s, are also periods where expected excess inflation was highest. It is also true that during these periods output was above trend.[30] On the other hand, during the period of stagnation during the 1980s, there were forecastable declines in inflation relative to trend along with below-capacity output.[31] The 1992–93 recession also pushed output below trend.

10.5.3   The Empirical Day-to-Day Rate Reaction Function

If we add and subtract long-run equilibrium inflation, π^*, from the right side of equation 5, we can express the relation for the target rate simply as

$$(7) \quad rs_t^0 = rs^* + (1 + \gamma^p)[E_t\{\pi_{t-j}^k\} - \pi^{*k}] + \gamma^{ip}[E_t\{ip_t - ip_t^*\}],$$

where rs^* $(= rrs^* + \pi^*)$ is the steady-state nominal interest rate, equal to the sum of the steady-state real rate and the steady-state inflation rate. Equation 7 together with equation 5 then determines the day-to-day rate. We first consider the two cases with forward-looking inflation and then turn to the Taylor specification.

Forward-Looking Inflation Gap

We estimate, using instrumental variables, the following equation for the day-to-day rate (obtained from substituting equation 7 into 5:

$$(8) \qquad rs_t = a + b_1[E_t[\{\pi_{t-j}^k\} - \pi^{*k}]$$
$$+ b_2[E_t\{ip_t - ip_t^*\}] + \sum_{i=1}^{k} d_i rs_{t-i} + \varepsilon_t.$$

We use as instruments for $E_t\{\pi_{t-j}^k\} - \pi^{*k}$ and $E_t\{ip_t - ip_t^*\}$, lagged values of these gap variables and also the orthogonalized time t innovations in the variables that the Bundesbank can observe contemporaneously (real commodity prices, the money supply, and the real exchange rate).[32] We found that $k = 3$

---

29. Formally, ip_t^* is the Beveridge-Nelson permanent component of output and is computed analogously to p_t^* (see note 28). See Rotemberg (1994) for Beveridge-Nelson decompositions of output and prices for U.S. data. See Clarida and Gali (1994) for an application of this technique to variety of aggregate series for OECD countries.

30. Output was above trend during the 1980 and 1981 in part because there were declines in trend capacity output, possibly due to the oil shocks.

31. The 1986 decline in oil prices likely also contributed to the forecastable decline in inflation.

32. Since cumulative expected inflation and cumulative expected output growth will in general depend on the current interest rate, we use instrumental variables. If there is no serial correlation in the error term, then the lagged independent variables are legitimate instruments. It is also legitimate to use orthogonalized values of the observable shocks as instruments since, by construction, the orthogonalized shocks are exogenous with respect to the current interest rate.

lags of the day-to-day rate is sufficient to eliminate serial correlation from the estimated reaction function.

Table 10.4 reports the results along with the implied estimates of the relation for the target rate rs_t^0, given by equation 5. The top panel reports the estimates using the year-ahead forecast of excess inflation as the relevant gap variable, and the bottom panel does the same using the infinite-horizon forecast. Overall, the results indicate that the Bundesbank responds significantly to expected inflation and output growth, and does so in the direction that one would expect. They also indicate that the day-to-day rate adjusts quickly to the target rate: only the first lagged interest rate enters significantly, and it does so with a coefficient that suggests reasonably fast adjustment.

The implied equation for the target rate is informative about the implications of our estimates for nature of Bundesbank policy. For the "year-ahead" inflation gap, this relation is given by

$$(9) \quad rs_t^0 = 6.06 + 0.78[E_t\{\pi_{t-j}^k\} - \pi^{*k}] + 0.64[E_t\{ip_t - ip_t^*\}].$$

The estimated equation for the infinite-horizon case is quite similar. The coefficient on the inflation gap falls in half, which simply reflects the fact that this gap variable is normally about twice the size of its counterpart in the year-ahead case (see figure 10.9).

We note first that the constant term in equation 9 gives an implied estimate of the steady-state nominal interest rate rs^* (compare equations 8 and 9), which is very close to the estimate of 6.28 obtained in section 10.5.2. Second, the estimates imply that a 1-percentage-point rise in expected excess inflation in-

Table 10.4   **The Bundesbank Reaction Function**

Twelve-Month Inflation Forecast
Dynamic Partial Adjustment Equation

rs_t =	0.57	+	$0.07(\pi_t^{12} - \pi_t^*)$	+	$0.06(ip_t - ip_t^*)$	+	$0.71rs_{t-1}$	+	$0.10rs_{t-2}$	+	$0.10rs_{t-3}$
	(0.12)		(0.03)		(0.02)		(0.07)		(0.08)		(0.07)

The sample is September 1974 to September 1993. Estimation is by instrumental variables. The instruments are a constant, $rs_{t-1}, rs_{t-2}, rs_{t-3}, (\pi_{t-2} - \pi_{t-2}^*), (ip_{t-2} - ip_{t-2}^*)$, and $e_t^{cp}, e_t^{ff}, e_t^m, e_t^{er}$. Box-Pierce $Q(36) = 47.88$, which is significant at the 0.09 level. $R^2 = 0.96$. Standard error of the estimate is 0.47.

Implied Equation for the Target Day-to-Day Rate
$$rs_t^0 = 6.06 + 0.78(p_t^* - p_t) + 0.64(ip_t - ip_t^*)$$

Infinite-Horizon Forecast
Dynamic Partial Adjustment Equation

rs_t =	0.53	+	$0.03(p_t^* - p_t)$	+	$0.06(ip_t - ip_t^*)$	+	$0.71rs_{t-1}$	+	$0.11rs_{t-2}$	+	$0.10rs_{t-3}$
	(0.11)		(0.01)		(0.01)		(0.07)		(0.08)		(0.07)

The instruments are a constant $rs_{t-1}, rs_{t-2}, rs_{t-3}, (p_{t-2}^* - p_{t-2}), (ip_{t-2} - ip_{t-2}^*)$, and $e_t^{cp}, e_t^{ff}, e_t^m, e_t^{er}$. Box-Pierce $Q(36) = 44.99$, which is significant at the 0.14 level. $R^2 = 0.96$. Standard error of the estimate is 0.47.

Implied Equation for the Target Day-to-Day Rate
$$rs_t^0 = 6.00 + 0.36(p_t^* - p_t) + 0.69(ip_t - ip_t^*)$$

Table 10.5   **The Bundesbank Reaction Function, Asymmetric Response to Expected Inflation and Disinflation**

Twelve-Month Inflation Forecast
Dynamic Partial Adjustment Equations

When $(\pi_t^{12} - \pi_t^{*12}) > 0$

$$rs_t = \underset{(0.13)}{0.53} + \underset{(0.08)}{0.15(\pi_t^{12} - \pi_t^{*12})} + \underset{(0.02)}{0.05(ip_t - ip_t^*)} + \underset{(0.07)}{0.71rs_{t-1}} + \underset{(0.08)}{0.10rs_{t-2}} + \underset{(0.07)}{0.09rs_{t-3}}$$

When $(\pi_t^{12} - \pi_t^{*12}) < 0$

$$rs_t = \underset{(0.13)}{0.53} + \underset{(0.06)}{0.03(\pi_t^{12} - \pi_t^{*12})} + \underset{(0.02)}{0.06(ip_t - ip_t^*)} + \underset{(0.07)}{0.71rs_{t-1}} + \underset{(0.08)}{0.10rs_{t-2}} + \underset{(0.07)}{0.09rs_{t-3}}$$

The sample is September 1974 to September 1993. Estimation is by instrument variables. The instruments are a constant, rs_{t-1}, rs_{t-2}, rs_{t-3}, $(\pi_{t-2} - \pi_{t-2}^*)$, $(ip_{t-2} - ip_{t-2}^*)$, and e_t^{cp}, e_t^{ff}, e_t^m, e_t^{er}. Box-Pierce $Q(36) = 54.64$, which is significant at the 0.03 level. $R^2 = 0.96$. Standard error of the estimate is 0.47.

Implied Equations for the Target Day-to-Day Rate

When $(\pi_t^{12} - \pi_t^{*12}) > 0$

$$rs_t^0 = 5.6 + 1.60(\pi_t^{12} - \pi_t^{*12}) + 0.56(ip_t - ip_t^*)$$

When $(\pi_t^{12} - \pi_t^{*12}) < 0$

$$rs_t^0 = 5.6 + 0.28(\pi_t^{12} - \pi_t^{*12}) + 0.56(ip_t - ip_t^*)$$

duces the Bundesbank to raise the target day-to-day rate by 78 basis points, while a 1-percentage-point increase in the output gap induces it to raise the day-to-day rate 64 basis points.[33] Thus, the Bundesbank does appear to condition policy on the state of the real economy, as our earlier analysis suggests.

One surprising feature of equation 9 is the implication that the Bundesbank raises the target rate by less than the increase in expected inflation. One possibility is that the policy rule is asymmetric with respect to inflation. That is, it may be the case that if output is at capacity, the Bundesbank does not ease much when expected inflation is below trend, but it tightens aggressively when expected inflation is above trend. In this case the low coefficient on the inflation gap could be due to the asymmetric policy response. We reestimated the feedback rule to allow the response to differ across positive and negative inflation gaps. The results support the asymmetry hypothesis.

Table 10.5 presents estimates of the asymmetric policy rule using the year-ahead measure of excess inflation. Results for the infinite-horizon case are very similar. Note that the response of the day-to-day rate to expected excess inflation is positive and significant when the gap is positive, while it is not significant when the gap is negative. The implied relation for the day-to-day rate is

$$(10) \quad rs_t^0 = \begin{cases} 5.60 + 1.60[E_t\{\pi_{t-j}^k\} - \pi^{*k}] \\ \quad + 0.56[E_t\{ip_t - ip_t^*\}], & \text{if } E_t\{\pi_{t-j}^k\} - \pi^{*k} \geq 0. \\ \\ 5.60 + 0.28[E_t\{\pi_{t-j}^k\} - \pi^{*k}] \\ \quad + 0.56[E_t\{ip_t - ip_t^*\}], & \text{if } E_t\{\pi_{t-j}^k\} - \pi^{*k} < 0. \end{cases}$$

33. Each of the gap variables is multiplied by one hundred, implying that the respective coefficients are in basis points.

When the inflation gap is positive, the Bundesbank raises the day-to-day rate 160 basis points in response to a 1% rise in expected excess inflation, implying a real rate increase of 60 basis. On the other hand, it barely responds when the inflation gap is negative. Allowing for an asymmetric policy response thus appears to resolve the puzzle. Another interesting feature of equation 10 is that, for the case of positive excess inflation, the estimated coefficients on the gap variables are very close to the ones Taylor used.[34] Thus, after allowing for our modifications, it is not an exaggeration to suggest that the Bundesbank policy rule during the post–Bretton Woods era bears a reasonable proximity to the rule that Taylor employs to characterize U.S. monetary policy under Greenspan.

As an informal way to judge both the fit and the implications of our estimated reaction function, figure 10.10 plots the estimated target day-to-day rate rs_t^0 against the actual rate rs_t for the linear policy rule described by equation 9. Figure 10.11 does the same for the asymmetric rule described by equation 10. In each case the target rate tracks the actual rate reasonably well, suggesting that the model provides a decent accounting of Bundesbank policy.

It is interesting to note that, during the mid- to late 1970s, policy was somewhat easier than the norm for the era predicted by the model, which is consistent with the narrative evidence. Specifically, the target rate was systematically above the actual rate over this period. Conversely, policy was somewhat tighter than the norm for the latter half of the sample. Particular episodes of relative tightness were late 1982 to early 1983, when the real economy was still experiencing the effects of a severe recession, and 1992–93, the approximate time of the breakup of the EMS. The relatively large gap between the actual and target rates during this latter period provides support for the view that the Bundesbank was being unusually tough prior to the EMS collapse.

Interestingly, the linear model portrayed in figure 10.10 suggests that policy was somewhat tougher than the norm during the mid-1980s, when the real economy was stagnating and inflation was low. As figure 10.11 suggests, however, this discrepancy may be due to the failure to allow for an asymmetric policy response during this period of below-trend inflation. The nonlinear model, in contrast, tracks this period reasonably well.

The Taylor Specification

We now reestimate the model using the difference between inflation over the past year and trend inflation as the relevant gap variable. We try two variations. The first follows Taylor strictly.[35] The second allows for partial adjustment.

---

34. The corresponding coefficients for Taylor's rule are 1.5 on the inflation gap and 0.5 on the output gap.

35. Because Taylor used quarterly data, we measure the output gap using the quarterly average of our monthly data. We also followed Taylor by assuming a deterministic trend for output. The results are not particularly sensitive to the method of detrending output, though allowing for a stochastic trend does seem to improve the fit.

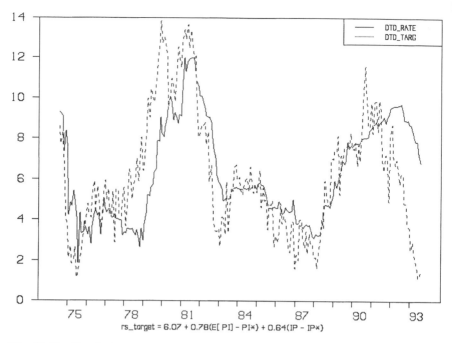

Fig. 10.10 Bundesbank day-to-day interest rate, target versus actual

Note: See equation 9.

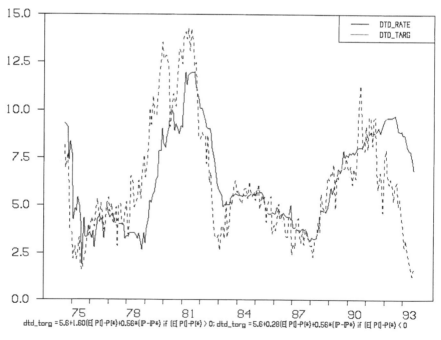

Fig. 10.11 Asymmetric response of day-to-day interest rates to inflation, target versus actual

Note: See equation 10.

Table 10.6   **Bundesbank Reaction Function: Taylor Rule Specification**

Taylor Rule

$$rs_t^0 = 6.35 + 0.71(\pi_t - \pi_t^*) + 0.20(ip_t - ip\tau_t)$$
$$\quad\;\;(0.12)\;\;(0.07)\qquad\qquad(0.03)$$

The sample is September 1974 to September 1993. Estimation is by OLS. Box-Pierce $Q(36) = 2{,}551.88$, which is significant at the 0.00001 level. $R^2 = 0.43$. Standard error of the estimate is 1.82. $IP\tau_t$ is the estimated trend in industrial production.

Taylor Rule with Partial Adjustment

$$rs_t = 0.33 + 0.01(\pi_t - \pi^*) + 0.04(ip_t - ip\tau_t) + 0.80rs_{t-1} + 0.11rs_{t-2} + 0.03rs_{t-3}$$
$$\quad\;(0.12)\qquad(0.02)\qquad\quad(0.01)\qquad\qquad(0.07)\qquad\;(0.09)\qquad\;(0.07)$$

The sample is September 1974 to September 1993. Estimation is by OLS. Box-Pierce $Q(36) = 50.03$, which is significant at the 0.06 level. $R^2 = 0.96$. Standard error of the estimate is 0.50. π_t is average inflation over previous twelve months. π^* is sample average inflation. $ip\tau_t - ip_t$ is deviation of deterministic trend ip from actual ip averaged over the previous three months.

Implied Equation for the Target Day-to-Day Rate
$$rs_t^0 = 6.6 + 0.15(\pi_t - \pi^*) + 0.84(ip_t - ip\tau_t)$$

Table 10.6 reports the results. The top panel presents estimates of the standard Taylor specification. The coefficients are of the right sign, though the coefficient on the inflation gap is too low to have the real rate move in the wrong direction. More significantly, there is strong evidence of residual serial correlation, suggesting the possibility of omitted variable bias. The bottom panel presents the estimates for the case of partial adjustment. Including the lagged day-to-day rate significantly reduces the residual correlation. On the other hand, the coefficient on the inflation gap is no longer significant.

Finally, figure 10.12 plots the implied target rates for the two Taylor specifications against the actual day-to-day rate. The top panel portrays the case with partial adjustment, while the bottom line portrays the standard specification. Overall, the results suggest that the basic Taylor specification does not work as well as our modified version.[36]

10.6   Concluding Remarks

Despite the public focus on monetary targeting, in practice German monetary policy involves the management of short-term interest rates, as it does in the United States. The targets, however, do provide a reference point for decision making. The key feature is that they provide a benchmark policy rule that is designed to meet a clearly articulated long-term inflation goal. While the Bundesbank can and often does deviate from this rule, it must always provide justification for doing so. By forcing this kind of focused discussion of Bundesbank decisions, the targeting provides some discipline on the policy process.

36. We also try a variation that uses the coefficients that Taylor specified for the United States. This specification does not improve the model's performance.

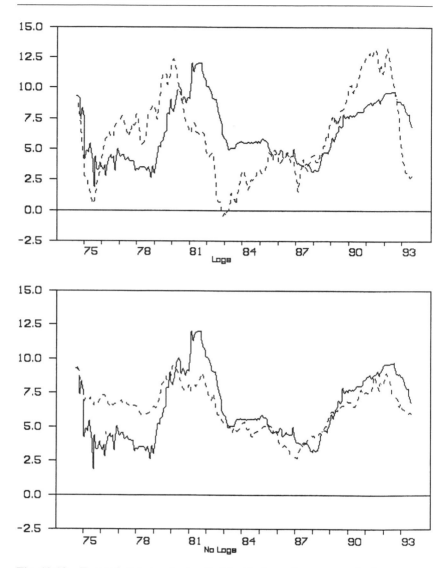

Fig. 10.12   Target interest rates implied by Taylor rules versus actual

Except during the mid- to late 1970s, the Bundesbank has aggressively adjusted interest rates to achieve and maintain low inflation. The goal of a low long-term inflation rate is paramount. However, from a variety of evidence, both informal and formal, we find that the performance of the real economy also influences Bundesbank decision making. It adopts a gradualist approach to disinflating, and it does ease when the real economy weakens. During these situations it often cites other factors in public announcements—concern about maintaining the stability of exchange rate regimes, for example. Our results suggest, however, that it is implicitly pursuing a countercyclical policy. In particular our formal analysis suggests that, for the most part, the Bundesbank has adjusted short-term interest rates according to a kind of modified Taylor rule: one that has the short-term rate adjust to anticipated inflation as opposed to past inflation, and that allows for an asymmetric response of the short-term rate to the inflation gap. In this respect there is a noteworthy parallel between the conduct of Bundesbank policy in the post–Bretton Woods era and the operation of the Federal Reserve Board since 1987.

Despite obvious success in maintaining a low long-term inflation rate, the Bundesbank has not been able to make disinflation a relatively painless process, as the recessions of the early 1980s and the early 1990s suggest. Why it has not reaped measurable gains from reputation building is a major puzzle, one that a number of economists have noted. As we discussed earlier, the Bundesbank's accommodation of inflation during the 1970s may have influenced public perceptions during the early 1980s, though it is doubtful that this could be the entire story. Further, since the Bundesbank aggressively pursued a low-inflation policy over the 1980s, this kind of explanation is less persuasive for the most recent recession. On the other hand, it is possible that reunification posed a special set of circumstances. Clearly, this general issue is an important topic for future research.

We conclude with a perhaps mundane but nonetheless potentially important lesson from the analysis. A current widely discussed issue is whether the monetary policy should be aimed at achieving zero inflation. We learn from the analysis that the Bundesbank has never tried to achieve exact price stability, and has instead focused on a goal of 2% long-run inflation. Concern about measurement error in the price index—specifically, possible overstatement of inflation due to imperfect adjustment for quality improvements—is the rationale provided for this objective. This measurement issue ought to be a key concern of monetary policymakers, as it appears it is becoming in the United States.

References

Ball, Laurence. 1994. What Determines the Sacrifice Ratio? In *Monetary Policy,* ed. N. Gregory Mankiw, 155–88. Chicago: University of Chicago Press.

Bernanke, Ben, and Alan Blinder. 1992. The Federal Funds Rate and the Transmission of Monetary Policy. *American Economic Review* 82:901–21.

Bernanke, Ben, and Ilyan Mihov. 1995. Measuring Monetary Policy. Princeton University, June. Mimeo.

Bernanke, Ben, and Frederic Mishkin. 1992. Central Bank Behavior and the Strategy of Monetary Policy: Observations from Six Industrialized Countries. *NBER Macroeconomics Annual* 7:183 227.

Blanchard, Olivier J. 1989. A Traditional Interpretation of Economic Fluctuations. *American Economic Review* 79:1146–64.

Christiano, Lawrence J., Martin Eichenbaum, and Charles Evans. 1996. The Effects of Monetary Policy Shocks: Evidence from the Flow of Funds. *Review of Economics and Statistics* 78 (February): 16–34.

Clarida, Richard, and Jordi Gali. 1994. Sources of Real Exchange Rate Fluctuations: How Important Are Nominal Shocks? *Carnegie-Rochester Conference Series on Public Policy* 41 (December): 1–56.

Deutsche Bundesbank. 1989. *Policy Practices and Procedures.* Frankfurt: Deutsche Bundesbank.

Eichenbaum, Martin, and Charles Evans. 1995. Some Empirical Evidence on the Effects of Monetary Policy on Exchange Rates. *Quarterly Journal of Economics* 110 (November): 975–1010.

Gali, Jordi. 1992. How Well Does the IS/LM Model Fit Post-War U.S. Data? *Quarterly Journal of Economics* 107 (May): 709–38.

Grilli, Vittorio, Donato Masciandaro, and Guido Tabellini. 1991. Central Bank Institutions and Policies. *Economic Policy.*

Issing, Otmar. 1995. Stability of Monetary Policy, Stability of the Monetary System: Experience with Monetary Targeting in Germany. Deutsche Bundesbank. Mimeo.

Kahn, George, and Kristina Jacobson. 1989. Lessons from West German Monetary Policy. *Federal Reserve Bank of Kansas City Economic Review* (April): 18–34.

Kim, Soyoung. 1994. Does Monetary Policy Matter in the G-6 Countries. Yale University. Mimeo.

Kim, Soyoung, and Nouriel Roubini. 1995. Liquidity and Exchange Rates: A Structural VAR Approach. New York University. Mimeo.

Kole, Linda, and Ellen Meade. 1994. Searching for the Holy Grail: An Examination of German Money Demand after Unification. Federal Reserve Board. Mimeo.

Neumann, Manfred J. M., and Jurgen Von Hagen. 1993. Germany. In *Monetary Policy in Developed Countries,* ed. Michele Fratianni and Dominick Salvatore. London: Greenwood Press.

Rotemberg, Julio. 1994. Prices, Output, and Hours: An Empirical Analysis Based on a Sticky Price Model. Massachusetts Institute of Technology. Mimeo.

Sims, Christopher A., and Tao Zha. 1994. Does Monetary Policy Generate Recessions? Using Less Aggregate Price Data to Identify Monetary Policy. Yale University. Mimeo.

Taylor, John. 1993. Discretion versus Policy Rules in Practice. *Carnegie-Rochester Conference Series on Public Policy* 38 (December): 195–214.

Trehan, Bharat. 1988. The Practice of Monetary Targeting: A Case Study of the West German Experience. *Federal Reserve Bank of San Francisco Economic Review* (spring): 30–44.

Tsatsaronis, Konstantinos. 1993. Bank Lending and the Monetary Transmission Mechanism: The Case of Germany. Mimeo.

Uctum, Merih. 1995. European Integration and Asymmetry in the EMS. Federal Reserve Bank of New York. Mimeo.

Von Hagen, Jurgen. 1994. Inflation and Monetary Targeting in Germany. University of Mannheim and Indiana University. Mimeo.

Woodford, Michael. 1994. Nonstandard Indicators for Monetary Policy. In *Monetary Policy,* ed. N. Gregory Mankiw, 95–115. Chicago: University of Chicago Press.

Comment   Rudiger Dornbusch

The paper by Clarida and Gertler (ClaGer for short) offers a revisionist view of the Bundesbank. The myth has been that of an institution fighting inflation, with little other concern, predominantly with an M3-oriented strategy. ClaGer make a good case that the Buba is no different from most other central banks, notably the Fed. They establish a reaction function with inflation and output gaps as the chief determinants of an interest rate–oriented policy. Amazingly, M3 plays *absolutely* no role in the story.

That rendition is nothing short of dramatic. After all, the Buba keeps talking about M3 and keeps getting entangled in the huge discrepancies between targeted M3 and the large departures of actual M3. I argue that ClaGer have done a great job in bringing Buba policy down to earth, but that they have not gone far enough. Whenever M3 goes wild, the Buba is mired in its own rhetoric. That is precisely when the Buba does *not* do the obvious, that is, cut rates in the midst of a no-inflation, serious-downturn situation. The first half of 1996 is a case in point.

I review briefly the Buba folklore, consider the ClaGer rendition, and move on to an attempt to reestablish some role for M3 in interpreting Buba policy mistakes. The point is, when common sense and adherence to M3 targets point in opposite directions, the Buba sometimes goes the wrong way.

The Folklore

The setting is shown in figure 10C.1, which reports German CPI inflation (for twelve-month periods). Three major inflation episodes are apparent. Coming out of the destructive experience of a hyperinflation, a monetary write-off in 1948, dollar dependence under Bretton Woods, and an unsuccessful encounter with supply-shock inflation, the Buba places great weight on a firm anchor. A premium is placed on a simple message that allows the Buba to tie its hands against any temptation to pursue a long-run inflationary strategy.

M3 is thought to offer precisely that assurance.

The relationship in question derives from a stable long-run M3 real money demand. The velocity of M3, other than for a 1% per year downward trend, is near-constant over the medium term. Accordingly, there is a relationship between the medium-term price level P^*, the level of potential output Y^*, trend velocity V^*, and the trend price level P^*:

$$(1) \qquad\qquad P^* = V^*M3/Y^*.$$

Such a relationship existed in the United States until Goodhart's law caught up with it; in Germany it is believed still to exist. Empirical evidence for various

Rudiger Dornbusch is the Ford Professor of Economics and International Management at the Massachusetts Institute of Technology and a research associate of the National Bureau of Economic Research.

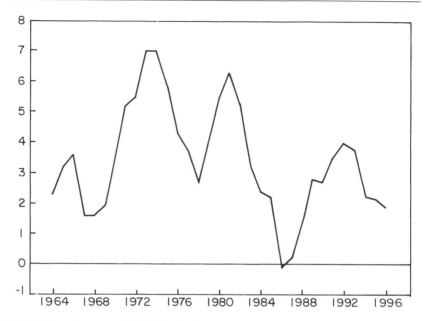

Fig. 10C.1   Germany: CPI inflation (percentage during the past twelve months)

OECD countries is reviewed in Hoeller and Poret (1991). In the case of Germany, as recently as 1995 the evidence of a stable M3 equation has been reviewed by the Buba (*Monthly Report*, July 1995) and the conclusion remains: yes, there is a stable demand for M3, and as a consequence, M3 targeting is the basis of a sound monetary strategy. "Most of the empirical studies now available show positive results. Hence German monetary policy makers can continue to count on lastingly stable money demand" (Deutsche Bundesbank 1995).

With a stable money-demand equation in hand, the Buba operates its policy by setting annual M3 growth corridors. The extraordinary claim of ClaGer is that this is just camouflage. A plain vanilla reaction function à la Taylor explains what goes on, M3 is just not there!

The Clarida-Gertler Rendition

The ClaGer paper reviews in careful detail the broad trends in Buba policy and then comes down to the hard work of identifying just what goes on. The central conclusion is that policy can be modeled as a reaction function. The short-term interest rate is expressed as a function of the discrepancy between actual and long-run target inflation and the output gap. There is also a dynamics to the rate setting, which I skip here. The real interest rate target level, R, that emerges is

$$(2) \qquad\qquad R = r^* + \alpha (\pi - \pi^*) + \beta gap,$$

where r^* is the long-run real interest rate (3%), while π and π^* are the forward-looking inflation forecast and the long-run equilibrium rate. There are important technical features in the modeling of the inflation deviation and the output gap—they are forward-looking using estimates of a variable autoregression (VAR) model, but that is not a central issue here. The focus rather is on the finding that inflation gaps and the output gap explain what the Buba does with interest rates; M3 is just not part of the story. (Not part of the story over and above the role in the VAR forecast.) Figures 10.10 and 10.11 show the target interest rate emerging from the reaction function as well as the actuals, and it is clear that the model works surprisingly well.

The details of the coefficient deserve attention. ClaGer experiment with asymmetries and their conclusion is this.

- The Buba responds to a 100-basis-point inflation shock with a 60-basis-point increase in real interest rates.
- A 100-basis-point favorable inflation surprise induces only a 28-basis-point cut in nominal interest rates or, equivalently, a 72-basis-point increase in real rates. Thus interest rate policy does not fully accommodate disinflation.
- A 100-basis-point increase in the output gap (measured by industrial production) includes a 64-basis-point increase in nominal and real interest rates.

A central question in this reaction-function setting is what the long-run or target level of inflation is. ClaGer find that the level of π^* is 3.2%. This is surprising because, at least since the 1980s, the rhetoric is 0–2%. Even so, they refer to their finding as "sensible" and note: "the steady-state inflation rate provides a measure of the long-run dimension of monetary policy. Since this number is a product of the steady-state money-growth rate that the policy rule generates, it is ultimately a choice variable of the Bundesbank."

Bundesbankers would be surprised to find that their long-run strategy implies a 3.2% inflation! The authors may have come to their unusual finding because their sample period includes the supply-shock period of the 1970s, where the Buba was taken by surprise and spent a long time with inflation rates that were out of sight. That argues for using the post–oil shock sample period, where the recognition is made explicitly that moderate inflation in long-run averages requires that any overshooting be followed by periods of undershooting. This point is particularly obvious in the 1995–96 discussion rendered in the *Monthly Reports*. There we read that, yes, inflation is safely below 2% but that is not an invitation for expansion. It has to be kept low and pushed down so that the long-run averages come out right. Some of this may be brinkmanship, but the fact is that Germany is in a slump and the Buba is not rushing out to give relief. In sum, modeling strategy around a target of 3.2% inflation is plainly a misreading of what the Buba is about, at least in the last decade.

M3 Matters

A second question about the reaction functions is just how successful they are. I note that, indeed, the major episodes of large rate changes are captured well. But as figure 10.11, for example, shows, there are major and persistent discrepancies between target and actual rates. Thus, in 1978–81 targets exceed actuals persistently, while in 1982–83 the converse is the case. Once again, in 1991–93 actuals exceed targets significantly. The figure shows that by 1993 the target nominal rate would have been below 2.5%! It is tempting to believe that M3 has to do with precisely these persistent discrepancies between the reaction-function prediction and the outcome. Consider, for example, the experience of the 1990s. ClaGer show large discrepancies of target and actual rates in 1993–93. Table 10C.1 shows large overshooting of M3 relative to target. Is it not tempting to consider that the Buba gave some weight to the M3 overshooting, and for that reason the reaction function, which does not contain M3, misfires?

It is tempting therefore to suggest a formulation well within the spirit of ClaGer but with a Buba special. The real interest rate equation might be stated as

(3) $R' = \gamma R + (1 - \gamma)M3\ Overshoot.$

In this fashion we capture the factors ClaGer identify in the Taylor-style rendition of the reaction function but at the same time leave room for the situation where M3 overshooting puts the Buba in a bind.

An episode along these lines is surely the early part of 1996. As figure 10C.2 shows, after a slow year of M3 growth, far below target, in 1996 M3 growth took off like a bat out of hell. The Buba is bewildered: the economy with low inflation and no growth needs stimulus, but M3 is running wild. What to do? The Buba is all tied in knots, hoping that M3 will slow down, the economy will recover, and M3 targeting can be kept alive.

European Monetary Union

Another direction to look, if we want to understand just how committed the Buba is to monetary targeting, is the setup for Europe's new monetary institutions. As Europe moves toward a common money, the operating instructions for the European Central Bank are being drafted. The Buba has weighed in heavily: predictably, with monetary targeting. The Buba has denounced inflation-targeting U.K.-style and has insisted on monetary-aggregates targeting. Specifically, Buba president Tietmeyer (1996) argued that stability of real money demand in Europe, outside Germany, was a fact: "As a result, a monetary aggregate strategy, in my judgment, is the most convincing concept for monetary policy in the monetary union. With its use, the European Central Bank could inherit the reputation of the Bundesbank. For a young institution such as ECB will be, this seems certainly attractive" (Tietmeyer 1996).

Table 10C.1   **Bundesbank M3 Targets and Outcomes**

	Target	Actual
1992	3.5–5.5	9
1993	4.5–6.5	7
1994	4.0–6.0	6
1995	4.0–6.0	2
1996	4.0–7.0	

Source: Deutsche Bundesbank 1995.
Note: Growth rate fourth quarter to fourth quarter.

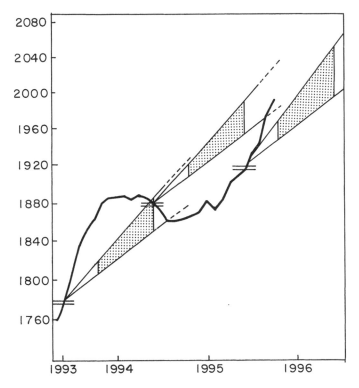

Fig. 10C.2   M3 growth targets

Of course, the short-run instability of M3 in Germany and the controversy over a stable real money demand in most countries on earth make it a bit hard to force all new partners into the same straitjacket. Whereas Tietmeyer was still all-out M3, the most recent struggle with M3 in early 1996 has cooled the enthusiasm somewhat. Thus Issing came out with a milder version, a mix of both inflation targeting and room for aggregates. In a significant weakening of the dogma, leaning far in the direction of the U.K. plea for monetary targeting as the new central bank culture, he notes: "In the end, the discussion about an optimal concept cannot be an Either-Or but must rather a combination of monetary aggregates strategy and inflation targeting" (1996, 8; see also König 1996).

The point remains: M3 has been there, is there, and is not about to disappear. The German saving public (*die Sparer*) have been brought up to trust in the simple quantity theory, and they are not ready to believe in a new institution *and* new operating instructions all at once.

It is appropriate to end on a quote from the *Zauberlehrling* of Goethe: "Herr, die Not is gross, die ich rief die Geister, werd ich nun nicht los."

References

Deutsche Bundesbank. 1995. *Annual Report.* Frankfurt: Deutsche Bundesbank.
Hoeller, P., and P. Poret. 1991. Is *P** a Good Indicator of Inflationary Pressures in OECD Countries? *OECD Economic Studies,* no. 17, 7–30.
Issing, Otmar. 1996. Speech to the Bavarian Assembly. *Deutsch Bundesbank Auszuge aus Presseartikeln,* no. 30, May 5, 1996, 8.
König, Reiner. 1996. The Bundesbank's Experience in Monetary Targeting. In *Monetary Policy Strategies in Europe,* ed. Deutsche Bundesbank. Munich: Verlag Wahlen.
Tietmeyer, Hans. 1996. Speech to the Colloquium on Globale Finanzmarkte und EWWU, Goethe Universität, Frankfurt. *Deutsche Bundesbank Auszuge aus Presseartikeln,* no. 27, April 4, 1996, 4.

Contributors

Andrew B. Abel
Department of Finance
The Wharton School
University of Pennsylvania
2315 Steinberg-Dietrich Hall
3620 Locust Walk
Philadelphia, PA 19104

Laurence Ball
Department of Economics
Johns Hopkins University
Baltimore, MD 21218

Olivier J. Blanchard
Department of Economics
Massachusetts Institute of Technology
Cambridge, MA 02139

Marta Campillo
Department of Economics
Boston University
270 Bay State Road
Boston, MA 02215

David Card
Industrial Relations Section
Firestone Library
Princeton University
Princeton, NJ 08544

Richard Clarida
Department of Economics
Columbia University
International Affairs Bldg., Room 1020
New York, NY 10027

J. Bradford De Long
Department of Economics
University of California
549 Evans Hall
Berkeley, CA 94720

Rudiger Dornbusch
Department of Economics
Massachusetts Institute of Technology
Cambridge, MA 02139

Martin Feldstein
President and Chief Executive Officer
NBER
1050 Massachusetts Avenue
Cambridge, MA 02138

Benjamin M. Friedman
Department of Economics
Harvard University
Cambridge, MA 02138

Mark Gertler
Department of Economics
New York University
269 Mercer Street, 7th Floor
New York, NY 10003

Dean Hyslop
Department of Economics
University of California
2263 Bunche Hall
405 Hilgard Avenue
Los Angeles, CA 90024

Alan B. Krueger
Woodrow Wilson School
Princeton University
Princeton, NJ 08544

Owen Lamont
Graduate School of Business
University of Chicago
1101 East 58th Street
Chicago, IL 60637

N. Gregory Mankiw
Department of Economics
Harvard University
Cambridge, MA 02138

Jeffrey A. Miron
Department of Economics
Boston University
270 Bay State Road
Boston, MA 02215

Maurice Obstfeld
Department of Economics
University of California
549 Evans Hall
Berkeley, CA 94720

Christina D. Romer
Department of Economics
University of California
549 Evans Hall
Berkeley, CA 94720

David H. Romer
Department of Economics
University of California
549 Evans Hall
Berkeley, CA 94720

Matthew D. Shapiro
Department of Economics
University of Michigan
Ann Arbor, MI 48109

John Shea
Department of Economics
University of Maryland
College Park, MD 20742

Robert J. Shiller
Cowles Foundation for Research in
    Economics
Yale University
30 Hillhouse Avenue, Room 23a
New Haven, CT 06520

Douglas Staiger
Kennedy School of Government
Harvard University
79 JFK Street
Cambridge, MA 02138

James H. Stock
Kennedy School of Government
Harvard University
79 JFK Street
Cambridge, MA 02138

John B. Taylor
Department of Economics, Landau
    Center
Stanford University
Stanford, CA 94305

Mark W. Watson
Woodrow Wilson School
Princeton University
Princeton, NJ 08544

Name Index

415

Subject Index

Akaike information criterion (AIC), 228, 233

Bayesian information criterion (BIC), 221, 228, 233

Carter administration, 271–72
CBI. *See* Central bank independence (CBI)
Central bank: proposed European Central Bank, 325–26; reforms in New Zealand and France, 324–25
Central bank, Germany: Bundesbank Board, 366; Central Bank Council, 366; daily policy management, 370; design and jurisdiction of, 366–67; independence of, 366; inflation policy of Bundesbank, 363; institutions of Bundesbank, 365–71; monetary targets, 367; policy (1973–78), 372–75; policy (1979–83), 375–76; policy (1983–89), 376–77; policy (1990–93), 377
Central bank independence (CBI): association with inflation, 339–62; defined, 337
Central bank money (CBM), Germany, 370
Consumption: allocation with inflation, 129–39
Consumption, retirement: with traditional welfare gain, 131–36; welfare effects of price changes in, 129–30

Data: construction of matched Current Population Survey panels, 105–7; construction using Nexis newspaper article abstracts, 283–85
Data sources: analysis of inflation effects on

labor market, 72, 73–74; for analysis of reporting of wage changes, 83; to estimate NAIRU based on Phillips curve, 206; for term "shortage," 283–85
Deadweight loss: from distortion caused by inflation, 129; imposed by capital taxation, 149; from life-cycle consumption distortion, 129–30
Deutsche Bundesbank Act (1957), 366
Discount window, German, 371
Disinflation: change in unemployment with, 179–84; effects on NAIRU, 171–74, 188–92; interaction with labor market variables, 176–79; Volcker's policy of, 258, 272, 274
Dynamic inconsistency, 309, 314–15, 319, 331–32

Economic performance: German (1980s to present), 364; German central bank attention to, 378
Economy, U.S.: effects of Great Depression on, 250–52, 255–57; legacy of Keynes (1960s), 252–57; supply shocks as cause of inflation (1970s), 267–70, 276–77
European Central Bank (ECB), proposed structure, 325–26
European Monetary System (EMS): collapse (1992), 377; role of Germany in, 366–67

Federal Reserve Board: Burns's policy, 258, 262–65, 272–73; Volcker's disinflation policy, 258, 272, 274
France: monetary institution reform, 324–25